Using Quicken® 6 for DOS

LINDA A. FLANDERS

Publisher: Lloyd J. Short

Associate Publisher: Rick Ranucci

Product Development Manager: Thomas H. Bennett

Book Designer: Scott Cook

Production Team: Jeff Baker, Claudia Bell, Jodie Cantwell, Paula Carroll, Michelle Cleary, Denny Hager, Bob LaRoche, Joy Dean Lee, Laurie Lee, Jay Lesandrini, Cindy L. Phipps, Linda Seifert, Sandra Shay, Susan Shepard, Suzanne Tully, Phil Worthington

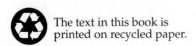
The text in this book is printed on recycled paper.

CREDITS

Title Manager
Shelley O'Hara

Production Editor
Fran Blauw

Editors
Jo Anna Arnott
William A. Barton
Donald R. Eamon

Technical Editor
J. Scott Avery, CPA

Senior Acquisitions Editor
Chris Katsaropoulos

Composed in *Cheltenham* and *MCPdigital*
by Que Corporation

To Scott, Jade, Jordan, and Ali, who continue to give me love and support.
And to Ed, who, in his own way, challenged me to do this.

Linda A. Flanders is a Certified Public Accountant and holds a Bachelor of Science degree in accounting from Indiana University. She has worked in public accounting for Arthur Andersen & Co. and in private accounting for Mayflower Group, Inc., where she specialized in taxation. She currently operates a small individual tax practice. She is the author of *Using TurboTax: 1992 Edition*, *CheckFree Quick Reference*, *Quicken 5 Quick Reference*, *Using Microsoft Money*, and *Using QuickBooks*, all published by Que Corporation. She is also the author of *10 Minute Guide to Quicken 5* and coauthor of *The Best Book of Peachtree Complete III*, both published by Sams.

ACKNOWLEDGMENTS

Thanks to Rick Ranucci, associate publisher, and Chris Katsaropoulos, senior acquisitions editor, who show great faith in me.

Thank you to Shelley O'Hara, title manager, for her guidance and support.

And thank you to Fran Blauw, production editor, who worked many long, hard hours to make this a better book and to ensure its timeliness.

From behind the scenes, I want to thank Don Eamon and Jo Anna Arnott. And a special thanks to Bill Barton, for challenging me with his many questions and comments that, now and in the future, will make my work better.

CONTENTS AT A GLANCE

I Learning Quicken

II Getting the Most from Quicken

III Analyzing Your Finances with Quicken

IV Managing Quicken

V Putting Quicken To Use

Appendixes

Introduction

If you're like most people, your personal bookkeeping takes you hours and hours each month. You probably sit down three to four times a month to pay bills, each time gathering paperwork, writing checks, entering checks and deposits into your checkbook register, calculating your bank account balance, and addressing envelopes. Then, when your monthly bank statement arrives, you have to sit down once more to perform the tedious task of balancing your checkbook by checking off cleared transactions, adding outstanding deposits and checks, and performing the reconciling calculations. After you've endured all these ordeals, heaven forbid if *your* bank account balance does not agree with the bank's! That crisis means spending even more time trying to detect the error(s). All of these tasks just to keep your financial records in some semblance of order. But keeping your financial records in order is a task that *cannot* be overlooked nor trusted to a financial system that is outdated or ineffective.

If you invest your money in any type of securities, then you absolutely must keep track of your investments or you won't know if your investment strategies are paying off. If your focus is on income-producing investments, you need to monitor those investments to make sure that the income yields are maximized. If your focus is on growth investments, you need to monitor those investments to make sure that they are growing at a satisfactory level. No matter what your focus, you need to monitor your investments to make sure they don't dwindle away. Of course, you can entrust this process to your investment advisor or broker, but you'll want to be on top of things to make sure the experts are doing their job with *your* money.

Quicken is your solution to the boring and long process of bookkeeping and financial management and the necessary, but sometimes complex task of monitoring your investments. With Quicken, you can speed up your recordkeeping activities and have a little fun, too. By using screens that resemble what you're used to seeing on the desktop (checks and check Registers), you can quickly and easily enter your financial transactions, print checks, reconcile your bank account, create budgets, and generate reports so that you can analyze your finances more easily. Quicken's investment features help you track each of your investments so that you can easily manage your portfolio.

To truly have a handle on your finances, you must keep track of your income and expenses so that you know how much money is coming in and how much is going out. Quicken helps you do that. In order to make informed decisions about spending, you must know exactly where you are (financially) at any given time. If you want to take a vacation to Europe or buy a new car, for example, you immediately know what you can afford. Quicken helps you make these decisions by presenting the financial data that you need in a format that is meaningful to you. That's what this book is really about: making better financial decisions by using financial information—financial information that Quicken can help you collect, store, and use.

In this age of super technology, almost anything you do behind a desk can be accomplished with a computer. Bookkeeping and financial management are no exception. With a well-designed software package, you can perform all your financial activities, including tracking your investments, in far less time and with far less frustration.

If you are considering the installation of a personal or small-business accounting package like Quicken, if you have decided to install Quicken and want a little extra help, or if you already have begun using Quicken and want a reference source that goes beyond the information provided in the user's manual, *Using Quicken 6 for DOS* will help. This text includes a wealth of information about Quicken Version 6.0 and about managing your personal or small-business finances.

After you read this Introduction, you will know what Quicken Version 6.0 is and whether the program suits your needs. This Introduction also identifies the contents of each chapter.

What Is Quicken?

Quicken is a computer-based bookkeeping system you can use to manage your personal or business finances. Used in the simplest way, Quicken maintains your check register for you by deducting payments and adding deposits to your checking account balance. Quicken eliminates the possibility of you overdrawing your account because of an arithmetic error.

The real value of Quicken, however, stems from several other features the program provides. First, Quicken enables you to use your computer and printer to generate checks, which is a real time-saver if you find yourself writing many checks at home every month. Second, Quicken enables you to use the information stored in your Check Register to report on your income and expenses, track tax deductions, and compare your actual income and expenses to what you originally budgeted. Third, you can use Quicken to perform bookkeeping for most personal and business assets and liabilities, including personal investments, business receivables, personal credit lines and mortgages, and business payables. With these extra features, individuals can track and manage their finances closely, and many small businesses can use Quicken as a full-fledged accounting package. (Quicken enables you to generate personal and business income statements, balance sheets, and cash-flow statements.)

New Features in Quicken 6.0

If you've used earlier versions of Quicken, you'll want to know what Quicken 6.0 has in store for you. Quicken features new to Version 6.0 are indicated throughout this book by a special icon, just like the one in this margin. The following is a list of the new features in Quicken 6.0:

- *Graphing capability:* You can create on-screen graphs to compare your income with expenses, assets with liabilities, actual amounts with budget amounts, and your investment portfolio with investment results. Refer to Chapter 17, "Creating Graphs," to learn more about Quicken's new graphing capability.

- *Financial planning calculators:* There's not much you cannot do now that Quicken includes several financial planning calculators. In just seconds, you can calculate how much money you'll need for Billy's college education, how much you need to save for that early retirement, how feasible (or unfeasible) refinancing your home is, and the present or future value of investments. Refer to Chapter 18, "Financial Planning with Quicken," to learn how to use Quicken's new financial calculators.

- *QuickFill:* Here's a neat new feature—QuickFill. When you type a few characters in the Payee or Category field in the Register or the Write Checks screen, Quicken searches through the last three months of transactions in the Register or the Memorized Transaction list to find a matching payee or category. When Quicken finds a match, QuickFill fills in the rest of the transaction for you, based on the previous transaction. QuickFill also enters investment transaction information when you type characters in the Security or Action field in the Investment Register. See Chapters 5, 7, and 16 for discussions on QuickFill.

■ *IntelliCharge:* If you have a Quicken VISA card, you can set up an IntelliCharge account in Quicken and receive your statements on disk or by modcm. IntelliCharge enters the credit card transactions for you and even categorizes them. See Chapter 11, "Managing Your Credit Cards," for more on IntelliCharge.

■ *Quick Calendar:* You can use Quicken's new pop-up calendar, Quick Calendar, just to review dates, to go to a certain date in the Register or the Write Checks screen, or to paste a date in a Date field in a Quicken screen. Refer to Chapter 2, "Getting Around in Quicken," to learn how to access and use Quick Calendar.

■ *Copying and pasting transactions:* Now you can copy a transaction from the Register and paste it over an existing transaction or in an empty transaction line in the Register, or you can copy a check and paste it in a blank check or over an existing check. See Chapter 5, "Automating the Register," to learn how to copy and paste a transaction. See Chapter 7, "Automating Check Writing," to learn how to copy and paste checks.

■ *Amortize variable rate loans:* Using Quicken's updated loan calculator, you can amortize a loan with variable interest rates. You also can amortize loans in which you've made prepayments. See Chapter 10, "Tracking Your Net Worth, Other Assets, and Liabilities," to learn how to amortize variable rate loans and loans with prepayments.

■ *Field-specific help:* Now you can position the cursor on a specific field that you need help with and press F1 to display help for that field only. See Chapter 2, "Getting Around in Quicken," to see how this new feature works.

■ *Search for Quicken data files:* If you need to find a data file, you can have Quicken search the A, B, or C drive for all Quicken files. Chapter 19, "Managing Your Quicken Files," shows you how to search for Quicken data files.

■ *Receive electronic mail from CheckFree:* In the past, you've been able to send electronic mail to CheckFree. Now you can receive messages from CheckFree via your modem and Quicken. See Chapter 13, "Paying Bills Electronically," to learn how to check your CheckFree mailbox for messages.

■ *Return to a report after QuickZoom:* In the previous version of Quicken (which introduced the QuickZoom feature), you could not return to the report after you used QuickZoom to examine transaction detail in the Register. Now you can. See Chapter 12, "Creating and Printing Reports," to learn how.

■ *New assistants:* Quicken includes more assistants to help you perform tasks such as exporting tax information to TurboTax or other tax preparation programs, setting up an amortized loan payment, and setting up an investment account and entering investment transactions. Refer to Chapter 2, "Getting Around in Quicken," to learn how to use Quicken's new assistants.

■ *Import stock prices from Prodigy:* In the previous version of Quicken, you could import stock prices from an ASCII file into the Update Prices and Market Value window so that your security prices were updated. Now, you can save stock prices from Prodigy (which gets prices from its Dow Jones Service) to an ASCII file in Quicken's special import format. See Chapter 16, "Monitoring Your Investments," to learn how to import stock prices from Prodigy.

■ *New colors and background patterns:* So you won't get bored, Quicken 6.0 provides more colors and background patterns for you to choose from (if you have a color monitor). See Chapter 20, "Customizing Quicken," to learn how to change colors and background patterns.

■ *Accounts are easier to set up:* Accounts have never been difficult to set up in Quicken. The new version of Quicken makes it even easier, however, by giving you more information on-screen as you go through the steps in setting up an account. See Chapter 3, "Defining Your Accounts," to see how easy account setup really is.

■ *One-line Register view:* If you want your Register to be more concise so that you can see more transactions at once, you can use Quicken's new Register View option that compresses unselected transactions into one line instead of two. See Chapter 4, "Using the Register," to see how this option works.

■ *Vertical adjustments for laser checks:* With Quicken 6.0, you can line up your laser checks precisely with the new vertical adjustment feature. Chapter 6, "Writing and Printing Checks," shows you how to use this new feature.

■ *Interactive supplies order forms:* New on-screen order forms display catalog menus so that you can complete the order form in a few seconds. And if you decide to pay for your order by check, Quicken even offers to write the check for you. See Chapter 1, "Preparing To Use Quicken," to learn how to complete the supplies order form.

When To Use Quicken

Answering the question *When should I use Quicken?* depends on whether you are using the program for personal or small-business purposes. If you are considering Quicken for personal use, four factors indicate that Quicken represents a good investment of your time and money:

- When check-writing and checking-account recordkeeping take more time than you want to spend. Quicken does most of the work related to keeping your checkbook: recording transactions, writing checks, reconciling account balances, and maintaining the check register. Because Quicken does the work for you, the program saves you a tremendous amount of time.

- When you need to track your tax deductions carefully. Quicken tracks the amounts you spend on tax-deductible items. At the end of the year, totaling your charitable contribution deductions is as simple as printing a report.

- When you want to budget income and expense amounts and compare what you earn and spend with what you budgeted. Budgets, contrary to their reputation, are not equivalent to financial handcuffs that prevent you from enjoying life. Budgets are tools that enable you to identify your financial priorities. They help you monitor your progress in organizing your financial life so that you can meet your financial objectives. Quicken makes budgeting easy.

- When you want to monitor and track personal assets (such as investments) and personal liabilities (such as your mortgages and credit card debt).

If you are considering Quicken for business, three factors indicate that Quicken represents a good investment of your time and money and a reasonable accounting alternative:

- You do not need or want to use a small-business accounting package that requires double-entry bookkeeping. Bookkeeping for a small business should involve double-entry accounting to accurately record the activity of the business, however. Packages such as DacEasy, Peachtree, and others require that you use double-entry bookkeeping. Although this procedure is a powerful and valuable tool, if you are not familiar with double-entry bookkeeping, you probably can spend your time better in ways other than learning accounting methods. Quicken provides a single-entry, easy-to-use accounting system. Quicken's category and transfer accounts provide an easy way to meet this requirement without the added difficulty of entering transactions in journals and then posting transactions to a general ledger.

■ You do not need a fancy billing and accounts receivable system. Quicken enables you to perform recordkeeping for accounts receivable. If you have fewer than two dozen transactions a month, Quicken provides a satisfactory solution. If your transaction volume exceeds this amount, however, you may want to consider a full-fledged accounts receivable package that prepares invoices, calculates finance charges, and easily handles high volumes of customer invoices and payments. You may want to use QuickBooks, Intuit's new software for small businesses.

■ You do not need an automated inventory recordkeeping system. Although Quicken enables you to track other assets, such as inventory, the program does not enable you to track the number of units of these other assets—only the dollars. With inventory, however, you not only need to know the dollar value of inventory, you need to know the number of units of inventory. Suppose that you sell snow skis. You need to know how many pairs of skis you have as well as the dollar value of your ski inventory.

What This Book Contains

Using Quicken 6 for DOS is divided into 5 parts and 22 chapters. If you read the book from cover to cover, you may notice a little repetition in some places; repetition is inevitable because the book also serves as a reference.

Part I, "Learning Quicken," includes eight chapters that, as the title implies, help you learn the basics of Quicken so that you can perform most tasks.

Chapter 1, "Preparing To Use Quicken," guides you through the steps you need to take before you start using Quicken, including ordering any preprinted forms you will need, learning to use the system, choosing a starting date, and setting up Quicken to work with your printer. Chapter 1 describes each of these steps in detail.

Chapter 2, "Getting Around in Quicken," gives you a quick introduction to the mechanics of actually working with the program. You learn how to start the program, select menu options, tap Quicken's on-line help feature, use the built-in calculator, and learn about the new calendar feature. If you already have started using Quicken, you may want to skim this material.

Chapter 3, "Defining Your Accounts," walks you through the steps to set up your second and subsequent bank accounts. The chapter also describes a few basic concepts you need to know from the start if you will be using Quicken for more than just a single bank account.

Chapter 4, "Using the Register," explains the steps for using Quicken's fundamental feature: its Register. The chapter doesn't assume that you know anything about Quicken. Rather, you read a complete explanation of what the Register is, what information it contains, and how you use it. If you're a new user of Quicken or think you can use a little help with the basics, you'll get a lot out of this chapter.

Chapter 5, "Automating the Register," describes some of the special menu options, which, although not essential, can make the Quicken Register easier to use. When you're comfortable with the information covered in Chapter 4, spend some time in Chapter 5. Your time investment should pay rich dividends.

Chapter 6, "Writing and Printing Checks," describes one of Quicken's core features—the capability to print checks. The chapter includes instructions for completing the Write Checks screen, where you provide the information Quicken needs to print a check. You also learn how to record, review, edit, and print checks. Not everyone wants or needs to use Quicken to print checks, but if you do, Chapter 6 is the place to start after you understand the Quicken Register.

Chapter 7, "Automating Check Writing," describes how to use the special menu options available on the Write Checks screen to speed up the check-writing process. Although the information in Chapter 7 is not essential to writing checks, it will make writing and printing checks even faster.

Chapter 8, "Reconciling Your Bank Account," discusses one of the important steps you can take to protect your cash and the accuracy and reliability of your financial records. This chapter first reviews the reconciliation process in general terms and then describes the steps for reconciling your accounts in Quicken, correcting and catching errors, and printing and using the reconciliation reports that Quicken creates.

Part II, "Getting the Most from Quicken," shows you how to use Quicken to its maximum potential.

Chapter 9, "Organizing Your Finances," discusses one of Quicken's optional and most powerful features—the capability to categorize and classify your income and expenses. The categories make it easy to determine tax deductions, the amounts spent for various items, and the types of income that go into your bank accounts. The classes also enable you to look at specific groups of categories, such as expenses relating to specific clients, jobs, or properties. Chapter 9 defines Quicken's categories and classes, describes why and when you should use them, shows the predefined categories provided within Quicken, and explains how to use these categories. The chapter also outlines the steps for adding, deleting, and modifying your own categories and classes.

Chapter 10, "Tracking Your Net Worth, Other Assets, and Liabilities," describes some of the special features that Quicken Version 6.0 provides for personal use. You can track cash and other assets (such as real estate), as well as liabilities (such as a mortgage). Chapter 10 also describes how to use the loan calculator and Quicken 6.0's new features to amortize variable rate loans and loans that you have made prepayments on.

Chapter 11, "Managing Your Credit Cards," explains how to use Quicken's Credit Card Register to record credit card purchases and payments and reconcile your account against your credit card statements. And if you have a Quicken VISA card, Chapter 11 will show you how to set up an IntelliCharge account so that you can receive your credit card statements on disk or by modem.

Chapter 12, "Creating and Printing Reports," shows you how to sort, extract, and summarize the information contained in the Quicken Registers by using the Reports menu options. Quicken's reports enable you to gain better control over and insight into your income, expenses, and cash flow.

Chapter 13, "Paying Bills Electronically," describes how you can use Quicken to pay your bills electronically by using the CheckFree service. Electronic payment isn't for everybody, but if you're a Quicken user, you should at least know what's involved and whether it makes sense for you. Chapter 13 gives you this information.

Chapter 14, "Using Quicken To Prepare for Income Taxes," is a short chapter, but an important one. This chapter tells you how to make sure that the financial records you create with Quicken provide the information you will need to prepare your federal and state income tax returns. The chapter also briefly discusses the general mechanics of passing data between Quicken and an income tax preparation package, such as TurboTax.

Part III, "Analyzing Your Finances with Quicken," shows you how to use Quicken beyond the basics to help you analyze your finances through budgeting, monitoring investments, graphing financial results, and financial planning.

Chapter 15, "Budgeting with Quicken," discusses one of Quicken's most significant benefits—budgeting and monitoring your success in following a budget. This chapter reviews the steps for budgeting, describes how Quicken helps with budgeting, and provides some tips on how to budget more successfully. If you are not comfortable with the budgeting process, Chapter 15 should give you enough information to get started. If you find budgeting an unpleasant exercise, the chapter also provides some tips on making budgeting a more positive experience.

Chapter 16, "Monitoring Your Investments," describes the Investment Register feature that Quicken provides for investors. If you want to monitor your investments better, read through Chapter 16 to see the tools and options that Quicken provides specifically for managing investments.

Chapter 17, "Creating Graphs," describes the new Quicken 6.0 graph feature. If you want to see relationships between your income and expenses, assets and liabilities, actual and budget amounts, and investment portfolios, read Chapter 17 to learn about the various graphs that you can create on-screen.

Chapter 18, "Financial Planning with Quicken," explains how to use Quicken 6.0's new financial calculators: the investment planning calculator, the retirement planning calculator, the college planning calculator, and the refinance calculator. Quicken's financial calculators help you play out *what-if* scenarios to quickly see results.

Part IV, "Managing Quicken," shows you how to manage your Quicken files and customize the Quicken program.

Chapter 19, "Managing Your Quicken Files," describes how to take care of the files that Quicken uses to store your financial records. Chapter 19 describes how to back up and restore your Quicken files, how to make copies of the files, and how to purge from the files information you no longer need.

Chapter 20, "Customizing Quicken," describes the two ways you can customize, or fine-tune, Quicken's operation. One way is to use the commands under the main menu option **Set Preferences**. The other way is to start Quicken with parameters. This chapter describes both approaches.

Part V, "Putting Quicken To Use," moves away from the mechanics of using Quicken's features and talks about how to use Quicken as a financial-management tool.

Chapter 21, "Using Quicken for Home Finances," discusses how you can use Quicken for personal financial recordkeeping. Using any software, and particularly a financial-management program, is more than mechanics. This chapter answers questions about where Quicken fits in for home users, how Quicken changes the way you keep your personal financial records, and when you should use Quicken options.

Chapter 22, "Using Quicken in Your Business," covers some of the special techniques and procedures for using Quicken in business accounting. This chapter begins by discussing the overall approach to using Quicken in a business. Next, the following six basic accounting tasks are detailed: tracking receivables, tracking payables, tracking inventory, accounting for fixed assets, preparing payroll, and job costing.

Using Quicken 6 for DOS also provides two appendixes.

Appendix A, "Installing Quicken," discusses the hardware and software requirements to use Quicken and shows you how to install the Quicken program on your hard disk.

Appendix B, "Using QuickPay with Quicken," briefly describes the QuickPay payroll utility, how the utility works, and when it is an appropriate business solution. If you're preparing payroll by using Quicken, review this appendix to learn whether you should acquire the QuickPay program.

P A R T

I

Learning Quicken

O U T L I N E

Preparing To Use Quicken

Preparing to use Quicken is not difficult. If you are new to computers, however, a little hand-holding and emotional support never hurts. Chapter 1 walks you through the steps for preparing to use Quicken. Don't worry that you may not know enough about computers, Quicken, or computer-based accounting systems. Simply follow the instructions and steps described in this chapter.

In this chapter, you learn how to do the following:

- Choose a conversion date (the best date to start using Quicken to automate your finances)

- Start Quicken 6.0 for the first time and set up your Quicken system

- Set up Quicken to print to your printer

- Order check and other supplies from Intuit

Choosing a Conversion Date

Choosing a conversion date is another critical decision you must make before you can enjoy the advantages of an automated accounting system. The *conversion date* is the day on which you stop using your old manual system and begin using your new Quicken system. The less frequently you expect to use Quicken, the less important is the conversion date.

If you intend to use Quicken to organize your income tax deductions, calculate business profits, or plan budgets, designate a clean accounting cutoff point for the date you begin keeping records with Quicken. From the conversion date forward, Quicken handles all your accounting information. Before the conversion date, your old accounting system still provides your accounting information. Pick a natural cutoff date that makes switching from one system to another easy. Often the best time to begin a new accounting system is at the beginning of the year. All income and expense transactions for the new year then are recorded in the same place. Picking a good cutoff date may seem trivial, but having all your tax deductions for one year recorded and summarized in one place can save you much time and effort.

If you cannot start using Quicken at the beginning of the year, the next best time is at the beginning of a month. If you do start at the beginning of a month, you must combine your old accounting or recordkeeping information with Quicken's information to get totals for the year. When calculating tax deductions, for example, you must add the amounts Quicken shows to whatever your old system shows.

C P A
T I P   If you use data from both your manual system and your Quicken system to complete your income tax return, make sure that you keep adequate worksheets and documentation for any items you deduct. If audited, you want your documentation to show clearly that you added amounts from your manual system to your Quicken system to arrive at your deductions.

To start using Quicken at the beginning of the month, first take time to summarize your accounting information from the old system. Make sure that you don't record the same transaction (income received or an expense paid) twice or forget any altogether.

> **CAUTION:** Two common errors are possible after you choose an accounting cutoff date: You may record the same income or expense transaction in both systems and therefore count the transaction twice when you combine the two systems to get your annual totals. Or, you may neglect to record a transaction in one system because you think that you recorded it in the other system. Your records will be wrong if you make either error.

The worst time to begin using Quicken is in the middle of a month. With no natural cutoff point, you are even more likely than at the beginning of a month to count some transactions on both systems and to forget to record others in either system.

Perhaps you don't intend to use Quicken to summarize income and expense transactions or to monitor how closely you are sticking to a budget; all you really want is a tool to help you maintain your checkbook and produce checks. If so, the conversion date isn't so important.

Starting Quicken 6.0 the First Time

To start Quicken, press the letter Q at the DOS prompt. The first time you start Quicken, the program displays the Welcome to Quicken 6.0 screen (see fig. 1.1). This screen gives you the following choices for starting Quicken:

- Read the brief 10-minute overview.

- Create your own Quicken data file.

Select one of these first-time setup options by typing the number listed in front of the option. To select the **See an overview of Quicken** option, for example, press 1 and then press Enter. If you decide that you don't want an option you have selected, press Esc to halt the option. Press Esc again to display the Quicken main menu (see fig. 1.2).

The overview simply explains what Quicken is and shows you how the program works. If you're a new user of Quicken, take the time to go through the overview, which is a series of sample Quicken windows with explanations. If you want to stop the overview after it starts, press Esc twice. Quicken displays its main menu. Quicken also displays its main menu after you complete the overview.

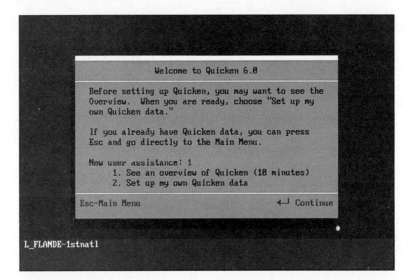

FIG. 1.1

The Welcome to Quicken 6.0 screen.

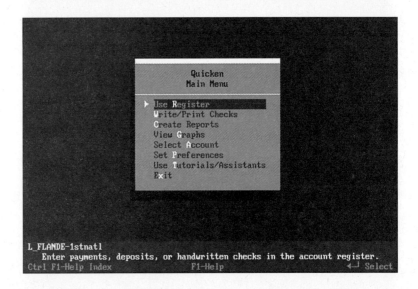

FIG. 1.2

The Quicken main menu.

The **Set up my own Quicken data** option explains the way Quicken organizes your financial records, accounts, and categories. Creating your own Quicken data tests your new knowledge. This option walks you through the steps for setting up a file for keeping your financial records with Quicken.

Describing these new-user options in detail here would be like describing how to use an on-line tutorial that describes how to use Quicken. Be sure to experiment with these tools, however. New users of Quicken may find them particularly helpful.

Setting Up Your Quicken System

You already may have set up your financial records if you selected the second option from the Welcome to Quicken 6.0 screen. If so, you can skip this entire section. If you haven't, you must set up the file, accounts, and categories you need to store and organize your financial records.

If you're new to Quicken, you can set up your records in one of two ways: by using a Quicken assistant or by using the **Select/Set Up File** command. If you have been using an earlier version of Quicken, you simply can convert your old Quicken data files. The sections that follow describe the steps for performing each task.

 You can use a mouse to select menu options and perform operations in Quicken 6.0. Using a mouse is explained in Chapter 2, "Getting Around in Quicken."

Setup for New Quicken Users

New users of Quicken have a choice of two methods for creating a data file in which to store financial records: a Quicken assistant called the File Assistant and the **Select/Set Up File** command. The File Assistant takes a tutorial approach to help you set up a file, an account, and the categories you want to use within that file. Based on information you enter in the initial assistant windows, Quicken sets up your file, account, and categories for you. Quicken requires more effort on your part when you use the **Select/Set Up File** command to create a data file.

The following steps describe how to set up a new file using the File Assistant:

1. From the Quicken main menu, select the **Use Tutorials/Assistants** command by pressing the letter T. Quicken displays the Use Tutorials/Assistants menu (see fig. 1.3).

2. Select the **Create New File** command from the Use Tutorials/ Assistants menu by pressing the letter F. Quicken displays the Create New File Assistant window (see fig. 1.4).

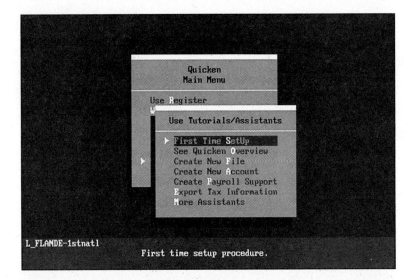

FIG. 1.3

The Use Tutorials/Assistants menu.

FIG. 1.4

The Create New File Assistant window.

NOTE   The Use Tutorials/Assistant menu also gives you access to the first-time setup options described previously in this section. To display the Welcome to Quicken 6.0 screen, select the **First Time Setup** command by pressing the letter S. To start the 10-minute overview without displaying the Welcome to Quicken 6.0 screen, select the **See Quicken Overview** command by pressing the letter O.

3. Press Enter to continue past the Create New File Assistant window. Quicken displays the Set Up an Account window (see fig. 1.5). You must enter specific information about the account you want to set up before you enter information to create the new file. Quicken accounts are similar to the accounts used in your finances, such as bank accounts, credit card accounts, and cash accounts. You learn more about accounts in Chapter 3, "Defining Your Accounts."

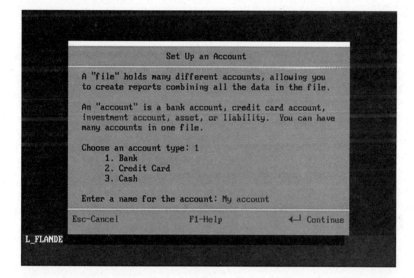

FIG. 1.5

The Set Up an
Account window.

The Set Up an Account window provides two fields that you must fill with information: an account name and an account type.

4. In the Choose an Account Type field, indicate whether the account is a bank account, a credit card account, or a cash account. If you are setting up a bank account, the account type is 1. Bank accounts are used to record transactions in a checking account or another type of account where you deposit and withdraw funds. Press Enter to move to the Enter a Name for the Account field.

5. Enter a description of the account in the Enter a Name for the Account field. The description can be up to 15 characters long and can use any characters except the following:

   [ ] / :

You can use spaces, too.

C P A
T I P

In describing your bank account, you may want to abbreviate the bank name and use the last four digits of the account number in order to distinguish among various accounts at the same bank. Standard Bank of Washington, account 9173526471, for example, becomes StdWash 6471. Standard Bank of Oregon, account 7386427389, becomes StdOre 7389. Standard Bank of Washington, account 9173533721, becomes StdWash 3721. This procedure enables you to separate different accounts at the same bank.

6. After you enter the account name and type, press Enter to display the Account Balance and Date window, shown in figure 1.6. Enter the starting account balance in the Balance field. If you are creating a bank account file, this amount is your current account balance according to your bank statement. You must enter a balance, even if it is 0.

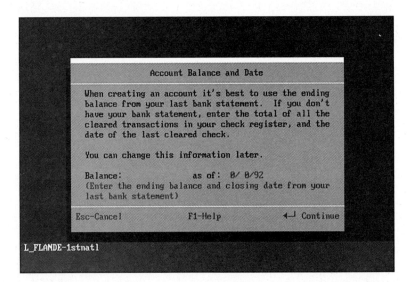

FIG. 1.6

The Account Balance and Date window.

CAUTION: When you enter the ending balance from your last bank statement as the starting balance in your bank account, you must include all uncleared transactions. In other words, you must include all transactions that have not cleared through your bank account by the current date (the date you start Quicken). If you overlook these transactions, you will have difficulty reconciling your account. You learn how to enter transactions in Chapter 4, "Using the Register."

7. Enter the date in the As Of field. The *as of* date is the day on which the balance you entered is correct. If you use the ending balance from your last bank statement, enter the bank statement date in the As Of field.

> **NOTE** You'll notice that in the Account Balance and Date window shown in figure 1.6, Quicken tells you to enter the total of all the cleared transactions in your check register if you don't have your latest bank statement. This may sound confusing. What Quicken means here is that you should go back in your checkbook register to the last check cleared through the bank. Enter that balance in the Balance field. Then enter the date of the last cleared check in the As Of field.

8. When you finish entering information for the Account Balance and Date window, press Enter.

   Quicken now displays the File Assistant window, shown in figure 1.7. The File Assistant window identifies the account type, the account name, the account balance, and the as of date.

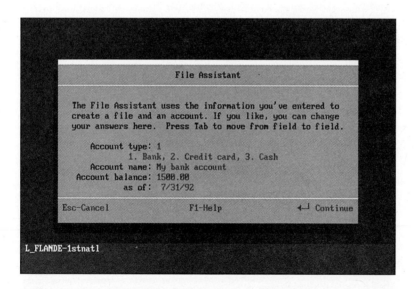

FIG. 1.7

The File Assistant window.

9. If any of the information displayed in the File Assistant window is incorrect, press the Tab key to move the cursor to the field you want to correct. Then replace the incorrect information by typing the correct entry.

10. When the information in the File Assistant window is correct, press Enter if the cursor is positioned in the last field (the As Of field) or press Ctrl-Enter or F10 if the cursor is positioned in any other field.

You haven't actually created a file yet. Rather, you have collected the information necessary for creating your first account in the Quicken file that you are about to create. Quicken now displays the File Assistant Note window, shown in figure 1.8. In the screens that follow, you are prompted for the information that Quicken needs to create a new file.

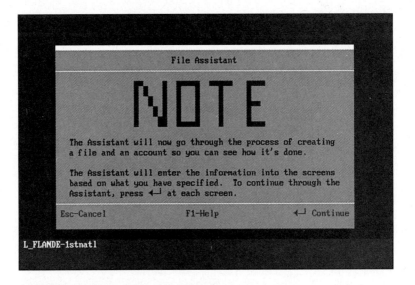

FIG. 1.8

The File Assistant Note window.

Follow these steps to create the new file:

1. From the File Assistant Note window, press Enter. Press Enter at each on-screen message until the Set Up New File window appears, as shown in figure 1.9.

   Quicken creates an eight-character name for the DOS file in which it stores your financial records. This name is based on the user name you gave during installation. As shown in figure 1.9, the author entered her name as *L FLANDERS*, so Quicken created a default file named *L_FLANDE*—a shortened version of her name.

2. If you want, type a different file name. Whatever you enter here, however, must be a valid DOS file name. If you are unsure about DOS file-naming conventions, see your DOS user's manual.

3. When the file name is correct, press Enter to move the cursor to the Location for File field.

By default, Quicken stores the file in the Quicken program directory—QUICKEN, unless you specified a different directory name when you installed the program.

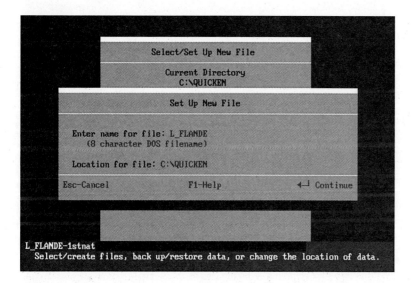

```
                  Select/Set Up New File

                    Current Directory
                      C:\QUICKEN

                    Set Up New File


  Enter name for file: L_FLANDE
        (8 character DOS filename)

  Location for file: C:\QUICKEN

  Esc-Cancel              F1-Help           ◄┘ Continue



  L_FLANDE-1stnat
    Select/create files, back up/restore data, or change the location of data.
```

The Set Up New
File window.

4. If you want, specify another directory in which to locate the new file by typing the complete path name of the desired directory. If you're unsure how to specify path names, see your DOS user's manual.

   If you're a new computer user, don't worry about specifying some other file name or directory. The defaults work fine.

5. When the new file's location is correctly specified, press Enter. Press Enter again at the on-screen message that follows, which tells you to select categories. Quicken displays the Standard Categories window (see fig. 1.10).

Now you must decide whether to use the standard categories defined by Quicken or to define your own categories. A *category* describes and summarizes common business and personal income and expenses— such as salary, insurance, utilities, and so on. Categories group your income and expenses so that Quicken can classify your transactions for reporting, budgeting, and income tax purposes. In simple terms, categories describe where your money comes from and where it goes. (Chapter 9, "Organizing Your Finances," describes Quicken's categories in more detail.)

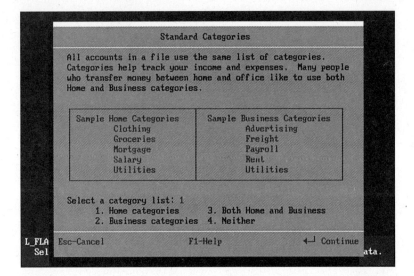

FIG. 1.10

The Standard
Categories
window.

Quicken includes two predefined sets of categories: Home and Business. If you want to use Quicken's categories, you can tell Quicken to use one of or both the predefined category lists.

> **CAUTION:** Now is the only time that you can choose to use one of the predefined category lists. After your data file is created, you cannot go back and select or change to another of these category lists. Be sure to select the category list that works best for you. If you plan to use Quicken in your business, make certain that you select Business categories instead of Home categories so that you don't need to completely modify the list to make it appropriate for business use.

6. Press 1 if you want to use Quicken's Home categories. Press 2 if you want to use Quicken's Business categories. If you want to use both, press 3. If you don't want to use either category, press 4 to select neither. When you select neither of the standard category lists, you must create your own list if you plan to use categories to classify your transactions in Quicken. Chapter 9, "Organizing Your Finances," explains how to add categories.

7. After you select the categories you want to use, press Enter. The File Assistant is ready to create the file.

To direct the File Assistant to create the account for your file, press Enter. Quicken's File Assistant then executes the Quicken commands that create the account according to the information the program has collected. Simultaneously, the File Assistant explains each step it performs and prompts you to press Enter to continue. When the File Assistant finishes creating the new account, the program returns you to Quicken's main menu.

After you create a file and your first account with the File Assistant, you may not need as much help the next time you set up a file. Instead, you can use the **Select/Set Up File** command. To set up a new file using this command, follow these steps:

1. From the Quicken main menu, select the **Set Preferences** command by pressing the letter P. Quicken displays the Set Preferences menu (see fig. 1.11).

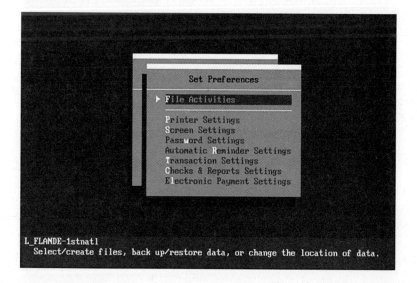

FIG. 1.11

The Set Preferences menu.

2. Select the **File Activities** command from the Set Preferences menu by pressing the letter F. Quicken displays the File Activities menu (see fig. 1.12).

3. Select the **Select/Set Up File** command by pressing the letter S. Quicken displays the Select/Set Up New File window (see fig. 1.13).

4. Use the up- and down-arrow keys to highlight the <Set Up New File> line in the window. Then press Enter. Quicken displays the Set Up New File window shown in figure 1.14.

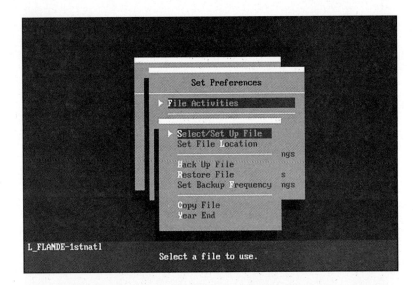

FIG. 1.12

The File Activities
menu.

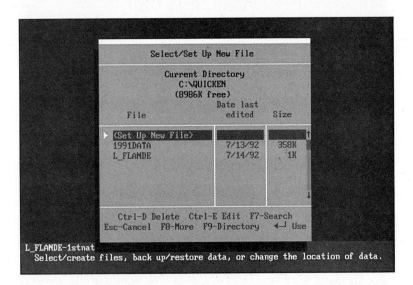

FIG. 1.13

The Select/Set
Up New File
window.

5. In the Enter Name for File field, enter the name you want for your
   financial records file. This name must be a valid DOS file name.
   Refer to your DOS user's manual if you have questions about DOS
   file-naming conventions.

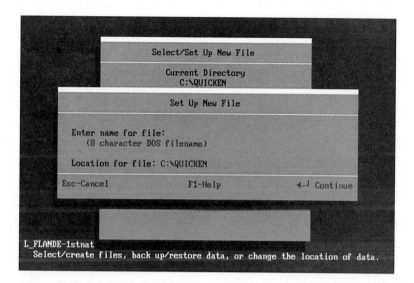

FIG. 1.14

The Set Up New File window.

6. When the file name is correct, press Enter or Tab to move the cursor to the Location for File field. By default, Quicken stores data files in the Quicken program directory. If you want the file stored in a different directory, enter that directory and path name.

7. When the file location is correct, press Enter. Quicken displays the Standard Categories window (see fig. 1.15).

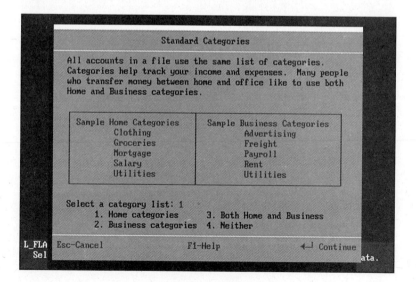

FIG. 1.15

The Standard Categories window.

8. Press 1 if you want to use Quicken's Home categories. Press 2 if you want to use Quicken's Business categories. If you want to use both, press 3. If you don't want to use either category, press 4. When you select neither of the standard category lists, you must create your own list if you plan to use categories to classify your transactions in Quicken. Chapter 9, "Organizing Your Finances," explains how to add categories.

9. When you have identified the categories you want, press Enter. Quicken redisplays the Select/Set Up New File window.

10. Use the arrow keys to highlight the new file that you just created. Then press Enter. Quicken displays the Set Up New Account window superimposed over the Select Account to Use window (see fig. 1.16).

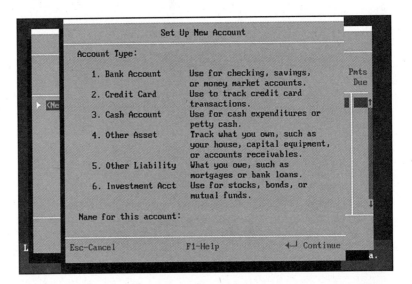

FIG. 1.16

The Set Up New Account window.

11. In the Account Type field, indicate whether the account is a bank account, credit card account, cash account, other asset account, other liability account, or an investment account by pressing the number listed for the account type you want to set up. (See Chapter 3, "Defining Your Accounts," for more information about these account types.) To set up a bank account, for example, press 1. Press Enter to move to the Name for This Account field.

12. Enter a description of the account in the Name for This Account field. The description can be up to 15 characters long and can use any characters except the following:

[ ] / :

You can use spaces, too. Press Enter to display the Starting Balance and Description window, shown in figure 1.17.

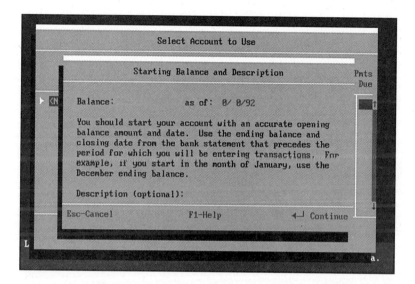

FIG. 1.17

The Starting Balance and Description window.

13. Enter the starting account balance. If you are creating a bank account file, this amount is your current account balance according to your records. For best results, use the ending balance from your last bank statement as the starting account balance. You must enter a balance, even if it is 0.

CAUTION: When you enter the ending balance from your last bank statement as the starting balance in your bank account, you must enter all uncleared transactions in the Bank Account Register. In other words, you must include all transactions that have not cleared through your bank account by the current date (the date you start using Quicken). If you overlook these transactions, you will have difficulty reconciling your account. You learn how to enter transactions in Chapter 4, "Using the Register."

14. Enter the date in the As Of field. The *as of date* is the day on which the balance you entered is correct. If you use the ending balance from your last bank statement, enter the statement date in the As Of field.

15. (Optional) Fill in the Description field to provide an additional 21 characters of account description.

16. After you enter information for the Starting Balance and Description window, press Enter. If you are setting up a bank account, Quicken displays the Source of Starting Balance window (see fig. 1.18). If you are setting up a credit card account, Quicken displays the Specify Credit Limit window so that you can enter your current credit limit for the account you set up. If you are setting up any other type of account, Quicken adds the account and goes to the Select Account to Use window, as shown in figure 1.19. Notice that the account you added now is listed in the Select Account to Use window.

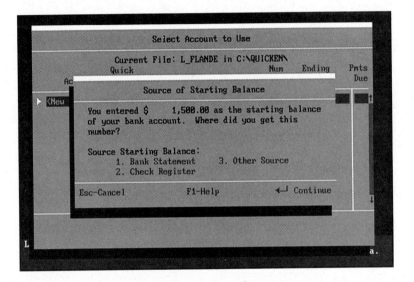

FIG. 1.18

The Source of
Starting Balance
window.

17. At the Source of Starting Balance window, tell Quicken from which source you determined your bank account's starting balance. Press the number that matches that of the source for the starting balance: 1 for **Bank Statement**, 2 for **Check Register**, or 3 for **Other Source**. Press Enter.

Quicken recommends that you use the ending balance from your latest bank statement as the starting balance and the statement cutoff date for the *as of* date. Quicken asks whether you want to change your starting balance if you selected **Check Register** or **Other Source** as the source for your starting balance. Press Y if you want to go back and change your starting balance. Press N if you don't want to change your balance. If you entered the starting balance from your bank statement, Quicken congratulates you with an on-screen message for having made the right decision. Press Enter from the congratulatory message to go to the Select

Account to Use window, where you can choose the bank account that you just created to start work in. Chapter 3, "Defining Your Accounts," tells you how to choose the account that you want to work in.

18. Press Esc three times to return to the Quicken main menu.

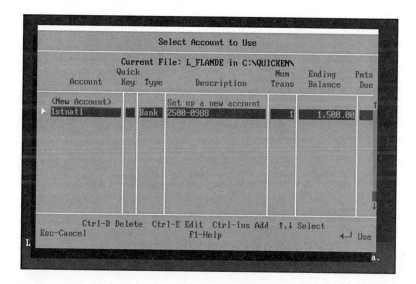

FIG. 1.19

The Select Account to Use window.

Setup for Current Quicken Users

If you have been using Quicken 5.0, your existing files are automatically updated when you install Quicken 6.0. Quicken 6.0 searches your QUICKEN5 directory (the directory where you installed Quicken 5.0) and converts those data files to the Quicken 6.0 format. Your Quicken 5.0 data files then are moved from the QUICKEN5 directory to the QUICKEN directory (the directory where you installed Quicken 6.0).

If you changed the location of your Quicken 5.0 data files to a directory other than QUICKEN5, Quicken will not be able to locate your Quicken 5.0 data files. To convert those data files to Quicken 6.0, you must update files as explained in the following procedure for Quicken 3.0 or Quicken 4.0 files.

If you have been using Quicken 3.0 or 4.0, you can update your existing data and use it to create your Quicken 6.0 data file.

NOTE You can update your Quicken 1.0 or 2.0 data also, but you need a special file-conversion utility from Intuit. Contact Intuit's customer service department and request the Quicken 2.0 Copy and Update utility.

To update a Quicken 3.0 or 4.0 file for use with Quicken 6.0, follow these steps:

1. Select the **Set Preferences** command from the Quicken main menu by pressing the letter P. Quicken displays the Set Preferences menu.

2. Select the **File Activities** command by pressing the letter F. Quicken displays the File Activities menu.

3. Choose the **Select/Set Up File** command by pressing the letter S. Quicken displays the Select/Set Up New File window.

4. If the Quicken 3.0 or 4.0 file isn't shown on the Select/Set Up New File window, press F9. Quicken displays the Set File Location window (see fig. 1.20).

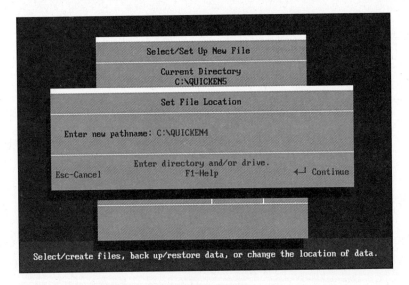

FIG. 1.20

The Set File Location window.

Enter the path for the Quicken 3.0 or 4.0 file in the Set File Location window. Suppose that the Quicken 4.0 file you want to convert to a Quicken 6.0 file is stored in the QUICKEN4 directory on the C drive. Type *quicken4* in the Enter New Pathname field and press Enter. Quicken redisplays the Select/Set Up New File window and lists the Quicken files in the specified directory.

5. Use the arrow keys to highlight the Quicken 3.0 or 4.0 file you want to convert to a Quicken 6.0 file. Press Enter. Quicken displays the message window shown in figure 1.21.

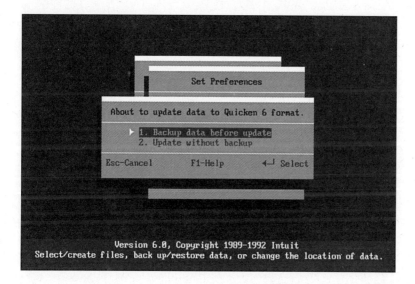

FIG. 1.21

The About To Update Data To Quicken 6 format message window.

6. Press 1 to back up data before the update if you want to keep a backup copy of your Quicken 3.0 or 4.0 data file before converting it to Quicken 6.0.

7. Quicken displays the Select Backup Drive window, shown in figure 1.22. You need to specify the drive to which you want Quicken to back up your Quicken 3.0 or 4.0 data file.

8. Insert your backup disk and type the appropriate drive letter. Press Enter to back up your Quicken 3.0 or 4.0 data file.

If you select option 2 at the About To Update Data To Quicken 6 Format window (**Update without backup**), Quicken displays a warning message stating that you won't be able to use your data file in Quicken 3.0 or 4.0 after it is updated to Quicken 6.0. If you're sure that you want to update your Quicken 3.0 or 4.0 data file without backing it up, type *yes* and press Enter. If you want to make a backup, press Esc to return to the message window shown in figure 1.21. Then select the **Backup data before update** option by pressing 1.

Quicken converts your Quicken 3.0 or 4.0 data file to Quicken 6.0 and displays the File Updated window shown in figure 1.23. Quicken tells you which categories weren't used in your Quicken 3.0 or 4.0 data file before the update procedure by placing an asterisk next to each unused category in the File Updated window. You learn about categories in Chapter 4, "Using the Register," and in more detail in Chapter 9, "Organizing Your Finances."

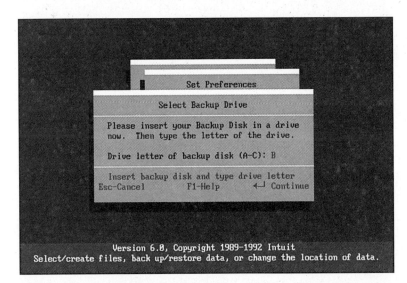

FIG. 1.22

The Select
Backup Drive
window.

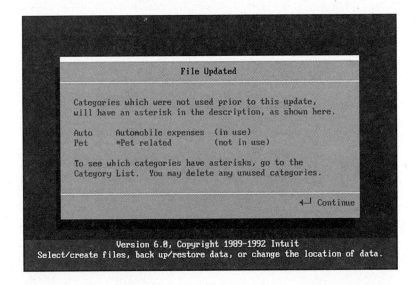

FIG. 1.23

The File Updated
window.

9. Press Enter. Quicken next displays the Select Account to Use window for the Quicken 3.0 or 4.0 file that you just updated. Use the up- and down-arrow keys to highlight the account you want to

use. Press Enter. Quicken displays the Register screen for the selected account. You now are ready to begin using your Quicken 3.0 or 4.0 data file in Quicken 6.0. Refer to Chapter 4, "Using the Register," to learn how to enter transactions in the Register.

Setting Your Printer

You want to be sure to set up Quicken for your printer before you go any further. If you identified your printer during installation, all you need to do is to describe how your computer and printer connect.

Specifying Printer Settings

To describe how your printer and computer connect, follow these steps:

1. Select the **Set Preferences** command from the main menu by pressing P. Quicken displays the Set Preferences menu.

2. Select the **Printer Settings** command from the Set Preferences menu by pressing P. Quicken displays the Printer Settings menu (see fig. 1.24).

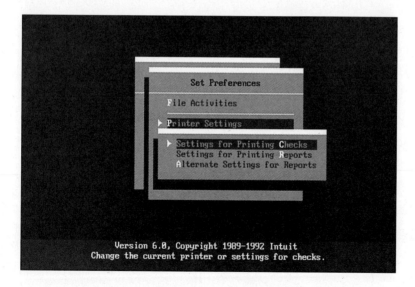

FIG. 1.24

The Printer Settings menu.

With Quicken, you can maintain three sets of printer configuration settings: one setting for printing checks, a primary setting for printing reports, and an alternate setting for printing reports.

3. Use the arrow keys to highlight the printer configuration setting you want to modify. Press Enter. If you select the **Settings for Printing Checks** option from figure 1.24, for example, Quicken displays the Check Printer Settings screen with the Select Check Printer window and Available Styles window overlaid on-screen (see fig. 1.25). If you select the **Settings for Printing Reports** or the **Alternate Settings for Reports** option from the Printer Settings menu, Quicken displays the appropriate windows to select report printing options.

Each printer configuration setting identifies the printer, describes the printer-to-computer connection, and controls how the printer operates.

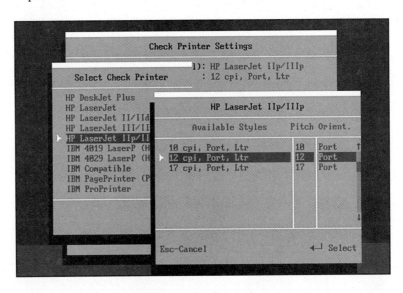

FIG. 1.25

The Check Printer Settings screen with the Select Check Printer and Available Styles windows overlaid.

4. Press Esc twice to remove the Select Check Printer and Available Styles windows. With these two windows gone, the full Check Printer Settings screen shows, as in figure 1.26.

5. Press the Tab or Enter key twice to move the cursor to the Print To field. This field tells Quicken which communications port to use to send checks and reports to the printer. The **PRN**, **LPT1**, **LPT2** and **LPT3** options refer to parallel ports. The **AUX**, **COM1**, and **COM2** options refer to serial ports.

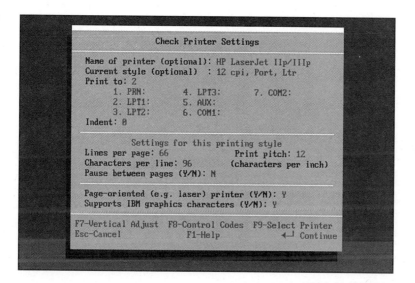

FIG. 1.26

The Check Printer
Settings screen.

6. Press the number that identifies the correct communications port. Press 1 to select **PRN**, for example. If you aren't sure which port your printer uses, follow the printer cable to the back of your computer. The socket the printer cable plugs into may be labeled.

T I P

If you can choose how your printer and computer communicate, choose a parallel port. Parallel connections enable the printer and computer to talk to each other at the same time—in parallel. This capability usually results in faster communication.

When you use a serial port, the computer can send information to the printer only when the printer is not sending information back to the computer and vice versa. With a serial port, your computer and printer take turns communicating with each other.

---

7. Save the printer settings by pressing Enter when the cursor is positioned in the Supports IBM Graphics Characters field. Or, press Ctrl-Enter or F10 when the cursor is positioned in any other field in the Check Printer Settings screen. Quicken redisplays the Set Preferences menu. Press Esc to return to the main menu.

If you selected an undefined printer, (None, Other Dot-Matrix, Other Laser, or Other PostScript from the Select Check or Report Printer window) you must follow these additional steps before saving your printer settings:

1. Type the name of the printer in the Name of Printer field.

2. Press Enter or Tab to move the cursor to the Print To field. Type the number that identifies the communications port that connects your printer and computer.

3. Press Enter or Tab to move the cursor to the Indent field. Use this field to tell Quicken how many characters from the left margin of the form or paper to begin printing.

   Each time Quicken begins printing a line, the copy starts that many characters to the right. Enter a number from 0 to 80, but be careful not to enter a number so large that Quicken doesn't have room to print. If you have a laser printer, you can use an indent setting equal to 0. If you own an impact printer, you can start with an indent setting equal to 0 also; you may need to increase this setting, however, if Quicken prints too close to the left side of your paper. If Quicken prints off the page on the right side of the paper, reduce your indent setting.

4. Press Enter or Tab to move to the Lines per Page field. Use this field to tell Quicken how many lines you want printed on a page. Quicken assumes that 6 lines equal an inch. If you use 11-inch paper, therefore, set this value to 66. If you use 14-inch paper, set this value to 84.

   To determine whether the Lines per Page setting is correct, compare where Quicken starts printing on successive pages. If the print doesn't start at the same distance from the top of each page, you must adjust the Lines per Page setting. The setting is too high if Quicken starts printing lower on the second page than on the first. The setting is too low if Quicken starts printing higher on the second page than on the first.

5. Press Enter or Tab to move to the Print Pitch field. Use this field to tell Quicken how many characters your printer prints per inch. Typical pitch, or characters per inch, settings are 10, 12, and 15. Check your printer manual to determine your printer's pitch. You also can use a ruler to measure the number of characters, including blank spaces, printed in 1 inch on a sample of the printer's output.

6. Press Enter or Tab to move to the Characters per Line field. Use this field to tell Quicken how many characters fit in a line. This setting usually equals 80 if your pitch setting is 10, or 96 if your pitch setting is 12.

7. Press Enter or Tab to move the cursor to the Pause between Pages field. Use this field to tell Quicken whether to stop after printing a full page so that you can insert a new piece of paper or adjust the printer. Press Y for Yes or N for No.

8. Press Enter or Tab to move to the Page-Oriented Printer field. To Quicken, printers that use individual sheets of paper are page-oriented, such as laser or inkjet printers. Use the Page-Oriented Printer field to tell Quicken whether your printer uses individual sheets of paper. Press Y for Yes or N for No.

9. Press Enter or Tab to move to the Supports IBM Graphics Characters field. Use this field to tell Quicken whether your printer supports the extended IBM character set. If this set is available on your printer, Quicken uses IBM graphics characters in the extended character set in headings on your reports. Press Y for Yes or N for No.

10. Press F8 to access the Printer Control Codes window. Figure 1.27 shows the Printer Control Codes window for setting print configurations for reports. The control codes vary, depending on whether you set the print configurations to print reports or checks. You use the Printer Control Codes window to enter the special sequences of letters, numbers, and other keyboard characters that instruct your printer to perform in a specific manner or print in a certain style, such as condensed print.

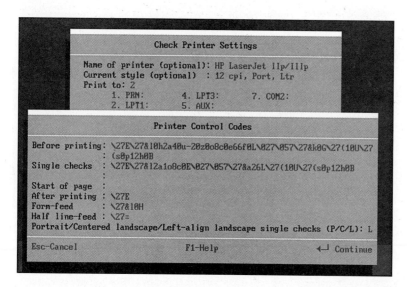

FIG. 1.27

The Printer Control Codes window for report print configurations.

To determine which printer control codes are appropriate for your printer, look them up in your printer manual. Type the control code Quicken must initially send to your printer in the Before Printing field. Press Enter or Tab to move the cursor to the Start of Page field, and type the control code Quicken must send to your printer as it starts a new page.

11. Press Enter or Tab to move the cursor to the After Printing field, and type the control code Quicken must send to your printer when it finishes printing. Press Enter or Tab to move the cursor to the Form-Feed field, and type the control code Quicken must send to advance your printer to the top of the next page. Press Enter or Tab to move the cursor to the Half Line-Feed field, and type the control code Quicken must send to advance your printer one line.

The last field on the Printer Control Codes window for printing checks tells Quicken how you feed single check forms through your printer (see fig. 1.28). Press P to feed the check form through the printer in normal portrait fashion. Press C to feed the check form through the printer in centered landscape fashion. Press L to feed the check form through the printer in left-aligned landscape fashion.

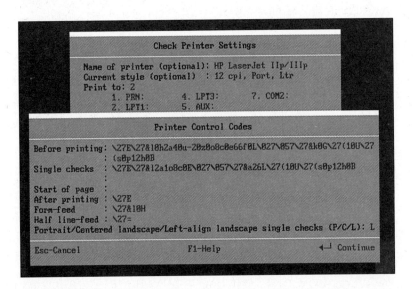

FIG. 1.28

The Printer Control Codes window for check print configurations.

12. Press Ctrl-Enter or F10 to return to the Check or Report Printer Settings screen.

13. To save the printer settings, press Enter when the cursor is positioned in the Supports IBM Graphics Characters field in the Check Printer Settings screen. Or, press Ctrl-Enter or F10 when the cursor is positioned in any other field. Quicken redisplays the Set Preferences menu. Press Esc to return to the main menu.

Identifying a New Printer

If you connect a different printer to your computer after the initial installation, you must identify the new printer. Follow these steps to identify your new printer to Quicken:

1. Select the **Set Preferences** command from the main menu by
   pressing the letter P. Quicken displays the Set Preferences menu.

2. Select the **Printer Settings** command from the Set Preferences
   menu by pressing the letter P. Quicken displays the Printer Settings menu.

   With Quicken, you can maintain three sets of printer configuration
   settings: one setting for printing checks, a primary setting for
   printing reports, and an alternate setting for printing reports.

3. Use the arrow keys to highlight the printer configuration setting
   you want to modify. Then press Enter.

   If you select the Settings for Printing Checks configuration from
   the Printer Settings menu, for example, Quicken displays the
   Check Printer Settings screen with the Select Check Printer window and Available Styles window overlaid on-screen.

4. Press Esc once so that just the Select Check Printer window is
   displayed (see fig. 1.29).

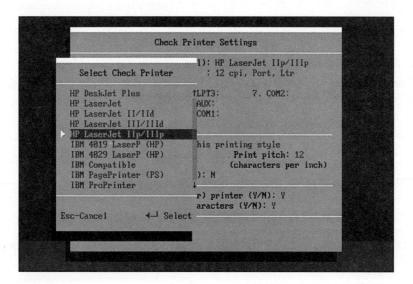

FIG. 1.29

The Check
Printer Settings
screen with the
Select Check
Printer window
displayed.

5. Use the arrow keys to highlight your printer, or type the first letter of your printer name to move quickly to the first printer name that starts with the same letter. Then use the down-arrow key to highlight your printer. Press Enter. Quicken displays the Available Style window.

6. Use the arrow keys to highlight the print style, pitch, and page orientation you want. If your printer has a variety of *fonts* (character sets), *pitches* (number of characters per inch horizontally), and *orientations* (direction in which text is printed on paper), highlight the exact style you want from the choices listed in the Print Style window. Press Enter to select that style. Quicken displays the Check Print Settings screen without the Select Printer and Available Style windows.

7. To save the printer settings, press Enter when the cursor is positioned in the Supports IBM Graphics Characters field, or press Ctrl-Enter or F10 when the cursor is positioned in any other field in the Check Printer Settings screen. Quicken redisplays the Set Preferences menu. Press Esc to return to the main menu.

Ordering Check Forms and Other Supplies

You don't need to print your checks with Quicken in order to benefit from the program, but Quicken's check-writing feature is a time-saver. The time saved, however, does not come cheaply. Expect to pay between $40 and $90 for 250 computer check forms. Usually, you will spend more for check forms in the course of a year than you originally spent for Quicken. Obviously, you want to make sure that you make the right decision about ordering checks. Two situations merit the expense of check forms: You write a great many checks at home or at work (more than two dozen each month), or you plan to use Quicken for a business and want the professional appearance of computer-printed checks.

T I P   You still will use manual checks—those you write by hand—even if you choose to use Quicken check forms. Home users, for example, need manual checks for trips to the grocery or the department store. And business owners need manual checks for unexpected deliveries that require immediate cash payments (when access to a computer is not available).

If you decide to use Quicken to print checks, you must order pre-printed check forms for every bank account for which you want computer-printed checks. The cheapest and easiest source of pre-printed check forms is Intuit, the manufacturer of Quicken. Intuit offers both laser and continuous-feed checks. You can order from Intuit other supplies that you may need, such as deposit slips, double-window envelopes, stationery, and so on.

Complete and mail the order form included in the Quicken package; Intuit prints checks with your name and address at the top of the check and the bank and account information at the bottom. Or, use Quicken 6.0's new Order Supplies feature, described in the following section, to generate an order form for the checks and any additional supplies you need.

When choosing a starting number for your computer checks, consider two points: First, start the computer-printed check form numbers far enough away from your manual check numbers so that the numbers don't overlap or duplicate; duplications may cause confusion in your record-keeping and reconciliations. Second, start your computer-printed checks with a number that quickly shows you whether you wrote a check manually or with Quicken.

**C P A
T I P**

Deciding Which Checks To Use

When you order preprinted checks, you make choices about size, style, or color, and you decide whether the check is multipart or has voucher stubs. Table 1.1 summarizes your options.

You are on your own when selecting the color, size, and lettering style of your check forms. The following discussion, however, offers some hints about choosing the number of parts your check form can have and about deciding whether you want a voucher stub (or a remittance advice) on your checks.

Table 1.1 Summary of Quicken Check Form Options

Name	Colors	Form Size (inches)	Number of Parts	Comments
Antique Standard	Tan	3 1/2 x 8 1/2	1	*Antique* refers to parchment background; printed three to a sheet.
Prestige Standard	Gray	3 1/2 x 8 1/2	1 or 2	You can choose blue, green, or maroon accent strip; printed three to a sheet.
Prestige Voucher	Gray	7 x 8 1/2	1 or 2	You can choose blue, green, or maroon accent strip; larger form size due to voucher stub.
Classic Standard	Blue or Green	3 1/2 x 8 1/2	1, 2, or 3	8 1/2 x 10 1/2 sheets—each with three check forms—fit into printer paper tray.
Classic Voucher	Blue or Gray	7 x 8 1/2	1, 2, or 3	Larger form size due to voucher stub.
Laser Voucher	Blue or Green	3 1/2 x 8 1/2	1 or 2	8 1/2-by-11-inch sheets—each with one check form—fit into printer paper tray.
Classic Wallet-Size	Blue or Green	2 5/6 x 6	1 or 2	Has a 2 1/2-inch check stub so that overall form width is 8 1/2 inches.
Antique Wallet-Size	Tan	2 5/6 x 6	1 or 2	Has a 2 1/2-inch check stub so that overall form width is 8 1/2 inches.

Printing checks with Quicken assures that you don't fall behind in entering your financial transactions. When you write manual checks, it's easy to put off entering transactions for those checks in Quicken. You may find that you have several transactions to enter in Quicken at one time if you let yourself fall behind.

C P A
T I P

The *number of parts* in a check refers to the number of printed copies. With a one-part check, only the actual check form that you sign is printed. With a two-part check, a copy is printed at the same time as the original. With a three-part check, you get two copies plus the original.

Multipart checks probably aren't necessary for most home uses. In a business, however, the second parts can be attached to paid invoices as a fast and convenient way of keeping track of which checks paid which invoices. The third copy of a check can be placed in a numerical sequence file to help you identify the payee more quickly than you can by using the check number alone.

If you use multipart checks, keep in mind that the check forms may wear out your impact printer's *head* (the points that strike the printer ribbon and cause characters to be printed). Check your printer's multi-part form rating by referring to your printer manual. Verify that your printer is rated for at least the number of parts you want to print.

The *voucher stub*, also called the *remittance advice*, is the blank piece of paper, about the same size as the check form, that is attached to the form. Voucher stubs give you extra space to describe, or *document*, the reason for the check. You can use this area to show any calculations involved in arriving at the total check amount. You may use the voucher stub space to describe how an employee's payroll amount was calculated, for example, or to define the invoices for which that check was issued. As with multipart checks, voucher stubs probably make more sense for business use rather than home use.

Using Quicken To Order Supplies

New in Quicken 6.0 is the **Order Supplies** option. This feature enables you to fill in an order form on-screen with the help of interactive menus. If you choose this option, Quicken displays the Intuit Catalog menu, which lists all the items you can order. Simply make the appropriate choices, and Quicken fills in the order form.

Filling In the Product Order Form

The following steps show you how to order checks or any other supplies by using Quicken's **Order Supplies** option:

1. Access the Register by pressing R from the Quicken main menu, or access the Write Checks screen by pressing W. The **Order Supplies** option is available only from the Register or the Write Checks screen.

2. From the Register or the Write Checks screen, press A to display the Activities menu, as shown in figure 1.30.

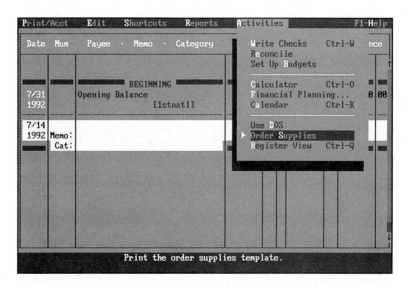

FIG. 1.30

The Activities menu.

3. From the Activities menu, press S to select the **Order Supplies** option.

   Quicken displays the Intuit Catalog menu and the Product Order form, as shown in figure 1.31.

4. Press the number of the item you want to order from the Intuit Catalog menu. To order checks, for example, press 1.

   Quicken takes you through a series of menus so that you can make choices about the item you are ordering. When you order checks, for example, you select from the following menus:

   Paper Form
   Size
   Number of Parts (when ordering Payroll/Voucher checks)
   Style
   Color

Figure 1.32 shows the menu to select the check style that you want to order.

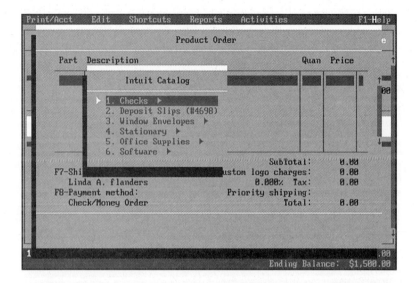

FIG. 1.31

The Product Order form and the Intuit Catalog menu.

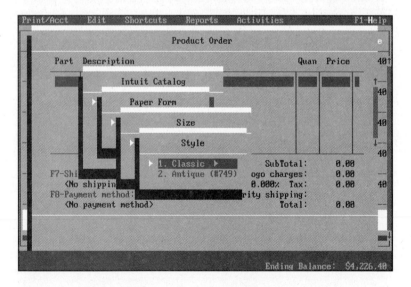

FIG. 1.32

The Style menu to select the check style that you want to order.

5. To make a selection, press the number next to the desired choice.

   After you make your selections, Quicken displays the Quantity and Price chart, as shown in figure 1.33.

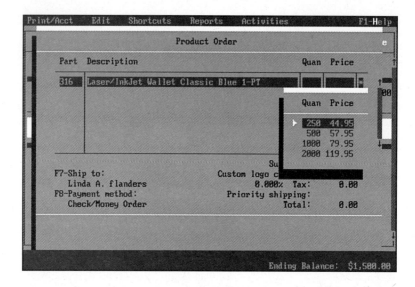

FIG. 1.33

The Quantity and
Price chart.

6. To tell Quicken how many items you want to order, use the arrow keys to highlight the desired quantity. Then press Enter. Quicken fills in the first line of the Product Order form with the item number, item description, quantity, and price (see fig. 1.34).

7. To order another item, use the down-arrow key to position the cursor on the next blank line of the Product Order form. Press Tab to redisplay the Intuit Catalog menu you saw in figure 1.31. Make your selections as described in the preceding steps.

   If you order preprinted checks or other preprinted items, such as deposit slips or stationery, Quicken prompts you for the information it needs after each item is entered in the Product Order form. When you order checks, for example, Quicken displays the Check Information window shown in figure 1.35.

8. Enter the name and account number to be printed on the checks and the check number you want Intuit to start with. Also specify whether you want a *custom* or *standard* logo printed on your checks. Intuit has a selection of hundreds of standard logos that they will print free on your Quicken checks. Standard logos are identified by number and are shown on the order form included in your Quicken 6.0 software package. A custom logo is a logo that

was designed specifically for you or your company. If you want to include your custom logo, you must attach a copy of the logo with your order. (Intuit charges $35 to print a custom logo on your checks or other items.)

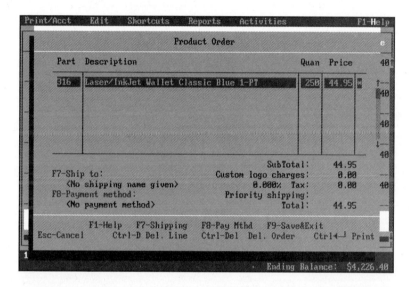

FIG. 1.34

A completed line on the Product Order form.

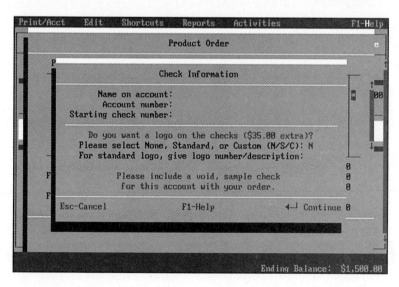

FIG. 1.35

The Check Information window.

When you finish ordering checks and supplies, you must tell Quicken where to ship the order and how you are paying for it.

9. To enter your shipping address, press F7 to display the Shipping Instructions window shown in figure 1.36.

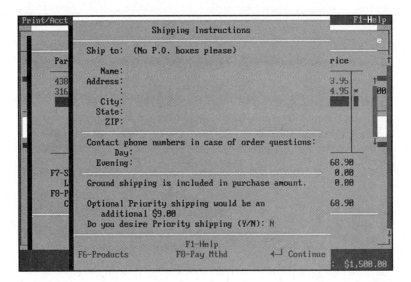

10. Enter your name, address, day and evening telephone numbers; and specify whether you want priority shipping. (Items are normally shipped UPS ground service and are delivered within three weeks from the date Intuit receives your order. If you need your order sooner, you can elect to have it shipped by 2nd Day Air service. If you select second-day shipping, Quicken enters the appropriate shipping charges on the Product Order form.)

11. When the Shipping Instructions window is complete, press F6 to return to the Product Order form, or press F8 to tell Quicken how you are paying for your order.

    Pressing F8 from the Product Order form or the Shipping Instructions window displays the Payment Method window (see fig. 1.37). Quicken enters the current order total at the top of the Payment Method window so that you can see how much your order costs.

12. Press the number, listed in the Payment Method field, that corresponds to the method of payment you want to use. If you are paying by MasterCard, for example, press 3. (If paying by credit card, you must complete the Credit Card Number, Expiration Date, and Name on Credit Card fields.) Press Ctrl-Enter or F10 when you complete the Payment Method window.

If you are paying for your order by check, Quicken can memorize a check transaction to Intuit for the amount of the order. Memorizing a check transaction is covered in Chapter 7, "Automating Check Writing."

You now have completed the Product Order form and are ready to print it.

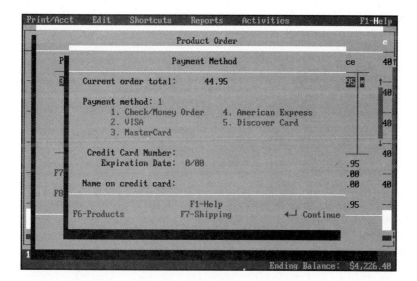

FIG. 1.37

The Payment
Method window.

Printing the Product Order Form

Before you print the Product Order form, make sure that Quicken is set up to work with your printer. When you installed Quicken 6.0, you told it which printer you use (see Appendix A). If you specified an undefined printer when you installed Quicken 6.0, you now must set up Quicken for your printer. See the earlier section in this chapter, "Setting Your Printer."

To print the Product Order form, follow these steps:

1. From the Product Order form screen, press Ctrl-Enter. Quicken displays the Print Supply Order Form window shown in figure 1.38.

   With Quicken, you can maintain three sets of printer configurations: a primary setting for printing reports (Rpt), an alternate setting for printing reports (Alt), and a setting for printing checks (Chk).

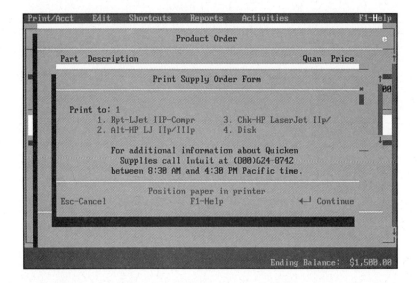

FIG. 1.38

The Print Supply
Order Form
window.

2. In the Print To field, press the number that matches that of the
   printer setting you want to use to print your Product Order form.
   Press 1, for example, to print using the primary setting for reports.
   You can print your order to a disk file, rather than to your printer,
   by pressing 4. If you choose to print to disk, Quicken requests
   three additional pieces of information: the file name, the number
   of lines to be printed to on a page, and the width of the page. For
   more information about printing to disk, refer to Chapter 12,
   "Creating and Printing Reports."

3. Press Enter to print the Product Order form. If you are paying for
   your order by check, Quicken displays the

   ```
   Create a Memorized Check to Intuit?
   ```

   message shown in figure 1.39. Press 1 to have Quicken memorize
   the check transaction for the amount of your order. Press 2 if you
   don't want to memorize the check transaction to Intuit. If you're
   new to Quicken and don't know about memorizing checks, just
   press 2 for now so that Quicken doesn't memorize the check. If
   you plan to print checks with Quicken, you can always write the
   check yourself, as you'll learn in Chapter 6. If you do want to ven-
   ture out and memorize the check, just press 1 to select the **OK to
   Memorize** option and Quicken memorizes the check for you.
   When you're ready to send in your order to Intuit, you'll need to
   recall the memorized check and print it so that you can send payment along with your order. See Chapter 7 to learn how memorized checks work and how to recall a memorized check when
   you're ready to write a check.

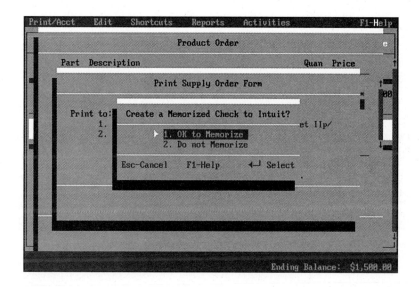

FIG. 1.39

The Create a
Memorized
Check to
Intuit?
message.

NOTE Memorized check transactions are a quick, easy way to
write checks for recurring transactions, such as your mortgage payment, rent, insurance premiums, and so on. When
you memorize a check transaction, Quicken stores the
check information in a list that you can use later to recall
the check. You don't have to retype the check each time.

After you print your Product Order form, you can mail it to Intuit. Be
sure to enclose your check or money order if you are paying by either
method.

Chapter Summary

This chapter described the steps you take in preparing to use Quicken:
choosing the conversion date, starting Quicken the first time, setting up
your Quicken system, setting your printer for Quicken, and ordering
checks and supplies. Now you are ready to begin using the system.
Before you start entering actual checks and deposits, writing checks, or
reconciling accounts, however, take a few minutes to peruse the next
chapter. Chapter 2 covers the basics of using Quicken and makes getting the most from Quicken that much easier.

Getting Around in Quicken

Quicken isn't difficult to use, especially if you begin with the operations described in this chapter. In this chapter, you learn how to do the following:

- Start Quicken
- Select menu options and move around in Quicken, using the keyboard and a mouse
- Use the Quicken screens to collect financial information
- Access the on-screen Help system
- Use Quicken's Calculator and Quick Calendar

Starting Quicken

In Chapter 1, "Preparing To Use Quicken," you learned how to start Quicken for the first time. You start subsequent Quicken sessions the same way, but you don't have to set up a new file or account each time. To start Quicken, follow these steps:

1. At the C:\ prompt, type *Q*.
2. Press Enter.

Quicken is loaded and displays the Quicken main menu, as shown in figure 2.1. The main menu is always your starting point when you begin a new Quicken session.

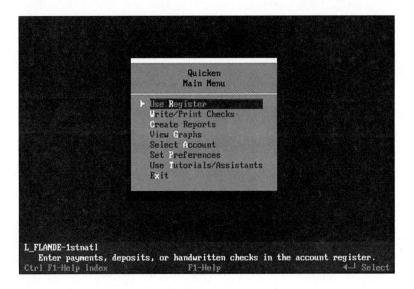

FIG. 2.1

The Quicken
main menu.

Using Quicken Menus

You instruct Quicken to perform various activities through the use of menus. The Quicken main menu lists the program's main areas and activities, called *options*. Following are the available main menu options and their functions:

Main Menu Option	Function
Use Register	Displays the Register for the account you are currently using. See Chapter 4, "Using the Register," for more about Register screens.
Write/Print Checks	Displays the Write Checks screen, where you write and print checks or write and transmit electronic payments. Refer to Chapter 6, "Writing and Printing Checks," for more about the Write Checks screen. See Chapter 13, "Paying Bills Electronically," for more about writing and transmitting payments.

Main Menu Option	Function
Create Reports	Displays the Reports menu so that you can select the type of report you want to create and print.
View Graphs	Displays various graphs menus so that you can create graphs of your income and expenses, net worth, budgeted and actual amounts, and investments. See Chapter 17, "Creating Graphs," for more about this option.
Select Account	Displays the list of accounts in the current file. You can select an account from this list, or you can add, edit, or delete accounts from the current file. See Chapter 3, "Defining Your Accounts," for more about working with accounts.
Set Preferences	Enables you to change Quicken's settings (including printer settings, screen settings, passwords, and so on) or to select another Quicken file to work with. Preferences are covered in various chapters in *Using Quicken 6 for DOS*.
Use Tutorials/Assistants	Provides an on-screen overview of the Quicken program and assists you in initiating first-time setup; creating new files, accounts, and payroll support; exporting tax information; amortizing loans; and setting up investment accounts. Using tutorials and assistants is explained in this chapter.
Exit	Saves your Quicken data in the current file and exits the program. Exiting Quicken is covered later in this chapter.

Selecting Menu Options

Quicken gives you four ways to select menu options:

- ▪ Typing the highlighted letter in the option name
- ▪ Clicking the left mouse button when the mouse pointer is positioned on the option name (see the section "Using a Mouse To Move Around in Quicken," later in this chapter)

■ Highlighting the option and pressing Enter

■ Using the shortcut keys

The first way to select an option from a menu is to press the letter that identifies the option. If you want to select the **Write/Print Checks** option from the main menu, for example, press W. Quicken displays the Write Checks screen (see fig. 2.2). To exit the screen and return to the main menu, press Esc.

The second way to select an option from a menu is to click the left mouse button when the mouse pointer is positioned on the option name. At the main menu, position the mouse pointer on the Write/Print Checks option name to select the Write/Print Checks option and display the Write Checks screen. To exit the screen and return to the main menu, click the right mouse button. (Pressing the right mouse button is the same as pressing Esc from the keyboard.)

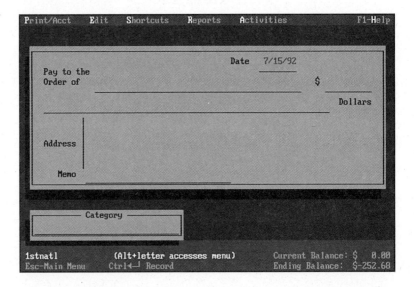

FIG. 2.2

The Write
Checks screen.

The third way to select menu options is to use the cursor-movement keys to highlight the appropriate selection. If you press the up- and down-arrow keys, the highlight bar moves up and down, respectively. When the bar highlights the option you want to select, press Enter.

At the top of each data-entry screen, such as the Write Checks screen, Quicken gives you access to other menus (refer to fig. 2.2). The Write Checks screen, for example, features a Print/Acct menu, an Edit menu, a Shortcuts menu, a Reports menu, and an Activities menu. Select one of these menus, and Quicken displays a list of menu options. The selection techniques described previously apply to these menus also. First, however, you must activate the menus and display the menu you want: Press the Alt key and the first letter of the menu name. To activate menus using a mouse, position the mouse pointer on the menu name and click the left mouse button. To select the Edit menu, for example, press Alt and the letter E (see fig. 2.3).

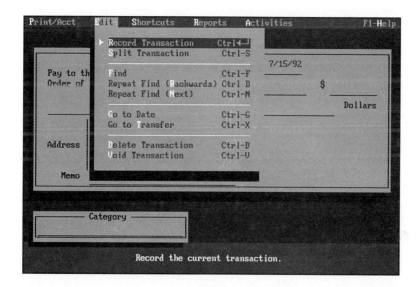

FIG. 2.3

The Edit menu.

The fourth way to select menu options is to use a shortcut key combination. Quicken shows you the shortcut keys (for example, Ctrl-D) to the right of each option on certain menus. Not every menu option has a shortcut key, but most options you use regularly do. To execute a shortcut, hold down the Ctrl key and press the appropriate letter key. One way to delete a check or deposit in the Register, for example, is to select the **Delete Transaction** option from the Edit menu and press Enter to confirm that you want the transaction deleted (refer to fig. 2.3). Or you can simply press the Ctrl and D keys to accomplish the same thing. (Chapter 5, "Automating the Register," describes the **Delete Transaction** option in detail.)

NOTE You can use a few shortcut keys from the main menu to select options or perform other tasks. Refer to table 2.1 for a list of those keys.

T I P   After you activate any menu, you can use the left- and right-arrow keys to display the other menus. If the Edit menu is displayed, for example, pressing the right-arrow key displays the Shortcuts menu (see fig. 2.4).

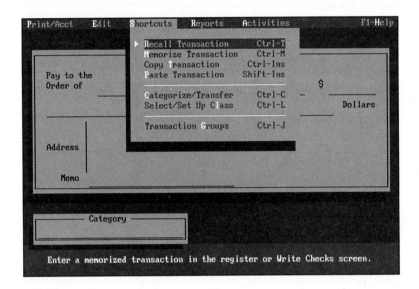

FIG. 2.4

The Shortcuts menu.

Table 2.1 lists and describes the shortcut keys for performing Quicken functions or selecting Quicken menu options. Many shortcut keys are available from any Noninvestment Register, the Write Checks screen, and report screens. A *Noninvestment Register* is any register used for accounts other than investment accounts. Investment accounts are explained in Chapter 16, "Monitoring Your Investments." Other shortcut keys are available only from the Investment Register. Some shortcut keys access other screens or perform Quicken functions from the main menu. The appropriate chapters of *Using Quicken 6 for DOS* more fully describe the menu options accessed by shortcut keys. For now, remember that shortcut keys are another way to execute menu options and that using these keys saves time.

Table 2.1 Shortcut Keys To Perform Quicken Functions or Access Menu Options

Shortcut Key	Function
Main Menu Shortcut Keys	
Ctrl-A	Goes to the Select Account To Use screen
Ctrl-B	Backs up all files and remains in Quicken
Ctrl-E	Backs up all files and exits Quicken
Ctrl-F or Ctrl-G	Goes to the Select/Set Up New File screen
Ctrl-O	Displays the Quicken Calculator
Ctrl-W	Goes to the Write Checks screen

Shortcut Key	Function
Noninvestment Registers, the Write Checks Screen, and Report Screens Shortcut Keys	
Ctrl-C	Selects or sets up a category or transfer
Ctrl-D	Deletes transaction or item
Ctrl-E	Edits account, category, class, or files
Ctrl-F	Finds transaction
Ctrl-B	Repeats Find (backwards)
Ctrl-N	Repeats Find (next)
Ctrl-G	Goes to Date
Ctrl-H	Accesses field-specific Help
Ctrl-I	Inserts a transaction
Ctrl-J	Selects or sets up a transaction Group
Ctrl-K	Displays Quick Calendar
Ctrl-L	Selects or sets up a class
Ctrl-M	Memorizes a transaction or report
Ctrl-O	Displays the Quicken Calculator

continues

Table 2.1 Continued

Shortcut Key	Function
Ctrl-P	Prints
Ctrl-Q	Changes view of Register
Ctrl-R	Goes to Register
Ctrl-S	Splits a transaction
Ctrl-T	Recalls a memorized transaction
Ctrl-V	Voids a transaction
Ctrl-W	Goes to the Write Checks screen
Ctrl-X	Goes to the transfer transaction
Ctrl-Z	Uses QuickZoom or redoes the last report
Ctrl-Ins	Copies a transaction
Shift-Ins	Pastes the copied transaction

Shortcut Key	Function

Investment Register Shortcut Keys

Ctrl-A	Selects account
Ctrl-C	Selects or sets up a category or transfer
Ctrl-D	Deletes transaction
Ctrl-E	Edits securities
Ctrl-F	Finds transaction
Ctrl-B	Repeats find (backwards)
Ctrl-N	Repeats find (next)
Ctrl-G	Goes to date
Ctrl-H	Displays price history
Ctrl-I	Inserts a transaction
Ctrl-J	Selects or sets up a transaction group
Ctrl-K	Displays Quick Calendar
Ctrl-L	Selects action
Ctrl-M	Memorizes a transaction
Ctrl-O	Displays the Quicken Calculator

Shortcut Key	Function
Ctrl-P	Prints
Ctrl-R	Goes to Investment Register
Ctrl-T	Recalls a memorized transaction
Ctrl-U	Updates prices
Ctrl-W	Goes to the Write Checks screen
Ctrl-X	Goes to the transfer transaction
Ctrl-Y	Displays Security list
Ctrl-Z	Redoes last report
Ctrl-Ins	Copies a transaction
Shift-Ins	Pastes the copied transaction

Changing the Menu Access

If you used Version 1.0, 2.0, 3.0, or 4.0 of Quicken before switching to Quicken 6.0, you know that you selected Quicken menu options in those versions differently than in the current version. (Quicken 5.0 uses the same menu style as Quicken 6.0.) In versions prior to Quicken 5.0, you selected main menu options by pressing numbers, and you selected pull-down menus from data-entry screens by pressing function keys. This type of menu access is called *function-keys access*. To select the **Use Register** option from the main menu of an earlier version of Quicken, for example, you pressed 1; to select the Edit pull-down menu from the Write Checks screen, you pressed F3. The default method used in Quicken 5.0 and 6.0 to select menu options is the Alt-keys access because you press letters to select menu options from menus and you press the Alt key to access pull-down menus.

If you feel more comfortable selecting menu options as you did in an earlier Quicken version, you can change the way Quicken 6.0 displays its menus to resemble that of the old method. To change Quicken 6.0's menu access, follow these steps:

1. From the Quicken main menu, select the **Set Preferences** option by pressing P. Quicken displays the Set Preferences menu, as shown in figure 2.5.

2. From the Set Preferences menu, select the **Screen Settings** option by pressing S. The Screen Settings menu appears (see fig. 2.6).

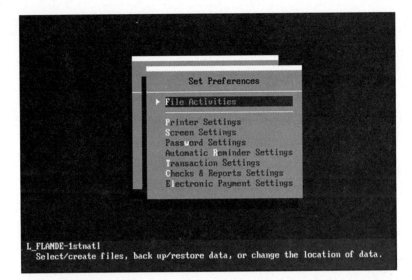

FIG. 2.5

The Set Preferences menu.

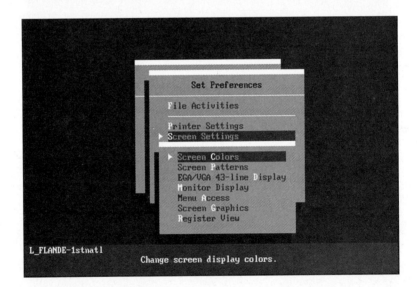

FIG. 2.6

The Screen Settings menu.

3. From the Screen Settings menu, select the **Menu Access** option by pressing A. Quicken displays the Menu Access window, as shown in figure 2.7.

4. Press 1 to select the function-keys menu access option. Press Enter. Quicken displays a message stating that the new menu display takes effect the next time you start Quicken. Press Enter to remove the message.

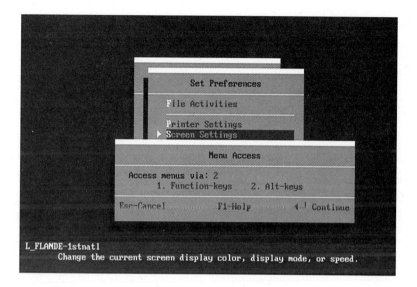

FIG. 2.7

The Menu Access window.

5. Press Esc until you return to the Quicken main menu, and press X to exit the program.

6. Restart Quicken by typing *Q* at the C:\QUICKEN> prompt.

When Quicken restarts, the main menu is displayed in function-key access style, as shown in figure 2.8.

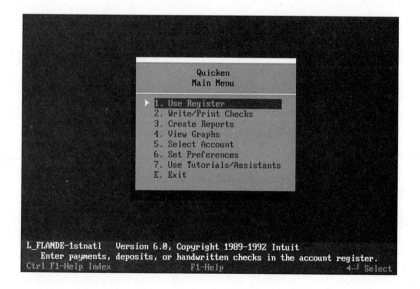

FIG. 2.8

The Quicken main menu in function-key access style.

NOTE When you install Quicken 6.0, the Alt-keys method is the default menu-access method. If you are upgrading to Quicken 6.0 from Version 3.0 or 4.0, Quicken 6.0 also uses the Alt-keys menu-access method as the default. However, if you changed the menu access in Version 5.0 of Quicken to function keys, when you install Quicken 6.0, the function-keys menu access method remains in use.

Using a Mouse To Move Around in Quicken

You can use a mouse in Quicken to move around screens and to select menu options. First, however, you must know the basic procedures of using a mouse.

Quicken works with any Microsoft-compatible mouse. If your mouse is installed properly, you should see a mouse *pointer* (cursor) on your screen. If you don't see the mouse pointer on your screen, check for the following problems:

- Your mouse is not properly installed. Test your mouse with other programs to see whether the mouse pointer appears on-screen and works properly. If not, reinstall the mouse with the mouse software.

- The cable connections may not be securely fastened to the correct port on your computer. Check your mouse manual to determine which port to use, and then check the connection. Make any necessary adjustments.

- Your PATH statement may not include the directory where you installed your mouse software. Check your PATH statement and edit as necessary. (Refer to your DOS manual for information on how to edit PATH statements.)

As you move the mouse on your desktop or on a mouse pad, the mouse pointer moves in the same direction on your screen. When you have moved the mouse pointer where you want it, you can perform one of the following procedures:

Click	Press and release the left mouse button once.
Double-click	Press and release the left mouse button twice in quick succession.

Drag   Hold down the left mouse button and move the mouse on your desktop or mouse pad. You use dragging to scroll through the Register, a list window, or a report screen using the vertical scroll bar. When you drag the scroll box within a vertical scroll bar, it moves the scroll box up or down so that your position within the Register, list window, or report screen changes. To drag the scroll box, hold down the left mouse button and move the mouse on your desktop. Then release the mouse button to place the scroll box you are "dragging" where you want it in the vertical scroll bar. The scroll bar and scroll box are explained next.

To scroll up and down in Quicken with a mouse, use the vertical scroll bar that appears on the right side of the screen (see fig. 2.9). The shaded scroll box indicates your location within a screen. If the scroll box appears in the middle of the scroll bar, for example, you are in the middle of a Register, screen, or report. The arrow keys at the top and bottom of the scroll bar (the *upper* and *lower scroll arrows*) control movement by one line or one transaction. To move up one transaction in a Register, for example, click the upper scroll arrow. To move down one transaction, click the lower scroll arrow.

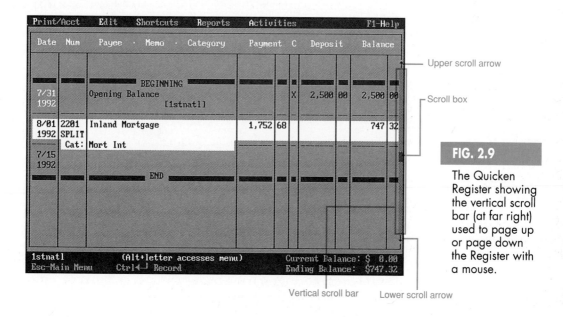

FIG. 2.9

The Quicken Register showing the vertical scroll bar (at far right) used to page up or page down the Register with a mouse.

In report screens, Quicken displays a horizontal scroll bar also, as shown in figure 2.10. The horizontal scroll bar enables you to move across wide reports that cannot fit on one screen. Like the vertical scroll bar, the horizontal scroll bar includes a shaded scroll box. A right scroll arrow and a left scroll arrow control movement right or left, respectively, by column.

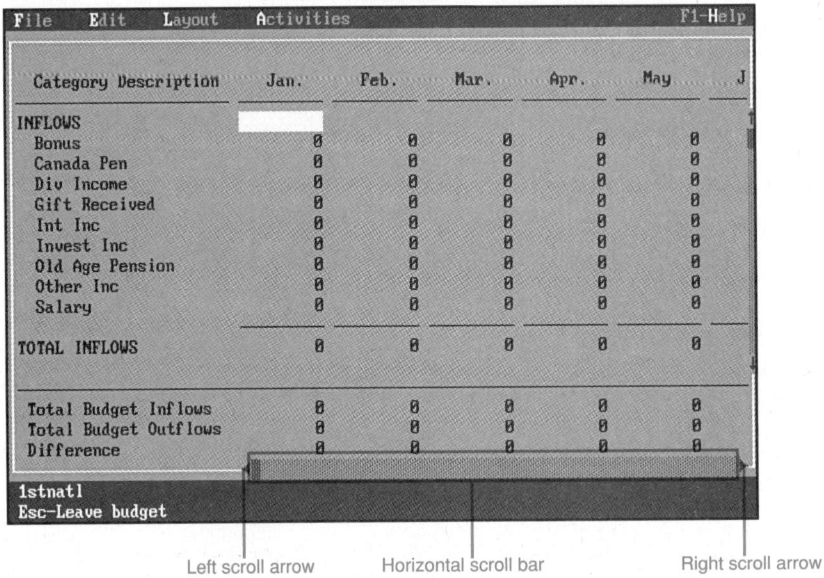

FIG. 2.10

A report screen showing the horizontal scroll bar (at the bottom) used to move right or left with a mouse.

To execute commands, position the mouse pointer on the command that appears at the bottom or top of a screen and click. Position the mouse pointer on **F1-Help**, for example, and click to execute this command.

Use the following mouse procedures to move around Quicken screens:

- ■ To move up or down the screen, click the vertical scroll bar above or below the scroll box.

- ■ To move up one transaction or line, click the upper scroll arrow.

- ■ To move down one transaction or line, click the lower scroll arrow.

- ■ To scroll a list, Register, or Help screen, drag the scroll box toward the bottom or the top of the vertical scroll bar. Alternatively, you can position the mouse pointer on the upper or lower scroll arrow and hold down the left mouse button.

- To move right or left in a report screen, click the horizontal scroll bar to the right or left of the scroll box.

- To move to a different position in the Register, list window, or report screen, drag the scroll box to a different position in the scroll bar.

 Throughout *Using Quicken 6 for DOS*, most Quicken activities are explained in terms of the keyboard. If you have a mouse, use the techniques described in the preceding section to select menu options and commands and to move around screens and windows.

Entering Data in Quicken

Collecting data on-screen involves moving between fields, entering and editing fields, and saving your work. Quicken gives you many ways to accomplish these tasks. These methods are explained in the following sections. To follow along on your computer, go to the Write Checks screen by selecting the **Write/Print Checks** option from Quicken's main menu.

Moving Between and Within Fields

Quicken gives you several ways to move between fields: You can move from field to field by pressing Enter. You can move to the next field by pressing Tab or to the preceding field by pressing Shift-Tab. You can move to different fields (as well as within the same field) by using the arrow keys; pressing Ctrl-Left arrow moves the cursor to the beginning of the preceding field, and pressing Ctrl-Right arrow moves the cursor to the beginning of the next field. You can move to any field by positioning the mouse pointer within the field and clicking the left mouse button. You also can use keys from the keyboard to move within a field, such as moving to the beginning of the current field or the end.

Table 2.2 summarizes the cursor-movement keys used to move between fields, as well as those used to move within a field. To practice using the cursor-movement keys in the Write Checks screen, try each key or key combination listed in table 2.2.

Table 2.2 Cursor-Movement Keys for Moving Between and Within Fields	
Key	**New Cursor Placement**
Enter	Next field
Tab	Next field
Shift-Tab	Preceding field
← or ›	One space to the left or right, according to the arrow
Ctrl-←	Beginning of preceding word within field
Ctrl-→	Beginning of next word within field
Home	Beginning of current field
End	End of current field
Home Home	First field
End End	Last field

Entering and Editing Data On-Screen

Entering data into a field or editing an existing field of data is as easy as moving between and within fields. To enter data into a field, simply type the appropriate characters. Whether Quicken accepts only numeric or alphabetic and numeric characters depends on the field in which you are entering the data. Refer to the chapters pertaining to the different screens for more information.

Usually, you type dollar amounts as numeric data by using the number keys on your keyboard or your numeric keypad. Do not enter the dollar symbol or any commas because Quicken adds these symbols for you. If an amount represents a negative number, however, do precede the number with a minus sign, as in –1.47. Quicken assumes that the number is an even dollar amount unless you use a decimal when entering the numerals. The entry *1245*, for example, displays as $1,245.00, and *12.45* displays as $12.45. Quicken does not place dollar signs before amounts in the Register, however.

If you make an error entering an amount, use the arrow keys to position the cursor on the numbers you want to change. You also can click the characters you want to change. You can use Home and End to move the cursor within a field, too. Press Home to move the cursor to the start of a field; press End to move the cursor to the end of a field. To delete numbers, use the Backspace or Del key. The Backspace key removes the number preceding the cursor location; the Del key removes the number at the cursor location. To delete the entire field, press Ctrl-Backspace.

Most of the remaining data stored in Quicken (that is, data other than dollar amounts) can be alphabetic, numeric, or both. Where alphabetic characters are allowed, you can use either upper- or lowercase characters. Practice typing the name of someone to whom you frequently write checks, such as the grocer or your cleaning person. You can use spaces, capital letters, numbers, and whatever else you want or need.

You can edit or change any entry in a text field. Retype the field's contents, or use the arrow keys or click the mouse to position the cursor on the characters you want to change. To delete characters, use the Backspace or Del key. To add characters to existing text, press the Ins key and type the new characters. To add characters to the end of existing text, use the right-arrow key or the mouse to position the cursor at the end of the text and type the remaining characters. As with numeric data, you can clear the field to start over by pressing Ctrl-Backspace.

Quicken has a special editing capability for changing date fields. By pressing the + (plus) key, you can add one day to the date; by pressing the – (minus) key, you can subtract one day. Try this feature by entering *1/1/93* in the Date field. Pressing + changes the date to 1/2/93 and pressing – changes the date to 12/31/92. If the date shows the month and year only—as in some places in the Quicken system—you can move the date ahead one month by pressing the + key and back one month by pressing the – key.

Quicken gives you several tools to help enter dates quickly. By pressing T, you enter the current system date. By pressing M, you enter the first date of the current month. By pressing H, you enter the last date of the current month. By pressing Y, you enter the first date of the year. Finally, by pressing R, you enter the last date of the year. The month and day of the Date field must be blank, however, for you to use these date-entering keys.

Table 2.3 summarizes the keys you can use to enter or edit date fields.

NOTE You can use Quicken's on-screen calendar, Quick Calendar, to enter a date in a Date field. See the section "Using Quick Calendar," later in this chapter, for information about using Quick Calendar to enter dates.

Table 2.3 Keys To Enter Dates or Edit Date Fields

Key	Function
+ (plus key)	Adds one day to the current date or one month to the current month/year shown
– (minus key)	Subtracts one day from the current date or one month from the current month/year shown
T	Enters the current system date
M	Enters the first day of the current month
H	Enters the last day of the current month
Y	Enters the first day of the current year
R	Enters the last day of the current year

Saving Your Work

When you finish entering data on-screen and want to keep the data, you have four ways to save your work:

- Press F10.
- Press Enter from the last field on-screen.
- Press Ctrl-Enter.
- Click the phrase `Ctrl ↵ Record` with the left mouse button.

After you record a check, Quicken displays a blank Write Checks screen for you to enter another check. After you record a transaction in the Register, Quicken displays the next empty transaction line in the Register for you to record another transaction.

Using Help

Quicken gives its users extensive on-screen assistance. If you encounter a problem carrying out any procedure, Quicken's Help system usually provides a solution. Help screens assist with Quicken menu options, screens, and specific fields.

Accessing the Help System

Think of Quicken's Help feature as a user's manual stored in your computer's memory. You can access this manual anywhere in Quicken by pressing F1. Quicken's Help feature is *context-sensitive*; that is, Help not only provides the manual but also opens it to the correct page. If you access Help from Quicken's main menu, for example, you receive information about the main menu options (see fig. 2.11).

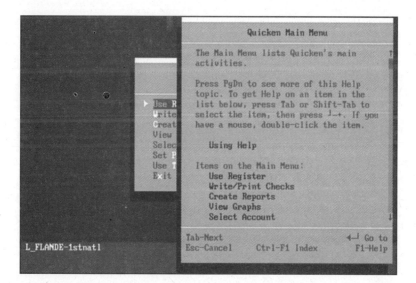

FIG. 2.11

Help for
Quicken's main
menu.

Often, the information you get when you press the Help key (F1) requires more than one screen. Use the PgDn and PgUp keys to access, respectively, the following or preceding pages of information. A Help screen usually refers the user to other Help topics, too. Quicken identifies these topics by displaying the topic name in black rather than blue letters. The Help screen for Quicken's main menu, as shown in figure 2.11, for example, refers you to **Using Help**, **Use Register**, **Write/Print Checks**, and so on. To view the Help screens for a referred topic, press Tab until the topic is highlighted, and press Enter. After you read the Help information, press Esc to return to the program. Quicken returns you to where you were when you pressed the Help key.

Using the Help Index and Table of Contents

Pressing F1 twice anywhere in Quicken accesses the Help Table of Contents screen, which organizes topics into related groups (see fig. 2.12).

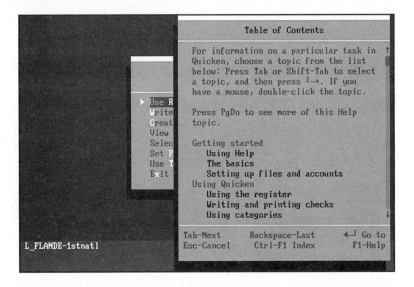

FIG. 2.12

The Help Table of Contents screen.

Pressing Ctrl-F1 from anywhere in Quicken, including the Help Table of Contents screen, accesses the Help Index screen, which lists all the Help topics available (see fig. 2.13). To select a topic, press Tab until the topic is highlighted, and press Enter. To access the Help Table of Contents screen from the Help Index, press F1.

Getting Field-Specific Help

Quicken 6.0 gives you context-sensitive Help, which enables you to access information for a particular field. This new feature is called *field-specific Help*. You can access it from any Quicken screen or window containing three or more data-entry fields.

To get help for a field, follow these steps:

1. Position the cursor on the field for which you want field-specific Help.

2. Press F1 or Ctrl-H. Quicken displays a Help screen with information that pertains to that field only.

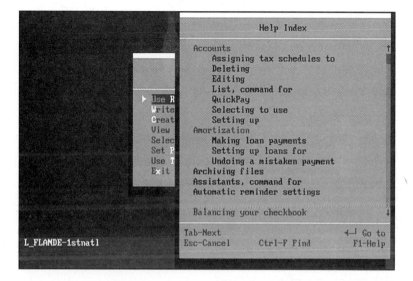

FIG. 2.13

The Help Index
screen.

Figure 2.14 shows the Help screen displayed after you press F1 from
the Category field in the Write Checks screen.

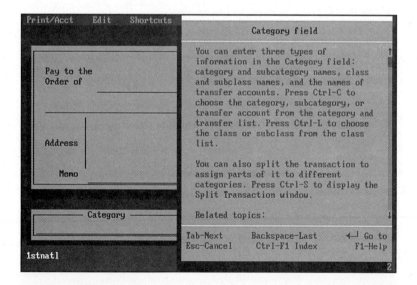

FIG. 2.14

The field-specific
Help screen for
the Category
field in the Write
Checks screen.

At the bottom of each field-specific Help screen, Quicken lists any related topics that you can access for more information. Press Tab to
highlight a related topic in the Help screen, and press Enter. From the
field-specific Help screen, you also can access Help for the entire
screen in which the field is located. Press the Backspace key, and Help
appears for the entire screen.

Exiting Help Screens

After you finish viewing a Help screen, press Esc to remove the screen. You return to the screen or window in which you were working before you accessed Quicken's Help system. If you use a mouse, click the Esc command in the information line at the bottom of the screen.

Using the Quicken Tutorials and Assistants

As you learned in Chapter 1, "Preparing To Use Quicken," Quicken's tutorials and assistants give you an overview of the Quicken program; help you set up your Quicken system; and help you create new files, new accounts, and payroll support.

Quicken 6.0 features new assistants to help you export tax information, amortize loan payments, set up your first investment account, and enter investment transactions. To use Quicken's tutorials and assistants, follow these steps:

1. From the Quicken main menu, select Use Tutorials/Assistants by pressing T. Quicken displays the Use Tutorials/Assistants menu, as shown in figure 2.15.

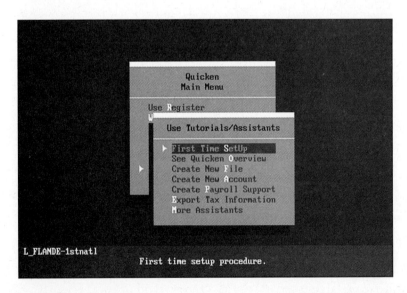

2. From the Use Tutorials/Assistants menu, highlight the menu option that identifies the area of Quicken you want to review. Then press Enter. Quicken begins the tutorial or displays the assistant screens.

3. To discontinue a tutorial or an assistant screen, press Esc to return to the main menu.

Finding Other Resources

Quicken is usually easy to use, but you may sometimes find yourself perplexed. To minimize the hassles and headaches that can come from learning a new program, consider several additional resources.

For a solid foundation in the program, read both the Quicken user's manual and this book—at least those chapters that apply to the program features you intend to use.

Talk to other Quicken users. They may be working through problems similar to yours and find helpful solutions. Formal and informal users' groups often are excellent support systems. Among those who may be able to direct you to Quicken users' groups are the people at the store where you purchased Quicken, the store or computer consultant who helps you with your hardware and software, or the CPA who prepares your tax return or annual financial statements.

Spend some time experimenting with the software. Try different transactions, explore the menus and screens, and study the reports. Such experimentation increases your confidence in the system; gives you experience working with actual business or family data; and, most important, confirms which operations accomplish which tasks.

Using the Calculator

Another of Quicken's tools is its on-screen calculator. You access the calculator by pressing the shortcut key combination Ctrl-O. Figure 2.16 shows the Calculator screen. Quicken's calculator is accessible from any Register screen, the Write Checks screen, or the report screens. You can access the calculator during bank account reconciliation and from the Quicken main menu as well.

Quicken verifies that Num Lock (*number lock*—a key on the keypad) is on when you access the calculator so that you can use the numeric keypad to enter numbers. If the Num Lock key is off, Quicken temporarily toggles the key on while you use the calculator.

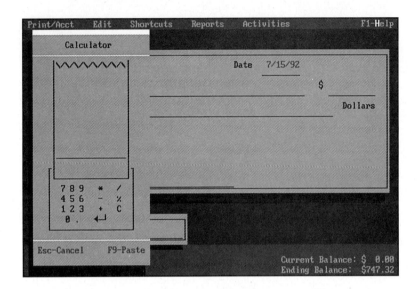

FIG. 2.16

The Calculator screen before entering numbers.

Using the Calculator's Math Functions

Use the on-line calculator as you do a regular calculator. To add three invoices for $12.87, $232.01, and $49.07 and subtract a $50 credit memo, for example, enter the following:

12.87 + 232.01 + 49.07 - 50

Press Enter or the equal sign on the regular keyboard. Quicken performs the calculation and displays the results, as shown in figure 2.17. The calculator "tape" shows both the numbers and the math operators. To clear the calculator tape, press C. (If you do not clear the calculator tape, Quicken saves the numbers and the math operators, and they reappear the next time you access the calculator.) When subtracting numbers, use the minus key on the regular keyboard or the numeric keypad.

To multiply numbers, use the asterisk from the numeric keypad or the regular keyboard. To multiply $232.01 by .25, for example, enter the following:

232.01 * .25

Press Enter or the equal sign on the regular keyboard to perform the calculation.

To divide numbers, use the slash key on the keyboard or the slash key from the numeric keypad. To divide $527.32 by 2, for example, enter the following:

527.32 / 2

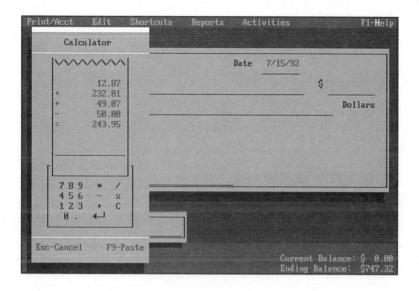

FIG. 2.17

The Calculator tape showing the numbers and the math operators.

Press Enter or the equal sign on the regular keyboard to perform the calculation.

The on-line calculator can add or subtract percentages also. To add 25 percent to 200 (add 25% of 200 to 200), for example, type *200 + 25%* and press Enter. Quicken calculates and displays the result, as shown in figure 2.18. Press Esc to exit the on-line calculator.

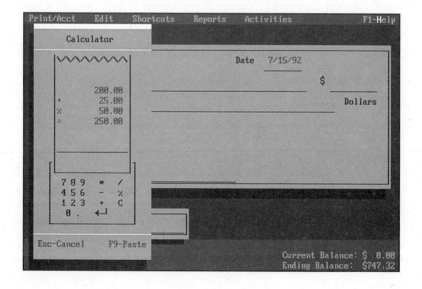

FIG. 2.18

Using the percent key with the Quicken calculator.

Pasting Calculator Results into Fields

If you are calculating an amount with Quicken's calculator to enter as a value in a field, you can paste the result from the calculator to that field. Pasting results from the calculator is the same as copying the result from the calculator into an amount field in Quicken.

To paste or copy a calculation from the calculator into a field, follow these steps:

1. Position the cursor in the field for which you want to calculate a value.

2. Press Ctrl-O to display the calculator.

3. Perform the calculation.

4. Press the F9 function key. Quicken removes the calculator from the screen and pastes the result into the field where the cursor was located when you pressed Ctrl-O.

Using Quick Calendar

Another new feature of Quicken 6.0 is Quick Calendar, an on-screen calendar. You can use Quick Calendar to review dates, to enter or paste a date into the Date field of the Register or the Write Checks screen, or to find a specific transaction.

To access Quick Calendar, as shown in figure 2.19, press Ctrl-K from the Register or the Write Checks screen. When you access Quick Calendar, Quicken highlights the current date in the calendar.

 You cannot access Quick Calendar from the Quicken main menu, from a Help screen, or from any window in Quicken that displays a list.

To exit Quick Calendar and remove it from the screen, press Esc. Quicken returns to the Register or screen in which you were working before you accessed Quick Calendar.

Selecting Dates in Quick Calendar

To select a specified date in Quick Calendar, simply move the highlight bar (by moving the cursor) to the desired date. To move the highlight bar within the current month in Quick Calendar, use the up-, down-, right-, and left-arrow keys. To change the month in Quick Calendar, use the PgDn key to scroll through future months or the PgUp key to scroll through past months.

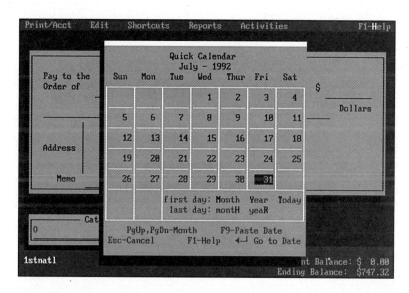

FIG. 2.19

The Quick Calendar.

TIP

Using the PgUp and PgDn keys to change the month in Quick Calendar may seem counter-intuitive. To move forward one month, you press PgDn; to move backward one month, you press PgUp. If this gets confusing, think of the calendar as a continuous-roll calendar. Future months are below the current month; therefore, you press PgDn to display a future month. Past months are above the current month; therefore, you press PgUp to display a past month.

Use the following keys to quickly select dates in Quick Calendar:

Key	Moves To
T	Today's date
M	First day of current month
Y	First day of current year
H	Last day of current month
R	Last day of current year

Finding Transactions with Quick Calendar

If you need to find a transaction made on a specific date, you can use Quick Calendar to locate and move to that transaction from the Register or the Write Checks screen.

To find a transaction with Quick Calendar, follow these steps:

1. From the Register or the Write Checks screen, press Ctrl-K to access Quick Calendar.

2. If the transaction you want to find took place in the current month, select the date of the transaction by using the up-, down-, right-, and left-arrow keys to highlight the date. If the transaction took place in a month other than the current one, use the PgUp and PgDn keys to change the month; then use the arrow keys to highlight the date.

3. Press Enter. Quicken goes to the first transaction with the selected date that is listed in the Register or at the Write Checks screen.

Pasting Quick Calendar Dates into Fields

You can use Quick Calendar to paste dates into the Date field in the Register or the Write Checks screen. To paste a date into a date field, follow these steps:

1. Press Ctrl-K to access Quick Calendar from the Register or the Write Checks screen.

2. Select the date you want to paste into the Date field.

3. Press the F9 function key. Quicken removes Quick Calendar from the screen and pastes the date from Quick Calendar into the Date field.

Using DOS from Quicken

While in Quicken, you may need to access DOS to format a floppy disk for backup or to list files in a directory. Instead of ending your Quicken session, you can access DOS directly from the Quicken program and return to Quicken afterward.

To access DOS from Quicken, follow these steps:

1. From a Register, the Write/Checks screen, or the Write/Invoices screen, press Alt-A to open the Activities menu.

2. Select the **Use DOS** option by pressing D. Quicken exits to DOS, where you can use DOS commands such as FORMAT or DIR.

3. To return to Quicken after you finish in DOS, type *exit* at the C:> prompt.

> **CAUTION:** Do not load a memory-resident utility while using DOS from Quicken; the utility may interfere with your Quicken files. A *memory-resident* utility is a program that remains in your computer's memory while you are working in other programs, such as Quicken.

Exiting Quicken

When you finish working in Quicken, you must exit the program. When you exit Quicken, it saves your work in the data file you are in when you leave the program. To exit Quicken, follow these steps:

1. Press Esc repeatedly to return to the main menu.

2. From the main menu, select **Exit** by pressing X. Quicken saves your data file and returns you to the DOS prompt.

> **CAUTION:** If you turn off your computer before exiting Quicken through the main menu, you may lose some of your data. Although Quicken reconstructs some files the next time you use the program, complete reconstruction of interrupted data files is not possible.

NOTE Be sure to keep backup copies of all your financial data to prevent losses due to system failure or power outages. Quicken's reminder system can help you remember to back up your files each time you exit Quicken. See Chapter 19, "Managing Your Quicken Files," to learn about Quicken's reminder system and about backing up your Quicken data.

If you want to back up your Quicken data file before you exit Quicken, you can press Ctrl-B from the main menu. Backing up your files before you exit also is explained in Chapter 19.

Chapter Summary

This chapter described the basics of getting around in Quicken: selecting menu options; using the mouse; entering data on-screen; and using Help, the Calculator, and Quick Calendar; as well as accessing DOS from Quicken. The chapter also provided additional tips for learning to use Quicken.

If you need to define more than one bank account to use with Quicken, you now should read Chapter 3. If you need only one bank account defined, you are ready to learn the fundamentals of actually working in Quicken: writing and printing checks, using Quicken's Register, and reconciling your bank account. These operations are covered starting in Chapter 4.

Defining Your Accounts

I f you followed the steps outlined in Chapter 1, "Preparing To Use Quicken," you already have defined one bank account as part of setting up your Quicken system, but you may want to define other bank accounts. You may, for example, have more than one checking account, one or two savings accounts, and even certificates of deposit for which you will keep records with Quicken. If you want to use Quicken to track more than one account, you need to define these accounts in Quicken. You then can use Quicken to record transactions in the accounts and track transfers between accounts.

You can add other Quicken account types (Credit Card, Cash, Other Asset, Other Liability, and Investment Accounts) to your Quicken file so that you can record and track all your financial activity—not just transactions that occur in a bank account. These account types are explained in general later in this chapter, and more specifically in later chapters. This chapter also gives you some tips on creating accounts— information that should make working with multiple accounts easy.

In this chapter, you learn how to do the following:

■ Add another bank account to your Quicken file

■ Edit and delete accounts

■ Select an account to use

Defining Account Types

Before you go any further, you should learn a little more about accounts and the types of accounts that you can use in Quicken. A Quicken account is similar to the accounts you use to keep track of your transactions—such as checking, savings, credit card accounts, and so on. You use other types of accounts to track the value of your assets and investments or the principal balance of your liabilities or debts. The types of accounts you can add and use in Quicken follow:

- *Bank accounts:* This is the most commonly used account type. Use bank accounts to set up your checking, savings, or money market accounts.

- *Credit card accounts:* These accounts keep track of your credit card activity, including purchases, payments, other credits, finance charges, and credit card fees. With Quicken 6.0, you can set up an IntelliCharge account to electronically track your Quicken VISA card activity. See Chapter 11, "Managing Your Credit Cards," to learn more about credit card accounts.

- *Cash accounts:* Cash accounts keep track of your cash expenditures, such as the cash you spend on vacations or dining out, or your business's petty cash fund. See Chapter 10, "Tracking Your Net Worth, Other Assets, and Liabilities," for more information on how to use cash accounts.

- *Other asset accounts:* Use this account type to record and track the value of the things you own, such as your home or auto, or your business's accounts receivable and fixed assets. You learn more about other asset accounts in Chapter 10, "Tracking Your Net Worth, Other Assets, and Liabilities."

- *Other liability accounts:* Use this account type to record and track the debts you owe, such as the mortgage on your home or the outstanding loan balance on your auto. For businesses, the other liability account type can be used to track accounts payable or a credit line with the bank. Refer to Chapter 10, "Tracking Your Net Worth, Other Assets, and Liabilities," for more on other liability accounts.

- *Investment accounts:* Use investment accounts to track your investments, such as stocks, bonds, and mutual funds. The investment account is an advanced feature in Quicken; therefore, you should be sure to read Chapter 16, "Monitoring Your Investments," and use the Quicken assistants from the Use Tutorials/Assistants menu to learn about these accounts. Using the Quicken assistants is explained in Chapter 2, "Getting Around in Quicken."

NOTE You need only one account to start using Quicken: your bank account—the account from which you write checks and make deposits. If you're just learning Quicken, don't worry about setting up more accounts right now. You can read Chapters 4 through 8 to learn how to enter transactions and write and print checks from your bank account. As you get up to speed with Quicken (which will happen before you know it!), start adding other accounts to your Quicken system to complete your financial picture.

Adding Another Account

You need to define or identify accounts for each account you want to track with Quicken. You defined only one bank account as part of setting up your Quicken system, but you can have as many as 255 accounts in a file, and you can have multiple files. (Files are discussed in more detail in Chapter 19, "Managing Your Quicken Files.")

This chapter explains how to add another account by using the **Select Account** option from the Quicken main menu. You also can use the **Create New Account** command on the Use Tutorials/Assistants menu, however.

NOTE If you used earlier versions of Quicken, you will notice that adding an account in Quicken 6.0 is easier than ever!

To set up another bank account, choose the **Select Account** option from Quicken's main menu (see fig. 3.1). Quicken displays the Select Account to Use window shown in figure 3.2. This window shows the bank account you defined as part of setting up your Quicken system.

You can access the Select Account to Use window from other screens in Quicken by pressing Ctrl-A.

T I P

To add another account, follow these steps:

1. Use the up- and down-arrow keys to highlight the <New Account> line in the Select Account to Use window and press Enter. The Set Up New Account window appears (see fig. 3.3). You also can press Ctrl-Ins to access the Set Up New Account window.

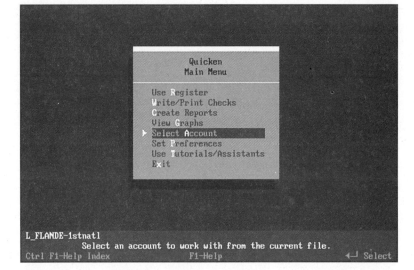

FIG. 3.1

Choosing the **Select Account** option from Quicken's main menu.

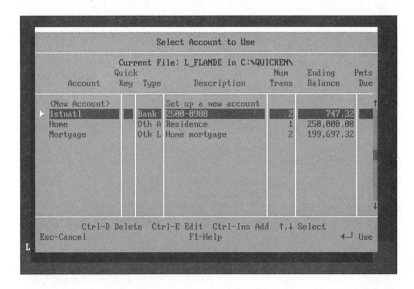

FIG. 3.2

The Select Account to Use window.

2. With the cursor in the Account Type field, press 1 to choose **Bank Account**. If you're adding up another account type, just press the number next to the account type that you want to add.

3. Move the cursor to the Name for This Account field. Type a name or short description of the account in the field. Use characters, letters, spaces, and any symbols except brackets ([]), a slash (/), or a colon (:).

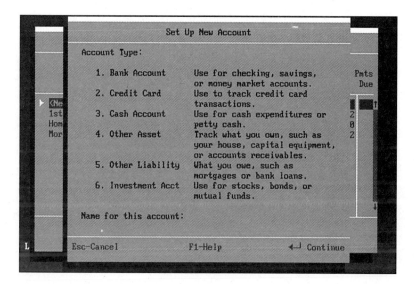

FIG. 3.3

The Set Up New
Account window.

Remember that you have only 15 spaces for the account name. Use
an abbreviation of the bank's name; First National could become
1stNatl, for example. This leaves room for the last four digits of the
account number. You then can distinguish accounts easily, as shown
by the following example:

T I P

> 1stNatl-1234 for a checking account
> 1stNatl-3272 for a savings account
> 1stNatl-7113 for CDs

4. When the Set Up New Account window is complete, press Enter.
   Quicken displays the Starting Balance and Description window as
   shown in figure 3.4.

5. In the Balance field, type the ending balance from your last bank
   statement and press Enter. Do not use commas or dollar signs
   when you enter the balance. If the starting balance for an account
   is zero, you must press 0.

6. Type the date of the balance amount in the As Of field using the
   MM/DD/YY format. If you entered the ending balance from your
   last bank statement in step 5, you should enter the bank statement date (the ending or cut-off date) in the As Of field. Remember that you can use the + (plus) and – (minus) keys to move the
   date ahead and back one day.

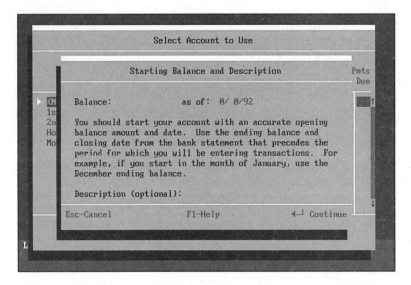

FIG. 3.4

The Starting
Balance and
Description
window.

7. (Optional) Move the cursor to the Description (optional) field.
Type a further description of the account, such as the account
number.

8. Press Enter to move to the Source of Starting Balance window that
you see in figure 3.5. Here, Quicken shows you the balance that
you entered as your starting balance and asks you for the source
of that balance.

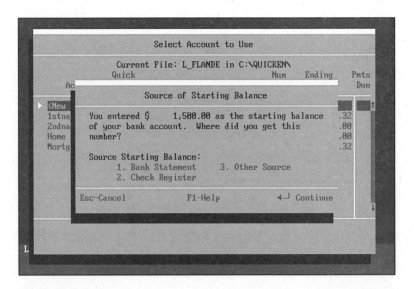

FIG. 3.5

The Source of
Starting Balance
window.

NOTE Although you can enter a starting balance for an account from any source, not just your bank statement, Quicken and this author recommend that you use the ending balance from your last bank statement as your starting balance. Make sure, however, that you reconciled your account with that statement before you rely on the amount the bank states that you have in your account.

> **CAUTION:** When you enter the ending balance from your last bank statement as the starting balance in your bank account, you must enter all uncleared transactions in your Quicken Bank Account Register. In other words, you must enter all transactions that have not been cleared through your bank account as of the current date (the date that you start Quicken). If you don't enter these transactions, you will have difficulty reconciling the account. You learn how to enter transactions in Chapter 4, "Using the Register."

9. In the Source Starting Balance field, type the number that corresponds to the source you used to enter the account's starting balance. Press 1 for **Bank Statement**, 2 for **Check Register**, or 3 for **Other Source**. Then press Enter.

Because Quicken recommends that you use the ending balance from your last bank statement as the starting balance and the statement cutoff date for the as of date, Quicken asks you if you want to change your starting balance if you selected the Check Register or other source as your source for the starting balance. Quicken displays the window shown in figure 3.6, for example, if you used your check register as the source for the starting balance. Press Y if you want to go back and change your starting balance, or press N if you don't want to change your starting balance.

If you entered your starting balance from your bank statement, Quicken congratulates you for making the right decision with the on-screen message shown in figure 3.7. Press Enter from the congratulatory message to go to the Select Account to Use window that you saw in figure 3.2. The bank account that you just added now is listed in the Select Account to Use window.

If you want to add more accounts, just repeat steps 1 through 9.

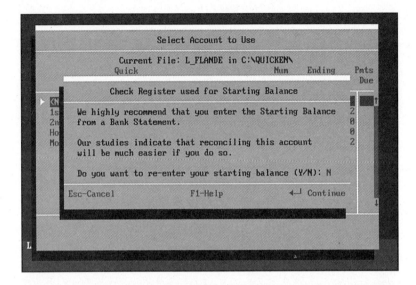

FIG. 3.6

The Check Register used for Starting Balance window.

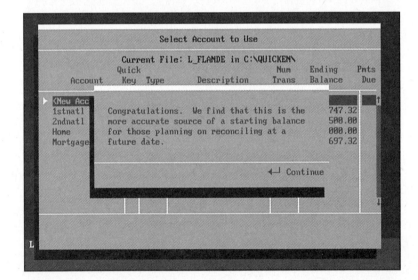

FIG. 3.7

The congratulatory message displayed when you use your bank statement as the source for a bank account's starting balance.

Deciding Which Accounts To Add

When you first set up accounts for Quicken, adding accounts can get out of hand. You may, for example, define Quicken accounts for every checking account you have, regardless of whether the account is active. You also may define Quicken accounts for each of your savings accounts, credit unions, money market accounts, and perhaps even accounts for certificates of deposit. Rather than indiscriminately defining accounts for every bank account you have, consider a few ideas and rules for determining which of your bank accounts also should be Quicken accounts:

- If you want to write checks on the account by using Quicken, you must define a Quicken account.

- If you want to use Quicken's reconciliation feature to explain differences between your records and the bank's, credit union's, or brokerage house's statement, you must define a Quicken account.

- If you have transactions in an account that you want to include in Quicken's tax deduction summaries or profit and loss statements, you must define a Quicken account. You may have charitable contributions or mortgage interest transactions in other bank accounts, for example.

Other factors can indicate that you probably do not need to define a bank, credit union, or brokerage house account as a Quicken account:

- If you do not have any deposits into or withdrawals from the account other than interest income or bank service fees, your monthly statement will suffice for your financial records.

- If you have only a handful of transactions a month—fewer than a dozen—and none represents an account transfer from or to an account for which you will use Quicken, you probably do not need to track the account in Quicken. This choice, however, is a matter of personal preference.

- If you otherwise would not track an account, you probably should not bother to put the account into Quicken—even if you have the best of intentions about becoming more diligent in your record-keeping.

If you want to measure your *net worth* (assets minus liabilities), you should add a Quicken account for each account that you have that represents an asset. You may have an account with only a few transactions per month, but with a large account balance, for example. If you don't set up a Quicken account for this account, the account balance, which represents an asset, will not be reflected in your net worth in Quicken Net Worth reports.

C P A
T I P

Editing Existing Accounts

You also can use the Select Account to Use window to edit the names and descriptions of existing accounts. You may do this, for example, if you originally described the account incorrectly. Or, you may want to edit an account name and description if you have transferred the account in total to a new account number or even a new bank. Maybe you moved from Denver to San Francisco and are using the same bank, but a different branch. Quicken does not, however, enable you to change the account type, balance, or as of date after you add the account. If these dates are wrong, you need to delete and then re-create the account.

To edit an account, follow these steps:

1. From the Quicken main menu, choose the **Select Account** option to display the Select Account to Use window. Or just press Ctrl-A from the Register or the Write Checks screen.

2. Use the up- and down-arrow keys to highlight the account you want to edit.

3. Press Ctrl-E. The Edit Account Information window appears, filled with the current information for the account (see fig. 3.8).

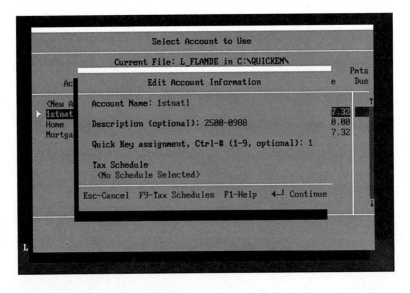

FIG. 3.8

The Edit Account Information window.

4. (Optional) Edit the bank account name in the Account Name field by typing over the existing characters or using the Backspace or Del key to remove characters.

5. (Optional) Move the cursor to the Description (optional) field to edit the bank account description.

6. (Optional) If you want to assign a quick key that you can use to easily move to another account, move the cursor to the Quick Key Assignment field. Press a number from 1 to 9 and press Enter.

> **T I P**
>
> If you assign a quick key to an account, you can switch to that account from the main menu, any Register, or the Write Checks screen. To switch to the account, press the Ctrl key in combination with the number that you assigned to the account in the Edit Account Information window. When you assign a quick key to an account, the quick key number appears next to the account name in the Select Account to Use window.

> **NOTE**
>
> The Edit Account Information window also enables you to attach a tax schedule and tax schedule line number to an account. If you do this, transactions that are transfers to and from an account are summarized so that you can more easily complete a particular line of a particular tax schedule. You can attach a tax schedule and line to an account by pressing the F9 function key to display the list of tax schedules. Refer to Chapter 14, "Using Quicken To Prepare for Income Taxes," for more information on attaching tax schedules to accounts and collecting income tax return data using Quicken.

7. Press Enter to save your changes to the account and return to the Select Account to Use window.

To edit additional accounts, repeat steps 1 through 7.

Deleting Accounts

You also can use the Select Account to Use window to delete accounts you no longer use. Perhaps you closed an account or decided that an account wasn't worth tracking with Quicken. To delete an account, follow these steps:

1. From the Quicken main menu, choose the **Select Account** option to display the Select Account to Use window. Or just press Ctrl-A from the Register or the Write Checks screen.

2. Use the up- and down-arrow keys to highlight the account that you want to delete.

3. Press Ctrl-D. The Deleting Account window appears, providing the name of the account to be deleted and alerting you to the permanence of the deletion (see fig. 3.9).

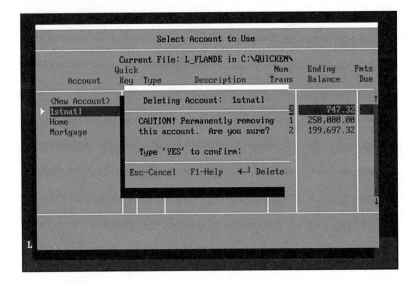

FIG. 3.9

The Deleting Account window.

4. Type *yes* and then press Enter to delete the selected account. If you do not want to delete the account, press Esc.

CAUTION: When you delete an account, you delete the account description and any transactions you have recorded in the account. Be sure that you really want to delete the account before taking the steps to do so.

Selecting an Account To Use

When you start working with multiple accounts, you need to tell Quicken which account you want to use. Suppose that you decide to use Quicken to track a savings and a checking account. Whenever you enter a savings account deposit, you need to make sure that you record the deposit in the savings account and not in the checking account.

Similarly, if you withdraw money from the checking account, you need to make sure that the withdrawal is correctly recorded in your checking account and not in the savings account. To record account activity correctly, you first must select the appropriate Quicken account to use.

To select an account to use, follow these steps:

1. From the Quicken main menu, choose the **Select Account** option to display the Select Account to Use window. Or just press Ctrl-A from the Register or the Write Checks screen.

2. Use the up- and down-arrow keys to highlight the account that you want to use.

3. Press Enter.

If you assigned a quick key to the account that you want to use, just press the Ctrl key in combination with the number that you assigned to that account. If you entered number 5 as the quick-key assignment for the account named *1stNatl*, for example, press Ctrl-5 to start using the 1stNatl account.

T I P

Entering all transactions for an account at one time is more efficient than entering them randomly. Consider collecting several transactions for an account and then recording them at one time.

T I P

Chapter Summary

In this chapter, you learned how to add other accounts—specifically bank accounts—and how to edit and delete existing Quicken accounts. You also learned how to select the account that you want to use in your Quicken file. With the information in the first three chapters, you should be ready to use Quicken. In essence, these first three chapters covered the details of getting started with Quicken—the things you need to do before you actually start working with the program.

The next five chapters in Part I, "Learning Quicken," describe the basics of using Quicken and cover such tasks as recording financial transactions with Quicken, printing Registers, writing and printing checks, reconciling your bank account, and so on. These chapters don't cover as much about business and personal accounting topics as they do about using the Quicken system. When you finish reading the chapters in this part of *Using Quicken 6 for DOS*, you will be well acquainted with the mechanics of using the Quicken program. That knowledge is essential to turning Quicken into a tool you can use for business or personal financial management.

Using the Register

Your checkbook, or check register, is your most fundamental
financial tool. You probably agree that your check register largely
summarizes your financial life. Money flows into your checking account
in the form of wages for a household or sales collections for a business.
Money flows out of the checking account to pay expenses.

Moving your check register to Quicken provides two major benefits.
First, Quicken does the arithmetic of deducting checks and withdrawals
and adding deposits—a trivial contribution until you remember the last
time an error in your arithmetic caused you to bounce a check. Second,
Quicken records each of your checking account transactions in the
Register so that you can use Quicken's Reports feature to summarize
and extract information from the Register—information that helps you
plan and control your finances more effectively.

Quicken's Register is the program's major component. Every other
program feature—writing checks, reconciling accounts, and printing
reports—depends on the Register. Every user works with Quicken's
Register directly by entering transactions into the Register and indi-
rectly by using the information stored in the Register. In fact, any of
the financial transactions you record can be entered directly into the
Quicken Register.

If you want to use Quicken to write and print checks, the **Write/Print Checks** option provides a convenient format for collecting the information Quicken needs to print checks.

This chapter describes the basics of using Quicken's Register, including the following:

- Understanding the Register screen
- Recording transactions in the Register
- Reviewing and editing Register transactions
- Printing the Register

Chapter 5, "Automating the Register," describes Quicken features that you can use to speed up your work in the Register and make using the Check Register even easier. Chapter 10, "Tracking Your Net Worth, Other Assets, and Liabilities," describes how you can use the Register to track other assets and even to track liabilities like your mortgage or other bank loans. Chapter 16, "Monitoring Your Investments," describes a special set of tools that Quicken provides for managing your investments. To track and monitor your investments, Quicken provides the Investment Register.

Accessing the Register

You select the **Use Register** option from Quicken's main menu to access the Register screen. You use this screen to record most of your checking account transactions—manual checks, deposits, interest, bank fees, and so on—that affect your checking account (see fig. 4.1).

T I P You can access the Register from the Write Checks screen by pressing Ctrl-R.

Understanding the Register Screen

The Register screen looks similar to the manual check register that you use. The Register includes a transaction line with fields to enter the following information:

Field	Records
Date	The date of the transaction.
Num	The check number. Or, you can use this field to enter *ATM* for *automatic teller machine transaction* or any other descriptive term for transactions that don't involve checks.
Payee	The person or firm you are paying. Or, in the case of a deposit, the source of the deposit.
Memo	An optional field to enter a check memo or description of the transaction.
Category	The category or subcategory assigned to the transaction. You learn more about categories in Chapter 9, "Organizing Your Finances."
Payment	The amount of the check or withdrawal.
C (Cleared)	Indicates whether the transaction has cleared the bank. You learn more about cleared transactions in Chapter 8, "Reconciling Your Bank Account."
Deposit	The amount of the deposit or bank credit.
Balance	Quicken calculates the balance in your account after the current transaction and enters the result here. You cannot make an entry in the Balance field.

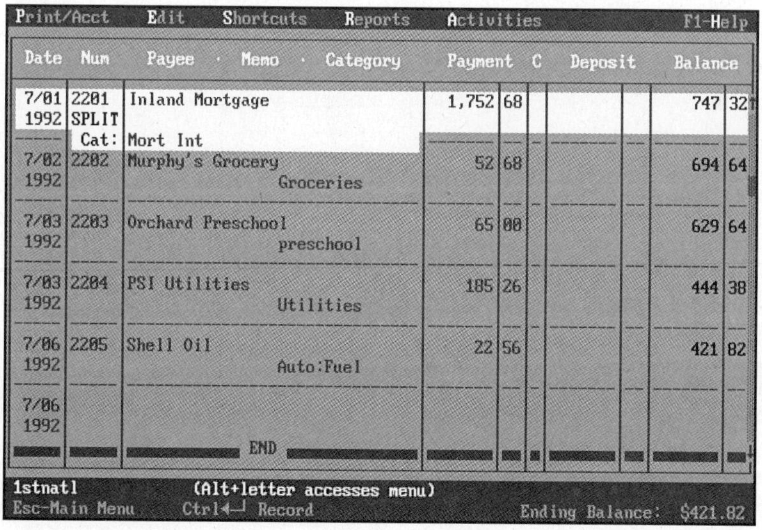

FIG. 4.1

The Register screen.

If you don't print checks using Quicken, you probably will enter all of your checking account transactions in the Register. If you do print checks with Quicken, you should enter check information in the Write Checks screen. You can print checks from information entered in the Register as well, however. When you enter and record a check in the Write Checks screen, Quicken records the transaction in the Register and updates the account balance. The steps for entering check information in the Write Checks screen are outlined in Chapters 6 and 7. The steps you take to record a transaction in the Register screen are described in the next section.

The Register screen can be broken down into three parts: the menu bar at the top of the screen, the actual Check Register, and the information lines at the bottom of the screen.

The menu bar shows the menus you can use from the Register screen to access commands: Print/Acct, Edit, Shortcuts, Reports, and Activities.

The second part of the Register screen is the actual Check Register you use to record account transactions. Take a minute to review the Register—it probably resembles the register you now use to record checks manually. (The fields are described later in the chapter.)

The third part of the Register screen contains the information lines at the bottom. These lines show the bank account name (checking) that you are using, information on what the Esc and Enter keys do, and the ending balance in the account.

Before you start recording transactions in the Register, you can use the information at the bottom of the Register screen to make sure that you have selected the correct account and to gauge the effect of the transactions you want to record (do you have enough money in your account to cover the checks that you need to write?).

Changing the Register View

When you start using Quicken, the Register is displayed using two lines of text for each transaction (other than the highlighted transaction). Figure 4.1 shows the Register in normal or two-line view. You can change the Register view so that each transaction takes up only one line in the Register. When you change the Register view, Quicken compresses each transaction line into one line. Don't worry, your data is safe, some of it is just hidden from view.

To change the Register view, follow these steps:

1. From the Register, press Alt-A to access the Activities menu shown in figure 4.2.

2. From the Activities menu, select the **Register View** option. You also can select the Register View option by pressing Ctrl-Q without accessing the Activities menu first.

Quicken changes the Register view so that each transaction takes up only one line of text (see fig. 4.3).

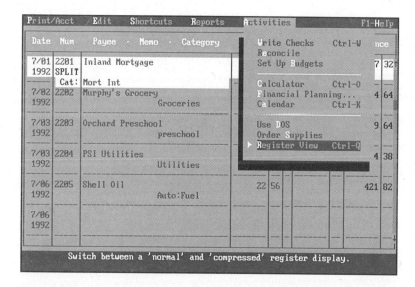

FIG. 4.2

The Activities menu.

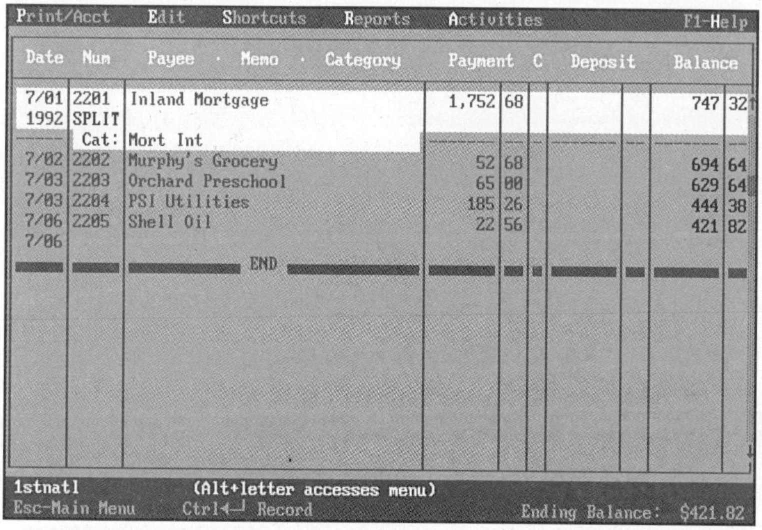

FIG. 4.3

Changing the Register view to one line per transaction.

T I P You can use the Ctrl-Q shortcut key to toggle between one-line and two-line Register views.

NOTE You cannot change the Register view in the Register for an investment account.

Moving Around the Register

As you get up to speed with Quicken, you will want to move through the Register quickly so that you can enter transactions as fast as possible or review prior transactions without having to move through the Register line by line. Use the following keys to help you move quickly and easily around the Register:

Press	To Move
↑	Up one transaction
↓	Down one transaction
PgUp	Up one screen of transactions
PgDn	Down one screen of transactions
Ctrl-PgUp	To the beginning of the preceding month
Ctrl-PgDn	To the beginning of the next month
Ctrl-Home or Home Home Home	To the beginning of the Register
Ctrl-End or End End End	To the end of the Register

To use the mouse to move around the Register, you use the *scroll bar*. The scroll bar is the vertical bar along the right edge of the Register with arrows at both ends. Using the scroll bar gives you three additional ways to move through the Register. To move to the preceding page of Register transactions, for example, you can click the up arrow at the top of the scroll bar. To move to the next page of Register transactions, you can click the down arrow at the bottom of the scroll bar.

You can move the portion of the Register that is on-screen by dragging the *scroll box*. The scroll box is the dark square on the scroll bar that shows you approximately which portion of the Register is currently displayed. To drag the scroll box, press the left mouse button and drag the scroll box up or down. You also can move to the preceding or next page of Register transactions by clicking the scroll bar above the scroll box to see the preceding page of transactions. Click the scroll bar below the scroll box to see the following page of transactions.

If you want to find a specific transaction, such as a check written to a particular payee or a check written on a certain date, Quicken includes **Find** and **Go to Date** options, which enable you to locate transactions in the Register quickly without having to scroll through months of transactions. To learn about these features, refer to Chapter 5, "Automating the Register."

Recording a Check

Recording a check in the Quicken Register closely parallels recording a check by hand in a paper checkbook register. The Register screen, however, makes the whole process easier. You can record any check in the Register, including checks you want to print. Typically, however, you record checks you have written previously by hand directly into the register. You record checks you want to print using the **Write/Print Checks** option, which is described in Chapter 6.

To record a check, follow these steps:

1. Select **Use Register** from Quicken's main menu if the Register is not displayed already. Quicken displays the Register screen. If you are working with more than one account, you may need to select the account first (see Chapter 3, "Defining Your Accounts").

2. Enter the check date in the Date field in the MM/DD/YY format.

NOTE You can change the way dates are entered and displayed by changing the transaction setting option called Enter Dates as MM/DD/YY or DD/MM/YY. By default, Quicken displays dates as MM/DD/YY; however, you can change the way dates are displayed (to DD/MM/YY) by changing this transaction setting option. If you change the transaction setting option, for example, dates are entered and displayed with the day first, followed by the month. August 18, 1992, for example, is entered and displayed as 18/08/92 instead of 08/18/92. See Chapter 20, "Customizing Quicken," to learn how to change this transaction setting.

The first time you use Quicken, the program fills the Date field with the system date. After you record your first transaction in the Register screen, Quicken fills the Date field with the last date you used. To edit the date, you have two choices. First, you can move the cursor to the month, day, or year you want to change and type over what already is showing on-screen. Or, you can use the special date-entry keys, such as the + (plus) and – (minus) keys, and the T, M, H, W, and R keys. (For more information on how these keys work, refer to Chapter 2, "Getting Around in Quicken.")

C P A
T I P

Businesses and individuals often receive discounts for paying bills early. Consider early payment in setting the check date. Not taking early payment discounts is an extremely expensive way to borrow money from the vendor. Suppose that a vendor normally requires payment within 30 days but allows a 2 percent discount for payments received within 10 days. If you pay within 30 rather than 10 days, you essentially pay the vendor a 2 percent interest charge for paying 20 days later. Because one year contains roughly 18 20-day periods, the 2 percent for 20 days equals approximately 36 percent annually.

Although you may need to "borrow" this money, you probably can find a much cheaper lender. As a rule of thumb, if a vendor gives you a 1 percent discount for paying 20 days early, you are borrowing the vendor's money at about an 18 percent annual interest rate if you do not pay early. A 3 percent discount works out to a whopping 54 percent a year.

3. Press Enter or Tab to move the cursor to the Num field. Enter the number of the check in this field. Checks you recorded in the Write Checks screen but have not printed show asterisks as check numbers.

   If you want to enter a check that you will want to print later, you can enter the check number as asterisks. The Write/Print Checks screen and option, however, provide a more convenient method of writing and printing checks. Refer to Chapter 6 for detailed information on Quicken's Write/Print Checks feature.

4. Press Enter or Tab to move the cursor to the Payee field. Enter the name of the person or business that you are writing the check to. You have space for up to 31 characters.

T I P

You can use the + (plus) key to enter the next check number or the – (minus) key to enter the check number before the last check number used. If the check number from the preceding transaction was 1892, for example, press the + (plus) key to enter 1893 as the check number in the next transaction line or press the – (minus) key to enter 1891 as the check number.

NOTE Quicken 6.0 includes the QuickFill feature, which searches through the last three months of transactions and the Memorized Transaction list for previous transactions that match the characters you type in the Payee field. When Quicken finds a matching transaction, QuickFill fills in the rest of the transaction for you. QuickFill is explained in more detail in the next chapter.

5. Press Enter or Tab to move the cursor to the Payment field. Enter the check amount, using up to 10 characters for the amount. You can enter a check as large as $9,999,999.99. The decimal point counts as one of the 10 characters but the commas do not.

6. Press Enter or Tab to reach the Cleared (C) field, which shows whether a transaction has been recorded by the bank. Use this field as part of *reconciling*, or explaining the difference between your check register account balance and the balance the bank shows on your monthly statement. To mark a transaction as cleared, enter an asterisk (*), the only character Quicken accepts here, in the C field. During reconciliation, Quicken changes the asterisk to an X (see Chapter 8, "Reconciling Your Bank Account").

7. (Optional) Press Enter or Tab twice to move the cursor through the Deposit field and to the Memo field. Use the Memo field to describe a transaction. You can use up to 31 characters to describe a transaction. If you are making several payments a month to the bank, the Memo field enables you to specify the house payment, the school loan, the hot tub, the boat, and so on.

8. (Optional) Press Enter or Tab to move the cursor to the Category field. You use this field to assign a category to a transaction. The category is used to classify expenses, such as utilities expense, interest expense, or entertainment. (Categories also are used to classify income, such as dividend income, interest income, wages, and so on.) Press Ctrl-C to access the Category and Transfer list, which contains the existing categories provided by Quicken or

those you have added previously (see fig. 4.4). Use the up- and down-arrow keys to highlight the category you want to assign to the check transaction and press Enter or double-click the category with the mouse.

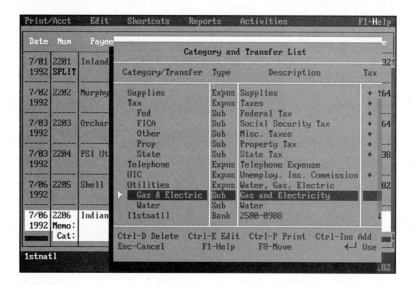

FIG. 4.4

Press Ctrl-C to see the Category and Transfer list.

NOTE You can assign more than one category to a single transaction. This is called *splitting a transaction.* You may need to do this if you are writing one check to a department store, for example, to pay for clothing, computer supplies, and cosmetics. Obviously, there is no one category that describes these different expenses. By splitting the transaction, you can assign three categories to the check transaction so that each expense is properly classified in your records. You learn how to split a transaction in the next chapter.

You also can use the Category field to describe the class into which a transaction falls. Categories and classes are described in Chapter 9, "Organizing Your Finances." Figure 4.5 shows a check to the Indianapolis Power Company. The category is Utilities.

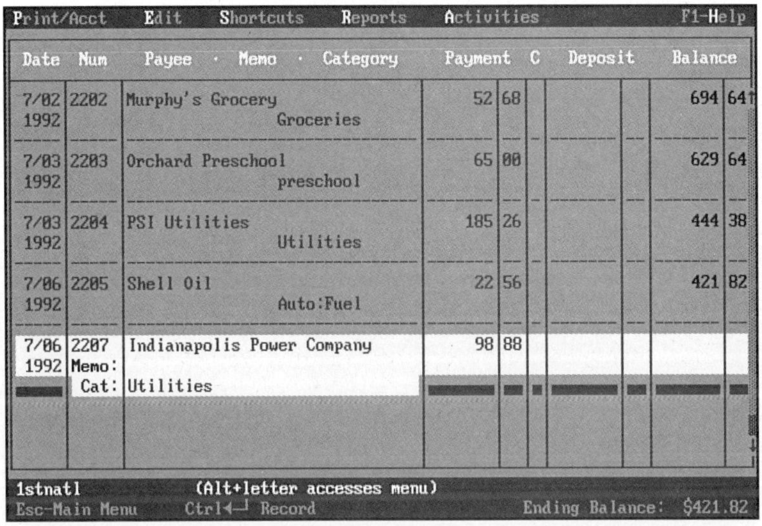

FIG. 4.5

A sample check
entered in the
Register.

T I P

6

Quicken provides a feature known as *QuickFill*, which you can use
when you know the category name. If you type enough of the category name to uniquely identify that name and press Enter, QuickFill
types the rest of the category name for you.

Suppose that you have a category named *Utilities*, and it is the only
category name that starts with the letter *U*. If you type a *U* in the
Category field and press Enter, QuickFill types the remaining letters
of the word—*tilities*. The only trick to the QuickFill feature is that
you need to type enough of the category name to uniquely identify it
from other categories in the Category and Transfer list.

Refer to Chapter 5, "Automating the Register," for more information
on QuickFill.

9. Record the transaction by pressing Enter when the cursor is on
   the last field, Category, or record the transaction while the cursor
   is on any transaction field by pressing Ctrl-Enter or F10. If you're
   using a mouse, record the check transaction by clicking the words
   Ctrl ⌐ Record at the bottom of the screen, in the information
   line.

If you press Enter when the cursor is in the last field (Category),
Quicken displays a prompt asking you to confirm that you want to
record the transaction. If you select **Record Transaction**, the transaction is recorded.

When you record a transaction, a flashing message in the lower left-hand corner of the screen says RECORDING. (If your computer is very fast, you can hardly read the message.) When Quicken finishes recording the transaction, your computer beeps and an empty row is added to the bottom of the Register, with the cursor positioned at the empty Date field. Because Quicken arranges checking account transactions by date, it rearranges transactions if you enter them in an order other than the order of their dates.

T   I   P   Speaking of the beep that you hear when you record a transaction, you'll be glad to know that you have the option of turning it off so that Quicken is silent when you record transactions. This is particularly attractive if you're entering several transactions at a time and are becoming annoyed with the constant beeping. You turn off the beep sound by going to the Beep When Recording and Memorizing field and pressing N. Turn to Chapter 20, "Customizing Quicken," to learn how to access transaction settings and turn off the beep sound.

Quicken also calculates the new Balance field when you record a transaction (see fig. 4.6). If the balance is too large for a positive or negative number to display, Quicken displays asterisks in the Balance field. Quicken uses negative numbers to indicate that you have overdrawn your account. If you have a color monitor, Quicken displays negative amounts in a different color.

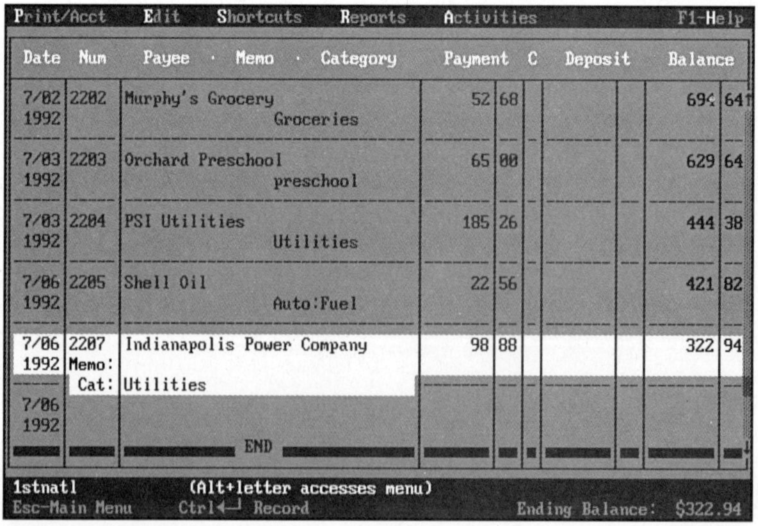

Print/Acct	Edit	Shortcuts	Reports	Activities			F1-Help

Date	Num	Payee · Memo · Category	Payment	C	Deposit	Balance
7/02 1992	2202	Murphy's Grocery Groceries	52 68			69< 64
7/03 1992	2203	Orchard Preschool preschool	65 00			629 64
7/03 1992	2204	PSI Utilities Utilities	185 26			444 38
7/06 1992	2205	Shell Oil Auto:Fuel	22 56			421 82
7/06 1992	2207	Indianapolis Power Company Memo: Cat: Utilities	98 88			322 94
7/06 1992		END				

1stnatl   (Alt+letter accesses menu)
Esc-Main Menu   Ctrl↵ Record   Ending Balance: $322.94

FIG. 4.6

The Register showing the new balance after a check is recorded.

Recording a Deposit

As you may expect, recording a deposit in the Quicken Register is like recording a deposit in your checkbook's paper register. To record a deposit in the Quicken Register, follow these steps:

1. Select **Use Register** from Quicken's main menu if the Register is not displayed already. Quicken displays the Register screen. If you are working with more than one account, you may need to select the account first (see Chapter 3, "Defining Your Accounts").

2. Enter the deposit date in the Date field in MM/DD/YY format. Remember that you can use the + (plus) and – (minus) keys to change the date one day at a time.

3. (Optional) Press Enter or Tab to move the cursor to the Num field. Enter the receipt number of the deposit in this field. Remember that you also can use the + (plus) and – (minus) keys to change the Num field one number at a time.

4. Press Enter or Tab to move the cursor to the Payee field. Enter a description of the deposit transaction. You have space for up to 31 characters. A business recording a deposit from a customer, for example, may describe the deposit by using the customer name, such as *Acme Manufacturing*. A home user recording a payroll deposit may describe the deposit as *Payroll Check*. Interest may be described as *October Interest Income*.

5. Press Enter or Tab three times to move the cursor through the Payment and C fields to the Deposit field. As with the Payment field, Quicken enables you to enter only numbers, with amounts under $9,999,999.99.

6. (Optional) Press Enter or Tab to move the cursor to the Memo field. Use this field to describe the transaction. You can use up to 31 characters to describe a transaction. A business, for example, may note the invoice number that a customer's deposit relates to. A home user may indicate the payroll period covered by a payroll check.

7. (Optional) Press Enter or Tab to move the cursor to the Category field to assign a category to the deposit transaction, such as *gross sales*, *wages*, or *interest income*. Press Ctrl-C to access the Category and Transfer list, which includes the existing categories provided by Quicken or those you have previously added. Use the up- and down-arrow keys to highlight the category you want to assign to the deposit transaction.

You also can use the Category field to describe the class into which a transaction falls. Categories and classes are described further in Chapter 9, "Organizing Your Finances." Figure 4.7 shows a deposit transaction for recording interest income.

8. Record the transaction by pressing Enter when the cursor is on the last field, Category, or record the transaction while the cursor is in any field by pressing Ctrl-Enter or F10. If you're using a mouse, record the transaction by clicking `Ctrl ↵ Record` at the bottom of the screen in the information line.

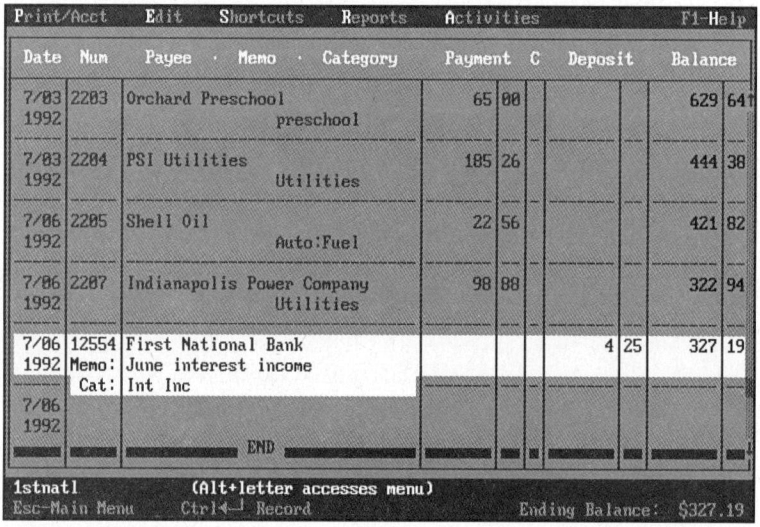

FIG. 4.7

A sample deposit recorded in the Register.

Print/Acct		Edit	Shortcuts		Reports		Activities					F1-Help
Date	Num	Payee	·	Memo	·	Category	Payment	C	Deposit		Balance	
7/03 1992	2203	Orchard Preschool				preschool	65	00			629	641
7/03 1992	2204	PSI Utilities				Utilities	185	26			444	38
7/06 1992	2205	Shell Oil				Auto:Fuel	22	56			421	82
7/06 1992	2207	Indianapolis Power Company				Utilities	98	88			322	94
7/06 1992	12554	First National Bank Memo: June interest income Cat: Int Inc							4	25	327	19
7/06 1992												
				END								

1stnatl   (Alt+letter accesses menu)
Esc-Main Menu   Ctrl↵ Record   Ending Balance: $327.19

If you press Enter when the cursor is in the last field (Category) Quicken displays a prompt asking you to confirm that you want to record the transaction. If you select **Record Transaction** by pressing 1, the transaction is recorded.

Recording Other Withdrawals

The steps for recording other withdrawals—such as automated teller machine transactions, wire transfers, and automatic payments—parallel the steps for recording a check. You enter the date, number, payee, payment amount, and, optionally, a memo description and a category. Record the withdrawal by pressing Enter when the cursor is in the Category field or by pressing Ctrl-Enter or F10 when the cursor is in any other transaction field.

CPA TIP

Consider the monthly service fees a bank charges when choosing a bank and in keeping minimum balances. Most banks charge monthly service fees of about $5. Some banks waive the $5 fee if you keep an average balance of $200 at all times in your account. The $5 a month translates into $60 a year. Because $60 in fee savings equals $60 in interest, the interest rate the bank pays people who keep their minimum balance at $200 is $60/$200 or 30 percent. The return is even better than that for most people because the interest income gets taxed, but the fee savings do not. Probably no other $200 investment in the world is risk-free and pays 30 percent interest.

Recording Transfers Between Accounts

You can use the Category field to record transfers from one account to another. Suppose that you are recording a check drawn on your checking account for deposit to your credit union account with the Acme Credit Union. The check is not an expense, so it should not be categorized as utilities, medical, insurance, or something else. It is a transfer of funds from one account to another. You can identify such transfers by entering the account name in brackets, as shown in figure 4.8.

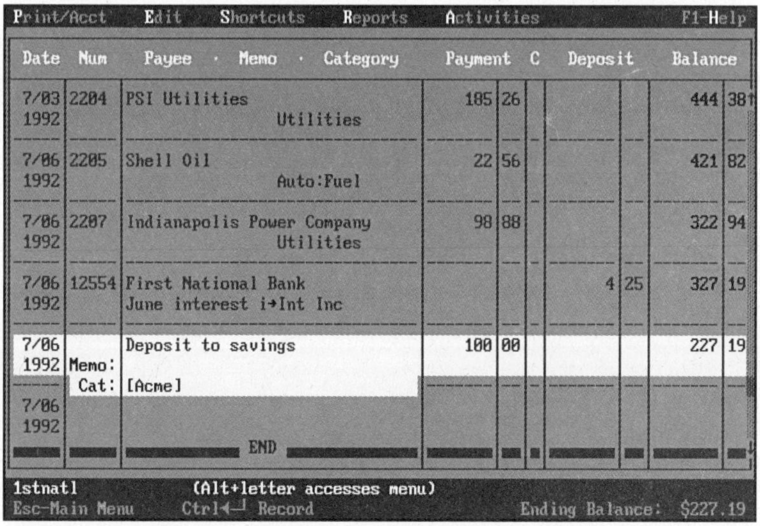

FIG. 4.8

The Category field completed to record a transfer between accounts.

Be sure that the account has been set up first before you try to transfer to or from the account. Quicken enables you to add categories, but not accounts, while you are using the Register.

TIP

When you press Ctrl-C, Quicken lists categories as well as accounts in the Category and Transfer list. Quicken lists categories first (income categories, then expense categories) followed by accounts. Accordingly, you also can press Ctrl-C to see accounts for transfers. Because the accounts are located at the end of the Category and Transfer List, you can access them more quickly by pressing the End key to reach the end of the list. Then use the up- and down-arrow keys to highlight the proper account, press Enter, and Quicken inserts the account name (enclosed in brackets, such as [Acme]) in the Category field in the Register.

If you record a transfer transaction, Quicken records the transaction in the Registers for both accounts. In the transaction shown in figure 4.8, a payment of $100 is recorded in the checking account and, at the same time, a deposit of $100 is recorded in the Acme savings account. Figure 4.9 shows the Register for the Acme savings account with the $100 deposit. You can toggle between the two Registers by pressing Ctrl-X.

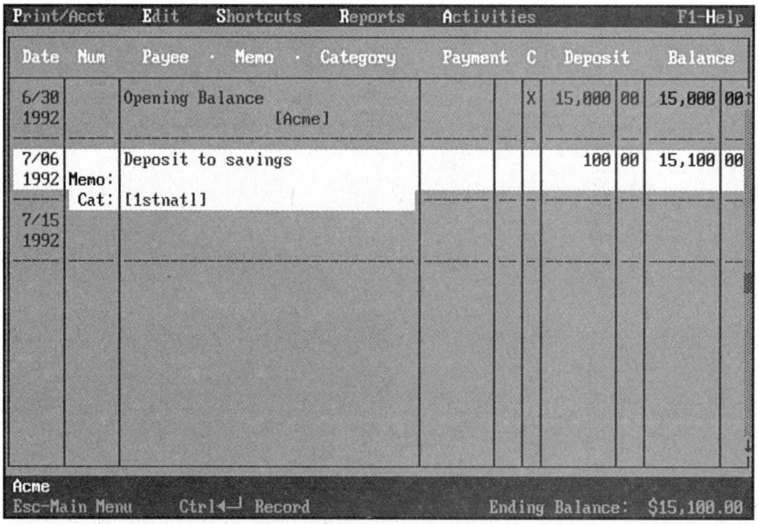

```
 Print/Acct    Edit    Shortcuts    Reports    Activities              F1-Help

  Date  Num   Payee  ·  Memo  ·  Category    Payment  C   Deposit    Balance

  6/30         Opening Balance                        X  15,000 00  15,000 00
  1992                        [Acme]

  7/06         Deposit to savings                        100 00    15,100 00
  1992 Memo:
       Cat: [1stnatl]

  7/15
  1992




 Acme
 Esc-Main Menu    Ctrl←┘ Record                   Ending Balance:  $15,100.00
```

FIG. 4.9

The other part of the transfer transaction shown in figure 4.8.

Entering Uncleared Transactions

You learned in Chapters 1 and 3 that you should enter the ending balance from your last bank statement as the starting balance in your Quicken bank account. This makes reconciling easy the next time you receive your bank statement and start to reconcile your bank account with Quicken.

However, using the balance from your last bank statement doesn't account for transactions that have occurred (before you started using Quicken) but have not been cleared through your bank. In order to accurately reflect your account balance in Quicken, you must enter all uncleared transactions from the date of your last bank statement to the date that you start using Quicken. If your last bank statement was dated 11/15/92, for example, and you started using Quicken on 12/01/92, then you must enter all transactions that occurred between 11/15/92 and 12/01/92 in addition to those transactions that occurred prior to 11/15/92 but did not show up on your last statement.

This chapter showed you how to enter check, deposit, and other withdrawal transactions in the Register, which is all you need to know to enter uncleared transactions. Just move to the last empty line in the Register and begin entering uncleared transactions like you enter any other transaction. Make sure that you enter the correct date, check number, or deposit number for each transaction. After you record the transaction by pressing Ctrl-Enter or F10 (or just Enter from the Category field of a transaction), Quicken sorts your transactions in the Register and places the transactions that you just entered in order by date.

Reviewing and Editing Register Transactions

You can review and edit transactions by accessing the Register at any time. You may want to review a transaction to make sure that you recorded the transaction correctly. You also may want to review a transaction to see whether you received a deposit or to see whether you remembered to pay a particular bill.

You can move from transaction to transaction in the Register screen in two ways—you can use the keyboard or you can use the mouse. You learned about moving around the Register using both the keyboard and mouse earlier in this chapter.

To edit a transaction in the Register, move to the transaction you want to change, edit the fields you want to change, and re-record the transaction by pressing Ctrl-Enter or F10, by pressing Enter while the cursor is in the Category field, or by clicking `Ctrl ↵ Record` at the bottom of the screen in the information line.

If you decide that you want to cancel changes that you have made to a transaction, you can do so any time before the changed transaction is recorded. To cancel the changes, press Esc. Quicken displays the Leaving Transaction window, as shown in figure 4.10. Press 2 to select the **Cancel changes and leave** option. Quicken enters the original information in the transaction and returns to the main menu.

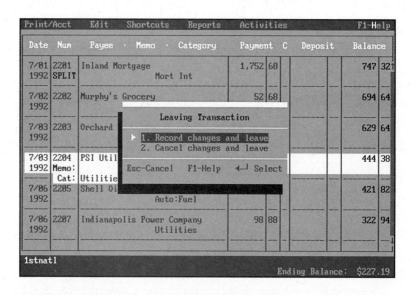

FIG. 4.10

The Leaving Transaction window.

Postdating Transactions

Postdating transactions means that you enter a future date for a check or deposit transaction. Traditionally, people use postdated checks as a way to delay a payment. The payee cannot or should not cash the check before the future date. With Quicken, you can use postdated transactions to delay checks being cashed. Perhaps more importantly, you can forecast your cash flows and balances by entering those checks and deposits that you know are in the future.

The steps for entering postdated transactions mirror those for entering regular transactions. The only difference, of course, is that the check or deposit date is in the future. When you enter postdated transactions,

Quicken calculates two account balances: the current balance, which is the account balance for the current date, and the ending balance, which is the account balance after the last postdated transaction. Quicken determines the current date by looking at the system date. If your computer's system date is incorrect, refer to your DOS user manual to learn how to set or reset the date in your system.

Figure 4.11 shows the 1stNatl Account Register with a postdated transaction. The ending balance, $2,675.93, incorporates all the transactions for the account, including postdated transactions. The current balance, $2,761.19, is the account balance at the current date.

Quicken identifies postdated transactions by drawing a double-dashed line between the current and previous transactions and the postdated transactions. In figure 4.11, notice the double-dashed line between the last two transactions.

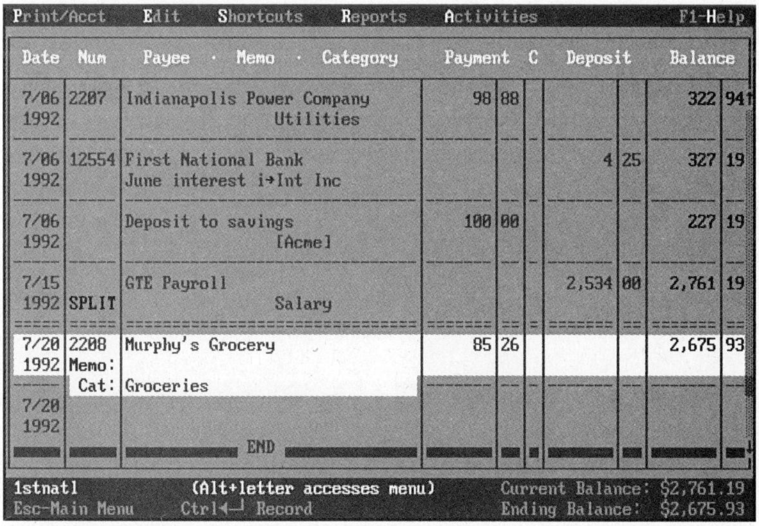

FIG. 4.11

The Register showing a postdated transaction, the current balance, and the ending balance.

Printing the Register

You will want to print a paper register each time you enter a group (perhaps more than five) of check and deposit transactions. A printed copy of the Register enables you to review checking account transactions without turning on your computer. It also can provide a way to recover your financial records if no backup files exist. (Chapter 19, "Managing Your Quicken Files," describes the steps for backing up your Quicken data files.)

To print the Register, follow these steps:

1. From the Register, select the Print/Acct menu by pressing Alt-P. Quicken displays the Print/Acct menu as shown in figure 4.12.

2. Select the **Print Register** option. Quicken displays the Print Register window (see fig. 4.13). You also can press Ctrl-P without first accessing the Print/Acct menu to display the Print Register window.

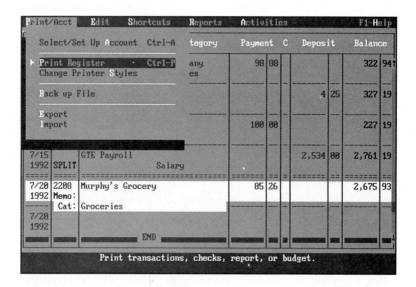

FIG. 4.12

The Print/Acct menu.

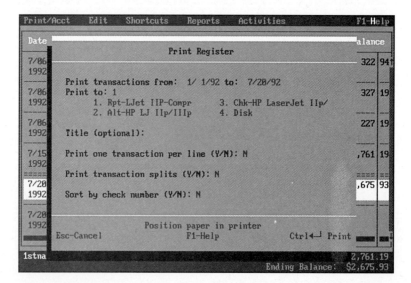

FIG. 4.13

The Print Register window.

3. Verify that your printer is set to use regular paper—not check forms.

4. In the Print Transactions From field, enter the date of the first check or deposit transaction you want printed on the Register. If you are printing only the transactions for the day's batch of transactions, enter the Print Transactions From date as the current date. If you are printing a copy of the month's transactions, enter the Print Transactions From date as the first day of the month. (Remember that the + (plus) and − (minus) keys change the date one day at a time, that the T letter key sets the date to the current system date, and that the M and H letter keys set the date to the first day and last day of the month.)

5. Press Enter or Tab to move the cursor to the To field. Enter the date of the last check or deposit transaction that you want included in the printed Register. If you are printing only the transactions for the day's batch of transactions, enter the To date as the current date. If you are printing a copy of the month's transactions, enter the To date as the last day of the month.

6. Press Enter or Tab to move the cursor to the Print To field. Use this field to specify which printer will print the Register. Quicken lists up to three printers you may have defined as part of the installation process, and it lists a fourth option—Disk. To specify the setting for the Print To field, type the number that corresponds to the printer you want to use.

   If you press 4 from the Print To field, you can create an ASCII file on disk. Quicken displays the Print To Disk window, which collects the file name you want to use for the ASCII file, the number of lines per page, and the page width. Enter the name you want Quicken to use for the ASCII file in the DOS File field. If you want to use a data directory different from the Quicken data directory, QUICKEN, you also can specify a path name. (See your DOS user's manual for information on path names.) Set the number of Register lines Quicken prints between page breaks in the Lines per Page field. If you are using 11-inch paper, the page length is usually 66 lines. Set the number of characters, including blanks, that Quicken prints on a line in the Width field. If you are using 8 1/2-inch paper, the Characters per Line figure usually is 80. Figure 4.14 shows the Print To Disk window.

7. (Optional) Press Tab or Enter to move the cursor to the Title (optional) field. Enter a special title or description you want Quicken to print at the top of each page of the Register. You may, for example, enter *August Check Register* for August's Register.

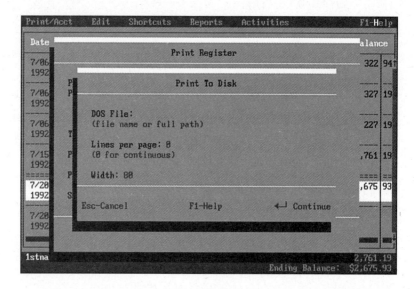

FIG. 4.14

The Print To Disk window.

8. (Optional) Press Enter or Tab to move the cursor to the Print One Transaction per Line field. Press Y if you want Quicken to print the Register in a compact form using only one line per transaction and using abbreviations for many of the fields.

9. (Optional) Press Enter or Tab to move the cursor to the Print Transaction Splits field. If you *split* transactions—you used more than one category for the transaction—you can have Quicken print each of those categories by pressing Y from this field (see Chapter 5, "Automating the Register," to learn about split transactions).

10. (Optional) Press Enter or Tab to move the cursor to the Sort by Check Number field. Usually, Quicken arranges the check and deposit transactions by date. You can, however, press Y to arrange transactions by the check numbers. If a check deposit does not have a number or has the same number as another transaction, Quicken uses the date as a secondary sorting tool.

11. When the Print Register window is complete and you are ready to print, press Ctrl-Enter.

Quicken generates a copy of the Register like that shown in figure 4.15 or figure 4.16. Figure 4.15 shows the Register when the Print One Transaction per Line field is set to the N default. Figure 4.16 shows the same Register when the field is set to Y.

```
                        Check Register
1stnatl                                        Page 1
7/15/92

Date    Num   Transaction        Payment     C    Deposit     Balance
....    .....  .................  ........    ..   ........    ........

7/01    2201  Inland Mortgage    1,752.68               747.32
1992 SPLIT
        cat:  Mort Int
7/02    2202  Murphy's Grocry       52.68               694.64
1992 memo:
        cat:  Groceries
7/03    2203  Orchard Preschool     65.00               629.64
1992 memo:
        cat:  preschool
7/03    2204  PSI Utilities        185.26               444.38
1992 memo:
        cat:  Utilities
7/06    2205  Shell Oil             22.56               421.82
1992 memo:
        cat:  Auto:Fuel
7/06    2207  Indpls Power Company  98.88               322.94
1992 memo:
        cat:  Utilities
7/06    12554 First National Bank              4.25     327.19
1992 memo:    June interest income
        cat:  Int Inc
7/06    Deposit to savings        100.00               227.19
1992 memo:
        cat:  [Acme]
7/15    GTE Payroll                         2,534.00  2,761.19
1992 SPLIT
        cat:  Salary
7/20    2208  Murphy's Grocery      85.26             2,675.93
1992 memo:
        cat:  Groceries
```

FIG. 4.15

The Register with
transactions
printed on
several lines.

```
                          Check Register

  1stnatl                                                        Page 1
  7/15/92

  Date     Num    Payee            Memo        Category      Amount   C    Balance
  ......   .....  ................  .........   ..........   ........  ..   .......

  7/1/92   2201 S Inland Mortgage              Mort Int     -1,752.68        747.32

  7/2/92   2202   Murphy's Grocery             Groceries      -52.68         694.64

  7/3/92   2203   Orchard Preschoo             preschool      -65.00         629.64

  7/3/92   2204   PSI Utilities                Utilities     -185.26         444.38

  7/6/92   2205   Shell Oil                    Auto:Fuel      -22.56         421.82

  7/6/92   2207   Indpls Pow                   Utilities      -98.88         322.94

  7/6/92   12554  First National B June inter  Int Inc          4.25         327.19

  7/6/92          Deposit to savin             [Acme]        -100.00         227.19

  7/15/92       S GTE Payroll                  Salary       2,534.00       2,761.19

  7/20/92  2208   Murphy's Grocery             Groceries      -85.26       2,675.93
```

FIG. 4.16

The Register with one transaction printed on each line.

C P A
T I P

At the end of each month, print a copy of the Register for the transactions you entered in that month. Store the Register with the bank statement for the month. That way, if you ever have questions about a previous month—or the bad luck to lose your Quicken data file—you can reconstruct transactions from previous months. You can discard the now redundant individual Registers that show each of the groups of transactions for the month. You don't need these with a copy of the entire month.

Chapter Summary

This chapter introduced you to Quicken's Register—the central repository of all your checking account information. The basics include knowing the components of the Check Register screen; using the Register to record checks, deposits, and other checking account transactions; reviewing and editing Register transactions; and printing the Register.

The next chapter describes Quicken features that you can use to make working in the Register more efficient and easier.

Automating the Register

This chapter can help you work more efficiently with Registers by describing the Quicken features you can use to enter transactions quickly and easily. These features can help you enter transactions quickly, search through your Register for specific transactions, or save and reuse information you record repeatedly in your Register. Editing features makes it easier for you to add, modify, and remove transactions; special shortcut options offer features that speed up the process of recording transactions.

In this chapter, you learn how to do the following:

- Use Quicken 6's new QuickFill feature to quickly fill in transaction information

- Delete and void transactions in the Register

- Insert a transaction in the Register

- Assign more than one category to a transaction by splitting the transaction

- Find transactions in the Register using the **Find** feature and the **Go to Date** option

- Work with memorized transactions

- Use transaction groups to enter groups of transactions that occur at the same intervals
- Switch between the Check Register and the Write Checks screen

Using QuickFill

Now you can enter transactions in the Register faster and easier than ever with the new QuickFill feature in Quicken 6. When you type a few characters in a field, Quicken searches the various lists and the Register (the last three months of transactions only) to find a matching entry in that particular field. When Quicken finds a match, the QuickFill feature fills in the rest of the transaction with the transaction information it found.

QuickFill works while entering transactions when you make an entry in the Payee field or the Category field in the Register or Write Checks screen. QuickFill also works when you enter investment transactions in the Investment Register. This chapter, however, is limited to a discussion of using QuickFill in a Noninvestment Register. See Chapter 16, "Monitoring Your Investments," to see how QuickFill works when entering investment transactions. See Chapter 7, "Automating Check Writing," to see how QuickFill works when writing checks from the Write Checks screen.

NOTE   QuickFill does not work when you edit an existing transaction.

QuickFill is turned on or activated by default. When you first start to use Quicken 6, this feature should already be working. Refer to the section "Deactivating QuickFill," later in this chapter, to learn how to turn on and off QuickFill.

Using QuickFill from the Payee Field

Quicken searches the Memorized Transaction List and the last three months of transactions in the Register when you type a few characters in the Payee field of a transaction, whether in the Register or the Write Checks screen. (You learn about using QuickFill from the Write Checks screen in Chapter 7.) When Quicken finds a transaction with the same payee name, QuickFill fills in the rest of the payee name from the transaction it found in the Memorized Transaction list or the previous transactions in the Register.

Follow these steps to use QuickFill from the Payee field:

1. In the empty transaction line of the Register, enter the date and transaction number as usual.

2. Type a few characters in the Payee field. Type *PS*, for example. Quicken searches the Memorized Transaction list and the last three months of transactions in the Register for a payee name that starts with *PS*. When Quicken finds the first transaction with the payee *PSI Utilities*, for example, QuickFill fills in the rest of the payee name.

3. If the payee name (*PSI Utilities*, in this example) is indeed the payee that you want to enter in the transaction, press Enter and QuickFill fills in the rest of the transaction information for that payee: the transaction amount, the Memo field (if used), and the category or subcategory exactly like the transaction that Quicken found.

If Quicken finds the matching transaction in the Memorized Transaction list, it displays <MEM> next to the payee name. If Quicken finds the matching transaction in the Register, the month and day (<month/day>) are displayed next to the payee name.

If QuickFill doesn't fill in the payee information that you want, keep typing characters in the Payee field or press Ctrl-+ (plus) or Ctrl-− (minus) to keep searching the Memorized Transaction list or the transactions in the Register for the correct transaction.

NOTE If more than one payee name exists in the Memorized Transaction list or previous transaction in the Register that begins with the characters that you type, QuickFill enters the transaction information for the first payee name found.

Figure 5.1 shows a transaction filled in by QuickFill from the Memorized Transaction list. Figure 5.2 shows a transaction filled from a transaction dated 7/2 in the Register.

After QuickFill fills in the transaction, you can edit any of the transaction fields necessary. When the transaction information is complete and as you want it, record the transaction by pressing Ctrl-Enter or F10.

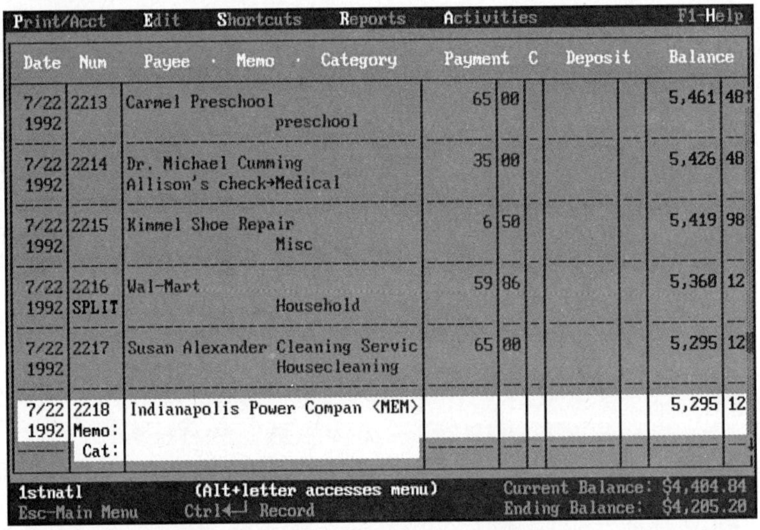

FIG. 5.1

A transaction filled in by QuickFill from the Memorized Transaction list.

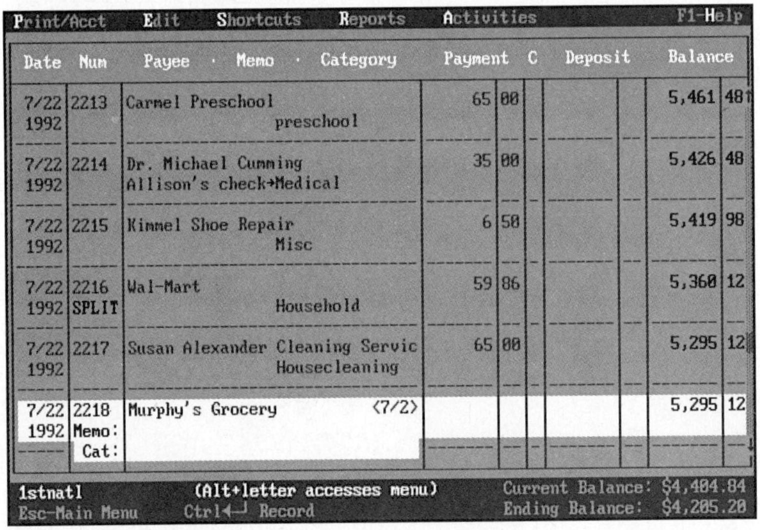

FIG. 5.2

A transaction filled in by QuickFill from a transaction in the Register.

Using QuickFill To Fill in the Category Field

QuickFill also works when you type a few characters in the Category field of a new transaction. (QuickFill does not work when editing an existing transaction.) QuickFill searches the Category and Transfer list and searches for the first category or transfer account that begins with the characters you type. If you want to enter a subcategory or a class, you can type a colon (:) after the category name is filled in and Quicken searches the subcategories under that particular category and enters the first subcategory that it finds. If you want to enter a class, you can type a slash (/) and a few characters after the category or subcategory name is filled in. Quicken then searches the Class list and enters the first class it finds that begins with the characters you type. Classes are explained in Chapter 9, "Organizing Your Finances."

To use QuickFill to fill in the Category field, follow these steps:

1. From the Category field for a new transaction in the Register, type a few characters of the category name that you want to assign to the transaction. Quicken searches the Category and Transfer list for the first category or transfer account that matches the characters you type.

   When Quicken finds a matching category or transfer account, QuickFill fills in the rest of the category or transfer account name.

2. If this is the category or transfer account that you want to assign to the transaction, press Enter to accept it.

   If the category or transfer account name filled in by QuickFill is not the one that you want, type a few more characters or press Ctrl-+ (plus) or Ctrl-- (minus) until Quicken finds the right name.

3. To enter a subcategory after QuickFill fills in the category name, press End to go to the end of the category name and type a colon (:). QuickFill fills in the first subcategory for the category that it just filled in. If the subcategory is not the one that you want, type a few more characters or press Ctrl-+ (plus) or Ctrl-- (minus) to find the next or preceding subcategory under the category. Press Enter to accept the subcategory.

4. To enter class information, type a slash (/) after the category or subcategory name that QuickFill filled in and type a few characters of the class name. QuickFill searches the Class list and fills in the first class that begins with the characters you type. To accept the class, press Enter. If the class is not the one that you want, type a few more characters or press Ctrl-+ (plus) or Ctrl-- (minus) to find the next or preceding class. To enter a subclass, type a colon after the class name and QuickFill fills in the first subclass for the class that it just filled in. Use the Ctrl-+ (plus) or Ctrl-- (minus) key to find the next or preceding subclass under the class. Press Enter to accept the subclass.

> **NOTE**
>
> If the category or class that you want to assign to a transaction is not in the Category and Transfer list or the Class list (because they're new), you can add a new category or class simply by typing the new name in the Category field. When you press Enter after the new category or class name, Quicken asks if you want to add it to the Category or Class list or select a category or class from the existing list. To add the category or class, select option 1, **Add to Category List or Add to Class List**, and go through the normal steps for adding categories and classes. You learn how to add a category and class in Chapter 9.

Deactivating QuickFill

If you don't want to use the QuickFill feature, perhaps because you have varied transactions that are rarely the same or because you feel more comfortable typing transaction information on your own, you can deactivate or turn off the QuickFill feature.

To deactivate QuickFill, follow these steps:

1. From the Quicken main menu, select the **Set Preferences** option. The Set Preferences menu appears.

2. Choose the **Transaction Settings** option. Quicken displays the Transaction Settings window (see fig. 5.3).

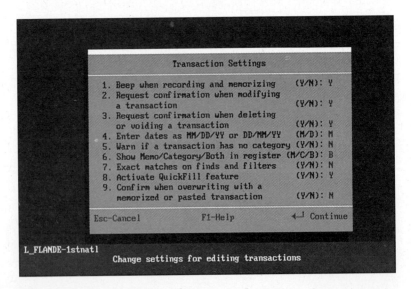

FIG. 5.3

The Transaction Settings window.

3. Press Tab seven times to move the cursor to option 8—the Activate QuickFill Feature field. If you use a mouse, you can get to option 8 a lot quicker by clicking the field for option 8.

4. Press N for this setting.

5. Press Ctrl-Enter or F10 to save the Activate QuickFill Feature setting.

6. Press Esc to return to the main menu.

The QuickFill feature now is turned off. You can go back and activate it again if you decide that you want to use it by pressing Y from the Activate QuickFill Feature field.

Deleting a Transaction from the Register

Quicken enables you to delete a transaction that you inadvertently entered twice, entered in the wrong account Register, and so on. When you delete a transaction, it is removed permanently from the Register.

> You should not delete transactions for manual checks or for checks that you have written with Quicken. When you delete a transaction, Quicken removes all record of the transaction. If the transaction involves a check, deleting the transaction removes the check information and leaves a gap in your check-numbering sequence. Void a check transaction that you want to remove because of a lost check, a check that you have stopped payment on, or an improperly printed check, but do not delete such checks. Information for voided transactions remains in the Register so that you can track each prenumbered check. You learn how to void a transaction in this chapter and how to void a check in Chapter 6, "Writing and Printing Checks."

C P A
T I P

You should delete a recorded transaction only under the following conditions:

- *You inadvertently enter a transaction that should not be entered at all.* If you enter a deposit transaction in the Register and subsequently do not make the deposit, for example, you should delete the transaction. Or, if you enter a transaction for a bank fee in the Register that is later rescinded by the bank, delete the bank fee transaction.

■ *You duplicate transaction information.* If you withdraw funds from an automatic teller machine and enter the transaction twice in the Register, for example, you should delete one of the two transactions.

■ *You enter a transaction in the wrong Quicken Register* (Quicken provides a Register for each account that you set up). If you enter a credit card payment (that you make manually) in the Register for your checking account but want to track your credit card purchases in the Credit Card Register, you should delete the transaction from the Checking Account Register and enter the credit card information in the Credit Card Register.

In all other cases, you should void or reverse transactions in the Register so that you have complete records of all of your check numbers and have established a proper *audit trail* (a history of each and every transaction) in the Register.

If you need to delete a transaction, follow these steps:

1. Access the Register for your checking account.

2. Use the keys listed in the section "Moving Around the Register" in Chapter 4 to highlight the transaction that you want to delete.

3. Select the Edit menu by pressing Alt-E (see fig. 5.4).

4. Select the **Delete Transaction** option from the Edit menu.

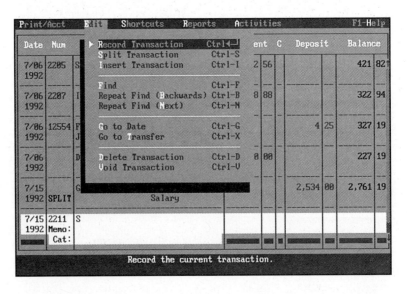

FIG. 5.4

The Edit menu.

Quicken displays the OK to Delete Transaction? window shown in figure 5.5.

The OK to Delete Transaction? window.

5. Press Enter to delete the transaction (because the **Delete transaction** option is highlighted), or press 2 if you don't want to delete the transaction.

When you delete a transaction, Quicken removes all transaction information from the Register.

NOTE

If you delete a transaction from one Quicken account that is part of a transfer transaction (where you transferred funds from one Quicken account to another), the corresponding transaction in the other account also is deleted.

If you try to delete a transaction that is part of a split transfer transaction, you must delete the transaction from the account where the transaction originated—in other words, the account that you entered the transfer transaction in.

To quickly find the corresponding transfer transaction, use the **Go to Transfer** option from the Edit menu. See the section "Using the Go to Transfer Option," later in this chapter.

Voiding a Transaction in the Register

You may need to void a check when you want to stop payment, when you lose a check and write another one to replace it, or when a check prints incorrectly and you have to print another. Note that you can choose to void a check from the Write Checks screen; however, when you select the **Void transaction** option from the Write Checks screen, Quicken takes you to the Checking Account Register and enables you to void the check transaction from there.

If you void a transaction that is part of a transfer from one account to another, voiding any part of the transaction also voids the other parts of the transaction—those recorded in the other Registers.

To void a check from the Checking Account Register, follow these steps:

1. Access the Register.

2. Use the keys listed in the section "Moving Around the Register" in Chapter 4 to highlight the transaction for the check that you want to void. If you are voiding a manual check that you have not yet entered in the Register, enter the date and check number in the last empty transaction line. Keep this transaction highlighted as you move to the next step.

3. Select the Edit menu by pressing Alt-E.

4. Select the **Void transaction** option from the Edit menu.

   Quicken displays the OK to Void Transaction? window shown in figure 5.6.

T I P   You can use the Ctrl-V shortcut key to select the **Void transaction** option.

5. Press Enter to void the transaction (because the **Void transaction** option is already highlighted), or press 2 if you decide not to void the transaction.

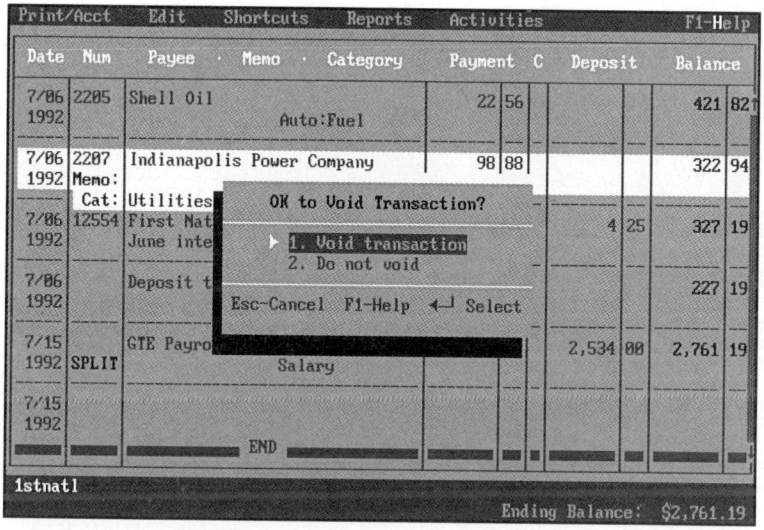

FIG. 5.6

The OK to Void
Transaction?
window.

Quicken enters the word VOID: in the Payee field before the payee
name and marks the transaction with an X in the Clear column so that
the transaction is not considered an uncleared item when you perform
your account reconciliation. Figure 5.7 shows the Register with a
voided check transaction.

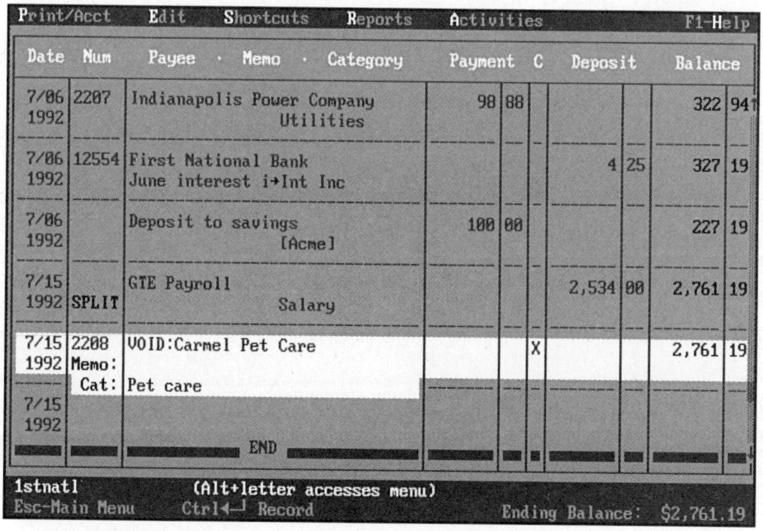

FIG. 5.7

The Register with
a voided check
transaction.

NOTE   When you void a check, Quicken erases the amount of the transaction and adjusts your checking account balance. Quicken also subtracts the amount of the voided check from the category that was originally assigned to the check transaction.

Inserting a Transaction in the Register

You can insert an empty transaction line anywhere in the Register. When you insert a line, Quicken inserts the transaction line above the currently highlighted transaction line. You can use this empty transaction line to record another transaction. Usually, transactions are recorded in the empty transaction line at the end of the Register, however.

To insert a transaction into the Register, follow these steps:

1. Access the Register.

2. Highlight the transaction line just below the place where you want to insert a transaction.

3. Select the Edit menu by pressing Alt-E.

4. Select the **Insert Transaction** option from the Edit menu. Quicken inserts an empty transaction line just above the highlighted line.

T I P   You can use the Ctrl-I shortcut key to select the **Insert Transaction** option.

NOTE   When you enter and record a transaction in an inserted transaction line, Quicken sorts the transactions and moves it, if necessary in proper date order. You therefore should not bother inserting transactions unless you insert them in the proper date order in the Register.

Splitting Transactions

In the last chapter, you learned how to enter transactions in the Register and how to assign a category to a single transaction. But what happens when you write a check for an expense that covers more than one category, such as the check you write to the bank to pay a mortgage payment that pays principal, interest, insurance, and property taxes? In this case, you need to *split the transaction*, or assign more than one category or subcategory to the transaction. (Subcategories further divide a category into second-, third-, fourth-level, and so on categories. You may want to divide the Utilities category so that you can track expenses for electricity, gas, and water, for example. Subcategories are explained in more detail in Chapter 9.

 NOTE You can split transactions when you write a check from the Write Checks screen or enter a manual check in the Register. Quicken enables you to assign up to 30 categories or subcategories to a single transaction.

A transaction line in the Register screen provides one field to assign a category or subcategory. Occasionally, however, you need to be able to break down a transaction into multiple categories, such as in the mortgage payment example. Selecting **Split Transaction** (Ctrl-S) from the Edit menu provides additional Category fields so that you can assign more than one category to a transaction or further describe a transaction.

To split a transaction, follow these steps:

1. From the Register, press Alt-E to display the Edit menu.

2. Select **Split Transaction** to display the Split Transaction window shown in figure 5.8.

You can press the shortcut key Ctrl-S to display the Split Transaction window to split a transaction. **T I P**

3. Enter the category name in the Category field for the first line in the Split Transaction window. You use this field in this window like the Category field in the Register screen. You also can use the Category field to record transfers to other accounts. The Split Transaction window gives you 30 lines in which to assign multiple categories to a transaction.

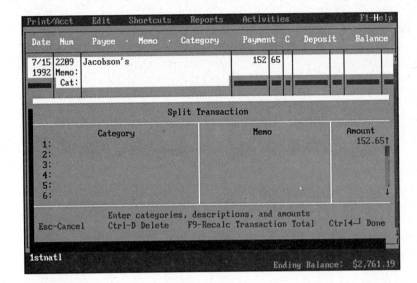

FIG. 5.8

The Split
Transaction
window.

> **NOTE**   Remember that Quicken provides defined Home and
> Business categories. You selected one of these lists
> when you set up your Quicken system (see Chapter 1,
> "Preparing To Use Quicken"). The Home Category list
> has descriptions for most general household expenses,
> and the Business Category list has general business
> income and expense categories. Press Ctrl-C to view
> and select from a list of the defined categories.

4. (Optional) Press Enter or Tab to move the cursor to the Memo
   field in the first line of the Split Transaction window. Type a description of the category or the amount in this field. The Memo
   field provides a 27-character space for further description of a
   transaction or an explanation of your category choice.

5. Press Enter or Tab to move the cursor to the Amount field. You
   use this field in two ways, depending on whether you select the
   Split Transaction option before or after you enter the payment or
   deposit amount in the Register screen.

   ■ If you select the **Split Transaction** option before you enter
     an amount in the Amount field, Quicken adds each of the
     amounts you enter in the Amount fields in the Split Transac-
     tion window. Quicken then takes the total of these amounts
     and enters that total in the Payment or the Deposit field of
     the Register screen. If the total of the split transaction
     amounts is negative, Quicken places the amount in the Pay-
     ment field; if the total is positive, Quicken places the amount
     in the Deposit field.

■ If you select the **Split Transaction** option after you enter the payment or deposit amount in the Register screen, Quicken copies the amount entered into the Split Transaction window into the first Amount field. When you enter the Register amount as a payment, Quicken copies the amount into the Split Transaction window as a negative number; when you enter the amount as a deposit, Quicken copies the amount into the Split Transaction window as a positive number. If you then overwrite the first Amount field in the Split Transaction window with another amount, Quicken calculates the difference between the Register screen amount and the amount you have entered and places this difference in the second Amount field in the Split Transaction window.

Usually, you want to enter dollar amounts in the Split Transaction window's Amount fields. You also can enter percentages. Quicken then uses these percentages to calculate the split amount and enters the result in the Amount field. If you enter a check for $150 in the Payment field of the Register, for example, and 30 percent of this should be entered in the first split transaction Amount field, you can just type *30%* in the Amount field. When you press Tab or Enter to move to the next field, Quicken calculates the number that equals 30 percent of $150 and enters this resulting value in the field.

T   I   P

6. Press Enter or Tab to move to the next line in the Split Transaction window. Repeat steps 3, 4, and 5 for each category and amount combination you want to record. You can record up to 30 category and amount combinations.

    If you use all 30 of the Split Transaction Amount fields, the sum of the split transaction amounts may not equal the Register amount. In this case, you must adjust manually the Register screen amount or one of the Split Transaction window amounts. You also can press F9 to recalculate the total of the amounts in the Amount fields in the Split Transaction window and to insert that total into the Payment or Deposit field in the Register.

7. When the categories and amounts in the Split Transaction window are complete, press Ctrl-Enter or F10 to save the information in the Split Transaction window and return to the Register.

8. After you return to the Register from the Split Transaction window, press Ctrl-Enter or F10 to record the split transaction in the Register. Quicken indicates that a transaction is split by displaying the word SPLIT below the check or transaction number (see fig. 5.9).

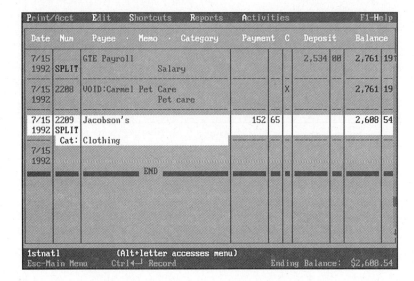

Print/Acct	Edit	Shortcuts	Reports	Activities			F1-Help

Date	Num	Payee · Memo · Category	Payment	C	Deposit	Balance
7/15 1992	SPLIT	GTE Payroll Salary			2,534 00	2,761 19
7/15 1992	2208	VOID:Carmel Pet Care Pet care		X		2,761 19
7/15 1992	2209 SPLIT Cat:	Jacobson's Clothing	152 65			2,608 54
7/15 1992		═══ END ═══				

1stnatl   (Alt+letter accesses menu)
Esc-Main Menu   Ctrl↵ Record   Ending Balance: $2,608.54

FIG. 5.9

Quicken identifies split transactions with the word SPLIT under the check or transaction number in the Num field.

If you split transactions, you may want to see the extra category names, memos, and amounts on the printed version of the Register. When you select **Print Register** from the Acct/Print menu, the Print Register window includes a Print Transaction Splits field that you can use to indicate whether you want to print the category, memo, and amounts for each line in a split transaction. (See Chapter 4 for more information on printing the Register.)

Entering Negative Amounts in Split Transactions

You can enter negative amounts in split transactions to represent withholdings for payroll checks or amounts deducted from a deposit, for example. To enter a negative amount in the Split Transaction window, just press the – (minus) key before you enter the amount. Figure 5.10 shows the Split Transaction window with negative amounts for a payroll check.

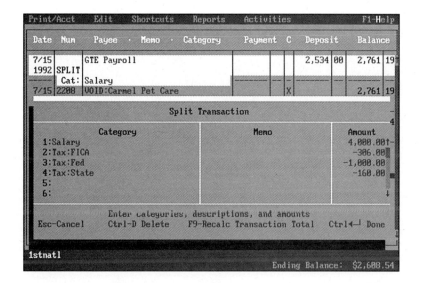

FIG. 5.10

The Split
Transaction
window with
negative
amounts.

Calculating Transaction Amounts in Split Transactions

When entering a split transaction, you can have Quicken calculate the transaction amount as you are entering lines in the Split Transaction window. To have Quicken calculate the transaction amount, follow these steps:

1. Enter the transaction information into the Register as usual, except for the amount.

2. For check or payment transactions, position the cursor on the blank Payment field. For deposit transactions, position the cursor on the blank Deposit field.

3. Press Ctrl-S to display the Split Transaction window.

4. Enter the information in the Split Transaction window. As you enter amounts, Quicken fills in the Payment or Deposit field with the total amount in the Split Transaction window.

5. When you have finished entering lines in the Split Transaction window, press Ctrl-Enter or F10 to return to the transaction in the Register. If you need to return to the Split Transaction window to make a change, just press Ctrl-S and make the necessary changes and then press Ctrl-Enter or F10 again. Quicken does not record the split transaction until you return to the Register and record the transaction from there (as in step 6).

6. Press Ctrl-Enter or F10 to record the split transaction and the transaction amount in the Register.

Editing Split Transactions

You can change the information in the Split Transaction window just as you can change any other transaction. To edit a split transaction, follow these steps:

1. Highlight the split transaction in the Register.

2. Press Ctrl-S to display the Split Transaction window.

3. Make any necessary changes to categories, memos, or amounts in the Split Transaction window. Press Ctrl-End to move to the last line in the Split Transaction window. Note that if you change an amount, the Split Transaction window may not balance (the total amount in the Split Transaction window will not equal the transaction amount in the Register). If necessary, you can press F9 to recalculate the transaction amount. Don't press F9 to recalculate if the amount in the Payment or Deposit field in the Register is the correct amount and you're just reallocating amounts to categories or subcategories in the Split Transaction window. To delete a line in the Split Transaction window, press Ctrl-D. To delete all lines, press Ctrl-D at each line.

4. After making changes in the Split Transaction window, press Ctrl-Enter or F10 to save the changes and to return to the split transaction in the Register.

5. Press Ctrl-Enter or F10 to record the changed split transaction.

Deleting Split Transactions

Just as you can delete transactions with only one category or subcategory assigned to it, you also can delete split transactions. Use the same discretion when deleting a split transaction that you use for deleting a transaction assigned to only one category or subcategory as explained in the section "Deleting a Transaction from the Register," earlier in this chapter.

You delete split transactions the same way you delete single-category transactions. To delete a split transaction, follow these steps:

1. Highlight the split transaction that you want to delete.

2. Press Ctrl-D to select the **Delete Transaction** option. Quicken displays the OK to Delete Transaction? window.

3. Press Enter to delete the split transaction (because the **Delete Transaction** option is highlighted), or press 2 if you decide that you don't want to delete the split transaction.

> **NOTE** If you try to delete a transaction that is part of a split transfer transaction (where one part of the split transaction transfers funds from one Quicken account to another), you must delete the transaction from the account where the transaction originated; in other words, the account that you entered the split transfer transaction in. Use the **Go to Transfer** option to locate the split transfer transaction (see the section "Using the Go to Transfer Option," later in this chapter). Once you've located the split transfer transaction, press Ctrl-S to open the Split Transaction window, highlight the transfer transaction, and press Ctrl-Del to delete the transaction. Quicken then deletes the corresponding transaction in the other account.

> **T I P** When you want to track your income and expenses closely, enter split transactions for payments to department stores, discount stores, and so on where you purchase different types of items. If you don't split the transaction to record a check to Wal-Mart where you buy hardware, cleaning supplies, office supplies, and so on, for example, and lump the total check transaction into one category, your expenses are not accurately reflected.

Undoing Split Transactions

After you have split a transaction, you can go back, undo the split, and assign only one category or subcategory to the transaction. Follow these steps to undo a split transaction:

1. Highlight the split transaction that you want to undo.

2. Press Ctrl-S to display the Split Transaction window.

3. Delete each line in the Split Transaction window by highlighting the line and pressing Ctrl-D.

4. After you have deleted all lines, press Esc to return to the transaction in the Register. Notice that Quicken removes the word SPLIT from the Num field.

5. Enter one category or subcategory in the Category field.

6. Press Ctrl-Enter or F10 to record the transaction.

Finding Transactions

You may write only a handful of checks and make only one or two deposits a month. Even with such low volumes, however, you soon will have several dozens of transactions in a Register. As you write more checks and make additional deposits, searching through your Register for specific transactions becomes more and more difficult. You may eventually want to know whether you recorded a deposit or paid a bill, or when you last paid a vendor. Quicken provides the **Find** option to locate specific transactions.

You can use the **Find** option from the Edit menu to search through the Register for transactions using the following transaction fields: Num, Payee, Payment, C (Cleared), Deposit, Memo, or Category. Quicken provides another option—the **Go to Date** option (also from the Edit menu)—to locate transactions using the Date field. You learn about finding transactions with specific dates later in the section "Using the Go to Date Option." You can look for transactions where the payee is *Stouffer's Office Supplies*, where the category is *Utilities*, or where the amount is *$88.44*, for example.

Using the Find Option

To quickly locate a specific transaction or group of transactions you recorded in the Register, follow these steps:

1. Press Alt-E to display the Edit menu, and then select the **Find** option or press the shortcut key Ctrl-F. Quicken displays the Transaction to Find window shown in figure 5.11.

2. (Optional) To search through the Register for a transaction with a specific check or transaction number, enter that number in the Num field.

3. (Optional) To search through the Register for checks to a certain payee or a deposit from a particular source, type the payee or source name in the Payee field.

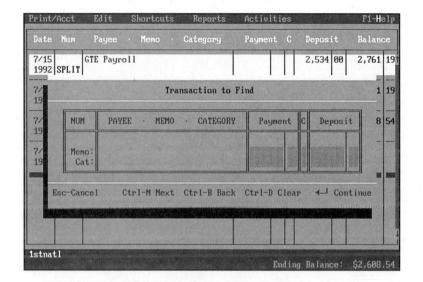

FIG. 5.11

The Transaction
to Find window.

4. (Optional) To search through the Register for a transaction equal
   to a specific amount, enter the amount in the Payment or the Deposit field. The amount you look for is called a *search argument*.

   If you enter an amount in the Payment field in the Transaction to
   Find window, Quicken searches through the checks in the Register for that amount. If you enter an amount in the Deposit field,
   Quicken searches for that amount among the deposits in the Register. If Quicken finds a transaction that matches your search
   argument, it highlights that transaction on the Register screen.

5. (Optional) To search through the Register for checks or deposits
   with a specific entry in the C field (X or *), enter that entry in the
   C field. You may want to perform this search to find cleared or
   outstanding transactions.

6. (Optional) To search through the Register for checks or deposits
   with a specific memo or description, type that memo or description in the Memo field.

7. (Optional) To search through the Register for checks or deposits
   assigned to a specific category or subcategory, enter the category
   or subcategory name in the Category field. Alternatively, you can
   press Ctrl-C to display the Category and Transfer list and select a
   category, subcategory, or transfer account from the list.

8. When you finish entering the search argument or arguments in the
   Transaction to Find window, press Ctrl-Enter or F10.

Quicken asks in which direction you want to search by displaying the Search Direction? window shown in figure 5.12. **Find backwards** (Ctrl-B) looks through transactions with dates earlier than the transaction highlighted in the Register. **Find next** (Ctrl-N) looks through transactions with dates later than the date of the transaction highlighted in the Register.

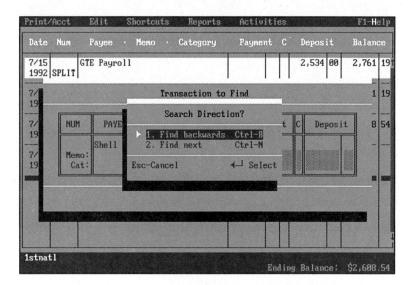

FIG. 5.12

The Search
Direction?
window.

9. Select **Find backwards** by pressing 1 or **Find next** by pressing 2.

Quicken searches for a transaction that exactly matches the information or search argument that you entered in the Transaction to Find window. If you enter an asterisk (*) in the C field, for example, Quicken searches for those transactions in the Register that you marked as cleared with an asterisk. If you enter *Chris Katz* in the Payee field, Quicken searches for transactions with the payee *Chris Katz*. Quicken does not recognize case; *CHRIS KATZ*, *chris katz*, and *cHRIS kATZ* are all exact matches from Quicken's perspective. If the Payee field is *Christopher Katz*, *C. Katz*, or *Mr. Chris Katz*, however, Quicken does not find the transaction.

If Quicken does not find a transaction that matches your search argument, the program displays the message No matching transactions were found, as shown in figure 5.13.

T I P   To clear the entries in the Transaction to Find window, press Ctrl-D.

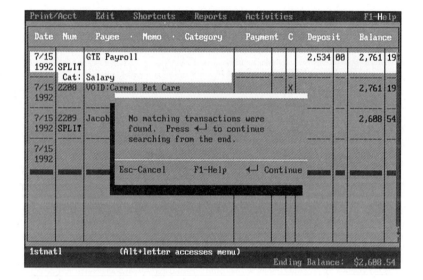

FIG. 5.13

The No matching transactions were found message.

Using Key-Word Matches

Key-word matches enable you to search a field that includes or excludes certain letters, characters, or series of characters. Key-word matches use three characters: the period (.), question mark (?), and . Periods are wild-card indicators that can represent any character, a group of characters, or even no characters. The question mark represents any character. The tilde identifies a word, character, or characters you want to exclude from your search. If you want to find transactions that don't include the word *Interest*, for example, enter the tilde character before the word interest (~*interest*) as the search argument. Table 5.1 summarizes what various search arguments do and do not find.

Combining Exact and Key-Word Matches

You can search transactions using more than one exact match or key-word argument. Figure 5.14 shows the Transaction to Find window set to search for transactions with the phrase *big national bank* in the Payee field and an asterisk (*) in the Cleared field.

If you use more than one exact match or key-word argument, the **Find** option locates any transactions that meet all arguments. With the Transaction to Find window shown in figure 5.14, for example, **Find** does not locate transactions with the phrase *big national bank* used in the Payee field unless the asterisk character also is used in the C field. **Find** also does not locate transactions with the asterisk character used in the C field unless the phrase *big national bank* also is used in the Payee field.

Table 5.1 Summary of Search Arguments Using Special Characters[*]

Argument	What It Finds	What It Does Not Find
..interest	interest car loan interest mortgage interest	car loan interest expense mortgage expense war loan
interest..	interest interest expense	car loan car loan interest mortgage expense mortgage interest war loan
..interest..	interest car loan interest interest expense mortgage interest	car loan mortgage expense war loan
~..interest	car loan interest expense mortgage expense war loan	interest car loan interest mortgage interest
~interest..	car loan car loan interest mortgage expense mortgage interest war loan	interest interest expense
~..interest..	car loan mortgage expense war loan	car loan interest interest interest expense mortgage interest
?ar loan	car loan war loan	car loan interest interest interest expense mortgage expense mortgage interest
~?ar loan	interest car loan interest interest expense mortgage expense mortgage interest	car loan war loan

[*]*For a sample list of memo descriptions containing the following: car loan, car loan interest, interest, interest expense, mortgage expense, mortgage interest, and war loan.*

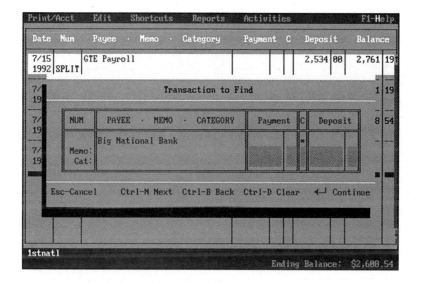

FIG. 5.14

Searching for transactions that include the phrase *big national bank* in the Payee field.

Repeating a Find Request

When Quicken executes a Find request, it selects the first transaction that meets the search argument or arguments you entered in the Transaction to Find window. If you were precise in specifying the exact match or key-word match, the first transaction Quicken finds may be the one you want. That transaction also could be similar to the one you want, but not an exact match, so Quicken gives you two additional **Find** options: **Repeat Find backwards** (Ctrl-B) and **Repeat Find next** (Ctrl-N). **Repeat Find backwards** (Ctrl-B) executes the find request already specified in the Transaction to Find window, and it looks through checks and deposits *before* the currently highlighted transaction. Similarly, **Repeat Find next** (Ctrl-N) executes the Find request already specified in the Transaction to Find window, but it looks through checks and deposits *after* the currently highlighted transaction.

Instead of thumbing through paid invoices, use the Quicken **Find** option to locate a transaction when a vendor is on the phone, alleging nonpayment. Simply type the vendor's name in the Transaction to Find window and search backward or forward through the Register. Quicken finds and highlights each transaction to this particular vendor in seconds.

C P A
T I P

Using the Go to Date Option

You may have wondered about the absence of a Date field in the Transaction to Find window that you worked with in the last section. Quicken provides the **Go to Date** option to search for transactions with a specific date.

To find a transaction by date in the Register, follow these steps:

1. From the Register, press Alt-E to display the Edit menu.

2. Select the **Go to Date** option from the Edit menu.

   Quicken displays the Go to Date window shown in figure 5.15.

T   I   P   You can press the shortcut key Ctrl-G to select the **Go to Date** option.

Quicken initially displays the current system date in the Go to Date field.

3. Change the date by typing the date you want over the default date. (You also can use the + and – special date entry keys to enter the date. If you don't remember how to use these keys, refer to Chapter 2, "Getting Around in Quicken").

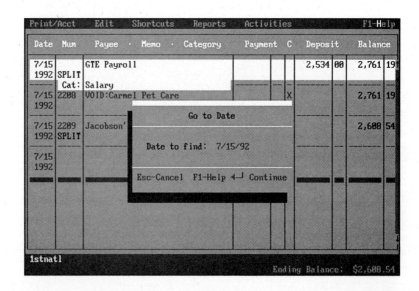

FIG. 5.15

The Go to Date window.

After you set the date you want, Quicken finds and displays the first transaction with the date you entered. If no transaction has the date you entered, the transaction with the date closest to that date is displayed.

Because Quicken arranges transactions in the Register by date, you do not need to specify a search direction for the **Go to Date** option. By comparing the date of the currently highlighted transaction to the date in the Go to Date field, Quicken determines which direction it needs to search. If the Go to date is earlier than the date of the highlighted transaction, Quicken looks through the previous transactions; if the Go to date is later than the date of the highlighted transaction, Quicken searches succeeding transactions.

Using the Go to Transfer Option

If the currently highlighted transaction is a transfer transaction, you can switch quickly to the corresponding transaction by using the **Go to Transfer** option. A *transfer transaction* is a transfer from one Quicken account to another account. Figure 5.16, for example, shows that the Deposit to Savings transaction is selected. By looking at the Category field, which displays [Acme], you can see that this is a transfer transaction. The name of the account to which the transfer is taking place is displayed in brackets in the Category field.

If you highlight the transfer transaction and select the **Go to Transfer** option by choosing it from the Edit menu or pressing Ctrl-X, Quicken displays the Account Register with the corresponding transaction selected. Figure 5.17 shows the corresponding transaction in the Savings Account Register. In the first account, 1stnatl, the transaction is a payment because it reduces that account balance. In the second account, Acme, the transaction is listed as a deposit.

If you use the **Go to Transfer** option from a split transaction, Quicken asks you to identify the category to which you want to go. With a split transaction, you can make transfers to more than one account. If you try to change a split transaction from one of the other Registers, Quicken tells you that the transaction was created through a transfer, and you must return to the original transaction to make changes.

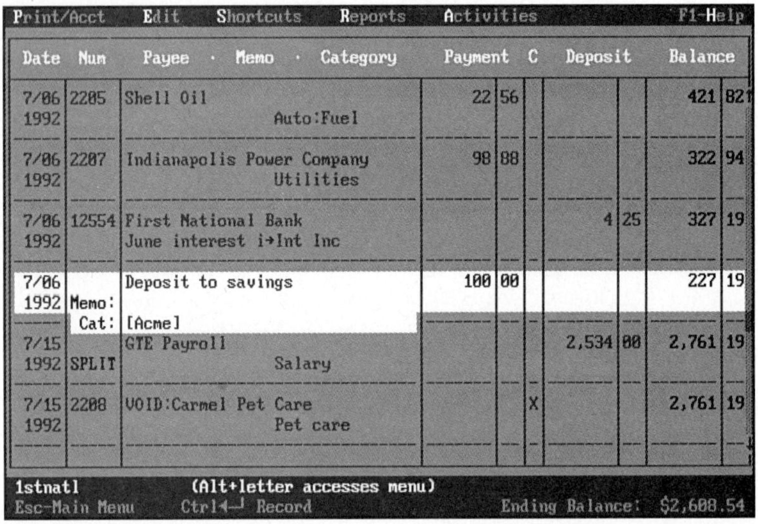

| Print/Acct | Edit | Shortcuts | Reports | Activities | | | F1-Help |

Date	Num	Payee · Memo · Category	Payment	C	Deposit	Balance
7/06 1992	2205	Shell Oil Auto:Fuel	22 56			421 82↑
7/06 1992	2207	Indianapolis Power Company Utilities	98 88			322 94
7/06 1992	12554	First National Bank June interest i→Int Inc			4 25	327 19
7/06 1992	Memo: Cat:	Deposit to savings [Acme]	100 00			227 19
7/15 1992	SPLIT	GTE Payroll Salary			2,534 00	2,761 19
7/15 1992	2208	VOID:Carmel Pet Care Pet care		X		2,761 19

1stnatl   (Alt+letter accesses menu)
Esc-Main Menu   Ctrl◄─┘ Record   Ending Balance: $2,608.54

FIG. 5.16

The Deposit to Savings transaction is part of a transfer.

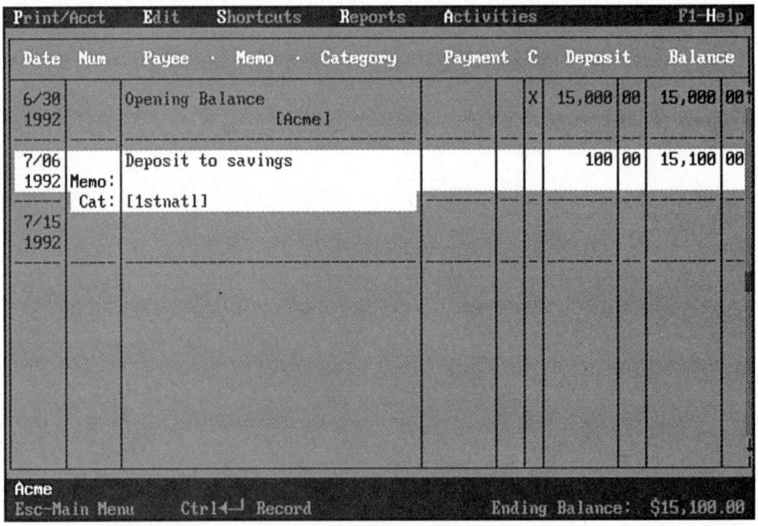

| Print/Acct | Edit | Shortcuts | Reports | Activities | | | F1-Help |

Date	Num	Payee · Memo · Category	Payment	C	Deposit	Balance
6/30 1992		Opening Balance [Acme]		X	15,000 00	15,000 00↑
7/06 1992	Memo: Cat:	Deposit to savings [1stnatl]			100 00	15,100 00
7/15 1992						

Acme
Esc-Main Menu   Ctrl◄─┘ Record   Ending Balance: $15,100.00

FIG. 5.17

The corresponding transfer transaction.

Working with Memorized Transactions

Quicken already may be fast enough for you. After all, it does not take that much time to type in the half dozen fields you enter to record a check or a deposit. But you can streamline your record-keeping further by using *memorized transactions*. A memorized transaction is information you save from one transaction so that you can recall it for other transactions.

Many of the checks you write and the deposits you make are similar or identical to previous checks and deposits. A household, for example, may record the mortgage check, the car payment check, the utility bill check, and the payroll deposit each month. A business may write checks for the monthly rent, payroll, and expenses like supplies or insurance.

Because so many Register transactions are largely the same every month, Quicken gives you the capability to store transaction information in a memorized transaction list. Rather than entering the information over and over, you can recall it from the list of memorized transactions.

Quicken can memorize any transaction that you enter into your system. You can memorize a transaction from any Quicken Account Register, including Investment Account Registers. Quicken stores memorized investment transactions in a separate memorized transaction list. In this section, you learn how to memorize and recall transactions in the Checking Account Register; you can use the same steps to memorize and recall transactions in any other Noninvestment Account Register. (You learn how to memorize check transactions in the Write Checks screen in Chapter 7 and how to memorize investment transactions in Chapter 16.)

Quicken saves the memorized transactions to the Memorized Transaction list when you memorize the following types of transactions:

- Checks
- Deposits
- Banking fees
- Interest earned
- Automatic teller machine transactions
- Any other transaction recorded in the following Account Registers: Bank, Credit Card, Cash, Other Asset, and Other Liability.

You can recall the memorized transaction from the Memorized Transaction list, and Quicken enters the transaction information in the Register. You can edit or delete a memorized transaction directly from the memorized lists.

C P A
T I P Memorized transactions provide a quick method to enter lengthy, split transactions that you always assign to the same categories or subcategories. A transaction to record your paycheck, for example, involves several split lines because you must assign categories for federal withholding, state withholding, FICA withholding, Medicare withholding, and so on, to each paycheck transaction. If you memorize a paycheck transaction and then recall it, Quicken enters the categories for you. You then simply change the amounts assigned to the categories, if necessary.

Memorizing a Transaction

To memorize a transaction in a Register, follow these steps:

1. Enter the transaction you want to memorize in the Register. You can enter as little or as much of the transaction that you want to memorize. If you want to memorize the payee and the category only, for example, enter only that information and continue with steps 2 through 4.

2. With the transaction still highlighted, press Alt-S to display the Shortcuts menu shown in figure 5.18.

3. Select the **Memorize Transaction** option from the Shortcuts menu.

T   I   P You can press the shortcut key Ctrl-M directly from the Register to select the **Memorize Transaction** option.

Quicken displays a message telling you the program will memorize the highlighted fields (see fig. 5.19).

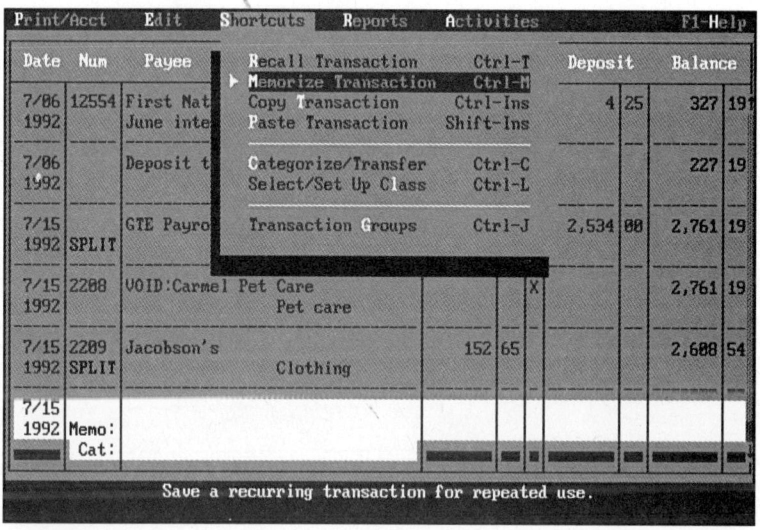

FIG. 5.18

The Shortcuts menu.

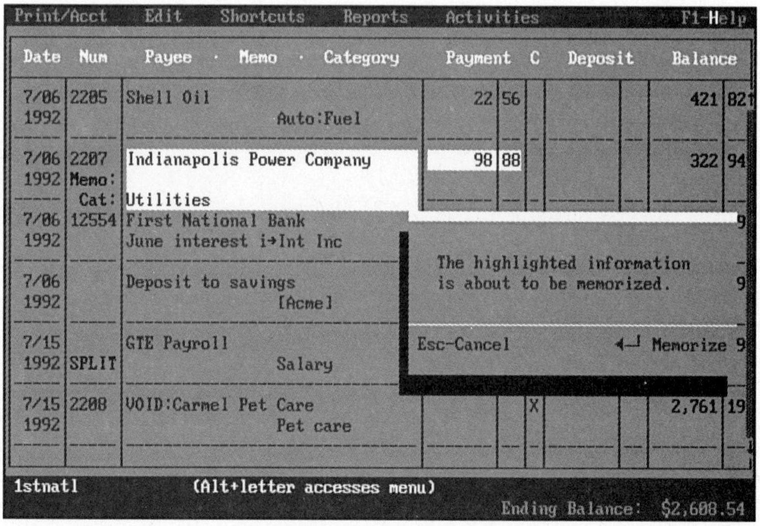

FIG. 5.19

The Quicken message telling you that the highlighted fields will be memorized.

4. To memorize the transaction, press Enter. Quicken memorizes the transaction and adds it to the Memorized Transaction list shown in figure 5.20. Press Esc if you do not want to memorize the transaction.

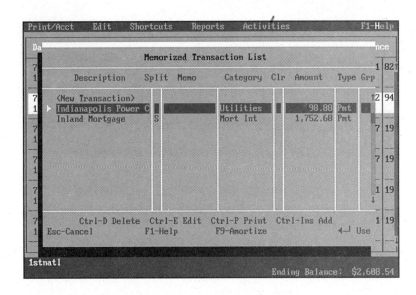

FIG. 5.20

The Memorized
Transaction list.

5. After Quicken memorizes the transaction information, you can complete the transaction, if necessary, and press Ctrl-Enter or F10 to record the transaction.

T I P   Quicken does not memorize the date of a transaction or the check or transaction number. When you recall a memorized transaction, Quicken enters the current date. You assign the check number when you enter or print a check transaction.

You do not have to record a transaction to memorize it. You can enter the transaction information, memorize it, and then press Ctrl-D to clear the transaction information from the Register. The memorized information remains in the Memorized Transaction list. You also can memorize transactions that you already have recorded.

To memorize a recorded transaction, follow these steps:

1. Highlight the transaction you want to memorize.

2. Press Ctrl-M to select the **Memorize Transaction** option.

   Quicken highlights the transaction information it is about to memorize. Quicken does not memorize the date, check number, or invoice number.

3. Press Enter to memorize the transaction.

Recalling a Memorized Transaction

After you have memorized a transaction, you can recall the transaction and record it in the Register. When you recall a transaction, Quicken enters the stored transaction information in the highlighted transaction.

To recall a memorized transaction in the Register, follow these steps:

1. From the Register, press Ctrl-End to highlight the blank transaction line at the end of the Register.

> **CAUTION:** If you recall a memorized transaction into a transaction line with a recorded transaction, Quicken replaces the existing transaction information with the recalled memorized transaction. You can set one of the transaction-setting options so that Quicken displays a confirmation message anytime you attempt to overwrite an existing transaction. To turn on this option, refer to Chapter 20, "Customizing Quicken," to learn about transaction-setting options.

2. Select the **Recall Transaction** option from the Shortcuts menu.

You can press the shortcut key Ctrl-T to select the **Recall Transaction** option.

T I P

Quicken displays the Memorized Transaction list with a list of the transactions that you have memorized.

3. Use the up- and down-arrow keys to highlight the transaction that you want to recall to the Register and press Enter.

Quicken enters the memorized transaction information into the Register.

4. Make any necessary changes to the transaction.

5. Press Ctrl-Enter or F10 to record the recalled transaction in the Register.

Editing a Memorized Transaction

You can change a memorized transaction at any time. You may want to do this if the amount of a memorized transaction changed, for example, or you want to change the category assigned to the memorized transaction.

To edit a memorized transaction, follow these steps:

1. Press Alt-T to select the **Recall Transaction** option and display the Memorized Transaction list.

2. Highlight the memorized transaction you want to edit and press Ctrl-E. Quicken displays the Edit/Setup Memorized Transaction window (see fig. 5.21).

3. Change the fields in the memorized transaction as necessary and then press Enter or F10.

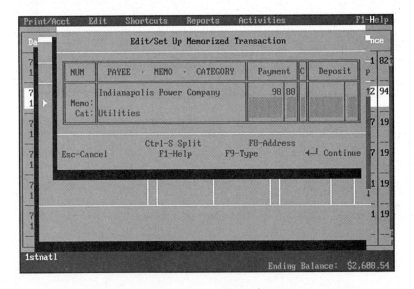

Deleting a Memorized Transaction

If you no longer use a memorized transaction, you can delete it from the list. You may want to delete a memorized transaction, for example, with the final payment on a house or car loan.

Follow these steps to delete a memorized transaction:

1. From the Register, press Ctrl-T to choose the **Recall Transaction** option and display the Memorized Transaction list.

2. Use the up- and down-arrow keys to highlight the memorized transaction you want to delete.

3. Press Ctrl-D. Quicken alerts you that you are about to delete a memorized transaction (see fig. 5.22).

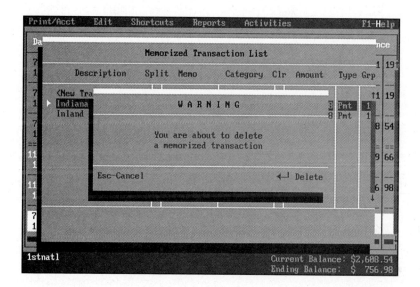

FIG. 5.22

Quicken's message that you are deleting a memorized transaction.

4. Press Enter to delete the memorized transaction, or press Esc if you do not want to delete the transaction from the memorized list.

Printing the Memorized Transaction List

Quicken also enables you to print a list of the transactions you have memorized. Most of the time, you will not need this feature. As long as Quicken is running, the Memorized Transaction list is at your fingertips simply by pressing Ctrl-T. One example of when you may want a printed list is for an annual review of transactions.

To print a copy of the Memorized Transaction list, follow these steps:

1. Press Ctrl-T to select the **Recall Transaction** option and display the Memorized Transaction list.

2. Press Ctrl-P. Quicken displays the Print Memorized Transaction List window, which you use to specify settings for printing the list. (This screen is like the Print Register screen that you saw in Chapter 4.)

3. Indicate which printer configuration you want to use (Rpt, Alt, Chk, or Disk). Quicken then prints the Memorized Transactions list (see fig. 5.23).

```
                    Memorized Transaction List

L FLANDE                                              Page 1
7/15/92

Payee/Memo/Category          Clr     Type        Amount
- - - - - - - - - - - - - -   - - -   - - - - - -  - - - - - -

Indianapolis Power Company           Payment      -98.88

  Utilities

Inland Mortgage                      Payment    -1,752.68
                         SPLITS

  Mort Int                                      -1,300.00
  Tax:Prop                                        -150.00
  [Mortgage]                                      -302.68
```

FIG. 5.23

A printed
Memorized
Transactions list.

C P A
T I P

Consider each of the transactions you now regularly record as candidates for the Memorized Transaction list: rent, house payment, utility payment, school loans, payroll deposits, bank service fees, and so on. The easiest time to memorize transactions is when you initially record a transaction, so every time you enter a transaction, ask yourself whether the transaction is one you will enter repeatedly. You also can memorize split transactions.

Copying and Pasting Transactions

Memorizing transactions is a quick, easy way to enter recurring transactions. If you want to enter a transaction that is the same as another transaction in the Register, but you don't want to memorize it (perhaps because it may only be used once), you can copy the transaction and then paste it in the empty transaction line or in the Register. You can replace transactions by pasting a copied transaction over an existing transaction. You also can copy and paste transactions from the Write Checks screen (see Chapter 7, "Automating Check Writing").

When Quicken copies a transaction, it is essentially memorizing the transaction information. This information is stored in Quicken and can be pasted in the same Register or any other Noninvestment Account Register. You can repaste the same transaction more than once. Quicken will not save the stored transaction information after you copy another transaction or exit the program, however.

To copy and paste a transaction in the Register, follow these steps:

1. Highlight the transaction in the Register that you want to copy.

2. Select the **Copy Transaction** option from the Shortcuts menu (see fig. 5.24). Quicken flashes a message in the bottom right corner of your screen that it is memorizing the transaction.

Print/Acct	Edit	Shortcuts	Reports	Activities		F1-Help

Date	Num	Payee			Deposit	Balance
			Recall Transaction	Ctrl-T		
			Memorize Transaction	Ctrl-M		
7/15		GTE Payro	▶ Copy Transaction	Ctrl-Ins	2,534 00	2,761 19
1992	SPLIT		Paste Transaction	Shift-Ins		
7/15	2208	VOID:Carm	Categorize/Transfer	Ctrl-C		2,761 19
1992			Select/Set Up Class	Ctrl-L		
7/15	2209	Jacobson'	Transaction Groups	Ctrl-J		2,608 54
1992	SPLIT					
11/01		Indianapolis Power Company		98 88		2,509 66
1992		Utilities				
11/01		Inland Mortgage		1,752 68		756 98
1992	SPLIT	Mort Int				
7/15		Memo:				
1992		Cat:				

Copy current transaction into buffer.

FIG. 5.24

The Copy Transaction option from the Shortcuts menu.

You can use the shortcut key Ctrl-Ins to select the **Copy Transaction** option.

T I P

3. Press Ctrl-End to move to the empty transaction line in the Register. Or, if you want to replace an existing transaction with the copied transaction, highlight the transaction that you want to replace.

4. Select the **Paste Transaction** option from the Shortcuts menu. Quicken enters (or pastes) the transaction information from the copied transaction into the highlighted transaction.

T I P   You can press the shortcut key Shift-Ins to select the **Paste Transaction** option.

If the transaction setting Confirm When Overwriting with a Memorized or Pasted Transaction is turned on, Quicken displays the OK to Overwrite Transaction? window before it replaces an existing transaction with the copied transaction (see fig. 5.25). To enter the copied trans-Esc. You learn how to work with transaction settings in Chapter 20, "Customizing Quicken."

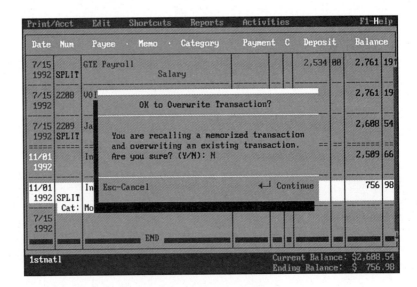

Using the Categories

You can assign a category or subcategory to a transaction by typing the category or subcategory name in the Category field or by using the **Categorize/Transfer** option from the Shortcuts menu. This option displays the Category and Transfer list so that you can find and assign a category, subcategory, or transfer account to a transaction. You also can use this option to add a new category or edit or delete an existing category. Adding, editing and deleting categories and subcategories is described in Chapter 9.

To find and assign a category or subcategory to a transaction, follow these steps:

1. From the Register, press Alt-S to display the Shortcuts menu.

2. Select the **Categorize/Transfer** option.

You can press the shortcut key Ctrl-C to select the **Categorize/ Transfer** option.

T I P

Quicken displays the Category and Transfer list with predefined categories, subcategories, and any accounts you may have created (see fig. 5.26).

```
Print/Acct    Edit    Shortcuts    Reports    Activities         F1-Help

 Date  Num   Payee                                                      e
                            Category and Transfer List
 7/15       GTE Pa                                                     191
 1992 SPLIT       Category/Transfer  Type      Description        Tax

 7/15 2288  VOID:C ► <New Category>           Set up a new category    119
 1992              Bonus            Inc    Bonus Income           ♦
                   Canada Pen       Inc    Canadian Pension       ♦
 7/15 2289  Jacobs Div Income       Inc    Dividend Income        ♦   54
 1992 SPLIT        Gift Received    Inc    Gift Received          ♦
                   Int Inc          Inc    Interest Income        ♦
11/01       Indian Invest Inc       Inc    Investment Income      ♦   66
 1992 Memo:        Old Age Pension  Inc    Old Age Pension        ♦
      Cat: Utilit  Other Inc        Inc    Other Income           ♦
11/01       Inland Salary           Inc    Salary Income          ♦   98
 1992 SPLIT        Auto             Expns  Automobile Expenses
                     Fuel           Sub    Auto Fuel
 7/15                Loan           Sub    Auto Loan Payment      ↓
 1992
                   Ctrl-D Delete  Ctrl-E Edit  Ctrl-P Print  Ctrl-Ins Add
                   Esc-Cancel     F1-Help      F8-Move        ←┘ Use
 1stnatl                                                              54
                                                                     .98
```

FIG. 5.26

The Category and Transfer list.

3. Select the category, subcategory, or account you want to assign to a transaction and press Enter. Quicken retrieves the category or account name from the list and enters it in the Category field.

You can use the PgUp, PgDn, Home, and End keys to move quickly through long lists of categories and accounts. Pressing PgUp displays the preceding page of categories in the list; pressing PgDn displays the next page of categories in the list; pressing Home displays the first page of categories, and pressing End displays the last page of categories. The Category and Transfer list also provides a scroll bar that mouse users can take advantage of for moving up and down the list. (Refer to Chapter 4's discussion of using the Register's scroll bar if you don't know how scroll bars function.)

NOTE Quicken does not require that you assign categories to transactions. If you want to track your income and expense so that you know where your money comes from and where it goes, however, you should assign a category to each transaction that you enter in Quicken. To ensure that you do assign a category to each transaction, you can turn on the transaction-setting option Warn If a Transaction Has No Category. When this transaction setting is turned on, Quicken displays a warning message each time you record a transaction without an assigned category. To learn how to turn on this transaction setting, refer to Chapter 20, "Customizing Quicken."

Using Transaction Groups

A *transaction group* contains recurring transactions that you simultaneously pay or add to a Register. Transaction groups can consist of one or many transactions. You may, for example, want to set up a transaction group for bills for which you don't receive invoices or statements, such as your rent or loan payments. You also may want to set up a transaction group for bills due at the same time each month, such as quarterly estimated tax payments and insurance premiums.

When you create a transaction group, you assign one or more memorized transactions to a group and then name it. You may, for example, set up a transaction group named *Monthly Bills*.

If you are using Billminder (see Chapter 20, "Customizing Quicken"), you'll be reminded at least three days before transaction groups are due by a message displayed at your computer's DOS prompt. Quicken also reminds you that you have transactions groups due by displaying a message at its main menu.

You'll find Quicken's reminder system great for prompting you to pay bills for which you do not receive an invoice, such as your rent, payroll taxes, and loan payments. Although Quicken gives you plenty of notice and prompting about transactions groups that are due, the program does not enter the transactions in the Account Register or the Write Checks screen for you. You must tell Quicken to enter the transactions from the group by recalling the transaction group.

After you set up a transaction group, you can add, delete, or change transactions in the group. You also can delete an entire transaction group.

Setting Up a Transaction Group

Before you can set up a transaction group, you must memorize the transactions that you want to include in the group. (You learned how to memorize transactions in "Memorizing a Transaction," earlier in this chapter.) You can include one or several memorized transactions in a transaction group. You also can include the same transaction in more than one group.

To set up a transaction group, follow these steps:

1. From the Register, select **Transaction Groups** from the Shortcuts menu. Or, press Ctrl-J.

    Quicken displays the Select Transaction Group to Recall window shown in figure 5.27.

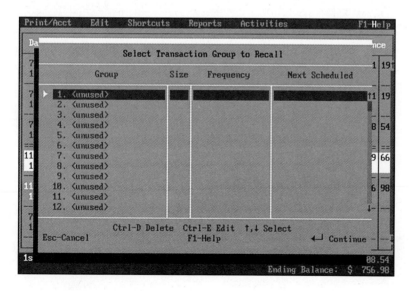

FIG. 5.27

The Select Transaction Group to Recall window.

2. Use the up- and down-arrow keys to highlight the first <unused> transaction group, and then press Enter.

3. Quicken displays the Describe Group window (see fig. 5.28).

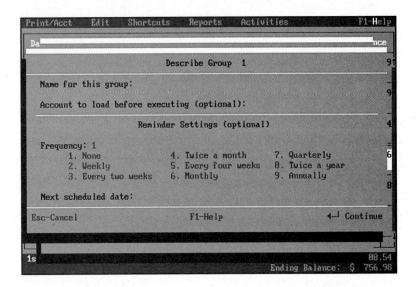

Print/Acct   Edit   Shortcuts   Reports   Activities   F1-Help

Da━━━nce

Describe Group 1   9

Name for this group:

Account to load before executing (optional):

Reminder Settings (optional)

Frequency: 1
   1. None   4. Twice a month   7. Quarterly
   2. Weekly   5. Every four weeks   8. Twice a year
   3. Every two weeks   6. Monthly   9. Annually

Next scheduled date:

Esc-Cancel   F1-Help   ←┘ Continue

1s   08.54
                                       Ending Balance: $ 756.98

FIG. 5.28

The Describe
Group window.

4. In the Name for This Group field, type a name for the transaction group that you are setting up and press Enter. You can include up to 20 characters in your transaction group names, which must be unique.

5. In the next field, Account To Load Before Executing (optional), enter the account name where the transactions should be recorded. This action causes the appropriate account to be selected before you recall the transaction group. If you work with only one account, you do not need to fill in this field.

6. Press Enter or Tab to move to the Frequency field. Set the frequency using one of the nine settings shown in figure 5.28: None, Weekly, Every two weeks, Twice a month, Every four weeks, Monthly, Quarterly, Twice a year, or Annually. Select the frequency you want by pressing the number that corresponds to the frequency listed in the Describe Group window. Quicken reminds you when transactions groups are due, based on your entry in this field. If you choose **None** from the Frequency list, Quicken does not remind you of this transaction group's due date.

7. If you set the frequency to something other than **None**, you also must set the next schedule date. Enter the date that the next

transaction group is due in the Next Scheduled Date field. If you're setting up a transaction group for checks that are due on the first of the month and today's date is October 15, for example, type 8/01/92. Quicken enters the current date. Use the + (plus) and – (minus) keys to change the date one day at a time. Or, you can type a new date.

8. When you complete the Describe Group window, press Ctrl-Enter or F10. Quicken displays the Assign Transactions to Group window, shown in figure 5.29. You now select the memorized transactions you want to include in the transaction group.

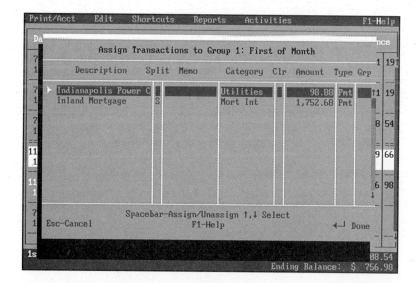

FIG. 5.29

The Assign Transactions to Group window.

9. Use the up- and down-arrow keys to highlight each transaction you want to include in the new transaction group. Press the space bar to include the transaction (Quicken enters the group number in the Grp field next to each transaction that you select). To unassign a transaction to a transaction group, highlight the transaction and press the space bar again.

10. When you finish selecting transactions to include in the new transaction group, press Ctrl-Enter or F10. Quicken enters the transaction group's name, the number of transactions in the group, frequency, and the next scheduled date in the Select Transaction Group to Recall window.

Recalling a Transaction Group

Quicken and Billminder remind you when a transaction group is due; however, Quicken does not enter the transaction group automatically. You must recall the transaction group so that Quicken enters all the group's transactions into the appropriate Account Register. Quicken then highlights the first transaction entered from the group so that you can make any necessary changes.

To recall a transaction group, follow these steps:

1. From the Register, press Ctrl-J to select **Transaction Groups** from the Shortcuts menu. Quicken displays the Select Transaction Group to Recall window.

2. Use the up- and down-arrow keys to highlight the transaction group name that you want to recall.

3. Press Enter to display the Transaction Group Date window shown in figure 5.30.

FIG. 5.30

The Transaction Group Date window.

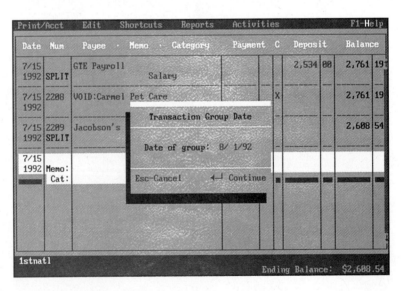

4. The date displayed in the Date of Group field represents the date you want Quicken to use when it enters the group's transactions. Quicken enters the current date. Or, you can type a new date or use the + (plus) or – (minus) key to increase or decrease the date one day at a time.

5. Press Enter to recall the transaction group.

Quicken enters and records the transactions to the appropriate Account Register and displays the Transaction Group Entered window that you see in figure 5.31.

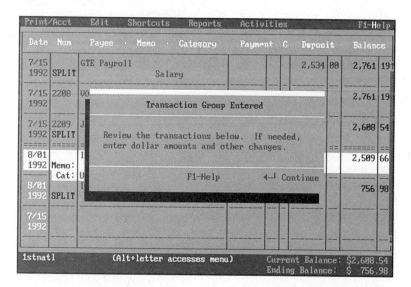

The Transaction Group Entered window.

6. Press Enter to remove the Transaction Group Entered window and highlight the first transaction so that you can make any necessary changes to it or the following transactions.

NOTE When you recall a transaction group that includes check transactions, Quicken enters the check transactions but does not print them. You'll need to print the checks, as you will learn in the next chapter.

Editing a Transaction Group

Because transaction groups segregate your checks into groups you pay together at one time, changes in payment due dates mean that you need to change the transaction group. If you refinance your mortgage, for example, the due date may change from the fifth to the fifteenth. If you have separate transaction groups for checks you write at the beginning of the month and those you write during the middle of the month, you may need to change your transaction groups.

You can change the following information for a transaction group: its name, the account in which Quicken enters transactions, the frequency, or the next scheduled date. You also can add or delete a transaction from an existing transaction group.

To edit a transaction group, follow these steps:

1. From the Register, press Ctrl-J to select the **Transaction Groups** option and display the Select Transaction Group to Recall window.

2. Use the up- and down-arrow keys to highlight the transaction group you want to edit.

3. Press Ctrl-E to display the View/Edit Standard Transaction Group window that contains the information you entered when you created the transaction group.

4. Type over the group name, select a new account, change the frequency, or enter a different next scheduled date.

5. Press Ctrl-Enter or F10 to go to the Assign Transactions to Group window.

6. Press the space bar to assign or unassign any transaction to the group. (You learn how to add or delete a transaction from a transaction group in "Adding and Deleting Transactions from a Transaction Group," later in this chapter.)

7. Press Ctrl-Enter or F10 to save the changes to the transaction group.

Deleting a Transaction Group

You can delete transaction groups that you no longer use. When you delete a transaction group, Quicken permanently removes the transaction group from the Select Transaction Group to Recall window, but does not delete the memorized transactions, which remain in the Memorized Transaction list.

To delete a transaction group, follow these steps:

1. From the Register, press Ctrl-J to select **Transaction Groups** from the Shortcuts menu.

   Quicken displays the Select Transaction Group to Recall window.

2. Use the up- and down-arrow keys to highlight the transaction group you want to delete.

3. Press Ctrl-D. Quicken warns you that you are about to permanently delete a transaction group.

4. Press Enter to delete the group. Press Esc to keep the transaction group in the list.

Adding and Deleting Transactions from a Transaction Group

You can add or delete transactions from an existing transaction group. You may, for example, want to add a new employee to or delete a former employee from your payroll transaction group.

To add to or delete a transaction from an existing transaction group, follow these steps:

1. Make sure that you have memorized the transaction you want to add or delete.

2. From the Register, press Ctrl-J to select the **Transaction Groups** option. Quicken displays the Select Transaction Group to Recall window.

3. Use the up- and down-arrow keys to highlight the transaction group for which you want to add or delete a transaction and press Ctrl-E.

4. Quicken displays the Describe Group window. Press Ctrl-Enter or F10 to move to the Assign Transactions to Group window.

5. Use the up- and down-arrow keys to highlight the memorized transaction you want to include in the transaction group or that you want to remove from the transaction group. Press the space bar to add or delete the transaction from the group.

6. Press Ctrl-Enter or F10 to add or delete the transaction from the group.

Switching from the Checking Account Register to the Write Checks Screen

Anytime you're working in the Checking Account Register (or any other Bank Account Register), you can access the Write Checks screen simply by pressing Ctrl-W. This is handy for switching back and forth from writing checks in the Write Checks screen to entering manual transactions or deposits in the Register.

Chapter Summary

In this chapter, you learned about Quicken features that make the Register easier and faster to work with. More specifically, you learned about Quicken 6's new QuickFill feature; how to insert, delete, and void transactions; how to find transactions; how to split transactions; and how to use memorized transactions and transaction groups.

In the next chapter, you learn how to write and print checks at the Write Checks screen.

Writing and Printing Checks

With Quicken's check-printing feature, you can write checks and pay bills faster and more efficiently than you ever thought possible. You can pay bills faster because Quicken provides a collection of shortcuts and timesaving techniques that automate and speed up check writing and bill paying. You can pay bills more efficiently because Quicken helps you keep track of the bills coming due and provides categories with which you can classify the ways you are spending your money.

The check-writing feature in Quicken is one of the program's most powerful tools. Writing checks with Quicken not only saves you valuable time, but spares you from having numerous opportunities to make clerical errors. When you write a check using Quicken, you simply enter the information in an on-screen check facsimile (the Write Checks screen), and Quicken takes it from there. The program records the check in the Checking Account Register, adjusts your account balance, and adds the transaction amount to the appropriate category, which you specify when you write a check. From this point, you only have to print the check, sign it, stick the check in an envelope (Intuit even provides window envelopes for checks), and mail it.

This chapter describes the basics of writing and printing checks with Quicken. Included in this chapter are discussions of the following topics:

- Accessing and understanding the Write Checks screen
- Moving around the Write Checks screen
- Writing and recording checks
- Reviewing and editing checks
- Positioning checks in your printer
- Printing and reprinting checks

Accessing the Write Checks Screen

Access the Write Checks screen when you want to do the following:

- Write checks
- Postdate checks
- Review checks that you have not printed
- Edit or delete checks that you have not printed
- Print checks

Before you access the Write Checks screen, you must select a bank account to use from the Select Account to Use window. You learned how to select accounts to use in Chapter 3, "Defining Your Accounts." You cannot write a check from any other type of account other than a bank account. The bank account that you use usually will be your checking account. If you attempt to access the Write Checks screen from an account other than a bank account, Quicken displays the message you see in figure 6.1. Press Enter from this message window and Quicken then takes you to the Select Account to Use window, where you can select a bank account.

To access the Write Checks screen, select the **Write/Print Checks** option from the Quicken main menu. Quicken displays the Write Checks screen you see in figure 6.2.

You can access the Write Checks screen by pressing Ctrl-W from the Quicken main menu or by pressing Ctrl-W from a Bank Account Register.

T I P

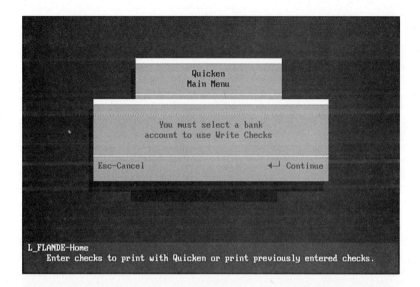

FIG. 6.1

The message Quicken displays when you try to access the Write Checks screen from an account other than a bank account.

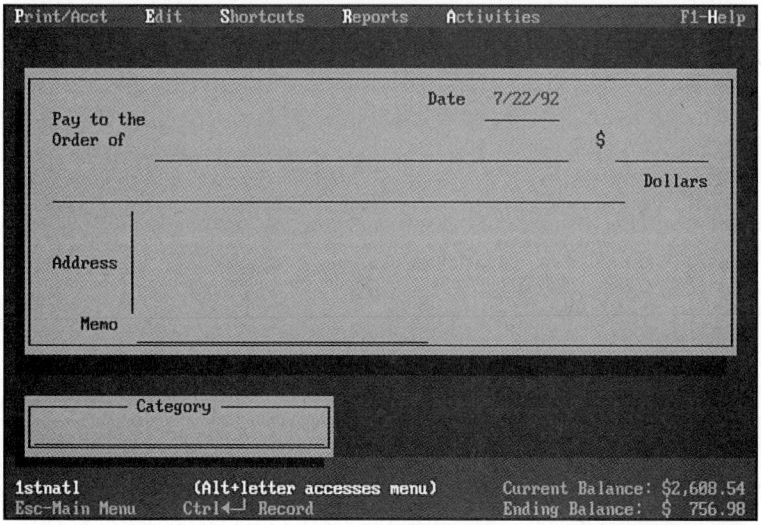

FIG. 6.2

The Write Checks screen.

Understanding the Write Checks Screen

You use the Write Checks screen to collect the information you use to print checks. After collecting the information, Quicken records the check in the Register for the bank account that you're using.

The Write Checks screen can be broken down into three parts: the menu bar at the top of the screen, the actual check, and the information lines at the bottom of the screen.

The menu bar shows the menus you use from the Write Checks screen to access commands. These menus should look familiar if you have worked with the Register screen: Print/Acct, Edit, Shortcuts, Reports, and Activities.

The second part of the screen is the actual check where you enter the date; payee; amount; memo (optional); and category, subcategory, or transfer account. Note that check numbers are not entered in the Write Checks screen; you specify the check numbers when you print checks. The steps for completing checks are described in the following section, "Writing a Check."

The third part of the Write Checks screen includes the information lines at the bottom of the screen. These lines show several pieces of information, including the account you are using, descriptions of what the Esc and Enter keys do, the total amount of checks to print, and the current and ending balance in the account. The *current balance* represents the balance in your account as of the current date. The *ending balance* represents the balance, taking into account any postdated checks you have written.

Moving Around the Write Checks Screen

The following keys help you move around the Write Checks screen quickly and easily.

Press	To Move
Enter or Tab	Forward one field
Shift-Tab	Backward one field
Home	Beginning of current field
Home Home	Beginning of first field in current check
End	End of current field

Press	To Move
End End	End of last field in current check
Ctrl- →	Forward one word within a field
Ctrl- ←	Backward one word within a field
PgUp	To the preceding check
PgDn	To the next check

Writing a Check

The mechanics of writing a check with Quicken closely resemble those for manually writing a check. The only real difference is that Quicken's Write Checks screen makes the process easier. With Quicken, writing a check means you simply complete the Write Checks screen. You fill in as many as seven fields: Date, Payee, Amount, Address, Message, Memo, and Category. After you write the check, you're ready to record and print the check.

Filling In the Check

To write a check, you take the following steps:

1. Select the **Write/Print Checks** option from Quicken's main menu. Or, if you're already in the Register screen, press Alt-A to display the Activities menu and select the **Write Checks** option. Or even more simply, just press Ctrl-W from the Register for the bank account that you want to use to write checks. Quicken displays the Write Checks screen as shown in figure 6.2.

2. Enter the date of the check in the Date field. Enter the date in the MM/DD/YY format (such as 12/11/92). The first time you write a check in the current Quicken session, the program fills the Date field with the system date (the current date according to your computer's internal memory). After you write your first check using the Write Checks screen, Quicken fills the Date field with the last date used. To edit the date, you have two choices. First, you can move the cursor to the part of the date—month, day, or year—that you want to change and type over the date already on-screen. Second, you can use the special date-editing keys, which are explained in detail in Chapter 2.

C P A
T I P

As mentioned in Chapter 4, businesses and individuals often receive discounts for paying bills early, so consider early payment in setting the check date. In effect, not taking early payment discounts is an extremely expensive way to borrow money from the vendor. Suppose that a vendor normally requires payment within 30 days but gives a two percent discount for payments received within 10 days. If you pay within 30 rather than 10 days, you pay the vendor a two percent interest charge for paying 20 days later. Because one year contains roughly 18 20-day periods, the two percent for 20 days equals approximately 36 percent annually.

Although you may need to borrow this money, you probably can find a much cheaper lender. As a rule of thumb, if a vendor gives you a one percent discount for paying 20 days early, you are borrowing money from him at about an 18 percent annual interest rate if you do not pay early. A three percent discount works out to a whopping 54 percent per year.

3. Press Enter or Tab to move the cursor to the Pay to the Order Of field. This field is where you enter the name of the person or business, called the *payee*, that the check pays. Type the name you want to appear on the check.

Quicken 6 has a new feature called *QuickFill* that makes entering payees and transactions fast and easy. When you type a few characters of the payee name, Quicken searches the Memorized Transaction list and the last three months of transactions in the Register for a transaction with a payee name that begins with the characters you type. When Quicken finds a payee, QuickFill fills in the rest of the payee name for you. If this is the payee that you want, press Enter and QuickFill fills in the rest of the check for you: the check amount; memo (if used in the transaction found); and category, subcategory, or transfer account. Refer to the next chapter, "Automating Check Writing," for more detailed information on QuickFill.

C P A
T I P

Because you have space for up to 40 characters, you should not have any problem fitting in the payee's name. In fact, you should have room to enter *and* and *or* payees. An *and* payee, for example, is *Robert Southern and Ronald Hamilton*. Both Southern and Hamilton must endorse such a check to cash it. An *or* payee is entered as *Robert Southern or Ronald Hamilton* and requires Southern *or* Hamilton to endorse the check to cash it.

4. Press Enter or Tab to move the cursor to the Amount field. The Amount field shows the amount of the check. You can use up to 10 characters to enter the amount. Quicken enables you to enter only numbers, commas, and decimal points in the Amount field. Quicken enters commas if you do not and if room is available for them. The largest value you can enter in the Amount field is 9999999.99. Because this number is difficult to read without commas (the number is $9,999,999.99), you probably will want Quicken to have enough room to insert commas. If you use some of the 10 characters for commas, the largest value you can enter is 999,999.99. When you complete the Amount field and press Enter, Quicken writes out the amount on the next line of the check—just as you do when writing a check manually. To save space, Quicken may abbreviate *hundred* as *Hndrd*, *thousand* as *Thsnd*, and *million* as *Mill*.

5. (Optional) Press Enter or Tab to move the cursor to the next field—the first line of the address block. The optional Address field provides five 30-character lines. If you use envelopes with windows and enter the payee's address in this field, the address shows in the envelope window. You save time that otherwise is spent addressing envelopes.

   Assuming that you are using the Address field, you need to type the payee's name on the first line. Quicken provides a shortcut for you. If you type ' (apostrophe) or " (quotation marks), Quicken copies the name from the Pay to the Order Of field. (Because the Pay to the Order Of field has space for 40 characters and the address lines have only 30 characters, this shortcut may cut off up to the last 10 characters of the payee's name.)

6. (Optional) If you set the check setting Extra Message Line on Check to Yes, press Enter or Tab to move the cursor to the Msg field. If this check setting is not Yes, no message line is displayed. To learn how to set the check setting so that the extra message line is displayed in the Write Checks screen, refer to Chapter 20, "Customizing Quicken."

   The message field, if displayed as shown in figure 6.3, gives you another 24 characters for additional information you want printed on the check, such as an account number for a credit card or a loan number for a mortgage. Because this information does not show through an envelope window, do not use the line for address information.

7. (Optional) Press Enter or Tab to move the cursor to the second line of the address block. Enter the street address or post office box.

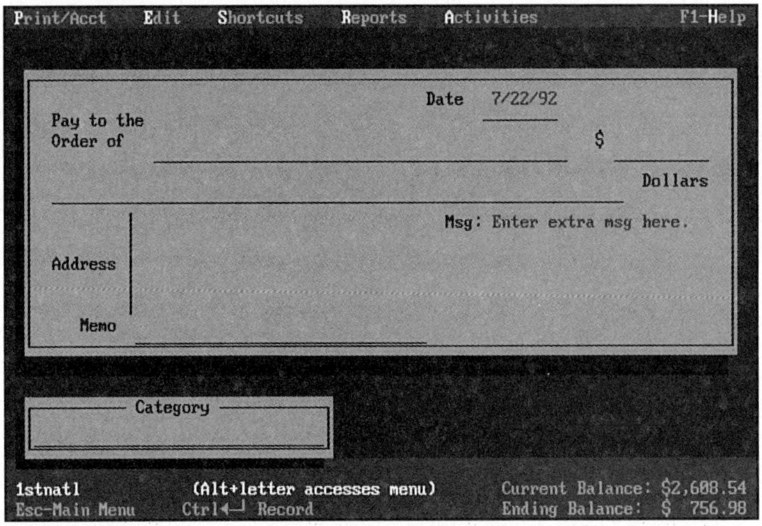

FIG. 6.3

The Write Checks screen with the extra message (Msg) line displayed.

8. (Optional) Press Enter or Tab to move the cursor to the third line of the address block. Enter the city, state, and ZIP code.

9. (Optional) Press Enter or Tab to move the cursor to the other address lines—there are five altogether—and enter any additional address information.

10. (Optional) Press Enter or Tab to move the cursor to the Memo field. You can use this field as you use the extra message line to further describe the check, such as *November rent*, or you can use the line to tell the payee your account number or loan number.

11. (Optional) Press Enter or Tab to move the cursor to the Category field. You use this field to assign a category or subcategory to a transaction so that you know what the check covers—such as utilities expense, interest expense, or entertainment. You also can use the Category field to describe the class into which a check falls. (Categories and classes are described in Chapter 9, "Organizing Your Finances.") And, you can use the Category field to enter another Quicken account if the check that you are writing represents a transfer of funds between your checking account and another account. (Transfer transactions were explained in Chapter 4, "Using the Register.") Quicken provides a listing of the most typical categories for home or business use to enable you to quickly categorize your most frequent transactions. You access the defined list by pressing Ctrl-C.

Quicken 6.0 provides a feature called *QuickFill*, which you can use after you have learned a few of the category names. If you type enough characters of a category name to uniquely identify the category and then press Enter, Quicken searches the Category and Transfer list to find the first category that begins with the characters you type. Suppose that you have a category named *Entertainment*, and that it is the only category name that starts with the three letters *Ent*. If you type *Ent* and press Enter, Quicken searches the Category and Transfer list until it finds a category that begins with *Ent*. When Quicken finds *Entertainment*, the QuickFill feature fills in the remaining letters of the category name for you—*ertainment*. You also can use QuickFill to enter an account name in the Category field when transferring money to another account. You learn more about using QuickFill to write checks in Chapter 7.

Recording a Check

After the check is complete, record the check by pressing Ctrl-Enter or F10. Or, you can press Enter if the cursor is positioned in the last field in the Write Checks screen. When you press Enter to record a check, Quicken displays the OK to Record Transaction? window, as shown in figure 6.4. Press 1 to record the check or press 2 if you decide that you don't want to record the check. Figure 6.5 shows a completed check at the Write Checks screen.

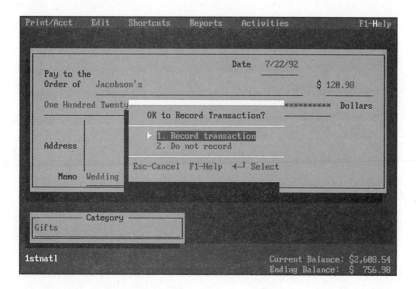

FIG. 6.4

The OK to Record Transaction? window.

```
 Print/Acct    Edit    Shortcuts    Reports    Activities              F1-Help

                                       Date    7/22/92
      Pay to the
      Order of    Jacobson's                                    $  120.98

      One Hundred Twenty and 98/100******************************* Dollars


      Address



          Memo   Wedding gift for cousin


                ─── Category ───
      Gifts
                                             Checks to Print:  $   120.98
 1stnatl            (Alt+letter accesses menu)  Current Balance: $2,487.56
 Esc-Main Menu     Ctrl⏎  Record                Ending Balance:  $   636.00
```

FIG. 6.5

A completed
check at the
Write Checks
screen.

Whichever method you choose to record a check, you briefly see
a flashing message in the lower left corner of the screen that says
RECORDING. (If you use a very fast computer, you may not be able to
read the message because it appears and disappears so quickly.) After
Quicken finishes recording the check, your computer beeps, and the
recorded check scrolls off the screen. A new, blank check that was hidden by the preceding check is left on-screen—ready to be completed.

T I P   You have the option of turning off the beep that you hear when you
record a check so that Quicken is silent. This is particularly attractive if you are entering several checks at a time and become annoyed
with the constant beeping. You turn off the beep sound through the
Beep When Recording and Memorizing transaction setting option.
Turn to Chapter 20, "Customizing Quicken," to learn how to access
transaction settings and turn off the beep sound.

Reviewing and Editing Checks

You can return to, review, and edit the checks you write with the
Write/Print Checks option until you print them. You can correct errors
in a payee's name, change the check amount, or change the category or

subcategory assigned to the check, for example. Suppose that you write a check to pay several bills from the same person or business— perhaps the bank where you have your mortgage, your car loan, and a personal line of credit. If you receive another bill from the bank, you may need to change the check amount.

You can use the PgUp, PgDn, Home, and End keys on the Write Checks screen to move through the checks you have written but not yet printed:

PgUp	Displays the preceding check
PgDn	Displays the next check
Home	Displays the first check
End	Displays the last check

Quicken arranges by date the checks you have written at the Write Checks screen but have not printed. Those checks with the earliest dates are listed first, followed chronologically by later checks. Checks with the same date are arranged in the order you entered them. To edit a check you already have recorded, press PgUp or PgDn to move to the check you want to change and then edit the appropriate fields.

NOTE Quicken does not store checks in the Write Checks screen after they have been printed. To review checks that have been printed, you must access the Register. Locate checks that you want to review in the Register by using the **Find** option or the **Go to Date** option that you learned about in Chapter 5, "Automating the Register."

If you decide that you don't want to print a check, you simply delete it. To delete the check, press Ctrl-D while the check is displayed. Or, you can select **Delete Transaction** from the Edit menu in the Write Checks screen. Chapter 7, "Automating Check Writing," explains how to delete checks.

Postdating Checks

Chapter 4, "Using the Register," talks about using postdated transactions. All the same reasons described there also apply to postdated checks. When writing checks with Quicken, however, postdating takes on an added feature. Quicken can review postdated checks for those that you should print. To do this, Quicken uses a built-in program called the *Billminder*. Billminder looks for postdated checks it thinks you should print. You are reminded of postdated checks and of transaction groups every time you turn on your computer. Quicken uses a pop-up message window (see fig. 6.6). You also are reminded of postdated checks and of transaction groups every time you start Quicken. Billminder displays a message at the bottom of the main menu screen, as shown in figure 6.7, telling you that you have checks to print or transaction groups due.

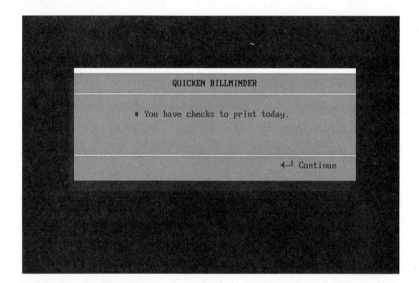

FIG. 6.6

The pop-up Billminder message window.

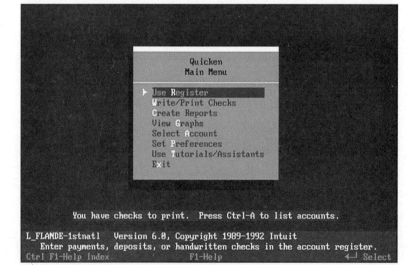

FIG. 6.7

The Billminder feature displays a reminder message at the bottom of the main menu screen.

If you enter postdated checks, Quicken adds the current account balance in the information lines at the bottom of the Write Checks screen. The current balance is the checking account balance—not including postdated checks.

Printing Checks

When you have your Quicken checks, you need to position them in your printer properly before you start printing. Aligning checks in your continuous-feed printer is easy with Intuit's patented automatic alignment feature; you no longer have to align by trial and error. Aligning laser checks is a snap with Quicken 6.0's new Vertical Check Adjustment feature.

Before you begin to print checks with Quicken, make sure that your system has been set up properly to print to your printer. Refer to Chapter 1, "Preparing To Use Quicken," to learn how to set up Quicken for your printer.

After you receive your checks from Intuit, review them carefully to ensure that they are free of printing errors. Most importantly, examine the bank account number to make sure that it is correct. If you find an error, return the checks immediately and have them reprinted. Unless the printing error was caused by wrong information submitted by you, your checks will be reprinted at no charge.	**C P A** **T I P**

Positioning Checks in Your Printer

Before you start printing checks, you should print a sample check to ensure that your checks are properly positioned and aligned in your printer and that the vertical print settings are correct. If you're using continuous-feed checks, use the sample checks that were enclosed in your Quicken software package to print a sample check. If you're using a laser or page-oriented printer, it's best to print a sample check on plain paper so that you don't waste any of your checks. You can use the sample check printed on plain paper as an overlay on your laser checks to see how the print lines up. You learn how to print both types of sample checks in this section.

NOTE After you go through the process of aligning checks by entering the vertical print settings and determining the proper horizontal positioning for checks, your printer will stay aligned and you will not need to repeat this process each time you print checks.

Printing a Sample Continuous-Feed Check

To print a sample continuous-feed check, follow these steps:

1. Make sure that you have at least one check to print. If not, you can write a sample check and then delete it later.

2. Insert the continuous-form checks into the printer as you would insert continuous-form paper.

3. From the Write Checks screen, press Alt-P to display the Print/Acct menu as shown in figure 6.8.

4. Select the **Print Checks** option from the Print/Acct menu. Quicken displays the Print Checks window that you see in figure 6.9.

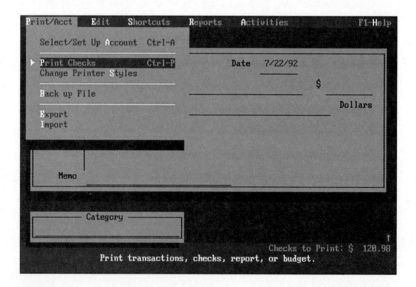

FIG. 6.8

The Print/Acct menu.

NOTE You can select the Print Checks option by pressing the shortcut key Ctrl-P directly from the Write Checks screen.

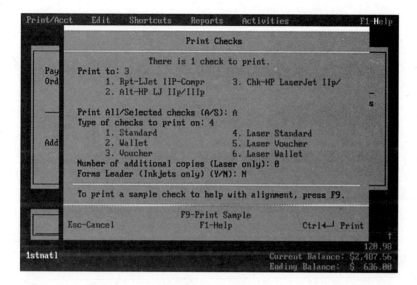

FIG. 6.9

The Print Checks window.

5. With the cursor positioned in the Print To field, select the printer you want to use by pressing 1, 2, or 3. If you described your printer when installing Quicken, you should see your printer name here. If you don't see it, refer to Chapter 1.

6. In the Type of Checks To Print On field, enter the number that corresponds to the continuous-feed check type you are using: 1 for **Standard**, 2 for **Wallet**, or 3 for **Voucher**.

7. Press F9 to print a sample check with the fields filled so that you can see how the print on a check lines up—both vertically and horizontally for continuous-feed checks or just vertically for laser checks.

   Quicken displays a Note window that tells you not to adjust your printer after the sample check prints and to follow Quicken's on-screen instructions to adjust your printer.

8. Press Enter to remove the Note window and begin printing the sample check. Figure 6.10 shows the sample check printed by Quicken.

The Date field is filled as XX/XX/XX. The Pay to the Order of field is filled with Payee. The Amount field is filled with XX,XXX.XX. The Memo field is filled with the phrase This is a void check.

Quicken also prints a *pointer line*, as shown in figure 6.10. The pointer line enables you to tell Quicken how the check form is aligned vertically.

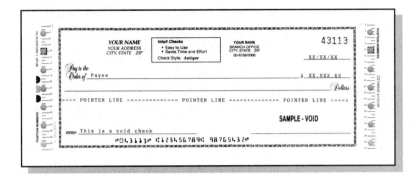

FIG. 6.10

A sample check.

After the sample check is printed, Quicken displays the Type Position Number window that you see in figure 6.11, which you can use to align the check form vertically. If the sample check printed correctly, press Enter.

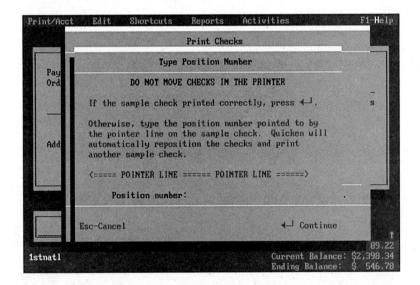

FIG. 6.11

The Type Position Number window to vertically align continuous-feed checks.

If the sample check did not print correctly, use Quicken's alignment feature by entering the number from the check form's pin-feed strips that the pointer line points to. (*Pin-feed strips* are the strips of holes on the sides of the check forms. Your printer uses these holes to move the check forms through the printer.) Only even numbers show on the pin-feed strips. The odd numbers are identified by hash marks. Press Enter after the pointer line number is entered and Quicken advances the checks in your printer and prints another sample check.

To align the check horizontally, manually adjust the check form in the printer to the right or left. You may decide, for example, that the print in the fields shown in figure 6.10 is a little too far to the left—perhaps an eighth of an inch. In that case, you manually move the check forms over to the left an eighth of an inch. Quicken prints the next check with its check form spaces filled an eighth of an inch to the right compared to the preceding check form.

When the checks are aligned properly in your printer, press Enter from the Type Position Number window to return to the Print Checks window.

NOTE When your continuous-feed checks are aligned properly, make note of their position in your printer so that you can align them correctly the next time you insert checks. Look for something on your printer that aligns with one of the position numbers on the edge of the checks (or mark your printer with a piece of tape to use as a guidepost).

If you entered a test check, be sure to delete it after your continuous-feed checks are aligned properly. Refer to the next chapter to learn how to delete a check.

Printing a Sample Laser Check

If you're using a laser printer, you will not use the F9 sample check feature to print a sample check. Rather, to print a sample laser check, use the Print command as if you are printing a check as usual. It's best to use plain paper to print a sample laser check so that you don't waste any of your preprinted laser checks.

To print a sample laser check, follow these steps:

1. Make sure that you have at least one check to print. If not, you can write a sample check and then delete it later.

2. Load regular paper into your laser printer.

3. From the Write Checks screen, press Alt-P to display the Print/Acct menu.

4. Select the **Print Checks** option from the Print/Acct menu. Quicken displays the Print Checks window.

You can select the **Print Checks** option by pressing the shortcut key Ctrl-P directly from the Write Checks screen.   **T I P**

5. With the cursor positioned in the Print To field, select the printer you want to use by pressing 1, 2, or 3. If you described your printer when installing Quicken, you should see your printer name here. If you don't see it, refer to Chapter 1.

6. Press Tab or Enter to position the cursor in the Print All/Selected Checks field. Press A to print all checks if there is only one check to print. Press S if more than one check to print. (You don't want to print all of your checks until the check alignment is correct.)

7. In the Type of Checks To Print On field, enter the number that corresponds to the laser check type you are using: 4 for **Laser Standard**, 5 for **Laser Voucher**, or 6 for **Laser Wallet**.

8. Press Ctrl-Enter to select the **Print** command from the Print Check window.

9. (Optional) If you pressed S from the Print All/Selected Checks field, Quicken displays the Select Checks to Print window. Use the up- and down-arrow keys to highlight the check that you want to print and press the space bar. To deselect a check to print, highlight the check and press the space bar again. Press Ctrl-Enter to continue.

   Quicken displays the Enter Check Number window that you see in figure 6.12. You tell Quicken what your next check number is in this window.

10. If the number that appears in the window is not the correct check number, press the + (plus) or – (minus) key to change the check number by one number at a time. When the check number is correct, press Enter.

    Quicken prints the check information on the first sheet of blank paper in your laser printer and displays the Did Check # Print Correctly? window that you see in figure 6.13.

11. Place the printed sheet over one of your preprinted check forms to check the alignment of the print. You should be able to see through to the preprinted check form quite easily to determine if the printed text is placed properly. If so, select the **Yes** option by pressing Enter from the Did Check # Print Correctly? window. If your check printed correctly, don't print another sample check. Delete the check transaction that you just printed from the Register by going to the Register and highlighting the check that you just printed. Press Ctrl-D and then press Enter to delete the transaction.

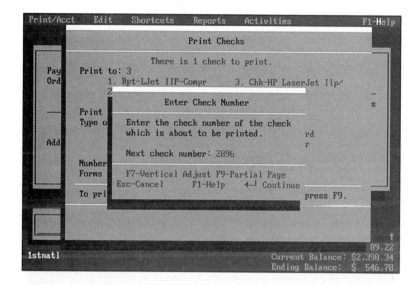

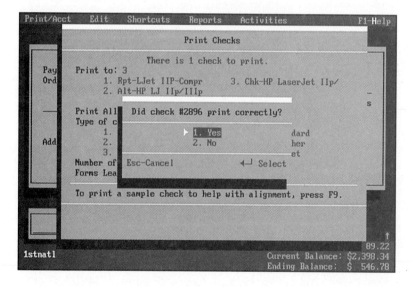

If your sample laser check did not line up properly, select the **No**
option from the Did Check # Print Correctly? window by pressing 2.
Quicken returns to the Print Checks window. You then need to adjust
the vertical alignment by following these steps:

1. Press Ctrl-Enter from the Print Checks window. Quicken displays
   the Enter Check Number window.

2. Press F7 to display the Vertical Check Adjustment window that you see in figure 6.14.

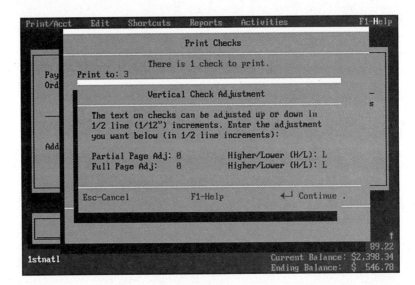

FIG. 6.14

The Vertical Check Adjustment window.

3. If you printed a full check page, position the cursor in the Full Page Adj field. Enter the number of half lines that you want to adjust the text on the check. Press Enter. (If you printed a partial page of checks, use the Partial Page Adj field to enter the number of half lines that you want to adjust the text by.)

4. Position the cursor in the Higher/Lower field and press H if you want the text adjusted higher on the check or L if you want the text adjusted lower.

5. Press Ctrl-Enter to save the vertical settings and return to the Enter Check Number window. Enter a check number and press Enter to print the second sample laser check.

Review the second sample check. If the vertical alignment is still off, select the **No** option from the Did Check # Print Correctly? window and perform steps 1 through 5. Be sure to delete any sample check transactions that Quicken records in the Register after you finish printing sample laser checks.

NOTE   If you've printed at least three sample laser checks and still are having trouble with alignment, call Intuit's technical support staff to get help adjusting your printer control code settings.

Printing Checks

Once your checks are positioned properly in your printer, you're ready to print a check. Printing checks with Quicken is fast, easy, and even fun. Just don't forget to sign your checks after they are printed. Signing checks is the one task that Quicken cannot perform for you.

To print checks, follow these steps:

1. Load the checks into your printer.

   If you are using a laser printer, place the check form sheets in the printer paper tray, as you would place regular sheets of paper. If your printer prints on the face-down side of the paper, for example, make sure that your laser checks are inserted face down. Be sure that your checks are positioned in the proper order according to check number (the sheet with check number 3456 comes before the sheet with check number 3459).

2. Press Ctrl-P to select the **Print Checks** option. Quicken displays the Print Checks window shown in figure 6.15. This window displays two messages that give you information about the checks ready to be printed and provides three fields for you to control the printing of your checks. The first two messages tell you how many checks you have to print, and, if relevant, how many checks are postdated. Figure 6.15 shows that you have one check to print.

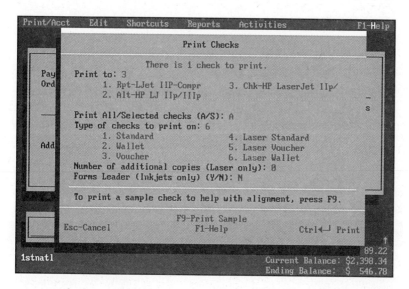

FIG. 6.15

The Print Checks window.

3. With the cursor positioned in the Print To field, select the printer you want to use by pressing 1, 2, or 3. If you described your printer when installing Quicken, you should see your printer name. If you don't see it, refer to Chapter 1.

4. Press Enter or Tab to move the cursor to the Print All/Selected Checks field. To print all the checks that you have written (but have not yet printed) at the Write Checks screen, leave this field set to A for **All**. To print only some of the checks, press S.

5. If you have postdated checks to print, Quicken displays the Print Checks Dated Through field next. This field accepts a date through which you want Quicken to print postdated checks.

   Suppose that today is 11/15/92 and that the checks waiting to be printed are dated 11/15/92, 11/16/92, and 11/17/92. If you set the date of this field to 11/16/92, Quicken prints the checks dated 11/15/92 and 11/16/92. Quicken does not, however, print the check dated 11/17/92. Use the + (plus) and – (minus) keys to change the date in the Print Checks Dated Through field.

6. Press Enter or Tab to move the cursor to the Type of Checks To Print On field. Then, specify the kind of check form:

Press	To Designate
1	Continuous-feed standard checks
2	Continuous-feed wallet checks
3	Continuous-feed voucher check
4	Laser checks
5	Laser voucher checks
6	Laser wallet checks

   If you are using a laser printer with multipart voucher checks, you need to specify the number of additional copies (up to 3) that should be printed in the Number of Additional Copies field.

7. (Optional) If you entered S in the Print All/Selected checks field, Quicken displays the Select Checks to Print window, from which you can select the checks you want to print (see fig. 6.16). To select a check you want to print, use the up- and down-arrow keys to highlight a check. When the check that you want to print is highlighted, press the space bar to select the check. To deselect a check previously marked for printing, highlight that check and press the space bar again.

8. After you select checks to print, press Enter to leave the Select Checks to Print window. Quicken then displays the Enter Check

Number window, asking you for the number of the next check to print (see fig. 6.17). The number of the next check is already displayed in the window.

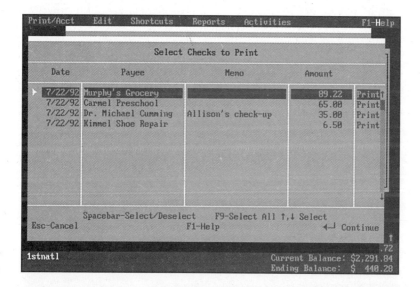

FIG. 6.16

The Select Checks to Print window.

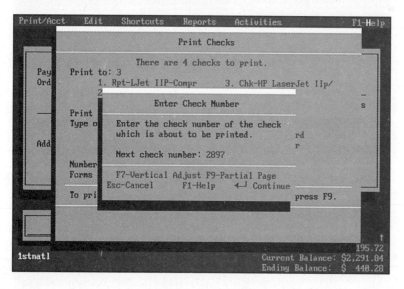

FIG. 6.17

The Enter Check Number window.

9. If the number Quicken displays is the same as the number that appears in the upper right corner of the next check form, press Enter to print the check. If the number Quicken displays is not

correct, type the correct check number. You also can use the + (plus) and – (minus) keys to change the number.

If you're using a laser printer, you can print to a partial page of checks (one or two checks left on the page). You first must tell Quicken how many checks there are on the page, however. To print to a partial page of checks, press F9 after you enter the correct check number in the Enter Check Number window. Quicken displays the Start Printing on Partial Page window that you see in figure 6.18.

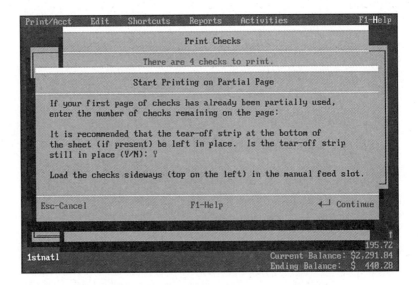

FIG. 6.18

The Start Printing on Partial Page window.

Type the number of checks remaining on the page in the first field (1 or 2). In the second field, indicate whether the strip at the bottom of the page is still intact by pressing Y or N. Follow the on-screen instructions for loading the partial page of checks into your printer and press Enter. Quicken returns to the Enter Check Number window.

CAUTION: If you are printing laser checks on a partial page, make sure that you tell Quicken how many checks are left on the page by pressing F9 from the Enter Check Number window. If you fail to do this, Quicken will assume that you are printing on a full page and your checks will not be printed correctly.

10. Press Enter to print the checks. Figure 6.19 shows a sample check to Jacobson's printed with the vertical and horizontal alignment correct. After Quicken finishes printing the checks, the program asks you if the checks printed correctly (see fig. 6.20). If each of your checks printed correctly, press Enter or 1 to select **Yes**.

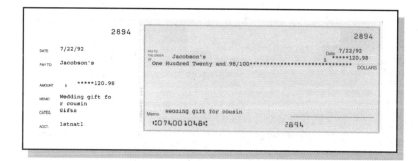

FIG. 6.19

A sample check made payable to Jacobson's.

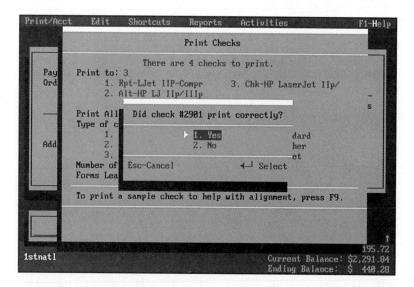

FIG. 6.20

Quicken asks whether the check printed correctly.

If one or more of your checks printed incorrectly—perhaps the alignment was not right or the check forms jammed in the printer halfway through printing—press 2 to answer **No**. Quicken asks for the number of the first check that printed incorrectly. Quicken then returns to the Print Checks window, and you repeat each of the Print Checks steps to reprint the checks that printed incorrectly. Quicken records in the Register only those checks that printed correctly.

C P A T I P Write *VOID* in large letters across the face of checks that Quicken incorrectly prints. This precaution prevents you and anyone else from later signing and cashing the checks.

Reprinting a Check

If you decide later, even after leaving the Print Checks screen, that you want to reprint a check, you can do so. Suppose that the original check somehow gets lost or destroyed. You still have to pay the person, so you need to reprint the check. Rather than reenter all the same information, you can reprint the original information. (If you lose a check, consider placing a stop-payment order with your bank.)

When you describe checks you want to print using the Write Checks screen, Quicken actually records the checks in the Register. Because Quicken hasn't assigned check numbers, however, asterisks are entered in the check number field in the Register. These asterisks indicate that the check is one that you have set up to print using the Write Checks screen (see fig. 6.21). When Quicken prints the checks, it replaces the asterisks with the actual check number.

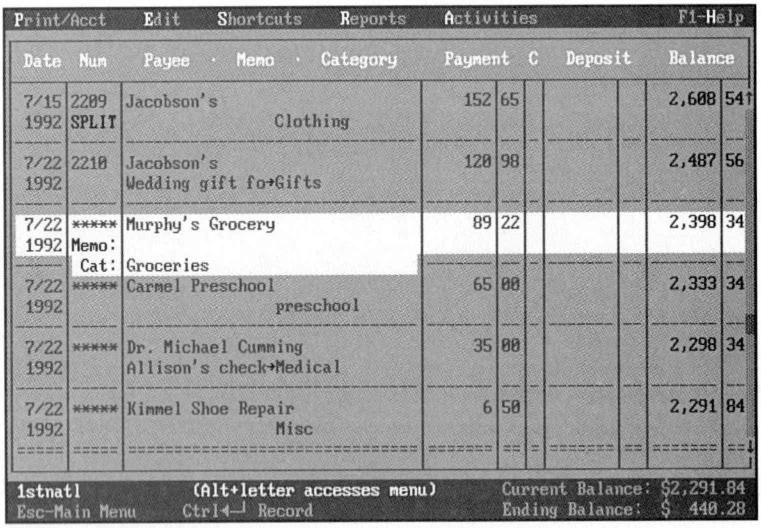
Print/Acct Edit Shortcuts Reports Activities F1-Help
Date Num Payee · Memo · Category Payment C Deposit Balance
7/15 1992 2209 SPLIT Jacobson's Clothing 152 65 2,608 54
7/22 1992 2210 Jacobson's Wedding gift fo→Gifts 120 98 2,487 56
7/22 1992 ***** Murphy's Grocery Memo: Cat: Groceries 89 22 2,398 34
7/22 1992 ***** Carmel Preschool preschool 65 00 2,333 34
7/22 1992 ***** Dr. Michael Cumming Allison's check→Medical 35 00 2,298 34
7/22 1992 ***** Kimmel Shoe Repair Misc 6 50 2,291 84
1stnatl (Alt+letter accesses menu) Current Balance: $2,291.84
Esc-Main Menu Ctrl←┘ Record Ending Balance: $ 440.28

FIG. 6.21

Quicken storing checks to be printed in the Register and identifying them by setting the check numbers to asterisks.

By itself, this bit of information isn't all that exciting, but it does enable you to trick Quicken into reprinting a check. All you need do is change a check's number to asterisks. Quicken then assumes that the check is one you want to print. To print the check after you have changed the number to asterisks, you follow the steps described earlier in "Printing Checks."

Chapter Summary

This chapter described the basics of writing and printing checks with Quicken. These basics include the components of the Write Checks screen; how to use the Write Checks screen to record and postdate checks; and how to review, edit, and print checks. The next chapter describes the Quicken features that you can use to make check-writing even easier.

Automating Check Writing

Y ou learned how to write a check at the Write Checks screen in the last chapter. This chapter describes how you can use features in Quicken to make check writing faster and easier. Most of the features you will learn about to automate check writing are the same as those for automating the Register (as you learned in Chapter 5). In fact, the only real difference between working with the Register and the Write Checks screen is that the screens are different; the menus and features are the same. If you're already familiar with the following Quicken features, you may want to skim this chapter:

- QuickFill

- Deleting and voiding transactions

- Splitting transactions

- Finding transactions using the **Find** option, the **Go to Date** option, and the **Go to Transfer** option

- Memorizing transactions

- Copying and pasting transactions

- Using categories

- Using transaction groups

If you're still not comfortable with the preceding Quicken features, read this chapter thoroughly so that you have the tools you need to make check writing fast and easy.

Using QuickFill

Writing checks is faster and easier than ever with Quicken's new QuickFill feature. When you type a few characters in a field, Quicken searches the various lists and the Register (the last three months of transactions only) to find a matching entry in that particular field. When Quicken finds a match, the QuickFill feature fills in the rest of the check with the transaction information that it found.

QuickFill works when you make an entry in the Payee field or the Category field in the Write Checks screen or the Register. See Chapter 5 to see how QuickFill works when entering transactions in the Register.

NOTE   QuickFill does not work when you edit an existing check.

QuickFill is turned on or activated by default. When you first start to use Quicken 6, this feature already should be working. Refer to Chapter 5 to learn how to turn on QuickFill if it's not active when you start Quicken.

Using QuickFill at the Payee Field

Quicken searches the Memorized Transaction list and the last three months of transactions in the Register when you type a few characters in the Payee field of the Write Checks screen. When Quicken finds a transaction with the same payee name, QuickFill fills in the rest of the payee name from the transaction it found in the Memorized Transaction list or the previous transactions in the Register.

Follow these steps to use QuickFill at the Payee field:

1. At the Write Checks screen, enter the check date as usual.

2. Type a few characters in the Payee field. Type *Ca*, for example. Quicken searches the Memorized Transaction list and the last three months of transactions in the Register for a payee name that starts with *Ca*. When Quicken finds the first transaction with the payee *Carmel Boyscouts*, for example, QuickFill fills in the rest of the payee name.

3. If the payee name (or in this example, *Carmel Boyscouts*) is indeed the payee that you want to enter in the transaction, press Enter and QuickFill fills in the rest of the transaction information for that payee: the transaction amount, the memo field (if used), and the category or subcategory exactly like the transaction that Quicken found.

If Quicken finds the matching transaction in the Memorized Transaction list, it displays <MEM> next to the payee name. If Quicken finds the matching transaction in the Register, it displays the month and day (<month/day>) next to the payee name.

If QuickFill doesn't fill in the payee information that you want, keep typing characters in the Payee field or press Ctrl-+ (plus) or Ctrl-− (minus) to keep searching the Memorized Transaction list or the transactions in the Register for the correct transaction.

> **NOTE** If more than one payee name exists in the Memorized Transaction list or more than one previous transaction exists in the Register that begins with the characters you type, QuickFill enters the transaction information for the first payee name found.

Figure 7.1 shows the payee name filled in by QuickFill from the Memorized Transaction list; figure 7.2 shows a check payee from a transaction dated 7/22 in the Register.

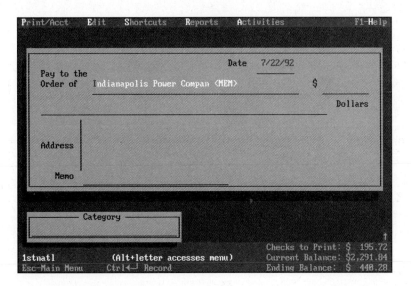

FIG. 7.1

A payee name filled in by QuickFill from the Memorized Transaction list.

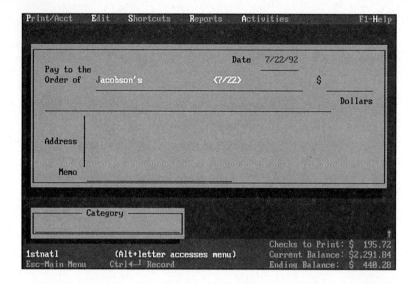

FIG. 7.2

A payee name filled in by QuickFill from a transaction in the Register.

4. After QuickFill fills in the check, you can edit any of the transaction fields necessary. When the correct entries are made to all of the check fields, record the check by pressing Ctrl-Enter or F10. Quicken records the checks and displays a blank check next.

Using QuickFill To Fill In the Category Field

QuickFill also works when you type a few characters in the Category field of a new check. (QuickFill does not work when editing an existing check.) QuickFill searches the Category and Transfer list and searches for the first category or transfer account that begins with the characters you type. If you want to enter a subcategory or a class, you can type a colon (:) after the category name is filled in. Quicken searches the subcategories under that particular category and enters the first one that it finds. If you want to enter a class, you can type a slash (/) and a few characters after the category or subcategory name is filled in. Quicken then searches the Class list and enters the first class it finds that begins with the characters you type. Classes are explained in Chapter 9, "Organizing Your Finances."

To use QuickFill to fill in the Category field, follow these steps:

1. At the Category field for a new check in the Write Checks screen, type a few characters of the category name that you want to

assign to the transaction. Quicken searches the Category and Transfer list for the first category or transfer account that matches the characters you type.

When Quicken finds a matching category or transfer account, QuickFill fills in the rest of the category or transfer account name.

2. If this is the category or transfer account that you want to assign to the transaction, press Enter to accept it.

If the category or transfer account name filled in by QuickFill is not the one that you want, type a few more characters or press Ctrl-+ (plus) or Ctrl-– (minus) until Quicken finds the right name.

3. To enter a subcategory after QuickFill fills in the category name, press End to go to the end of the category name and type a colon (:). QuickFill fills in the first subcategory for the category that it just filled in. If the subcategory is not the one that you want, type a few more characters or press Ctrl-+ (plus) or Ctrl-– (minus) to find the next or preceding subcategory under the category. Press Enter to accept the subcategory.

4. To enter class information, type a slash (/) after the category or subcategory name that QuickFill filled in and type a few characters of the class name. QuickFill searches the Class list and fills in the first class that begins with the characters you type. To accept the class, press Enter. If the class is not the one you want, type a few more characters or press Ctrl-+ (plus) or Ctrl-– (minus) to find the next or preceding class. To enter a subclass, type a colon after the class name, and QuickFill fills in the first subclass for the class that it just filled in. Use the Ctrl-+ (plus) or Ctrl-– (minus) key to find the next or preceding subclass under the class. Press Enter to accept the subclass.

> **NOTE** If the category or class that you want to assign to a check is not in the Category and Transfer list or the Class list (because they're new), you can add a new category or class simply by typing the new name in the Category field. When you press Enter after the you enter a new category or class name in the Write Checks screen, Quicken displays the Category Not Found window and asks if you want to add it to the Category or Class list or select a category or class from the existing list. To add the category or class, select option 1, **Add to Category List** or **Add to Class List**, and go through the normal steps for adding categories and classes. You learn how to add a category and class in Chapter 9.

Deactivating QuickFill

If you don't want to use the QuickFill feature, perhaps because you have varied checks that are rarely the same or because you feel more comfortable typing check information on your own, you can deactivate or turn off the QuickFill feature. Refer to Chapter 5, "Automating the Register," to learn how to deactivate QuickFill.

Deleting Checks

You can delete a check that you have written at the Write Checks screen as long as you have not printed the check yet. Once checks are printed, Quicken no longer stores them in the Write Checks screen. Printed check information is saved in the Register.

C P A
T I P
You should not delete a check that you have written and printed with Quicken. When you delete a check, Quicken removes all record of the transaction. Deleting the check removes the check information and leaves a gap in your check-numbering sequence. Void a check transaction that you want to remove because of a lost check, a check that you have stopped payment on, or an improperly printed check, but do not delete such checks. Information for voided transactions remains in the Register so that you can track each prenumbered check.

To delete a check from the Write Checks screen, follow these steps:

1. Use the PgUp and PgDn keys or the Home and End keys to display the check that you want to delete.

2. Select the Edit menu by pressing Alt-E (see fig. 7.3).

3. Select the **Delete Transaction** option from the Edit menu.

T I P
You can press the shortcut key Ctrl-D to select the **Delete Transaction** option.

Quicken displays the OK to Delete Transaction? window that you see in figure 7.4.

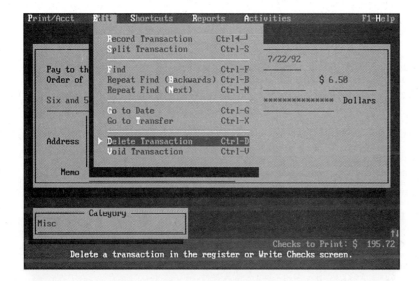

FIG. 7.3

The Edit menu.

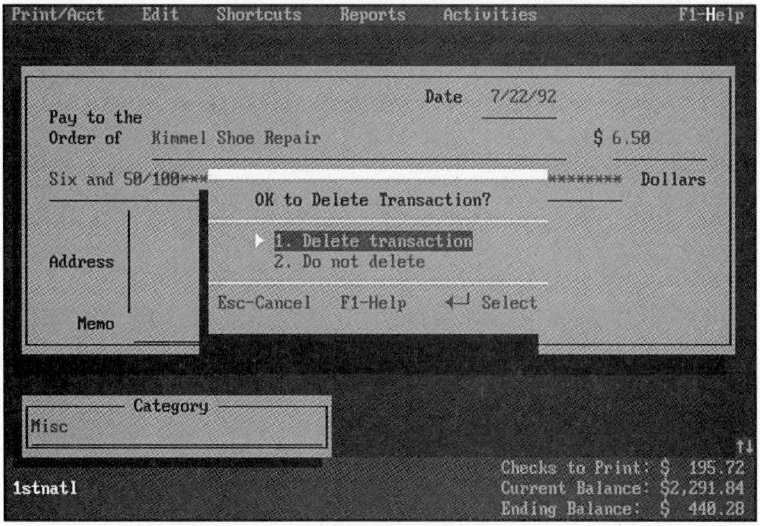

FIG. 7.4

The OK to Delete
Transaction?
window.

4. Press Enter to delete the transaction (the **Delete Transaction**
   option is highlighted), or press 2 if you don't want to delete the
   transaction.

When you delete a check, Quicken removes all check information from
the Write Checks screen and the Register.

Voiding Checks

You may need to void a check when you want to stop payment, when you lose a check and write another one to replace it, or when a check prints incorrectly and you have to print another. Note that when you choose to void a check from the Write Checks screen, Quicken takes you to the Checking Account Register and enables you to void the check transaction from there.

If you void a check transaction that is part of a transfer from one account to another, voiding any part of the transaction also voids the other parts of the transaction—those recorded in the other Registers.

To void a check from the Write Checks screen, follow these steps:

1. Use the PgUp and PgDn keys or the Home and End keys to display the check that you want to void.

2. Select the Edit menu by pressing Alt-E.

3. Select the **Void Transaction** option from the Edit menu.

T I P You can use the Ctrl-V shortcut key to select the **Void Transaction** option.

Quicken moves to the Register for the account from which you wrote the check and highlights the check that you are voiding. The OK to Void Transaction? window is displayed as seen in figure 7.5.

4. Press Enter to void the transaction (the **Void transaction** option is already highlighted), or press 2 if you decide not to void the transaction.

Quicken enters the word VOID: in the Payee field before the payee name and marks the transaction with an X in the Clear (C) column so that the transaction is not considered an uncleared item when you perform your account reconciliation.

5. Press Ctrl-W to return to the Write Checks screen.

Splitting Check Transactions

The Write Checks screen provides a field for assigning a category or subcategory to the check transaction. A check written to the power company may be assigned to the Utilities category, for example. A check written to pay for office supplies may be assigned to the Supplies category. Many transactions, however, fit into more than one category. When you need to assign a check to more than one category, use the **Split Transaction** option from the Edit menu. This option provides additional category fields and more space to assign categories and subcategories to a check.

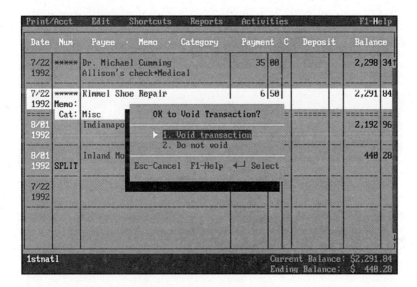

To split a check transaction, follow these steps:

1. Press Alt-E to display the Edit menu and select **Split Transaction** (or press Ctrl-S). The Split Transaction window appears (see fig. 7.6).

2. Enter the first category name in the Category field in line 1. You can use the Category field in the Split Transaction window in the same way that you use the Category field in the Write Checks screen. You also can use the Category field to record transfers to other accounts. Up to 30 lines are available on the Split Transaction window to assign categories, subcategories, or transfer accounts.

NOTE Quicken provides defined Home and Business categories. The Home Category list provides categories for most general household expenses, and the Business Category list includes general business income and expense categories. To access these categories, press Ctrl-C from the Category field in the Split Transaction window.

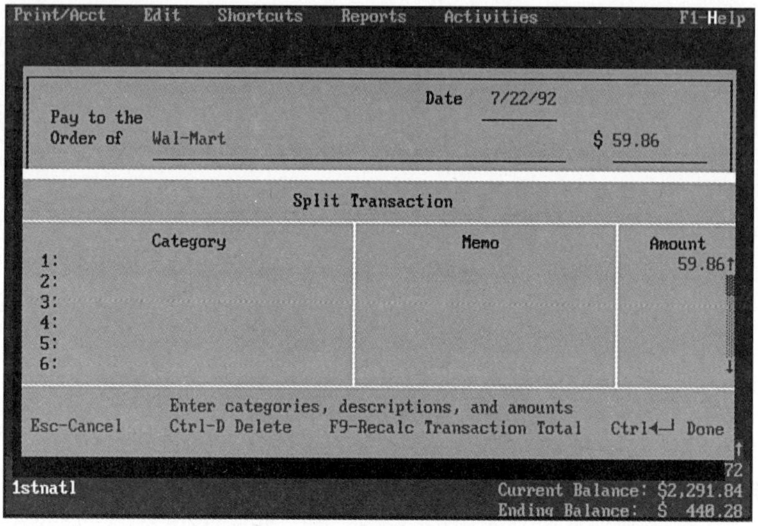

FIG. 7.6

The Split
Transaction
window.

3. (Optional) Press Enter or Tab to move the cursor to the Memo field. Type a description of the category or the amount. The Memo field provides a 27-character space you can use to describe a transaction, to explain why you selected a category, or to detail how you calculated the check amount.

4. Press Enter or Tab to move the cursor to the Amount field. You can use the Amount field in two ways, depending on whether you select **Split Transaction** before or after you enter the amount on the Write Checks screen.

   If you select **Split Transaction** before you make an entry in the Amount field on the Write Checks screen, Quicken adds each of the amounts you enter in the Amount field in the Split Transaction window. Quicken then enters this total in the $ field in the Write Checks screen.

   If you select **Split Transaction** after entering a check amount in the Write Checks screen, Quicken shows this amount in the first Amount field in the Split Transaction window. If you then enter a number in the first Amount field in the Split Transaction window, Quicken calculates the difference between the check amount in the Write Checks screen and the new amount you entered and then places this difference in the second Amount field in the Split Transaction window.

5. Press Enter or Tab to move to the next line of the Split Transaction screen. Repeat steps 2, 3, and 4 for each category and amount combination you want to record. You can record up

to 30 category and amount combinations. Figure 7.7 shows a completed Split Transaction window.

> **T I P**
>
> As noted in Chapter 5, you also can enter percents in the Split Transaction window's Amount fields. If you enter a check for $1,200 and 25 percent of this amount is to be entered in the first Split Transaction field, move the cursor to the field, type *25%*, and press Enter. When you press Tab or Enter to move to the next field, Quicken calculates the number that equals 25 percent of $1,200 and enters this value in the Amount field.

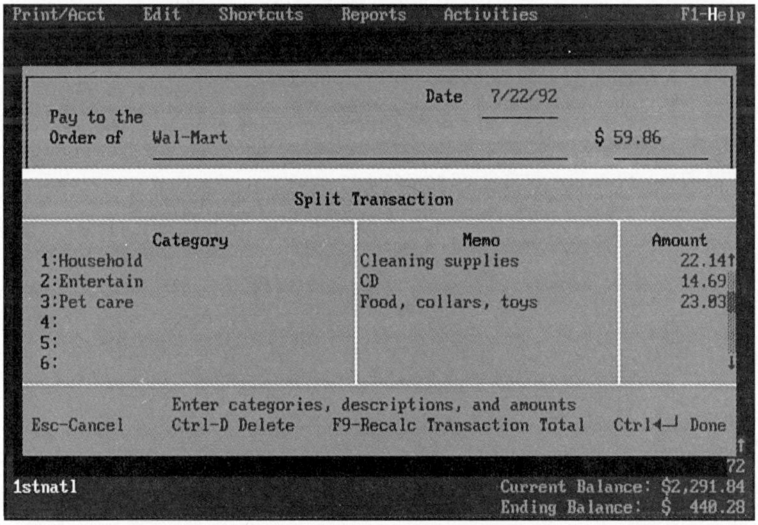

FIG. 7.7

A completed Split Transaction window.

If you use all 30 split transaction Amount fields, Quicken has nowhere to make the Write Checks screen amount equal to the total Split Transaction amount. You must manually adjust the Write Checks screen amount or one of the Split Transaction window amounts. You also can press F9 to total the Amount fields in the Split Transaction window and insert the total into the $ field in the Write Checks screen.

6. To leave the Split Transaction window and return to the Write Checks screen, Press Ctrl-Enter or F10.

7. After returning to the Write Checks screen, record the check. Quicken indicates a split transaction by displaying the word SPLIT below the Category field (see fig. 7.8).

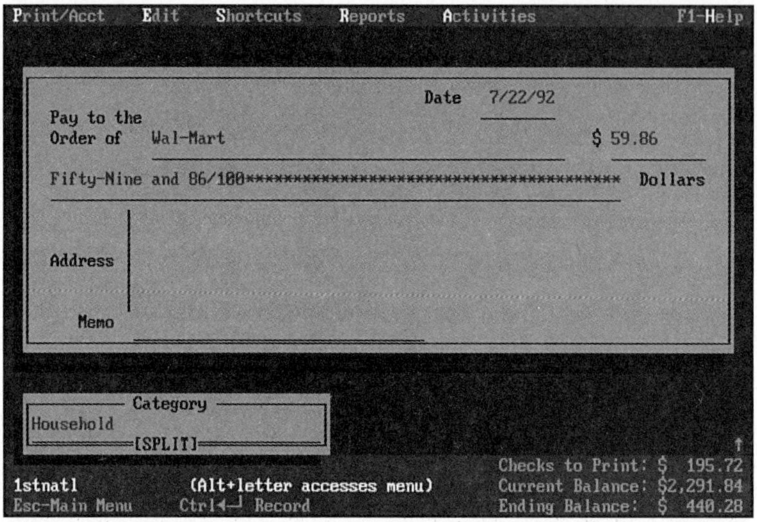

FIG. 7.8

Quicken identifies a split transaction with the word [SPLIT] below the Category field on the Write Checks screen.

```
  Print/Acct    Edit    Shortcuts    Reports    Activities              F1-Help

  ┌──────────────────────────────────────────────────────────────────────┐
  │                                        Date    7/22/92                 │
  │   Pay to the                                   _____                │
  │   Order of   Wal-Mart                                    $ 59.86       │
  │                                                                        │
  │   Fifty-Nine and 86/100*********************************** Dollars     │
  │                                                                        │
  │                    │                                                   │
  │   Address          │                                                   │
  │                    │                                                   │
  │   Memo             │                                                   │
  └──────────────────────────────────────────────────────────────────────┘

  ┌─────── Category ───────┐
  │Household               │
  │ ────────[SPLIT]────────│                            Checks to Print: $  195.72
  └────────────────────────┘                                                    ↑
  1stnatl              (Alt+letter accesses menu)       Current Balance: $2,291.84
  Esc-Main Menu      Ctrl◄┘ Record                      Ending Balance:  $  440.28
```

T I P   If you use check forms with vouchers and enter individual invoices and invoice amounts in the Split Transaction window, Quicken prints this information on the voucher. Vendors then can record your payments correctly, and you no longer have to spend time trying to explain which invoice a check pays. Remember that room is available on the voucher only for the first 15 lines in the Split Transaction window. If you use all 30 lines in the Split Transaction window, only half of the split transaction detail appears.

Calculating Check Amounts in Split Transactions

You can calculate the amount that you want to write a check for by using the Split Transaction window. Perhaps you have several invoices from the same vendor, but each invoice represents a different type of expense that you want to assign to different categories. You can use the Split Transaction window to assign the categories, enter the amounts, and calculate the total amount to enter as the check amount in the Write Checks screen. (Calculating transaction amounts in split transactions is explained in Chapter 5.) Use the same steps to calculate check amounts in split transactions in the Write Checks screen.

Editing, Deleting, and Undoing Split Transactions

The procedures for editing, deleting, and undoing a split transaction in the Write Checks screen are the same as those for the Register. Refer to Chapter 5 to learn how to edit, delete, and undo a split transaction.

Finding Checks

After you write a large volume of checks, you may need to find a check to review or edit. Quicken's **Find** option enables you to locate a check (that you have written but not printed) in the Write Checks screen quickly and easily.

Using the Find Option

One way to search through unprinted checks is to use an exact match. An *exact match* means that you look for a check that has a payee, an amount, a category, or another piece of check information exactly equal to what you want. The amount you are looking for is known as a *search argument*.

To search through checks you created but didn't print, follow these steps:

1. Press Alt-E to display the Edit menu and select the **Find** option (or press Ctrl-F). The Transaction to Find window shown in figure 7.9 appears.

2. Perform one or more of the following searches:

   To search through the Write Checks screen for checks with a specific entry in the Payee field, enter the name of the payee in the Payee field.

   To search for checks equal to a specific amount, enter the amount in the Payment field. Quicken searches through the unprinted checks for the amount you entered. The amount you are looking for is the *search argument*.

   To search for unprinted checks with a specific memo, enter the memo you are looking for in the Memo field.

   To search for unprinted checks assigned to a specific category, enter the category name assigned to the check you are looking for in the Category field.

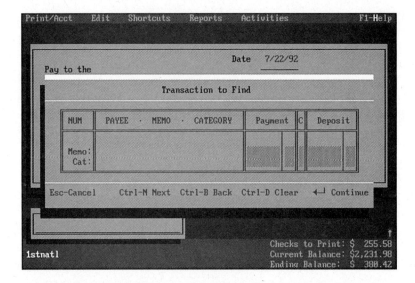

FIG. 7.9

The Transaction
to Find window.

Do not enter an amount in the Num, C, or Deposit fields. Although these fields appear on the Transaction to Find screen, these amounts do not appear in the Write Checks screen. Therefore, you cannot use these fields to find checks written at the Write Checks screen.

3. After you enter the search arguments, press Ctrl-Enter or F10. Alternatively, press Enter when the cursor is in the Category field.

Quicken asks in which direction you want to search by displaying the screen shown in figure 7.10. You have two options: **Find backwards** and **Find next**. **Find backwards** (Ctrl-B) searches through checks dated earlier than the check displayed in the Write Checks screen. **Find next** (Ctrl-N) searches through checks dated later than the check displayed in the Write Checks screen.

4. Select **Find backwards** or **Find next**.

Quicken searches for the exact words you type. If you enter *75* in the Payment field, for example, Quicken searches for checks equal to $75.00. If you type *mortgage* in the Memo field, Quicken looks for checks with *mortgage* in this field. Because Quicken's search isn't case sensitive, *Mortgage*, *MORTGAGE*, and *mortgage* are all exact matches from Quicken's perspective. If the Memo field reads *May mortgage*, however, Quicken does not find the check.

If Quicken finds a check that matches the search argument, it displays the check in the Write Checks screen. If Quicken does not find a check that matches the search argument, the program displays the message No matching transactions were found (see fig. 7.11).

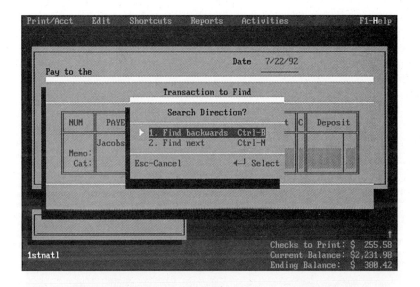

Quicken asks whether you want to search through checks dated before or after the currently displayed check.

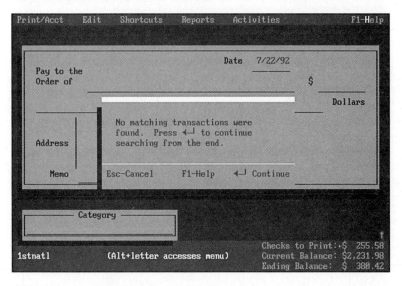

The No matching transactions were found message.

Finding Key-Word Matches

Key-word matches enable you to search based on a field that includes or excludes certain letters, characters, or series of characters. Key-word matches use three special characters: periods (.), question marks (?), and tildes (~). Periods act as wild-card indicators that can represent any character, group of characters, or even no character. The question mark can represent any one character. The tilde character identifies a word, character, or group of characters to exclude from the search. Refer to table 5.1 in Chapter 5 for a summary of the special characters Quicken uses to find key-word matches in Write Checks screen fields.

Combining Exact Matches and Key-Word Matches

You can search by using more than one exact match or key-word search argument. Figure 7.12, for example, shows the Transaction to Find window to search for checks using *big national* in the Payee field and *mortgage* in the Memo field. The same techniques that work for searching through the Register also work for searching through unprinted checks. For more information about key-word matches, refer to Chapter 5.

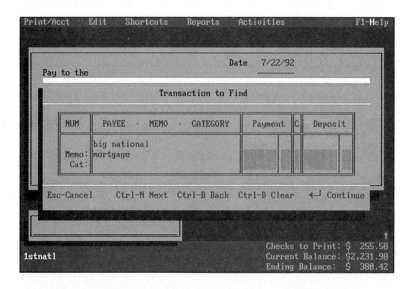

FIG. 7.12

Using key-word matches on the Transaction to Find screen.

If you use more than one match test, Quicken locates only the checks that meet all the tests. In the example in figure 7.12, Quicken does not locate checks with the phrase *big national* in the Payee field unless the word *mortgage* is in the Memo field and vice versa.

Repeating a Search

When executing a Find request, Quicken selects the first check that matches the search arguments you entered. If you were precise in specifying the exact match or key-word match, the first check Quicken finds may be the one you want. Because the first check Quicken finds often is not the one you want, however, Quicken gives you two other Find options: **Repeat Find (backwards)** and **Repeat Find (next)**. **Repeat Find (backwards)** executes the Find request already specified on the Transaction to Find window; it searches through checks dated earlier than the currently displayed check. Similarly, **Repeat Find (next)** executes the Find request already specified on the Transaction to Find window; it searches through checks dated later than the currently displayed check.

Using the Go to Date Option

To search for a specific day's checks, select the **Go to Date** option from the Edit menu or press Ctrl-G. Quicken displays the Go to Date window as shown in figure 7.13.

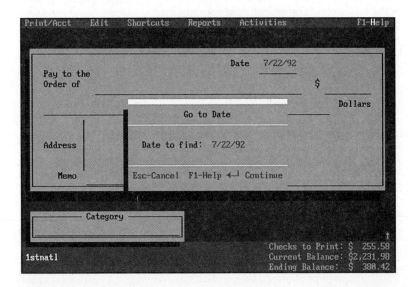

FIG. 7.13

The Go to Date window.

Initially, Quicken displays the current system date in the Go to Date window. To specify a date for the search, type the date you want over the default date. You also can use the + (plus) and – (minus) keys to move the date forward or backward one day at a time.

After you specify a date and press Enter, Quicken finds and displays the first check with the date you entered. If no check with the entered date is found, Quicken displays the check with the date closest to the entered date.

Because Quicken arranges all checks by the check date, you do not need to specify a search direction when using the **Go to Date** option. By comparing the date on the currently displayed check to the date you enter, Quicken determines the direction to search. If the date for which you want to search falls before the date on the current check, Quicken looks through the previous checks. If the date you want to search for falls after the date on the current check, Quicken looks through checks dated after the current check.

Using the Go to Transfer Option

You can select the **Go to Transfer** option from the Edit menu or press Ctrl-X to go to the transfer transaction related to the currently displayed check. If you entered the transfer account in the Category field, recorded the check, and then executed the **Go to Transfer** option, Quicken accesses the Account Register for the corresponding transaction and highlights the transfer transaction. Pressing Ctrl-X again returns you to the transaction in the Register for the account that you wrote the check from. Usually, you enter an account here because you're transferring money from a checking account to another bank account by writing a check. To review account transfers, see Chapters 4 and 5.

Using Memorized Check Transactions

To speed the check-writing process, you can memorize recurring check transactions from the Write Checks screen. Many checks you write probably are similar from week to week and month to month. For a household, you may write a mortgage check, a car loan check, a utility bill check, and so on. For a business, you may write weekly payroll checks to employees and monthly checks to major vendors. Because checks often are similar, Quicken enables you to store check information in a special list known as the *Memorized Transactions list.* Instead of re-entering the same information, you can reuse transaction information. The **Memorize Transaction** option is valuable if you address checks, because you do not have to re-enter the payee's address every time you write a check.

Memorizing a Check Transaction

If you have read Chapter 5, "Automating the Register," you already know about using memorized transactions in the Register. The **Memorize Transaction** option works similarly in the Write Checks screen. Therefore, if you feel well versed in the mechanics of memorized transactions, skip or skim the next few paragraphs. The only substantive difference between memorized transactions in the Register and memorized transactions for unprinted checks in the Write Checks screen is that if you memorize an unprinted check, Quicken memorizes the address information. (Address information doesn't appear in the Register.)

To memorize a check transaction, follow these steps:

1. Use the PgUp and PgDn keys or the Home and End keys to display the check you want to memorize in the Write Checks screen (see fig. 7.14).

2. Press Alt-S to display the Shortcuts menu, and then select the **Memorize Transaction** option or just press Ctrl-M. Quicken alerts you that the marked information is about to be memorized (see fig. 7.15).

3. To complete the memorization process, press Enter. Quicken saves a copy of the check in the Memorized Transaction list.

Recalling a Check Transaction

You can select **Recall Transaction** by pressing Ctrl-T to complete the Write Checks screen by using information from memorized transactions. Suppose that you use the **Memorize Transaction** option to memorize the monthly cleaning payment shown in figure 7.15. When you need to pay Susan Alexander Cleaning Services again, select **Recall Transaction** from the Shortcuts menu or press Ctrl-T. Either approach displays the Memorized Transaction list shown in figure 7.16. The Memorized Transaction list shows all memorized transactions (except memorized investment transactions). You want to recall, however, only those transactions that show Chk in the Type column. Chk indicates that the transaction was memorized from the Write Checks screen. Chk transactions include information that appears only in the Write Checks screen, such as the address data and the extra message line.

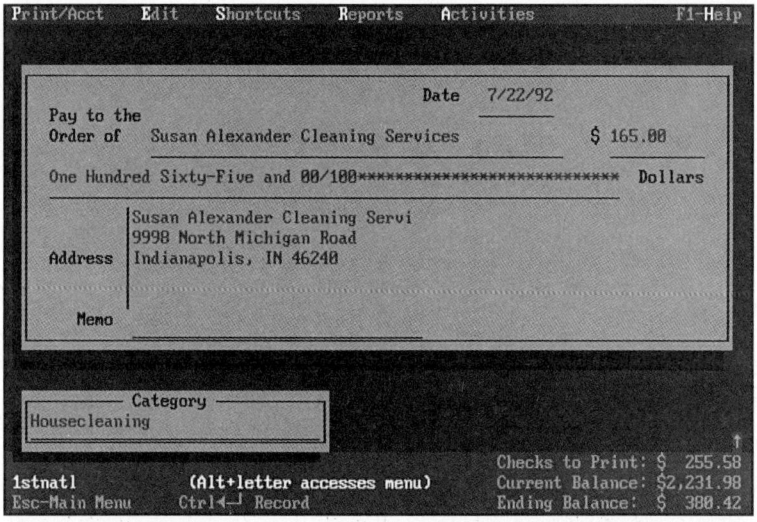

FIG. 7.14

Memorizing a monthly house-cleaning or janitorial check.

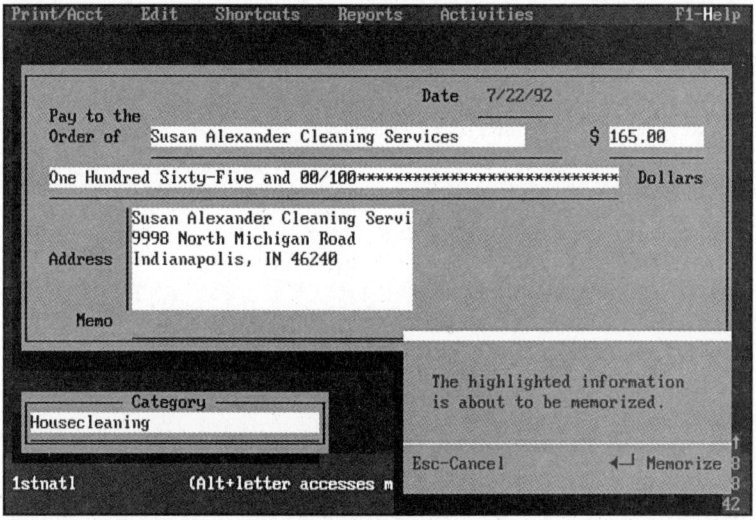

FIG. 7.15

Quicken telling you that the marked informa-tion is about to be memorized.

Figure 7.16 shows some of the information saved as part of the Memo-rize Transaction operation. The address information and message also are saved, but the address and message do not show in the Memorized Transaction list.

The Memorized Transaction list is sorted by payee. For each payee, Quicken shows whether the transaction is a split transaction, the memo (if any), the category assigned to the memorized transaction, whether the memorized transaction has cleared the bank, the transaction amount, the transaction type (Chk, Pmt, Dep, and so on) and to which transaction group (if any) the memorized transaction belongs. Transaction groups are described later in the chapter.

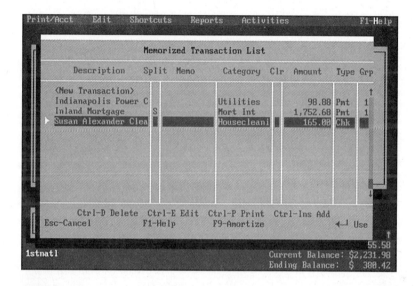

FIG. 7.16

The Memorized Transaction List.

NOTE If you memorize a split check transaction, Quicken displays a message window that asks if you want to memorize the split amounts as amounts or as percentages of the check amount. To answer the message, press A if you want the actual amounts memorized or press P to memorize the percentages. This feature is handy if a memorized check amount varies, but the split is always based on the same percentages.

To recall a memorized check transaction, follow these steps:

1. Select the Write/Print Checks option from the main menu or press Ctrl-W to access the Write Checks screen.

2. Press Alt-S to display the Shortcuts menu and select the **Recall Transaction** option, or press Ctrl-T. Quicken displays the Memorized Transaction list.

3. Use the up- and down-arrow keys to highlight the memorized check that you want to recall to the Write Checks screen.

4. Press Enter. Quicken uses the memorized transaction to fill the Write Checks screen.

5. Edit the information from the memorized check, if necessary.

6. Press Ctrl-Enter or F10 to record the check.

Editing a Memorized Check Transaction

Over time, the check information you memorize may need to be up-dated. Updating check information, however, doesn't present a prob-lem. To edit a memorized transaction, follow these steps:

1. Press Alt-S to display the Shortcuts menu and select the **Recall Transaction** option (or press Ctrl-T). Quicken displays the Memo-rized Transaction list.

2. Highlight the transaction you want to edit and press Ctrl-E. Quicken displays the Edit/Setup Memorized Transaction window (see fig. 7.17).

3. Change the fields as necessary and then press Ctrl-Enter or F10.

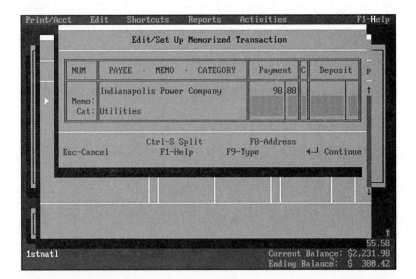

FIG. 7.17

The Edit/Setup Memorized Transaction window.

Deleting a Memorized Check Transaction

At some point, the original reasons you had for memorizing a transac-tion may no longer apply. Eventually, you may pay off the mortgage or car loan, children may outgrow the need for day care, or you may choose to stop spending money on an item, such as club dues or cable television.

You can use the **Recall Transaction** option to delete memorized transactions from the Memorized Transaction list. To delete a transaction from the list, follow these steps:

1. Press Alt-S to display the Shortcuts menu and select the **Recall Transaction** option (or press Ctrl-T). Quicken displays the Memorized Transaction list.

2. Use the up- and down-arrow keys to highlight the transaction you want to delete.

3. After you highlight the transaction to delete, press Ctrl-D. Quicken alerts you that you are about to delete a memorized transaction (see fig. 7.18).

4. To delete the memorized check transaction, press Enter. If you decide not to delete the memorized transaction, press Esc.

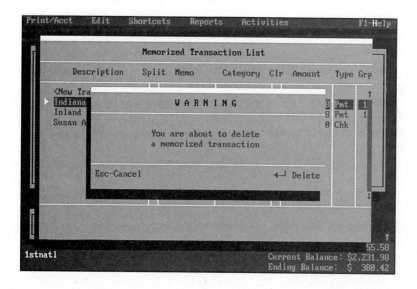

FIG. 7.18

The message warning that you are about to delete a memorized transaction.

Printing the Memorized Transaction List

Quicken enables you to print lists of memorized transactions. Assuming that you entered payee addresses, a printed list of memorized transactions can act as a directory of the people and businesses to whom you write checks.

To print a list of memorized checks and other transactions, follow these steps:

1. Press Alt-S to display the Shortcuts menu and then select the **Recall Transaction** option (or press Ctrl-T). The Memorized Transaction List screen appears.
2. Press Ctrl-P. Quicken displays the Print Memorized Transaction list window, which is similar to the Print Checks window described in Chapter 6. Specify the printer setting you want to use to print the report.
3. Indicate the printer you want to use and press Enter. Quicken prints the list (see fig. 7.19).

```
                 Memorized Transaction List

L FLANDE                                             Page 1
7/22/92

    Payee/Memo/Category         Clr   Type       Amount
----------------------------    ---  -------   ---------

Indianapolis Power Company           Payment      -98.88

    Utilities

Inland Mortgage                      Payment   -1,752.68
                        SPLITS

    Mort Int                                   -1,300.00
    Tax:Prop                                     -150.00
    [Mortgage]                                   -302.68

Jacobson's                           Payment     -152.65
                        SPLITS

    Clothing                                     -127.65
    Cosmetics                                     -25.00
```

FIG. 7.19

The printed Memorized Transaction List.

CPA TIP

Consider as candidates for the Memorized Transaction list each check you regularly write using Quicken: rent, house payment, utility payment, school loans, and so on. Using the **Memorized Transaction** option saves you time you otherwise spend typing, finding addresses, and describing checks.

Copying and Pasting Check Transactions

If there is a single check that you want to copy, but you don't feel the need to memorize it and make it part of the Memorized Transaction list, now with Quicken 6.0 you can copy that check and paste it in a blank check or an existing check in the Write Checks screen.

When Quicken copies a check, it is essentially memorizing the check information. This information is stored in Quicken and can be pasted in a blank check or an existing check in the Write Checks screen. You can repaste the same check more than once. Quicken will not save the stored check information after you copy another check or exit the program, however.

To copy and paste a check in the Write Checks screen, follow these steps:

1. Use the PgUp and PgDn keys or the Home and End keys to display the check that you want to copy.

2. Select the **Copy Transaction** option by pressing Ctrl-Ins. Quicken flashes a message in the bottom right corner of your screen that it is MEMORIZING the transaction.

3. Display a blank check or, if you want to replace an existing check with the copied check, display the check that you want to replace.

4. Press Shift-Ins to select the **Paste Transaction** option. Quicken enters (or pastes) the check information from the copied check into the currently displayed check.

If the Confirm When Overwriting with a Memorized or Pasted Transaction setting is turned on, Quicken displays the OK to Overwrite Transaction? message before it replaces an existing check with the copied check. To proceed and enter the copied check over the existing check, press Enter. Otherwise, press Esc. You learn how to work with transaction settings in Chapter 20, "Customizing Quicken."

Using Categories

You can assign a category or subcategory to a check by typing the category or subcategory name in the Category field or by using the **Categorize/Transfer** option from the Shortcuts menu. This option displays the Category and Transfer list so that you can find and assign a category, subcategory, or transfer account to a check. You also can use this option to add a new category or edit or delete an existing category. Adding, editing, and deleting categories and subcategories is described in Chapter 9, "Organizing Your Finances."

To find and assign a category or subcategory to a check, follow these steps:

1. From the Write Checks screen, press Alt-S to display the Shortcuts menu. Then select the **Categorize/Transfer** option.

T I P You can press the shortcut key Ctrl-C to select the Categorize/Transfer option.

Quicken displays the Category and Transfer list with predefined categories, subcategories, and any accounts you may have created (see fig. 7.20).

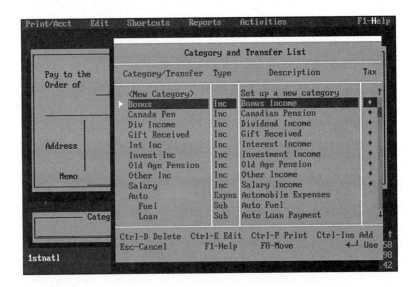

FIG. 7.20

The Category
and Transfer List.

2. Highlight the category, subcategory, or account you want to assign to the check and press Enter. Quicken retrieves the category or account name from the list and enters it in the Category field.

You also can use the PgUp, PgDn, Home, and End keys to move quickly through long lists of categories and accounts. Pressing PgUp displays the preceding page of categories in the list; pressing PgDn displays the next page of categories in the list; pressing Home displays the first page of categories, and pressing End displays the last page of categories. The Category and Transfer list also provides a scroll bar that mouse users can take advantage of for moving up and down the list. (Refer to Chapter 2, "Getting Around in Quicken," if you don't know how scroll bars function.)

Using Check Transaction Groups

The capability of recalling a single memorized check saves time, but Quicken provides you with another option: you can recall sets of memorized transactions, or *transaction groups*. Transaction groups enable you to recall several memorized checks at the same time. Rather than repeatedly using **Recall Transaction** to retrieve checks from the Memorized Transaction list, you can recall an entire group of checks in one step.

Using transaction groups is explained in Chapter 5, "Automating the Register," including setting up a transaction group, recalling a trans- action group, editing and deleting transaction groups, adding a new transaction to a group, and deleting a transaction from a group. Using transaction groups at the Write Checks screen works the same way. In fact, when you're at the Write Checks screen and select the **Transac- tion Groups** option from the Shortcuts menu, Quicken takes you to the Register so that you can set up or recall a transaction group from there.

Switching To the Register from the Write Checks Screen

Anytime you're working in the Write Checks screen, you can quickly switch to the Register for the account that you're writing checks from by pressing Ctrl-R.

Chapter Summary

This chapter showed you how to speed up your check writing using QuickFill, memorized transactions, and transaction groups. You learned how to copy and paste a check transaction and how to quickly find transactions using the **Find** option, the **Go to Date** option, and the **Go to Transfer** option.

In the next chapter, we'll wrap up Part I of *Using Quicken 6 for DOS* by showing you how to reconcile your bank account. The hours and hours you've spent doing this task in the past will turn into minutes when you reconcile your account with Quicken!

Reconciling Your Bank Account

Reconciling your bank account regularly is one of the most important steps you can take to protect your cash and the accuracy and reliability of your financial records, but most people probably don't reconcile—except out of a sense of guilt or frustration. The work is tedious and usually aggravating as you search, often futilely, for the transaction that explains the difference between the bank's records and your personal records. Fortunately, Quicken provides a fast and easy method of reconciliation.

In this chapter, you learn how to do the following:

- Reconcile a bank account using Quicken
- Mark transactions as cleared
- Print and use reconciliation reports
- Correct and catch reconciliation errors

Reviewing the Reconciliation Process

Reconciling a bank account is not difficult. You probably already understand the mechanics of the reconciliation process. For those readers who are a bit rusty with the process, however, the next few paragraphs briefly describe how reconciliation works.

To reconcile a bank account, you perform three basic steps:

1. Review the bank statement for new transactions and errors. You want to verify that you have recorded each transaction correctly.

2. Find the transactions not recorded by the bank or cleared, and total these transactions.

3. Verify that the difference between your Quicken Register balance and the bank balance equals the total of the uncleared transactions. If the totals don't agree, you need to repeat steps 1 and 2.

 NOTE If you still find the process confusing, examine your monthly bank statement. The back of your current bank statement probably explains the whole process step by step.

Reviewing the Bank Statement

The first step in reconciling an account is to review the bank statement. First, find any new transactions that the bank recorded and that you now need to record. These transactions may include bank service fees, overdraft charges, and interest income. You need to record these transactions in the Register before you proceed with the reconciliation.

For each transaction, confirm that the checking account transaction recorded in the Register and on the bank statement are the same amount. If you find a transaction not recorded in both places for the same amount, review the discrepancy and identify the incorrect transaction.

C P A
T I P   Carefully review each canceled check for authenticity. If a check forger successfully draws a check on your account, you can discover the forgery by reviewing canceled checks. As Appendix D explains, you need to find forgeries if you hope to recover the money.

Checking Cleared Transactions

The second step in checking account reconciliation is to calculate the total dollar value of those transactions that have not cleared the bank. By adding up all checks that have not cleared (usually known as *outstanding checks*) and also all deposits (usually known as *deposits in transit*), you calculate an amount that represents the logical difference between the bank's records and your records.

Usually, the mechanics of this step work in the following way: you look through the bank statement to identify checks and deposits that have cleared, and then mark cleared transactions in the Register. After you mark all the cleared transactions in the Register, adding up all transactions that haven't cleared is a simple matter.

Verifying that Balances Correspond

The final step is a quick one: you verify that the difference between the Quicken Register balance and the bank statement balance is the total of the transactions that *have not* cleared. If you have correctly performed steps 1 and 2 in the reconciliation process, the balance in your Quicken Register and the ending bank balance should differ by the total of all transactions not yet cleared. If the two amounts don't differ by precisely this amount, you must repeat steps 1 and 2 until you locate and correct the error.

Using Quicken To Reconcile Your Account

Quicken makes reconciling a bank account easier by automating the steps and doing the arithmetic for you. To reconcile an account, follow these steps:

1. Select the **Reconcile** option from the Activities menu at the Write Checks or Register screen.

NOTE The first time you use Quicken to reconcile your account, a brief message is displayed telling you what the **Reconcile** option does and that you should read the chapter in the Quicken manual to learn about reconciling. Press Enter to remove the message and continue with the reconciliation process.

Quicken displays the Reconcile Register with Bank Statement window that you see in figure 8.1.

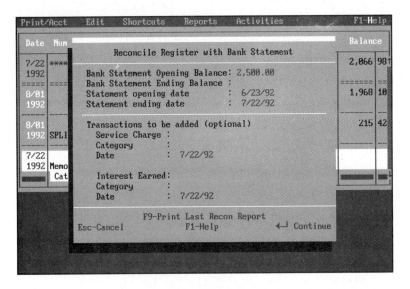

FIG. 8.1

The Reconcile Register with Bank Statement window.

2. In the Bank Statement Opening Balance field, type the bank statement balance shown at the start of the period the statement covers if the balance differs from the one shown. This number appears on your bank statement. If this is your first time to reconcile your account with Quicken, the opening balance that you entered when you added the account to your system is entered as the bank statement opening balance.

> **NOTE**   Remember, Quicken strongly recommends that you use the ending balance from your last bank statement as the opening balance in a new bank account. Therefore, if you used the ending balance as your opening balance, the opening balance that Quicken enters in the Bank Statement Opening Balance field should be correct.

If this is not your first time to use Quicken to reconcile your bank account, Quicken uses the ending balance per your bank statement from the last time you reconciled your account as the opening bank statement balance.

If the opening bank statement balance that Quicken enters in the Reconcile Register with Bank Statement window does not agree with the opening balance on your bank statement, be sure to read the section "Adjusting Opening Balance Differences," later in this chapter.

If you normally keep a large account balance, you should have an interest-bearing checking account. You should not keep your money in an account that doesn't earn interest.

C P A
T I P

Before you close your current account and open a new one, however, review the fees your bank charges for each type of account. Weigh the interest factor against the fee schedule to determine the most beneficial account type for your business. If your bank does not offer interest-bearing accounts to businesses, you may want to deposit excess cash into a savings or money market account. Remember that you can set up savings and money market accounts in your Quicken system and use the Reconcile feature to balance each account.

3. Press Enter or Tab to move the cursor to the Bank Statement Ending Balance field and type the bank statement balance shown at the end of the period the bank statement covers. This number also appears on your bank statement.

4. Press Enter or Tab to move to the Statement Opening Date field. Type the date shown on your bank statement as the opening or starting date.

5. Press Enter or Tab to move to the Statement Ending Date field. Type the date shown on your bank statement as the ending date.

NOTE After you have reconciled your account using Quicken, the next time you reconcile, Quicken automatically enters dates in the Statement Opening Date and Statement Ending Date fields based on the dates you entered the first time you reconciled. If these dates differ, just change them by typing a new date or using the + (plus) or – (minus) key to change the date one day at a time.

6. Press Enter or Tab to move the cursor to the Service Charge field. If you have not recorded monthly service fees, record these fees now by entering the appropriate amount in the Service Charge field.

7. (Optional) Press Enter or Tab to move the cursor to the Category field. If you entered an amount in the field and want to assign the charge to a category, enter the appropriate category name in the Category field. (Remember that you can access the Category and Transfer list by pressing Ctrl-C and select a category from the list.)

8. Press Enter or Tab to move the cursor to the Interest Earned field. If you have not recorded monthly interest income on the account, record the interest earned by entering the appropriate amount in the Interest Earned field.

9. (Optional) Press Enter or Tab to move the cursor to the Category field. If you entered an amount in the Interest Earned field and want to assign the income to a category, enter the appropriate category name here.

10. (Optional) Press F9 to print the last reconciliation report before you start reconciling. This is your last chance to print this report. After you start reconciling your account, the data from the last reconciliation report will be overwritten.

    If you select to print a reconciliation report by pressing F9, Quicken displays the Print Reconciliation Report window. See the section "Printing a Reconciliation Report," later in this chapter, to learn how to complete this window and print a report.

11. Press Ctrl-Enter or F10 when the Reconcile Register with Bank Statement window is complete. Quicken displays the Transaction List window, which shows each bank account transaction (see fig. 8.2).

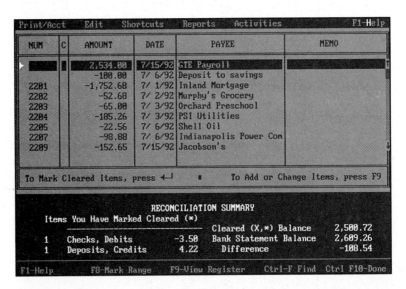

FIG. 8.2

Bank account transactions shown in a list.

12. Mark checks and deposits that have *cleared* (were recorded by) the bank. To mark an item as cleared, use the up- and down-arrow keys to highlight the transaction you want to mark. Press Enter to

mark the highlighted transaction as cleared and move to the next transaction. Quicken enters an asterisk (*) in the Cleared column. To unmark a transaction, highlight the transaction that you want to unmark and press the space bar to remove the asterisk.

To mark a range of transactions as cleared, press F8. The Mark Range of Check Numbers as Cleared window appears (see fig. 8.3). You use this screen to specify that all transactions with check numbers in the indicated range should be marked as cleared.

As you mark transactions, the reconciliation summary in the Transactions List window shows the numbers and dollar amounts of the check and deposit transactions you marked as cleared, the cleared transaction total, the ending balance, and the difference between the total and the balance. You are finished with the reconciliation when the difference between the cleared balance and the bank statement balance equals zero.

FIG. 8.3

The Mark Range of Check Numbers as Cleared window.

13. (Optional) To correct transactions you entered incorrectly in the Register, press F9 to redisplay the same information in an abbreviated form of the standard Register. Edit the transactions in the Register in the usual manner. To change the displayed screen back to the Transaction list, press F9 again. (Chapter 5 describes how to edit transactions in the Quicken Register.)

Figure 8.4 shows sample transactions as they appear in the Register.

14. When the difference between the cleared balance and the bank statement balance is zero, press Ctrl-F10 to indicate that you are finished with the reconciliation. When you press Ctrl-F10, Quicken changes each asterisk (*) in the C field to an X, and asks whether you want to print a reconciliation report (see fig. 8.5).

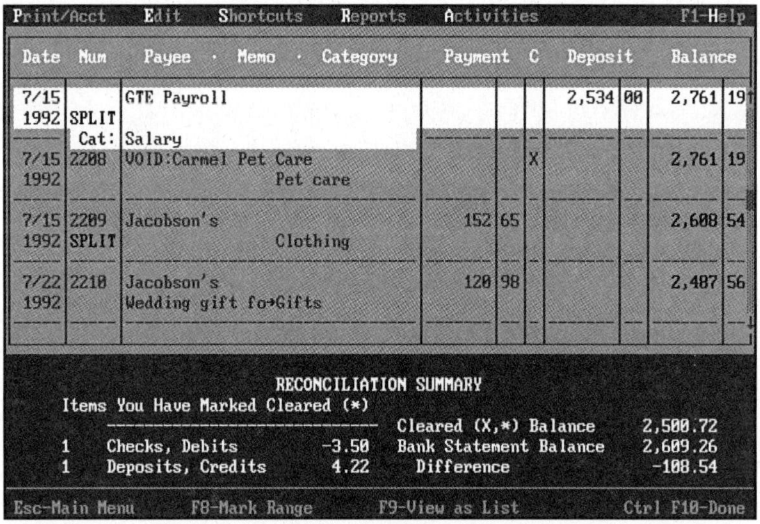

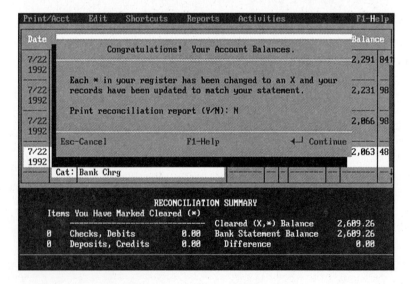

FIG. 8.4

Checking account transactions shown in the Register.

FIG. 8.5

Quicken congratulates you when your account balances.

C P A
T I P

If you understand double-entry bookkeeping, you probably recognize that Quicken uses the labels *debit* and *credit* incorrectly from your perspective. Do not be confused by this usage. The reconciliation summary uses the terms from the bank's perspective to help people who do not understand double-entry bookkeeping.

You can leave the reconciliation process at any time by pressing Esc. When you press Esc, Quicken displays the Reconciliation is Not Complete window that you see in figure 8.6. Press 2 to select the **Leave reconciliation (your work will be saved)** option. Quicken then returns to the Register you were in before you began the reconciliation. Any work you have done (entering balances, service charges, marking checks, and so on) is saved so that, when you return to the reconciliation, you can proceed at the point you left.

If you don't want to leave the reconciliation after you have pressed Esc, just press Enter to select the **Proceed to next reconciliation step** option.

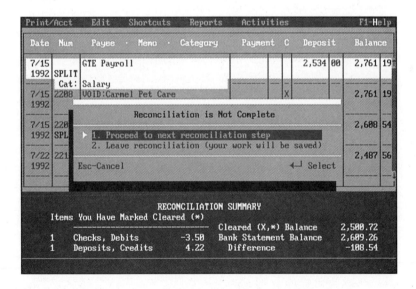

FIG. 8.6

The Reconciliation is Not Complete window.

Printing Reconciliation Reports

Many people like to keep printed records of their reconciliations. Printed copies of the reconciliation report show how you reconciled your records with the bank, indicate all checks and deposits still outstanding, and show all transactions that cleared the bank in a given month—information that may be helpful if you subsequently discover that the bank made an error or that you made a reconciliation error.

Printing the Report

To print a reconciliation report, follow these steps:

1. Press Y (from the screen shown in figure 8.5) to print a reconciliation report. The Print Reconciliation Report window shown in figure 8.7 appears.

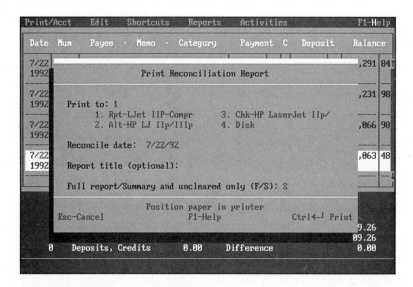

FIG. 8.7

The Print Reconciliation Report window.

2. Complete the Print To field by pressing 1 for the report printer, 2 for the alternate report printer, 3 for the check printer, or 4 to print to a disk file. (If you used printer names on the Printer Settings screen, you see those printer names on the Print Reconciliation Report screen.)

If you choose to print an ASCII file to disk, select Disk (by pressing 4) from the Print Reconciliation Report window. Quicken then displays the Print to Disk window requesting three additional pieces of information: the file name, the number of lines per page, and the width (see fig. 8.8). In the DOS File field, enter the name you want Quicken to use for the created ASCII file. To use a data directory other than QUICKEN, enter the drive and directory you chose, such as C:\QUICKEN\PRNT_TXT. Next, enter the number of lines per page—usually 66. Finally, enter the width of the page (80), or, if you are using a condensed mode, you may enter a larger number, such as 132.

FIG. 8.8

The Print To Disk window.

3. Press Enter or Tab to move the cursor to the Reconcile Date field and enter the date you performed the reconciliation. Type the date or use the + (plus) or – (minus) key to change the date one day at a time.

4. (Optional) Press Enter or Tab to move the cursor to the Report Title field, and then enter a report title for the reconciliation report. You may want to use the month and year to distinguish one report from another.

5. Press Enter or Tab to move the cursor to the Full Report/Summary and Uncleared Only field. This field enables you to choose how much detail shows on the reconciliation report. The default is **Summary**, because **Full** includes all the details on every transaction you mark as cleared. Respond to the Full Report/Summary and Uncleared Only field by pressing F for **Full** or S for **Summary**.

6. Verify that the printer is turned on and loaded with paper. Press Ctrl-Enter or F10 to print the reconciliation report. Quicken warns you if the printer is not ready.

Reviewing the Reconciliation Report

The printed reconciliation report includes three distinct components: the Reconciliation Summary, the Cleared Transaction Detail, and the Uncleared Transaction Detail. (If you select **Summary**, only the first and third parts of the reconciliation report print.)

The Reconciliation Summary report, shown in figure 8.9, essentially restates the reconciliation summary shown at the bottom of the abbreviated Register screen that you saw in figure 8.2. The reconciliation summary has two sections:

- Bank Statement—Cleared Transactions
- Your Records—Uncleared Transactions

The first section calculates the ending balance according to the bank statement by subtracting the cleared checks and adding the cleared deposits from the beginning bank balance. The second section calculates the ending Register balance by subtracting the outstanding checks and adding the deposits in transit from the ending bank balance.

The Reconciliation Summary report isn't a report you read—rather, the report documents how you reconciled the account. For this reason, you don't actually need to spend time reviewing this report unless, for some reason, you need to go back later and explain to the bank what the balance should be or you need to see which transactions were outstanding when you reconciled.

If you print a full transaction report, the Cleared Transaction Detail section of the reconciliation report shows each of the cleared checks and payment transactions and each of the cleared deposits and other credit transactions you marked with an asterisk as part of the most recent reconciliation. The report does not include transactions you marked as cleared in some prior reconciliation.

The Cleared Transaction Detail section includes most of the information related to a transaction, including the transaction date, the check or transaction number, the payee name or transaction description, any memo description, and the amount. Checks and payments are displayed as negative amounts because these amounts decrease the account balance. Deposits are displayed as positive amounts because these amounts increase the account balance. Because of space constraints, some Payee, Memo, and Category field entries are truncated on the right. The total amount and number of cleared transactions in the Cleared Transaction Detail section support the data shown in the first section of the Reconciliation Summary section.

```
                        Reconciliation Report

    1stnatl                                           Page 1
    7/22/92

                        RECONCILIATION SUMMARY

        BANK STATEMENT -- CLEARED TRANSACTIONS:

    Previous Balance:                             2,500.00
                                                 --------------
        Checks and Payments:        9 Items      -2,433.21
        Deposits and Other Credits: 3 Items       2,542.47
                                                 --------------
    Ending Balance of Bank Statement:  2,609.26


        YOUR RECORDS -- UNCLEARED TRANSACTIONS:

    Cleared Balance:                              2,609.26
                                                 --------------
    Checks and Payments:            7 Items       -541.56
    Deposits and Other Credits:     0 Items          0.00
                                                 --------------
    Register Balance as of  7/22/92:              2,067.70
                                                 --------------
    Checks and Payments:            0 Items          0.00
    Deposits and Other Credits:     0 Items          0.00
                                                 --------------
    Register Ending Balance:                      2,067.70


    Uncleared Checks and Payments

    7/22/92  2211  Jacobson's Wedding gift fo    Gifts        -120.98
    7/22/92  ***** Murphy's Grocery              Groceries     -89.22
    7/22/92  ***** Carmel Preschool              preschool     -65.00
    7/22/92  ***** Dr. Michael Cumm Allison's Check  Medical   -35.00
    7/22/92  ***** Kimmel Shoe Repa              Misc           -6.50
    7/22/92  ***** Wal-Mart                      Household     -59.86
    7/22/92  ***** Susan Alexander               Housecleaning -165
                                                             --------
    Total Uncleared Checks and Payments          7 Items     -541.56


    Uncleared Deposits and Other Credits                     --------
    Total Uncleared Deposits and Other Credits   0 Items        0.00

                                                           ===========
    Total Uncleared Transactions                 7 Items     -541.56
```

FIG. 8.9

The printed
Reconciliation
Summary report.

The Uncleared Transaction Detail section of the reconciliation report, shown in figure 8.9, is identical to the Cleared Transaction Detail report except that the still uncleared transactions for your checking account are summarized. The report is broken down into transactions dated prior to the reconciliation date and transactions dated subsequent to the reconciliation date.

Like the Cleared Transaction Detail section of the report, the Uncleared Transaction Detail section includes most of the information related to a transaction, including the transaction date, the check or transaction number, the payee name or transaction description, any memo description, and the amount. Checks and payments are shown as negative amounts because they decrease the account balance. Deposits are shown as positive amounts because they increase the account balance. The total amount and total number of uncleared transactions in the Uncleared Transaction Detail section support the data shown in the second section of the Reconciliation Summary report.

Creating Balance Adjustment Transactions

If you cannot *reconcile* an account—that is, if the difference amount shown in the reconciliation summary equals any number other than zero—the difference may be due to a difference in the opening balance that Quicken shows in the Reconcile Register with Bank Statement window and the opening balance shown on your bank statement. Quicken handles these differences by adjusting the opening balance difference. Quicken handles any other differences (not arising from an opening balance difference) by creating a balancing adjustment.

Adjusting Opening Balance Differences

If you changed the amount in the Bank Statement Opening Balance field in the Reconcile Register with Bank Statement window to match the opening balance on your bank statement, Quicken shows the opening balance difference in the reconciliation summary (see figure 8.10).

The following three reasons can cause your Quicken opening balance to differ from your bank statement's opening balance:

■ You are reconciling your account with Quicken for the first time, so Quicken is using the opening balance you entered when you set up your checking account as the bank statement opening balance.

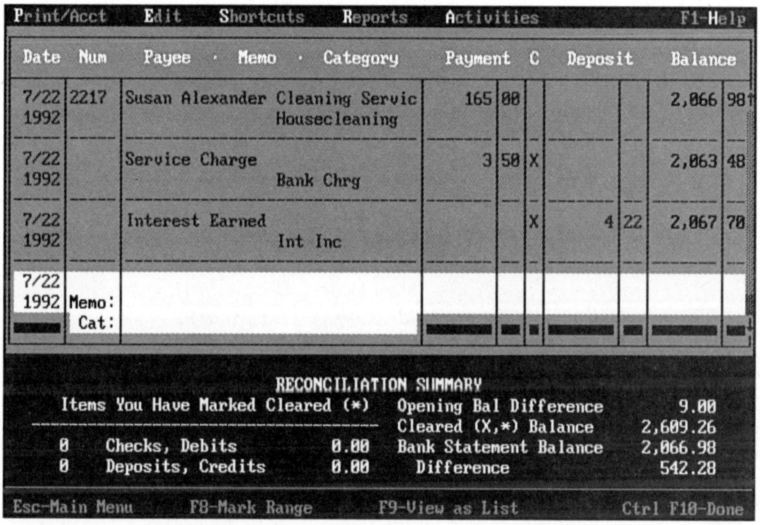

```
 Print/Acct    Edit    Shortcuts    Reports    Activities         F1-Help

  Date  Num    Payee  ·  Memo  ·  Category    Payment  C  Deposit    Balance

  7/22 2217  Susan Alexander Cleaning Servic    165 00              2,066 98↑
  1992                      Housecleaning

  7/22       Service Charge                       3 50 X            2,063 48
  1992                      Bank Chrg

  7/22       Interest Earned                           X     4 22   2,067 70
  1992                      Int Inc

  7/22
  1992 Memo:
       Cat:

                          RECONCILIATION SUMMARY
       Items You Have Marked Cleared (*)     Opening Bal Difference      9.00
  ─────────────────────────────────────     Cleared (X,*) Balance   2,609.26
        0      Checks, Debits      0.00      Bank Statement Balance  2,066.98
        0      Deposits, Credits   0.00      Difference                542.28

 Esc-Main Menu      F8-Mark Range       F9-View as List        Ctrl F10-Done
```

FIG. 8.10

The opening balance difference in the reconciliation summary.

If the opening balance that you entered when you set up your checking account did not account for uncleared checks written before you started your Quicken system (because you did not enter previous transactions), then your bank's opening balance differs from the opening balance in your account by the amount of uncleared checks.

Assume, for example, that you set up your checking account on November 1 and entered the opening balance shown in your manual checkbook register—$3,500. If, however, you had written three checks totaling $500 that had not cleared the bank by November 1, your opening bank statement balance would be $500 greater, or $4,000.

The opening balance difference remains until you enter all uncleared transactions and adjust Quicken's opening balance to agree with the amount that actually was in your checking account the day you started using Quicken (in this example, you adjust the opening balance to $4,000). You can enter uncleared transactions without leaving the reconciliation by pressing F9 to access the Register. Note that Quicken can do an automatic opening balance adjustment at the end of the reconciliation process; however, don't let Quicken make this adjustment unless you agree with the amount. In this section, you learn how to make opening balance adjustments when you complete the reconciliation process.

■ You did not enter previous transactions before you began using Quicken. When you later entered these previous transactions, you changed the opening balance in the Checking Account or Bank Account Register to reflect your checking account's balance on the first day of the year. The opening balance difference remains until you mark previous transactions as cleared. To do this, leave the reconciliation and go to the Register.

For each cleared transaction, type an *X* in the C (cleared) field. Because all previous transactions may not have cleared the bank, you should review your bank statements, beginning with the first of the year, to account for all numbered checks and deposits.

■ You are not using the most current bank statement, or you have not reconciled a previous month's statement. Reconcile your account first against the earliest monthly statement, and then reconcile your account against each subsequent statement.

When you press Ctrl-F10 to finish a reconciliation when there is an opening balance difference, Quicken displays the Create Opening Balance Adjustment window that you see in figure 8.11.

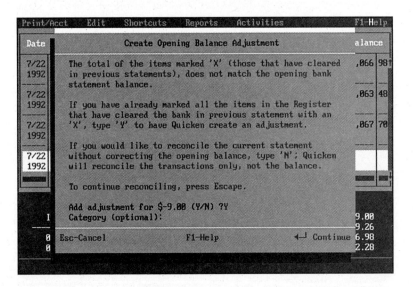

FIG. 8.11

The Create Opening Balance Adjustment window.

If you have exhausted all efforts at locating the opening balance difference, you can have Quicken create an adjustment to your opening balance. Press Y to create the adjustment; press N if you don't want to adjust the opening balance but want to finish the reconciliation.

To categorize an opening balance adjustment transaction (press Ctrl-C to see a Category and Transfer list), enter a category name in the optional Category field.

Press Ctrl-Enter or F10 to create the opening balance adjustment.

Adjusting for Other Differences

If other differences arise (other than an opening balance difference) at the completion of the reconciliation, as a last resort you may want to make a *balance adjustment*. A balance adjustment means that Quicken creates a transaction that forces the difference amount to zero. You can make a balance adjustment by pressing Esc from the Register screen before you have reduced the difference between the cleared balance and the bank statement balance to zero. Quicken then displays the Reconciliation is Not Complete window that you saw in figure 8.6.

The Reconciliation is Not Complete window identifies two options: **Proceed to next reconciliation step** and **Leave reconciliation (your work will be saved)**. If you select the second option, Quicken returns to the main menu.

If you select the first option, Quicken displays the window shown in figure 8.12. This window informs you of the magnitude of the problem and possible causes. If you still want to create an adjustment transaction, follow these steps:

1. Press Enter to adjust for the difference.

    The Adding Balance Adjustment Entry window appears (see fig. 8.13). This window alerts you that the adjustment is about to be made and suggests that you may want to reconsider the decision.

2. To make the adjustment, press Y for **Yes**. If you do not want to make the adjustment, press N for **No**. To leave this screen and return to the abbreviated Register screen, press Esc.

3. (Optional) To categorize an adjustment transaction (press Ctrl-C to see a Category and Transfer list), enter a category name in the optional Category field.

Quicken next tells you that the Register has been adjusted to agree with the bank statement balance and displays a window you can use to print the reconciliation report, as shown in figure 8.14. To print a reconciliation report, press Y for **Yes**. The Print Reconciliation Report window appears, which you use as described previously in this chapter to print the reconciliation report. Figure 8.15 shows a sample adjustment transaction.

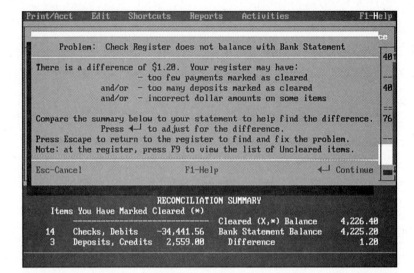

FIG. 8.12

The Problem:
Check Register
Does Not
Balance with
Bank Statement
window.

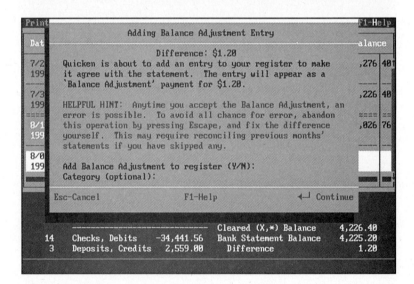

FIG. 8.13

The Adding
Balance Adjust-
ment Entry
window.

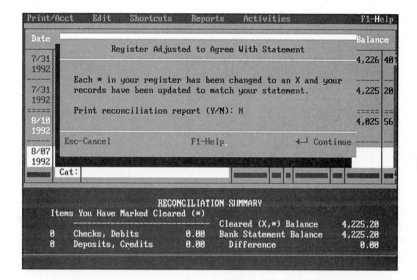

```
Print/Acct    Edit    Shortcuts    Reports    Activities         F1-Help
Date                                                            Balance
           ┌───────────────────────────────────────────────────┐
7/31       │         Register Adjusted to Agree With Statement  │ 4,226 40
1992       │                                                    │
           │  Each * in your register has been changed to an X and your │
7/31       │  records have been updated to match your statement.│ 4,225 20
1992       │                                                    │
====       │  Print reconciliation report (Y/N): N              │ ===== ==
8/10       │                                                    │ 4,025 56
1992       │  Esc-Cancel          F1-Help          ← Continue   │
           └───────────────────────────────────────────────────┘
8/07
1992    Cat:

                        RECONCILIATION SUMMARY
        Items You Have Marked Cleared (*)
        ────────────────────────────────────────────────
            0    Checks, Debits      0.00   Cleared (X,*) Balance    4,225.20
            0    Deposits, Credits   0.00   Bank Statement Balance   4,225.20
                                            Difference                   0.00
```

FIG. 8.14

The Register Adjusted to Agree With Statement window.

```
Print/Acct    Edit    Shortcuts    Reports    Activities         F1-Help
Date  Num   Payee · Memo · Category      Payment  C  Deposit   Balance
7/29        Prudential Eq               2,400 00  X            4,251 40
1992             [Prudential Eq]
7/29        Value Line Inco                       X    25 00   4,276 40
1992             [Value Line In→
7/31  2220  American Heart Association     50 00  X            4,226 40
1992             Charity
7/31        Balance Adjustment              1 20  X            4,225 20
1992 Memo:
     Cat: Misc
8/07
1992              END

1stnatl           (Alt+letter accesses menu)
Esc-Main Menu     Ctrl← Record              Ending Balance:  $4,225.20
```

FIG. 8.15

A sample adjustment transaction created by Quicken.

			Although Quicken provides the adjustment feature, you probably should not use it because it camouflages errors in the Register. As a result, you never really can be sure where the error occurred. The difference amount equals a number other than zero because you are missing one or more transactions in the Register or because you incorrectly marked a transaction as cleared, or perhaps you transposed some numbers (such as typing *$87.00* as *$78.00*). The difference also may occur because someone has forged checks or embezzled from your account. If you cannot reconcile the account, make sure that the previous month's reconciliation resulted in a difference equal to zero. If the previous month's reconciliation shows a difference other than zero, you must reconcile that month, and perhaps the months prior to that one, before you can get the current month's difference to be displayed as zero.
C	**P**	**A**	
T	**I**	**P**	

Catching Common Errors

You easily can make several errors when recording transactions in a checking account; these errors may make reconciling an account difficult or even impossible. At times, a general search for errors may not be as helpful as looking for certain kinds of errors; the next few sections identify (and explain tricks for catching) some of the more common errors.

Transposing Numbers

Transposing numbers is a frequent error in recording any financial transaction. People accidentally transpose two of the numbers in an amount. If the difference is divisible by 9, a transposition error is likely. You may write a check for $32.67, for example, and record the check as $23.67 or $32.76. This error appears obvious, but is surprisingly easy to make and often difficult to catch. When you review each transaction, you see all the correct numbers; however, the numbers are arranged in a slightly different order.

When searching for transposed numbers, you can focus on the decimal places of the transaction where the transposition error may have occurred. Table 8.1 summarizes by amounts where the transposition error may have occurred.

Table 8.1 Possible Locations of Transposition Errors

Error Amount	Decimal Places of Transposition
$.09 to $.72	In cents. For example, $.12 versus $.21 or $1.19 versus $1.91.
$.90 to $7.20	Between the dollar decimal position immediately to the left of the decimal place and the cents decimal position to right of the decimal place. For example, $32.56 versus $35.26 or $2,004.56 versus $2,005.46.
$9.00 to $72.00	Between the two positions immediately to the left of the decimal place. For example, $1,423 versus $1,432 or $281 versus $218.
$90 to $720	Between the second and third positions immediately to the left of the decimal place. For example, $1,297 versus $1,927 or $1,124 versus $1,214.

Forgetting To Record Transactions

The most common mistake is forgetting to record transactions. In a personal checking account, these omissions often include decreases in the account (for example, automated teller machine withdrawals) and increases in the account, such as interest income. In a business checking account, manual checks seem to be a common culprit; you tear out a blank check for a purchasing trip and subsequently forget to record the check.

If the amounts differ because of one transaction, identifying the missing transaction can be as easy as finding a transaction on the bank statement that equals the difference. Also, examine the sequence of checks to see whether any are missing.

Entering Payments as Deposits or Deposits as Payments

Another error is to enter a payment transaction as a deposit transaction or a deposit transaction as a payment transaction. This error, until found, can be particularly frustrating. If you look at the Register, you see that every transaction is recorded, and every number is correct.

An easy way to find such an error is to divide the error by half and see whether the result equals some transaction amount. If the result does match a transaction amount, you may have incorrectly recorded the transaction. Suppose that you currently have a difference of $1,234.56 between the Register and the bank statement balances. If you divide $1,234.56 by 2, you get $617.28. If you see a $617.28 transaction in the Register, verify that you recorded this transaction in the correct column. If you recorded a $617.28 payment as a deposit or if you recorded a $617.28 deposit as a payment, the difference will equal twice the transaction amount, or $1,234.56.

Offsetting Errors

You may have more than one error in your account, and these errors may partially offset each other. Suppose that you forgot to record an automated teller machine withdrawal of $40, and then made a transposition error in which you recorded a deposit as $216 instead of the correct amount of $261. The difference equals $5, which is the combined effect of both transactions and is calculated as the following:

$$-40 + (261 - 216) = \$5$$

Although the difference seems small, you actually have two large errors in the account.

With offsetting errors, remember that when you find one of the errors, you may feel that you are moving further away from the goal of a zero difference. Do not get discouraged if one minute you are $5 away from completing the reconciliation, and the next minute, you are $50 away from completing the reconciliation. Clearly, you are making progress if you find errors—even if the difference grows larger.

Chapter Summary

This chapter explained how to reconcile your account with Quicken. You learned about the reconciliation process, how to mark transactions that have cleared, how to print a reconciliation report, how to adjust for differences, and how to detect errors.

The next chapter begins Part II of *Using Quicken 6 for DOS*, "Getting the Most from Quicken." In Part II, you learn how to organize your finances using categories and classes, track your net worth, manage your credit cards, create and print reports, pay bills electronically, and use Quicken to prepare for income taxes. More specifically, in the next chapter you learn more about categories and classes.

Getting the Most from Quicken

P A R T

II

OUTLINE

Organizing Your Finances

Many of the previous chapters in *Using Quicken 6 for DOS* mention Quicken's categories. *Categories* enable you to summarize the information in a Register, track tax deductions, and monitor the money flowing into and out of accounts. The previous discussions of Quicken's categories, however, were rather superficial. In fact, so far this book has only touched on the power of categories.

This chapter, however, goes into depth on the subject of categories and how you can use categories to organize your finances and track your income and expenses. This chapter describes—and tells you why and when to use—categories, and shows the predefined categories Quicken provides for business and home use.

This chapter also describes the steps for adding, deleting, and editing categories you create and how to take categories one step further by creating subcategories. A *subcategory* further divides a category into smaller categories that provide a more detailed accounting of your income and expenses.

Finally, this chapter covers a related tool, Quicken's *classes* and *subclasses*. Classes and subclasses add a second dimension to categories by enabling you to classify which project, job, client, and so on, that a particular income or expense item belongs to.

More specifically, in this chapter, you learn how to do the following:

- Add categories and subcategories to the Category and Transfer list

- Specify categories as tax-related

- Edit and delete categories and subcategories

- Assign subcategories to transactions

- Change categories to subcategories and vice versa

- Merge categories and subcategories

- Print the Category and Transfer list

- Add classes and subclasses

- Edit and delete classes and subclasses

- Assign classes and subclasses to transactions

Working with Categories

To review briefly, categories enable you to group *income* and *expense* items that flow into and out of accounts. Income or deposits into an account may stem from earned wages from a full-time job, interest income, dividends, revenues from a part-time business, and so on. Expenses or payments can stem from rent, food, transportation, clothing, part-time business expenses, and so on. By grouping each payment from and each deposit into an account, Quicken easily adds the totals for each kind of payment and deposit. You then can see exactly how much each category contributes to the cash flow. You may find, for example, that cash flows into and from your account are like the cash flows summarized in table 9.1.

Table 9.1 Personal Cash Flows

Deposits	Amount
Wages from job	$35,000
Interest	$ 500
Dividends	$ 500
Business revenue	$ 4,300
Total Deposits	$40,300

Withdrawals	Amount
Housing	$18,000
Food	$ 4,000
Transportation	$ 3,000
Clothing	$ 2,500
Business Expenses	$ 1,500
Total Withdrawals	$29,000
Cash Flows	$11,300

C P A
T I P

Not all cash inflows represent income and not all cash outflows represent an expense. If you sell stock, for example, the proceeds from the sale are not considered income. Income from the sale is determined by subtracting the cost basis of the stock from the net sales proceeds (if the result is negative, you incur a loss). Medical insurance reimbursements also are not considered income, but rather they offset your medical expense. If you pay $100 to a doctor, for example, you enter a transaction in the Register for $100 and assign the Medical category to the transaction. If you later receive $80 reimbursement from your medical insurance company, the $80 is not income, but rather it offsets the $100 medical expense transaction that you previously entered. Your net medical expense is $20 ($100 – $80).

If you pay $15,000 for a car, this is not considered an expense. You should enter a transaction in your Bank Account Register for the $15,000 check you write to the car dealer, but assign an account to the transaction, instead of a category. In this example, you probably would set up an Other Asset account for your new automobile (perhaps called *Auto*) and enter the Other Asset account in the Category field. In essence, this transaction transferred funds from your bank account to another asset account (the account called *Auto*). Transfer transactions like this are explained in Chapter 4.

The information shown in table 9.1 is valuable because categorizing your inflows and outflows is the first step in beginning to manage personal or business finances. Categories enable you to do the following:

- Track and tally income tax deductions for individual retirement accounts, mortgage interest deductions, charitable contributions, and so on.

- Break down checking account deposits and payments into groups of similar transactions so that you can summarize income and expenses.

- Budget income and expenses and compare budgeted amounts with actual amounts.

If you want to use Quicken for a business, the predefined categories enable you to prepare most of the reports you need for managing business finances. These reports include the following:

- A business profit and loss statement that resembles and performs most of the calculations required to complete the federal income tax form Schedule C. The Schedule C form reports the profits or losses from a business or profession.

- Income and cash-flow statements on a monthly and annual basis that enable you to understand cash flows and measure business profits or losses.

- Employee payroll checks and payroll reports.

If any of the reports listed look like benefits you want to enjoy as part of using Quicken, you will want to use Quicken's categories. How involved or complicated the use of these categories becomes depends on your goals.

NOTE The Quicken program does not require that you assign a category to transactions. If you want to make sure that you do assign a category to all your transactions so that your income and expenses are accurately accounted for, you can turn on the Warn If a Transaction Has No Category transactions setting. When this transaction setting is turned on, Quicken displays a message each time you attempt to record a transaction in the Register or Write Checks screen without a category. You must confirm that you do not want to assign a category to the transaction before you can record the transaction. To learn how to turn on the Warn If a Transaction Has No Category transaction setting, refer to Chapter 20.

If you want your Quicken system to track each item of income and each expense, make sure that you assign a category, subcategory, or another Quicken account to every transaction that you enter. Turning on the Warn If a Transaction Has No Category transaction setting will help you remember to do this.

C P A
T I P

Building a List of Categories

The information you want to track determines the various categories you will want to use to group similar payments or deposits. Three basic rules apply when building a list of categories:

- If you want to use categories for tallying and tracking income tax deductions, you need a category for each deduction.

- If you want to use categories to summarize cash inflows and outflows, you need a category for each income or expense account you want to use in the summaries.

- If you want to use categories to budget—so that at a later date, you can compare what you budgeted and what you actually spent—you need a category for each comparison you want to make.

Creating Categories for Tax Deductions

If you want to use categories for tallying and tracking income tax deductions, you need a category for each deduction. If you deduct contributions to your IRA (Individual Retirement Accounts), mortgage interest, and state and local taxes, you need categories for each of these deductions. The following list shows the itemized deductions you may want to track to prepare a personal income tax return more easily. The list is based on the federal income tax form, Schedule A.

Sample Personal Tax Deduction Categories
Medical and dental*
Medical and dental—other*
State and local income taxes
Real estate taxes
Other taxes, including personal property taxes

Sample Personal Tax Deduction Categories

Deductible home mortgage interest paid to financial institutions

Deductible home mortgage interest paid to individuals

Deductible points

Deductible investment interest

Contributions by cash or check

Contributions other than by cash or check

Casualty or theft losses

Moving expenses**

Unreimbursed employee expenses**

Union dues, tax preparation fees, investment publications, and fees

Individual retirement account contributions

Other miscellaneous expenses

---

* *The first medical expense category includes prescription medicines and drugs, insulin, doctors, dentists, nurses, hospitals, and medical insurance premiums. The second includes items like hearing aids, dentures, eyeglasses, transportation, and lodging.*

** *This itemized deduction must be supported by an additional tax form. Therefore, you also want to consider setting up the individual amounts that need to be reported on that form as categories.*

The following list shows the income and deduction categories you may want to use to prepare a business income tax return. This list is based on the Schedule C federal income tax form.

Income Categories

Gross receipts or sales

Sales returns and allowances

Cost of goods sold*

Rental/interest

Other income

---

* *The cost of goods sold must be calculated or verified by using Part III of Schedule C.*

Deduction Categories

Advertising

Bad debts from sales or services

Bank service charges

Car and truck expenses

Commissions

Depletion

Depreciation**

Dues and publications

Employee benefit programs

Freight

Insurance

Interest—mortgage

Interest—other

Laundry and cleaning

Legal and professional services

Office expense

Pension and profit-sharing plans

Rent on business property

Repairs

Supplies

Taxes (payroll and business)

Travel

Meals and entertainment

Utilities and telephone

Wages

Wages—job credit

Other deductions

* *This deduction amount must be supported by an additional tax form; consider setting up as categories the individual amounts reported on the second form.*

C P A
T I P

If you plan to take the home office deduction, make sure that you have adequate support for the expenses that you show on the home office supporting tax schedule. Consider using split transactions to allocate utilities, mortgage or rent payments, cleaning, and so on between business and personal use. Once you determine the percentage that applies to your home office, you can split transactions using percentages as explained in Chapter 5.

Creating Income and Expense Categories

If you want to use categories to summarize cash inflows and outflows, you need a category for each income or expense account you want to use in the summaries. To account for your work expenses and a spouse's work expenses, you need categories for both sets of expenses.

Creating Budget Categories

If you want to use categories to budget—so that at a later date, you can compare what you budgeted with what you actually spent—you need a category for each comparison you want to make. To budget entertainment expenses and clothing expenses, you need categories for both.

Completing the List

By applying these three rules, you can build a list of the categories you want to use. As an aid in creating the list, figure 9.1 shows the category list that Quicken provides for home use. Figure 9.2 shows the category list Quicken provides for business use.

Consider these lists as starting points. The predefined Personal, or Home, category list provides a long list of income and expense categories that you may find useful for your home finances. Depending on the situation, some categories you don't need may be provided, and other categories you do need may be missing. Similarly, the predefined Business list provides income and expense categories you may find useful in business accounting. If you apply the rules described previously for devising categories, you may have no problem when using the predefined lists as starting points for constructing a category list that works well for you.

```
                         Category and Transfer List
HOME                                                         Page 1
7/22/92

                                        Tax
        Category        Description     Rel Tax Schedule & Line
        --------------  --------------  --- --------------------------------

        INCOME
        ------

        Bonus           Bonus Income      *  W-2:Salary
        Canada Pen      Canadian Pension  *
        Div Income      Dividend Income   *  Schedule B:Dividend income
        Gift Received   Gift Received     *
        Int Inc         Interest Income   *  Schedule B:Interest income
        Invest Inc      Investment Income *
        Old Age Pension Old Age Pension   *
        Other Inc       Other Income      *
        Salary          Salary Income     *  W-2:Salary

        EXPENSE
        -------

        Auto            Automobile Expenses
          Fuel          Auto Fuel
          Loan          Auto Loan Payment
          Service       Auto Service
        Bank Chrg       Bank Charge
        Charity         Charitable Donations  *  Schedule A:Cash charity contribut
        Childcare       Childcare Expense
        Christmas       Christmas Expenses
        Clothing        Clothing
        Dining          Dining Out
        Dues            Dues
        Education       Education
        Entertain       Entertainment
        Gifts           Gift Expenses
        Groceries       Groceries
        Home Rpair      Home Repair & Maint.
        Household       Household Misc. Exp
        Housing         Housing
        Insurance       Insurance
        Int Exp         Interest Expense      *
        Invest Exp      Investment Expense    *  Schedule A:Investment man. fees
        Medical         Medical & Dental      *  Schedule A:Medicine and drugs
        Misc            Miscellaneous
        Mort Int        Mortgage Interest Exp *  Schedule A:Home mortgage interest
        Other Exp       Other Expenses        *
        Recreation      Recreation Expense
        RRSP            Reg Retirement Sav Plan
        Subscriptions   Subscriptions
        Supplies        Supplies              *
        Tax             Taxes                 *  Schedule C:Taxes and licenses
          Fed           Federal Tax           *  W-2:Federal Withholding
          FICA          Social Security Tax   *  W-2:FICA
          Other         Misc. Taxes           *
          Prop          Property Tax          *  Schedule A:Real estate tax
          State         State Tax             *  W-2:State Withholding
        Telephone       Telephone Expense
        UIC             Unemploy. Ins. Commission  *
        Utilities       Water, Gas, Electric
          Gas & Electric Gas and Electricity
          Water         Water

        BANK
        ----

        1stnatl
```

FIG. 9.1

The category list that Quicken provides for personal or home use.

After you complete the list, review the categories for any redundancies produced by two of the rules calling for the same category. For home use of Quicken, for example, you can add a category to budget for monthly individual retirement account (IRA) contributions. You also can add a category to tally IRA payments because these payments represent potential tax deductions. Because both categories are the same, cross one category off the list.

```
                         Category and Transfer List

BUSINESS                                                          Page 1
7/22/92

                                              Tax
       Category          Description          Rel Tax Schedule & Line
-----------------  -------------------------  ---  --------------------------------

INCOME
------

Gr Sales           Gross Sales                 *   Schedule C:Gross receipts
Other Inc          Other Income                *
Rent Income        Rent Income                 *   Schedule E:Rents received

EXPENSE
-------

Ads                Advertising                 *   Schedule C:Advertising
Car                Car & Truck                 *   Schedule C:Car and truck expenses
Commission         Commissions                 *   Schedule C:Commissions and fees
Freight            Freight                     *   Schedule C:Other business expense
Int Paid           Interest Paid               *   Schedule C:Interest expense, othe
L&P Fees           Legal & Prof. Fees          *   Schedule C:Legal and professional
Late Fees          Late Payment Fees           *   Schedule C:Other business expense
Office             Office Expenses             *   Schedule C:Office expense
Rent Paid          Rent Paid                   *   Schedule C:Rent on other bus prop
Repairs            Repairs                     *   Schedule C:Repairs and maintenanc
Returns            Returns & Allowances        *   Schedule C:Returns and allowances
Tax                Taxes                       *   Schedule C:Taxes and licenses
Travel             Travel Expenses             *   Schedule C:Travel
Wages              Wages & Job Credits         *   Schedule C:Wages paid

BANK
----

1stnatl
```

FIG. 9.2

The category list that Quicken provides for business use.

Sometimes, however, overlapping or redundant categories are not as easy to spot. A tax deduction you need to calculate may be only a small part of a budgeting category, or a budgeting amount you need to calculate may be only a portion of a tax-deduction category. You need to detail categories so that each represents separate tax deduction or budgeting categories.

Categories act as building blocks you use to classify data the way you want it. You can use the following categories to calculate the tax-deduction amounts and the budgeted amounts shown in table 9.2:

> Mortgage interest
> Mortgage principal
> Mortgage late-payment fees
> Credit card late-payment fees
> Property taxes

Table 9.2 Personal Budget and Tax Amounts

Amounts	Categories Used
Late fees (a budgeted amount)	Mortgage late-payment fees Credit card late-payment fees
Housing (a budgeted amount)	Mortgage principal Mortgage interest Property taxes
Mortgage interest (deduction)	Mortgage interest Mortgage late-payment fees
Property taxes (deduction)	Property taxes

Setting Up Categories

When you create files, you can choose to use the defined Home or
Business categories from the Standard Categories window as the
foundation of the Category and Transfer list (see fig. 9.3).

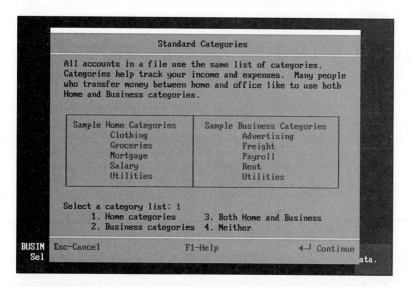

```
                        Standard Categories

 All accounts in a file use the same list of categories.
 Categories help track your income and expenses.  Many people
 who transfer money between home and office like to use both
 Home and Business categories.

    Sample Home Categories      Sample Business Categories
           Clothing                    Advertising
           Groceries                   Freight
           Mortgage                    Payroll
           Salary                      Rent
           Utilities                   Utilities


    Select a category list: 1
         1. Home categories      3. Both Home and Business
         2. Business categories  4. Neither

 BUSIN  Esc-Cancel              F1-Help              ◄─┘ Continue
 Sel                                                          ata.
```

FIG. 9.3

The Standard
Categories
window to set
up categories.

If you select Home categories, Quicken copies its predefined list of
Home categories (as shown in fig. 9.1) to the Category and Transfer list
in your file. If you select Business categories, Quicken copies its predefined list of Business categories that you saw in figure 9.2 to your list.
Even if you select to use one of the predefined category lists, however,
you may need to modify the category list.

<table>
<tr><td>

C   P   A

T   I   P

</td><td>

Quicken enables you to specify which categories are tax-related (a taxable income item or a tax-deductible expense). To help you identify tax-related items, review last year's tax return. Taxable income items usually are found on page 1 of Form 1040 (Federal Individual Income Tax Return). Schedule A of Form 1040 lists deductible itemized expenses, including medical expenses, mortgage interest, charitable contributions, moving expenses, investment expenses, and so on. Call a CPA if you have specific questions when trying to identify a potential tax-deductible expense.

</td></tr>
</table>

Adding Categories

You can add categories in two ways:

■ Access the Category and Transfer list and select the <New Category> line.

■ Type the new category name in the Category field while entering a transaction.

Both methods are described here, and you can pick the method you find most convenient.

Using the Category and Transfer List

To add categories from the Category and Transfer list, follow these steps:

1. Press Alt-S to access the Shortcuts menu from the Register or Write Checks screen. Remember, you can access the Register or Write Checks screen from the main menu.

2. Select the **Categorize/Transfer** option from the Shortcuts menu or use the shortcut key Ctrl-C. The Category and Transfer list appears, as shown in figure 9.4.

3. Press Home to highlight the <New Category> line, and then press Enter. Quicken displays the Set Up Category window shown in figure 9.5. You also can press Ctrl-Ins to display the Set Up Category window.

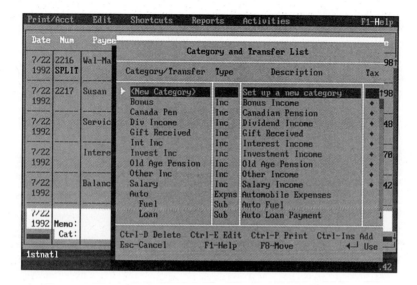

FIG. 9.4

The Category
and Transfer list.

NOTE

The Category and Transfer list is where Quicken stores all
the categories, subcategories, and transfer accounts in your
Quicken file. Quicken provides a separate Category and
Transfer list for each file.

The Category and Transfer list not only lists the categories,
subcategories, and transfer accounts, but also shows the
category type (income or expense), the account type (bank,
cash, investment, and so on), the category or account description, and whether the category or subcategory is tax-
related.

You can use the Category and Transfer list to select a
category, subcategory, or transfer account to assign to a
transaction. You also can use the list to add, edit, or delete
categories and subcategories, change a category to a subcategory (and vice versa), and print a hard copy of the
Category and Transfer list.

4. Type the category name you want to use in the Name field. Category names can contain up to 15 characters, and can include any
character except the following:

   [ ] : /

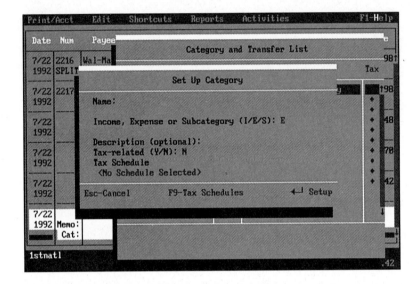

FIG. 9.5

The Set Up
Category
window.

5. Press Enter or Tab to move the cursor to the Income, Expense, or Subcategory field. Press I if the category that you are adding represents an income category, or E if the category is for an expense item. If you're adding a subcategory, press S (adding subcategories is covered later in this chapter).

6. (Optional) Press Enter or Tab to move the cursor to the Description field. You can use up to 25 characters to describe the category.

7. (Optional) Press Enter or Tab to move the cursor to the Tax-Related field. The Tax-Related field determines whether the category that you are adding is a taxable income or tax-deductible expense item. If you specify that a category is tax-related by pressing Y from the Tax-Related field, Quicken includes that category in tax reports. Tax reports then can be used to accumulate transactions that are assigned to tax-related categories to help you prepare your personal or business income tax return. If you specify a category as tax-related, go to step 8; otherwise, go to step 9.

8. (Optional) If you are setting up a category to report a specific kind of taxable income or tax deduction, press F9. The Tax Schedule window appears, listing two dozen common tax schedules (see fig. 9.6). Use the up- and down-arrow keys to highlight the tax schedule that the category pertains to. If, for example, you're adding a category for an itemized deduction, such as tax preparation fees, highlight Schedule A in the Tax Schedule window and press Enter to select it.

After you select a tax schedule, Quicken displays the Tax Line window so that you can indicate which line of the schedule the category will be shown on (see fig. 9.7). The items in the Tax Line window depend on the tax schedule selected. Use the up- and down-arrow keys to highlight the line that you want to select and press Enter. In the example, you would select the **Tax preparation fees** option.

For some tax schedules, such as Schedule C, Schedule K-1, and Form W-2, Quicken lists a tax line for your spouse. Also, these schedules and forms can be filed in duplicate. If, for example, you and your spouse own separate businesses and therefore file separate Schedule Cs to report the income and expenses of the businesses, you can assign certain categories to one copy of Schedule C and others to another copy of Schedule C. When you select one of these schedules or forms from the Tax Schedule window and then select a tax line, Quicken displays the Schedule Copy Number window shown in figure 9.8. Indicate which copy of the schedule or form (1 to 16) that the category you are adding relates to.

After you have selected a tax schedule and tax line for a tax-related category, Quicken returns to the Set Up Category window that you saw in figure 9.5.

9. When the Set Up Category window is complete, press Ctrl-Enter or F10 to save the category information and add the category to the Category and Transfer list. Quicken inserts the new category name in its proper alphabetical order.

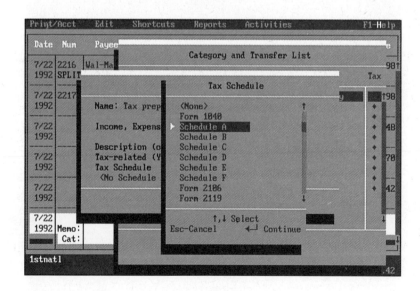

FIG. 9.6

The Tax Schedule window.

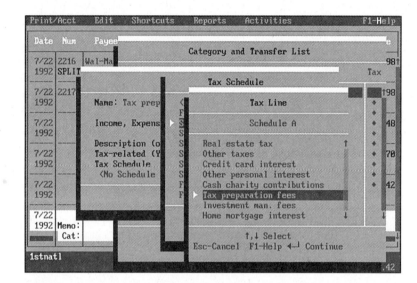

FIG. 9.7

The Tax Line window.

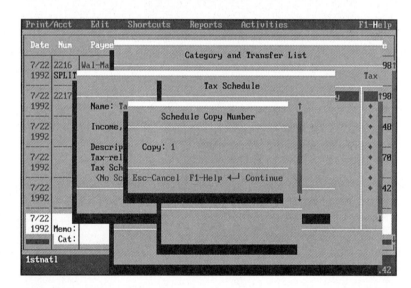

FIG. 9.8

The Schedule Copy Number window.

Adding a Category as You Enter a Transaction

You can shortcut the entire process of adding a category by typing the new category in the Category field as you are entering a transaction. To add a category using this shortcut method, follow these steps:

1. Move the cursor to the Category field in the Write Checks screen, the Register screen, or the Split Transactions window (accessed by pressing Ctrl-S).

2. Type the new category name in the Category field. If the category doesn't already exist, the Category Not Found window appears (see fig. 9.9).

3. To add the category, press 1 to select the **Add to Category List** option. The Set Up Category window appears, which you complete as discussed in steps 4 through 9 of the preceding procedure.

If you choose the **Select from Category List** option, Quicken displays the Category and Transfer list that you saw in figure 9.4 and highlights the category that comes closest to the name you entered.

Generally, you have plenty of room for as many categories as you need. The precise maximum number, however, depends on the computer's available memory, the length of the category names and descriptions, and the other information stored in memory. You usually have room for about 150 categories with 384K of memory and more than 1,000 categories with 512K of memory.

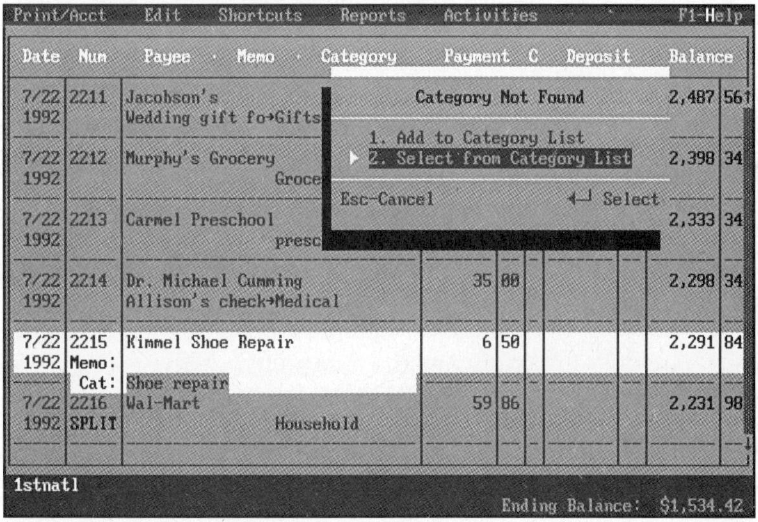

FIG. 9.9

The Category Not Found window.

Deleting a Category

You also may want to delete categories—either because you don't use a particular category or because you added the category incorrectly. Deleting categories is even easier than adding categories.

To delete a category, follow these steps:

1. Press Alt-S to access the Shortcuts menu from the Write Checks or Register screen.

2. Select **Categorize/Transfer** from the Shortcuts menu, or use the shortcut key Ctrl-C. Quicken displays the Category and Transfer list.

3. Use the up- and down-arrow keys or the PgUp, PgDn, Home, and End keys to highlight the category that you want to delete. Pressing Home moves you to the beginning of the list; pressing End moves you to the end of the list.

4. When the item you want to delete is highlighted, press Ctrl-D. A warning message appears, telling you that you are about to permanently delete a category.

5. To remove the category from the category list, press Enter. If you don't want to remove the category, press Esc.

After you delete a category, you cannot use the category unless you add the category again. If you assigned previous transactions to the deleted category, Quicken removes the category from the Category field (the Category field becomes blank). You need to return to the Register and assign a new category to any blank Category field. (Chapters 4 and 5 explain how to use the Register.)

Editing a Category

You also can edit a category. Suppose that you run a business and use Quicken to account for, among other things, the wages you pay. Further, suppose that the Wages category was always used for employees working in Washington state. If you create a new category named *OR_WAGES* to account for the wages you pay to employees working in Oregon, you may want to change the name of the Wages category to *WA_WAGES* to reflect the change in the significance of the account.

The steps for editing a category roughly parallel the steps for adding one. To edit a category, follow these steps:

1. Press Alt-S to access the Shortcuts menu from the Write Checks or Register screen.

2. Select **Categorize/Transfer** from the Shortcuts menu, or use the shortcut key Ctrl-C. The Category and Transfer List window appears.

3. Use the up-arrow, down-arrow, PgUp, PgDn, Home, or End key to highlight the category that you want to edit. Pressing Home moves you to the beginning of the list; pressing End moves you to the end.

4. Press Ctrl-E. The Edit Category window appears, as shown in figure 9.10.

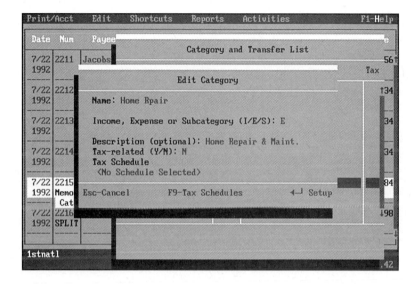

FIG. 9.10

The Edit Category window.

5. (Optional) Retype or edit the category name you want to use in the Name field.

6. (Optional) Press Enter or Tab to move the cursor to the Income, Expense, or Subcategory field. If necessary, change the Income, Expense, or Subcategory field by pressing I for income, E for expenses, or S for subcategory.

7. (Optional) Press Enter or Tab to move the cursor to the Description field. If necessary, retype or edit the existing description.

8. (Optional) Press Enter or Tab to move the cursor to the Tax-Related field. If necessary, change the Tax-Related field.

9. (Optional) Press F9 to display the Tax Schedule window. Use the up- and down-arrow keys to highlight the appropriate schedule. Press Enter. Quicken displays the Tax Line window. Use the up- and down-arrow keys to highlight the appropriate line of the schedule and press Enter. Next, type the schedule number (1 to 16) in the Schedule Copy Number window. Press Enter to return to the Edit Category window.

10. To save the changes to the category, press Ctrl-Enter or F10.

Using Subcategories

If you decide to use categories as building blocks to classify your income and expenses, you need to know about subcategories. Taking the first row of the data from table 9.2, suppose that you create a category called *LateFees* to track late-payment fees. You then can set up two subcategories of the category *LateFees* called *LMortgage* for late mortgage fees and *LCredit* for late credit card fees (the *L* stands for *late*.) Then, when you record a transaction to pay late fees on your mortgage, you can assign the subcategory *LMortgage* to the transaction. When you record a transaction for late fees on your credit card, assign the subcategory *LCredit* to the transaction. You can design reports so that all your subcategories are shown or just the categories.

When only categories are shown, Quicken shows the sum of all transactions assigned to their subcategories as the category total. In the example, you could show a subcategory line for *LMortgage* and *LCredit* to see just how much was spent on late fees for each, or you could lump both the *LMortgage* and *LCredit* subcategories together and show their total in the category line *LateFees*. Figure 9.11 shows a cash flow report where subcategories were used.

Assigning Subcategories to Transactions

Subcategories are assigned to transactions in much the same way that categories are assigned in the Category field of the Register or Write Checks screen. When you assign a subcategory, however, you first must enter the category that the subcategory falls under.

To assign a subcategory to a transaction, follow these steps:

1. At the Register or Write Checks screen, move to the Category field.

2. Enter the primary income or expense category. Enter the category by typing the first few characters, and QuickFill takes over and fills in the rest of the category name. If the category that QuickFill enters is not the one you want, press Ctrl-+ (plus) or Ctrl-– (minus) to enter the next or preceding category from the Category and Transfer list. You also can press Ctrl-C to display the Category and Transfer list, highlight the category that you want to assign to the transaction, and press Enter.

```
                        CASH FLOW REPORT
                   7/ 1/92 Through 7/31/92
  L_FLANDE-Bank,Cash,CC Accounts                        Page 1
  7/22/92
                                     7/ 1/92-
                Category Description    7/31/92
        ----------------------  --------------------
  INFLOWS
     Int Inc                           8.47
     Salary                        4,000.00
                                   ----------
  TOTAL INFLOWS                    4,008.47

  OUTFLOWS
     Auto:
        Fuel                 22.56
                          ----------
     Total Auto                       22.56
     Bank Chrg                         3.50
     Clothing                        127.65
     Cosmetics                        25.00
     Entertain                        14.69
     Gifts                           120.98
     Groceries                       141.90
     Housecleaning                   165.00
     Household                        22.14
     LateFees:
        LCredit             6.50
        LMortgage          22.50
                          ----------
     Total LateFees                   29.00
     Medical                          35.00
     Misc                              6.50
     Mort Int                        600.00
     Pet care                         23.03
     preschool                       130.00
     Tax:
        Fed              1,000.00
        FICA               306.00
        Prop                52.98
        State              160.00
                          ----------
     Total Tax                     1,518.98
     Utilities                       284.14
     Outflows - Other                533.28
     TO Mortgage                     100.00
                                   ----------
  TOTAL OUTFLOWS                    3,903.35

                                   ----------
  OVERALL TOTAL                       105.12
                                   ==========
```

FIG. 9.11

Using subcategories gives you the capability of showing greater detail.

3. After the appropriate category is entered in the Category field, type a colon after the category name. QuickFill fills in the first subcategory for the category that you entered. If the subcategory that QuickFill enters is not the one you want, type the first few letters of the subcategory name or press Ctrl-+ (plus) to enter the next subcategory. You also can type the subcategory name or press Ctrl-C to display the Category and Transfer list, highlight the subcategory that you want to assign, and press Enter.

4. If the rest of the transaction is complete, press Ctrl-Enter or F10 to record the transaction and the category and subcategory assigned to the transaction.

Figure 9.12 shows a recorded transaction with a subcategory assigned in the Category field.

```
Print/Acct   Edit   Shortcuts   Reports   Activities              F1-Help

Date  Num   Payee  ·  Memo  ·  Category    Payment  C  Deposit    Balance

7/22         Interest Earned                        X      4 22   3,067 40↑
1992                        Int Inc

7/22         Balance Adjustment            533 28 X                2,534 12
1992

7/22  2218   Inland Mortgage                22 50                   2,511 62
1992  Memo:
====  Cat:  LateFees:LMortgage       ======== == ======== ==   ======== ==
7/25  2219   Visa                             6 50                  2,505 12
1992                        LateFees:LCred→

7/22
1992                         END

1stnatl          (Alt+letter accesses menu)   Current Balance:  $2,511.62
Esc-Main Menu    Ctrl◄┘ Record                Ending Balance:   $2,505.12
```

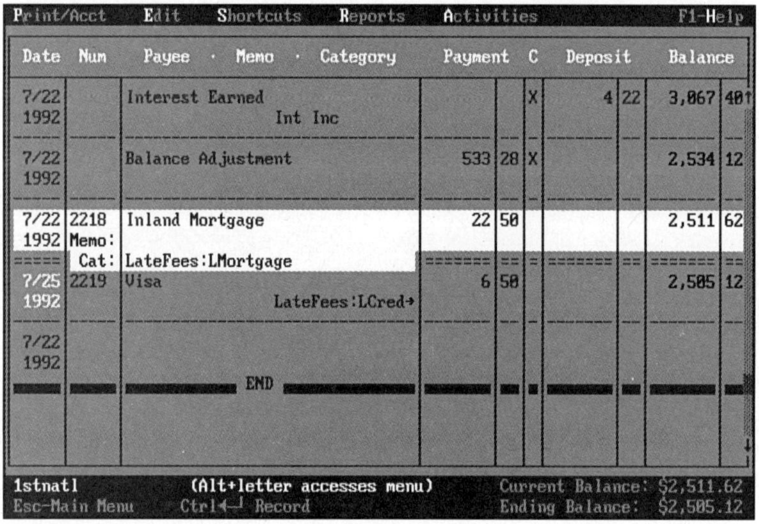

FIG. 9.12

A recorded transaction with a subcategory assigned in the Category field.

Adding Subcategories

You add a subcategory to the Category and Transfer list in much the same way you add a category. You can add the subcategory directly to the Category and Transfer list, or you can type the new subcategory name in the Category field of a transaction and select the **Add to Category List** option that Quicken presents when it doesn't find the subcategory in the list.

Using the Category and Transfer List

To add a subcategory to the Category and Transfer list, follow these steps:

1. Press Alt-S to access the Shortcuts menu from the Register or Write Checks screen.

2. Select the **Categorize/Transfer** option from the Shortcuts menu or use the shortcut key Ctrl-C. The Category and Transfer list appears.

3. Use the up- and down-arrow keys or the PgUp and PgDn keys to highlight the category that you want to add a subcategory to. Press Ctrl-Ins to display the Set Up Category window.

4. Type the subcategory name you want to use in the Name field. Subcategory names can include up to 15 characters and can include any character except the following:

   [ ] : /

5. Press Enter or Tab to move the cursor to the Income, Expense, or Subcategory field. Press S for Subcategory.

6. (Optional) Press Enter or Tab to move the cursor to the Description field. You can use up to 25 characters to describe the subcategory.

7. (Optional) Press Enter or Tab to move the cursor to the Tax-Related field. The Tax-Related field determines whether the subcategory that you are adding is a taxable income or tax-deductible expense item. If you specify that a subcategory is tax-related, Quicken includes that subcategory in tax reports. Tax reports then can be used to accumulate transactions that are assigned to tax-related categories and subcategories to help you prepare your personal or business income tax return.

8. (Optional) If you are setting up a subcategory to report a specific kind of taxable income item or tax deduction, press F9. The Tax Schedule window appears, listing two dozen common tax schedules. Use the up- and down-arrow keys to highlight the tax schedule that the category pertains to. Press Enter to select it.

After you select a tax schedule, Quicken displays the Tax Line window so that you can indicate which line of the schedule the subcategory will be shown on in your return. The items in the Tax Line window depend on the tax schedule selected. Use the up- and down-arrow keys to highlight the line that you want to select and press Enter.

For some tax schedules, such as Schedule C, Schedule K-1, and Form W-2, Quicken lists a tax line for your spouse. Also, these schedules and forms can be filed in duplicate. When you select one of these schedules or forms from the Tax Schedule window and then select a tax line, Quicken displays the Schedule Copy Number window. Indicate which copy of the schedule or form (1 to 16) that the subcategory you are adding relates to.

After you have selected a tax schedule and tax line for a tax-related subcategory, Quicken returns to the Set Up Category window.

9. When the Set Up Category window is complete, press Ctrl-Enter or F10 to save the subcategory information and add the subcategory to the Category and Transfer list. Quicken inserts the new subcategory name in its proper alphabetical order under its parent category.

Adding a New Subcategory as You Enter a Transaction

To add a subcategory from the Category field as you are entering a transaction, follow these steps:

1. Move the cursor to the Category field in the Write Checks screen, the Register screen, or the Split Transactions window (accessed by pressing Ctrl-S).

2. Enter the category that you want to add a subcategory to. Type a colon after the category name.

3. Type the name of the new subcategory. Because the subcategory doesn't already exist, the Category Not Found message appears.

4. To add the subcategory, press 1 to select the **Add to Category List** option. The Set Up Category window appears, which you complete as discussed in steps 4 through 9 of the procedure for adding subcategories.

If you choose the **Select from Category List** option, Quicken displays the Category and Transfer list and highlights the subcategory that comes closest to the name you entered.

Editing and Deleting Subcategories

You can edit a subcategory at any time. When you change a subcategory name, all previous transactions assigned to that subcategory also are changed. To edit a subcategory, follow the same steps for editing a category as explained earlier in this chapter.

You also can delete a subcategory if you no longer need it. When you delete a subcategory, Quicken permanently removes it from the Category and Transfer list. Previous transactions assigned to the subcategory that you subsequently delete are merged into the parent category. If, for example, you assign transactions to the subcategory *Movies*, under the category *Entertainment*, and then delete the subcategory, Quicken assigns all those transactions to the category *Entertainment*.

To delete a subcategory, follow the same steps for deleting a category as explained earlier in this chapter.

Rearranging Categories and Subcategories

Once you have established your category list and added categories and subcategories, you can change categories to subcategories and vice versa. The **Move** option from the Category and Transfer list enables you to change a category to a subcategory (*demote* a category), change a subcategory to a category (*promote* a subcategory), or move a subcategory underneath another category (so that it has a different parent category). You may decide to make the category *Auto Fuel* a subcategory of the category *Auto*, for example. The **Move** option enables you to make this change and Quicken changes the previous transactions assigned to these categories.

Changing a Category to a Subcategory

To change a category to a subcategory (demote a category), follow these steps:

1. Press Alt-S to access the Shortcuts menu from the Register or Write Checks screen.

2. Select the **Categorize/Transfer** option from the Shortcuts menu or use the shortcut key Ctrl-C. The Category and Transfer list appears.

3. Use the up- and down-arrow keys or the PgUp and PgDn keys to highlight the category that you want to change to a subcategory.

4. Press F8 to select the **Move** option. Quicken moves the category to the top of the Category and Transfer list and places a colon (:) in front of the category name to show that it now can be moved (changed).

5. Use the up- and down-arrow keys to move the category name to the category (target category) it is to be a subcategory for. Quicken displays the category name next to the target category name. In the preceding example, after completing this step, the category will appear like this:

```
Auto : Auto Fuel
```

6. Press Enter to change the category to a subcategory. Quicken places the new subcategory beneath the target category name in the Category and Transfer list.

Changing a Subcategory to a Category

To change a subcategory to a category (promote a subcategory), follow these steps:

1. Press Alt-S to access the Shortcuts menu from the Register or Write Checks screen.

2. Select the **Categorize/Transfer** option from the Shortcuts menu or use the shortcut key Ctrl-C. The Category and Transfer list appears.

3. Use the up- and down-arrow keys or the PgUp and PgDn keys to highlight the subcategory that you want to change to a category.

4. Press F8 to select the **Move** option. Quicken moves the sub-category name to the same line as its parent category name, separated by a colon (:) to show that the subcategory can be moved or changed.

5. Press Home to move the subcategory to the top of the Category and Transfer list.

6. Press Enter, and Quicken changes the subcategory to a category and positions the new category alphabetically in the Category and Transfer list.

Merging Categories and Subcategories

You can merge one category or subcategory into another. You may want to merge the Int Inc (Interest income) category into the Invest Inc (Investment income) category if you find that you are not really using the former category, for example.

When you merge two categories or subcategories, Quicken assigns the category or subcategory name that you retain (in this case, Invest Inc) to each transaction that was assigned to the merged category or subcategory (Int Inc).

Before you can merge a category into another category, you first must change the category that you want to merge to a subcategory. To merge a subcategory into another subcategory, make the subcategory that you want to merge a subcategory of the subcategory that you want to retain. If, for example, you have a subcategory named *Condo Exp* and want to merge it with a subcategory named *Condo Repairs*, you first must make the subcategory *Condo Exp* a subcategory of *Condo Repairs*. Figure 9.13 shows how categories and subcategories are listed in the Category and Transfer list. Notice how categories and subcategories appear—in outline format with a category listed first, followed by its subcategory (indented to the right). A subcategory of a subcategory is indented to the right a little farther.

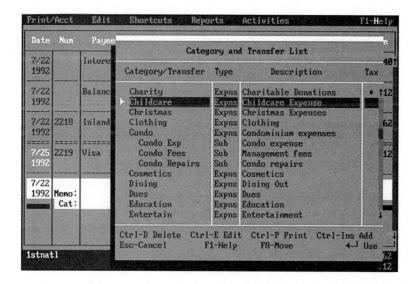

FIG. 9.13

Categories and subcategories appear in outline format in the Category and Transfer list.

To merge a category or subcategory, follow these steps:

1. Press Alt-S to access the Shortcuts menu from the Register or Write Checks screen.

2. Select the **Categorize/Transfer** option from the Shortcuts menu or use the shortcut key Ctrl-C. The Category and Transfer list appears.

3. Use the up- and down-arrow keys or the PgUp and PgDn keys to highlight the category or subcategory that you want to merge into another category or subcategory.

4. If you want to merge a category into another category, you first must change the category that you want to merge to a subcategory. If you want to merge a subcategory into another subcategory, make the subcategory that you want to merge a subcategory of the one you want to retain. Follow the steps explained in the preceding section to change a category or subcategory to a subcategory.

5. Once the category or subcategory that you want to merge is changed to a subcategory of the category or subcategory that you want to retain, delete it by pressing Ctrl-D.

   Quicken displays the warning message that you are about to delete a subcategory and that all transactions currently assigned to the subcategory will be merged into the parent category or subcategory.

6. Press Enter to delete the subcategory and merge it into its parent category or subcategory.

Printing a Category and Transfer List

When you select **Categorize/Transfer** from the Shortcuts menu, a list of categories and accounts appears. Occasionally, you may want a printed copy of this list. You also may want to review the list with a tax advisor at his office to verify that you are tracking all tax deduction categories, or you may want to keep a paper copy of the list as an aid to entering transactions.

To print a copy of the Category and Transfer list, follow these steps:

1. Press Alt-S to access the Shortcuts menu from the Write checks or Register screen.

2. Select **Categorize/Transfer** or use the shortcut key Ctrl-C. The Category and Transfer list appears.

3. Press Ctrl-P. The Print Category and Transfer List window appears, as shown in figure 9.14. This window, which resembles the Print Register window, provides fields to select the printer settings you want to use.

4. Indicate the printer settings you want to use—press 1 for the first setting, 2 for the second setting, and so on. Next, press F10 or Ctrl-Enter. Quicken prints a copy of the Category and Transfer list.

For help in completing the Print Category and Transfer List window, refer to the discussion in Chapter 4 on printing a Register. The Print Register window, which you use to print a Register, works the same way as the Print Category and Transfer List window.

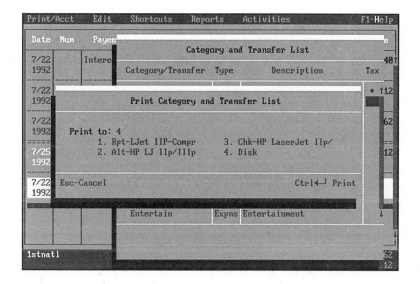

FIG. 9.14

The Print Category and Transfer List window.

Working with Classes

Categories and subcategories group revenues and expenses by the type of transaction. Income transactions may be categorized as gross sales, other income, and so on, for example. Expense transactions may be categorized as car and truck expenses, supply expenses, utilities, and so on. But you may want to slice the data in other ways. You also may want to see income or expenses by job or project, by salesperson or product line, and by geographic location or functional company areas.

Classes add a second dimension to the income and expense summaries that categories provide. Nonbusiness use of Quicken probably does not require this second dimension. Business owners, however, can find Quicken's classes a powerful way to view financial data from a second perspective.

Besides using two categories—Product and Service—to track income, you can use classes to determine which salespeople actually are booking the orders. With three salespeople, use these three classes: Joe, Bill, and Sue. Besides seeing the sales of company products and company services, you also can see things such as the sales Bill made, the product sales Joe made, and the service sales Sue made. In effect, you have two perspectives on this income—the kind of income (which appears as a product or service) and salespeople (which appears as Joe, Bill, or Sue). Table 9.3 shows these perspectives.

Table 9.3 Two Perspectives on Income

Kind of Income	Salespeople Booking Orders		
	Joe	Bill	Sue
Product	Joe's product sales	Bill's product sales	Sue's product sales
Service	Joe's service sales	Bill's service sales	Sue's service sales

Defining a Class

The first step in using classes is to define the classes you want to use. The classes you choose depend on how you need or want to view the financial data you collect with Quicken. Unfortunately, giving specific advice on picking appropriate classes is difficult and Quicken does not provide predefined lists of classes (as it does for categories). Classes usually are specific to the particular personal or business finances. You can, however, follow one rough rule of thumb: look at the kinds of questions you currently ask but cannot answer by using categories alone. A real estate investor may want to use classes that correspond to individual properties. A law firm may want to use classes that represent each of the partners or each client. Other businesses have still different views of financial data. After you define the classes you want to use, you are ready to add the classes in Quicken. You can add as many classes as you want.

To add classes, follow these steps:

1. Press Alt-S to access the Shortcuts menu from the Write Checks or Register screen.

2. Choose the **Select/Set Up Class** option from the Shortcuts menu. The Class list appears (see fig. 9.15). You also can press the shortcut key Ctrl-L to display the Class list.

3. Highlight the <New Class> line at the top of the list and press Enter. The Set Up Class window appears (see fig. 9.16).

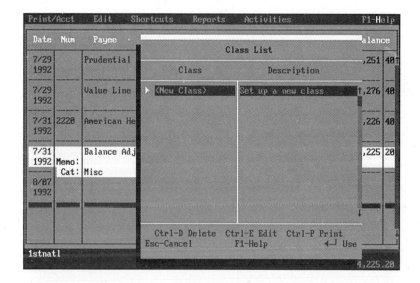

FIG. 9.15

The Class list.

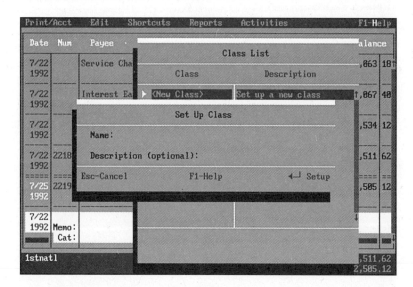

FIG. 9.16

The Set Up Class window.

4. Type the name you want to use for the class. Class names can contain up to 15 characters, including spaces. You cannot use the following characters:

    : [ ] /

5. (Optional) Press Enter or Tab to move the cursor to the Description field. Type a description for the class.

6. To save the class, press Ctrl-Enter or F10. Quicken adds the class to the Class list in alphabetical order.

Editing and Deleting Classes

If you start defining classes, you also need to know how to edit and delete these classes. The classification scheme you use undoubtedly can change over time. Suppose that you are a real estate investor and you use classes to track properties. You probably buy and sell properties over a period of time. Alternatively, if you are a bookkeeper for a law firm, the lawyers working at the firm probably change over a period of time. Both of these examples indicate a need for editing classes. The steps for editing and deleting are simple and familiar if you previously edited or deleted categories.

To edit a class, follow these steps:

1. Press Alt-S to access the Shortcuts menu from the Write Checks or Register screen.

2. Choose **Select/Set Up Class** from the Shortcuts menu. The Class list appears. You also can press the shortcut key Ctrl-L to display the Class list.

3. Use the up- and down-arrow keys to highlight the class you want to edit.

4. Press Ctrl-E. Quicken displays the Edit Class window, as shown in figure 9.17.

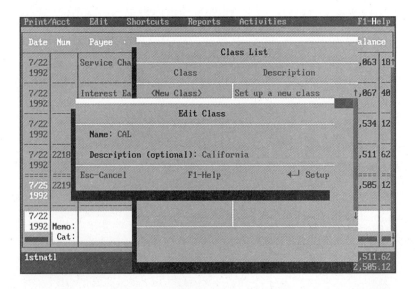

FIG. 9.17

The Edit Class window.

5. (Optional) If necessary, retype or edit the class name.

6. (Optional) Press Enter or Tab to move to the Description field. If necessary, retype or edit the class description.

7. To save the changes to the class, press Ctrl-Enter or F10.

To delete a class, follow these steps:

1. Press Alt-S to access the Shortcuts menu from the Write Checks or Register screen.

2. Choose **Select/Set Up Class** from the Shortcuts menu. The Class list screen appears. You also can press the shortcut key Ctrl-L to display the Class list.

3. Use the up- and down-arrow keys to highlight the class that you want to delete.

4. Press Ctrl-D. Quicken warns you that you are about to permanently delete a class.

5. Press Enter to complete the deletion or press Esc to cancel the deletion.

Using Subclasses

If you use classes to add another dimension to the reporting and recording process, you also may want to use subclasses. *Subclasses* are classes within classes. If you use a geographical scheme to create classes, the classes may be states. Within each state, you may choose to use subclasses corresponding to portions of the state. *Washington*, a class, may have the subclasses *Eastern Washington* and *Western Washington*, for example. *California*, another class, may have the subclasses *Northern California* (excluding the Bay Area), *Bay Area*, *Southern California* (excluding Los Angeles County), and *Los Angeles County*. You enter, edit, and delete subclasses by following the same procedures as for classes.

Subclasses are helpful for sales taxes based on a state, county, or city with different tax rates for each jurisdiction, or if you must report sales within each jurisdiction.

C P A
T I P

Assigning Classes and Subclasses to Transactions

You use the Category field in the Write Checks or Register screen or Split Transaction window to assign classes to transactions. Quicken does not prompt you to assign classes to transactions, so if you want to use classes, be sure that you remember to assign them after you assign a category.

To assign a class to a transaction, follow these steps:

1. After the category or subcategory is entered into the Category field, type a slash (/).

2. Type the class name or press Ctrl-L to display the Class list and select a class from the list. If, for example, you want to record the income category *SALES* and the California class *CAL* for a transaction, type *SALES/CAL* in the Category field. The same QuickFill feature described previously in this book also applies to classes. If you type enough of a class name for Quicken to identify the class, QuickFill completes the entry for you.

3. If the rest of the transaction is complete, press Ctrl-Enter or F10 to record the transaction and the class assignment.

If you use subclasses, enter the primary class, a colon, and then the subclass. If, for example, the class *CAL* has the subclass *NORTH*, you can record sales for Northern California by typing *SALES/CAL:NORTH* in the Category field.

If you have more then one subclass—classes within classes within classes—you also separate the additional subclasses with colons.

C P A
T I P

The Quicken user's manual describes a series of ways you can use classes. For the most part, the ideas are good. Some accounting problems exist with many of the manual's suggestions. From the start, think about these problems so that you don't go to a great deal of work and then find you wasted time. The basic problem with classes is that they don't give you a way to budget. You cannot, for example, budget by classes. This may not seem too important to you right now, but before you begin to use classes, review Chapter 15. Business users also will probably benefit by reading Chapter 22.

Chapter Summary

Quicken's categories and classes give you a means to organize your finances to give you the information that you need. This chapter described how you can modify Quicken's defined categories; how to add, edit, and delete categories; and how you use subcategories. This chapter also defined classes; described when to use the class features; and detailed the steps for adding, editing, and deleting classes.

In the next chapter, you learn how to complete your financial picture by adding other asset accounts and liability accounts. Once you have established these accounts, Quicken easily can determine your *net worth* (assets minus liabilities).

Tracking Your Net Worth, Other Assets, and Liabilities

Quicken was originally designed as an electronic check register for writing and recording checks. The newer releases of Quicken, Versions 3.0, 4.0, 5.0, and now 6.0, however, can do much more than keep track of your checking account. You can maintain financial records for any asset or liability by using Quicken's familiar check-register format.

Assets are personal or business resources that have lasting value. For individuals, assets include such items as a house, cars, furniture, and investments. For businesses, assets include money owed by customers (accounts receivable), inventory held for resale, and any fixtures or equipment used in the business. *Liabilities* are debts—any money you owe others. For individuals, liabilities include mortgages, car loans, credit card debts, and income taxes. For businesses, liabilities include amounts owed suppliers (accounts payable), wages payable to employees, and loans from banks and leasing companies.

The benefits of using Quicken to track your other assets (in addition to bank accounts) and your liabilities are similar to the benefits derived from tracking bank accounts. By carefully tracking your other assets, you know what those assets currently are worth and why they may have changed in value. By carefully tracking your liabilities, you maintain a firmer control over your debts, which helps you make regular payments, and you have concrete records showing why the amounts of your debts have changed. With both your assets and your liabilities carefully documented this way, you can use Quicken to generate a report that states your personal or business financial net worth. (The only drawback to tracking your other assets and your liabilities is the additional effort you expend keeping track. In many cases, however, the benefits you realize more than merit this effort.)

In essence, using Quicken to track all your assets, as well as your liabilities, gives you a complete picture of your entire financial state in one place. You not only have a powerful record-keeping tool for your cash inflows and outflows, but also all the information you need to determine your overall financial health, or *net worth*, within easy access.

This chapter describes generally how to use Quicken to keep records of your other assets and your liabilities. You are told why and how to use Quicken to generate net-worth reports, or *balance sheets*, also. (If Quicken's record-keeping possibilities intrigue you, read Chapters 16, 21, and 22 for more information.)

Specifically, this chapter teaches you how to do the following:

- Set up accounts for other assets and liabilities
- Record assets and liabilities and track their values
- Record assets and liabilities using transfer transactions
- Use Quicken's Loan Calculator to calculate loan payments or principal balances
- Amortize memorized loan payments on fixed-rate loans or variable-rate loans
- Recall memorized loan payments
- Update Cash Account balances
- Measure your net worth by creating a net-worth report, or balance sheet

If you have used earlier versions of Quicken, you will discover that adding an account in Quicken 6.0 is easier than ever.

Setting Up Accounts for Other Assets and Liabilities

You must set up a Quicken account for each asset or liability for which you want to keep computer records. You can track any asset or liability you want. Only one limit or restriction exists: You can keep a maximum of only 255 accounts within a single Quicken file. You must remember, however, that any accounts you want grouped on a single balance sheet must be set up within the same file. Typically, this restriction means that all your business accounts must be kept in one file and all your personal accounts in another file.

After you create a Quicken file, take the following steps to set up your accounts:

1. Choose the **Select Account** option from Quicken's main menu. Quicken displays the Select Account to Use window, as shown in figure 10.1.

2. To add a new account, select **<New Account>** from the Select Account to Use window. Quicken displays the Set Up New Account window, as shown in figure 10.2.

3. With the cursor in the Account Type field, type the number of the account type you are adding. This can be in an asset account or a liability account.

   Quicken lists four asset account types: Bank Account, Cash Account, Other Asset, and Investment Account. If the asset is a bank account, choose account type 1 (you learned about bank accounts in Chapter 3). If the asset is cash, such as that in your wallet or in the petty cash box, choose account type 3. If the account is an investment, choose account type 6. (Refer to Chapter 16 for specifics on defining an investment account.) For any other asset—accounts receivable, real estate, and so on—choose account type 4.

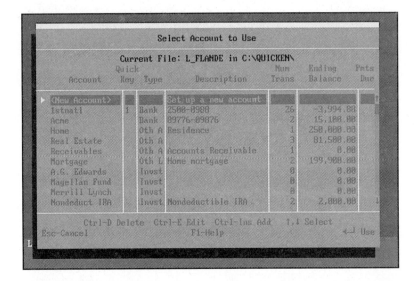

FIG. 10.1

The Select
Account to Use
window.

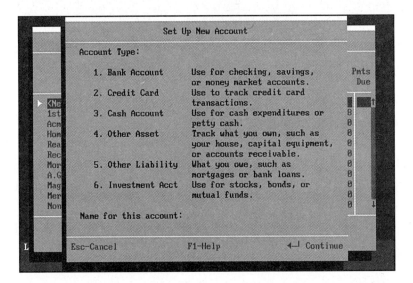

FIG. 10.2

The Set Up New
Account window.

Quicken lists two liability account types: Credit Card and Other
Liability. If the liability is the balance on your VISA or MasterCard
account, choose account type 2 (you learn about credit card accounts in the next chapter); otherwise, choose account type 5.

4. Press Enter or Tab to move the cursor to the Name for This Account field. Enter a description of the account. The Name field can

contain up to 15 characters and can include any character except the following:

[ ] / :

You can use spaces also.

5. Press Ctrl-Enter or F10 to display the Starting Balance and Description window, as shown in figure 10.3

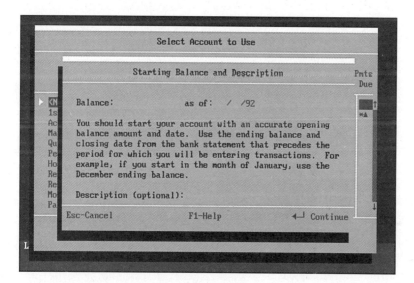

FIG. 10.3

The Starting Balance and Description window.

6. With the cursor in the Balance field, enter the starting balance for the account. (You learned how to enter the starting balance for a bank account in Chapters 1 and 3.) To set up a starting balance for an asset or liability, enter the amount here. Assets can be listed at their original costs or their current fair market values. Liabilities are listed at their current balances. If the starting balance is zero, you must enter *0* in the Balance field; you cannot leave the Balance field blank.

7. Press Enter or Tab to move the cursor to the As Of field. Enter the date on which the balance you entered is correct.

8. (Optional) When you set up a credit card account, Quicken displays the IntelliCharge field. See Chapter 11 for complete information about setting up credit card accounts and IntelliCharge.

9. (Optional) Press Enter or Tab to move the cursor to the Description field. Fill in the Description field with up to an additional 21 characters of account description.

10. (Optional) When you set up a credit card account, Quicken asks for the credit limit on your card.

After you enter the information for your new asset or liability account, Quicken adds the account to the Select Account to Use window. Quicken then organizes all accounts alphabetically within each account type. The account types are listed in the same order as on the Set Up New Account window. Thus, the first accounts listed are Bank Accounts, followed by Credit Card, Cash, Other Asset, and Other Liability accounts; Investment Accounts are listed last.

Recording Assets and Liabilities

After you initially set up an account—whether an asset or a liability account—you can maintain it in one of two ways: record transactions directly in the Register, or use transfer transactions.

Recording Transactions in the Register

Select an account by choosing the **Select Account** option from Quicken's main menu. Quicken displays the Select Account to Use window. Use the up- and down-arrow keys to highlight the account you want to update or revise and press Enter. After you select an account, you can use the Register to enter transactions that increase or decrease your balance, just as you do in your Quicken checking account.

Figure 10.4 shows how the Register may look for a major real-estate asset (a personal residence). This Other Assets Register is almost identical to the regular Bank Account Register and is used the same way. Transaction amounts that decrease the asset account balance are recorded in the Decrease field of the Register (the Payment field on the bank-account version of the Register screen). Transaction amounts that increase the asset account are recorded in the Increase field of the Register (the Deposit field on the bank-account version). The total Real Estate account balance is displayed in the bottom right corner of the screen. If you have *postdated transactions*—transactions with dates in the future—the current balance also is shown.

In the example in figure 10.4, the opening balance of $100,000 shows what you may originally have paid for your home. The two subsequent transactions—one for the addition of a new family room and the other for a new backyard swimming pool—show what changed the value of your home. By keeping these records, you can better keep track of the value of your home and any reasons for changes in its value.

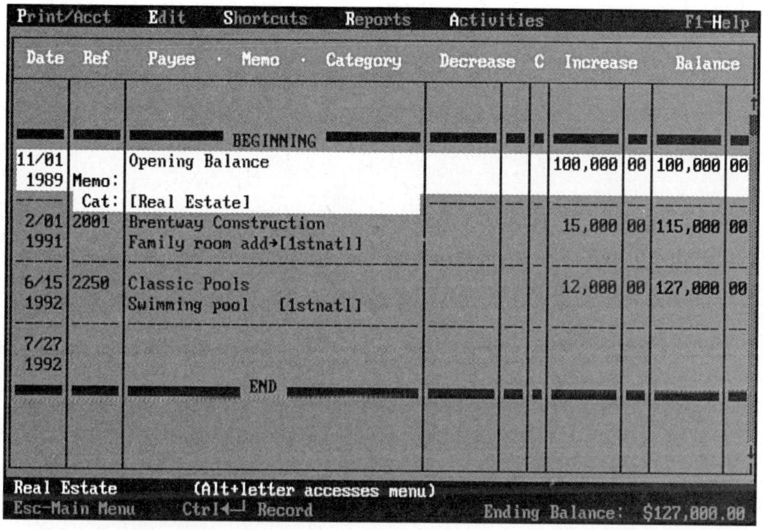

```
 Print/Acct    Edit    Shortcuts    Reports    Activities        F1-Help

  Date  Ref   Payee  ·  Memo  ·  Category    Decrease  C  Increase    Balance


 ━━━━━ ━━━ ━━━━━━━━━━ BEGINNING ━━━━━━━━━━━━ ━━━━━━━ ━ ━━━━━━━ ━━━━━━━
 11/01       Opening Balance                            100,000 00 100,000 00
 1989  Memo:
       Cat: [Real Estate]
 2/01  2001  Brentway Construction                       15,000 00 115,000 00
 1991        Family room add→[1stnatl]

 6/15  2250  Classic Pools                               12,000 00 127,000 00
 1992        Swimming pool   [1stnatl]

 7/27
 1992
 ━━━━━ ━━━ ━━━━━━━━━━━━━ END ━━━━━━━━━━━━━━ ━━━━━━━ ━ ━━━━━━━ ━━━━━━━

 Real Estate       (Alt+letter accesses menu)
 Esc-Main Menu     Ctrl←┘ Record              Ending Balance:  $127,000.00
```

FIG. 10.4

A Real Estate Account Register used to record the value of a personal residence.

When working with an Other Assets Register, you can access the same menu options as from the Bank Account Register, except that **Update Account Balances** replaces **Reconcile** on the Activities menu. (See "Updating Account Balances," later in this chapter.)

Figure 10.5 displays a Register for tracking what you owe on a loan, such as a business credit line or a home mortgage. The Other Liability Register also mirrors the Bank Account Register in appearance and operation. Transaction amounts that increase the amount owed are recorded in the Increase field of the Register. (On the bank-account version of the Register screen, this field is labeled Payment.) Transaction amounts that decrease the amount owed are recorded in the Decrease field of the Register. (On the bank-account version of the Register, this field is labeled Deposit.) The total liability balance is shown in the bottom right corner of the screen. If you have postdated transactions, the current balance also is shown. You do not use the C field when tracking a liability account.

In the example in figure 10.5, the opening balance of $80,000 shows what you may have borrowed originally on a mortgage. The subsequent transaction—the July mortgage payment—shows the reduction in the outstanding loan balance stemming from the principal portion of the July loan payment.

When working with the Other Liability Register, the menu options available are the same as when you work with the Bank Account Register, except that the **Update Account Balance** option from the Activities menu replaces the **Reconcile** option for bank accounts.

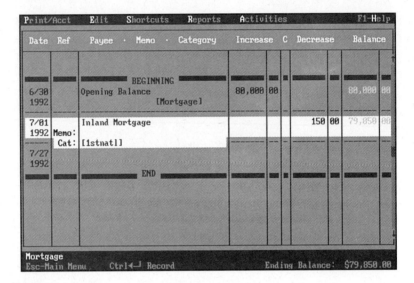

FIG. 10.5

The Register used
to track the
outstanding
balance on a
mortgage loan.

 NOTE Only the principal reductions are recorded in the Register
for a loan or mortgage. The interest portion is reported as
interest expense and should be assigned to a category set
up for mortgage interest (Mort Int).

Using Transfer Transactions

Entering transactions directly into a Register is one way to maintain
correct account balances for another asset or liability account. You
can, however, choose a second way to maintain correct account balances for other assets and liabilities. Quicken enables you to enter an
account name in the Category field on the Write Checks and Register
screens. Quicken then uses the information from the checking-account
transaction to record the appropriate transaction in one of the other
asset or liability accounts.

If you write a check to the bank or company that holds your mortgage
and enter the account name for your mortgage (for example, *Mortgage*)
in the Category field (in the Write Checks screen or the Checking Account Register) to show the principal portion of the payment, Quicken
records a corresponding decrease in your mortgage liability account.
This decrease is equal to the principal portion of the payment made
from your checking account. When you enter an account name in the
Category field for a transaction, Quicken places that account name in

brackets ([Mortgage]) to show that the transaction is a transfer transaction. The portion of your payment that pays interest is assigned to the mortgage interest category (see fig. 10.6).

Figure 10.6 shows a $1,000 check written to First National Bank for a mortgage payment. The transaction is split to allocate a portion of the payment to the mortgage liability account ([Mortgage]) and mortgage interest (Mort Int). (You learned about split transactions in Chapters 5 and 7.) The principal amount of this payment that is applied to the current mortgage balance is $100. (The remainder of the payment is mortgage interest.) When you record the check, Quicken records a corresponding $100 decrease in your Mortgage account.

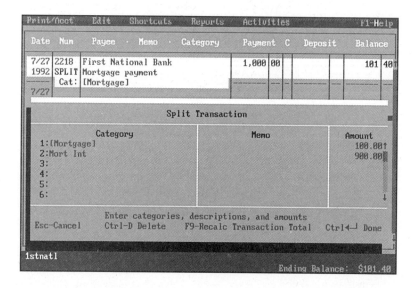

A convenient way to move between different parts of the same transfer transaction is to use the **Go to Transfer** option from the Edit menu. You can use the shortcut key Ctrl-X to go to a transfer transaction, too. After you record a mortgage payment in the Check Register, you may want to look at the liability account for your mortgage to see how much your outstanding balance is.

Using the Loan Calculator

Quicken includes a tool for loan payment and balance record-keeping: a Loan Calculator. You can use this calculator in two ways: to calculate loan payments and to calculate the interest and principal portions of memorized loan payments.

Calculating Loan Payments

Probably the simplest use of the Loan Calculator is to calculate loan payments. If you know the loan amount, annual interest rate, number of years the loan will be outstanding, and the number of payments made annually, Quicken can calculate the payment amount. The Loan Calculator also can produce a payment, or *amortization*, schedule. An amortization schedule shows what portion of your payments goes to paying interest and what portion goes to reducing the principal balance of the loan.

With Quicken 6.0, you can select the type of calculation to make with the Loan Calculator. The calculator no longer is limited simply to calculating a loan payment. Now you can calculate the principal amount outstanding when you know the annual interest rate, number of years the loan will be outstanding, the number of payments made annually, and the payment amount.

To calculate loan payments or the principal amount of a loan, and to produce a payment schedule, follow these steps:

1. From any Register or Write Checks screens, select the Activities menu (see fig. 10.7).

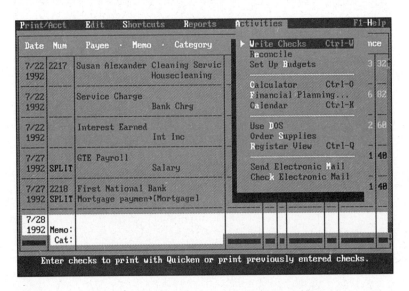

FIG. 10.7

The Activities menu.

2. Select the **Financial Planning** option from the Activities menu. Quicken displays the Financial Planning menu, as shown in figure 10.8.

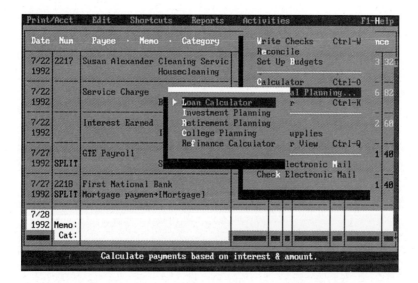

FIG. 10.8

The Financial
Planning menu.

3. From the Financial Planning menu, select **Loan Calculator**.
Quicken displays the Loan Calculator and places a check mark
next to the variable to be calculated (Principal or Regular Payment), as shown in figure 10.9. (In the figure, the check mark
appears next to the Regular Payment field. To have Quicken
calculate the principal amount of the loan instead of the regular
payment, press F8 to move the check mark to the Principal field.
Press F8 again to re-mark the Regular Payment field.)

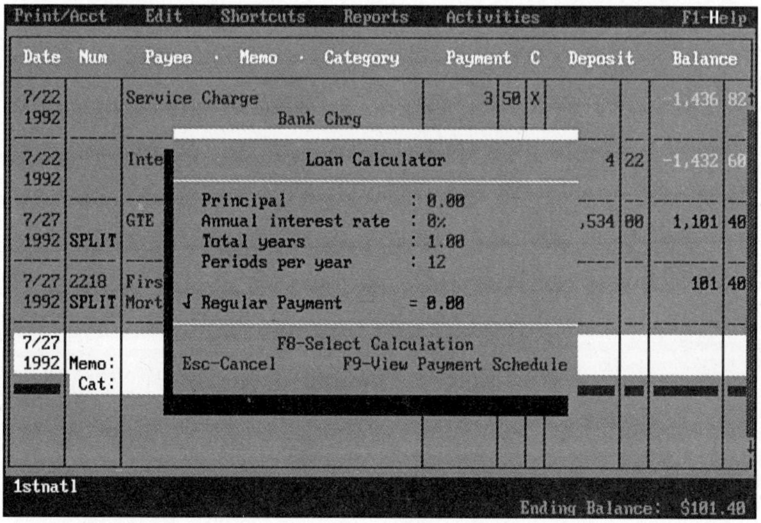

FIG. 10.9

The Loan
Calculator.

4. ***Important:*** Skip this step if you are calculating the principal amount of a loan. To calculate a loan's regular payment (the check mark appears next to the Regular Payment field), start with the cursor in the Principal field. Enter the amount of the balance of the loan in the Principal field. If you are calculating the principal amount of a loan (the check mark appears next to the Principal field), Quicken does not accept an entry in the Principal field; go to step 5.

5. Press Enter or Tab to move the cursor to the Annual Interest Rate field and enter the annual interest rate. If the annual loan interest rate is 12.5 percent, for example, type *12.5.*

> **CAUTION:** Don't mistake the annual percentage rate (APR) for the annual interest rate. The APR encompasses all the costs of obtaining credit and includes not only interest charges but loan fees and other borrowing costs as well. The APR, which is required by truth-in-lending laws, provides a way to compare the overall cost of obtaining a loan. The APR, however, shouldn't be used to calculate the loan payment.

6. Press Enter or Tab to move the cursor to the Total Years field. Enter the number of years you must make payments. If the loan is a 5-year car loan, for example, press 5. If the loan is a 30-year mortgage, type *30.*

7. Press Enter or Tab to move the cursor to the Periods per Year field. Enter the number of payments you must make each year. Typically, because most payments must be made monthly, this number is *12* and is already entered.

8. ***Important:*** Skip this step if you are calculating the regular payment of a loan. To calculate the principal amount of the loan (the check mark appears next to the Principal field), press Enter or Tab to move to the Regular Payment field. Enter the amount of your loan payment in the Regular Payment field. If you are calculating the regular payment amount (the check mark appears next to the Regular Payment field), no entry is allowed in the Regular Payment field; go to step 9.

9. Press Enter after you enter the value for the last field on the Loan Calculator. Quicken calculates the loan payment amount in the Regular Payment field or the principal amount in the Principal

field. Figure 10.10 shows the monthly payment on a $12,000 loan with 12.5 percent interest and 4 years of monthly payments to be $318.96. Figure 10.11 shows the principal amount of a loan to be $198,850.98 when the regular loan payment is $1,600.00 per month for 30 years and the annual interest rate is 9 percent.

10. (Optional) To produce a payment schedule for the loan, press F9 after you have finished calculating the Regular Payment or Principal amount. Quicken displays the Approximate Payment Schedule window, depicted in figure 10.12. The Approximate Payment Schedule window shows the approximate interest and principal portions of each loan payment and the loan balance after the payment. To move up and down in the payment schedule, use the PgUp and PgDn keys. Or use the mouse on the scroll bar. You can use the Home and End keys also: Home displays the first page of the payment schedule, and End displays the last page of the payment schedule.

The Loan Calculator, showing the monthly payment on a 4-year, 12.5 percent, $12,000 loan.

11. (Optional) To print a copy of the payment schedule, press Ctrl-P. Quicken displays the Print Payment Schedule window, which is similar to the Print Checks window described in Chapter 6. Indicate the printer you want to use and press Enter. Quicken prints the schedule.

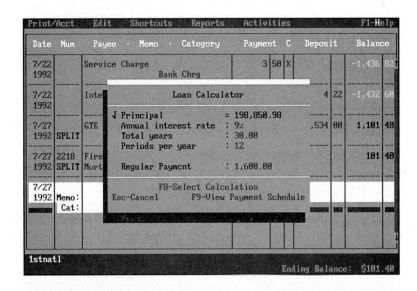

FIG. 10.11

The Loan Calculator, showing the principal amount on a 30-year, 9 percent loan with regular payments of $1,600 per month.

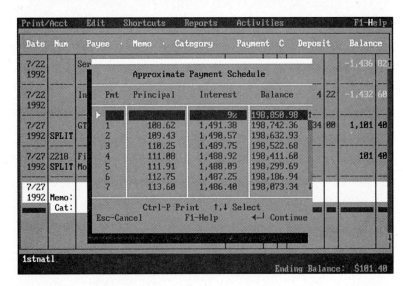

FIG. 10.12

The Approximate Payment Schedule window.

C P A
T I P

If you are uncertain how big a mortgage you can afford when buying a home, use the Loan Calculator to help you determine what amount you actually can afford. To calculate the principal amount, enter into the appropriate Loan Calculator fields the amount you decide that you can spend for housing from your monthly income (Regular Payment) and the current annual interest rate. Then, if you want to pay less interest over the life of the mortgage and pay off the mortgage balance sooner, use 15 years as the total years to pay. If you cannot afford the monthly mortgage payments for a 15-year loan, use 30 years. With this information, you can calculate the total principal amount, which gives you a better idea of what to look for in a mortgage.

Quicken normally calculates an arrangement known as a *payment in arrears*, or an *ordinary annuity*. These terms mean that the payment is made at the end of the payment period, as is the case with loan payments. With some loans, however, payments are made at the beginning of the period. This beginning-of-the-month arrangement is known as a *payment in advance*, or an *annuity due*. To convert a payment-in-arrears payment to a payment-in-advance payment, divide the payment amount Quicken calculates by the following factor:

(1 + (annual interest rate/periods in a year))

To convert the $318.96 payment in arrears to a payment in advance on a 12.5 percent loan (.125), make the following calculation:

$318.96/(1 + (.125/12))

This calculation produces a result of $315.67.

Amortizing Memorized Loan Payments

You also can use the Loan Calculator with memorized loan payments. In effect, using the payment schedule information, you can memorize not only the loan payment amount, but also the loan interest expense and loan principal reduction associated with each payment.

With Quicken 6.0, you can amortize and memorize the payment schedule information for loans with variable interest rates and prepayments. The interest rate on a fixed-rate loan remains constant throughout the loan period and cannot be adjusted unless you refinance the loan. The interest rate on a *variable-rate* loan, however, fluctuates throughout the loan period to correspond with another factor, such as Treasury Bill interest rates or the prime lending rate. Loan *prepayments* are payments you make in addition to required payments. If your mortgage payment is $850 per month, for example, and you pay $900 every month, you're making a $50 prepayment of principal each month that you pay $900 instead of the required $850.

If you want some additional assistance with amortizing loan payments, Quicken 6.0 provides a new assistant, the Amortize Loan Assistant, to help. To use the assistant, select the **Use Tutorials/Assistants** option from the Quicken main menu. Then select **More Assistants** to display the Select Tutor/Assistant window. From here, just highlight the Amortize assistant and press Enter. Follow the Amortized Loan Assistant's on-screen instructions to set up a loan for amortization and to learn how to record payments on a loan.

Amortizing and Memorizing a Loan Payment on a Fixed-Rate Loan

To amortize and memorize the payment-schedule information for a fixed-rate loan, follow these steps:

1. Record a loan payment in the Register for the account that you write your loan payment from or the Write Checks screen. Loan payments are recorded as split transactions because you allocate a portion of the payment to a liability account (to decrease the principal balance of the loan) and to the interest category. There may be other allocations made for loan payments, such as property taxes, insurance, and so on. You learned how to split transactions in Chapters 5 and 7.

2. Use the Split Transaction window (press Ctrl-S) to assign the liability account and the interest expense category to the transaction.

The first item in the Split Transaction window must be the liability account you use to track the principal balance (such as *[Mortgage]*). The second item must be the expense category you use to track interest expense (such as *Mort Int* for mortgage interest). You can use all other lines in the Split Transaction window to allocate the remainder of the loan payment to property taxes, insurance, and so on. Figure 10.13 shows the Split Transaction window for a loan payment, broken down into the principal amount, mortgage interest, property taxes and insurance. Chapter 5 shows you how to split a transaction.

3. Memorize the loan payment by pressing Ctrl-M. (You learned about memorizing transactions in Chapters 5 and 7. The procedure is the same when memorizing loan payments.)

4. Press Alt-T to display the Memorized Transaction List (see fig. 10.14).

5. Use the up- and down-arrow keys to highlight the loan payment transaction you memorized in step 3.

6. Press F9. Quicken displays the Set Amortization Information window (see fig. 10.15).

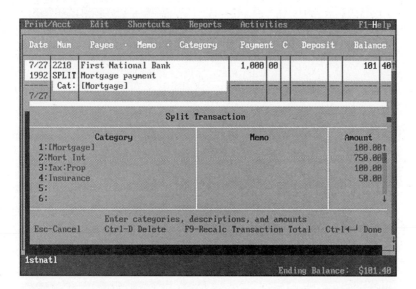

FIG. 10.13

The Split Transaction window for a mortgage payment.

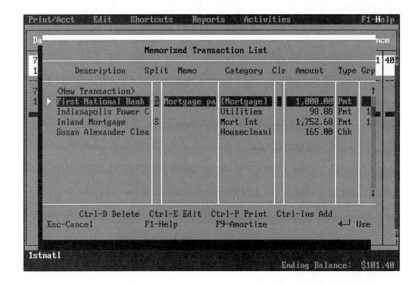

FIG. 10.14

The Memorized Transaction list.

7. With the cursor in the Regular Payment field, enter the usual loan payment amount if it is different than the amount shown. (Quicken enters the regular payment amount from the memorized transaction.)

8. Press Enter or Tab to move the cursor to the Annual Interest Rate field. Enter the annual interest rate.

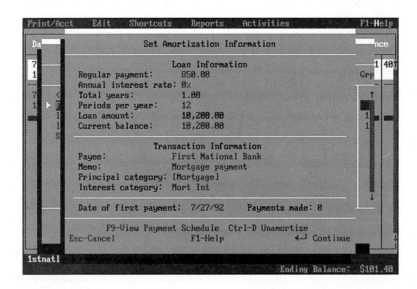

FIG. 10.15

The Set Amortization Information window.

9. Press Enter or Tab to move the cursor to the Total Years field. Enter the number of years you must make payments.

10. Press Enter or Tab to move the cursor to the Periods per Year field. Enter the number of payments you must make each year if different than 12.

11. After the appropriate information is entered in all four fields, press Enter. Quicken calculates the loan balance and displays this amount in the Loan Amount field. Figure 10.16, for example, shows each payment on a $105,639.59 loan at 9 percent interest with 30 years of monthly payments to be $850.00.

> **CAUTION:** A slight rounding error of a penny or two may occur when performing calculations with the Loan Calculator.

12. If you have already made payments on this loan, enter the current outstanding principal balance in the Current Balance field. The current, or outstanding principal, balance is not the same as the original loan amount (the amount in the Loan Amount field) if any payments have been made.

> **NOTE** You can use the Loan Calculator to determine the current outstanding principal balance of a loan. Use the calculator as explained in the preceding sections, and press F9 to view the Approximate Payment Schedule (refer to fig. 10.12). Use the up- and down-arrow keys to move through the Approximate Payment Schedule until you come to the payment number of the loan you currently are paying. The amount shown in the Balance field is the outstanding principal balance after the current payment has been made.

13. To change any fields in the Transaction Information section, press Enter or Tab to move the cursor to the field you want to change and type the new entry. (The Transaction Information section of the Set Amortization Information window already is filled in for you based on the categories and accounts you assigned in the Split Transaction window for the memorized loan payment.)

14. Press Enter or Tab to move the cursor to the Date of First Payment field. Enter the date you made or will make the first loan payment.

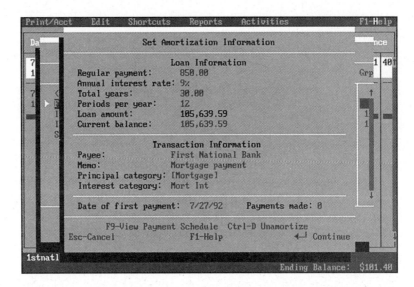

FIG. 10.16

The loan amount, given an $850 monthly payment on a 30-year, 9 percent loan.

15. Press Enter or Tab to move the cursor to the Payments Made field. Enter the number of payments you have made (zero if you have not yet made any payments). As you make payments on the loan, Quicken updates the number of payments listed in the Payments Made field.

16. Press Ctrl-Enter or F10 to return to the Memorized Transaction list. An *A* (for *amortized*) appears in the Split column of the memorized loan payment in the Memorized Transaction list.

17. Press Esc to return to the Register or the Write Checks screen.

Amortizing and Memorizing a Loan Payment on Variable-Rate Loans and Prepayments

Amortizing a memorized loan payment on a variable-rate loan differs only slightly from amortizing a memorized loan payment on a fixed-rate loan. The difference lies in how you set up the amortization. For variable-rate loans, you set up the amortization as if payments for the loan were starting today, with no previous payments made. (You set up the amortization this way regardless of how many payments you have actually made.)

To amortize and memorize the payment schedule information for a variable-rate loan and prepayments, follow these steps:

1. Follow steps 1 through 6 in the preceding section to amortize a memorized fixed-rate loan payment.

2. At the Set Amortization Information window, enter the usual loan payment amount in the Regular Payment field if different than the amount shown.

3. Press Enter or Tab to move the cursor to the Annual Interest Rate field, and enter the current annual interest rate.

4. Press Enter or Tab to move the cursor to the Total Years field. Enter the number of years you must make payments.

5. Press Enter or Tab to move the cursor to the Periods per Year field. Enter the number of payments you must make annually. (Again, this entry typically is *12*.)

6. After the appropriate information is entered into all four fields, press Enter. Quicken calculates the loan balance and displays this amount in the Loan Amount field. If you already have made payments on this loan, the current, or outstanding principal, balance is not the same as the original loan amount (the amount in the Loan Amount field).

7. Press Enter or Tab to move to the Current Balance field. Enter the current outstanding principal balance in the Current Balance field if it is different from what Quicken displays in the Loan Amount field.

8. To change any of the fields in the Transaction Information section, press Enter or Tab to move the cursor to the field you want to change, and type the new entry. (The Transaction Information section of the Set Amortization window is filled in for you based on the categories and accounts you assigned in the Split Transaction window for the memorized loan payment.)

9. Press Enter or Tab to move the cursor to the Date of First Payment field. Enter the date of the next payment you will make.

10. Press Enter or Tab to move the cursor to the Payments Made field and enter zero (*0*). (Regardless of the number of payments you may already have made, you always enter zero in the Payments Made field when amortizing a memorized loan payment on a variable-rate loan or a loan on which you have made prepayments.)

11. Press Ctrl-Enter or F10 to return to the Memorized Transaction list. An *A* (for *amortized*) appears in the Split column of the memorized loan payment in the Memorized Transaction list.

12. Press Esc to return to the Register or the Write Checks screen.

Recalling Amortized Loan Payments

After you have amortized a memorized loan payment, you can recall your record of the loan whenever you want to record a new payment. Quicken keeps track of which payment is being made—the first payment, the second payment, the third payment, and so on. Quicken then uses the payment schedule information to split the payment amount between the loan's principal reduction and the interest expense. After you have recalled a memorized loan payment and recorded new payments as many times as you initially indicated that payments were left, Quicken removes the loan from the Memorized Transaction list.

To recall an amortized loan payment, follow these steps:

1. From an empty transaction line in the Register or a blank check in the Write Checks screen, press Ctrl-T. The Memorized Transaction list is displayed.

2. Use the up- and down-arrow keys to highlight the memorized loan payment and press Enter.

T I P

If QuickFill is activated, type only the first few characters of the payee name in the Payee field. Quicken searches the Memorized Transaction list for a transaction with a payee name that begins with the characters you type. QuickFill then fills in the rest of the memorized transaction for you. Refer to Chapter 5 to learn more about QuickFill.

Quicken displays the Use Amortize Transaction window for the memorized loan payment, as shown in figure 10.17.

3. To change any of the information in the Use Amortize Transaction window, press Enter or Tab to move to the field you want to change, and type a new entry. Here you tell Quicken whether you're making additional prepayments on the loan (in the Additional Prepayment field) or whether the interest rate has changed on a variable-rate loan (in the Current Interest Rate field). When you change the current interest rate, Quicken recalculates the payment amount for you and enters the result in the Regular Payment Amount field.

4. After the appropriate information is entered in all the fields of the Use Amortize Transaction window, press Ctrl-Enter. Quicken enters the transaction information in the Register or the Write Checks screen.

5. Press Ctrl-Enter or F10 to record the transaction.

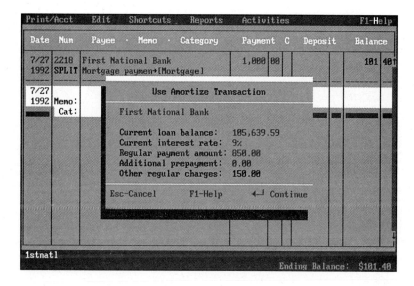

FIG. 10.17

The Use Amortize
Transaction
window.

T I P

When Quicken prepares an approximate payment schedule, the
program makes certain necessary assumptions. Quicken assumes,
for example, that you always make the payment on the same day of
the month; that each month has the same number of days; and that
interest on your loan is calculated, or *compounded*, only at the time
each payment is made. Obviously, however, these assumptions do
not always match reality. You may not always remember to pay a
loan on the same day each month, for example. Or the mail may be
delayed. That fact that not every month has the same number of
days also can alter your payment schedule. Your bank may even
have some special way of calculating interest. The result of such
discrepancies is that the split between interest and principal turns
out to be slightly incorrect—perhaps by a few pennies or perhaps
even by several dollars. To deal with this problem, update the loan
account balance at the end of each year by using the **Update Account Balances** option on the Activities menu. Any such discrepancies should be assigned to a category for interest expense.

Undoing Recalled Loan Payments

If you make a mistake and record a loan payment you didn't actually
make, you must reverse the payment so that Quicken keeps an accurate count of the loan payments you have made. (Remember that every

time you recall a memorized loan payment, Quicken increases the number in the Payments Made field by one.)

To undo a recalled loan payment, follow these steps:

1. From the Register or the Write Checks screen, press Ctrl-T to display the Memorized Transaction list.

2. Use the up- and down-arrow keys to highlight the memorized loan payment you mistakenly recalled.

3. Press F9 to display the Set Amortization Information for the memorized loan payment.

4. Position the cursor in the Payments Made field, and type the number of payments made before you mistakenly recalled the memorized loan payment.

5. Position the cursor in the Current Balance field and type the correct current balance. (If you changed the interest rate or entered a prepayment in the Use Amortize Transaction window when you mistakenly recalled the memorized loan payment, you must change the Current Balance amount back to that of the outstanding principal balance before you recalled the memorized loan payment.)

6. Press Ctrl-Enter. Quicken displays a warning that you are about to change the amortization information. Press Enter to change the amortization information, or press Esc to cancel the changes.

7. After you have changed the amortization information, go to the recalled transaction in the Register or the Write Checks screen and delete the transaction for the memorized loan payment you mistakenly recalled. You learned how to delete transactions from the Register in Chapter 5.

Reviewing Tips for Working with Other Assets and Liabilities

All Quicken Registers work essentially the same way, regardless of account type. A few tips and techniques, however, can help you in using Quicken to account for your other assets and liabilities. These tips and techniques include hints on dealing with the nuances and subtleties of cash accounts. They also cover using the **Update Account Balances** option with cash accounts. (Credit card accounts have their own nuances and subtleties, but these account types are not explained in this chapter. Chapter 11 describes how to use credit card accounts in Quicken to manage your credit card debts.)

Dealing with Cash Accounts

The **Cash Account** option works well when you want to keep complete, detailed records of miscellaneous cash outlays. (*Miscellaneous cash outlays* are all those paid out of pocket with actual currency rather than with a check, such as $5 for stamps, $12 for lunch, $7.50 for parking, and so on.) Often, you don't really need this level of control or detail. But when you do want such detailed records, the cash account type gives you just the tool you need for the job. (As Quicken warns you with an on-screen message, however, you cannot use the **Write/Print Checks** option with this type of account.)

> The cash account type is a convenient way for businesses to keep track of petty-cash expenditures and reimbursements. Even very large businesses can benefit by using Quicken for petty-cash accounting.
>
> **T I P**

Figure 10.18 shows a Cash Account Register (called *Petty Cash*), which is almost identical to the Bank Account Register. Money flowing in and out of the account is recorded in the Spend and Receive fields. (In the Bank Account Register, money flowing out of the account is recorded in the Payment field and money flowing into the account is recorded in the Deposit field. In the Other Assets and Other Liability Account Registers, money flowing into and out of the account is recorded in the Increase and Decrease fields.)

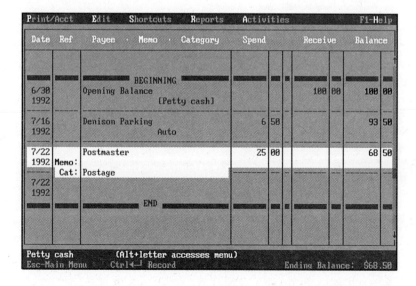

FIG. 10.18

A Cash Account Register (*Petty Cash*).

As with the Other Assets and Other Liability Account Registers, the C field usually is not used. You can use this column, however, to match receipts against entries to indicate that you have backup records. Press C in this field to show that you have entered a cash transaction from an actual receipt.

Updating Account Balances

The **Update Account Balance** option replaces **Reconcile** on the Activities menu at the Registers for Cash Accounts and for Other Asset and Other Liability accounts. The **Reconcile** option was explained in Chapter 8. (On the Activities menu at the Credit Card Account Register, **Pay Credit Card Bill** replaces **Reconcile**. The **Pay Credit Card Bill** option is described in Chapter 11.) Figure 10.19 shows the Cash Account Activities menu.

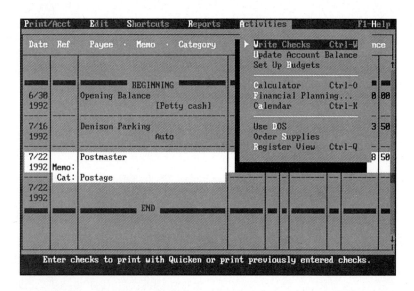

FIG. 10.19

The Cash
Account
Activities menu.

Selecting the **Update Account Balance** option from a Register gives you a window with which to reconcile, or adjust, an account. Suppose that the Register you use to keep track of your petty cash or pocket cash shows $68.50 as the on-hand cash balance, but the actual balance is $61.88. To update your account, use the Update Account Balance window to record an adjustment, as shown in figure 10.20.

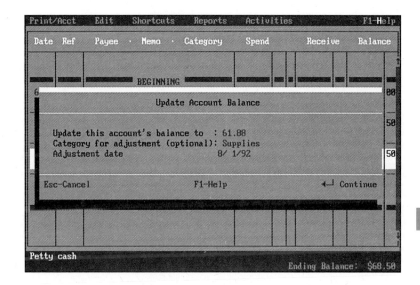

To update or adjust an account balance, follow these steps:

1. From the Cash Account Register, press Alt-A to display the Activities menu.

2. Choose Update Account Balance from the Activities menu. Quicken displays the Update Account Balance window.

3. Enter the amount to which the account balance should be adjusted in the Update this Account's Balance To field.

4. (Optional) Press Enter or Tab to move the cursor to the Category for Adjustment field. Enter the category to which you want to assign the difference between the old and new account balances. You can use a miscellaneous category or, if you know exactly what the difference stems from, use that category.

5. Press Enter. Quicken makes the adjustment transaction to update the account balance. (Remember that you can press Ctrl-C to see the Category and Transfer list.) Figure 10.21 shows the adjustment transaction created by the Update Account Balance transaction so that the account balance is now $61.88.

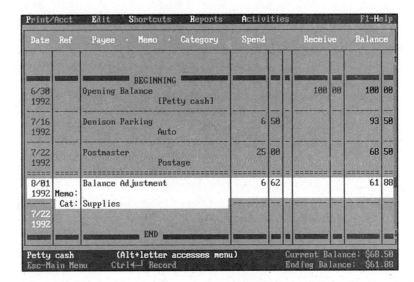

Date	Ref	Payee · Memo · Category	Spend		Receive		Balance	
		BEGINNING						
6/30 1992		Opening Balance [Petty cash]			100	00	100	00
7/16 1992		Denison Parking Auto	6	50			93	50
7/22 1992		Postmaster Postage	25	00			68	50
8/01 1992	Memo: Cat:	Balance Adjustment Supplies	6	62			61	88
7/22 1992								
		END						

Petty cash   (Alt+letter accesses menu)   Current Balance: $68.50
Esc-Main Menu   Ctrl↵ Record   Ending Balance: $61.88

FIG. 10.21

The adjustment transaction to update the Cash Account balance to the actual balance.

C P A
T I P

Often you don't really know which category explains the difference between the old and new account balances. The discrepancy may be caused by transactions you forgot to record or recorded incorrectly. Essentially, what you are trying to do at the Update Account Balance window is to correct or record erroneous or missing transactions. If you cannot decide which category to record in the Category for Adjustment field, enter the category that you use most frequently with this Register. If most of your petty-cash transactions involve postage payments, for example, enter *postage* in the Category for Adjustment field.

CAUTION: You cannot guess or estimate tax-deduction amounts. *Do not*, therefore, use the method described in the preceding tip to increase your tax deductions. The Internal Revenue Service may disallow deductions that cannot be supported with evidence as to the exact type and amount of the deduction.

Dealing with Credit Card Accounts

Chapter 11, "Managing Your Credit Cards," explains how to use credit card accounts to track your credit card activity, reconcile your credit card accounts, and pay your credit card bills.

Measuring Your Net Worth

A balance sheet is one traditional tool individuals and businesses use to measure net worth. The balance sheet lists all your assets and liabilities. The difference between assets and liabilities is called *owner's equity*, or *net worth*. A balance sheet differs from reports such as income statements and cash-flow reports, which summarize financial activity occurring over a certain period of time. A balance sheet provides a "snapshot" of your personal or business finances at a particular moment in time.

> Before you create a balance sheet, make certain that all your asset and liability accounts are located within the same Quicken file.   **T I P**

Creating a balance sheet with Quicken is a two-step process. First, you must set up an account for each of your assets, with a beginning balance amount for each asset that is equal to the asset's cost or value. Generally, *assets* are items you have paid for that have lasting value. *Personal assets* include such items as the cash in your wallet, the surrender value of a life insurance policy, any investments, your home, and durable personal items such as your car and furniture. *Business assets* usually include cash, accounts receivable, inventory, and other property and equipment.

The second step in creating a balance sheet is to set up accounts for all your liabilities, recording the balance owed on each liability. *Liabilities* are amounts you currently owe other people, banks, or businesses. *Personal liabilities* encompass such items as credit card balances, income taxes, car loans, and mortgages. *Business liabilities* usually include accounts payable, wages and salaries owed employees, income and payroll taxes, and bank credit lines and loans.

C P A
T I P   Determine the cost or market value of all your assets and liabilities as of the same date. The cost or market value information must be accurate for your net worth calculation also to be accurate. Use only one method for appraising your assets or liabilities: either original cost or fair market value. Mixing the different methods can yield inaccurate results. Note also on your opening balances whether you used original cost or fair market value to determine these appraisals. If you use fair market value, be sure to document the source you used to make your estimate of fair market value.

After you enter the costs or market values of all your assets and liabilities, you can generate a report that calculates your net worth by subtracting your liabilities from your assets. The desired result, of course, is for the difference to be a positive one. Whether you are determining your net worth as a business or an individual, you want the net worth amount to grow larger in time, because this amount acts as a financial cushion should you ever experience fiscal difficulties.

Figure 10.22 shows an example of a personal balance sheet, or net-worth statement, created by Quicken. At the top of the page, Quicken lists each asset account and its balance as of a specific date. Below the asset accounts, Quicken lists each liability account and its balance as of a specific date. The difference between assets and liabilities is *total net worth*. In figure 10.22, the net-worth amount is $49,769.90.

A business balance sheet looks essentially the same, although the assets and liabilities listed usually are different. Chapter 12 describes how to print a business balance sheet, as well as each of Quicken's other reports.

Chapter Summary

In this chapter, you learned how easy it is to use Quicken for nearly all your personal or small-business accounting needs. The chapter described how Quicken can help you keep records on such assets as real estate or accounts receivable and on liabilities such as mortgage loans. For more information on Quicken's accounting capabilities, refer to Chapters 16, 21, and 22. Chapter 16 describes Quicken 6.0 features that can help you monitor your investments. Chapter 21 describes how to use Quicken for your home finances. Chapter 22 describes how to use Quicken as a business accounting package.

```
                          Personal Net Worth
                            As of 7/27/92
 L_FLANDE-All Accounts                                        Page 1
 7/27/92
                                              7/27/92
                          Acct                Balance
          ------------------------------------ -------------
          ASSETS
            Cash and Bank Accounts
              1stnatl                          101.40
              Acme                             350.00
              Petty cash                        68.50
                                              -------------
            Total Cash and Bank Accounts       519.90

            Other Assets
              Real Estate                    127,000.00
              Receivables                         0.00
                                              -------------
            Total Other Assets              127,000.00

            Investments
              Nondeduct IRA                   2,000.00
                                              -------------
            Total Investments                 2,000.00

                                              -------------
          TOTAL ASSETS                      129,519.90

          LIABILITIES
            Credit Cards
              VISA                               0.00
                                              -------------
            Total Credit Cards                   0.00

            Other Liabilities
              Mortgage                        79,750.00
                                              -------------
            Total Other Liabilities          79,750.00

                                              -------------
          TOTAL LIABILITIES                  79,750.00

                                              -------------
          TOTAL NET WORTH                    49,769.90
                                              =============
```

FIG. 10.22

An example of a
personal balance
sheet.

Chapter 11 describes how to set up, use, reconcile and pay a credit
card account. If you use Quicken's VISA card, you also will learn how to
track your credit card activity through statements received on disk or
through a modem.

Managing Your Credit Cards

I f you're like most people, you use several credit cards to purchase merchandise. Now that many service providers such as doctors, lawyers, and dentists are accepting credit as payment, you may be making even more credit purchases.

The more you purchase on credit and the more credit cards you use, the more important managing your credit becomes. With Quicken, you can set up individual credit card accounts that help you record and keep track of purchases, payments, and finance charges. Credit card accounts also can help you track a line of credit from your bank.

Now with Quicken 6.0, you can set up an IntelliCharge account to use with your Quicken VISA card. *IntelliCharge* is a new service that updates your Credit Card Register automatically by disk or modem. When you use IntelliCharge, you avoid entering credit transactions in your Credit Card Register; IntelliCharge does that for you. In this chapter, you learn how to set up an IntelliCharge account and receive your statement on disk or by modem. You also learn how to review and categorize your credit transactions.

If you're interested in obtaining a Quicken credit card, fill out the application form enclosed in your Quicken 6.0 package.

T I P

If you pay the balance on your credit card bills each month, you probably don't need to set up a credit card account. Instead, enter the payment transaction in the Register for the account that you use to pay your credit card bill and split the transaction to assign multiple categories to the transaction (see Chapters 5 and 7 to learn how to split transactions). If you don't pay your credit card balance each month, setting up a credit card account will help you manage your credit transactions.

C P A
T I P

The balance carried on your credit cards is a liability. If you want all liabilities reflected in your net worth, set up a credit card account so that these liabilities appear in Net Worth or Balance Sheet reports.

In this chapter, you learn how to do the following:

- Set up a credit card account

- Track credit card activity in a credit card account

- Reconcile your credit card account

- Pay your credit card bills

- Set up an IntelliCharge account

- Update your IntelliCharge account with statements received on disk or by modem

Using a Credit Card Account

If you always pay your credit card in full every month, you do not need to use the Credit Card Register, unless you want to track exactly where and when charges are made. You don't need to use the Credit Card Register because you usually can record the details of your credit card spending when you record the check payment to the credit card company. Also, because the credit card balance always is reduced to zero every month, you do not need to keep track of the balance.

The steps involved in using the Credit Card Register to perform record-keeping for your credit cards parallel the steps for using any other Register: set up an account, enter transactions, and then reconcile the account.

Setting Up a Credit Card Account

First, you set up the account and record the beginning balance. (Because you are working with a liability, the beginning balance is what you owe.)

To set up a credit card account, follow these steps:

1. Choose the **Select Account** option from Quicken's main menu. Quicken displays the Select Account to Use window shown in figure 11.1.

2. To add a new credit card account, select **<New Account>** from the Select Account to Use window. Quicken then displays the Set Up New Account window shown in figure 11.2.

3. With the cursor in the Account Type field, press 2 to select the Credit Card account type.

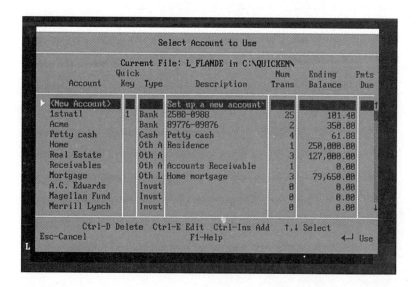

Select Account to Use						
Current File: L_FLANDE in C:\QUICKEN\						
Account	Quick Key	Type	Description	Num Trans	Ending Balance	Pmts Due
<New Account>			Set up a new account			
1stnatl	1	Bank	2500-0988	25	101.40	
Acme		Bank	89776-09876	2	350.00	
Petty cash		Cash	Petty cash	4	61.88	
Home		Oth A	Residence	1	250,000.00	
Real Estate		Oth A		3	127,000.00	
Receivables		Oth A	Accounts Receivable	1	0.00	
Mortgage		Oth L	Home mortgage	3	79,650.00	
A.G. Edwards		Invst		0	0.00	
Magellan Fund		Invst		0	0.00	
Merrill Lynch		Invst		0	0.00	

Ctrl-D Delete   Ctrl-E Edit   Ctrl-Ins Add   ↑,↓ Select
Esc-Cancel   F1-Help   ↵ Use

FIG. 11.1

The Select Account to Use window.

4. Press Enter or Tab to move the cursor to the Name for This Account field. Enter the name of the credit card, such as MasterCard, VISA, Discover, and so on. The Name for This Account field can contain up to 15 characters, and you can use any character except the following:

   [ ] / :

   You can include spaces.

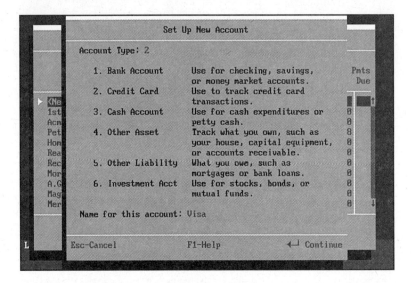

FIG. 11.2

The Set Up New
Account window.

5. Press Ctrl-Enter or F10 to display the Starting Balance and Description window shown in figure 11.3.

6. With the cursor in the Balance field, enter the outstanding credit
   card balance as of the date you are setting up the credit card account. If the credit card balance is zero, you must enter *0* in the
   Balance field (you cannot leave the Balance field blank).

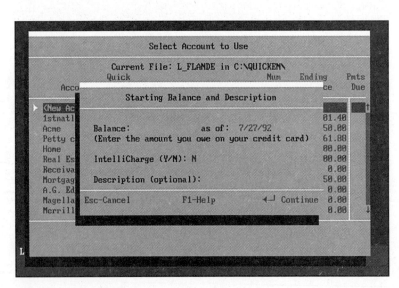

FIG. 11.3

The Starting
Balance and
Description
window.

7. Press Enter or Tab to move the cursor to the As of field. Enter the date on which the balance you entered is correct.

8. (Optional) If you use Quicken's VISA card and want to set up the credit card account to receive statements by disk or modem, press Y from the IntelliCharge field. Refer to "Using the IntelliCharge Account," later in this chapter, to learn more about setting up IntelliCharge accounts.

9. (Optional) Press Enter or Tab to move the cursor to the Description field. Fill in the Description field to provide an additional 21 characters of account description. Here, you may want to enter the credit card account number.

10. Press Ctrl-Enter when the Starting Balance and Description window is complete.

11. Quicken next displays the Specify Credit Limit window and asks for the credit limit on your card (see fig. 11.4). Enter your credit limit, if desired, and press Enter.

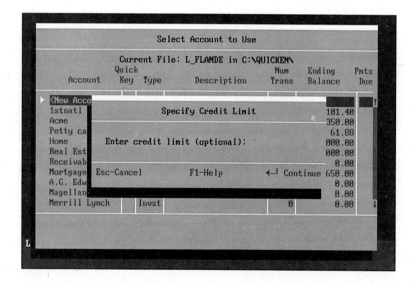

FIG. 11.4

The Specify Credit Limit window.

When you finish entering information for the new credit card account, Quicken adds the account to the Select Account to Use window.

Tracking Credit Card Activity

To track your credit card activity, you simply enter all credit card transactions into your Credit Card Register. Credit card purchases are entered directly into your credit card account. Credit card payments are entered into the Bank Account Register that you use to pay bills when you reconcile your credit card statement.

As with the Other Asset and Liability Registers, some minor differences exist between the Bank Account Register and menu options and the Credit Card Register and menu options. The Charge field in the Credit Card Register is where you record each use of your credit card. The Payment field is where payments to the credit card company are recorded. If you fill in the Credit Limit field when you set up the credit card account, Quicken shows the credit remaining in the lower right corner of the screen above the Ending Balance field. Figure 11.5 shows the Credit Card Register.

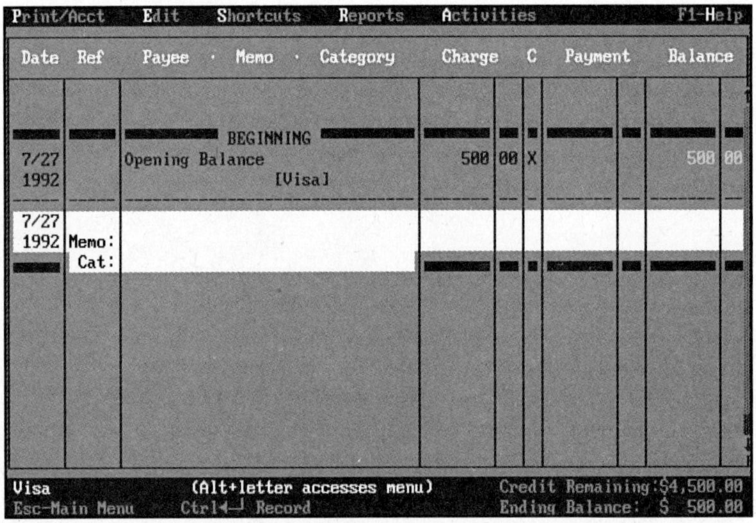

FIG. 11.5

The Credit Card Register.

Enter credit card transactions the same way that you enter transactions in the Bank Account Register. Refer to Chapters 4 and 5 to review the techniques for entering transactions into the Bank Account Register.

If your credit card allows for cash advances, don't make the mistake of assuming that the cash you receive avoids interest charges for 30 days. Cash advances begin accruing interest on the day the cash is advanced to you. If you are in a bind for cash, take out the cash advance, but pay it back as soon as possible to avoid excessive interest charges.

If you receive a cash advance from your credit card, record the advance in the Charge field. If you also use a cash account to track your cash expenditures (as explained in Chapter 10), enter the name of that account in the Category field for the transaction. Then, the cash advance that you receive also is entered in your cash account.

C P A
T I P

Reconciling Your Credit Card Account

When you receive your credit card statement each month, you should review it carefully to make sure that you have entered all credit purchases in the Credit Card Register. It is also a good idea to review your statement in order to uncover unauthorized uses of your credit card. You may find that the statement contains credit purchases that you or your spouse did not make.

Before you pay your credit card bill, you should reconcile your statement balance with the balance in your Quicken Credit Card Register. After you successfully reconcile your credit card statement, Quicken gives you the option of paying the entire credit card account balance or making a partial payment.

To reconcile your credit card account, follow these steps:

1. From the Credit Card Register, press Alt-A to access the Activities menu shown in figure 11.6.

2. From the Activities menu, select the **Reconcile/Pay Credit Card** option. Quicken displays the Credit Card Statement Information window shown in figure 11.7.

3. Enter the charges plus cash advances shown on your statement in the Charges, Cash Advances field and press Enter.

4. In the Payments, Credits field, enter the amount of payments plus credits shown on your credit card statement and press Enter.

5. In the New Balance field, type the balance due as shown on your credit card statement and press Enter. This is the balance due after charges plus cash advances, minus payments plus credits.

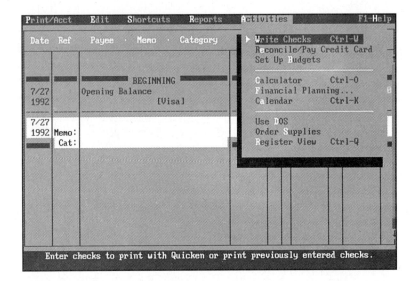

FIG. 11.6

The Activities menu.

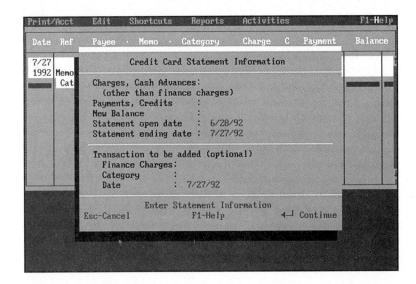

FIG. 11.7

The Credit Card Statement Information window.

6. In the Statement Open Date field, type the opening date on the credit card statement and press Enter.

7. In the Statement Ending Date field, type the closing date on the credit card statement and press Enter.

8. (Optional) In the Transactions to be Added section of the Credit Card Statement Information window, enter any finance charges

that appear on your credit card statement in the Finance Charges field. Quicken will enter a credit card transaction in your Credit Card Register for finance charges.

9. Press Enter to move to the Category field and enter the category that you want to assign to the finance charge transaction that Quicken enters, like *Int Exp* (for *interest expense*). Press Enter.

   You can press Ctrl-C to display the Category and Transfer list to select a category from the list. Quicken's new QuickFill feature also works from the Category field when you type the first few characters of the category name (see Chapter 5 for more information on QuickFill).

> Avoid credit card interest and finance charges. With the Tax Reform Act of 1986, deductions for consumer or personal interest are no longer allowed for federal and most state income tax returns. What's more, credit card annual interest rates are usually 18 percent to 21 percent (or if you are considered a high risk, even more). Consequently, with the lost tax deduction and high interest costs, carrying credit card balances that accrue interest doesn't make sense.
>
> **C P A**
> **T I P**

10. Enter the date that the finance charges were charged to your credit card account in the Date field.

11. When the Credit Card Statement Information window is complete, press Ctrl-Enter to continue with the reconciliation.

    Quicken displays the Transaction List window, which shows each credit card account transaction (see fig. 11.8).

12. Mark charges and payments that have *cleared* (were recorded by) the credit card company. To mark an item as cleared, use the up- and down-arrow keys to highlight the transaction you want to mark. Press Enter to mark the highlighted transaction as cleared and move to the next transaction. Quicken enters an asterisk in the cleared column. To unmark a transaction, highlight the transaction that you want to unmark, and press the space bar to remove the asterisk.

    To mark a range of transactions as cleared, press F8. The Mark Range of Dates as Cleared window appears. You use this window to specify that all transactions with dates within the indicated range should be marked as cleared.

As you mark transactions, the Reconciliation Summary in the Transactions List window shows the number and dollar amount of the charge and payment transactions you marked as cleared, the cleared transaction total, the statement balance, and the difference between the two. You are finished with the reconciliation when the difference between the Cleared Balance and the Statement Balance equals zero.

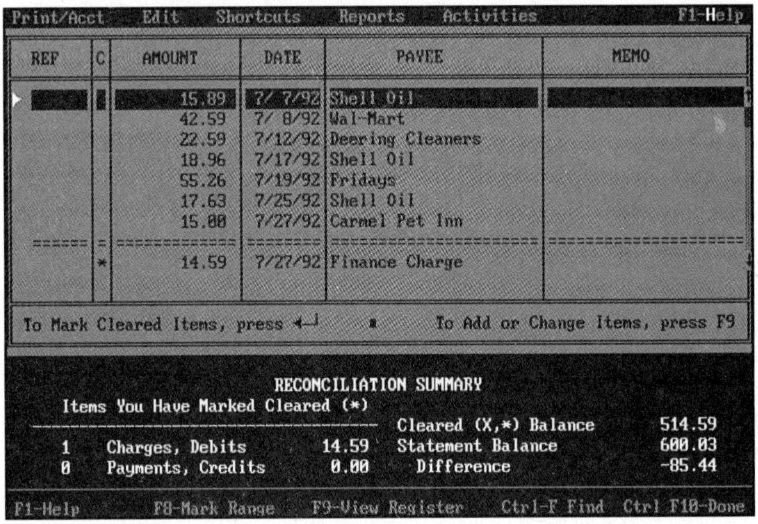

FIG. 11.8

Credit card account transactions shown in a list.

```
Print/Acct    Edit    Shortcuts    Reports    Activities              F1-Help

 REF   C    AMOUNT      DATE          PAYEE                   MEMO

             15.89   7/ 7/92 Shell Oil
             42.59   7/ 8/92 Wal-Mart
             22.59   7/12/92 Deering Cleaners
             18.96   7/17/92 Shell Oil
             55.26   7/19/92 Fridays
             17.63   7/25/92 Shell Oil
             15.00   7/27/92 Carmel Pet Inn
======  = ============= ========                     ===========================
        *    14.59   7/27/92 Finance Charge

To Mark Cleared Items, press ←┘      ■    To Add or Change Items, press F9

                         RECONCILIATION SUMMARY
      Items You Have Marked Cleared (*)
      ───────────────────────────────────── Cleared (X,*) Balance    514.59
        1     Charges, Debits      14.59   Statement Balance        600.03
        0     Payments, Credits     0.00    Difference              -85.44

F1-Help        F8-Mark Range    F9-View Register    Ctrl-F Find   Ctrl F10-Done
```

13. (Optional) To correct transactions you entered incorrectly in the Credit Card Register, press F9 to redisplay the same information in an abbreviated form of the standard Register. Edit the transactions in the Register in the usual manner. To change the screen back to the Transaction list, press F9 again.

14. When the difference between the Cleared Balance and the Statement Balance is zero, press Ctrl-F10 to indicate that you are finished with the reconciliation. Quicken displays the Make Credit Card Payment window shown in figure 11.9. The next section explains how to pay your credit card bill after you have reconciled your credit card statement.

If the difference does not equal zero and you press Ctrl-F10 to complete the reconciliation, Quicken displays an Adjusting Register To Agree with Statement window. To accept Quicken's adjustments, enter a category to assign to the adjustment transaction in the Category field and press Enter. To cancel, press Esc.

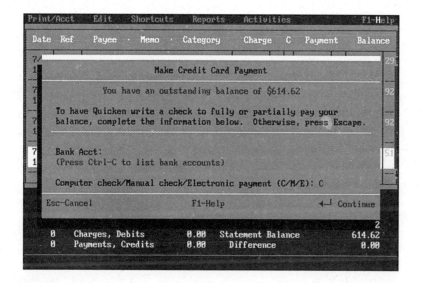

FIG. 11.9

The Make Credit Card Payment window.

NOTE Chapter 8 gives tips on finding and correcting reconciliation errors for a bank account. These tips also apply to reconciling a credit card statement.

You can leave the reconciliation process at any time (even when the difference between the cleared balance and the statement balance *is not* zero, by pressing Esc. When you press Esc, Quicken displays the Reconciliation is Not Complete window. Press 2 to select the **Leave reconciliation (your work will be saved)** option. Quicken then returns to the Credit Card Register. Any work you have done (entering balances, finance charges, marking transactions, and so on) is saved so that when you return to the reconciliation you can proceed from the point you left.

If you don't want to leave the reconciliation after you've pressed Esc, just press Enter to select the **Proceed to next reconciliation step** option.

Balancing your credit card account keeps you alert to unauthorized credit transactions. Your credit card number can be used for purchases made by telephone because no signature is required. All that an unauthorized user needs is your account number, expiration date, and your current address to make a credit purchase by telephone.

**C P A
T I P**

If you do not monitor your credit card statements on a timely basis, you may not be aware of violated usage until several thousands of dollars have been charged. Most credit card companies protect you against unauthorized credit transactions. You must inform them within a certain time period for their safeguards to take effect, however.

Paying Your Credit Card Bill

Now that you've reconciled your credit card statement, you're ready to pay your credit card bill. You can choose to pay the entire balance, to make a partial payment, or to pay nothing at all.

To pay your credit card bill, follow these steps:

1. From the Make Credit Card Payment window shown in figure 11.9, in the Bank Acct field, enter the bank account that you want to use to pay your credit card bill. Press Ctrl-C to display the Account list that you see in figure 11.10. Use the up- and down-arrow keys to highlight the bank account that you want to use to pay your credit card bill and press Enter to select the account. Quicken returns to the Make Credit Card Payment window.

    NOTE   If you don't want to pay your credit card bill, press Esc from the Make Credit Card Payment window. Quicken returns to the Credit Card Register.

2. Move the cursor to the Computer Check/Manual Check/Electronic Payment field. Press C if you want to write a check at the Write Checks screen and print a check using Quicken. Press M if you want to write a manual check and have Quicken enter the check transaction in the Register, or press E to pay your credit card bill electronically through CheckFree (see Chapter 13 to learn how to make electronic payments through CheckFree).

3. Press Ctrl-Enter or F10. If you selected to write a computer check, Quicken displays the Write Checks screen and fills in the check with the outstanding balance amount in the Amount field and the category that you assigned in the Category field. You fill in the credit card company name in the Payee field.

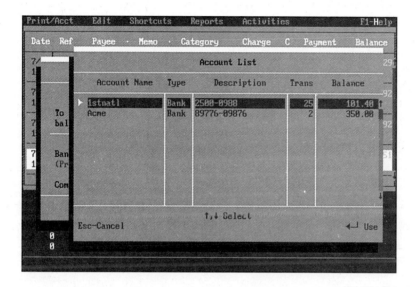

FIG. 11.10

The Account list.

If you want to make a partial payment instead of paying the outstanding balance, move to the Amount field and change the amount to whatever you want to pay. Press Ctrl-Enter or F10 to record the check in the Write Checks screen.

If you selected to write a manual check, Quicken displays the Register and fills in the transaction with the outstanding balance amount in the Payment field and the category that you assigned in the Category field.

If you want to make a partial payment instead of paying the outstanding balance, move to the Payment field and change the amount to the amount you want to pay. Press Ctrl-Enter or F10 to record the transaction in the Register.

If you selected to pay your credit card bill electronically, Quicken displays the Write Checks screen and fills in the outstanding balance in the Amount field and the category that you assigned to the transaction in the Category field. As with computer checks, you can change the Amount field to make a partial payment instead of paying the outstanding balance. Press Ctrl-Enter or F10 to record the electronic check in the Write Checks screen.

Using the IntelliCharge Account

IntelliCharge is a service that you can use in Quicken 6.0 to track your Quicken VISA card activity. (If you don't have a Quicken VISA card, don't set up an IntelliCharge account; IntelliCharge accounts only work with Quicken credit cards.) With IntelliCharge, you receive your monthly credit card statements on disk or by modem. With your credit card statement on disk or downloaded by modem, your credit card activity is instantly recorded in your IntelliCharge account. Credit transactions are not only recorded, but also are assigned automatically to categories according to Intuit's standard credit card category list.

Setting Up an IntelliCharge Account

Before you can begin using IntelliCharge to record your credit card transactions, you must set up a credit card account as an IntelliCharge account. Setting up an IntelliCharge account is similar to setting up a regular credit card account.

To set up an IntelliCharge account, follow these steps:

1. Choose the **Select Account** option from Quicken's main menu. Quicken displays the Select Account to Use window.

2. To add a new credit card account, select **<New Account>** from the Select Account to Use window. Quicken then displays the Set Up New Account window.

3. With the cursor in the Account Type field, press 2 to select the Credit Card account type.

4. Press Enter or Tab to move the cursor to the Name for This Account field. Enter the name of the credit card, like Quicken VISA, Quicken, or just VISA. The Name for This Account field can contain up to 15 characters, and you can use any character except the following:

   [ ] / :

   You can include spaces.

5. Press Ctrl-Enter or F10 to display the Starting Balance and Description window.

6. In the Balance field, enter zero (0). Enter zero even if you have an outstanding credit card balance.

7. Move to the As Of field and enter the date that you are setting up your IntelliCharge account.

8. Move to the IntelliCharge field and press Y to set up the credit card account as an IntelliCharge account.

9. When you press Y in the IntelliCharge field, Quicken changes the Description field in the Starting Balance and Description window to the Account Number field. Move to the Account Number field

and enter the account number of your Quicken VISA card (enter the 16-digit account number). Make sure that you enter the correct account number from your card or your latest Quicken VISA statement.

10. When the Starting Balance and Description window is complete, press Ctrl-Enter or F10.

    Quicken next displays the IntelliCharge Account Information window shown in figure 11.11.

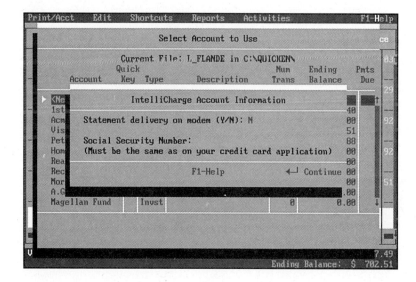

11. In the Statement Delivery on Modem field, press Y if you want to download your Quicken VISA statements by modem. Leave the setting at N if you want to receive your statements on disk. Press Enter.

12. Enter your Social Security number in the Social Security Number field and press Enter. Make sure that this is the same number that you entered when you filled out your Quicken VISA application.

13. If you chose to receive your statements on disk, skip to step 17. If you chose to receive your statements by modem, Quicken displays the IntelliCharge Phone Number and Password window shown in figure 11.12.

14. In the Enter the IntelliCharge Phone Number field, enter the local access number for the CompuServe network through which IntelliCharge downloads your statements. Press Enter. If you don't have this number, call 1-800-848-8980 and press 2 at the prompt.

The system will ask for the speed of your modem and your telephone number (from which you are calling). The system then gives you the CompuServe network number nearest you.

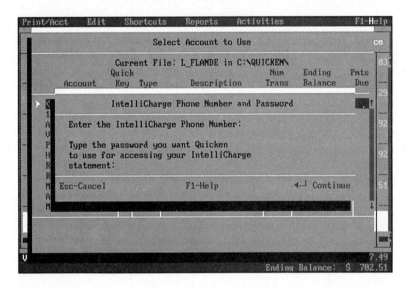

FIG. 11.12

The IntelliCharge
Phone Number
and Password
window.

NOTE   You do not have to have a CompuServe membership in order to use IntelliCharge.

15. (Optional) Move to the Type the Password... field and enter a password to prevent unauthorized access to your Quicken VISA statement file. Passwords can be eight characters in length, but must include at least four, nonblank characters.

16. When the IntelliCharge Phone Number and Password window is complete, press Ctrl-Enter. Quicken displays the Specify Credit Limit window.

17. Enter your Quicken VISA card limit, if desired, and press Enter. If you don't want to enter your limit, press Enter to continue.

Quicken adds your IntelliCharge account to the Select Account to Use window.

Converting a Credit Card Account to IntelliCharge

If you already have a credit card account set up in Quicken for your Quicken VISA card, you will need to convert the account to an IntelliCharge account if you want to receive your statements on disk or downloaded by modem. You may remember that in previous versions of Quicken, IntelliCharge imported transactions into the Register with asterisks (*) in the C (Cleared) field. You then had to use the **Reconcile** option to mark the transactions that appeared on your statement as cleared. In Quicken 6.0, once you convert your regular credit card account to an IntelliCharge account, transactions are reconciled as they are imported into the Register, with an X in the C (Cleared) field.

To convert a regular credit card account to an IntelliCharge account, follow these steps:

1. Choose the **Select Account** option from Quicken's main menu. Quicken displays the Select Account to Use window.

2. Use the up- and down-arrow keys to highlight the regular credit card account that you want to convert to an IntelliCharge account and press Ctrl-E.

   Quicken displays the Edit Account Information window shown in figure 11.13.

3. Move to the IntelliCharge field and press Y.

4. When you change the IntelliCharge field to Y, Quicken replaces the Description field with the Account Number field. If you had not entered your Quicken VISA card account number in the Description field before, enter the account number of your Quicken VISA card (enter the 16-digit account number) in the Account Number field. Make sure that you enter the correct account number from your card or your latest Quicken VISA statement.

5. Press Ctrl-Enter or F10. Quicken displays the IntelliCharge Account Information window.

6. Follow steps 11 through 17 in the preceding section to complete the IntelliCharge Account Information window and subsequent windows.

When you update your new IntelliCharge account the first time, the asterisks (*) in the C (Cleared) field of any old transactions will be changed to Xs.

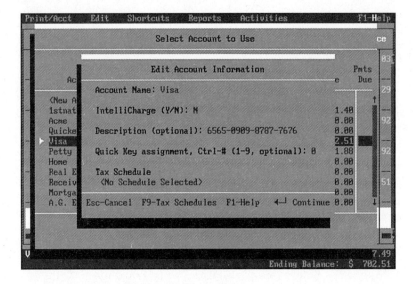

FIG. 11.13

The Edit Account
Information
window.

Updating Your IntelliCharge
Credit Card Account

Updating your IntelliCharge credit card account is the same as entering credit card transactions in a regular credit card account, except that IntelliCharge enters the transactions for you, either from a disk file or by modem. Every month, Intuit sends you your Quicken VISA card statement. If you choose to receive your statements on disk, Intuit mails a disk or file that contains your credit card activity (credit card purchases, cash advances, finance charges, credit, and payments) during the current statement period. If you choose to download your statement information by modem, Intuit makes an electronic statement available each month for you to download by modem to your Quicken system. After credit card transactions from the IntelliCharge statement are read by Quicken, they are displayed in the IntelliCharge Statement window so that you can review them and mark any transactions for edit or further review in the Register. After your review, transactions are recorded in the Credit Card Register.

The following sections explain how to receive your Quicken VISA card statements on disk and by modem, how to review transactions in the IntelliCharge Statement window, and how to record credit card transactions in the Register.

Receiving Your Statement on Disk

The disk file that Intuit sends you each month contains the current period activity for your Quicken VISA card. Information included in the disk file includes current credit purchases, cash advances, finance charges, credits, and payments. Normally, you enter these transactions yourself in the Credit Card Register. When you receive this information on disk, however, you quickly can import the credit card transactions into your IntelliCharge credit card account.

To receive your statement on disk and update your IntelliCharge account, follow these steps:

1. Access the Register for your IntelliCharge credit card account.

2. Press Alt-A to display the Activities menu.

3. Select the **Get IntelliCharge Data** option from the Activities menu. Quicken displays the Get IntelliCharge Data window (see fig. 11.14).

4. Insert the disk that contains your Quicken VISA card statement file into drive A or B.

5. In the Statement Disk Drive field, type the drive that you inserted your disk into (A or B) and press Enter. Quicken displays the Updating Account window. Each of your credit card transactions are displayed as Quicken reads them from the disk. You cannot make changes to any of these transactions as they are being read from the disk. After the transactions are entered in the IntelliCharge Statement window, however, you can review them and mark transactions that you want to edit (you can edit them after they are recorded in the Credit Card Register).

6. As you learn later in this chapter, IntelliCharge assigns categories to your credit card transactions. If IntelliCharge determines that a category should be assigned to a transaction that you do not have set up in the Category and Transfer list, you are given the following options:

   Option 1: Add it to the Category List

   Option 2: Select from Category List

   If you select option 1, Quicken displays the Set Up Category window so that you can enter the information for the new category. If you select option 2, Quicken displays the Category and Transfer list so that you can select another category to assign to the transaction.

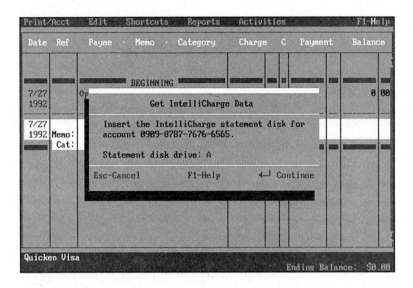

FIG. 11.14

The Get
IntelliCharge
Data window.

7. After all credit card transactions are read from the disk file,
    Quicken displays the IntelliCharge Statement window that shows
    the date, payee, amount, and category for each credit card trans-
    action.

The next step in updating your IntelliCharge account is to review all the
transactions in the IntelliCharge Statement window to make sure that
they match your records and that the category assigned to each transaction is appropriate. See the section "Reviewing Credit Card Transactions," later in this chapter, for more information on reviewing the
transactions in the IntelliCharge Statement window.

Receiving Your Statement by Modem

Receiving your Quicken VISA card statement by modem is similar to
receiving your statement on disk, except that you download the statement file instead of manually inserting a disk file into your computer's
disk drive. The file that you download contains the current period
activity for your Quicken VISA card. Information included in the file
includes current credit purchases, cash advances, finance charges,
credits, and payments. Normally, you enter these transactions yourself
in the Credit Card Register. When you download this information, however, you quickly can import the credit card transactions into your
IntelliCharge credit card account.

To receive your statement by modem and update your IntelliCharge account, follow these steps:

1. Access the Register for your IntelliCharge credit card account.

2. Press Alt-A to display the Activities menu.

3. Select the **Get IntelliCharge Data** option from the Activities menu. Quicken displays the Get IntelliCharge Data window as shown in figure 11.15.

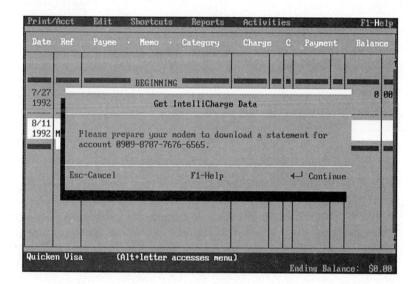

FIG. 11.15

The Get IntelliCharge Data window.

4. Turn on your modem and make sure that your telephone line is plugged in. Press Enter to initialize your modem and download your statement file.

5. Quicken displays the Updating Account window. Each of your credit card transactions is displayed as Quicken reads them from the downloaded file. You cannot make changes to any of these transactions as they are being downloaded from the disk. After the transactions are entered in the IntelliCharge Statement window, however, you can review them and mark transactions that you want to edit (you can edit them after they are recorded in the Credit Card Register).

6. As you learn later in this chapter, IntelliCharge assigns categories to your credit card transactions. If IntelliCharge determines that a category should be assigned to a transaction that you do not have set up in the Category and Transfer list, you are given the following options:

Option 1: Add it to the Category List

Option 2: Select from Category List

If you select option 1, Quicken displays the Set Up Category window so that you can enter the information for the new category. If you select option 2, Quicken displays the Category and Transfer list so that you can select another category to assign to the transaction.

7. After all credit card transactions are read from the downloaded file, Quicken displays the IntelliCharge Statement window that shows the date, payee, amount, and category for each credit card transaction.

The next step in updating your IntelliCharge account is to review all the transactions in the IntelliCharge Statement window to make sure that they match your records and that the category assigned to each transaction is appropriate. See the next section for more information on reviewing the transactions in the IntelliCharge Statement window.

Reviewing Credit Card Transactions

After you receive your IntelliCharge statement, whether on disk or by modem, you need to review your credit card transactions to make sure that they match your records and that the categories assigned by IntelliCharge are appropriate. You can review credit card transactions in the IntelliCharge Statement window, which is displayed after transactions are read from the disk file or the downloaded file.

From the IntelliCharge Statement window, you can mark items for further review. When you mark a transaction for further review, Quicken places five question marks (?????) in the Ref field of the transaction in the Credit Card Register. To mark a transaction for further review, use the up- and down-arrow keys to highlight the transaction and mark it in the IntelliCharge Statement window and press the space bar. Press the space bar again to unmark the transaction.

IntelliCharge assigned categories to your credit card transactions according to Intuit's standard Credit Card Category list (see the section "Assigning Categories to IntelliCharge Transactions," later in this chapter, for more information on how IntelliCharge assigns categories). You can change the category that IntelliCharge assigned to a transaction in the IntelliCharge Statement window. To change the category, use the up- and down-arrow keys to highlight the transaction with the category you want to change and press Ctrl-C. Quicken displays the Category and Transfer list that you can use to select a category for the credit card transaction.

To delete a category assigned to a transaction, use the up- and down-arrow keys to highlight the transaction with the category you want to delete and press Ctrl-D.

Recording Credit Card Transactions in the Register

When you are finished reviewing the credit card transactions in the IntelliCharge Statement window, you're ready to record the transactions in the Credit Card Register.

To record the credit card transactions, press Ctrl-Enter. Quicken records the transactions in the Credit Card Register and displays the Make Credit Card Payment window. Follow the steps in the section "Reconciling Your Credit Card Account" to complete the Make Credit Card Payment window and pay your Quicken credit card bill. If you don't want to make a credit card payment at this time, press Esc.

> **NOTE** If a transaction appears in your IntelliCharge statement that does not match your records, you can dispute the item by contacting Primerica Bank immediately (800-772-2221). You also must notify the bank, in writing, of any disputed item.
>
> Mark disputed items in the IntelliCharge Statement window. After you record the credit card transactions from the IntelliCharge Statement window to your Credit Card Register, use the Find feature (Ctrl-F) to locate the disputed transaction in the Register. Quicken inserts five question marks (?????) in the Ref field of marked transactions, so you can use ????? as your search argument in the Num field (this corresponds to the Ref field in a Credit Card Register) of the Transaction to Find window.

Assigning Categories to IntelliCharge Transactions

This section explains how IntelliCharge assigns categories to your credit card transactions. Because you don't assign the categories yourself, you should understand how IntelliCharge assigns categories.

The first time that you use IntelliCharge to update your credit card account, transactions are categorized by IntelliCharge according to Intuit's standard Credit Card Category list. (The standard Credit Card Category list is contained in the file INTELLIC.CAT on your Quicken 6.0

program disks and copied to your hard disk when you install Quicken.) After the first time you update your credit card account, if you change any of the assigned categories (by pressing Ctrl-C from the IntelliCharge Statement window), IntelliCharge learns how you prefer your transactions to be categorized by scanning the Credit Card Register. IntelliCharge looks for a payee that matches the payee in the transaction in the current statement. When it finds a matching payee, it assigns the category assigned to the previous transaction (the one you changed) to the current transaction. IntelliCharge copies the category from the most recent transaction with a matching payee.

If IntelliCharge finds a matching payee in a split transaction, it copies the category information from the first line in the Split Transaction window.

If IntelliCharge does not find a matching payee in the Credit Card Register, it assigns a category to the new credit card transaction from its own list of credit card categories.

 NOTE Remember that you can change the category that IntelliCharge assigns to a credit card transaction by highlighting the transaction in the IntelliCharge Statement window and pressing Ctrl-C to display the Category and Transfer list.

Chapter Summary

In this chapter you learned how to use Quicken's credit card accounts to manage your credit card activity. You learned how to set up a credit card account, how to enter credit transactions, and how to reconcile your credit card account and pay your credit card bill. You also learned about Quicken 6.0's new IntelliCharge account, how to receive your IntelliCharge statements on disk or by modem, and how to review and categorize IntelliCharge transactions.

The next chapter shows you how to create and print Quicken reports. All of the work that you've done so far in Quicken is meaningless unless you create reports that show you the results of your work. Quicken provides you with several types of reports that can help you assess your financial condition.

Creating and Printing Reports

When you collect information about your finances in a Quicken file, you essentially construct a database. With a database, you retrieve and summarize the information that database contains. With a financial database, you can determine your cash flows, net income or loss, tax deductions, and net worth. You do need a way to arrange, retrieve and summarize the data, however, and within Quicken, this need is met with the variety of reports that the program provides.

This chapter describes the nine report options available from the Reports menu. You access the Reports menu by selecting **Create Reports** from the main menu or **Reports** from the Activities menu at any Register or the Write Checks screen. Figure 12.1 shows the Reports menu.

The first three options on the Reports menu display menus of different types of reports that you can create. Figure 12.2 shows the Personal Reports menu. Figure 12.3 shows the Business Reports menu. Figure 12.4 shows the Investment Reports menu.

The fourth option, **Memorized Reports**, enables you to memorize reports that you have created so that you can easily go back and regenerate the report again. The next four options on the Reports menu enable you to create custom reports, as discussed later in the section "Creating Custom Reports."

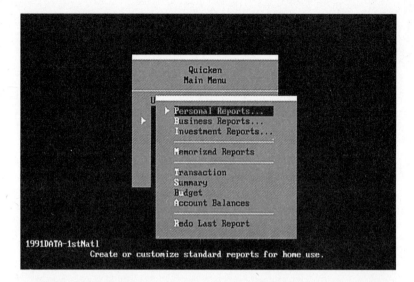

FIG. 12.1

The Reports menu.

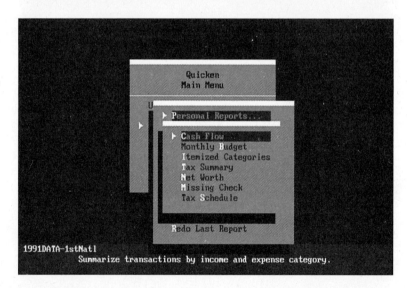

FIG. 12.2

The Personal Reports menu.

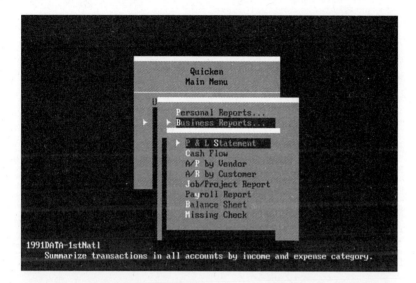

FIG. 12.3

The Business
Reports menu.

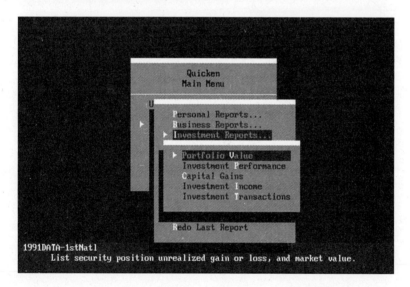

FIG. 12.4

The Investment
Reports menu.

The last option from the Reports menu, **Redo Last Report** (new to Quicken 6.0) enables you to regenerate the last report you created.

In this chapter, you learn how to do the following:

- Create and print reports in general

- Create and print each Quicken report

- Use the QuickZoom feature to investigate data in a report

- Redo the last report created

- Edit reports by changing titles, accounts used in reports, and the categories or transactions covered by reports

- Change the layout of reports

- Memorize reports

- Create customized reports

- Print reports to a disk file

Reviewing Report Printing Basics

No matter which Quicken report you want to print, you need to take the same basic steps. To print any report, you complete the following steps:

1. Select the **Create Reports** option from Quicken's main menu. Quicken displays the Reports menu. You also can access the Reports menu by pressing Alt-R from any Register or the Write Checks screen.

2. From the Reports menu, select the menu option for the report you want to print. If, for example, you want to print a personal cash flow report, select the **Personal Reports** option from the Reports menu. If you want to print a profit and loss statement, select the **Business Reports** option.

   When you select the **Personal Reports**, **Business Reports**, or **Investment Reports** option from the Reports menu, Quicken displays a second menu that lists the types of reports you can print. If you select the **Personal Reports** option, for example, Quicken displays the Personal Reports menu shown in figure 12.2. From this second menu, use the up- and down-arrow keys to highlight the report that you want to print and press Enter.

3. Quicken displays the window you use to create the report. The Cash Flow Report window is shown in figure 12.5, but this window closely resembles other windows that you use to print several of the reports. (Later in this chapter, you learn how to complete the individual report window for each separate report.)

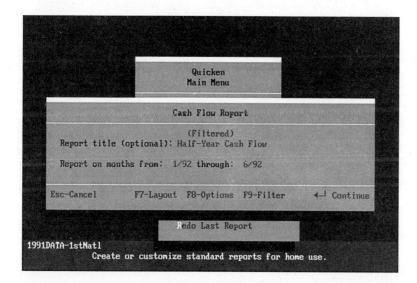

4. (Optional) Enter a report title.

   If you don't enter a report title, Quicken names the report using the menu option. The report produced when you select the **Cash Flow** option, for example, is named *Cash Flow Report*. The report created when you select the **Monthly Budget** option is named *Monthly Budget Report*.

5. (Optional) Press Enter or Tab to move the cursor to the Report on Months From and Through fields. Set up the time frame the report should cover by entering the starting month and year and the ending month and year you want included in the report. If you don't enter these dates, the report covers January of the current year through the current month. (Remember that you can use the special date-editing keys described in Chapter 2 to change dates.)

6. Press Ctrl-Enter or F10. Quicken creates the report that you selected and displays it on your screen.

   You can use the cursor-movement keys to see different portions of the report. You also can use the Home and End keys to see the first and last pages of the report. Or, you can use the mouse to scroll through the report by clicking the vertical or horizontal scroll bar. (See Chapter 2, "Getting Around in Quicken," to learn how to use a mouse to scroll report screens.)

7. When you are ready to print the report, press Ctrl-P. Quicken displays the Print Report window shown in figure 12.6. This window enables you to specify where you want the report printed.

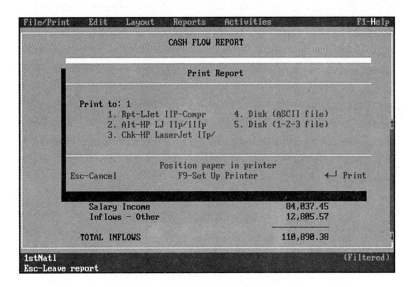

FIG. 12.6

The Print Report window.

8. In the Print To field, press 1 for printer 1, 2 for printer 2, and so on. If you select printer 1, 2, or 3 in the Print Report window, press Ctrl-Enter or F10 to begin printing the report.

NOTE Once you have created a report and the report is displayed on your screen, you can remove the report without printing it by pressing Esc. Quicken returns to the report window.

If you select 4 in the Print To field, Quicken prints an ASCII file. *ASCII files* are standardized text files that you can use to import a Quicken report into a word processing program, such as WordPerfect or Microsoft Word. Before creating the ASCII file, Quicken uses the Print To Disk window to request three pieces of information (see fig. 12.7).

Complete the following steps in the Print to Disk window:

1. (Optional) In the DOS File field, enter a name for Quicken to use for the ASCII file. To use a data directory other than the Quicken data directory, QUICKEN, you can specify a path name. (See your DOS users' manual for information on path names.)

2. (Optional) In the Lines Per Page field, set the number of report lines between page breaks. If you are using 11-inch paper, the page length usually is 66 lines.

3. (Optional) In the Width field, set the number of characters (including blanks) that Quicken prints on a line. If you are using 8 1/2-inch paper, the characters-per-line setting usually is 80. Figure 12.7 shows the completed Print To Disk window with the file name CASHFL.TXT. Press Ctrl-Enter or F10 from the Print to Disk window to begin printing the selected report to the disk file that you specified.

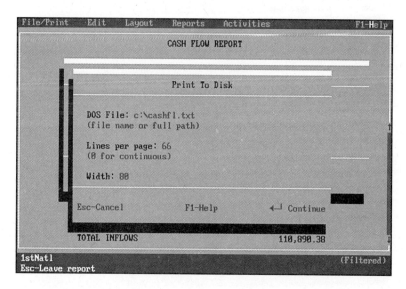

FIG. 12.7

The completed
Print To Disk
window.

If you press 5 to select the **Disk (1-2-3 file)** option from the Print To field in the Print Report window, Quicken displays the Print to Lotus File window. (1-2-3 is a popular spreadsheet program published by Lotus Development Corporation.) You need to complete one more step.

To create a 1-2-3 file, Quicken requests the name of the file you want to create using the Print to Lotus File window. As with the ASCII file creation option, if you want to use a data directory other than QUICKEN, you can specify a path name. (You don't have to worry about the correct file extension. Quicken adds the extension for you.)

Press Enter from the Print to Lotus File window to begin printing the selected report to the disk file that you specified.

NOTE You can customize all reports that you create to include transactions for certain payees, with certain memos, assigned categories, or classes. This is called *filtering* a report. Press F9 from the report window to access the Filter Transactions window. Filtering reports is explained later in this chapter.

You also can change the appearance of reports by setting report options such as the report organization (income and expense basis or cash-flow basis), whether transfers are included, whether unrealized gains from investment accounts are included, how amounts are displayed (rounded to the nearest dollar or including cents), and so on. Press F8 from the report window to access the Report Options window. You learn how to set report options in the section "Setting Report Options," later in this chapter.

You can change the layout of a report by pressing F7 from the report window to access the Create Summary or Create Transaction Report windows. You can change the report title, date range, row headings, column headings, and the accounts used in the report. Changing the report layout is covered in the section "Changing the Report Layout," later in this chapter.

Tracking Personal Finances with Personal Reports

You can select from seven reports in the Personal Reports menu. To create any of these reports, you need to complete the window that appears when you select a report from the Personal Reports menu.

The Cash Flow Report

Figure 12.8 shows an example of a personal cash flow report. The *cash flow* report shows the total cash inflows and outflows, by category. The personal cash flow report can show transfers to and from other accounts (however, the report in figure 12.8 does not show transfers). The report includes transactions from all the bank, cash, and credit card accounts in the current Quicken file.

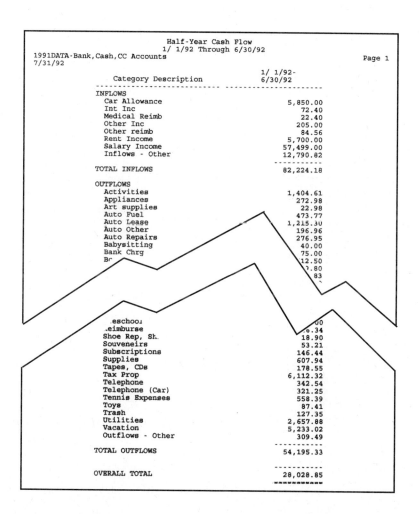

```
                    Half-Year Cash Flow
                  1/ 1/92 Through 6/30/92
 1991DATA-Bank,Cash,CC Accounts                          Page 1
 7/31/92
                                        1/ 1/92-
           Category Description          6/30/92
 ------------------------------   --------------------------
 INFLOWS
     Car Allowance                       5,850.00
     Int Inc                                72.40
     Medical Reimb                          22.40
     Other Inc                             205.00
     Other reimb                            84.56
     Rent Income                         5,700.00
     Salary Income                      57,499.00
     Inflows - Other                    12,790.82
                                        ----------
 TOTAL INFLOWS                          82,224.18

 OUTFLOWS
     Activities                          1,404.61
     Appliances                            272.98
     Art supplies                           22.98
     Auto Fuel                             473.77
     Auto Lease                          1,215.30
     Auto Other                            196.96
     Auto Repairs                          276.95
     Babysitting                            40.00
     Bank Chrg                              75.00
     Br                                     12.50
                                            .80
                                            .83

     .eschool                               .00
     .eimburse                            .34
     Shoe Rep, Sh.                         18.90
     Souveneirs                            53.21
     Subscriptions                        146.44
     Supplies                             607.94
     Tapes, CDs                           178.55
     Tax Prop                           6,112.32
     Telephone                            342.54
     Telephone (Car)                      321.25
     Tennis Expenses                      558.39
     Toys                                  87.41
     Trash                                127.35
     Utilities                          2,657.88
     Vacation                           5,233.02
     Outflows - Other                     309.49
                                        ----------
 TOTAL OUTFLOWS                         54,195.33

                                        ----------
 OVERALL TOTAL                          28,028.85
                                        ==========
```

FIG. 12.8

The personal
cash flow report.

The cash flow report can be extremely valuable. This report shows the various categories of cash flowing into and out of your personal banking accounts, cash accounts, and credit card accounts. If you question why you seem to have a bigger bank balance than usual or you always seem to run out of money before the end of the month, this report provides some answers.

The Monthly Budget Report

The *monthly budget* report shows actual income and expenses and budgeted income and expenses over a specified period. The monthly budget report also shows the comparison between the actual and budgeted amounts and calculates the difference (how much over or under budget you are, by category). This report includes transactions from all the bank, cash, and credit card accounts within the current Quicken file. Figure 12.9 shows the Monthly Budget Report window.

To produce a monthly budget report, you need to have first set up your budget. Refer to Chapter 15, if you need information on setting up a budget. Chapter 15 also shows you an example of a monthly budget report.

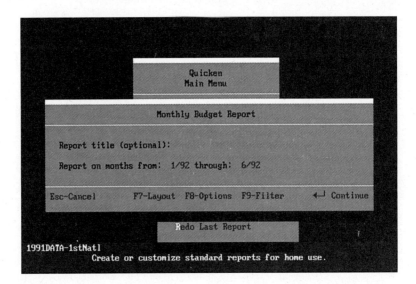

FIG. 12.9

The Monthly Budget Report window.

The Itemized Category Report

The *itemized category* report shows each transaction in the current Quicken file, sorted and subtotaled by category. This type of report provides a convenient way to see the detailed transactions that add up to a category total. The Itemized Category Report window works like the other report windows.

You can replace the default report title, *Itemized Category Report*, with a more specific title, such as *Personal Itemized Category Report*, by using the optional Report Title field. You also can specify a range of months to be included on the report. Figure 12.10 shows part of a sample itemized category report. (The defaults have been changed in this figure to customize the report titles.)

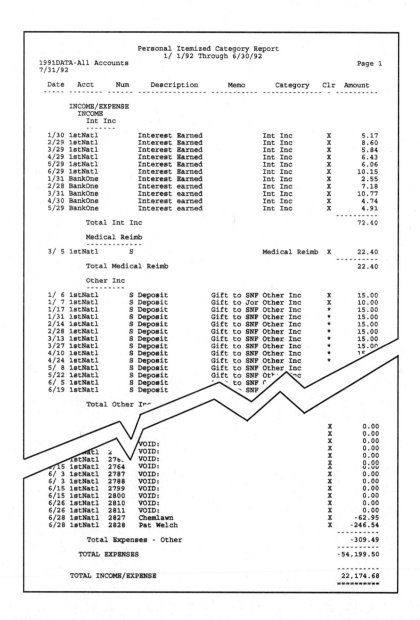

```
                    Personal Itemized Category Report
                        1/ 1/92 Through 6/30/92
    1991DATA-All Accounts                                    Page 1
    7/31/92

    Date  Acct    Num    Description      Memo      Category   Clr  Amount
    ----- ------- -----  -----------      ------    --------   ---  -------

            INCOME/EXPENSE
              INCOME
                Int Inc
                --------
    1/30 1stNatl         Interest Earned            Int Inc    X      5.17
    2/29 1stNatl         Interest Earned            Int Inc    X      8.60
    3/29 1stNatl         Interest Earned            Int Inc    X      5.84
    4/29 1stNatl         Interest Earned            Int Inc    X      6.43
    5/29 1stNatl         Interest Earned            Int Inc    X      6.06
    6/29 1stNatl         Interest Earned            Int Inc    X     10.15
    1/31 BankOne         Interest Earned            Int Inc    X      2.55
    2/28 BankOne         Interest earned            Int Inc    X      7.18
    3/31 BankOne         Interest earned            Int Inc    X     10.77
    4/30 BankOne         Interest earned            Int Inc    X      4.74
    5/29 BankOne         Interest earned            Int Inc    X      4.91
                                                                 ----------
            Total Int Inc                                          72.40

            Medical Reimb
            -------------
    3/ 5 1stNatl       S                     Medical Reimb  X      22.40
                                                                 ----------
            Total Medical Reimb                                  22.40

            Other Inc
            ---------
    1/ 6 1stNatl       S Deposit   Gift to SNF Other Inc   X      15.00
    1/ 7 1stNatl       S Deposit   Gift to Jor Other Inc   X      10.00
    1/17 1stNatl       S Deposit   Gift to SNF Other Inc   *      15.00
    1/31 1stNatl       S Deposit   Gift to SNF Other Inc   *      15.00
    2/14 1stNatl       S Deposit   Gift to SNF Other Inc   *      15.00
    2/28 1stNatl       S Deposit   Gift to SNF Other Inc   *      15.00
    3/13 1stNatl       S Deposit   Gift to SNF Other Inc   *      15.00
    3/27 1stNatl       S Deposit   Gift to SNF Other Inc   *      15.00
    4/10 1stNatl       S Deposit   Gift to SNF Other Inc   *      15.00
    4/24 1stNatl       S Deposit   Gift to SNF Other Inc   *      15
    5/ 8 1stNatl       S Deposit   Gift to SNF Other Inc
    5/22 1stNatl       S Deposit   Gift to SNF Ot
    6/ 5 1stNatl       S Deposit        to SNF
    6/19 1stNatl       S Deposit           SNF

            Total Other In


                                                    X       0.00
                                                    X       0.00
                                                    X       0.00
                                                    X       0.00
                 atl   2      VOID:                 X       0.00
            1stNatl  276     VOID:                  X       0.00
    /15 1stNatl  2764    VOID:                      X       0.00
    6/ 3 1stNatl  2787    VOID:                     X       0.00
    6/ 3 1stNatl  2788    VOID:                     X       0.00
    6/15 1stNatl  2799    VOID:                     X       0.00
    6/15 1stNatl  2800    VOID:                     X       0.00
    6/26 1stNatl  2810    VOID:                     X       0.00
    6/26 1stNatl  2811    VOID:                     X       0.00
    6/28 1stNatl  2827    Chemlawn                  X     -62.95
    6/28 1stNatl  2828    Pat Welch                 X    -246.54
                                                        ----------
            Total Expenses - Other                       -309.49
                                                        ----------
            TOTAL EXPENSES                            -54,199.50

                                                        ----------
            TOTAL INCOME/EXPENSE                       22,174.68
                                                        ==========
```

FIG. 12.10

A sample
itemized
category report.

The itemized category report resembles the cash flow report in purpose and information, except that the itemized category report does not include account transfers. If you want to see your cash inflows and outflows grouped and summarized by category, this is the report you want.

The Tax Summary Report

The *tax summary* report shows all the transactions assigned to categories you marked as tax-related. Transactions are sorted and subtotaled by category. The Tax Summary Report window works like the other report windows, enabling you to give the tax summary report a more specific title or to include only transactions from specified months. Figure 12.11 shows a page from a sample tax summary report.

The tax summary report is a handy tax-preparation tool to use at the end of the year. This report summarizes the taxable income items and the tax deductions you need to report on your federal and state income tax returns. (The report, however, summarizes only tax deductions paid with those bank accounts, cash accounts, and credit card accounts you choose to track with Quicken. If you have two checking accounts, write tax-deductible checks using both accounts, and track only one of the accounts with Quicken, you are missing half of your deductions.)

The Net Worth Report

A *net worth* report shows the balance in each of the accounts in your Quicken file on a particular date. If the file includes all your assets and liabilities, the resulting report is a balance sheet that provides one estimate of your financial net worth. *Net worth* is the difference between your total assets and total liabilities. If you own more assets than liabilities, you have a positive net worth. If you own fewer assets than liabilities, you have a negative net worth. (Balance sheets are described in Chapter 10. Figure 12.12 shows the Net Worth Report window.

The Net Worth Report window differs from other personal report windows because you cannot enter a range of dates; you can enter only one date. The net worth report does not report on activity for a period of time but provides a snapshot of certain aspects of your financial condition—the account balances in your Quicken file—at a point in time. Figure 12.13 shows a sample net worth report.

Monitoring your net worth probably is more important than most people realize. Over the years that you work, one of your financial goals may be to increase your net worth. During your retirement years, you probably will look to your net worth to provide income and security. Your net worth, for example, may include investments that produce regular interest or dividend income. Your net worth also may include your personal residence, completely paid for by the time you retire.

```
                          Personal Tax Summary Report
                            7/ 1/92 Through 7/31/92
L_FLANDE-All Accounts                                              Page 1
7/31/92

   Date   Acct    Num     Description    Memo     Category   Clr  Amount
   -----  -------- -----   -------------- --------- --------- --- --------

          INCOME/EXPENSE
           INCOME
             Int Inc
             -------
   7/ 6 1stnatl  2208    First National B June intere Int Inc    X     4.25
   7/22 1stnatl           Interest Earned             Int Inc    X     4.22
                                                                   ---------
                Total Int Inc                                          8.47

             Salary
             ------
   7/15 1stnatl           S GTE Payroll               Salary     X  4,000.00
   7/27 1stnatl           S GTE Payroll               Salary     *  4,000.00
                                                                   ---------
                Total Salary                                       8,000.00

             _DivInc
             -------
   7/ 6 Merrill  Div      Time Warner                _DivInc           50.00
   7/29 Value Li DivX     Value Line Inco            _DivInc           25.00
                                                                   ---------
                Total _DivInc                                         75.00
                                                                   ---------
             TOTAL INCOME                                          8,083.47


           EXPENSES
             Charity
             -------
   7/19 1stnatl  2219    March of Dimes               Charity        -50.00
   7/31 1stnatl  2220    American Heart A             Charity        -50.00
                                                                   ---------
                Total Charity                                       -100.00

             Medical
             -------
   7/22 1stnatl  2214    Dr. Michael Cumm Allison's c Medical        -35.00
                                                                   ---------
                Total Medical                                        -35.00

             Mort Int
             --------
   7/ 1 1stnatl  2201 S Inland Mortgage              Mort Int    X   -550.00
   7/27 1stnatl  2218 S First National B             Mort Int        -750.00
                                                                   ---------
                Total Mort Int                                    -1,300.00

             Tax:
             ----

               Fed
               ---
   7/15 1stnatl           S GTE Payroll              Tax:Fed     X -1,000.00
   7/27 1stnatl           S GTE Payroll              Tax:Fed     * -1,000.00
                                                                   ---------
                  Total Fed                                       -2,000.00

               FICA
               ----
   7/15 1stnatl           S GTE Payroll              Tax:FICA    X   -306.00
   7/27 1stnatl           S GTE Payroll              Tax:FICA    *   -306.00
                                                                   ---------
                  TOTAL FICA                                       -612.00

               Prop
               ----
   7/ 1 1stnatl  2201 S Inland Mortgage              Tax:Prop    X    -52.98
   7/27 1stnatl  2218 S First National B             Tax:Prop       -100.00
                                                                   ---------
                  Total Prop                                       -152.98

               State
               -----
   7/15 1stnatl           S GTE Payroll              Tax:State   X   -160.00
   7/27 1stnatl           S GTE Payroll              Tax:State   *   -160.00
                                                                   ---------
                  Total State                                      -320.00
                                                                   ---------
                Total Tax                                         -3,084.98
                                                                   ---------
             TOTAL EXPENSES                                       -4,519.98

                                                                   ---------
          TOTAL INCOME/EXPENSE                                     3,563.49
                                                                   =========
```

FIG. 12.11

A sample tax
summary report.

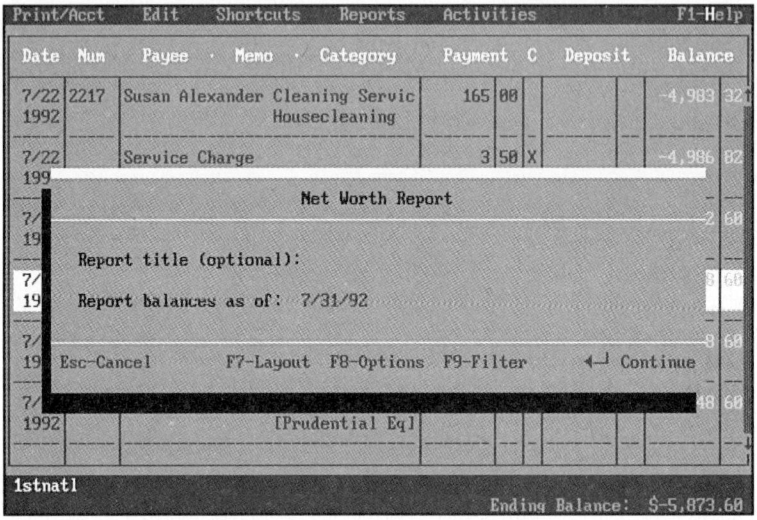

FIG. 12.12

The Net Worth Report window.

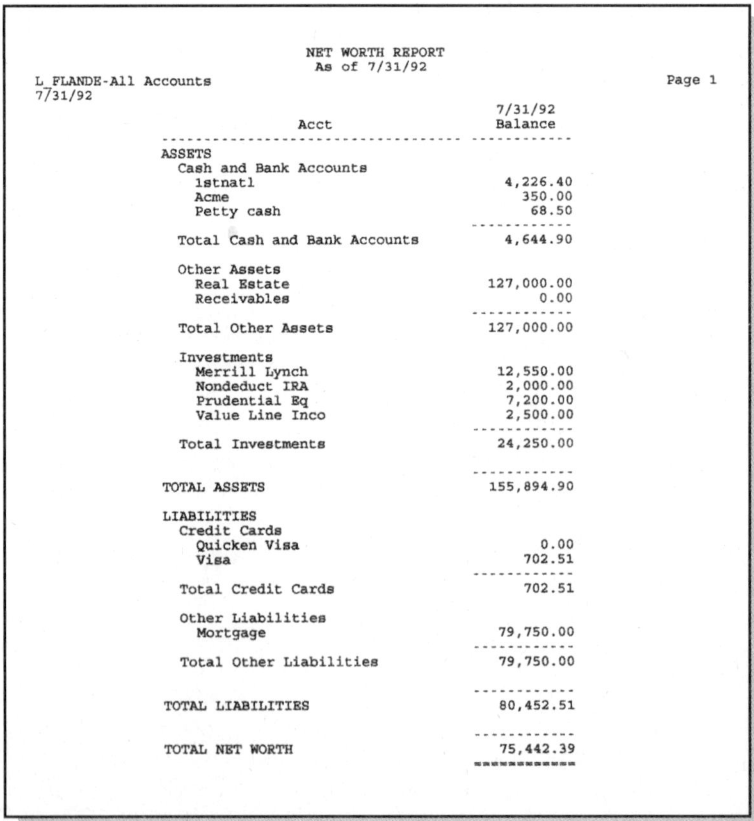

NET WORTH REPORT
As of 7/31/92

L_FLANDE-All Accounts
7/31/92

Page 1

Acct	7/31/92 Balance
ASSETS	
Cash and Bank Accounts	
1stnatl	4,226.40
Acme	350.00
Petty cash	68.50
Total Cash and Bank Accounts	4,644.90
Other Assets	
Real Estate	127,000.00
Receivables	0.00
Total Other Assets	127,000.00
Investments	
Merrill Lynch	12,550.00
Nondeduct IRA	2,000.00
Prudential Eq	7,200.00
Value Line Inco	2,500.00
Total Investments	24,250.00
TOTAL ASSETS	155,894.90
LIABILITIES	
Credit Cards	
Quicken Visa	0.00
Visa	702.51
Total Credit Cards	702.51
Other Liabilities	
Mortgage	79,750.00
Total Other Liabilities	79,750.00
TOTAL LIABILITIES	80,452.51
TOTAL NET WORTH	75,442.39

FIG. 12.13

A sample net worth report.

The Missing Check Report

The *missing check* report displays a list of all checking account transactions in check number order with any gaps in the check number sequence identified. To request a missing check report, you use the Missing Check Report window shown in figure 12.14. The Missing Check Report window works just like the other report windows. Figure 12.15 shows a sample missing check report on-screen with a missing check—number 2206—identified.

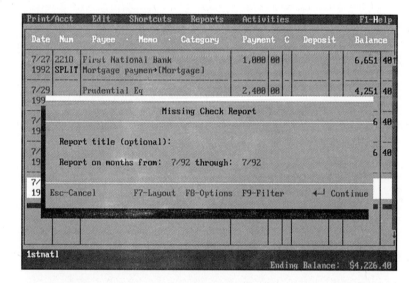

FIG. 12.14

The Missing Check Report window.

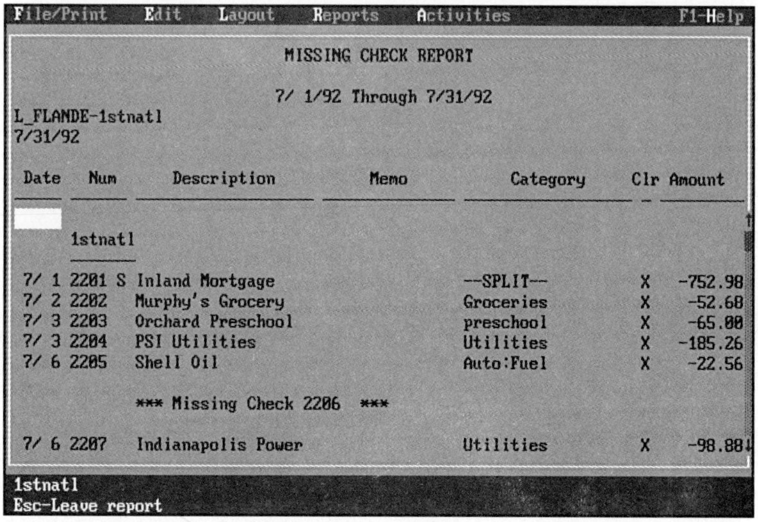

FIG. 12.15

The Missing Check Summary displayed on-screen.

The Tax Schedule Report

The *tax schedule* report summarizes tax-related categories in a way that makes it easy to prepare every common income tax schedule. Using category information, Quicken adds up the transactions that go on each line of each tax schedule. To create a tax schedule report, fill in the Tax Schedule Report window, which works like the other report windows. Chapter 14 describes and illustrates this handy report.

Tracking Your Business Finances with Business Reports

The Business Reports menu, shown in figure 12.3, provides eight reports. To create a business report, select the report that you want to create from the Business Reports menu and then complete the report window with an optional title and the date range that you want the report to cover. (The eighth report in the Business Reports menu is the missing check report. This report mirrors the missing check report from the Personal Reports menu already described in "The Missing Check Report.")

The P & L (Profit and Loss) Statement

The *P & L (profit and loss statement)* shows the total income and expenses by category for all accounts on a monthly basis. Data from transactions from any of the accounts in the current Quicken file are included, but transfers between accounts are not. Figure 12.16 shows the Profit & Loss Statement window. Like most of the report windows, you have two options: to use your own report title or the default title and to specify the months to be included in the report or to use the default (from January of the current year to the current date). Figure 12.17 shows a sample profit and loss statement.

Unless a business makes money (profits), it cannot keep operating for very long. Accordingly, business owners and managers must monitor profits. The profit and loss statement provides the means to do so.

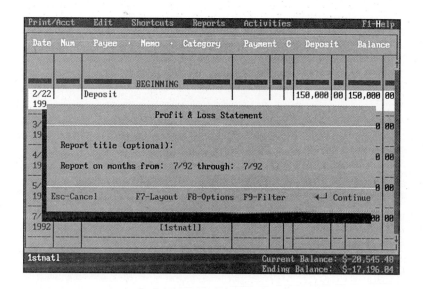

FIG. 12.16

The Profit & Loss Statement window.

```
                   Business Profit & Loss Statement
                      7/ 1/92 Through 7/31/92
BUSINESS-All Accounts                                         Page 1
7/31/92
                                        7/ 1/92-
                  Category Description   7/31/92
              --------------------------  ------------
              INCOME/EXPENSE
                INCOME
                  Gr Sales                19,500.00
                                          ------------
                TOTAL INCOME              19,500.00

                EXPENSES
                  Computer Supply            150.56
                  D23 Labor                6,753.00
                  D23 Land                10,400.00
                  D23 Materials            3,456.00
                  Payroll:
                    Comp FICA    117.80
                    Comp FUTA     14.60
                    Comp MCARE    26.83
                    Gross      1,825.00
                                ------------
                  Total Payroll            1,984.23
                  Expenses - Other             0.00
                                          ------------
                TOTAL EXPENSES            22,743.79

                                          ------------
                TOTAL INCOME/EXPENSE      -3,243.79
                                          ============
```

FIG. 12.17

A sample profit and loss statement.

C P A
T I P

The profit and loss statement is one of your business's most used and important financial reports. It reports your net income or net loss for a specific time period (month, quarter, year, and so on). Remember that the sales revenue shown on the profit and loss statement is not the same as cash inflow from sales for the period and that the expenses shown do not necessarily reflect the cash outflows of your business for the period. Create a cash flow report to show the cash position of your business.

The Cash Flow Report

A *cash flow* report resembles a profit and loss statement. This report includes all bank, cash, and credit card accounts and shows the money received (*inflows*) and the money spent (*outflows*) by category for each month. The cash flow report also shows transfers between accounts.

Like the Profit & Loss Statement window, the Cash Flow Report window provides fields for you to enter the range of months that you want the cash flow report to cover. You can enter your own report title for Quicken to print on the cash flow report in place of the default title, *Cash Flow Report*.

Figure 12.18 shows a sample cash flow report. The difference between this report and the profit and loss statement is that transfers to other accounts are shown on the cash flow report and the cash flow report groups cash inflows together and cash outflows together. The difference between cash inflows and outflows is the overall total, which may be positive or negative.

Cash flow is just as important as profits—particularly over shorter time periods. Besides making money, businesses need to have cash to purchase inventory or equipment, to have as working capital while they wait for customers to pay their bills, and to pay back loans from banks and vendors. The cash flow report, which summarizes your cash inflows and outflows by category and account, provides a method for monitoring your cash flow—and for pinpointing problems that arise.

```
                          Business Cash Flow Report
                           7/ 1/92 Through 7/31/92
    BUSINESS-Receivables                                       Page 1
    7/31/92
                                              7/ 1/92-
                  Category Description         7/31/92
                  -------------------      ------------------
    INFLOWS
        FROM Payroll-FICA                       235.60
        FROM Payroll-FUTA                        14.60
        FROM Payroll-FWH                        198.00
        FROM Payroll-MCARE                       53.66
        FROM Payroll-SWHIN                       45.89
        FROM Receivables                     15,000.00
                                           -----------
    TOTAL INFLOWS                            15,547.75

    OUTFLOWS
        D23 Labor                             6,753.00
        D23 Land                             10,400.00
        D23 Materials                         3,456.00
        Payroll:
          Comp FICA              117.80
          Comp FUTA               14.60
          Comp MCARE              26.83
          Gross               1,025.00
                              ----------
        Total Payroll                         1,984.23
        Outflows - Other                          0.00
                                           -----------
    TOTAL OUTFLOWS                           22,593.23
                                           -----------
    OVERALL TOTAL                            -7,045.48
                                           ===========
```

FIG. 12.18

A sample business cash flow report.

The A/P by Vendor Report

Because Quicken uses what is called *cash-basis accounting*, expenses are recorded only when you actually pay the bill. By not paying bills, or even paying bills late, your net income or profit and your net cash flow may look better. The problem, of course, is that this concept is clearly illogical. Just because you haven't paid a bill by the end of the month doesn't mean that the bill shouldn't be considered in assessing the month's financial performance. To partially address this shortcoming, Quicken provides the A/P (Unprinted Checks) by Vendor report, which enables you to see which bills have not been paid.

The *A/P by vendor* report lists all the unprinted checks, sorted and subtotaled by payee. (*A/P* is an abbreviation for *accounts payable*—the unpaid bills of a business.) Figure 12.19 shows the A/P (Unprinted Checks) by Vendor window. You do not enter a date or a range of dates in this window, but you can enter a substitute report title for Quicken to use instead of the default report title, *A/P (Unprinted Checks) by Vendor Report*.

Figure 12.20 shows a sample A/P by vendor report. Two vendor totals appear: one for Mark Stephens and another for Susan Lane. Quicken subtotals unprinted checks with the exact payee names. If you type the payee name differently for different checks, the payee is not recognized by Quicken as the same payee, and the amounts are not subtotaled. If you plan to use this report (or the A/R by customer report described next), use the Memorized Transaction feature. When you use this feature, the payee name is identical for each transaction.

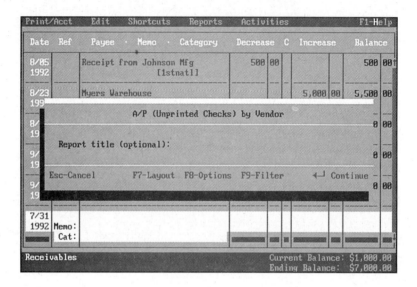

FIG. 12.19

The A/P (Unprinted Checks) by Vendor window.

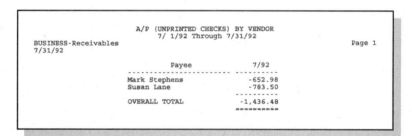

FIG. 12.20

A sample A/P by vendor report.

The A/R by Customer Report

The *A/R by customer* report shows the transactions in all of the other asset accounts, sorted and subtotaled by payee. The report, however, does not include transactions marked as cleared—those transactions marked with an asterisk (*) or X in the C field of the Register. (*A/R* is an abbreviation for *accounts receivable*—the amounts your customers owe.) The A/R by Customer window is very similar to the A/P by Vendor window shown in figure 12.19. You can enter a title to replace the default report title, *A/R by Customer Report*.

After you enter a report title in the A/R by Customer window, press Enter. Quicken displays the Select Categories to Include window (see fig. 12.21).

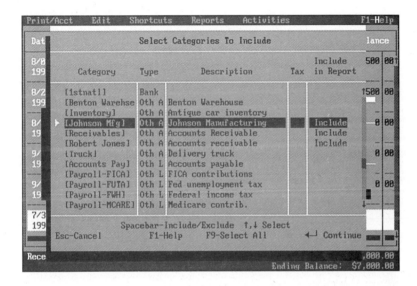

FIG. 12.21

The Select Categories to Include window.

Quicken lists all of your accounts in the Select Categories to Include window. You should include only receivable accounts in the A/R by customer report. Figure 12.21 shows three receivable accounts marked for inclusion. To include or exclude accounts, follow these steps:

1. Use the up- and down-arrow keys to highlight the account that you want to include or exclude.

2. Press the space bar. The space bar acts as a toggle switch, alternately marking the account for inclusion or exclusion.

3. (Optional) To select all the accounts, press F9.

Figure 12.22 shows a sample A/R by customer report.

For businesses that extend customer credit—which is what you do anytime you allow a customer to "buy now, pay later"—monitoring the amounts the customers owe is essential to profits and cash flows. Unfortunately, some customers don't pay unless you remind them several times, some customers frequently lose invoices and then forget that they owe you, and sometimes customers never receive your bill. To make sure that these small problems don't become big cash-flow problems, you can use the A/R by customer report.

```
                              A/R by Customer Report
                              7/ 1/92 Through 7/31/92
         BUSINESS-Selected Accounts                                Page 1
         7/31/92
                                                7/92-
                              Payee             7/92
                    --------------------------- -----------
                    Benton Manufacturing         1,500.00
                    Invoice #89-87               1,000.00
                    Invoice #89-90               2,500.00
                    Johnson Manuacturing       -15,000.00
                    Johnson Manufacturing       18,500.00
                    Myers Warehouse              5,000.00
                    Opening Balance                  0.00
                    Receipt from Johnson Mfg      -500.00
                                                -----------
                    OVERALL TOTAL               13,000.00
                                                ===========
```

FIG. 12.22

A sample A/R by customer report.

T I P   Good collection procedures usually improve cash flows dramatically, so consider using the customer-aging report as a collection guide (see Chapter 22 to learn how to create an aging report). You may, for example, want to telephone any customer with an invoice 30 days past due, and you may want to stop granting additional credit to any customer with invoices more than 60 days past due, and—in the absence of special circumstances—you may want to initiate collection procedures for any customer with invoices more than 90 days past due.

The Job/Project Report

The *job/project* report shows category totals by month for each month in the specified date range. The report also shows account balances at the end of the last month. (If you are using classes, the report shows category totals by class in separate columns across the report page.) The Job/Project Report window is just like many of the other report windows, such as the Profit & Loss Statement window shown in figure 12.16. Figure 12.23 shows a sample job/project report. (Refer to Chapter 22 for more information on job costing.)

The Payroll Report

The *payroll* report shows the total amounts paid to individual payees when the transaction category starts with payroll. (The search argument used is *payroll*. See the discussions of exact and key-word matches in Chapters 5 and 7 for more information.) The payroll report includes transactions from all accounts. The Payroll Report window works just like the other report windows.

Figure 12.24 shows a sample payroll report. (Refer to Chapter 22 for more information on preparing payroll with Quicken.)

```
                        JOB/PROJECT REPORT
                       7/ 1/92 Through 7/31/92
BUSINESS-All Accounts                                    Page 1
7/31/92

  Category Description    Illinois      Indiana       Ohio
  --------------------   ----------   ----------   ----------
INCOME/EXPENSE
  INCOME
    Gr Sales              5,000.00    18,500.00     1,500.00    3,500.00    28,500.00
                         ----------   ----------   ----------  ----------  ----------
  TOTAL INCOME            5,000.00    18,500.00     1,500.00    3,500.00    28,500.00

  EXPENSES
    Computer Supply           0.00         0.00         0.00      150.56       150.56
    D23 Labor                 0.00     6,753.00         0.00        0.00     6,753.00
    D23 Land             10,400.00         0.00         0.00        0.00    10,400.00
    D23 Materials             0.00         0.00     3,456.00        0.00     3,456.00
    Payroll:
      Comp FICA               0.00         0.00         0.00      117.80       117.80
      Comp FUTA               0.00         0.00         0.00       14.60        14.60
      Comp MCARE              0.00         0.00         0.00       26.83        26.83
      Gross                   0.00     1,825.00         0.00        0.00     1,825.00
                         ----------   ----------   ----------  ----------  ----------
    Total Payroll             0.00     1,825.00         0.00      159.23     1,984.23
    Expenses - Other          0.00         0.00         0.00        0.00         0.00
                         ----------   ----------   ----------  ----------  ----------
  TOTAL EXPENSES         10,400.00     8,578.00     3,456.00      309.79    22,743.79

                         ----------   ----------   ----------  ----------  ----------
  TOTAL INCOME/EXPENSE   -5,400.00     9,922.00    -1,956.00    3,190.21     5,756.21
                         ==========   ==========   ==========  ==========  ==========
```

FIG. 12.23

A sample job/ project report.

```
                        PAYROLL REPORT
                       7/ 1/92 Through 7/31/92
BUSINESS-All Accounts                                    Page 1
7/31/92
                                                      OVERALL
  Category Description  Mark Stephens  Susan Lane       TOTAL
  --------------------  -------------  ----------   ----------
INCOME/EXPENSE
  EXPENSES
    Payroll:
      Comp FICA             55.80         62.00        117.80
      Comp FUTA              6.60          8.00         14.60
      Comp MCARE            12.33         14.50         26.83
      Gross                825.00      1,000.00      1,825.00
                        -----------   ----------   ----------
    Total Payroll          899.73      1,084.50      1,984.23
                        -----------   ----------   ----------
  TOTAL EXPENSES           899.73      1,084.50      1,984.23

                        -----------   ----------   ----------
  TOTAL INCOME/EXPENSE    -899.73     -1,084.50     -1,984.23
                        ===========   ==========   ==========
```

FIG. 12.24

A sample payroll report.

C P A T I P

At the end of the calendar year, create a payroll report to help you complete your W-2 forms. Make sure that the time period covered by the report is for the full calendar year (1/1/92 to 12/31/92, for example). The payroll report shows the total gross wages paid to each employee and his or her total withholdings (federal, social security, state, local, and so on).

A W-2 form must be sent by January 31 of the following calendar year to each person that you employed at any time during the previous calendar year.

The Balance Sheet

The *balance sheet* report shows the account balances for all accounts in the current Quicken file at a specific point in time. If the file includes accounts for all your assets and liabilities, the resulting report is a balance sheet that shows the net worth of your business. (Chapter 10 describes balance sheets in more detail.) Figure 12.25 shows the Balance Sheet window. Figure 12.26 shows an example of a business balance sheet.

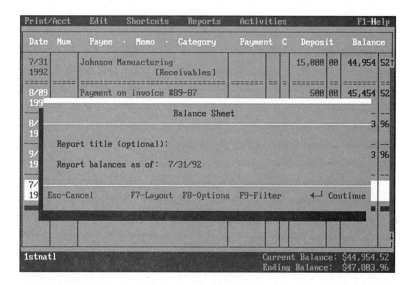

FIG. 12.25

The Balance
Sheet window.

Even for small businesses, balance sheets are important reports. Because a balance sheet shows what a business owns and what it owes, balance sheets give an indication of the financial strength or weakness of a business. The smaller the total liabilities amount in relation to the total assets amount, for example, the stronger the business. Alternatively, the larger the total liabilities in relation to the total assets, the weaker the business. As a result of these and similar financial insights, banks usually require a balance sheet in order to evaluate loan applications from businesses.

```
                          BALANCE SHEET
                          As of 7/31/92
BUSINESS-All Accounts                                     Page 1
7/31/92
                                          7/31/92
              Acct                        Balance
    -----------------------------  ----------------------------
    ASSETS

        Cash and Bank Accounts
        1stnatl
            Ending Balance           124,954.52
            plus: Checks Payable       1,436.48
                                     ------------
            Total 1stnatl                             126,391.00
                                                      ------------
        Total Cash and Bank Accounts                  126,391.00

        Other Assets
            Benton Warehse                                  0.00
            Inventory                                  30,000.00
            Johnson Mfg                                 2,500.00
            Receivables                                 9,500.00
            Robert Jones                                1,000.00
            Truck                                      12,000.00
                                                      ------------
        Total Other Assets                             55,000.00

                                                      ------------
    TOTAL ASSETS                                      181,391.00
                                                      ============

    LIABILITIES & EQUITY

        LIABILITIES
            Checks Payable                              1,436.48

        Other Liabilities
            Accounts Pay                                  150.56
            Payroll-FICA                                  235.60
            Payroll-FUTA                                   14.60
            Payroll-FWH                                   198.00
            Payroll-MCARE                                  53.66
            Payroll-SDI                                     0.00
            Payroll-SUI                                     0.00
            Payroll-SWHIN                                  45.89
                                                      ------------
        Total Other Liabilities                          698.31

                                                      ------------
    TOTAL LIABILITIES                                   2,134.79

    EQUITY                                            179,256.21
                                                      ------------
    TOTAL LIABILITIES & EQUITY                        181,391.00
                                                      ============
```

FIG. 12.26

An example of a balance sheet.

C P A
T I P

The balance sheet report measures the value of your business as of one moment in time—the date you entered in the Report Balances As Of field in the Balance Sheet window. *Asset amounts* represent values based on original cost—not replacement costs or earning power (unless you entered any amount other than original costs for assets in Quicken). *Liabilities* represent the legal claims of creditors who have loaned you money or goods or services that have been provided to you that you have not yet paid for. *Owner's equity*, or *net worth*, represents a claim resulting from the capital invested by the owners of the business and past profits retained in the business.

Tracking Your Investments with Quicken's Investment Reports

The Investment Reports menu provides five report options (see fig. 12.4). As with personal and business reports, the basic steps for printing an investment report are straightforward. To print any of the five reports, select the report that you want to print from the Investment Reports menu, complete the appropriate report window, and then print the report. You may want to review Chapter 16 before you attempt to print investment reports.

The Portfolio Value Report

A *portfolio value* report shows the estimated market values of each of the securities in your Quicken investment accounts on a specific date. To estimate the market values, Quicken uses each security's individual *price history* (a list of prices on certain dates). Quicken determines which price to use by comparing the date that you enter in the report window to use as the value date to the dates that have prices in the price history. Ideally, Quicken uses a price for the same date as the date you specify. When the price history does not contain a price for the same date specified, Quicken uses the price for the date closest to that date.

To create a portfolio value report, complete the Portfolio Value Report window shown in figure 12.27. You can enter a report title, and you need to enter a date in the Report Value As Of field. You can specify that the information on the report be summarized by account, security type, and investment goal. You also can specify whether the report should include the current account, all accounts, or only selected accounts, by using a window like the one shown in figure 12.21. Figure 12.28 shows an example of a portfolio value report.

The Investment Performance Report

Investment performance reports help you measure how well or how poorly your investments are doing. These reports look at all the transactions for a security and calculate an annual rate of return—in effect, the interest rate—an investment has paid you. To generate an investment performance report, you use the report window shown in figure 12.29.

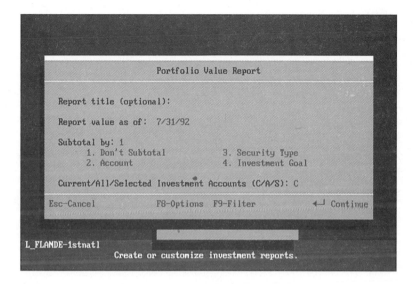

FIG. 12.27

The Portfolio Value Report window.

```
                    PORTFOLIO VALUE REPORT
                       As of 7/31/92
L_FLANDE-Merrill Lynch                                    Page 1
7/31/92

             Security    Shares  Curr Price  Cost Basis  Gain/Loss   Balance
             --------    ------  ----------  ----------  ---------   -------
Pepsi                    100.00        35 *   3,500.00       0.00   3,500.00
Time Warner              100.00        90 *   9,000.00       0.00   9,000.00
-Cash-                    50.00     1.000        50.00       0.00      50.00
                                             ----------  ---------   -------
Total Investments                            12,550.00       0.00  12,550.00
                                             ==========  =========  ========
```

FIG. 12.28

A sample of the portfolio value report.

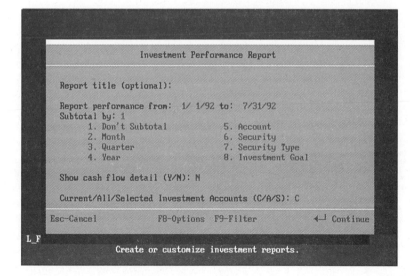

FIG. 12.29

The Investment Performance Report window.

The report window enables you to use a custom title for the report. The window also requires that you enter dates into the Report Performance From and To fields. These dates tell Quicken for which time frame you want to calculate investment returns. The report window also enables you to subtotal rates of return by different time periods, by account, by security, by security type, or by investment goals. You also can specify whether you want rates of return calculated for just the current account, for all accounts, or for selected accounts. Quicken notifies you if one or more of the total return calculations cannot be completed and displays the value as NA. Figure 12.30 shows an example of an investment performance report.

FIG. 12.30

A sample Investment Performance report.

```
                        PERFORMANCE REPORT BY SECURITY
                          1/ 1/92 Through 7/31/92
   L_FLANDE-Merrill Lynch                                      Page 1
   7/31/92
                                                  Avg. Annual
                        Description                Tot. Return
   ------------------------------------------     -----------

      Total Pepsi                                      0.0%

      Total Time Warner                                6.7%
```

The Capital Gains (Schedule D) Report

The *capital gains* report attempts to print all the information you need to complete the federal income tax form, Schedule D. Taxpayers use Schedule D to report capital gains and losses. To generate a capital gains report, use the Capital Gains (Schedule D) Report window shown in figure 12.31.

Most of the fields in the Capital Gains Report window should be familiar to you, and the fields that also appear on the other investment report windows are not described here. Two fields do deserve mention, however: the Subtotal by and the Maximum Short-Term Gain Holding Period (Days) fields. Although income tax laws currently in effect treat short-term capital gains the same as long-term capital gains, Congress may change this treatment. Accordingly, Quicken enables you to subtotal by short-term and long-term gains and losses.

Currently, gains and losses that stem from the sale of capital assets held for more than one year are considered long-term. The Maximum Short-Term Gain Holding Period field enables you to change the default number of days Quicken uses to determine whether a gain or loss is long-term, however. Figure 12.32 shows an example of a capital gains report by security.

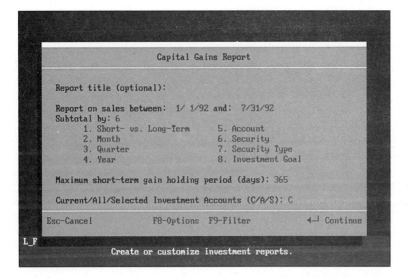

Capital Gains Report

Report title (optional):

Report on sales between: 1/ 1/92 and: 7/31/92
Subtotal by: 6
    1. Short- vs. Long-Term   5. Account
    2. Month   6. Security
    3. Quarter   7. Security Type
    4. Year   8. Investment Goal

Maximum short-term gain holding period (days): 365

Current/All/Selected Investment Accounts (C/A/S): C

Esc-Cancel   F8-Options F9-Filter   ⏎ Continue

L_F

Create or customize investment reports.

```
                       CAPITAL GAINS REPORT BY SECURITY
                            1/ 1/92 Through 7/31/92
    L_FLANDE-Merrill Lynch                                        Page 1
    7/31/92

        Security    Shares   Bought    Sold   Sales Price  Cost Basis  Gain/Loss
    ------------  --------  --------  -------- -----------  ----------  ---------

                  Time Warner
                  -----------
    Time Warner       100   6/30/91  7/31/92    10,250.00    9,000.00   1,250.00
                                               -----------  ----------  ---------
                  Total Time Warner             10,250.00    9,000.00   1,250.00
                                               ===========  ==========  =========
```

The Investment Income Report

The *investment income* report summarizes all the income transactions you recorded in one or more of the investment accounts. To generate the report, use the report window shown in figure 12.33. Figure 12.34 shows an example of the report.

Realized gains and losses result when the investment is actually sold and cash is received. A realized gain or loss is calculated by comparing the cash received upon sale with the original cost of the investment. *Unrealized gains and losses* result when the cost of the investment is compared with the market value to determine what the gain or loss would have been if the investment had been sold.

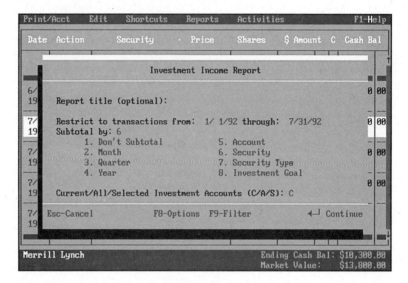

FIG. 12.33

The Investment Income Report window.

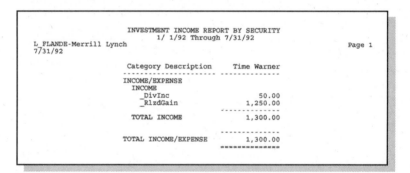

FIG. 12.34

A sample investment income by security report.

The Investment Transactions Report

The *investment transactions* report lists each of the investment transactions in the Register. To create the report, use the Investment Transactions Report window which is just like the window shown in figure 12.33. As with many of the other report windows, Quicken enables you to enter an optional title, specify the time frame the report should cover, indicate whether you want transactions subtotaled according to some convention, and to decide which accounts you want included in the report. Figure 12.35 shows an example of the investment transactions report by security.

```
                    TRANSACTIONS REPORT BY SECURITY
                      1/ 1/92 Through 7/31/92
 L_FLANDE-Merrill Lynch                              Page 1
 7/31/92

 Date Action   Secur   Categ    Price   Shares  Commssn   Cash
 ---- ------   -----   -----    -----   ------  -------   ----

      Pepsi
      -----
 7/06 BuyX    Pepsi             35      100             -3,500.00  3,500.00
                      [1stnatl]                         3,500.00            3,500.00
                                                       ----------  ---------- ----------
      Total Pepsi                                           0.00   3,500.00   3,500.00

      Time Warner
      -----------
 7/06 Div     Time Warne _DivInc                           50.00              50.00

 7/31 Sell    Time Warne        104     100    150.00   9,000.00  -9,000.00
                      _RlzdGain                          1,250.00            1,250.00
                                                       ----------  ---------- ----------
      Total Time Warner                                 10,300.00  -9,000.00  1,300.00
                                                       ----------  ---------- ----------
      OVERALL TOTAL                                     10,300.00  -5,500.00  4,800.00
                                                       ==========  ========== ==========
```

FIG. 12.35

A sample investment transactions by security report.

Creating Custom Reports

The Reports menu includes four custom reports that you can create in Quicken; transaction, summary, budget, and account balances (see fig. 12.1). You can use any one of these custom report options as a template to create a specific report to meet your needs. You can create a summary report by using the Reports menu's custom **Summary** option, which doesn't have a specific purpose the way other Quicken reports have. The profit and loss statement, for example, is a summary type report because it summarizes transactions and shows account totals instead of individual transactions. The custom **Transaction** report option on the Reports menu lists transactions in the current account, all accounts, or selected accounts. Quicken can list transactions by payee; category; class; account; or a time period such as week, month, quarter, and so on. You can create a custom budget report by using the **Budget** report option. This option enables you to compare actual amounts by category against monthly budget amounts. The last custom report option, **Account Balances**, enables you to list balances for all your accounts, selected accounts, or just the current account. Balances are listed based on intervals that you specify.

When you select a custom report option like **Transaction**, Quicken displays the Create Transaction Report window. Quicken displays the Create Summary Report window when you select the **Summary** report option. These create report windows are the same windows that are displayed when you press F7 (to change the report layout) from the report windows that you saw when you learned to create standard reports earlier in this chapter. If you choose the **F7-Layout** option by pressing F7 from the personal Cash Flow Report window, Quicken displays the Create Summary Report window. Because the cash flow report is a summary report (because it summarizes transactions instead of listing individual transactions), you use the Create Summary Report window to change the layout of the cash flow report.

Likewise, if you choose **F7-Layout** from the personal Itemized Categories Report window, Quicken displays the Create Transaction Report window. Because the itemized categories report is a transaction report (because it lists individual transactions instead of summarizing transactions and showing totals only), you use the Create Transaction Report window to change the layout of the itemized cash flow report. You learn more about changing report layouts later in this chapter in the section "Changing the Report Layout." For now, remember that the custom reports that you are about to read about are the basis for all other Quicken reports.

Creating Transaction Reports

You may want to view your Register transactions in some order other than chronologically by date. You may find value in sorting and summarizing transactions by the payee or by time periods such as a week or month, for example. The transaction report enables you to see your account transactions in any of these ways.

To create a transaction report, follow these steps:

1. Select the **Transaction** report option from the Reports menu shown in figure 12.1. Quicken displays the Create Transaction Report window (see fig. 12.36.)

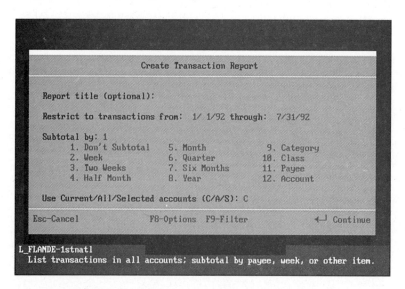

FIG. 12.36

The Create Transaction Report window.

2. (Optional) Enter a report title. If you don't enter a report title, Quicken names the report *Transaction Report*.

3. (Optional) Press Enter or Tab to move the cursor to the Restrict To Transactions From and Through fields. Enter the time frame the report should cover by entering the starting and ending dates you want included in the report. If you don't enter these dates, the report covers from January of the current year through the current date.

4. (Optional) Press Enter or Tab to move the cursor to the Subtotal By field. Pick one of the 12 subtotal options by typing the number that appears to the left of the option.

5. (Optional) Press Enter or Tab to move the cursor to the Use Current/All/Selected Accounts field. Here, you determine whether to include just the current accounts' transactions, just the selected accounts' transactions, or all the accounts' transactions. If you choose just selected accounts, Quicken displays the Select Accounts to Include window.

6. (Optional) Press F8 (Options) to access the Report Options window. Complete the Report Options window as described later in this chapter in the section "Setting Report Options."

7. (Optional) Press F9 (Filter) to access the Filter Report Transactions window. Complete the Filter Report Transactions window as described later in this chapter in the section "Filtering Reports."

8. When the Create Transaction Report window is complete, press Ctrl-Enter or F10. Quicken generates and displays the report on-screen.

9. When you are ready to print the report, press Ctrl-P. Quicken displays the Print Report window shown in figure 12.6. The Print Report window enables you to specify to where you want the report printed. Follow the steps outlined in the section "Reviewing Report Printing Basics," earlier in this chapter, to learn how to complete the Print Report window.

Creating Summary Reports

Like a transaction report, a summary report extracts information from the financial database you create using Quicken's Registers. A summary report, however, gives you totals by category, class, payee, or account, in addition to any of the other subtotals you request. With this type of report, you also can select the accounts to include.

To print a summary report, you follow essentially the same steps you follow to create a transaction report, except that you select the **Summary** report option from the Reports menu. Quicken then displays the Create Summary Report window, which you use to specify how the custom report should appear (see fig. 12.37). Refer to the steps for completing the Create Transaction Report window in the preceding section, "Creating Transaction Reports," to learn how to complete the Create Summary Report window.

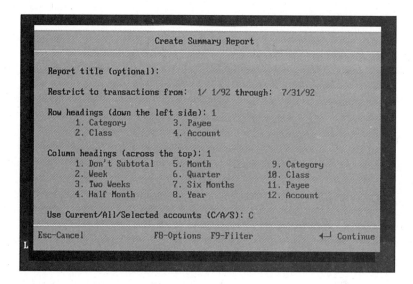

Creating Budget Reports

Chapter 15 describes budgeting as a fundamental tool that businesses and individuals can use to better manage their finances. One of the ongoing steps in using a budget as a tool is to compare the amount you spent with the amount you planned to spend, or budgeted. Quicken's Option report option on the Reports menu enables you to create customized budget reports tailored to your business or personal needs.

To print a budget report, you follow the same steps you use when creating transaction, summary, or account balances reports. Select the **Budget** report option from the Reports menu. Quicken then displays the Create Budget Report window, which you use to specify how the custom report should appear. Refer to the steps for completing the Create Transaction Report window in the preceding section to learn how to complete the Create Budget Report window.

Creating Account Balances Reports

You can use the eighth option on the Reports menu to create customized account balances reports. If you have extensive investments with several brokers, for example, and you want a report that specifies only those accounts, you can create this report (or a specialized version of this report). Figure 12.38 shows the Create Account Balances Report window that you use to construct customized account balances reports.

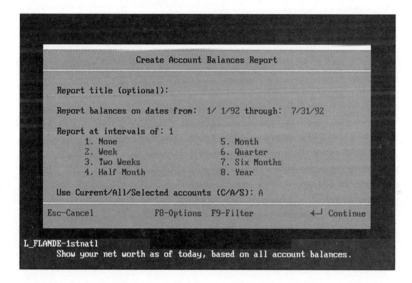

```
                     Create Account Balances Report

    Report title (optional):

    Report balances on dates from:  1/ 1/92 through:  7/31/92

    Report at intervals of: 1
             1. None              5. Month
             2. Week              6. Quarter
             3. Two Weeks         7. Six Months
             4. Half Month        8. Year

    Use Current/All/Selected accounts (C/A/S): A

  Esc-Cancel           F8-Options  F9-Filter            ←┘ Continue

L_FLANDE-1stnatl
       Show your net worth as of today, based on all account balances.
```

FIG. 12.38

The Create Account Balances Report window.

The basic steps you follow for creating an account balances report are the same as for any of the other custom reports. You select the **Account Balances** report option from the Reports menu, and Quicken displays the Create Account Balances Report window. Follow these steps to create an account balances report:

1. In the Report Title field, type a report title of up to 34 characters and press Enter. If you leave this field blank, Quicken supplies the title *Account Balances Report*.

2. The Report Balances on Dates From and Through fields are slightly different from the Restrict to Transactions From and Through fields in other custom report windows. The account balances report shows the account balances at a specific point in time. This field sets a boundary around the points in time for which an account balances report is generated. Type the dates that cover the time period to show account balances and press Enter.

3. The Report at Intervals Of field determines the points in time for which an account balances report is generated. The start of the first interval is the first day of the year. Assuming that the Report Balances on Dates From field is 1/1/92, the first account balances column is for 1/1/92. The next date depends on the interval. If the interval is weekly, the second column is 1/7/92. If the interval is biweekly, the second column is 1/14/92. If the interval is by half month, the second column is 1/15/92, and so on. The report shows account balances for each interval between the From and Through dates. The last column of the report shows the account balances on the Through date. In the Report at Intervals Of field, type the number that corresponds to the interval you want to use and press Enter.

    If the Report at Intervals Of field is set to 1 for **None**, the only point in time for which the account balances report is generated is the date entered in the Through field.

4. As with the other custom reports, the Use Current/All/Selected Accounts field enables you to determine which account balances are reported on the account balances report. Press C to designate just the current account; press S to designate only the selected accounts; press A to designate all accounts. If you choose only selected accounts, Quicken displays the Select Accounts to Include window. Use the up- and down-arrow keys to highlight the accounts that you want to include in the report and press the space bar to mark the account as included. Use the space bar as a toggle to designate **Include** or **Detail** next to the account. If you select **Detail**, Quicken shows the class or security detail for that account. Press Enter when you are finished selecting accounts. Quicken returns to the Create Account Balances Report window.

5. When the Create Account Balances Report window is complete, press Ctrl-Enter or F10 to display the report on-screen.

Viewing Reports On-Screen

You have learned how to create Quicken reports so that they are displayed on your screen. Most reports that you display, however, are too wide or too long to fit entirely within the boundaries of your screen. Table 12.1 lists the keys you can use to view reports on your screen.

Table 12.1 Report-Viewing Keys

Press	To View
Tab or →	Next column to the right
Shift-Tab or ←	Preceding column to the left
Ctrl- →	One screen to the right
Ctrl- ←	One screen to the left
PgUp	Up one screen
PgDn	Down one screen
Home	Far left column, current row
End	Far right column, current row
Home Home	Top left corner of report
End End	Bottom right corner of report

NOTE You can use the **Full Column Width** option from the report Layout menu to display transaction reports in full-width columns so that you can see more transaction detail. Refer to "Changing the Report Layout," later in this chapter, for more information on displaying full-width columns.

You also can use your mouse to scroll report screens by clicking the scroll box on the vertical or horizontal scroll bar. See Chapter 2 to learn more about using a mouse to scroll report screens.

Re-creating the Last Report

The last item on the Reports menu is the **Redo Last Report** option. This option enables you to display the last report that you created without having to select the report from the menu. This option is particularly useful if you last created a customized report by changing the layout, setting report options, and filtering report transactions. By selecting the **Redo Last Report** option, Quicken displays the last report, as you created it.

To re-create the last report, follow these steps:

1. Create any Quicken report. Exit the report screen by pressing Esc. Then continue with your work in Quicken.

2. From the main menu, select the **Create Reports** option to display the Reports menu. From the Register or the Write Checks screen, press Alt-R to display the Reports menu.

3. From the Reports menu, select the **Redo Last Report** option. You also can press Ctrl-Z to select this option. Quicken completes the appropriate report window and displays the report that you last created.

Customizing Reports

You learned how to create standard reports by selecting the report option from the Reports menu and completing the report's Create Report window. What if, for example, you want to report over different dates than you're allowed to enter in the Create Report window, or if you want to restrict transactions to those with a particular payee or assigned to certain categories? You can customize each standard Quicken report. The available options vary among report types.

You can customize reports so that Quicken provides the exact information that you want and exactly how you want to see this information. You can use the following Quicken options to customize a report from the report window (see fig. 12.39):

- F7-Layout
- F8-Options
- F9-Filter

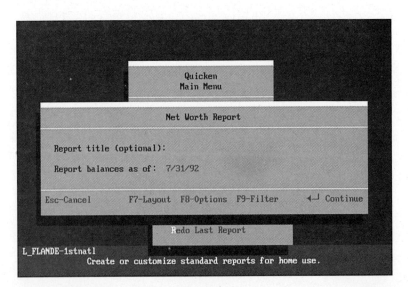

FIG. 12.39

The Net Worth Report window with customizing options.

Quicken displays all available customizing options at the bottom of the window that you use to create the report. Remember that report windows are displayed when you select the report that you want to create from the Personal, Business, or Investment Reports menu. When you select **F7-Layout**, Quicken displays one of the four custom report windows (Transaction, Summary, Budget, or Account Balances), depending on the type of report that you are creating. When you press F7 from the Net Worth Report window, for example, Quicken displays the Create Account Balances Report window because the net worth report is a report that shows account balances as of some point in time.

When you select **F8-Options**, Quicken displays the Report Options window like the one you see in figure 12.40. The report options Quicken enables you to change depend on the type of report you are creating.

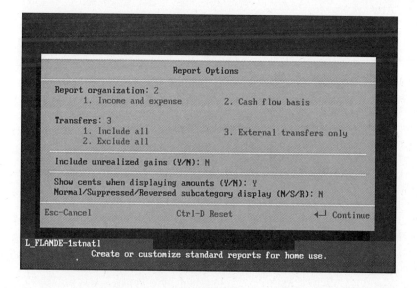

FIG. 12.40

The Report Options window to set report options for the personal cash flow report.

The last customizing option, **F9-Filters**, also can be selected from the report window that you use to create the report. When you select **F9-Filters**, Quicken displays the Filter Transactions window (see fig. 12.41). Filtering transactions enables you to limit the transactions included in the report. You can restrict reports to transactions meeting specific criteria; select which accounts and classes to include in reports; and include only those transactions with amounts below, equal to, or above certain amounts.

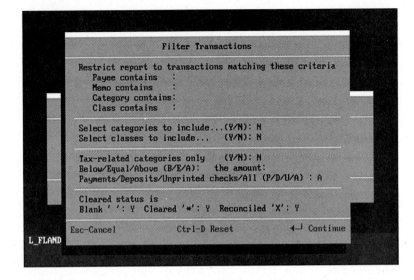

The Filter
Transactions
window to filter
transactions for
the personal cash
flow report.

Changing the Report Layout

You can change the report layout by changing titles, the date range
of transactions to include, the row and column headings, and the
accounts used in the report. To change the report layout, select **F7-
Layout** from the report window that you use to create the report. When
you press F7, Quicken displays the Create Summary Report window like
the one you saw in figure 12.37. The create report window displayed
will be the same create report window displayed to create custom reports (Summary, Transaction, Budget, or Account Balances).

Depending on the type of report you are customizing, Quicken enables
you to change the layout of the report by changing the following
settings:

■ *Report Title:* You can enter the title that you want to appear at the
top of the report. The title can include numbers, letters, and other
characters (up to 39 characters). If you don't enter a title, Quicken
uses the report type title, such as *Cash Flow Report* or *Net Worth
Report.*

■ *Restrict to Transactions From and Through:* By entering dates, you
determine the transactions covered by the report. If you want the
report to cover transactions for August 1992 only, for example,
type *8/1/92* in the From field and *8/31/92* in the Through field.
You can use the + (plus) and − (minus) keys in these fields to
change the date one day at a time.

■ *Row Headings:* You can select the item that you want to report on. Press the number that corresponds to the item on which you want to report. Press 1 for **Category**, 2 for **Class**, and so on. The item that you select determines the text that appears down the left side of the report. If you select to report on categories, for example, Quicken includes all the category names as row headings in the report.

■ *Column Headings:* You select how the report is subtotaled. When the report is created, Quicken includes a separate column for each column heading you select. Type the number that corresponds to the column heading you want to use. Press 1 for **Don't Subtotal** (Quicken includes a single column), 2 for **Week**, 3 for **Two Weeks**, and so on.

■ *Use Current/All/Selected Accounts:* You can determine which accounts you want to include in the report. Press C to include only the current account. Press A to include all accounts in the current Quicken file. For investment reports, selecting all accounts includes all investment accounts only. Or, press S to select the accounts that you want to include. When you choose to select the accounts to include, Quicken displays the Select Accounts to Include window. You learned how to complete the Select Accounts to Include window in the section "The A/P by Vendor Report," earlier in this chapter.

> **NOTE** All the options to change the report layout are not included in every Create Report window. Options available depend on the type of report you are creating. When you are creating an investment report, the **F7-Layout** option is not available from the report window used to create the report.

After you complete the Create Report window, press Ctrl-Enter or F10 to return to the original report window. From the report window, you can select to set report options (by pressing F8) or filter transactions (by pressing F9). Or, you can go ahead and create the report on-screen by pressing Ctrl-Enter or F10.

When the report is displayed on-screen, you can use the following options from the Edit menu to change some of the options you set to change the report layout:

■ Set Title & Date Range

■ Accounts

You can use the Layout menu to change other options you set to change the report layout:

- Row Headings
- Column Headings

Setting Report Options

Quicken enables you to set report options to change the appearance of reports, including report organization and what transaction information is included. To set report options, select **F8-Options** from the report window that you use to create the report. When you select **F8-Options**, Quicken displays the Report Options window.

Depending on the type of report you are customizing, Quicken enables you to design the report by changing the following settings:

- *Report Organization:* You can organize reports on an income and expense basis or a cash flow basis. If you select **Income and expense** by pressing 1, the report totals income, expenses, and transfer transactions in separate sections of the report. If you select **Cash flow basis** by pressing 2, the report groups and totals inflows (including transfers into the accounts) and outflows (including transfers out of the accounts).

- *Transfers:* For summary and transaction reports, you can select to include all transfers from and to the accounts included in the report by pressing 1, to exclude all transfers by pressing 2, or to include external transfers only by pressing 3 (where the corresponding transfer transaction is recorded in an account that is not included in the report).

- *Include Unrealized Gains:* You can include (by pressing Y) or exclude (by pressing N) unrealized gains from investment accounts in the report. Unrealized gains result when the cost of the investment is compared with the market value to determine what the gain or loss would have been if the investment had been sold.

- *Show Totals Only:* In transaction reports, enables you to show the totals for transactions—not the detail. Press Y for totals only or N to show transaction detail.

- *Show Split Transaction Detail:* In transaction reports, you can include the detail from split transactions in the report by pressing Y. Note that transaction reports automatically show split transaction detail if you set transaction filters or total the report by category or class.

■ *Memo/Category Display:* In transaction reports, you can select to include columns for the memo only by pressing 1, for the category only by pressing 2, or for both the memo and category by pressing 3. By default, Quicken includes a column for both.

■ *Show Cents When Displaying Amounts:* By pressing N, you can round report totals to the nearest dollar.

■ *Normal/Suppressed/Reversed Subcategory Display:* These options control how subcategories and subclasses are displayed in reports. Press N for **Normal** to indent subcategories under their main category. Press S for **Suppressed** to omit subcategories and subclasses in reports. The amounts from subcategories and subclasses then are combined into the total for the main category and class. Press R for **Reversed** to group the items in the report first by subcategory or class, with the main category and class grouped under them.

 NOTE All the report options are not included in every Report Options window. Report options available depend on the type of report that you are creating. Some investment reports include fewer report options.

After you complete the Report Options window, press Ctrl-Enter or F10 to return to the original report window. From the report window, you can select to change the report layout (by pressing F7) or filter transactions (by pressing F9). Or, you can go ahead and create the report on-screen by pressing Ctrl-Enter or F10.

When the report is displayed on-screen, you can use the following options from the Layout menu to change any of the report options you set in the Report Options window:

■ Show/Hide Cents

■ Show/Hide Split

■ Other Options

Filtering Report Transactions

Quicken report filters enable you to specify which transactions to include in a report. To filter transactions, select **F9-Filter** from the report window that you use to create the report. When you select **F9-Filter**, Quicken displays the Filter Transactions window like the one shown in figure 12.41.

You can use a variety of fields in the Filter Transactions window to include or exclude transactions in or from a report. To filter transactions, follow these steps:

1. From the Filter Transactions window, press Enter or Tab to move through the various fields on-screen.

   The Payee Contains field enables you to instruct Quicken to include or exclude a certain payee or transaction description from a transaction report based on exact or key-word matches. (Chapters 5 and 7 describe the mechanics of exact and key-word matches.) If you leave this field blank, you do not affect transactions being included or excluded from the report.

   The Memo Contains field works like the Payee Contains field, except that Quicken compares the Memo Contains field entry to the transactions' Memo field entries. This field affects the transactions included or excluded on the report, as does the Payee Contains field. Using this field is optional.

   The Category Contains field enables you to instruct Quicken to include or exclude transactions assigned to certain categories based on exact or key-word matches. If you leave this field blank, the transactions being included or excluded from the report are not affected.

   The Class Contains field works like the Category Contains field, except that Quicken compares the Class Contains field entry to entries in the transactions' classes. Like the Category Contains field, this optional field affects the transactions included or excluded on the report.

   The Select Categories to Include field enables you to specify an entire set of categories to be included in a report. Press Y to select categories. Quicken displays the Select Categories to Include window (after you press Ctrl-Enter or F10 from the Filter Transactions window) shown in figure 12.42. (Leave the setting at N if you don't want to select the categories to include in the report.)

   When you first access the Select Categories to Include window, Quicken marks all categories to include in the report. To select specific categories to include, first press F9 to unmark all categories. Then use the up- and down-arrow keys to highlight the categories that you want to mark or include in the report, and press the space bar. The space bar acts as a toggle switch, alternately marking the category for inclusion or exclusion.

   The Select Classes to Include field enables you to specify an entire set of classes to be included in a report. If you press Y from this field, Quicken displays the Select Classes To Include window (after you press Ctrl-Enter or F10 from the Filter Transactions window) that you can use to mark individual classes you want included in a report (see fig. 12.43).

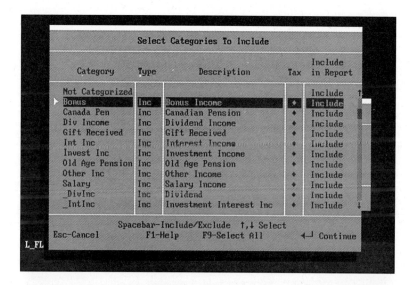

FIG. 12.42

The Select Categories To Include window.

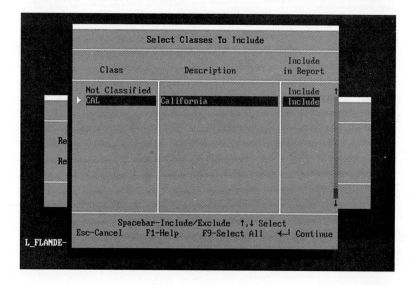

FIG. 12.43

The Select Classes To Include window.

To include a class, use the up- and down-arrow keys to highlight the class you want to include and press the space bar. The space bar acts as a toggle switch, alternately marking the class for inclusion and exclusion. To select all classes, press F9.

The Tax-Related Categories Only field enables you to include each of the categories you marked as tax-related when initially defining the category. (Chapter 9 describes how to identify a category as tax-related.)

The Below/Equal/Above field and the The Amount field enable you to include transactions in a report based on the transaction amount. Using these two fields, you tell Quicken that you want transactions included in your report only when the transaction amount is less than, equal to, or greater than some amount. Press B to indicate below, E to indicate equal, or A to indicate above. Enter the amount you want transaction amounts compared to in the The Amount field. If you want to include only transactions over $25, for example, press A for above and type *25* in the The Amount field.

The Payments/Deposits/Unprinted Checks/All field enables you to include only certain types of transactions. To include only payments, press P; to include only deposits, press D; to include only unprinted checks, press U; to include all transactions, press A. You can use this report filter to determine your cash flow requirements. If you have entered all your bills and want to know the total, press U for unprinted checks. Your report tells you the total cash required for all unpaid bills.

The Cleared Status Is field enables you to include transactions on a report based on the contents of the C field in the Register. The C field shows whether a transaction has been marked as cleared. Three valid entries exist for the C field: *, X, and nothing. As the Filter Report Transactions window shows, you include transactions in a report by pressing Y in the Blank, *, or X fields. You also can exclude transactions by pressing N for No next to the same three fields.

2. (Optional) If you start modifying these fields and then want to reset them to the original values, press Ctrl-D.

3. When you complete the Filter Transactions window, press Ctrl-Enter or F10 to return to the report window. (If you pressed Y in the Select Categories To Include or the Select Classes To Include field, the Select Categories To Include or the Select Classes To Include windows are displayed next.)

Using QuickZoom

QuickZoom enables you to examine the transaction detail behind an amount in a report while the report is displayed on-screen. If, for example, you create a cash flow report and want to see the transaction detail behind the amount shown for the category *Charity* (for charitable donations), you can use QuickZoom to search the Register for all transactions that make up the total amount shown in the report. QuickZoom then displays a list of those transactions. After you examine the transaction detail, you can return to the report.

 NOTE You can use the **QuickZoom** option in noninvestment reports only. You cannot use QuickZoom in account balances type reports, such as the net worth report or the balance sheet.

Examining Transaction Detail

To use QuickZoom to examine transaction detail in a report, follow these steps:

1. With the report displayed on your screen, highlight the report amount that you want to examine. Suppose that you had just displayed a report and want to know the detail behind the salary amount shown. You would highlight the amount in the Salary line by using the arrow keys.

2. Press Alt-F to display the File/Print menu.

3. From the File/Print menu, select the **QuickZoom** option. You also can press Ctrl-Z to select **QuickZoom**.

4. For summary or budget type reports, Quicken displays a Transaction List window (see figure 12.44). For transaction type reports, Quicken goes to the Register and highlights the Register entry for the transaction.

5. If you want to see the Register entry for a transaction listed in the Transaction List window, highlight the transaction and press F9. Quicken goes to the Register and highlights that transaction. From here, you can make any necessary changes or return to the report (see the next section).

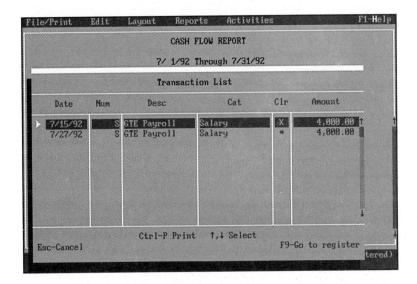

FIG. 12.44

The Transaction
List window.

Returning to a Report After QuickZoom

In Quicken 5.0, when you used QuickZoom to examine transaction detail for an amount in a report, you were unable to go back to the report
after you viewed transactions in the Register. With Quicken 6.0, you can
go right back to the report by pressing Ctrl-Z from the Register. The
Ctrl-Z shortcut key selects the **Redo Last Report** option.

Editing Reports On-Screen

If you already have created a report and it is displayed on-screen, you
don't have to go back to the report window to change the report layout, set report options, or filter transactions. You can change the report on-screen by using the menu options displayed at the top of the
report screen. The menu options available from report screens follow:

- *File/Print:* Includes options to print reports, memorize reports,
  and use QuickZoom. The File/Print menu is shown in figure 12.45.

- *Edit:* Includes options to set the report title and date range; filter
  transactions; and select which accounts, categories, and classes
  are included in the report. The Edit menu is shown in figure 12.46.

■ *Layout:* Includes options to change the appearance and format of the report, such as the row and column headings, whether amounts are rounded, whether the detail in split transactions is shown, which transactions are displayed and which are hidden, and so on. Figure 12.47 shows the Layout menu.

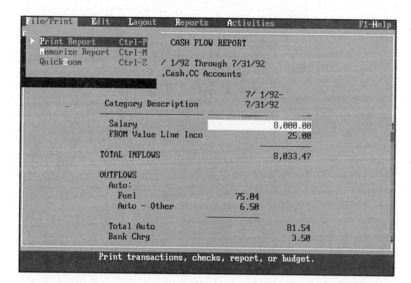

FIG. 12.45

The File/Print menu.

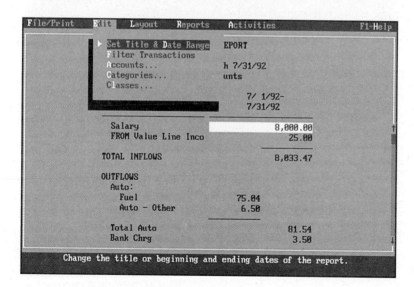

FIG. 12.46

The Edit menu.

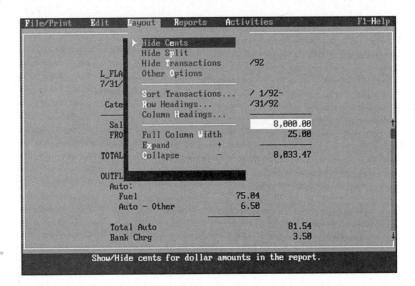

FIG. 12.47

The Layout menu.

Two other menu options are included in the report screen; Reports and Activities. The Reports menu is the same one that you see in figure 12.1, except that it does not include the **Redo Last Report** option. You can select to create any other type of report from the report screen currently displayed.

The Activities menu enables you to go to the Register or the Write Checks screen from the report screen or to use the Quicken Calculator while the report is still displayed.

You already have learned how to customize reports by using the **F7-Layout**, **F8-Options**, and **F9-Filter** options from the report window. Many of the options available from the menu at the top of the on-screen report enable you to set the same report settings that you set using F7, F8, or F9. The menu makes customizing and editing reports easier because you can do it directly from the report screen instead of going back to the various windows to change the layout, set options, and filter transactions. Because you have learned about most of these options in previous sections in the chapter, not every menu option is explained here. Menu options that you have not learned about are explained in the following sections.

Hiding/Showing Transactions in Reports

If you are creating a noninvestment transaction report, such as the itemized category report or the tax summary report, you can select to omit or display transaction detail. In transaction reports, Quicken displays the date, account, transaction number, description, memo, category, whether the transaction has cleared, and the amount for each transaction included in the report. If you select to hide transaction detail, Quicken displays only the description and the amount for each transaction. You easily can switch your report back to full transaction detail by selecting the **Show Transactions** option. The **Hide Transactions** option is useful if you want a more concise transaction report that still lists the individual amounts and overall totals of transactions.

> **NOTE** The **Hide Transactions** and **Show Transactions** options shown in the Layout menu alternate, depending on the option last chosen. If transaction detail is shown in your report, for example, the option that appears in the Layout menu is **Hide Transactions**. If you select the **Hide Transactions** option to hide transaction detail, Quicken changes the option in the Layout menu to **Show Transactions**.

To hide transaction detail, follow these steps:

1. With the transaction report displayed on-screen, press Alt-L to access the Layout menu.

2. Select the **Hide Transactions** option from the Layout menu. Quicken searches transactions and displays only the description and amount of each transaction.

To show transaction detail again, follow these steps:

1. With the transaction report with hidden transactions displayed on-screen, press Alt-L to access the Layout menu.

2. Select the **Show Transactions** option from the Layout menu. Quicken searches transactions and redisplays detail for each transaction.

Sorting Transactions in Reports

For noninvestment transaction reports, you can change how transactions are ordered in the report. You can sort transactions by account, date, check number, or amount. If you selected to have the report subtotaled (if you selected the **F7-Layout** option when you were creating the report), you can change the way that transactions are sorted within each subtotaled group.

To sort transactions in a report, follow these steps:

1. With the transaction report that you want to sort displayed on-screen, press Alt-L to access the Layout menu.

2. Select the **Sort Transactions** option from the Layout menu. Quicken displays the sort options shown in figure 12.48.

3. Use the up- and down-arrow keys to highlight the sort option that you want to use to sort transactions and press Enter. Quicken searches transactions and redisplays the report in the sort order you selected.

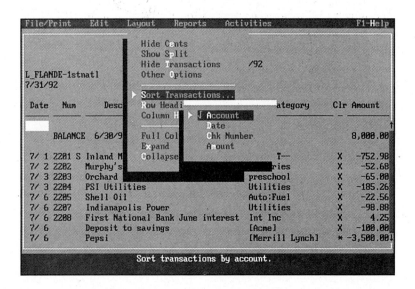

FIG. 12.48

The sort options available to sort transactions in a report.

Changing Report Columns

The Layout menu's **Full Column Width** option controls whether Quicken uses full-width columns or half-width columns for reports that list transactions. By default, Quicken displays reports in half-width columns so that you can see all transaction detail on your screen. The basic rule is to use columns wide enough to display the information you want to see. If, for example, the descriptions or memos in a report are cropped because the columns are too narrow, use full column widths.

To display a report with full-width columns, follow these steps:

1. With the transaction report displayed on-screen, access the Layout menu by pressing Alt-L.

2. From the Layout menu, select the **Full Column Width** option. Quicken uses full-width columns and changes the option name to **Half Column Width**.

To change the report back to half-width columns, simply perform the steps above and select the **Half Column Width** option.

Summarizing Rows in Reports

The **Expand** and **Collapse** options from the Layout menu work together and enable you to change the way that report rows are summarized. **Collapse** summarizes the detail for a row heading in summary, budget, or account balance reports without changing the report totals. If you want to present Total Inflows in a cash flow report as just one line, for example, you can collapse the row heading and Quicken reduces the Total Inflows section of the report to a single line.

NOTE   You cannot use the **Collapse** option to summarize report rows in transaction reports.

To summarize a row in a report, follow these steps:

1. With the report displayed on your screen, highlight the row heading that you want to summarize. Figure 12.49 shows a report before summarizing a row heading.

2. Select the **Collapse** option from the Layout menu. Or, press the – (minus) key to select the **Collapse** option. Quicken displays one line for the row heading that you selected. Figure 12.50 shows the same report after the row heading is collapsed.

If you want to return any detail in a report that is summarized or collapsed, you can use the **Expand** option. To expand report detail, follow these steps:

1. Highlight the row heading that you previously collapsed and want to expand.

2. Select the **Expand** option from the Layout menu. Or, press the + (plus) key to select the **Expand** option. Quicken displays the detail for the row in the report.

NOTE When you collapse a category within a section of a report, Quicken moves the category to the end of the section, removes the category name, and replaces it with a *hidden* title. If you collapse the Salary Income category in the Inflows section of a cash flow report, for example, Quicken moves the category to the end of the Inflows section and replaces the *Salary Income* title with the title *Inflows - Hidden*).

```
                                  NET WORTH REPORT
                                   As of 7/31/92
         L_FLANDE-All Accounts                                          Page 1
         7/31/92
                                                     7/31/92
                                    Acct              Balance
                                                  ------------
         ASSETS
           Cash and Bank Accounts
             1stnatl                               4,226.40
             Acme                                    350.00
             Petty cash                              68.50
                                                  ------------
           Total Cash and Bank Accounts            4,644.90

           Other Assets
             Real Estate                          127,000.00
             Receivables                               0.00
                                                  ------------
           Total Other Assets                     127,000.00

           Investments
             Merrill Lynch                         13,800.00
             Nondeduct IRA                          2,000.00
             Prudential Eq                          7,200.00
             Value Line Inco                        2,500.00
                                                  ------------
           Total Investments                       25,500.00
                                                  ------------
         TOTAL ASSETS                             157,144.90

         LIABILITIES
           Credit Cards
             Quicken Visa                              0.00
             Visa                                    702.51
                                                  ------------
           Total Credit Cards                        702.51

           Other Liabilities
             Mortgage                              79,750.00
                                                  ------------
           Total Other Liabilities                79,750.00
                                                  ------------
         TOTAL LIABILITIES                         80,452.51
                                                  ------------
         TOTAL NET WORTH                           76,692.39
                                                  ============
```

FIG. 12.49

A sample report showing a row heading before it has been collapsed.

Memorizing Reports

If you have spent considerable time customizing a report to include the specific information in a particular format, you will want to save the report settings so that you don't have to customize the report again. Quicken enables you to memorize a customized report so that you simply can select it from a list the next time you want to use it.

```
                        NET WORTH REPORT
                         As of 7/31/92
 L_FLANDE-All Accounts                                   Page 1
 7/31/92
                                        7/31/92
                          Acct          Balance
           -----------------------------  ------------
           TOTAL ASSETS                    157,144.90
           LIABILITIES
              Credit Cards
                 Quicken Visa                   0.00
                 Visa                         702.51
                                        ------------
              Total Credit Cards            702.51

              Other Liabilities
                 Mortgage                 79,750.00
                                        ------------
              Total Other Liabilities    79,750.00

                                        ------------
           TOTAL LIABILITIES             80,452.51

                                        ------------
           TOTAL NET WORTH               76,692.39
                                        ============
```

FIG. 12.50

A sample report showing a row heading after it has been collapsed.

When you memorize a report, Quicken saves all report settings and transaction filters, but doesn't save dates or data. If you customize your January profit and loss statement to include certain accounts and categories and show the report information in a certain order, when you memorize the report, Quicken stores only the report settings that indicate which accounts and categories to include and how to format the information. The program does not save the January dates or data in the memorized report. You therefore can recall the memorized report and create your February profit and loss statement, using the same report settings that you specified for the January report. In essence, the memorize report option prevents you from having to reinvent the wheel every time you need a report.

Memorizing a Report

You memorize a report after you customize the report and the report is displayed on-screen. You can, however, memorize a report from the report window, the Create Report window, the Report Options window, or the Filter Transactions window.

To memorize a report, follow these steps:

1. Create the report you want to memorize.

2. Press Ctrl-M. Quicken displays the Memorizing Report window shown in figure 12.51.

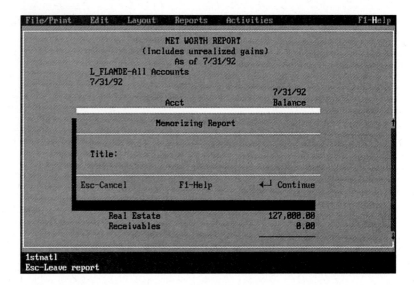

FIG. 12.51

The Memorizing
Report window.

3. Type a unique title for the report in the Title field, which Quicken uses to identify the report, but does not display as the report's title.

4. Press Enter to memorize the report.

Recalling a Memorized Report

You easily can recall a memorized report with the exact report settings you specified before you memorized it. To recall a memorized report, follow these steps:

1. Select the **Memorized Reports** option from the Reports menu. Quicken displays the Memorized Reports list shown in figure 12.52.

2. Highlight the memorized report you want to recall to the screen and press Enter. Quicken displays the Memorized Report window as shown in figure 12.53. Quicken enters the memorized report title.

3. Type over the title if you want to change it.

4. Change the Report on Months From or Through field in the Memorized Report window as necessary.

5. Press Ctrl-Enter or F10 to display the memorized report.

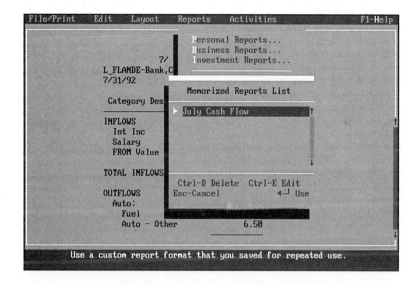

FIG. 12.52

The Memorized
Reports list.

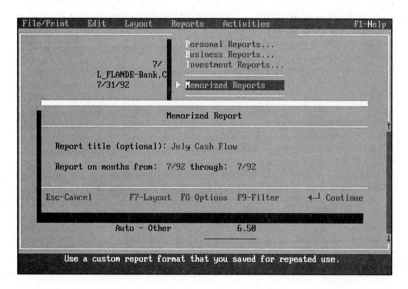

FIG. 12.53

The Memorized
Report window.

Editing and Deleting Memorized Reports

You can change a memorized report's title or delete a memorized report at any time. To change the title of a memorized report, follow these steps:

1. Select the **Memorized Reports** option from the Reports menu. Quicken displays the Memorized Reports List window.

2. Highlight the memorized report you want to edit and press Ctrl-E.

3. Quicken displays the Rename Memorized Report window that you see in figure 12.54.

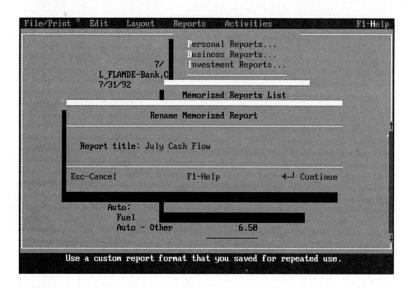

FIG. 12.54

The Rename
Memorized
Report window.

4. Type the new title in the Report Title field and press Ctrl-Enter to save the changes.

To delete a memorized report, follow these steps:

1. Select the **Memorized Reports** option from the Reports menu. Quicken displays the Memorized Reports List.

2. Highlight the memorized report that you want to delete and press Ctrl-Del. Quicken displays a warning that you are about to permanently delete a memorized transaction.

3. Press Enter to delete the memorized report or press Esc if don't want to delete the memorized report.

Chapter Summary

This chapter reviewed the basics of printing any Quicken report and detailed the steps and tricks for printing each of Quicken's personal, business, investment, and custom reports. These reports use the information stored in your Quicken file to provide you with a wealth of financial information that you can use to better manage your personal or business finances.

In the next chapter, you learn how to pay your bills electronically through CheckFree. If you have a modem and are ready to give up the process of hand-writing or printing checks, you will benefit by Quicken's electronic bill-payment feature and CheckFree.

Paying Bills Electronically

Quicken enables you to use CheckFree, an electronic bill payment service, to pay bills. By using Quicken and a modem, you can send payment instructions to CheckFree Corporation. Your payment instructions include all the information CheckFree needs to actually pay the bill: who you owe the money to, when the bill needs to be paid, how much you owe, and so on. CheckFree Corporation then either draws a check on or electronically transfers funds from your bank account to whomever you owe the money.

Paying bills electronically isn't for everyone. By getting one more party involved in the bill-paying process, you just may make this process more complicated. For Quicken users who have a modem and who want to stop printing checks, however, electronic payment is appealing.

This chapter explains how to perform the following tasks:

- Set up your system for electronic payment through the CheckFree service

- Identify the people you plan to pay by setting up payees

- Edit and delete payees

- Set up fixed payments

■ Pay bills electronically

■ Issue stop-payment requests

■ Make payment inquiries

■ Send and receive electronic mail to or from CheckFree

Setting Up Your System for Electronic Payment

To begin using electronic bill paying, you need to complete three steps. First, you need to complete the CheckFree paperwork. Second, you need to activate the electronic payment feature in Quicken so that Quicken knows that you want to use CheckFree. When you activate the electronic payment feature, you also must configure the modem and select the account(s) you use to pay bills electronically. Third, you need to set up the payees (the persons or companies that you will pay electronically). Performing these steps is easy. Completing this part of the work should take no more than a few minutes.

Completing the CheckFree Paperwork

Before you begin using the CheckFree service, you need to complete the CheckFree service form (see fig. 13.1). The form is self-explanatory. You need to tell CheckFree Corporation how much memory your computer has; give CheckFree some personal information, including your Social Security number, name, address, and so on; and provide CheckFree with a credit card account number so that CheckFree can charge your credit card account if it—acting on your payment instructions—overdraws the account. (For security reasons, use a security code—similar to what you use for automated teller machines— to gain access to your account.)

After you provide this basic information, you also need to tell CheckFree which phone lines you are using, specify which account number/security code you plan to use to gain access to the CheckFree system, and sign an authorization so that CheckFree can deduct funds from your bank account. (If you don't choose an account number or security code, CheckFree creates one for you.)

CheckFree®

CONFIDENTIAL

CHECKFREE SERVICE FORM

(To receive CheckFree service, please complete this form and return the top copy in the enclosed postage paid envelope as soon as possible. As with all CheckFree data, the information on this form is handled with the strictest security. Please print all information.)

IMPORTANT

PLEASE ATTACH A VOIDED CHECK FROM YOUR PAYMENT ACCOUNT TO THE TOP OF THIS FORM.

YOUR EQUIPMENT AND SOFTWARE

How much RAM does your computer have? _____ 384 _____ 512 _____ more than 512
What disk size do you require? _____ 3¼ _____ 5¼
With what type of software will you be using CheckFree? _____ Quicken 5.0 for DOS _____ Quicken for Windows

PERSONAL IDENTIFICATION

Your social security number _____ _____ - _____ - _____
(CheckFree Systems Identification Number)

Name _____
　　　　　　Last　　　　　　　　　First　　　　　　　　　Middle

Current Address _____
　　　　　　Street　　　　　　City　　　　　State　　　Zip

CREDIT CARD INFORMATION

CheckFree requires an account number for at least one credit card, should an overdraft occur. CheckFree reserves the right to charge the account only for the purpose of overdraft protection.

MasterCard or Visa Account Number _____ Exp. _____

COMMUNICATIONS INFORMATION

Home Phone (_____) _____ - _____　　Work Phone (_____) _____ - _____
Circle number from which you will be transmitting.

CHECKFREE PERSONAL SECURITY CODE

Your CheckFree personal security code is a four digit number which you may choose yourself. You will need to enter this number in your Quicken software and use it as a password to run your software. My number is [| | |]. If you have no number preference, leave the space provided blank and CheckFree will assign a number for you. We will give you this number at the same time you receive your CheckFree network access telephone number.

Date _____　　Signature _____
Your use of the CheckFree service signifies that you have read and accepted all of the terms and conditions of the CheckFree service printed on the back of this form.

CHECKFREE BANK REGISTRATION

Note: Checking accounts with credit unions and money markets occasionally require special handling. If your account is with either type of institution, please call 1-800-882-5280 before you send in this form and ask for a "Financial Institution Check." We'll advise you if any special action is required.

I, _____
　　(Last Name)　　　　(First Name)　　　　(Middle Initial)

authorize my bank to post my bill payment transactions from CheckFree to my account as indicated below. I understand that I am in full control of my account. If at any time I decide to discontinue service, I will simply call or write CheckFree to cancel service.

_____
(Bank Name)

_____
(Street Address)

_____
(City)　　　　　　　(State)　　　　　　(Zip)

_____
Customer Signature

Return the top copy of this entire form to CheckFree in the postage paid envelope provided and retain the bottom copy for your records. Also,

DON'T FORGET TO PROVIDE A VOIDED CHECK WITH THIS FORM AND RETURN BOTH ITEMS TO CHECKFREE.

Return to CheckFree in the enclosed postage paid envelope.

►CheckFree®

Q50/Q51

FIG. 13.1

The CheckFree service form.

After you complete the CheckFree service form, attach a voided check to the form and then mail the form to Intuit. To mail the form, use the business reply envelope included for returning the CheckFree service form. Intuit forwards the service form to CheckFree Corporation. In a few days, CheckFree sends you a confirmation letter that confirms or assigns the account number/personal security code, gives you the telephone number to use for CheckFree transmissions, and the fastest *baud rate*—the transmission speed—you can use for sending payment information.

Activating the Electronic Bill Payment Feature

After you receive the confirmation letter from CheckFree, you can activate Quicken's electronic bill payment feature, which basically tells Quicken that you are going to use the CheckFree service.

To activate the electronic bill payment feature in Quicken, follow these steps:

1. From the Quicken main menu, select the **Set Preferences** option. Quicken then displays the Set Preferences menu.

2. From the Set Preferences menu, select the **Electronic Payment Settings** option. Quicken displays the Electronic Payment Settings menu (see fig. 13.2).

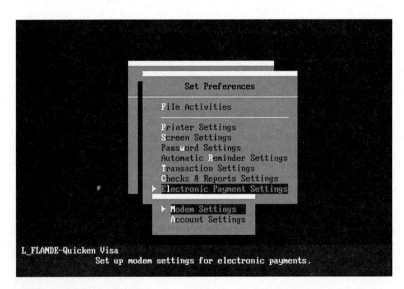

FIG. 13.2

The Electronic Payment Settings menu.

You need to do two things when activating the electronic bill payment feature: configure the modem and set up the bank accounts you plan to use to make the payments.

Configuring Your Modem

You must configure your modem so that you can transmit information to CheckFree through your modem and so that CheckFree can transmit confirmations and other information back to you.

To configure the modem, complete these steps:

1. From the Electronic Payment Settings menu shown in figure 13.2, select the **Modem Settings** option. Quicken displays the Electronic Payment Settings window shown in figure 13.3.

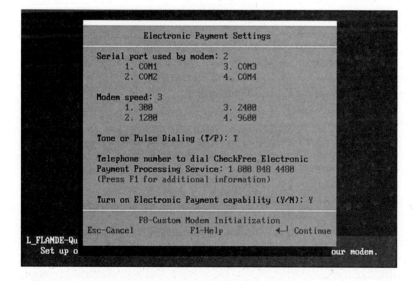

```
                    Electronic Payment Settings

        Serial port used by modem: 2
                1. COM1              3. COM3
                2. COM2              4. COM4

        Modem speed: 3
                1. 300              3. 2400
                2. 1200             4. 9600

        Tone or Pulse Dialing (T/P): T

        Telephone number to dial CheckFree Electronic
        Payment Processing Service: 1 800 848 4480
        (Press F1 for additional information)

        Turn on Electronic Payment capability (Y/N): Y

                    F8-Custom Modem Initialization
        Esc-Cancel          F1-Help              ← Continue
L_FLANDE-Qu
    Set up o                                      our modem.
```

FIG. 13.3

The Electronic Payment Settings window.

2. With the cursor positioned in the Serial Port Used by Modem field, enter the number of the serial port that the modem uses: 1 for serial communications port 1; 2 for serial communications port 2; and so on. If you don't know the serial communications port the modem uses, follow the cable that connects the modem to the computer and see whether the socket in which the modem cable plugs is labeled. The socket may be labeled with something like *COM1* or *Serial 1*.

3. Press Enter or Tab to move the cursor to the Modem Speed field. Pick the fastest modem speed setting that both CheckFree and your modem support. The CheckFree confirmation letter gives the

modem speed settings that CheckFree supports. The modem users' manual indicates the transmission speeds the modem is capable of running.

4. Press Enter or Tab to move the cursor to the Tone or Pulse Dialing field. Press T if the telephone service is tone; press P if the telephone service is pulse. If you aren't sure, refer to your monthly telephone bill or call the telephone company.

5. Press Enter or Tab to move the cursor to the Telephone Number to Dial field. Enter the telephone number given in the confirmation letter you receive from CheckFree. Include any special characters you want to dial. If you have call waiting, for example, *70 may turn off call waiting. You can start the dialing with *70 so that the beep a call-waiting call makes doesn't interfere with data transmission. You can use a comma to insert a pause. Quicken ignores any spaces and parentheses you enter.

6. At the Turn on Electronic Payment Capability field, press Y for Yes.

7. (Optional) If the modem is not Hayes-compatible, you need to give Quicken the initialization codes the modem uses to access the telephone line and get a dial tone. The odds are that the modem is Hayes-compatible, so you probably don't have to worry about the codes. If the modem isn't Hayes-compatible, press F8 from the Electronic Payment Settings window. The Custom Modem Initialization window appears (see fig. 13.4). Enter the initialization code that Quicken needs to send to the modem to access the telephone line and get a dial tone. The modem users' manual gives this initialization code.

Identifying CheckFree Bank Accounts

After you complete the Electronic Payment Settings window, you are ready to identify the CheckFree bank account or accounts. Essentially, here you identify only the bank accounts to use for electronic payment. You cannot use a credit card, other asset, other liability, or investment account for electronic payment—only bank accounts.

In Quicken, you cannot select an account to use for electronic payment until the Electronic Payment Settings window is filled out and the Turn on Electronic Payment Capability field is set to Y.

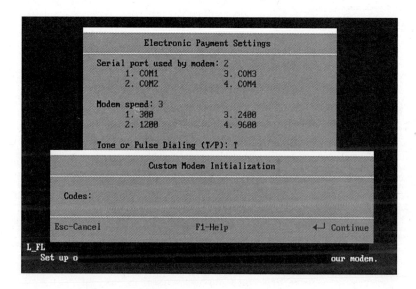

FIG. 13.4

The Custom Modem Initialization window.

To set up a bank account for electronic payment, follow these steps:

1. From the Electronic Payment menu, select the **Account Settings** option. Quicken then displays the Set Up Account for Electronic Payment window shown in figure 13.5. Because you can set up only bank accounts for electronic payment, Quicken lists only bank accounts in the window.

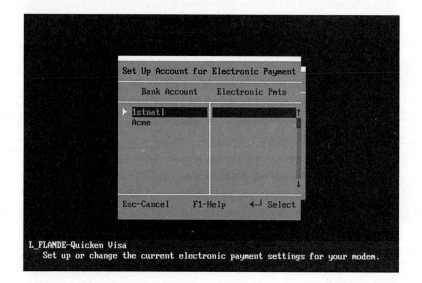

FIG. 13.5

The Set Up Account for Electronic Payment window.

2. Use the up- and down-arrow keys to highlight the bank account that you want to select and press Enter.

   For each account that you select, Quicken displays a message that asks whether you want to set up the account for electronic payment.

3. Press Y for Yes and press Enter. Quicken displays the Electronic Payment Account Settings window (see fig. 13.6).

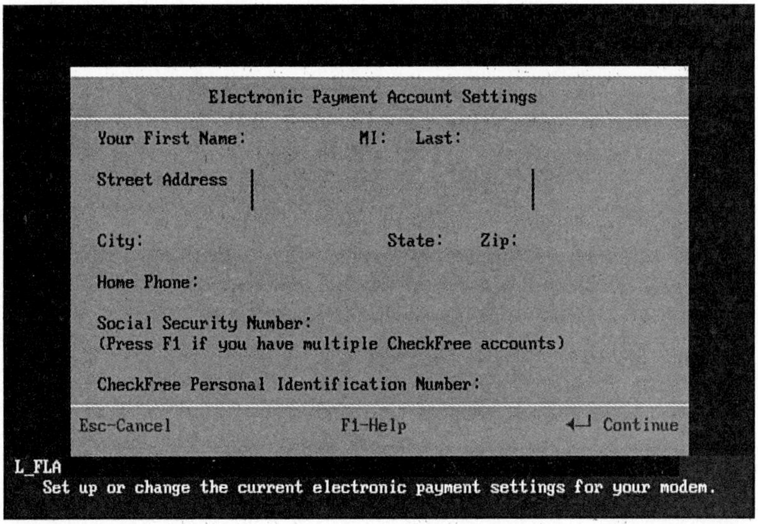

FIG. 13.6

The Electronic Payment Account Settings window.

4. With the cursor positioned in the Your First Name field, enter your first name.

5. Move the cursor to the MI field and enter your middle initial.

6. Move the cursor to the Last field and enter your last name.

7. Move the cursor to the Street Address field and enter the appropriate information.

8. Move the cursor to the City field and enter the name of the city or town in which you live.

9. Move the cursor to the State field and enter the two-character abbreviation for your state. If you don't know the two-character abbreviation, enter the first letter of the state name and press Enter. Quicken displays a list of valid state abbreviations from which you can choose the state's abbreviation.

10. Move the cursor to the Zip field and enter your ZIP code. Quicken validates the entry against a list of valid ZIP codes. If Quicken doesn't recognize what you enter, but you know the code is correct anyway, press Ctrl-Z to force Quicken to accept the ZIP code.

11. Move the cursor to the Home Phone field and enter your home phone number, including the area code. You don't have to include the punctuation characters, such as hyphens and parentheses; Quicken adds these characters after you press Enter.

12. Move the cursor to the Social Security Number field and enter your Social Security number, or the alternative identification number assigned by CheckFree. If you previously set up more than one bank account for electronic bill paying, which means that you filled out more than one CheckFree Service Agreement form, CheckFree gives you identifying numbers based on your Social Security number for each account. Enter this identifying number here.

13. Move the cursor to the CheckFree Personal Identification Number field and enter the account number/security number or PIN number from the CheckFree confirmation letter.

14. After the Electronic Payment Account Settings window is complete, press Ctrl-Enter. Quicken redisplays the Set Up Account for Electronic Payment window. The account you set up now is marked as *enabled* for electronic payment. When you subsequently select the enabled account to use, Quicken adds several more menu options that you can use for processing electronic payments.

Setting Up Your Payees

To pay a bill electronically, you need to collect and store information about each person or company you plan to pay so that CheckFree Corporation can process payments to the appropriate person or business. To set up a payee, just add the payee to the electronic payee list. From the Electronic Payee list, you can edit a payee or delete a payee to whom you no longer make payments.

Adding a Payee

Before you can make an electronic payment to a payee, you must add the payee to the Electronic Payee list. To add a payee, follow these steps:

1. From the main menu, select the **Write/Print Checks** option. Quicken displays the electronic payment version of the screen (see fig. 13.7).

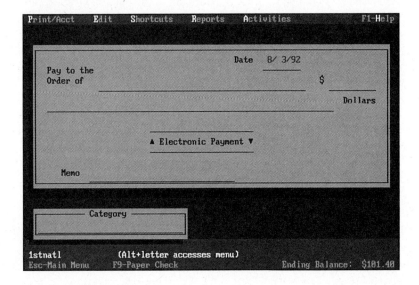

The electronic payment version of the Write/Print Checks screen.

2. Press Ctrl-Y to access the Electronic Payee list. You also can press Alt-S to access the Shortcuts menu and then choose the **Electronic Payee List** option from this menu. Either way, Quicken displays the Electronic Payee list shown in figure 13.8.

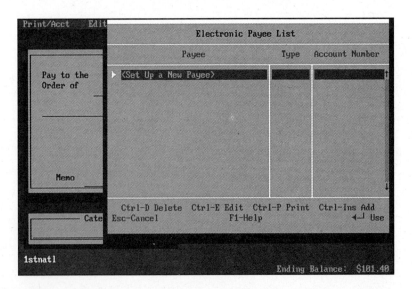

The Electronic Payee List.

3. To add a payee to the list, highlight the <Set Up a New Payee> line and press Enter. The Set Up Electronic Payee window appears (see fig. 13.9).

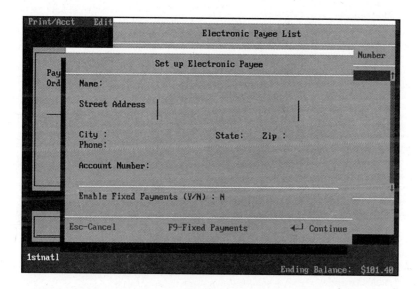

FIG. 13.9

The Set Up Electronic Payee window.

4. Move the cursor to the Name field and enter the complete name of the person or company you want to pay. In this field, you can add up to 28 characters.

5. Move the cursor to the Street Address field and enter the mailing address for sending payments to the payee.

6. Move the cursor to the City field and enter the name of the payee's city or town.

7. Move the cursor to the State field and enter the two-character abbreviation for the payee's state. If you don't know the two-character abbreviation, enter the first letter of the state name and press Enter. Quicken displays a list of valid state abbreviations from which you can pick the correct abbreviation.

8. Move the cursor to the Zip field and enter the payee's ZIP code. Quicken validates the entry against a list of valid ZIP codes. If Quicken doesn't recognize the code you enter even though you know the code is correct, press Ctrl-Z to force Quicken to accept the ZIP code.

NOTE Entering the payee name, address, phone number, and account number accurately is important because CheckFree uses this information to make payments to the payee.

9. Move the cursor to the Phone field and enter the person's or company's phone number, including the area code. You don't have to include punctuation, such as hyphens and parentheses; by default, Quicken adds these characters when you press Enter.

10. Move the cursor to the Account Number field and enter the account number the person or business uses to identify you.

11. (Optional) If you want to set up a fixed payment to the payee that you are setting up, move the cursor to the Enable Fixed Payments field and press Y. Fixed payments are explained in "Setting Up Fixed Payments."

12. After the Set Up Electronic Payee window is complete, check to make sure that the information is correct and then press Enter. The Electronic Payee List appears. To define additional electronic payees, repeat steps 3 through 12.

Editing and Deleting Payees

As on other lists in the Quicken system, you can press Ctrl-D to delete a payee from the Electronic Payee list, you can press Ctrl-E to edit a payee on the Electronic Payee list, and you can press Ctrl-P to print a list of electronic payees. The only difference between working with electronic payees and accounts, categories, classes, and so on, is that you cannot edit or delete an electronic payee if an untransmitted transaction exists for this payee. You learn more about untransmitted transactions later in this chapter.

Setting Up Fixed Payments

 Now, with Quicken 6.0, you can set up a payee to receive fixed payments from CheckFree. You also can edit an existing payee to receive fixed payments. *Fixed payments* are recurring payments, to the same payee, for the same amount, at a fixed interval (weekly, monthly, quarterly, and so on). After you set up a fixed payment to a payee, CheckFree makes the payment for you, based on the intervals that you specify. You may want to set up fixed payments, for example, for your mortgage, rent payment, insurance premiums, and so on. After you set up a fixed payment, you don't have to remember to transmit payment information to CheckFree; CheckFree remembers to make the payment for you.

Setting Up a Fixed Payment

To set up a fixed payment, follow these steps:

1. Access and complete the Set Up Electronic Payee window from the account Register that you want CheckFree to use to make payments. Or highlight an existing payee from the Electronic Payee list and press Ctrl-E to display the Edit Electronic Payee window.

2. Move to the Enable Fixed Payments field of the Set Up Electronic Payee or the Edit Electronic Payee window and press Y and then Enter. You also can press F9 to set up a fixed payment. Quicken displays the CheckFree Fixed Payments window shown in figure 13.10.

3. In the Payment Amount field, enter the amount of the fixed payment and press Enter.

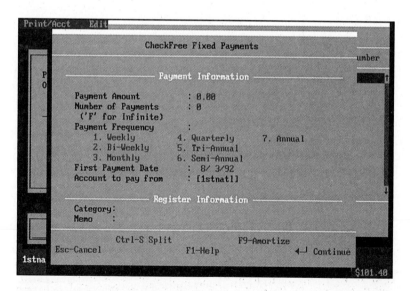

FIG. 13.10

The CheckFree Fixed Payments window.

4. Enter the number of payments (1 to 500) due to the payee in the Number of Payments field. If you owe 48 payments on your car loan, for example, and have already made 5, press enter *43* in the Number of Payments field.

5. Move to the Payment Frequency field and press the number that corresponds to how frequently payments are made (1 for **weekly**, 2 for **biweekly**, 3 for **monthly**, and so on).

6. Move to the First Payment Date field and enter the date that you want CheckFree to make the first payment. Use the + (plus) or – (minus) key to change the date one day at a time.

> **CAUTION:** Because many persons or businesses are not set up to handle electronic funds transfers, these kinds of payments are mailed by CheckFree from Ohio. If the payee's location is your home town, then the payment may take an extra day or two to reach the payee from Ohio. Schedule all CheckFree payments early enough to allow for delays in the mail system.

Quicken enters the account that you selected to pay this payee from in the Account to Pay From field. Quicken does not enable you to change this field.

7. Move to the Category field and enter the category that you want to assign to the fixed payment transaction. If necessary, press Ctrl-C to display the Category and Transfer list and select a category from the list. To assign more than one category to the fixed payment transaction, press Ctrl-S to open the Split Transaction window. Fill in the Split Transaction window as usual (see Chapters 5 and 7 to learn how to split transactions). If you are setting up a fixed payment for an amortized loan (see step 10), be sure that you enter the principal category on the first line in the Split Transaction window and the interest category on the second line.

8. (Optional) If you want to enter a memo to the fixed payment transaction, move to the Memo field and enter the additional information.

9. (Optional) If the fixed payment that you are setting up is a payment on a fixed-rate loan, you may want to memorize the amortized payment schedule so that Quicken allocates the proper principal and interest amounts to each payment. To set up a fixed payment for an amortized loan, press F9. Quicken displays the Set Amortization Information window. Fill in the Set Amortization Information window as you do for any other loan payment. See Chapter 10 to learn about amortizing loan payments.

10. After the CheckFree Fixed Payments window is complete, press Ctrl-Enter to return to the Set Up Electronic Payee window.

11. Press Ctrl-Enter or F10. Quicken displays a note that it first must connect to CheckFree to make fixed payments. To authorize CheckFree to begin making fixed payments to the payee that you just set up, press Enter. Quicken initializes the modem and transmits fixed payment information immediately to CheckFree. CheckFree, however, cannot make a payment until the first payment date that you specified in the CheckFree Fixed Payments window.

When you set up a fixed payment to a payee, Quicken enters the transaction in the Register and inserts the word FIXED in the Num field. After CheckFree makes the fixed payment and Quicken receives confirmation from CheckFree that the payment was made, the word FIXED is replaced with E-PMT (for electronic payment).

Editing a Fixed Payment

If you want to change the payment information for a fixed payment, you can do so from the Electronic Payee list.

To edit fixed payment information, follow these steps:

1. From the Register for the account that you use to make electronic payments, press Ctrl-Y to display the Electronic Payee list.

2. Use the up- and down-arrow keys to highlight the payee for the fixed payment and press Ctrl-E. The Edit Electronic Payee window appears, as shown in figure 13.11.

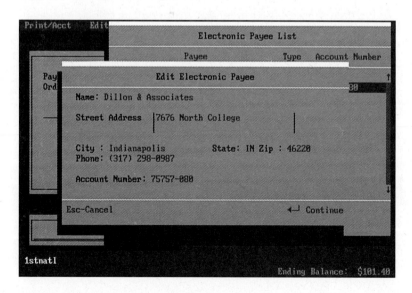

FIG. 13.11

The Edit Electronic Payee window.

3. From the Edit Electronic Payee window, press F9 to display the CheckFree Fixed Payments window.

4. Move to the field that you want and make the necessary changes.

5. After the changes are complete, press Ctrl-Enter. Quicken initializes the modem and immediately transmits the changes to the fixed payment information to CheckFree.

Deleting a Fixed Payment

If you no longer want to make fixed payments to a payee, you can delete the fixed payment information at any time. You cannot delete a fixed payment, however, that was already made and confirmed (E - PMT appears in the Register for these transactions). To delete a payment that was already made, use a stop payment request, as explained in a following section of this chapter.

To delete a fixed payment, follow these steps:

1. From the Register for the account that you use to make electronic payments, press Ctrl-Y to display the Electronic Payee list.

2. Use the up- and down-arrow keys to highlight the payee for the fixed payment and press Ctrl-E. Quicken displays the Edit Electronic Payee window.

3. Press Tab or Enter repeatedly to move to the Enable Fixed Payments field and press N to disable fixed payments.

4. Quicken displays a message that asks you to confirm that you want to cancel fixed payments. Press Enter to confirm.

5. Quicken initializes the modem and immediately transmits instructions to CheckFree to cancel fixed payments to the payee. Quicken also deletes from the Register all transactions (for the payee that you set up the fixed payment to) that show the FIXED message in the Num field.

Paying Bills and Transmitting Mail

Paying bills electronically closely resembles the process of writing and printing checks with Quicken. For this reason, this chapter doesn't repeat the discussions of Chapters 6 and 7, which cover how you write and print checks with Quicken. Instead, this section concentrates on different parts of the process. (If you haven't used the Quicken Write/ Print Checks feature, you may want to review Chapters 6 and 7 before continuing in this chapter.)

After you set up for electronic payment and identify the people you will pay, you can begin paying bills electronically. For each bill you want to pay, take the following steps:

1. From Quicken's main menu, select the **Write/Print Checks** option. (Before you select this option, make sure that you selected the bank account that you use to make electronic payments). Quicken displays the electronic payment version of the Write Checks screen.

2. Complete the electronic payment version of the Write Checks screen in the same way you complete the regular version of the screen, except for the following differences:

    ■ Rather than typing the payee's name, select the payee from the electronic payee list. To display the electronic payee list, press Ctrl-Y. To use one of the electronic payees shown on the list, use the up- and down-arrow keys to highlight the payee that you want to pay and press Enter. You also can use Quicken's new QuickFill feature to enter an electronic payee (see Chapter 7 for more information about QuickFill).

    ■ Rather than track unprinted checks, Quicken shows the checks to transmit in the lower right corner of the screen.

3. After the Write Checks screen is complete, press Ctrl-Enter or F10.

The check that contains the electronic payment scrolls off the screen, leaving behind an *empty* check that you can use to complete another electronic payment. Until you begin transmitting the electronic payments, you can edit these payments just as you do any other check you write at the Write Checks screen.

You also can enter and edit electronic payments by using the Quicken Register. Quicken identifies electronic payment transactions in the Quicken Register by displaying >>>>> in the Num field.

Transmitting Payment Information to CheckFree

After you enter the electronic payments, you can transmit the electronic payments so that CheckFree Corporation can pay them. To transmit the electronic payments, follow these steps:

1. Turn on the modem.

   Quicken first attempts to initialize the modem and then retries the modem twice. If a problem is encountered, a message appears that says Quicken was unable to initialize the modem. Make sure that your modem is connected properly and turned on. If Quicken continues to have a problem initializing your modem, refer to the users' manual for your modem or call Intuit's technical support staff.

2. From the Write Checks screen, press Alt-P to access the Print/Acct menu and select the **Transmit Payments** option (see fig. 13.12).

   Quicken displays the window shown in figure 13.13, which tells you how many payments you have to transmit.

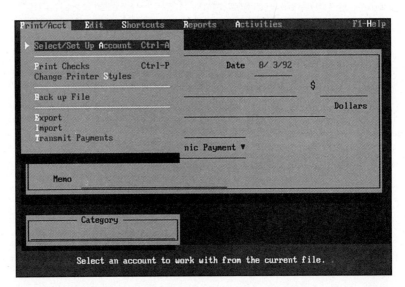

FIG. 13.12

The electronic payment version of the Print/Acct menu.

3. If you are ready to transmit, press Enter. Or, if you want to review the payments that are ready to be transmitted, press F9, and Quicken displays the Preview Transmission to CheckFree window.

This window lists the payments Quicken will transmit. After you do transmit the payments, CheckFree sends confirmation numbers back to Quicken for each transmitted payment. Confirmation numbers are stored in the Memo field of each transaction.

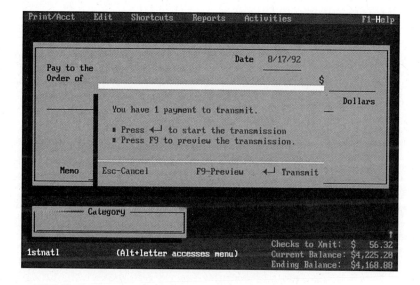

```
 Print/Acct    Edit    Shortcuts    Reports    Activities          F1-Help

                                    Date    8/17/92
    Pay to the
    Order of                                                 $
                                                                      Dollars
    _____                 You have 1 payment to transmit.        _

                             ▪ Press ↵ to start the transmission
                             ▪ Press F9 to preview the transmission.


    Memo        Esc-Cancel            F9-Preview    ↵ Transmit


              ----- Category -----
    _____
    |                                    |
    |_____|
                                                              ↑
    1stnatl           (Alt+letter accesses menu)   Checks to Xmit:  $   56.32
                                                   Current Balance: $4,225.20
                                                   Ending Balance:  $4,168.88
```

FIG. 13.13

The window that tells you how many payments you have to transmit.

Issuing a Stop Payment Request

You can use Quicken to issue stop payment requests on electronic payments you transmitted previously. To issue a stop payment request, follow these steps:

1. Turn on the modem.

2. Access the Register for the account that you use to make electronic payments.

3. Highlight the transaction in the Register on which you want to stop payment.

4. Press Alt-E to access the Edit menu.

5. Select the **Transmit Stop Payment Request** option from the Edit menu.

6. Quicken asks you to confirm the stop payment. Press Y for Yes. Quicken immediately transmits the request to CheckFree. If the transmission is successful, Quicken marks the transaction as Void.

Obviously, as with stop payment requests issued directly to the bank, you need to make the request before the transaction is processed.

Making an Electronic Payment Inquiry

You can ask about a payment you transmitted previously. Suppose that you receive a telephone call from someone who wants to know whether you have sent them a check yet. You can make an electronic payment inquiry to check the status of this particular payment.

To make an electronic payment inquiry, follow these steps:

1. Turn on the modem.

2. Access the Register for the account that you use to make electronic payments.

3. Highlight the transaction in the Register that you want to inquire about. Electronic payments are marked with >>>>> in the Num field.

4. Press Alt-E to access the Edit menu.

5. Select the **Electronic Payment Inquiry** option from the Edit menu.

6. Quicken displays the details of the transmitted payment, including the account number, the payment date, the date the transaction was transmitted to CheckFree, and the confirmation number you received from CheckFree. This window also indicates whether you can stop payment (if at least five days still remain between the transmission date and the payment date). Quicken also asks whether you want to send an inquiry message to CheckFree regarding the transaction.

7. Press Y if you want to send a payment inquiry to CheckFree. Quicken displays the Transmit Inquiry to CheckFree window.

8. Complete the Transmit Inquiry to CheckFree window and press Ctrl-Enter to send the payment inquiry to CheckFree.

Sending Electronic Mail to CheckFree

You also can send an electronic message to CheckFree. You may want to send a message to inquire about your CheckFree account or to respond to an inquiry from CheckFree.

To send an electronic mail message to CheckFree, follow these steps:

1. Turn on the modem.

2. Press Alt-A to access the Activities menu and select the **Send Electronic Mail** option. The Transmit Inquiry to CheckFree window appears (see fig. 13.14).

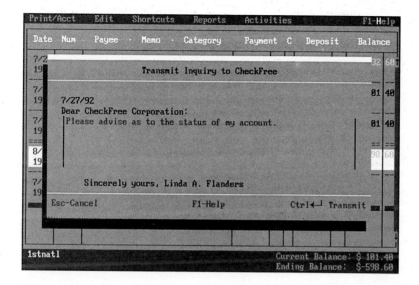

FIG. 13.14

The Transmit
Inquiry to
CheckFree
window.

3. Type the message to CheckFree just as you type a message with a word processor. You can type messages up to five lines in length. CheckFree wraps the end of the line to the following line so that you don't need to press Enter at the end of each line.

4. After you type the message, press Ctrl-Enter. Quicken initializes the modem and transmits the message to CheckFree.

Receiving Electronic Mail from CheckFree

With Quicken 6.0 you can receive electronic mail from CheckFree that you can read from the Register or the Write Checks screen.

To receive electronic mail messages from CheckFree, follow these steps:

1. Turn on the modem.

2. Press Alt-A to access the Activities menu and select the **Check Electronic Mail** option.

3. Quicken initializes the modem and transmits instructions to check your electronic mailbox for messages.

4. Quicken displays all messages in chronological order. Press F10 to read the next page or F9 to read the previous page. Press PgUp or PgDn to move up or down one message screen at a time.

Chapter Summary

This chapter described Quicken's electronic payment capability. You learned how to set up your system to make electronic payments, how to set up payees, how to use Quicken 6.0's new fixed payment feature, and how to pay bills electronically. You also learned how to transmit electronic messages to CheckFree and how to receive electronic mail from CheckFree (new to Version 6.0).

In the following chapter, you learn how to make tax time less hectic by using Quicken to accumulate tax data in reports that you can use easily to prepare your return. You also learn how to export tax data to tax preparation programs, such as TurboTax and TaxCut.

Using Quicken To Prepare for Income Taxes

A basic accounting requirement for businesses and individuals is to complete the required federal income tax forms at the end of the year to report income and expenses. Although everyone knows that taxes are inevitable, not everyone organizes financial activities so that tax time is not a surprise. With Quicken, you can designate categories and subcategories as tax-related and accumulate your tax information in seconds. Whether you prepare your own income tax return or hand your tax information to a paid tax accountant, Quicken alleviates the burden of gathering tax data.

The beginning of this chapter explains how to use categories for income tax purposes. Some Quicken users also want to know how to export the income tax deduction data inside Quicken to external income tax preparation packages such as TurboTax. The mechanics of exporting income tax data also are covered in this chapter.

Using Categories

The basic rule for using categories (and subcategories) to accumulate your tax data is to set up a category or subcategory for each taxable income item or tax deduction that you have. And the best way to do this is by reviewing your last two income tax returns to determine which of these items you have. If you make charitable contributions each year and itemize your deductions, you'll want to make sure that you have a category set up (and designated as tax-related) to assign to charitable contribution transactions. If you want to track a taxable income item or tax deduction item in more detail, you can use subcategories and designate the subcategories as tax-related. Chapter 9 describes how to create and use categories and subcategories and how to designate a category or subcategory as tax-related.

If you don't itemize your deductions (because the total of your itemized deductions does not exceed the standard deduction amount), then it's not necessary to designate the charitable contribution category as tax-related.

The following examples may help you to better understand how to use categories and subcategories. Real estate investors complete the Schedule E tax form; farmers complete the Schedule F tax form; sole proprietors complete the Schedule C tax form; partnerships complete the Schedule 1065 tax form; and corporations complete one of the three corporate income tax forms: 1120-A for small corporations, 1120S for S Corporations, and 1120 for all other corporations.

C P A
T I P   *S Corporations* are corporations that have elected to be treated as partnerships for income tax purposes. The income from the S Corporation is not taxed to the S Corporation, but rather to its shareholders.

If you live in a state with income taxes, you also may need to complete an equivalent state income tax form. Make sure that you or an accountant can easily prepare the tax return with the information Quicken produces. (The more time the accountant takes, the more money you pay to have the accountant to prepare the return.)

You also can work with categories that you need to combine with other categories to calculate an entry on a tax form. Suppose that you are a sole proprietor and own a restaurant. Although total wages goes on one line of the Schedule C tax form, you may want to track several categories of wages (subcategories), including waitresses, dishwashers, cooks, bartenders, and so on. Here, you have several wage subcategories that must be added to calculate the wages amount that goes on the tax form. The Tax Schedule report can help you accumulate data from more than one subcategory.

If you are using Quicken for a sole proprietorship and you hold and resell inventory, you need Part III of the Schedule C form to calculate the cost of goods sold and the inventory balances. You can use the periodic inventory approach described in Chapter 22 to produce the information for Part III of the Schedule C form.

If you are using Quicken for a partnership or a corporation, you must report asset and liability amounts on the tax return. You also want to verify that Quicken provides the data necessary to complete these lines of the tax return. The easiest approach probably is to set up accounts to track each asset and liability that appears on the tax return. Another approach is to use accounts that you can combine to calculate the total asset or liability figure that needs to be entered on the tax return.

Sole proprietors must consider one other thing: you may need to complete more than one Schedule C form. You cannot aggregate a series of dissimilar businesses and report the consolidated results on one Schedule C. If you own a tavern, practice law, and run a small manufacturing business, you must complete three Schedule C forms: one form for the tavern, one form for the law practice, and still another form for the manufacturing firm. Quicken can handle this situation, but you need to account for each business that needs a separate Schedule C in a separate Quicken file. (Chapter 19, "Managing Your Quicken Files," explains how to set up and select different Quicken files.)

When you use Quicken's categories, extracting the information you need to complete a tax form is simple. You just print the report that summarizes the categories that track income tax deductions. For individuals, the Tax Summary report is valuable; for businesses, the Profit and Loss statement is valuable.

C P A
T I P

Although tax forms give most of the general information about the kinds of expenses, the instructions and regulations made by the IRS may require that you gather additional information. One example is that the business usage of a vehicle owned by a business is subject to different limitations, which are not necessarily found in Quicken. Consult a tax advisor when you encounter questionable areas.

Exporting Quicken Data into Tax Preparation Programs

You can import the financial data you collect and store in Quicken directly into several popular income tax preparation packages. TurboTax, for example, imports Quicken data if you follow general steps. Even if you don't have TurboTax, you still may be able to apply the same general steps discussed in this section to export Quicken data to other tax preparation packages.

And now with Quicken 6.0, it's easy to export your Quicken data to a file that you can use in TurboTax, Taxcut, or other tax preparation packages. Quicken provides the Export Tax Schedule assistant, which you use to create a Tax Schedule report, and then to export the information from the report to a file you can import into your tax preparation program.

To export your Quicken data to a tax preparation program using the Export Tax Schedule assistant, follow these steps:

1. From the Quicken main menu, select the **Use Tutorials/Assistants** option.

   Quicken displays the Use Tutorials/Assistants menu, as shown in figure 14.1.

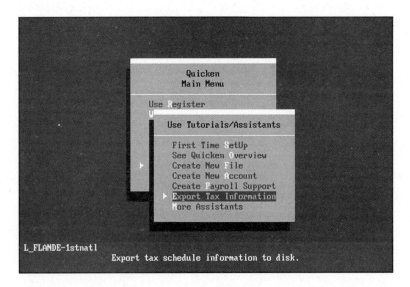

The Use Tutorials/Assistants menu.

2. Select the **Export Tax Information** option. Quicken displays the
   Export Tax Schedule Assistant window, shown in figure 14.2. Read
   the message that appears and press Enter to continue.

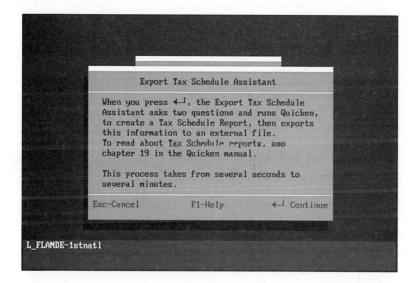

Export Tax Schedule Assistant

When you press ←⏎, the Export Tax Schedule
Assistant asks two questions and runs Quicken,
to create a Tax Schedule Report, then exports
this information to an external file.
To read about Tax Schedule reports, see
chapter 19 in the Quicken manual.

This process takes from several seconds to
several minutes.

Esc-Cancel   F1-Help   ←⏎ Continue

L_FLANDE-1stnatl

FIG. 14.2

The Export Tax
Schedule
Assistant
window.

3. In the assistant's next window, you're asked to enter the year that
   you want the Tax Schedule report to cover. When you enter a
   year, Quicken includes transactions through and including 1/1/*xx*
   to 12/31/*xx*. In the next field, the assistant asks for the beginning
   date for the capital gains information that you want to export.
   This date tells Quicken the earliest purchase date of any stock
   that you may have sold during the year.

4. Press Ctrl-Enter or F10 to continue. Next, you must enter the DOS
   file name that you want Quicken to use to name the file that it
   exports the Tax Schedule report data to. You can include a full
   path in the DOS File field. Make sure that your file name meets the
   criteria for DOS file names (consult your DOS manual if you need
   help).

5. After you enter the DOS file name, press Enter to continue with
   the exporting process.

   Quicken's Export Tax Schedule assistant sets up the transaction
   dates for the Tax Schedule report and displays the Choose
   Accounts to Include window superimposed over the Select
   Accounts to Include window (see fig. 14.3).

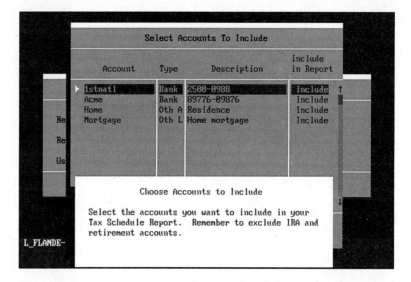

FIG. 14.3

The Choose Accounts to Include and the Select Accounts to Include windows.

6. Press Enter to remove the Choose Accounts to Include window so that you can choose the accounts you want Quicken to use to accumulate tax data. You will want to include all of your bank, cash, and credit card accounts so that Quicken picks up tax-related transactions from these accounts. You should not include your IRA or retirement account, however, because IRA and retirement contributions are reflected in the account where you made the contribution.

   Initially, all the accounts in the Select Accounts to Include window are marked to be included in the Tax Schedule report. To exclude an account, use the up- and down-arrow keys to highlight the account you want to exclude and press the space bar. You use the space bar as a toggle switch to mark transactions to include or exclude.

7. After you have selected the accounts you want Quicken to include in the Tax Schedule report, press Enter. Quicken's Export Tax Schedule assistant goes through some steps to include those accounts in the Tax Schedule report, and then displays the Choose Investment Accounts to Include window superimposed over the Select Accounts to Include window, as seen in figure 14.4 (Quicken includes only investment accounts in this window). Press Enter to remove the Choose Investment Accounts to Include window.

   Use the up- and down-arrow keys to highlight the investment account you want to include in the Tax Schedule report and press the space bar to include or exclude transactions. When you're finished selecting investment accounts, press Enter.

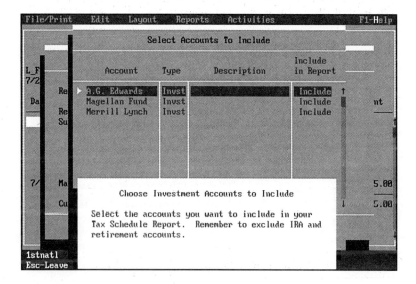

FIG. 14.4

The Choose
Investment
Accounts to
Include screen
and Select
Accounts to
Include window.

The assistant searches through the investment accounts that you selected to include tax-related transactions. If no transactions are found, a message to that effect is displayed (press Enter to remove the message, and the assistant continues with the exporting process).

The assistant continues to accumulate tax-related data and create and export the Tax Schedule report to an external file that can be used by TurboTax or other tax preparation programs. When the process is complete, the Quicken Export Tax Schedule assistant displays an ending message telling you that the Tax Schedule report was exported and is ready to be imported into TurboTax, Taxcut, or other tax preparation programs (see fig. 14.5).

After the Tax Schedule report is exported to an external file, exit Quicken and follow the instructions in your TurboTax or other tax preparation software manual for importing the data contained in the disk file that you just created. (For this information and for other help with TurboTax, you may want to read *Using TurboTax: 1993 Edition*, published by Que Corporation).

NOTE You don't have to use the Export Tax Schedule assistant to export tax data. You can create the Tax Schedule report (as explained in Chapter 12, "Creating and Printing Reports"), and then select the **Disk (tax file)** option from the Print Report window by pressing 6.

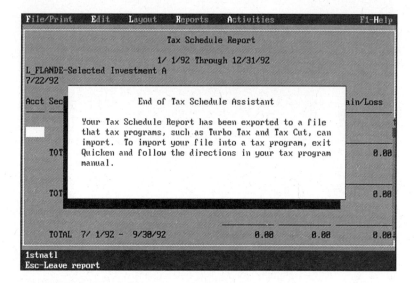

FIG. 14.5

The End of
Tax Schedule
Assistant screen.

Chapter Summary

This chapter described the basic steps to take to ensure that Quicken produces the data necessary to complete federal and state income tax returns. The steps are neither complex nor difficult. You are required from the very beginning, however, to use categories that enable you to summarize income and expense data correctly.

The next chapter begins Part III of *Using Quicken 6 for DOS*, "Analyzing Your Finances with Quicken." In this part, you learn how to create a budget with Quicken, how to use investment accounts to monitor your investments in stocks, bonds, mutual funds, and so on, and how to use two new features in Quicken 6.0: graphs and financial calculators.

Analyzing Your Finances with Quicken

P A R T

III

O U T L I N E

Budgeting with Quicken

Budgeting has an undeserved bad reputation because people tend to think of a budget as financial handcuffs—an obstacle to enjoyment and a drag on financial freedoms. Actually, nothing is further from the truth. Budgeting is a simple tool with astonishingly positive benefits for businesses and households. Budgets represent game plans that calibrate, or specify, what you need to do to succeed in business or personal financial life.

Because one of Quicken's most significant benefits is the capability of monitoring your financial success through budgeting, this chapter reviews the three steps of budgeting, describes how Quicken helps budget more effectively, and provides some tips on how to budget successfully.

In this chapter you learn the definition of budgeting and how to do the following tasks:

- Set financial goals
- Enter and edit budget data in Quicken's budgeting spreadsheet
- Change the spreadsheet layout
- Print, export, and import budget data

Defining Budgeting

Budgeting consists of the following three steps:

1. You need to set business or personal financial goals.

2. You then use the list of goals as a guide to developing a financial game plan, or budget.

3. Finally, you use the budget to monitor your spending to determine how closely you are progressing toward your business or personal goals.

Setting Your Goals

Budgeting begins with identifying goals in business or life. You are on your own here. When building a list of goals, however, keep the following two things in mind:

■ Keep the goals general.

■ Involve other people, particularly those who have to live within the budget, in setting the goals.

By stating the goals in more general terms, you don't start with built-in constraints and conflicts. Suppose that your goal is to live in an opulent fashion where the weather is warm and sunny. With this goal, you have a world of choices and an incredible range of prices. If the goal is to live in a mansion in Beverly Hills, you are limiting yourself. Living in a Beverly Hills mansion is one way—but not the only way—to live in an opulent fashion where the weather is warm and sunny. Keep your options open as you build a list of life goals, and you are more likely to get more of the things you want out of life and to achieve more in your business.

A second point about setting goals is to involve other people, because people who work together to build a list of goals later also work together to achieve the goals. Working together also produces better goal lists.

The United States Air Force and many businesses play a game called *desert survival*. This game demonstrates the results of a group that works to make decisions. You pretend that a plane on which you are a passenger crashes in the desert. You are 30 miles off course and at least that far from civilization; the temperature is over 100 degrees in the shade, and you can salvage about 15 or 20 items before the plane bursts into flames. First, you decide by yourself whether to stay with the wreckage or start toward civilization and which of the items you want to keep. Next, you repeat the analysis in groups of four or five people, and this time the entire group must agree on the plan and which items to keep. An interesting point about the game—and the reason that this whole issue applies to budgeting—is that in almost every case, when people make the decisions together, they dramatically increase the chance of survival of all the members of the group.

Making the wrong budgeting decision may not cost you your life or your business, but the moral of the desert survival game still applies. Whether you budget personal or business finances, you build better goal lists when you involve more people. Your spouse may end up discovering an option not previously considered. A daughter may announce that she is no longer interested in piano lessons or business school. A partner may point out a subtle flaw you overlooked.

After you finish setting your goals, write them down. Don't limit yourself to just financial goals. You may have financial goals, such as accumulating the down payment for a new car or taking a special vacation. You also may have nonfinancial goals, such as spending more time with the family or beginning a recreational or charitable activity.

Designing a Game Plan

After you build a list of goals, you are ready to create a game plan to achieve these goals. As you work through the details, you undoubtedly will modify the goals and make compromises. If you describe the goals in general terms and include everybody's good ideas, you come up with a detailed list of the costs of pursuing and achieving your business or personal goals.

At this stage, you decide how much money you are going to spend on entertainment or a vacation, how much you can spend on housing, and other issues. As a rough yardstick to use to build a detailed game plan, table 15.1 summarizes, on the average, what percent of income most people spend in various spending categories. This list comes from the July 1990 issue of *Survey of Current Business*, which is published by the U.S. Department of Commerce. The survey is dated, but because the results show as percentages of total income, the data is still valid for planning and comparison purposes.

Table 15.1 Average Spending Based on After-Tax Income

Spending Category	Percent
Durable Goods	
Motor vehicles and parts	5.43
Furniture and household equipment	4.50
Other durables	2.29
Nondurable goods	
Food	15.74
Clothing and shoes	5.38
Gasoline and oil	2.13
Other nondurables	6.57
Services	
Housing	14.34
Utilities	5.46
Transportation	3.47
Medical care	12.12
Other Services	14.71
Interest	2.74
Savings	5.12

If you are budgeting for a business, you can visit the local public library to obtain similar information. Dun and Bradstreet and Robert Morris Associates annually publish financial information on businesses grouped by industry and business size. For business or personal budgeting, however, don't interpret the averages as anything other than general guidelines. Seeing other companies spending numbers can provide a useful perspective on your spending but your goals should determine the details of your financial game plan.

After you finish setting your goals, write your spending game plan. Now that you know how much time and money you can allocate to each goal, you often can expand the list of goals to include estimates of costs and time. Table 15.2 lists a set of sample personal goals, and table 15.3 lists a set of sample business goals. Table 15.4 shows an example of an annual personal budget with monthly breakdowns supporting the goals from table 15.2. Table 15.5 shows an example of an annual business budget that supports the goals from table 15.3.

Table 15.2 Sample Personal Budget Goals

Goal	Cost	Timing
Visit Egypt	$5,000	1995
Start fishing again	$50	ASAP
Prepare for retirement	$100,000	2025
Spend time with family	$0	ASAP

Table 15.3 Sample Business Budget Goals

Goal	Cost	Timing
Generate 20% more annual sales	$20,000	over year
Pay down credit line	$5,000	year-end
Make profits of $25,000	$25,000	over year
Provide higher quality service	$0	ASAP

Table 15.4 Sample Budget To Support Personal Goals

Personal Budget	Annual	Monthly
Income	$25,000	$2,083
Outgo		
Income taxes	$1,750	$146
Social Security	1,878	156
Rent	6,000	500
Other housing	3,000	250
Food	4,800	400
Transportation	2,500	208
Vacation, recreation	1,200	100
Fishing gear	50	4
Clothing	1,250	104

continues

Table 15.4 Continued

Personal Budget	Annual	Monthly
Savings—IRA	500	42
Other	1,200	100
Total Expenses	24,628	2,052
Leftover/Contingency	373	31

Table 15.5 Sample Budget To Support Business Goals

Business Budget	Annual	Monthly
Sales	$125,000	$10,417
Expenses		
Materials	$30,000	$2,500
Labor	30,000	2,500
Rent	12,000	1,000
Transportation	12,500	1,042
Supplies	12,000	1,000
Legal/Accounting	1,200	100
Other	2,100	175
Total Expenses	99,800	8,317
Profits	25,200	2,100

Notice a few things about the relationships between the goals and budget. First, some goals represent plateaus you can achieve almost immediately; other goals may take longer to achieve. Second, some goals on the list don't directly affect the budget. Third, some expenditures don't tie to formal, or stated, goals but still represent implied goals. You do not, for example, list feeding the children or staying in business, but these actions may be your most important goals.

Monitoring Your Progress

The third and final step in budgeting relates to monitoring your progress in achieving personal or business goals. On a periodic basis—every month or quarter—compare the amount you budgeted to spend with the amount you actually spent. Often, people view these comparisons as negative, but the idea is that, when following a budget, you are moving toward your goals. If you get through the first month of the year and are operating under the budget shown in table 15.4, for example, you can compare what you spent with your budget. If you see from the numbers on the budget that you are having difficulty setting aside extra money for the trip to Egypt and to contribute to an individual retirement account, you know that your spending or your goals need to change.

Using Quicken To Budget

Quicken provides three features that enable you to budget more effectively for personal finances and for small businesses: categories, the budget spreadsheet, and reporting.

Using Categories

With categories, you can assign each check that you record a spending category, such as housing, contribution, entertainment, or taxes. You also can assign an income category to each of the deposits you record, such as wages, gross sales, or interest income. The steps and benefits of using categories are discussed in greater detail in Chapter 9, "Organizing Your Finances." By assigning the category into which every check and deposit you record belongs, you can produce reports that summarize and total the inflows and outflows—by category—for a specific period. Figure 15.1 shows an example of a Quicken cash flow report.

If you decide to tap the power of budgeting, reports like the one shown in figure 15.1 are invaluable. The report shows what you actually spend. What you actually spend can be compared to what you budgeted. When the actual spending matches the budgeted spending, you know you are following your financial game plan. When the spending doesn't match the budget, you know you are not following the game plan.

Creating Budgeting Reports

Quicken also enables you to enter any amount budgeted for a category. With this information, Quicken calculates the difference, or *variance*, between the total spent on a category and the budgeted amount for a category. Quicken performs the arithmetic related to monitoring how closely you follow the budget and how successfully you are marching toward your life goals. Figure 15.2 shows an example of a Quicken budget report. Chapter 12 shows you how to generate a budget report like the report shown in figure 15.2.

```
                        CASH FLOW REPORT
                   7/ 1/92 Through 7/31/92
        L_FLANDE-Bank,Cash,CC Accounts              Page 1
        7/27/92

          Category Description              7/ 1/92-7/31/92
          --------------------              --------------------
          INFLOWS
            Int Inc                                    8.47
            Salary                                 8,000.00
            ----------
          TOTAL INFLOWS                             8,008.47
          OUTFLOWS
            Auto:
              Fuel                 75.04
              Auto - Other          6.50
                                 --------
            Total Auto                                81.54
            Bank Chrg                                  3.50
            Clothing                                 127.65
            Cosmetics                                 25.00
            Dining                                    55.26
            Drycleaning                               22.59
            Entertain                                 14.69
            Finance chg                               14.59
            Gifts                                    120.98
            Groceries                                141.90
            Housecleaning                            165.00
            Household                                 64.73
            Insurance                                 50.00
            Medical                                   35.00
            Misc                                       6.50
            Mort Int                               1,300.00
            Pet care                                  38.03
            Postage                                   25.00
            preschool                                130.00
            Tax:
              Fed               2,000.00
              FICA                612.00
              Prop                152.98
              State               320.00
                                 --------
            Total Tax                              3,084.98
            Utilities                                284.14
            TO Mortgage                              250.00
                                              -----------
          TOTAL OUTFLOWS                            6,041.08
                                              -----------
          OVERALL TOTAL                             1,967.39
                                              ==========
```

FIG. 15.1

A sample cash flow report, by category.

```
                        BUDGET REPORT
                   7/ 1/92 Through 7/31/92
L_FLANDE-All Accounts                               Page 1
7/27/92

                       7/ 1/92         -        7/31/92
Category Description   Actual       Budget       Diff
-------------------    --------     -------     --------
INCOME/EXPENSE
  INCOME
    Int Inc               8.47         8.00        0.47
    Salary            8,000.00     8,000.00        0.00
                      --------     --------     --------
TOTAL INCOME          8,008.47     8,008.00        0.47

EXPENSES
  Auto:
    Fuel                75.04        75.00        0.04
    Auto - Other         6.50         7.00       -0.50
                      -------      --------     --------
Total Auto              81.54        82.00       -0.46
Bank Chrg                3.50         4.00       -0.50
Clothing               127.65       128.00       -0.35
Cosmetics               25.00        25.00        0.00
Dining                  55.26        55.00        0.26
Drycleaning             22.59        23.00       -0.41
Entertain               14.69        15.00       -0.31
Finance chg             14.59        15.00       -0.41
Gifts                  120.98       121.00       -0.02
Groceries              141.90       142.00       -0.10
Housecleaning          165.00       165.00        0.00
Household               64.73        65.00       -0.27
Insurance               50.00        50.00        0.00
Medical                 35.00        35.00        0.00
Misc                     6.50         7.00       -0.50
Mort Int             1,300.00     1,300.00        0.00
Pet care                38.03        38.00        0.03
Postage                 25.00        25.00        0.00
preschool              130.00       130.00        0.00
Tax:
  Fed                2,000.00     2,000.00        0.00
  FICA                 612.00       612.00        0.00
  Prop                 152.98       153.00       -0.02
  State                320.00       320.00        0.00
                      --------     --------     --------
Total Tax            3,084.98     3,085.00       -0.02
Utilities              284.14       284.00        0.14
                     ---------    ---------     --------
TOTAL EXPENSES       5,791.08     5,794.00       -2.92
                     ---------    ---------     --------

TOTAL INCOME/EXPENSE 2,217.39     2,214.00        3.39

                     =========    =========     ========
```

FIG. 15.2

A sample budget report.

TIP You can create graphs of the actual and budgeted data with Quicken's new **View Graphs** option from the main menu. Refer to Chapter 17, "Creating Graphs," to learn how to create on-screen graphs to compare the actual data to budgeted data.

Setting Up Budgets

To print budget reports, you first need to enter the budget amounts that Quicken uses for actual-to-budget comparisons. Quicken provides a spreadsheet screen in which you enter budgeted amounts for each category and subcategory.

To use Quicken's budgeting spreadsheet to set up a budget, these steps:

1. From the Register or the Write Checks screen, select the **Set Up Budgets** option from the Activities menu (see fig. 15.3).

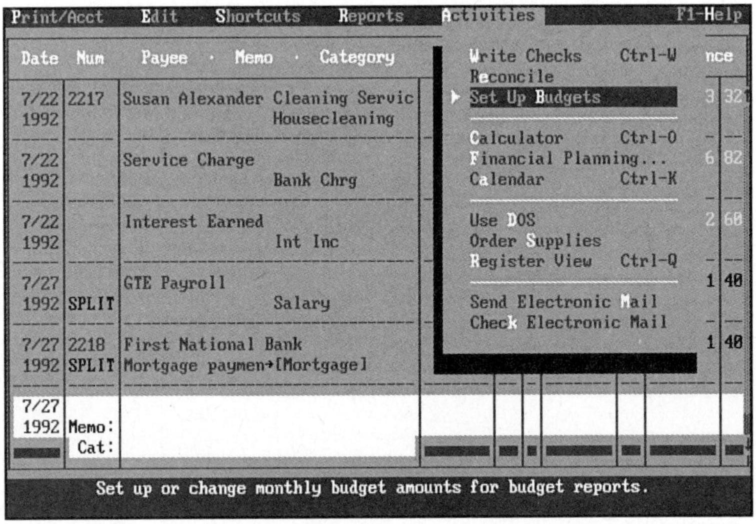

FIG. 15.3

The Set Up Budgets option from the Activities menu.

Quicken displays the budgeting spreadsheet screen that you see in figure 15.4. The budget spreadsheet shows a menu at the top of the screen that includes the File, Edit, Layout, and Activities names.

```
 File   Edit   Layout   Activities                         F1-Help

  Category Description    Jan.     Feb.     Mar.     Apr.     May     J

 INFLOWS
   Bonus                    0        0        0        0        0     1
   Canada Pen               0        0        0        0        0
   Div Income               0        0        0        0        0
   Gift Received            0        0        0        0        0
   Int Inc                  0        0        0        0        0
   Invest Inc               0        0        0        0        0
   Old Age Pension          0        0        0        0        0
   Other Inc                0        0        0        0        0
   Salary                   0        0        0        0        0
   _DivInc                  0        0        0        0        0
   _IntInc                  0        0        0        0        0
   _LT CapGnDst             0        0        0        0        0

   Total Budget Inflows     0        0        0        0        0
   Total Budget Outflows    0        0        0        0        0
   Difference               0        0        0        0        0

 1stnatl
 Esc-Leave budget
```

FIG. 15.4

The budgeting
spreadsheet
screen.

2. Enter monthly budgeted amounts for each category and, optionally, subcategories and account transfers on the category list. Use
   the up- and down-arrow keys to move up or down a monthly column, or use the Tab key to move right across the category rows.
   Pressing Shift-Tab moves you to the left in a category row. See
   "Entering and Editing Budget Data," later in this chapter, to learn
   how to enter or edit budgeted amounts in the budgeting spreadsheet.

3. After you enter the budgeted amounts, press Esc to leave the budgeting spreadsheet. The budget data then is saved.

Changing the Spreadsheet Layout

By default, Quicken assumes that you want to budget on a monthly
basis, so the spreadsheet displays a column for each month, but you
also can budget on a quarterly and monthly basis by pressing Alt-L to
display the Layout menu (see fig. 15.5). Use the down-arrow key to
highlight the layout that you want to select (**Quarter** or **Year**) and then
press Enter. Quicken changes the spreadsheet to the layout that you
select.

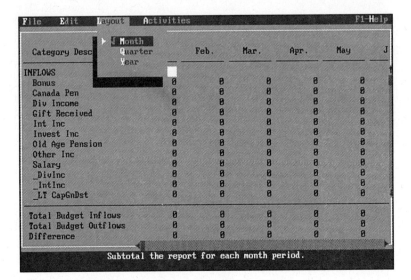

FIG. 15.5

The Layout menu
from the budget-
ing spreadsheet
screen.

Entering and Editing Budget Data

One way to enter budgeted amounts is directly into the spreadsheet by moving the cursor to the budget amount you want to enter, such as childcare expenses for January, and then typing the new budget figure. A second way to enter budget amounts is to copy amounts into the spreadsheet by using one of the Edit menu options. Figure 15.6 shows the Edit menu available on the budget spreadsheet screen. Using the Edit menu options, you can enter budget data in a variety of ways. You can enter budget data based on your actual income and expenses over a specified period of time, for example. Or, you can fill in one column or row and have Quicken copy the budget data that you entered into other columns or rows. You also can specify whether you want to enter budget data for subcategories and transfer accounts. The following sections describe the options from the Edit menu that you can use to enter data into the budgeting spreadsheet.

Entering Budget Data from Actual Data

If you want to set up a budget based on actual income and expense amounts, you can use the **AutoCreate** option from the Edit menu. **AutoCreate** copies actual data from a specified time period into the budgeting spreadsheet. You can tell Quicken to enter rounded values in the budget or to use averages for the period that you specify.

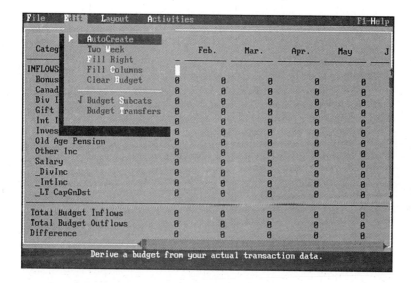

FIG. 15.6

The Edit menu from the budgeting spreadsheet screen.

To enter budget data from actual data, follow these steps:

1. Access the budgeting spreadsheet screen, as explained in the previous section, "Setting Up Budgets."

2. Press Alt-E to display the Edit menu.

3. From the Edit menu, select the **AutoCreate** option. Quicken displays the Automatically Create Budget window that you see in figure 15.7.

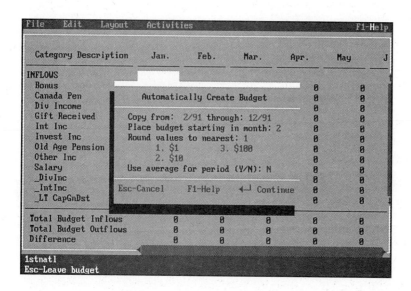

FIG. 15.7

The Automatically Create Budget window.

4. Enter the date range of the actual monthly figures you want to copy in the Copy From and Through fields.

5. Press Enter or Tab to move to the Place Budget Starting in Month (or period) field. Identify the first budgeting month or period in which you want to place the first copied number.

6. To indicate how Quicken rounds copied values before using them as the new budgeted amounts, move the cursor to the Round Values to Nearest field, and select a rounding option: 1 to round to the nearest dollar, 2 to round to the nearest 10 dollars, and 3 to round to the nearest 100 dollars.

7. To tell Quicken to calculate the average for the copied actual amounts and use the result as the budgeted amount, move the cursor to the Use Average for Period field and press Y.

8. To enter the budgeted amounts in the budgeting spreadsheet from the actual data, press Ctrl-Enter or F10.

Budgeting for Items that Occur Every Two Weeks

The Edit menu's **Two Week** option enables you to budget amounts that occur every two weeks, such as salary paid biweekly. To use this handy option, take the following steps:

1. Access the budgeting spreadsheet screen.

2. Highlight the amount field for the category for which you want to set up a two-week budget amount.

3. Select the **Two Week** option from the Edit menu. Quicken displays the Set Up 2 Week Budget window that you see in figure 15.8. In the Category field, Quicken enters the category name for the amount field that you selected in step 2.

4. Enter the dollar amount that you want to budget in the Enter the Amount field. Press Enter.

5. Enter the starting date for the first two-week interval in the Every 2 Weeks Starting field.

6. Press Ctrl-Enter or F10 to set up the two-week budget amount.

Filling in Rows and Columns

The **Fill Right** option from the Edit menu copies the highlighted budget amount to each field to the right in the current row. If you highlight, for example, the January entertainment expense budget amount field, which is set to $25, and then you select the **Fill Right** option, Quicken copies 25 to the entertainment expense budgets fields for February, March, April, May, and so on.

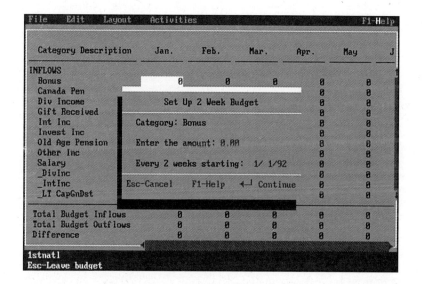

FIG. 15.8

The Set Up 2 Week Budget window.

The **Fill Columns** option from the Edit menu works like the **Fill Right** option except that **Fill Columns** doesn't copy a single budget amount. **Fill Columns** copies a column of budget amounts to the columns to the right of that column. If you highlight one of the budget amounts in the July column, for example, and then select the **Fill Columns** option, Quicken copies the budgeted figures in the July column to the August, September, October, November, and December budget columns.

Clearing the Budget Spreadsheet

If you want to clear all data from the budget spreadsheet and start over, you can select the **Clear Budget** option from the Edit menu. When you select **Clear Budget**, Quicken displays a warning that you are about to clear all budget amounts. To clear budget amounts, press Enter. If you decide that you don't want to clear the budgeted amounts from the budget spreadsheet, press Esc.

Budgeting Subcategories and Transfers

The Edit menu's last two options—**Budget Subcats** and **Budget Transfers**—control whether rows for budgeting subcategories and budgeting account transfers appear in the budget spreadsheet. Both the **Budget**

Subcats and **Budget Transfers** options are toggle switches that alternately turn on and turn off the display of these extra subcategory and account transfer rows. If the budget spreadsheet doesn't show subcategories, for example, just select the **Budget Subcats** option to display subcategories. If you later decide that you want the subcategories hidden, select the **Budget Subcats** option again.

> **T I P** The budget spreadsheet screen's Activities menu provides a subset of the options found on the Register and Write Checks screens' Activities menus. If you press Alt-A to display the Activities menu, you see three options on the Activities menu: **Register**, **Write Checks**, and **Calculator**. You probably already know how these options work. Select the **Register** option to display the Register screen. Select the **Write Checks** option to display the Write Checks screen. Finally, select the **Calculator** option to display the on-line 10-key calculator that Quicken provides.

Printing, Exporting, and Importing Budget Data

The budget spreadsheet's File menu provides three options: **Print Budgets**, **Export Budget**, and **Import Budget** (see fig. 15.9). The first File menu option, **Print Budgets**, prints a copy of the budget spreadsheet. When you select this option, Quicken displays a Print Budget window that looks like and works like the Print Register window described in Chapter 4.

The second and third File menu options, **Export Budget** and **Import Budget**, enable you to move data between Quicken and other application programs. **Export Budget** creates a QIF file that stores the information contained in the budget spreadsheet. **Import Budget** imports a QIF file that stores budget information and uses the information to fill in the budget spreadsheet screen. When you select the **Export Budget** or **Import Budget** option, Quicken displays a window you use to name the QIF file. Exporting, importing, and QIF files are discussed in greater detail in Chapter 19, "Managing Your Quicken Files."

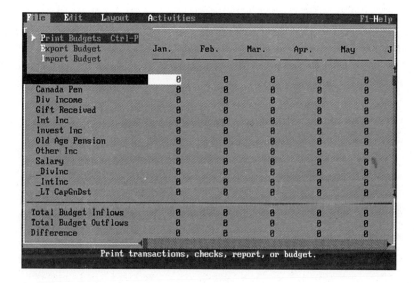

FIG. 15.9

The File menu
from the
budgeting
spreadsheet
screen.

Reviewing Tips for Successful Budgeting

Even if you started out listing personal or business goals, involved the
entire family or company in the process, and created a budget compatible with stated and implied goals, you can take other precautions to
succeed in budgeting. These precautions include paying yourself first,
recognizing after-tax shares, providing for unplanned or emergency
events, and using zero-based budgeting.

Paying Yourself First

Families need savings to provide cushions for financial emergencies,
money for major expenditures, such as a home or a child's education,
and the means for financial support during retirement. Small businesses need savings to provide funds for expanding the business,
for replacing assets, and for unexpected delays in collecting from
customers.

You always have bills to pay, however, and you have to resist a great
number of financial temptations. Reaching the end of the month with
extra money is difficult—which is why you need to pay yourself first.
For many people, paying yourself first is the only way to successfully
save money.

Figure 15.10 shows the amount you ultimately accumulate if you put away $25 a month and earn 10 percent interest, assuming various income tax rates. (The logic behind including income taxes is that if you earn $100 in interest and are taxed on the money at the 28 percent tax rate, for example, you need to withdraw $28 of the $100 to pay income taxes.)

	Ultimate Savings accumulated at $25 of savings per month assuming 8% annual interest			
Years	Marginal Income Tax Rates			
	0%	15%	28%	31%
5	$1,837	$1,781	$1,734	$1,723
10	4,574	4,280	4,044	3,992
15	8,651	7,788	7,124	6,980
20	14,726	12,711	11,228	10,916
25	23,776	19,622	16,699	16,100
30	37,259	29,323	23,990	22,926
35	57,347	42,938	33,709	31,917

FIG. 15.10

Saving $25 a month adds up.

If you save $50 a month, double the amounts shown in the figure. If you save $100, quadruple the amounts shown in the table, and so on.

C P A
T I P

If you save money for retirement, try to use options like individual retirement accounts (IRAs) and 401(k) plans. Figure 15.10 shows that when you save $25 a month for 35 years in one of these investment vehicles where you pay 0 percent income tax, you end up with roughly twice as much as you would if you were paying a 28 or 31 percent income tax on the interest income. (If you are saving for retirement, refer to Chapter 18, which discusses how to estimate how much you should save for retirement.)

Eventually, you do pay income taxes on the money you contributed to a 401(k) or IRA if you received a tax deduction for the contribution. You also pay income taxes on earnings accumulated in the account over the years. You don't need to begin withdrawing monthly, however, until you're 70 1/2 years old and, even if you begin withdrawing at the earliest possible date—age 59 1/2—you have a good chance of paying at a lower rate.

Recognizing After-Tax Shares of Bonuses and Raises

A second important budgeting consideration in personal and business situations is recognizing that if you receive an extra $1,000 as a bonus, raise, or windfall, you cannot spend the entire $1,000. For 1992, a 6.2 percent Social Security tax is levied on earned income up to $55,500. Another 1.45 percent Medicare tax is levied on earned income up to $130,200. You also must pay all federal income taxes of 15, 28, or 31 percent, plus all state income taxes. You may even have other expenses that, like income taxes, decrease your take-home share of any bonus or windfall, such as an automatic contribution to a deferred compensation plan or charity to which you have made a donation commitment. Totaled, you typically need to deduct at least 20 percent and as much as 60 percent from any bonus or windfall to figure out what you have available for spending.

Allowing for Unplanned and Emergency Expenses

Unfortunately, people lose jobs, cars break down, and children get sick. Over the time period a budget covers, all kinds of unforeseen and unplanned events occur that can cost you money. If you can afford to, the best approach is to budget and set aside a little money each month to cover these unexpected expenses.

Budget planners use several rules of thumb in determining how much emergency savings is enough. If your primary reason for emergency savings is in case you lose a job—because you are well-insured for medical, disability, and life claims—the following is an approach you should use:

- Consider the length of time you need to find a new job. (A traditional rule of thumb says that you need a month for every $10,000 of annual salary. If, for example, you make $10,000 a year, figure on one month. If you make $50,000 a year, figure on five months.)

- Take the salary you would have earned over the period of unemployment and subtract any unemployment benefits or severance pay you receive.

- Reduce that remainder by the income taxes you do not pay and all amounts you do not save because you have no income.

To illustrate, suppose that you take as long as six months to find a job. You currently earn $2,500 a month; you get half a month's severance pay if you lose your job; unemployment amounts to $100 a week; and you pay 6.2 percent Social Security tax, 1.45 percent Medicare tax, and a 15 percent income tax. You then can calculate the emergency savings as:

$$((6*\$2,500) - (26*\$100) - \$1,250)*(1 - 6.2\% - 1.45\% - 15\%) = \$8,625$$

Using Zero-Based Budgeting

Large businesses use zero-based budgeting with success, and individuals and smaller businesses also can use this method successfully. Basically, *zero-based budgeting* means that although you spent money on some category last year, you should not necessarily spend money on the same category this year.

Looking at what you spent last year can provide a valuable perspective, but determine the present year's spending by this year's goals. Saying, "Well, last year I spent $500 on furniture, and therefore I should spend $500 this year," is dangerous. Your house or apartment may not have room for more furniture. What about the dues for the athletic club you haven't used for months or years or the extra term life insurance you bought when the kids were living at home? What about the advertising money you spent to attract your first customers? Budgeting and spending amounts as you have in the past is easy to do, even when new goals, lifestyles, or businesses have meanwhile made the expense unnecessary.

Chapter Summary

This chapter outlined the budgeting process, told why budgeting is important in managing personal and business finances, described how Quicken helps with the process, and provided some tips on how to budget and manage finances more successfully. With this information as a background, you should be able to decide whether you want to use the budgeting tools that Quicken provides.

In the following chapter, you learn how to use investment accounts to track investments in stocks, bonds, mutual funds and so on. Quicken's investment accounts are an advanced feature in the program, so, if you want to use Quicken to monitor investments, pay particular attention to Chapter 16.

Monitoring Your Investments

Quicken provides features that enable you to monitor and report on your investments. Quicken provides a Register specifically for investments, several menu options that make monitoring and managing your investments easier, and a series of investment reports. Together, these tools enable you to monitor investment transactions, measure performance, track market values, and create reports for income tax planning and preparation.

This chapter describes how to prepare to monitor your investments with Quicken and how to track mutual funds and other investments using the Quicken Investment Register. To save you from reviewing material you already know, the chapter does not explain the parts of the Investment Register that also are part of the other Quicken Registers that you have examined in previous chapters. If you are not well-acquainted with the basics of using Quicken, refer to the first section of this book, "Learning Quicken."

In this chapter, you learn how to do the following:

■ Set up an investment account

■ Work with mutual fund accounts

■ Work with investment accounts that track brokerage accounts or individual securities

■ Use securities lists

■ Update investment accounts for market values

■ Reconcile an investment account

Preparing To Monitor Investments

To monitor investments with Quicken, you need to set up an investment account. When you set up an investment account in Quicken, you must specify whether the account is a mutual fund. If the account is not a mutual fund account, you can use the account to track a variety of securities or to have it maintain a cash balance. The *mutual fund account* is a simplified investment account that you use for a single mutual fund. The *securities and cash account* is a more powerful investment account that you use for other investments and investment groups.

The basic difference between the two accounts is difficult to grasp. If you learn the difference now, however, you will find it much easier to decide when to set up mutual fund accounts and when to set up securities and cash accounts.

The mutual fund account keeps track of the market value and the number of shares you hold of a single fund. The securities and cash account keeps track of the market value of multiple securities, the shares, and the cash balance. (The cash balance usually represents the money with which you buy additional stocks, bonds, and so on.)

Given these distinctions, the easiest approach is to set up a mutual fund account for each mutual fund investment you hold, set up a securities and cash account for each brokerage account you hold, and set up a securities and cash account for any collection of individual investments that you want to track and manage together in one Register (for example, if you just want to track your investment in IBM stock, set up a securities and cash investment account named *IBM*). As you work with the Quicken investment options, you will be able to fine-tune these suggestions.

T I P

A *mutual fund* is an open-end management company that pools the money of many investors and uses it to establish a portfolio of securities. The securities of the investors are managed by an investment advisor or portfolio manager.

If you don't want to manage your own portfolio by making decisions as to which securities to buy and sell, invest in a mutual fund. Large mutual funds usually hire the best investment advisors available.

If you want to diversify your portfolio, a mutual fund is an excellent vehicle for spreading your money to a variety of securities. When a single company's stock held in the fund declines, the impact on the total value of the mutual fund's portfolio is less because the fund's portfolio is made up of many securities. Also, security values that decline are offset by those securities that are appreciating in value.

Transaction costs when buying and selling shares in a mutual fund are often less than commission costs when buying and selling individual securities through a broker.

NOTE Because Quicken's investment accounts are one of the more advanced features in the program, the new version, Quicken 6.0, includes new assistants that help you set up your investment accounts and enter transactions in the Investment Register. To use the investment assistants, select the **Use Tutorials/Assistants** option from the main menu. Then select the **More Assistants** option from the Use Tutorials/Assistants menu. Next, you see options to select two separate assistants: one for setting up investment accounts and the other for entering transactions. Highlight the assistant that you want to use and press Enter. Follow the investment assistant's on-screen instructions to move through the steps in the tutorials.

To set up either type of investment account, follow these steps:

1. Choose the **Select Account** option from Quicken's main menu. Quicken displays the Select Account to Use window, shown in figure 16.1.

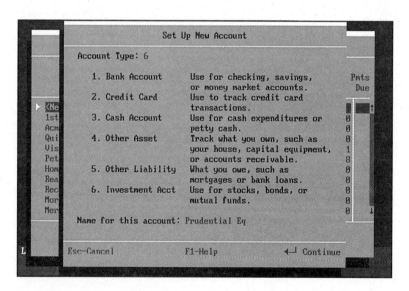

```
                    Select Account to Use

            Current File: L_FLANDE in C:\QUICKEN\
              Quick                        Num    Ending   Pmts
     Account  Key  Type   Description     Trans   Balance  Due
 ▶ <New Account>          Set up a new account
   1stnatl    1  Bank▲ 2500-0988            25     101.40    ↑
   Acme          Bank  89776-09876           2     350.00
   Quicken Visa  CCrd▲ 0909-8787-7676-6565   1       0.00
   Visa          CCard 6565-0909-8787-7676   9     702.51
   Petty cash    Cash  Petty cash            4      61.88
   Home          Oth A Residence             1  250,000.00
   Real Estate   Oth A                       3  127,000.00
   Receivables   Oth A Accounts Receivable   1       0.00
   Mortgage      Oth L Home mortgage         3   79,650.00
   Nondeduct IRA Invst Nondeductible IRA     2    2,000.00  ↓

      Ctrl-D Delete  Ctrl-E Edit  Ctrl-Ins Add  ↑,↓ Select
 Esc-Cancel                  F1-Help                  ↵ Use
```

FIG. 16.1

The Select
Account to Use
window.

2. Highlight the <New Account> line in the Select Account to Use
   window and press Enter. Quicken displays the Set Up New Account window, shown in figure 16.2.

3. Press 6 in the Account Type field to indicate that this is an investment account.

```
                    Set Up New Account

 Account Type: 6

      1. Bank Account    Use for checking, savings,      Pmts
                         or money market accounts.       Due
      2. Credit Card     Use to track credit card
                         transactions.
      3. Cash Account    Use for cash expenditures or     0
                         petty cash.                      0
      4. Other Asset     Track what you own, such as      0
                         your house, capital equipment,   1
                         or accounts receivable.          0
      5. Other Liability What you owe, such as            0
                         mortgages or bank loans.         0
      6. Investment Acct Use for stocks, bonds, or        0
                         mutual funds.                    0
                                                          0
 Name for this account: Prudential Eq

 Esc-Cancel                  F1-Help              ↵ Continue
```

FIG. 16.2

The Set Up New
Account window.

4. Press Enter or Tab to move the cursor to the Name for This Account field and enter a description of the account. The account name can be up to 15 characters and can contain any characters except the following: [ ] / : . You can include spaces in the account name.

5. Press Enter or Tab to display the Investment Account Type and Description window, shown in figure 16.3.

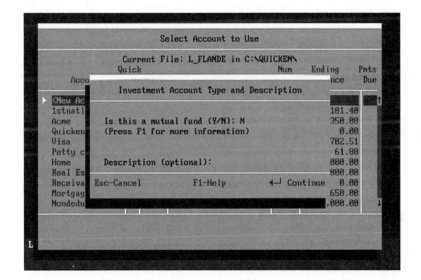

FIG. 16.3

The Investment Account Type and Description window.

6. In the first field, press Y if the account is a mutual fund. Leave the setting at N if the account is a securities and cash account.

7. Press Enter or Tab to move the cursor to the Description field. The Description field provides 21 spaces for additional investment description.

8. When you complete the Investment Account Type and Description window, press Ctrl-Enter or F10.

   If you are setting up a mutual fund account and have set the Is This a Mutual Fund field to Y, Quicken displays the Set Up Mutual Fund Security window (see fig. 16.4). The account description appears in the Name field.

   If you set the Is This a Mutual Fund field to N, you don't need to complete steps 8 through 12.

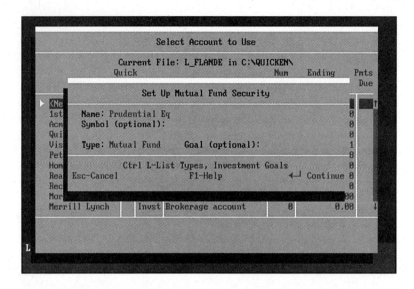

FIG. 16.4

The Set Up
Mutual Fund
Security window.

9. (Optional) Enter the mutual fund symbol in the Symbol field if you plan to import price data from another file. With Quicken 6.0, you can import stock prices from Prodigy to a file that you can import to your investment account.

The symbol that you enter in the Symbol field should be whatever you use to identify the mutual fund in the other file. For more information on this process, refer to "Updating Your Investment Records for Market Values" and "Importing Stock Prices," later in this chapter.

10. In the Type field, specify the type of mutual fund: Bond, CD, Mutual Fund, or Stock. Press Ctrl-L to see an on-screen list of the valid types, and select an item from the list.

If the type of mutual fund is not listed, you can select to add a type to the list. You may, for example, want to add T-Bill, Tax-Free Bond, Option, Unit Trust, and so on. Quicken handles a total of 16 security types. To add a type to the list, highlight the <Set Up New Type> line and press Enter. Quicken displays the Set Up Security Type window.

In the Type field, describe the new security type using up to 15 characters. Then press Enter. In the Price Display field, indicate whether you want the price calibrated in fractional (when the price is a multiple of 1/16) or decimal units. Press 1 for **Decimal** or 2 for **Fraction**. When the Set Up Security Type window is complete, press Ctrl-Enter or F10 to add the security type to the Security Type list. Then, select the new security type from the list.

> **NOTE** You can edit an existing security type by pressing Ctrl-E from the Security Type list. You also can delete a security type that you no longer use by pressing Ctrl-D.

11. (Optional) In the Set Up Mutual Fund Security window, specify an investment goal in the Goal field: College Fund, Growth, High-Risk Income, or Low-Risk Income. To see an on-screen list of goals, press Ctrl-L and select an item from the list. If the goal that you have for your investment does not appear on the list, you can add a new goal by selecting the <Set Up New Goal> line and typing the new goal description (up to 15 characters) in the Set Up Investment Goal window.

    The Type and Goal fields don't significantly affect the way Quicken processes information. (The Type field does dictate whether share prices are recorded using decimal or fractional numbers.) Quicken uses the Type field to sort securities alphabetically within type in the Update Prices window when you enter security prices from the newspaper. When securities are sorted by type, it's much easier for you to enter prices. You can use the Type and Goal fields to sort and organize information on reports. How to define different investment types and goals is discussed later in the chapter.

12. After you complete the Set Up Mutual Fund Security screen, press Ctrl-Enter or F10.

Repeat steps 1 through 7 for each securities and cash account you choose to set up. For each mutual fund account you establish, repeat steps 1 through 12.

After you have created an investment account, you are ready to use the Register to record initial balances, changes in the investment balance due to purchases or sales, and fluctuations in the market value. The next two sections explain how to use the investment accounts you have created. Because mutual fund accounts are easier to work with than securities and cash accounts, consider starting with the next section even if most of your investment recordkeeping pertains to stocks and bonds.

Working with Mutual Fund Accounts

Using Quicken to monitor a mutual fund investment consists of recording your starting balance and periodically recording changes in the balance due to the purchase of additional shares or the redemption of shares. To put things in perspective, you record the same information that appears on your mutual fund statements. By recording the information in the Quicken Register, however, you can use the information in several calculations that show how you really are doing with your investments.

The first step in working with a mutual fund is to record the initial purchase. To record the initial purchase of a mutual fund, follow these steps:

1. From the Quicken main menu, select the **Select Account** option to display the Select Account to Use window.

2. Highlight the mutual fund for which you want to record an initial balance and press Enter. Quicken displays the Create Opening Share Balance window (see fig. 16.5). The easiest way to set up a mutual fund balance is to follow steps 1 through 5. If, however, you want reports that accurately summarize the complete history of a mutual fund investment, skip steps 3, 4, and 5 and enter each of the mutual fund transactions you make.

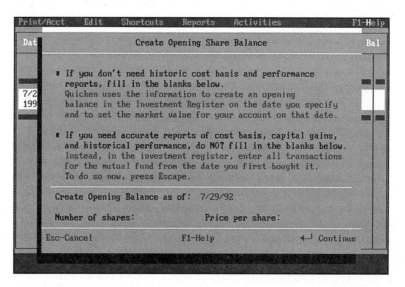

FIG. 16.5

The Create Opening Share Balance window.

3. Enter the date that you want to begin recording the opening share balance in the Create Opening Balance As Of field.

4. Move the cursor to the Number of Shares field and enter the number of shares that you now own.

5. Move the cursor to the Price per Share field and enter today's price per share for the mutual fund. You don't need to enter a dollar sign. If the price happens to be a whole number, you don't need to enter a decimal point and two zeros after the price. (You can find price per share information in many local newspapers and in daily financial newspapers such as *The Wall Street Journal*.)

By default, stock and bond prices use fractions. A stock price may be 7 1/8 and a bond price may be 97 1/8. Other investment prices, such as mutual funds and certificates of deposit, use decimals. A mutual fund price, for example, may be 14.02.

6. When the Create Opening Share Balance window is complete, press Ctrl-Enter or F10. Quicken displays the Register into which you can record investment transactions (see fig. 16.6).

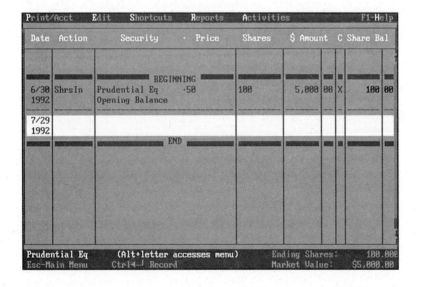

FIG. 16.6

The Mutual Fund Investment Register with the opening mutual fund balance.

After you have set up the initial mutual fund investment balance, you are ready to record a wide variety of transactions: purchases, sales, dividends, and so on. The basic process of recording each type of investment transaction is the same.

To record transactions in the Mutual Fund Account Register, follow these steps:

1. Enter the date of the transaction in the Date field. You can use the + (plus) and – (minus) keys to change the date one day at a time.

2. Move the cursor to the Action field and choose the type of action that best describes the transaction you're recording.

To choose from a list of actions, press Ctrl-L when the cursor is positioned on the Action field. Alternatively, choose the **Select Action** option from the Shortcuts menu. The Action list shown in figure 16.7 appears. When you choose from the Action list, specific action descriptions appear in submenus. Table 16.1 summarizes the general actions and describes the specific actions that fall into the general category.

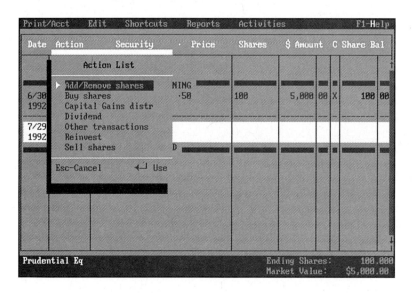

FIG. 16.7

The Action list.

After you learn the various mutual fund actions, consider using the QuickFill feature from the Action field; type just enough of the action for Quicken to uniquely identify it, and then press Enter. QuickFill completes the rest of the action for you. See Chapter 5, to learn how QuickFill works.

You must enter an account for any action that involves transferring money into or out of an account (always indicated with an X at the end of the action name). If you don't want to record a transfer account, use ShrsIn or ShrsOut, because these options don't require you to enter an account.

If you have questions about transferring money between accounts, refer to Chapter 4. Chapter 4 describes the logic and mechanics of transferring money between bank accounts. The same principles apply to transferring money between an investment account and a bank account.

3. Quicken enters the mutual fund name in the Security field. Move the cursor to the Price field and enter the price per share of the mutual fund. When entering a price, you can use up to three decimal places (for example, $11.594). In the Price field, you can use the + (plus) key to increase the price by $.125 and the – (minus) key to decrease the price by $.125.

4. Move the cursor to the Shares field and enter the number of shares involved in the transaction. You can use up to four decimal places when entering the number of shares. Press Enter or Tab to leave the Shares field, and Quicken calculates the Amount field. (Quicken calculates the Amount field by multiplying the price times the number of shares.)

5. (Optional) Move the cursor to the Memo field and enter a further description of the transaction.

6. (Optional) When you enter a purchase or sale transaction (BuyX or SellX), Quicken displays the Comm/Fee field. Enter into the Comm/Fee field any commission or brokerage fee you paid to execute the transaction. When you press Tab or Enter, Quicken adjusts the dollar amount of the transaction to include the commission or fee amount and enters the result in the XferAmt field. For a BuyX transaction, Quicken adds the commission or fee. For a SellX transaction, Quicken subtracts the commission or fee. If you enter the share price, number of shares, and dollar amount of the transaction, Quicken fills in the Comm/Fee field itself, if the Amount field doesn't equal the Price field multiplied by the Shares field. In this case, Quicken uses the Comm/Fee field to store the difference between what you entered as the dollar amount and the calculated result (price times the number of shares).

7. (Optional) Move the cursor to the Account field and record the bank account from which you withdrew the cash to purchase the mutual fund shares or the account in which you deposited cash from the sale of mutual fund shares, receipt of dividends, or receipt of capital gains distributions. Remember that you can display the Select Account to Use screen by pressing Ctrl-C. You also can use the QuickFill feature; type enough of the account name for Quicken to uniquely identify the account and then press Enter.

8. To record the transaction, press Ctrl-Enter or F10.

Figure 16.8 shows a sample transaction recording the purchase of additional shares of a mutual fund.

Table 16.1 Investment Actions for Mutual Fund Accounts

Action	Description
Add/Remove Shares	
ShrsIn	Investment shares transferred into the account
ShrsOut	Investment shares transferred out of the account
Buy Shares	
BuyX	Purchase investment shares with cash transferred into the account
Capital Gains Distr	
CGLongX	Cash received from a long-term capital gain transferred out of the account
CGShortX	Cash received from a short-term capital gain transferred out of the account
Dividend	
DivX	Cash received from a dividend transferred out of the account
Other Transactions	
Reminder	Reminder note tied to future date (Billminder reminds you about these notes)
StkSplit	Increase or decrease in number of shares because of a stock split
Reinvest	
ReinvDiv	Reinvest cash dividends or interest by purchasing more investment shares
ReinvInt	Reinvest interest by purchasing more investment shares
ReinvLg	Reinvest long-term; capital gains distribution by purchasing more investment shares
ReinvSh	Reinvest short-term capital gains distribution by purchasing more investment shares
Sell Shares	
SellX	Sell investment shares, but transfer cash received out of the investment account

Although the preceding eight steps illustrate only one type of investment transaction, the steps for recording other kinds of investment transactions are identical. The key is to choose the correct action description. The following paragraphs describe when to choose particular actions when executing mutual fund transactions.

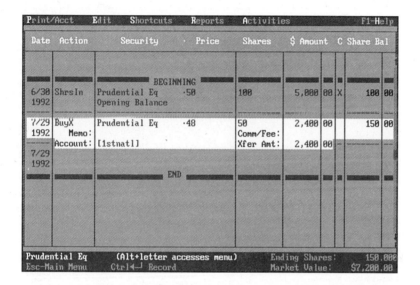

Print/Acct	Edit	Shortcuts	Reports	Activities			F1-Help

Date	Action	Security	·	Price	Shares	$ Amount	C	Share Bal

BEGINNING

| 6/30 1992 | ShrsIn | Prudential Eq Opening Balance | ·50 | 100 | 5,000 00 | X | 100 00 |

| 7/29 1992 | BuyX Memo: Account: | Prudential Eq [1stnatl] | ·48 | 50 Comm/Fee: Xfer Amt: | 2,400 00 2,400 00 | | 150 00 |

| 7/29 1992 | | | | | | | |

END

Prudential Eq	(Alt+letter accesses menu)	Ending Shares:	150.000
Esc-Main Menu	Ctrl↵ Record	Market Value:	$7,200.00

FIG. 16.8

A sample transaction recorded in the Mutual Fund Account Register.

The action descriptions of the mutual fund transactions you most often execute are BuyX for purchases or SellX for sales. If you invest in an income-oriented fund, you probably have monthly dividend or income payments. Record the monthly dividend or income payments as DivX if you withdraw the money from the fund. If you reinvest the dividends by buying more fund shares, record the dividend payments as ReinvDiv. Or, if you reinvest interest by buying more fund shares, record the interest payments as ReinvInt.

At the end of the year, the fund will make a capital gain distribution, which you record as CGLongX or CGShortX if you withdraw the money and as ReinvLg or ReinvSh if you reinvest the capital gains by buying more shares. (At this time, the income tax treatment for long- and short-term capital gains is identical; however, this may change.) When the mutual fund reports the capital gain, the statement should indicate whether the gain is long-term or short-term.

Occasionally, you may need to choose the StkSplit action, which adjusts the number of shares without changing the dollar amount. A StkSplit transaction does not require entries in the Price, Shares, or Amount fields. StkSplit records the date on which a certain number of new shares equals a certain number of old shares. The first number equals the number of new shares; the second number equals the number of old shares.

Suppose that the Prudential Equity mutual fund declares a stock split in which each old share is converted into one new share. Figure 16.9 shows just such a stock split transaction in which you receive one new share for every old share. You also can use this approach to record nontaxable stock dividends. When you receive a 10 percent stock dividend, for example, record the stock dividend as a 1.1:1 stock split.

Both Stock Split and Reminder are under Other Transactions in the Action list.

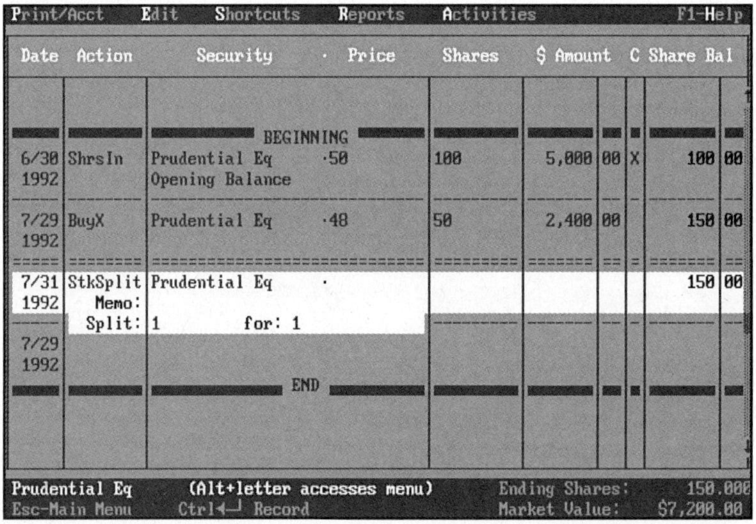

FIG. 16.9

A stock split transaction in the Mutual Fund Account Register.

The last action description used with mutual fund transactions is the Reminder option. Reminder transactions don't have a share or dollar amount—only the Security and Memo fields are filled. You can use the Reminder option in two ways: to make notes in your Investment Register and to remind yourself about certain transactions through the Quicken Billminder feature. The Billminder feature displays messages that alert you to Reminder transactions (just as Billminder displays messages that alert you to unprinted checks and scheduled transaction groups). To turn off a Reminder transaction, mark the transaction as cleared by entering an * or X in the C field.

C P A
T I P

If you buy mutual fund shares, you should know the difference between *load funds* and *no load funds*. You usually purchase load funds through a broker, who charges an up-front commission that can run from 3 percent to 10 percent. The commission is compensation for the salesperson who placed the order and helped you select the fund. Even though you may need the help of a broker in selecting a fund and placing an order, you should be aware that you can save yourself the commission (which means you're ahead from the start) by choosing a no-load mutual fund.

Research shows that on the average, load funds perform no better than no-load funds. Therefore, many investors see no reason to choose a load fund over a no load fund. No-load funds deal directly with their customers, which means the customer pays no commission. To find a no-load mutual fund, flip through *The Wall Street Journal* and look for mutual fund advertisements that specify no load. T. Rowe Price, Vanguard, and Scudder are large investment management companies that offer families of no-load mutual funds.

Working with Securities and Cash Accounts

If you have worked with the mutual fund version of the Investment Register, you quickly can adapt to the securities and cash version. The Securities and Cash Account Register tracks the number of shares you hold in the account of each individual security and any extra cash you are holding because you have just sold (or plan to purchase) a security. This process mirrors the way many brokerage accounts work: your account can have a cash component and a component detailing stock, bond, and certificate of deposit investments.

The steps for using the Securities and Cash Account Register mirror those for using the Mutual Fund Register. To use the Security and Cash Account Register, follow these steps:

1. From the Quicken main menu, choose the **Select Account** option to display the Select Account to Use window.

2. Highlight the investment account for which you want to record an initial balance and press Enter (you must define a securities and cash account before selecting the account). Quicken displays the

regular version of the Investment Register screen with the First-time Setup window (see fig. 16.10). The First-time Setup window informs you that you need to add shares by entering a ShrsIn transaction. You enter a ShrsIn transaction later in this process.

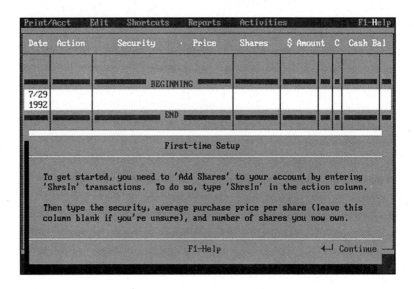

FIG. 16.10

The First-Time Setup window.

3. To continue past the First-time Setup window, press Enter. Quicken displays the Securities and Cash Account Register. Position the cursor in the Date field and enter the purchase date of the first security you want to record in the Register.

4. Move the cursor to the Action field and press Ctrl-L to display the Action list. Alternatively, choose the Select Action option from the Shortcuts menu. Choose the action that best describes the transaction you are recording. When Quicken lists the specific actions that fall into the general category, choose the appropriate action.

Table 16.2 summarizes the general and specific actions for the securities and cash account version of the Investment Register. In essence, this list is an expanded version of the investment actions available for mutual fund accounts. The list is expanded because you can hold cash in a securities and cash account. When a transaction involves cash, you need to tell Quicken whether you are transferring the cash out of the account or leaving the cash in the account.

Table 16.2 Investment Actions for Securities and Cash Accounts

Action	Description
Add/Remove shares	
ShrsIn	Investment shares transferred into the account
ShrsOut	Investment shares transferred out of the account
Buy shares	
Buy	Purchase investment shares with cash in the investment account
BuyX	Purchase investment shares with cash transferred into the account
Capital Gains distr	
CGLong	Cash representing a long-term capital gain received into the account
CGLongX	Cash received from a long-term capital gain transferred out of the account
CGShort	Cash representing a short-term capital gain received into the account
CGShortX	Cash received from a short-term capital gain transferred out of the account
Dividend	
Div	Cash received representing a dividend
DivX	Cash received from a dividend transferred out of the account
Interest	
IntInc	Cash received representing interest income
MargInt	Cash paid on margin loan interest using cash in account
Other transactions	
MiscExp	Pay for expenses, using cash from the account
MiscInc	Receive miscellaneous income
Reminder	Reminder note tied to future date (Billminder reminds you about these notes)
RtrnCap	Cash received that represents return of initial capital investment

continues

Table 16.2 Continued

Action	Description
StkSplit	Increase or decrease in number of shares because of a stock split
Reinvest	
ReinvDiv	Reinvest cash dividends or other income interest by purchasing more shares
ReinvInt	Reinvest interest by purchasing more shares
ReinvLg	Reinvest long-term capital gains distribution by purchasing more shares
ReinvSh	Reinvest short-term capital gains distribution by purchasing more shares
Sell Shares	
Sell	Sell investment shares and leave cash received in the investment account
SellX	Sell investment shares, but transfer cash received out of the investment account
Transfer Cash	
XIn	Cash transferred into the investment account
XOut	Cash transferred out of the investment account. (If you don't want to record a transfer account, use ShrsIn or ShrsOut, because these options don't require you to enter an account.)

5. Move the cursor to the Security field and enter the name of the security you are recording. If you have not used the security name before (which is the case the first time you record the security), Quicken displays the Security Not Found window (see fig. 16.11). The Security Not Found window lists two options: **Add to Security List** and **Select from Security List**.

After you define a security, you can use QuickFill. To use the QuickFill feature, type enough of the security name to uniquely identify the security and press Enter. Quicken searches the Security list for a security name that begins with the characters you type and enters the full security name in the Security field for you. See Chapter 4, for more information on using QuickFill.

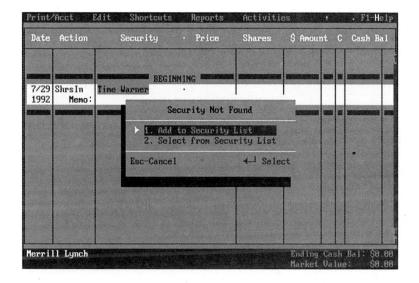

FIG. 16.11

The Security Not
Found window.

6. If you entered a new security in step 5, press 1 (or highlight **Add
   to Security List**) to add the new security. Quicken displays the Set
   Up Security window which is similar to the Set Up Mutual Fund
   Security window shown in figure 16.4. Entering the security symbol in the Symbol field is optional. (You use security symbols for
   importing price data from a separate ASCII file or from Prodigy, a
   process described later in this chapter.) Define the type of investment by moving the cursor to the Type field, pressing Ctrl-L, highlighting the current investment type, and pressing Enter. Define
   the investment goal by moving the cursor to the Goal field, pressing Ctrl-L, highlighting the investment goal, and pressing Enter.
   When the Set Up Security window is complete, press Ctrl-Enter or
   F10 to return to the Investment Register.

   If the security name you entered in step 4 has been defined,
   press 2 to choose the **Select from Security List** option. Quicken
   displays the Security list, shown in figure 16.12. The Security list
   shows the securities you have previously defined. Use the up- and
   down-arrow keys to highlight the security you want to select and
   press Enter.

7. Move the cursor to the Price field and enter the per share price of
   the security.

   For investments without an actual share price, you can enter the
   Price field value as 1 (representing one dollar) and subsequently
   enter the number of shares as the number of dollars of the investment. For investments that have a share or unit price, enter that
   figure in the Price field.

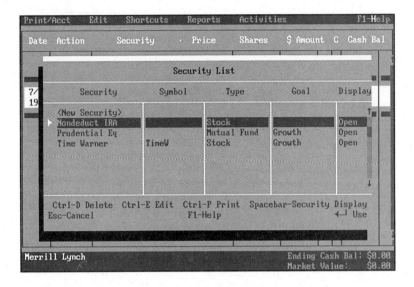

FIG. 16.12

The Security List.

By default, stock and bond prices use fractions. A stock price may be 6 7/8. A bond price may be 98 1/8. Other prices, such as mutual funds and certificates of deposit, use decimals. A mutual fund price, for example, may be 13.02. As noted earlier in the chapter, you can use the + and – keys to increase and decrease the price of a security. The + key increases the price 1/8, or .125, and the – key decreases the price 1/8, or .125.

You easily can find stock share prices in the business section of the newspaper. Other securities' prices, however, can be more difficult to determine. Some securities, such as money market funds and nonnegotiable certificates of deposit, don't have a share price. In these cases, enter the price as 1 (representing one dollar). The number of shares will equal the number of dollars' worth of the security you hold.

For other investments, such as bonds and negotiable certificates of deposit, the price shows as a percent. A bond price may be 98 3/8, which indicates that the bond is 98 3/8 percent of its face value. (Usually the face value of a bond is $1,000.) A negotiable certificate of deposit price may be 100.971, which indicates that the certificate of deposit is worth 100.971 percent of its face value. (Negotiable certificates of deposit are available in a wide variety of denominations—usually less than $100,000.)

As a general rule, enter the security price using whatever form appears in the newspaper or on your brokerage statement. Then, enter the number of shares as the value that, when multiplied by the share price, equals the total dollar value of the investment.

8. Move the cursor to the Shares field and enter the number of shares or units of the transaction. You can use up to four decimal places when entering the number of shares. When you press Enter or Tab to leave the Shares field, Quicken calculates the Amount field.

   You can enter any two of the three fields—Price, Shares, and Amount—and Quicken will calculate the third field. If you enter all three fields and the price times the number of shares does not equal the amount, Quicken puts the difference in the Comm/Fee field.

9. (Optional) Move the cursor to the Memo field and enter a further description of the transaction.

10. (Optional) If you enter a purchase and sales transaction, Quicken displays the Comm/Fee field. Move the cursor to the Comm/Fee field and enter any commission or brokerage fee you paid to execute the transaction. When you press Tab or Enter, Quicken calculates the XferAmt field by adding the transaction amount and the commission or fee.

11. If the action isn't ShrsIn or ShrsOut, move the cursor to the Account field and record the bank account you tapped for cash to purchase the investment. Remember that you can display the Select Account to Use screen by pressing Ctrl-C. Alternatively, you can use Quicken's QuickFill feature; type enough of the account name to uniquely identify the account and press Enter. Quicken finishes typing the name for you.

12. Record the transaction by pressing Ctrl-Enter or F10. Quicken displays the standard message window and asks whether you want to record the transaction. Press Enter to record the transaction.

Figure 16.13 shows several sample transactions in the Investment Register. The first transaction records the transaction to record existing securities at the time the investment account is set up. The second transaction records an additional purchase of securities in the brokerage account. The third transaction shows the receipt of dividends from one of the securities held in the brokerage account.

To record each transaction, follow the steps listed in the preceding paragraphs. Notice that the securities and cash account version of the Register (as compared to the mutual fund version) does not track share balances. However, the securities and cash account version of the Register tracks the cash you have available to purchase additional investments.

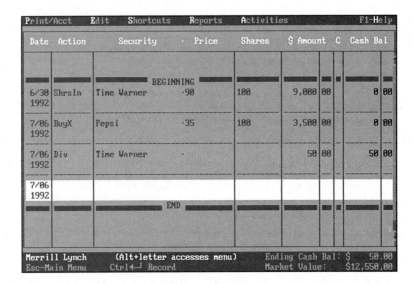

Print/Acct	Edit	Shortcuts	Reports	Activities				F1-Help

Date	Action	Security	Price	Shares	$ Amount	C	Cash Bal
		═══ BEGINNING ═══					
6/30 1992	ShrsIn	Time Warner	·90	100	9,000 00		0 00
7/06 1992	BuyX	Pepsi	·35	100	3,500 00		0 00
7/06 1992	Div	Time Warner	·		50 00		50 00
7/06 1992							
		═══ END ═══					

Merrill Lynch   (Alt+letter accesses menu)   Ending Cash Bal: $ 50.00
Esc-Main Menu   Ctrl◄┘ Record   Market Value: $12,550.00

FIG. 16.13

Sample transactions recorded in the securities and cash account version of the Register.

T I P

You can memorize investment transactions just like transactions you memorize in other Quicken Registers. To memorize an investment transaction, highlight the transaction and press Ctrl-M. When you memorize an investment transaction, Quicken stores the transaction in the Memorized Investment Transactions window (see fig. 16.14), accessed by pressing Ctrl-T to select the **Recall Transaction** option. Refer to Chapter 5, to learn more about memorizing transactions.

You also can set up investment transaction groups to quickly enter group transactions that you want to record at regular intervals. Transaction groups for investment transactions are set up the same way that you set up transaction groups for regular transactions from a Bank Account Register, Credit Card Register, and so on. Refer to Chapter 5, to learn how to use transaction groups.

Working with the Investment Register

The preceding sections of this chapter describe the fundamentals of working with the Quicken investment accounts, mutual fund, and securities and cash accounts. You can set up mutual fund accounts, create securities and cash accounts, and record transactions in the Register.

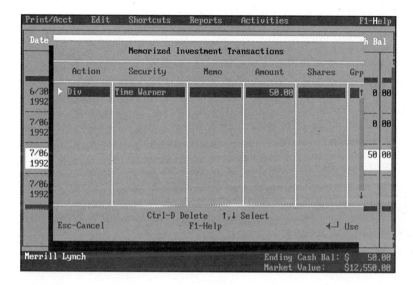

FIG. 16.14

The Memorized
Investment
Transactions
window.

The remaining sections of this chapter describe how to work with the
Quicken securities lists. You learn how to define your own investment
types and goals; how to update your investment records because of
changes in market values; and how to reconcile your investment
records with those provided by the mutual fund company, brokerage
house, or bank. The last section in the chapter offers tips on investments and investment recordkeeping that may save you headaches and
money.

You should try to plan your security transactions to minimize the
amount of net capital gain realized each year. If you are in a net
capital gain position, consider selling other securities that are in a
loss position. You can offset capital gains with capital losses to
minimize, or eliminate, your net gain position. Capital losses offset
capital gains dollar for dollar. You may not, however, deduct more
than $3,000 of capital losses against ordinary income. Be mindful of
your net capital loss position before entering into transactions
resulting in losses. Capital losses can be carried over to future years.

C P A
T I P

Working with the Security Lists

When working with the Securities and Cash Account Register, you can add securities to the list that Quicken maintains. Although this approach may be all you ever need, Quicken's **Security List** option enables you to work with the securities list before entering transactions in the Register. This option is helpful when, for example, you know that over the coming months you will be purchasing shares of several companies. The **Security List** option saves you time by enabling you to define the securities before you purchase them.

You can access the security list by pressing Alt-S, and then select the **Security List** option from the Shortcuts menu (see fig. 16.15). Alternatively, you can press Ctrl-Y. Either method produces the Security List window, shown in figure 16.16. From this list, you can add, edit, delete, and print lists of securities. You also can use the security list to access windows that enable you to add, edit, and delete investment types and goals.

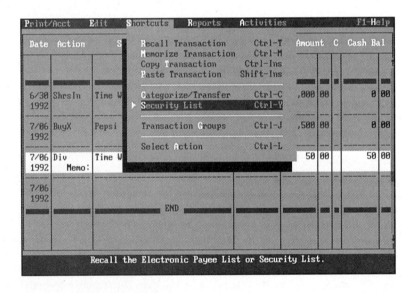

FIG. 16.15

The Shortcuts menu from the Investment Register.

Adding a Security

To add a security to the securities list, follow these steps:

1. Press Ctrl-Y to display the Security List window.

2. Use the up- and down-arrow keys to highlight the <New Security> line, and then press Enter. Quicken displays the Set Up Security window.

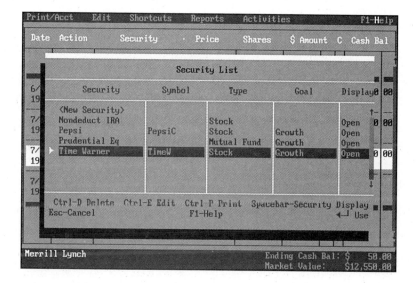

FIG. 16.16

The Security List
window.

3. Enter the security name in the Name field. You can enter a maximum of 18 characters.

4. (Optional) Enter the security symbol in the Symbol field. (You use security symbols for importing price data from a separate ASCII file—a process described later in the chapter.) You can enter a maximum of 12 characters.

5. To define the investment type, move the cursor to the Type field, press Ctrl-L, highlight the investment type in the Security Type list, and press Enter.

   Alternatively, if you want to define a new investment type, move the cursor to the Type field, press Ctrl-L, and select the <Set Up New Type> line from the Security Type list. Quicken displays the Set Up Security Type window. To define a new security type, describe the security type in the Type field and indicate whether you want the price calibrated in fractional or decimal units. You can have up to 16 security types. Only six security types fit in the Security Type list at one time, so if you use more than six security types, press PgUp and PgDn to see the first and last parts of the type list.

   The Type field is optional and has no effect on recordkeeping, other than determining the form in which a security price is shown. The Type field enables you to enter another piece of information about your investment. Quicken provides several investment types that you may find valuable: Bond, CD, Mutual Funds, and Stock. You may, however, have another piece of data that is more important to collect and store. If you are investing money based on the advice of several investment advisors, for example, you can keep track of which advisor suggested which security. Or, if you invest in several different industries, such as utilities, transportation, banking, and computers, you can keep track of the industry of individual issuers.

You also can edit and delete security types. To delete a security type, press Ctrl-D when the security you want to delete is highlighted in the Security Type list. Quicken warns you that a security type is about to be deleted and alerts you if the type is in use. If you want to delete the security type, press Enter. Press Esc if you don't want to delete the security type.

To edit a security type, press Ctrl-E when the security you want to edit is highlighted in the Security Type list. Quicken displays the Set Up Security Type window, which you use as described in the preceding paragraph to change the security type name or the price calibration.

6. To define the investment goal, move the cursor to the Goal field in the Set Up Security window, press Ctrl-L, highlight the current investment type from the Goal list, and press Enter. Investment goals describe the purpose of an investment, such as retirement, college, down payment, and so on.

   To define a new investment goal, move the cursor to the Goal field, press Ctrl-L, and select the <Set Up New Goal> line and press Enter. Quicken displays the Set Up Investment Goal window. To define a new investment goal, describe the goal in the Goal field. As is the case with the Security Type list, only six goals fit on the Goal list at one time. Use the PgUp and PgDn keys to view the first and last parts of the goal list. You can have up to 16 investment goals.

   The Goal field is optional and has no effect on the way that you track or monitor a particular investment. Like the Type field, the Goal field enables you to record another piece of information about your investment. Quicken provides several investment goals that you may find valuable. You may, however, have another piece of information that is more important to collect and store. Rather than using the Goal field to describe the investment, for example, you can use the Goal field to categorize how you want to spend the money you make on the investment. In that case, you can choose other goals, such as Retirement, Vacation, Emergency, and so on.

You also can edit and delete investment goals. To delete an investment goal, press Ctrl-D when the goal you want to delete is highlighted on the Goal list. Quicken warns you that a goal is about to be deleted and alerts you if the goal is in use.

To edit a goal (to change the title of a goal), press Ctrl-E when the goal is highlighted in the Goal list. Quicken displays the Edit Investment Goal window, which you use to edit the name. After you edit the goal name, press Enter to return to the Goal list.

7. When the Set Up Security window is complete, press Ctrl-Enter or F10. Quicken adds the new security to the Security List window.

Deleting a Security

Even if you are a long-term investor, you eventually will decide to sell a certain stock or bond and never purchase that security again. Because there is no reason to clutter your securities list, Quicken enables you to delete securities in which you no longer invest.

To delete a security from the Securities List window, follow these steps:

1. To display the Security List window, press Ctrl-Y from the Investment Register.

2. Use the up- and down-arrow keys to highlight the security that you want to delete.

3. Press Ctrl-D. Quicken alerts you that the security is about to be deleted permanently. Press Enter to delete the security or press Esc if you don't want to delete the security.

When a security is in use, Quicken presents a message that the security is in use and cannot be deleted at this time.

Editing a Security

As you know, Quicken stores four pieces of information about a security in the Securities list: name, symbol, type, and goal. Over time, one or more of these elements may change. When changes in the name, symbol, type, or goal occur, you can edit the security.

To edit a security on the securities list, follow these steps:

1. Press Ctrl-Y from the Investment Register to display the Security List window.

2. Use the up- and down-arrow keys to highlight the security that you want to edit.

3. Press Ctrl-E. Quicken displays the Set Up Security window. The process for editing a security mirrors the process of adding a new security. If you have questions about how to complete the Set Up Security window, refer to the steps that describe how to add a new security.

Printing the Security List

To print a list of the securities on the securities list, follow these steps:

1. Press Ctrl-Y from the Investment Register to display the Security List window.

2. Press Ctrl-P when the Security List window is displayed. Quicken displays the Print Security List window, which is similar to the Print Register window.

3. Complete the Print Security List window as you would the Print Register window: Indicate which printer setting you want to use, and then press Enter.

Hiding a Security

You also can hide certain securities so that they don't appear on Quicken's investment reports. Suppose that you don't want your children (who print out reports of investments for their college education) to see your retirement savings balance. You can hide the investments that you don't want them to see.

To hide a security, follow these steps:

1. Press Ctrl-Y from the Investment Register to display the Security List window.

2. Highlight the security you want to hide and press the space bar. Quicken changes the display setting to **Never**.

Follow the same process to "unhide" the security. The space bar acts as a toggle between three choices: **Open**, **Never**, and **Always**. **Always** causes a security to appear in the Update Prices and Market Value window (even if you no longer own the security). **Open** causes a security to appear as long as you own it. **Never** causes the security to never appear in the Update Prices and Market Value window. (You learn about the Update Prices and Market Value window in the next section of this chapter.)

Updating Your Investment Records for Market Values

One of the most common investment recordkeeping activities is tracking the market value of your investments. Quicken provides several tools that enable you to update your investment records and determine the overall market value of your investments.

To record the market value of an investment manually, follow these steps:

1. Access the Register that records the transactions for an investment. (The Register may be a Mutual Fund Account Register or a securities and Cash Account Register, depending on the investment.)

2. Press Alt-A to access the Activities menu. Figure 16.17 shows the Activities menu from the Investment Register.

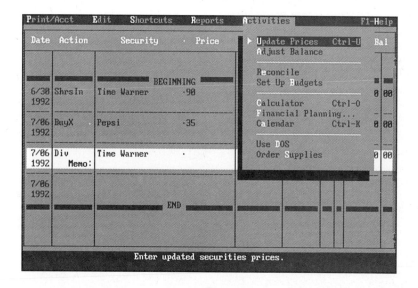

The Activities menu from the Investment Register.

3. Select the **Update Prices** option or press Ctrl-U. Quicken displays the Update Prices and Market Value screen, shown in figure 16.18.

4. Use the up- and down-arrow keys to highlight the security whose price you want to update.

5. With the cursor positioned on the Mkt Price field, enter the current market price. You also can use the + and – keys to increase or decrease the price by 1/8 or .125.

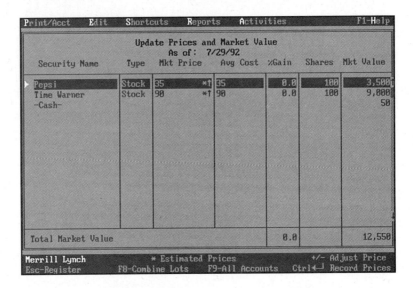

FIG. 16.18

The Update
Prices and
Market Value
screen.

6. Repeat steps 3 and 4 for each security in the Update Prices and
   Market Value screen. If you want to update investments in your
   other accounts, press F9 to display a complete list of your securities in all investment accounts.

T I P

To combine lots of securities that you hold, press F8 from the Update Prices and Market Value screen. Quicken combines lots of securities that you hold and lists them alphabetically. If, for example, you
bought 100 shares of Eli Lilly stock on 4/8/89, 200 shares on 12/7/90,
and 500 shares on 7/18/91, Quicken normally lists each lot or purchase of shares separately in the Update Prices and Market Value
screen. If you want to combine lots of Eli Lilly stock (and all other
securities that you hold), press F8. Quicken combines all 800 shares
of your Eli Lilly stock into one line in the Update Prices and Market
Value screen. Press F8 again to redisplay individual purchases or
lots.

After you record the change in the market price, Quicken asks you
whether it is OK to record the new prices and whether the system date
is appropriate. If so, press Enter. To change the date, use the + and –
keys to change to the date of record. Otherwise, F9 acts as a toggle
between the current Investment Register and all accounts. Press Esc to
return to the Investment Register from the Update Prices and Market
Value screen.

The Update Prices and Market Value screen shows several pieces of data with which you are familiar: the security name, the type, the market price, the number of shares, and the total market value. Two additional fields also appear: Avg Cost and %Gain. The Avg Cost field shows the average unit cost of all the shares or units of a particular security that you currently hold. The %Gain field shows the percentage difference between the total cost and the total market value of all the shares you currently hold. A negative percentage indicates a loss.

To view a date other than the current date in the Update Prices and Market Value screen, press Ctrl-G. Quicken displays the Go to Date window where you can enter a new date to use to view the market value of securities.

T I P

Creating a Price History for a Security

When you record security prices using the Update Prices and Market Value screen, you create a price history for each security.

To see the price history for the currently selected security when you are in the Update Prices and Market Value screen, follow these steps:

1. Press Alt-S to access the Shortcuts menu (see fig. 16.19).

2. From the Shortcuts menu, select the **Price History** option or press Ctrl-H. Quicken displays the Price History For window, shown in figure 16.20, which lists each of the price updates you entered for the security. The dates shown in the price history are the system dates on which you recorded new security prices.

You can request reports that show the market value of your investments on different dates. (Chapter 12 discusses Quicken's reports in detail.) Quicken uses the security prices from the price history to prepare these reports. If you want to see market values as of June 1, for example, Quicken uses the securities prices from the price history that are on or before June 1. For this reason, you may want to update security prices regularly. However, with the Update Prices and Market Value screen, you add a price to the price history for the current date.

To add to the price history a price for some date other than the current system date, select the <New Price> line in the Price History for window. Quicken displays the New Price For window, shown in figure 16.21, with the date filled in as the current system date. Enter the correct date and price. To record the date and price combination, press Enter.

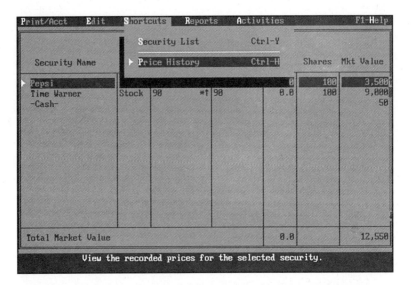

FIG. 16.19

The Shortcuts menu from the Investment Register.

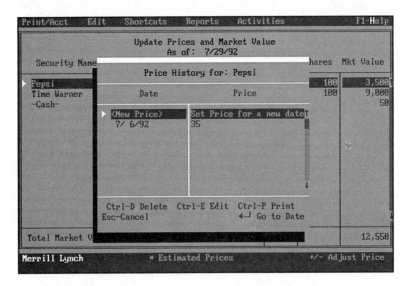

FIG. 16.20

The Price History for: window.

You likewise can edit or delete a price from the price history of a particular investment. Use Quicken's standard key combinations: Ctrl-D to delete and Ctrl-E to edit. The changes you make will be reflected on the Update Prices and Market Value screen after you complete the entry of new or updated information.

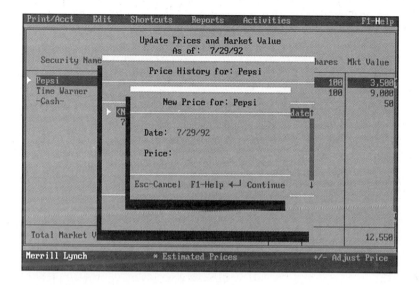

FIG. 16.21

The New Price
for: window.

Importing Stock Prices

You also can import price history data from an ASCII text file. The steps
aren't difficult, as long as the ASCII text file looks the way Quicken ex-
pects it to. The file needs to contain at least two pieces of information:
the security symbol and the price in decimal form. You also can (optionally) include a third piece of information: the date. The three pieces
of information that make up a price must be together on a single line,
must be separated by commas, and must not contain any embedded
spaces. Quicken can import the data even if one or more of the elements are enclosed in quotation marks. If the price history does not
include a date, Quicken uses a default date that you specify as part of
the import operation. All of the following, for example, can be imported
as price history data:

```
TIMEW,105.25,8/06/92
TIMEW,105.25
"TIMEW",105.25,"8/06/92"
"TIMEW","105.25","8/06/92"
```

NOTE   Now, with Quicken 6.0, you can import stock prices from
Prodigy's Dow Jones Service to an ASCII file in Quicken's
special import format. To save stock prices to a file, refer to
your Prodigy Users' Manual. Then perform the following
steps to import stock prices from the Prodigy file.

To import price history data, access the Update Prices and Market Value screen and follow these steps:

1. Press Alt-P to display the Print/Acct menu (see fig. 16.22).

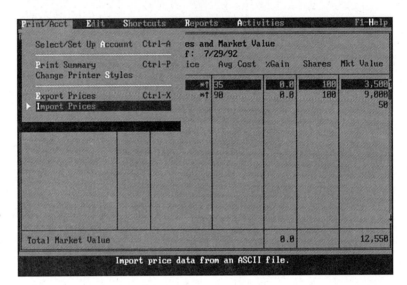

FIG. 16.22

The Print/Acct menu from the Update Prices and Market Value screen.

2. Select the **Import Prices** option. Quicken displays the Import Price Data window (see fig. 16.23).

3. In the DOS File field, enter the file name and extension of the ASCII text file that contains the price history information you want to import. If the ASCII file is not in the current directory, also specify the drive and directory where the ASCII file can be found.

4. Press Enter or Tab to move to the Date field. Enter the date that should be used as the default price date in case a date is not specified in the ASCII text file.

5. When the Import Price Data window is complete, press Enter. Quicken imports the price history data contained in the ASCII text file and updates the appropriate security price histories.

NOTE   You also can export security prices from the Update Prices and Market Value screen to an ASCII file for use in other programs. To export prices, select the **Export Prices** option from the Print/Acct menu or just press Ctrl-X. Quicken enables you to export prices for all securities listed in the Update Prices and Market Value screen or selected securities.

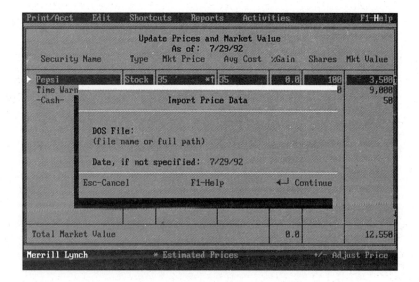

FIG. 16.23

The Import Price
Data window.

Returning to the Investment Register

After you finish updating the prices and market values of your securities, just press Esc to return to the Investment Register. Your work in the Update Prices and Market Value screen will be saved.

Reconciling Your Investment Accounts

Quicken enables you to reconcile mutual fund and securities and cash accounts. For the most part, the steps for reconciling these account types parallel the steps for reconciling other Quicken accounts. There are, however, a few minor differences.

In a mutual fund account, you reconcile the shares in the account—not the dollars. The basic process of reconciling a mutual fund account closely resembles the process described in Chapter 8 for reconciling bank accounts.

To reconcile a mutual fund account, follow these steps:

1. Press Alt-A to access the Activities menu from the Investment Register and select the **Reconcile** option. The Reconcile Mutual Fund Account window appears (see fig. 16.24).

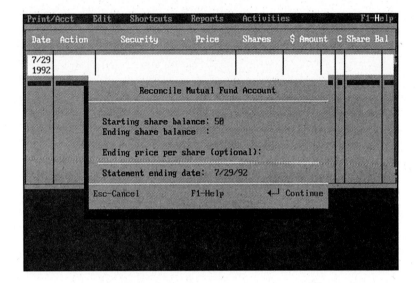

FIG. 16.24

The Reconcile Mutual Fund Account window.

2. Enter the starting and ending shares balance from your mutual fund statement.

3. (Optional) Move the cursor to the Ending Price per Share field and enter the ending share price that appears on your statement. Press Enter.

4. In the Statement Ending Date field, type the ending date that appears on your statement.

5. Press Ctrl-Enter or F10 when the Reconcile Mutual Fund Account window is complete. Quicken displays the abbreviated Mutual Fund Transaction list next (see fig. 16.25).

6. Mark the transactions in the transaction list that correspond to the transactions appearing on the mutual fund statement.

   You can mark transactions individually by using the space bar to toggle the * character in the C field. Alternatively, press F8 to mark a range of transactions, and Quicken asks you to indicate cleared transactions between two dates. Pressing F9 toggles between the **Reconcile** option and the Investment Register that you are reconciling. Quicken records a balance adjustment in the Investment Register to balance the account.

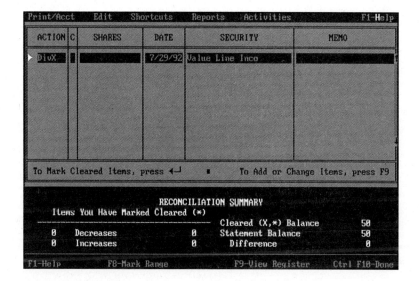

FIG. 16.25

The Mutual Fund Account Transaction List window.

7. When the difference between the Cleared Balance and the Statement Balance equals zero, press Ctrl-F10.

As with the process of reconciling bank accounts, the basic idea is that the difference in shares between your records and the mutual fund's records should stem only from transactions that (for reasons of timing) have not yet appeared on the mutual fund statement.

In a securities and cash account, you reconcile the cash balance. Predictably, this process parallels that for reconciling a bank account. (The cash balance in a securities and cash account also may be a bank account.) To reconcile the cash balance, enter the beginning and ending statement balances in the Reconcile Investment Account window (see fig. 16.26). Just as for a bank account, mark the transactions that have cleared the cash account, using an abbreviated transaction list (see fig. 16.27). Use the space bar to toggle, and mark transactions that have cleared with an asterisk.

If you want to reconcile an account but have questions about the mechanics of the reconciliation process, refer to Chapter 8. The basic principles described there also apply to investment accounts.

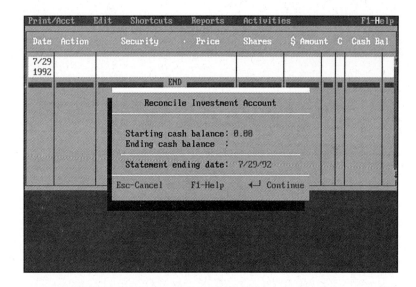

FIG. 16.26

The Reconcile Investment Account window.

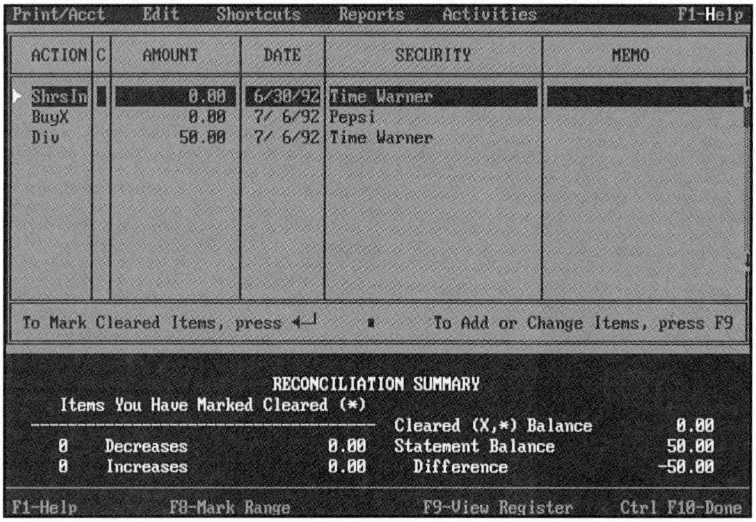

FIG. 16.27

The Securities and Cash Account Transaction List window.

Adjusting Investment Account Balances

If you don't want to reconcile your account, you may want to use the **Adjust Balance** option that appears on the Activities menu from the Investment Register. If the investment is a securities and cash account, Quicken displays the Adjust Balance menu, which lists options for adjusting the cash balance or the share balance (see fig. 16.28). Select the balance you want to adjust. Figure 16.29 shows the Adjust Cash Balance window.

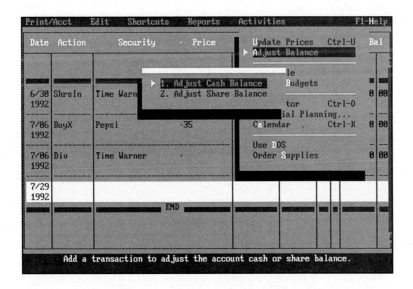

FIG. 16.28

The Adjust Balance menu.

To update the cash balance in the account, follow these steps:

1. Access the Adjust Cash Balance window.

2. In the first field, enter the current cash account balance.

3. Move the cursor to the Adjust Balance As Of field and enter the date for which the cash adjustment transaction should be recorded.

4. When the Adjust Cash Balance window is complete, press Ctrl-Enter or F10 to update the cash balance.

Figure 16.30 shows the Adjust Share Balance window accessed by selecting the Adjust Share Balance option from the Adjust Balance menu.

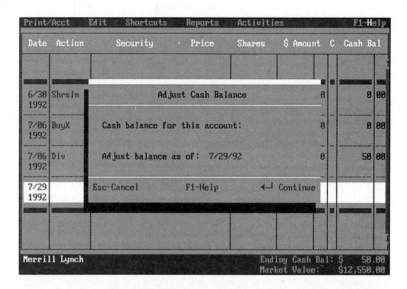

FIG. 16.29

The Adjust Cash
Balance window.

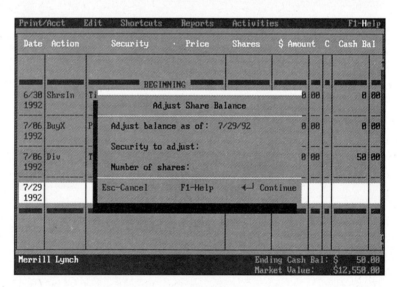

FIG. 16.30

The Adjust Share
Balance window.

To update the share balance for a specific security, follow these steps:

1. At the Adjust Share Balance window, enter the date for which the share adjustment transaction should be recorded in the Adjust Balance As Of field.

2. Move the cursor to the Security to Adjust field and enter the name of the security whose share balance needs to be adjusted. You also can press Ctrl-Y to select the security from the security list.

3. Move the cursor to the Number of Shares field and enter the number of shares of the security as of the date in the Adjust Balance As Of field.

4. When the Adjust Share Balance window is complete, press Ctrl-Enter or F10 to update the share balance.

If the investment is a mutual fund account, Quicken does not display the Adjust Balance menu. Quicken displays the mutual fund version of the Adjust Share Balance window (see fig. 16.31).

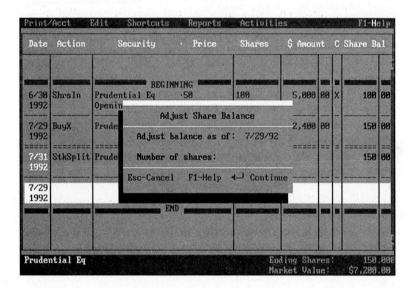

FIG. 16.31

The mutual fund version of the Adjust Share Balance window.

Mutual funds sometimes reinvest the interest on dividend income. Accordingly, with each interest or dividend payment, you may need to update or adjust the share balance.

To update the share balance for a specific security, follow these steps:

1. In the Adjust Share Balance window, enter the date for which the share balance adjustment transaction should be recorded.

2. Move the cursor to the Number of Shares field. Enter the current share balance of the mutual fund.

3. When the Adjust Share Balance window for the mutual fund is complete, press Ctrl-Enter or F10 to update the share balance.

Although the **Adjust Balance** option enables you to forgo the work of reconciling an account, this option has disadvantages. As Chapter 8 points out, the purposes of reconciling include catching errors, recording forgotten transactions, and discovering fraudulent transactions. By not reconciling an account, you miss out on significant benefits.

Tips on Investments and Investment Recordkeeping

Earlier sections of this book explained the procedural details of using Quicken; this section covers three additional tips.

First, you should know that Quicken applies the *first-in, first-out* (often called FIFO) method of recordkeeping. This means that when you sell shares of Apple Computer, for example, Quicken assumes that the shares you sell are the first shares that you bought.

The FIFO assumption conforms with Internal Revenue Service regulations. The problem with FIFO is that often the first shares you bought were the least expensive. This means that when you calculate the actual taxable gain by subtracting the original purchase price from the sales price, you end up calculating the largest possible gain and, as a result, you incur higher income taxes.

You can use another method, called *specific identification*, to record the sales and purchases of investments. Specific identification requires that you record all purchases of a particular stock as different investments, or lots. When you sell shares of Apple Computer, for example, you actually sell the shares from a specific lot. The obvious tax-saving opportunity results from picking the lot with the highest purchase price, because doing so minimizes your gain or maximizes your loss. (See your tax advisor for specific details.) To keep your tax-planning options open, set up each lot as a separate security.

Second, if you record meticulously the transactions that affect an investment, you can use one of Quicken's investment reports (the performance report) to measure the actual rate of return an investment produces. Although most individual investors are not accustomed to measuring the performance of their investments, you will find doing so an invaluable exercise. Too often, individual investors don't get to measure the performance of stocks a broker recommends, of a mutual fund an advertisement touts, or the bonds a financial planner suggests. But with the Quicken performance report, which is described in Chapter 12, you have a convenient way to calculate precisely how well or how poorly an investment has performed. Investment performance information can help you make better investment decisions.

Finally, there is more to investing than just recordkeeping. Despite the fact that Quicken provides an excellent recordkeeping tool, understanding how the tool works is not the same as understanding investments. To better understand investments, read *A Random Walk Down Wall Street*, by Burton G. Malkiel, a Princeton economics professor. You should be able to find the most recent edition in any good bookstore.

Chapter Summary

This chapter described how to monitor your investments using Quicken's investment accounts. The chapter listed the steps for tracking mutual funds with Quicken and the steps for tracking other investments, such as stocks, bonds, and certificates of deposit. You also learned how to import stock prices from ASCII files and how to reconcile your investment accounts.

In the next chapter, you learn about a new Quicken feature—graphing. You learn how Quicken analyzes your financial data and puts it into graph format so that you can view your income and expenses, assets and liabilities, actual and budget amounts, and your investments on a relative basis.

Creating Graphs

In previous chapters, you learned how to enter transactions and write checks, track your assets and liabilities, create budgets, and monitor your investments. In Chapter 12, "Creating and Printing Reports," you learned how to produce reports so that you could analyze the information and data that you enter in Quicken. Creating reports is an excellent way to summarize your financial information, but now, with Quicken 6.0, not the only way. With Quicken 6.0, you can create on-screen graphs to show relationships between your income and expenses, assets and liabilities, actual and budget amounts, and individual investments and total portfolio. If you have an installed graphics card, you can create any one of 21 different graphs. You can create graphs in just seconds based on the transactions that you enter and categorize, the account balances, budgeted data, and investment transactions entered.

In the case of your finances, it is sometimes easier to assess your financial situation when you can see a graph (picture) that shows an overview or summary of your finances. Graphs show you, for example, the relationship of individual expense categories to your total expenditures. You therefore can quickly see what percentage each individual expense category is to your total expenses. Although reports show you information in a format that is useful in financial analysis, graphs are a visual means for analysis that sometimes have more effect than a list of categories or accounts in a report.

In this chapter, you learn how to do the following:

■ Identify each graph format that Quicken creates (double-line graphs, line graphs, pie charts, and stacked bar graphs)

- Set up Quicken to display graphs
- Create income and expense, net worth, budget, and investment graphs
- Filter graph transactions

Overview of Quicken Graphs

Depending on the type of graph you select to create, Quicken displays the following graph formats:

- Double-bar graphs
- Line graphs
- Pie charts
- Stacked bar graphs

Quicken decides which graph format to create when you select a graph type.

Each of these graph formats compares financial information or shows information in a different way. In the following sections, you learn about the different graph formats and what they represent. Each graph that you create includes a *legend* (the box located in the upper right corner of the graph screen) that tells you what each line, bar, or piece of pie represents.

Double-Bar Graphs

Quicken creates *double-bar* graphs, like the one you see in figure 17.1, to compare data. The items the graphs compare appear as bars and are shown on the horizontal axis, side by side. The dollar amounts or values of the items being compared are shown on the vertical axis. In figure 17.1, you see the comparison of income to expenses. Income for the month is about $8,000, and is greater than expenses for the month, which are about $6,000. The box in the upper right corner of the graph shows that one bar in the graph represents income and the other represents expenses.

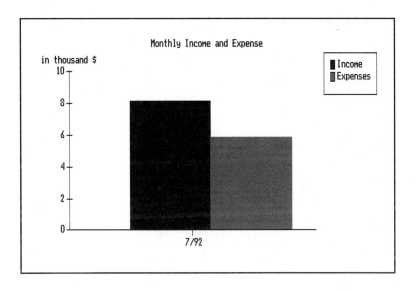

FIG. 17.1

A sample double-bar graph.

Line Graphs

The *line* graph format shows net values over time. Net values result when you select graph options like monthly assets less liabilities, monthly income less expense, and monthly actual less budget. Figure 17.2 shows a line graph that shows the net value of monthly assets less liabilities over the first six months of the year.

You can use line graphs to analyze trends over a period of time. If, for example, you are *overspending* (your expenses are greater than your income on a monthly basis), the line graphs show the trend of overspending over a specified period of time. Perhaps in January the deficit is $200, in February it's $300, and in March it's up to $500. A line graph shows an upward moving line that quickly tells you that your overspending problem is not dissipating but rather accelerating. News presented to you in this format, hopefully, will cause you to act to solve the problem.

C P A
T I P

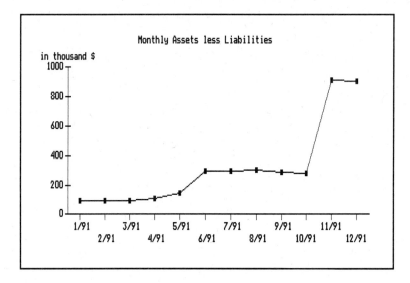

FIG. 17.2

A sample line graph that shows net value of assets less liabilities over time.

Pie Charts

Pie charts show the composition of each individual item to the whole. Pie charts show you what the composition of an individual item is to the total items. If you graph your income composition, for example, you see the percentage that your salary contributes to your total income from all sources. You can use a pie chart like the one shown in figure 17.3 to help you determine whether you are spending too much in a particular expense category or earning too little as compared to your total income.

Stacked Bar Graphs

A *stacked bar* graph shows trends (like the line graph). Stacked bar graphs show two trends simultaneously, however (see fig. 17.4). First, the graph show the composition of items in the stacked bar, such as the composition of total expenses. In this case, each income item is represented by a different color or pattern within each bar. That's why this graph format is called *stacked bar*—it stacks the items that comprise the whole in a single bar. Stacked bar graphs also show how items are comprised to the whole, over time. In figure 17.4, you see how the composition of income changes over a period of six months.

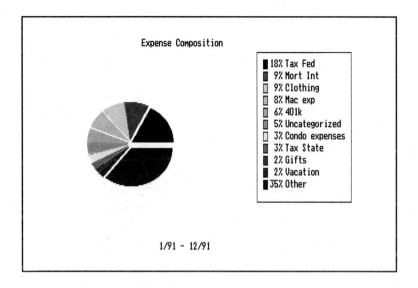

FIG. 17.3

A sample pie
chart that shows
how individual
expenses
make up total
expenses.

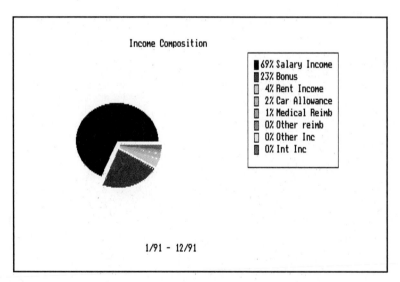

FIG. 17.4

A stacked bar
graph showing
the composition
of items and how
that composition
changes over
time.

Setting Up Quicken To Display Graphs

Before you can create and display graphs with Quicken, you must tell
Quicken the graphics driver that you are using. If you forget to set up

Quicken for your graphics driver, the first time you attempt to create a graph, Quicken displays the appropriate window for you to select the graphics driver you are using.

To set up Quicken to display graphs, follow these steps:

1. From the Quicken main menu, select the **Set Preferences** option. Quicken displays the Set Preferences menu.

2. From the Set Preferences menu, select the **Screen Settings** option. Quicken displays the Screen Settings menu.

3. From the Screen Settings menu, select the **Screen Graphics** option. Quicken displays the Graphics Drivers Options window that you see in figure 17.5.

   You first must tell Quicken whether to make the text in a graph larger or the graph area larger.

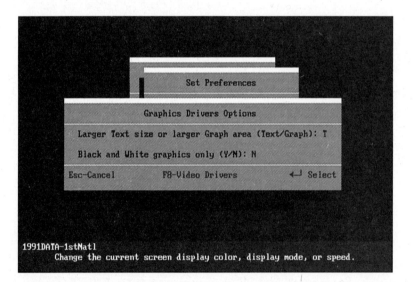

FIG. 17.5

The Graphics Drivers Options window.

4. Press T to make the text larger or G to make the graph area larger and press Enter. Quicken enables you to change this setting from the graph window that you use to create a graph.

   If you have a color monitor but want to show graphics in black and white only, press Y from the Black and White Graphics Only field. When you display graphics in black and white, Quicken uses patterns instead of colors to distinguish different bars, lines, or pie pieces in graphs. Press N if you want Quicken to display graphics in color.

5. Press F8 to display the Select Graphics Driver window shown in figure 17.6. Highlight the graphics driver that you have installed and press Enter to return to the Graphics Drivers Options window.

6. When the Graphics Drivers Options window is complete, press Ctrl-Enter or F10. Quicken returns to the Screen Settings menu. Press Esc twice to return to the main menu.

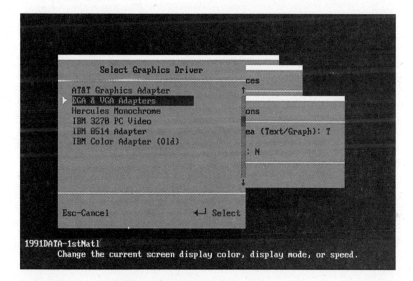

FIG. 17.6

The Select Graphics Driver window.

Creating Graphs

This section explains how to create and display graphs, in general. You learn how to access the View Graphs menu, select a graph option, display the graph, and remove the graph from your screen. The next section in this chapter explains how to create each individual graph to analyze your income and expenses, net worth, budget versus actual data, and investments.

To create a graph, follow these steps:

1. From the Quicken main menu, select the **View Graphs** option.

   Quicken displays the View Graphs menu shown in figure 17.7.

2. Use the up- and down-arrow keys to highlight the type of graph you want to create and press Enter.

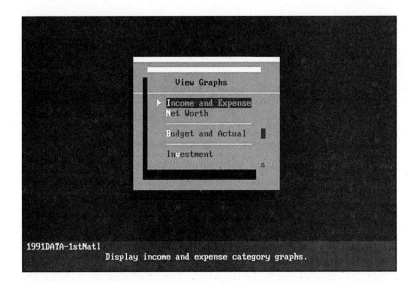

FIG. 17.7

The View Graphs menu.

Quicken displays the Income and Expense Graphs menu, the Net Worth Graphs menu, the Budget and Actual Graphs menu, or the Investment Graphs menu. Figure 17.8 shows the Income and Expense Graphs menu.

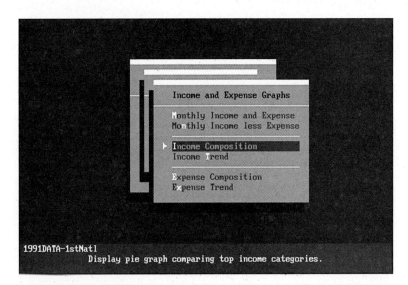

FIG. 17.8

The Income and Expense Graphs menu.

3. Use the up- and down-arrow keys to highlight the graph option that you want to select and press Enter. From the Income and Expense Graphs menu that you see in figure 17.8, for example, you can choose one of six graph options: **Monthly Income and Expense**, **Monthly Income less Expense**, **Income Composition**, **Income Trend**, **Expense Composition**, and **Expense Trend**.

After you choose a graph option, Quicken displays the graph window labeled with the option you selected. In figure 17.9, Quicken displays the Income Composition graph window that appears if you chose the **Income Composition** option from the Income and Expense Graphs window.

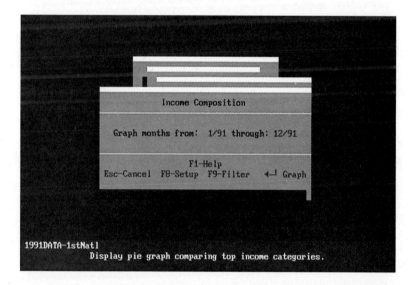

FIG. 17.9

The Income Composition graph window.

4. In the graph window, enter the dates that you want to limit transactions to. If you want to see only your income composition for the first six months of the year, for example, enter *1/92* in the Graph Months From field and *6/92* in the Through field. You can use the + (plus) and – (minus) keys to change the day or month by one.

Other graph types that you select present other graph settings such as whether to include unrealized gains; the date to use to graph balances as of; whether to show only income categories, only expense categories, or both; or whether to display balances by security, account, type, or goal. Graph settings are explained in more detail later in this chapter when you learn to create each type of Quicken graph.

5. (Optional) From the graph window, choose the **F8-Setup** option to display the Graphics Drivers Options window. Here, you can tell Quicken whether to make the text in a graph larger or the graph area larger. Press T to make the text larger or G to make the graph area larger. You probably will not need to set this option until after you have displayed a graph to see whether the text or graph area needs to be adjusted.

   If you have a color monitor but want to show graphics in black and white only, press Y from the Black and White Graphics Only field. When you display graphics in black and white, Quicken uses patterns instead of colors to distinguish different bars, lines, or pie pieces in graphs. Press N if you want Quicken to display graphics in color.

   If you haven't already set up Quicken for your graphics driver, from the Graphics Drivers Options window, you can select **F8-Video Drivers** to display the Select Graphics Driver window. Highlight a graphics driver and press Enter to return to the Graphics Drivers Options window.

   When the Graphics Drivers Options window is complete, press Ctrl-Enter or F10 to return to the graph window.

6. (Optional) If you want to filter graph transactions, choose **F9-Filter** from the graph window. *Filtering transactions* enables you to restrict the transactions included in the graph; to include certain categories and classes; to include the current account, all accounts, or select accounts; and so on. You learn about filtering graph transactions later in this chapter.

7. When the graph window is complete, press Ctrl-Enter or F10 to display the graph on your screen.

8. When you are finished reviewing the graph, press Esc to remove the graph from your screen and return to the graph window used to create the graph.

Creating Income and Expense Graphs

You can use income and expense graphs to analyze the items that make up your total income, expense items that make up your total expenses, spending habits, and your spending and earning trends. You also can use these graphs to compare your total income to expenses. Common questions you can answer by creating income and expense graphs follow:

■ By what margin is my income more than my expenses?

■ Am I overspending?

■ What sources make up my total income?

■ Has my income increased over time?

■ What expenses make up my total expenses?

■ Have my expenses increased or decreased over time?

After you create each income and expense graph, you will be able to answer these questions, and more.

Quicken provides six different graphs you can create to analyze your income and expenses:

Graph	Description
Monthly Income and Expense	A bar graph of your monthly income and monthly expenses over a specified period of time.
Monthly Income Less Expense	A line graph of your income minus expenses (net income) by month over a specified period of time.
Income Composition	A pie chart showing each individual income source as a pie piece that makes up your total income (the pie) over a specified period of time.
Income Trend	A stacked bar graph of your monthly income categories over a specified period of time.
Expense Composition	A pie chart (like the Income Composition graph) showing each expense that makes up your total expenses over a specified period of time.
Expense Trend	A stacked bar graph of your monthly expense categories over a specified period of time.

Income and expense graphs are created from the categories that you assign to transactions. Subcategories are not included in graphs. If you assigned categories to transactions, Quicken includes the subcategory totals within the categories that it graphs.

This section shows you how to create each type of graph. You can change the transactions that Quicken includes in graphs by using the **Filter** option (see "Filtering Graph Transactions," later in this chapter).

The Monthly Income and Expense Graph

The *Monthly Income and Expense* graph helps you to determine how your income compares to your expenses, on a monthly basis, over time. To create a Monthly Income and Expense graph, follow these steps:

1. Access the Income and Expense Graphs menu as explained in "Creating Graphs," earlier in this chapter.

2. Press Enter to select the **Monthly Income and Expense** graph option from the Income and Expense Graphs menu.

   Quicken displays the Monthly Income and Expense graph window, which is similar to the Income Composition graph window shown in figure 17.9.

3. In the Graph Months From field, type the starting month and year that you want the graph to cover. Type the ending month and year in the Through field. You can use the + (plus) and – (minus) keys to change the dates by one month at a time.

4. Press Ctrl-Enter or F10 to display the Monthly Income and Expense graph.

The Monthly Income and Expense graph compares income and expenses over time and tells you if you aren't earning enough to cover expenses or vice versa (spending too much in relation to your income).

The Monthly Income Less Expense Graph

Use the Monthly Income Less Expense graph to help you see the trend of your net income (income less expenses) over time. To create a Monthly Income Less Expense graph, follow these steps:

1. Access the Income and Expense Graphs menu as explained in "Creating Graphs," earlier in this chapter.

2. Select the **Monthly Income less Expense** graph option from the Income and Expense Graphs menu. Quicken displays the Monthly Income Less Expense graph window.

3. In the Graph Months From field, type the starting month and year that you want the graph to cover. Type the ending month and year in the Through field. You can use the + (plus) and – (minus) keys to change the dates by one month at a time.

4. Press Ctrl-Enter or F10 to display the Monthly Income Less Expense graph (see fig. 17.10).

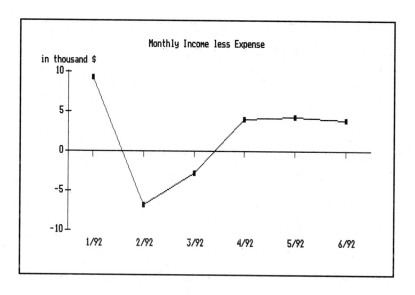

FIG. 17.10

The Monthly
Income Less
Expense graph.

From the Monthly Income Less Expense graph, you can see your *net income* (income minus expenses) trend over a period of time. If your income is greater than your expenses, the line in the graph appears above the horizontal axis; if your expenses are greater than your income, the line in the graph appears below the horizontal axis (negative values). Lines appearing as negative values should be a red alert that you need to take some action to stop your overspending trend.

The Income Composition Graph

The Income Composition Graph helps you see from what sources your total income is derived. To create an Income Composition graph, follow these steps:

1. Access the Income and Expense Graphs menu as explained in "Creating Graphs," earlier in this chapter.

2. Select the **Income Composition** graph option from the Income and Expense Graphs menu. Quicken displays the Income Composition graph window.

3. In the Graph Months From field, type the starting month and year that you want the graph to cover. Type the ending month and year in the Through field. You can use the + (plus) and – (minus) keys to change the dates by one month at a time.

4. Press Ctrl-Enter or F10 to display the Income Composition graph, which is similar to the graph shown in figure 17.3.

The Income Composition graph, displayed as a pie chart, is fairly self-explanatory. From this graph, you can see the relative contribution of each income source to your total income. Perhaps you see that your salary is the greatest contributor to your income or that you have no sources of income other than your salary. If that's the case, you may want to find a way to supplement your income to hedge against job loss or a layoff.

The Income Trend Graph

The *Income Trend* graph is a stacked bar graph that shows you two things: the composition of your income and the growth trend of your income over time. To create an Income Trend graph, follow these steps:

1. Access the Income and Expense Graphs menu as explained in "Creating Graphs," earlier in this chapter.

2. Select the **Income Trend** graph option from the Income and Expense Graphs menu. Quicken displays the Income Trend graph window.

3. In the Graph Months From field, type the starting month and year that you want the graph to cover. Type the ending month and year in the Through field. You can use the + (plus) or – (minus) key to change the dates by one month at a time.

4. Press Ctrl-Enter or F10 to display the Income Trend graph, which is similar to the graph shown in figure 17.4.

The Income Trend graph shows how your income is comprised and your income trend over time. The composition of your income is represented by each stacked bar that appears in the graph. Each item of income is shown in a different color or pattern within the bar. With the Income Trend graph, you easily can see your income patterns over a specified period of time. If you see that your income is decreasing, you should investigate the reasons. The stacked bar will show you if the decrease is a result of a salary decrease, declining investment income (such as interest and dividends), and so on.

The Expense Composition Graph

Use the Expense Composition graph to see what items make up your total expenses and the relationship of each expense to the total. To create an Expense Composition graph, follow these steps:

1. Access the Income and Expense Graphs menu as explained in "Creating Graphs," earlier in this chapter.

2. Select the **Expense Composition** graph option from the Income and Expense Graphs menu. Quicken displays the Expense Composition graph window.

3. In the Graph Months From field, type the starting month and year that you want the graph to cover. Type the ending month and year in the Through field. You can use the + (plus) and – (minus) keys to change the dates by one month at a time.

4. Press Ctrl-Enter or F10 to display the Expense Composition graph, which is similar to the graph shown in figure 17.3.

The Expense Composition graph shows each individual expense as it comprises your total expenses. From this graph, you can see how you are spending your money. This is a quick way to see just which expenses are out of line with other expenses. You may find that some *discretionary* expenses (expenses that are not fixed, such as your mortgage, rent, insurance premiums, and so on) make up a greater portion of your total expenses than they should. These types of expenses are the easiest to modify—you can eat out less, rent a movie instead of going to the theater, buy fewer clothes, watch for sales, and so on.

The Expense Trend Graph

An *Expense Trend* graph shows you the trend in your spending over time. You can see if spending is increasing at a rapid, steady, or declining rate. To create an Expense Trend graph, follow these steps:

1. Access the Income and Expense Graphs menu as explained in "Creating Graphs," earlier in this chapter.

2. Select the **Expense Trend** graph option from the Income and Expense Graphs menu. Quicken displays the Expense Trend graph window.

3. In the Graph Months From field, type the starting month and year that you want the graph to cover. Type the ending month and year in the Through field. You can use the + (plus) and – (minus) keys to change the dates by one month at a time.

4. Press Ctrl-Enter or F10 to display the Expense Trend graph.

The Expense Trend graph shows how your expenses are comprised and your spending trend over time. The composition of your expenses is represented by each stacked bar that appears in the graph. Each expense category is shown in a different color or pattern within the bar. With the Expense Trend graph, you easily can see your spending patterns over a specified period of time. If you see that your spending is increasing, you should investigate the reasons. The stacked bar will show you if the increase is a result of a fixed expense increase (like an increased mortgage payment due to a variable-rate change) or an increase in discretionary expenses such as clothing, entertainment, dining out, and so on.

Creating Net Worth Graphs

You can use *net worth* graphs to analyze the assets that make up your total assets, the liabilities that make up your total liabilities, and how your assets and liabilities have changed over time. You also can use net worth graphs to compare your total assets to your total liabilities. Common questions that you can answer by creating net worth graphs follow:

■ Do I have more assets than liabilities?

■ How has my *net worth* (assets minus liabilities) changed over time?

■ What assets make up my total assets?

■ Have my assets increased over time?

■ What liabilities make up my total liabilities?

■ Have my liabilities increased or decreased over time?

After you create each net worth graph, you'll be able to answer these questions, and more.

Net worth graphs are created from the account balances in your Quicken file.

This section shows you how to create each type of graph. You can change the transactions that Quicken includes in graphs by using the **Filter** option (see "Filtering Graph Transactions," later in this chapter, for more information).

Quicken provides six different graphs you can create to analyze your net worth:

Graph	Description
Monthly Assets and Liabilities	A bar graph of your monthly asset balances and monthly liability balances over a specified period of time.
Monthly Assets Less Liabilities	A line graph of your net worth by month over a specified period of time.
Asset Composition	A pie chart that shows each individual asset as a pie piece that makes up your total assets (the pie) as of a specified date.
Asset Trend	A stacked bar graph of your total asset balances, by month, over a specified period of time.
Liability Composition	A pie chart (like the Asset Composition graph) that shows each liability that makes up your total liabilities as of a specified date.
Liability Trend	A stacked bar graph of your total liability balances, by month, over a specified period of time.

The Monthly Assets and Liabilities Graph

The Monthly Assets and Liabilities graph compares your total assets to your total liabilities over time. To create the Monthly Assets and Liabilities graph, follow these steps:

1. Access the Net Worth Graphs menu as explained in "Creating Graphs," earlier in this chapter.

2. Select the **Monthly Assets and Liabilities** graph option from the Net Worth Graphs menu shown in figure 17.11.

   Quicken displays the Monthly Assets and Liabilities graph window shown in figure 17.12.

3. In the Graph Ending Balances for Months field, type the starting month and year that you want the graph to cover. Type the ending month and year in the Through field. You can use the + (plus) and – (minus) keys to change the dates by one month at a time.

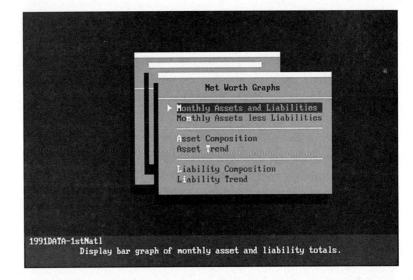

FIG. 17.11

The Net Worth
Graphs menu.

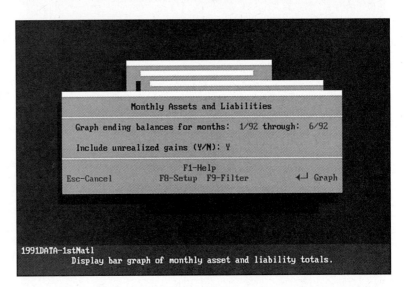

FIG. 17.12

The Monthly
Assets and
Liabilities graph
window.

4. Press Enter or Tab to move to the Include Unrealized Gains field.
Press N if you don't want Quicken to include the unrealized gains
and losses from changes in the value of your securities in your
investment accounts. Keep the setting at Y if you do want to include unrealized gains and losses in the graph.

5. Press Ctrl-Enter or F10 to display the Monthly Assets and Liabilities graph (see fig. 17.13).

The Monthly Asset and Liabilities graph compares assets and liabilities over time. Hopefully, you will see that your assets are greater than your liabilities so that you have a positive net worth. If your liabilities are greater than your assets, you have a negative net worth and will find it difficult to decrease your liabilities without some future infusion of income or other funds.

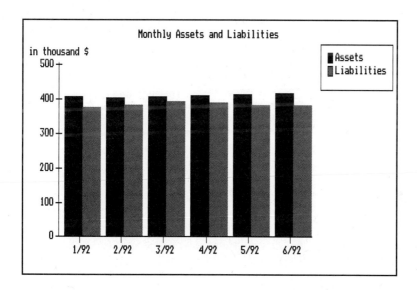

FIG. 17.13

The Monthly Assets and Liabilities graph.

The Monthly Assets Less Liabilities Graph

The *Monthly Assets Less Liabilities* graph is a line graph that charts your *net worth* (assets minus liabilities) over time. Hopefully, you see an increase when you create this graph. To create the Monthly Assets Less Liabilities graph, follow these steps:

1. Access the Net Worth Graphs menu as explained in "Creating Graphs," earlier in this chapter.

2. Select the **Monthly Assets less Liabilities** graph option from the Net Worth Graphs menu. Quicken displays the Monthly Assets Less Liabilities graph window.

3. In the Graph Ending Balances for Months field, type the starting month and year that you want the graph to cover. Type the ending month and year in the Through field. You can use the + (plus) and – (minus) keys to change the dates by one month at a time.

4. Press Enter or Tab to move to the Include Unrealized Gains field. Press N if you don't want Quicken to include the unrealized gains and losses from changes in the value of your securities in your investment accounts. Keep the setting at Y if you do want to include unrealized gains and losses in the graph.

5. Press Ctrl-Enter or F10 to display the Monthly Assets Less Liabilities graph, which is similar to the graph shown in figure 17.2.

The Monthly Assets Less Liabilities graph shows your *net worth* (assets minus liabilities), by month, over time. If your net worth is positive, the line in the graph appears above the horizontal axis; if your net worth is negative, the line appears below the horizontal axis. Ideally, your net worth should grow as you accumulate assets and pay off liabilities, so you should see an upward-moving line above the horizontal axis.

The Asset Composition Graph

The *Asset Composition* graph is a pie chart that shows how your assets are composed and the relationship of each asset to the total assets. To create an Asset Composition graph, follow these steps:

1. Access the Net Worth Graphs menu as explained in "Creating Graphs," earlier in this chapter.

2. Select the **Asset Composition** graph option from the Net Worth Graphs menu. Quicken displays the Asset Composition graph window.

3. In the Graph Balances As Of field, type the date you want to use to show balances. Quicken uses this date to look for account balances and uses the balances found on that particular date in the graph. You can use the + (plus) and – (minus) keys to change the dates by one day at a time.

4. Press Enter or Tab to move to the Include Unrealized Gains field. Press N if you don't want Quicken to include the unrealized gains and losses from changes in the value of your securities in your investment accounts. Keep the setting at Y if you do want to include unrealized gains and losses in the graph.

5. Press Ctrl-Enter or F10 to display the Asset Composition graph.

The Asset Composition graph, displayed as a pie chart, is fairly self-explanatory. From this graph, you can see the relative contribution of each of your assets to your total assets.

The Asset Trend Graph

Hopefully, the value of your assets grows over time. Creating an *Asset Trend* graph helps you see if your assets are increasing, remaining steady, or decreasing. You also can see how your assets are comprised. To create an Asset Trend graph, follow these steps:

1. Access the Net Worth Graphs menu as explained in "Creating Graphs," earlier in this chapter.

2. Select the **Asset Trend** graph option from the Net Worth Graphs menu. Quicken displays the Asset Trend graph window.

3. In the Graph Ending Balances for Months field, type the starting month and year that you want the graph to cover. Type the ending month and year in the Through field. You can use the + (plus) and – (minus) keys to change the dates by one month at a time.

4. Press Enter or Tab to move to the Include Unrealized Gains field. Press N if you don't want Quicken to include the unrealized gains and losses from changes in the value of your securities in your investment accounts. Keep the setting at Y if you do want to include unrealized gains and losses in the graph.

5. Press Ctrl-Enter or F10 to display the Asset Trend graph (see fig. 17.14).

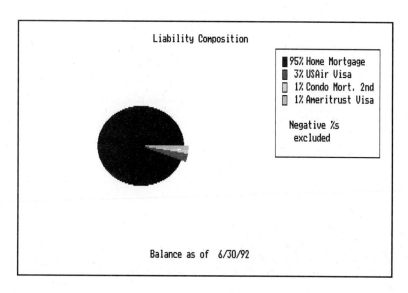

The Asset Trend graph.

The Asset Trend graph shows how your assets are comprised and your asset trend over time. The composition of your assets is represented by each stacked bar that appears in the graph. Each asset is shown in a different color or pattern within the bar. With the Asset Trend graph, you easily can see how the value of your assets changes over time.

The Liability Composition Graph

To see how your liabilities are comprised, you can create a *Liability Composition* graph displayed as a pie chart. With this graph, you see the relationship between each of your liabilities to your total liabilities. To create a Liability Composition graph, follow these steps:

1. Access the Net Worth Graphs menu as explained in "Creating Graphs," earlier in this chapter.

2. Select the **Liability Composition** graph option from the Net Worth Graphs menu. Quicken displays the Liability Composition graph window.

3. In the Graph Balances As Of field, type the date that you want to use to show balances. Quicken uses this date to look for account balances and uses the balances found on that particular date in the graph. You can use the + (plus) and − (minus) keys to change the dates by one day at a time.

4. Press Ctrl-Enter or F10 to display the Liability Composition graph (see fig. 17.15).

The Liability Composition graph shows each individual liability as it comprises your total liabilities.

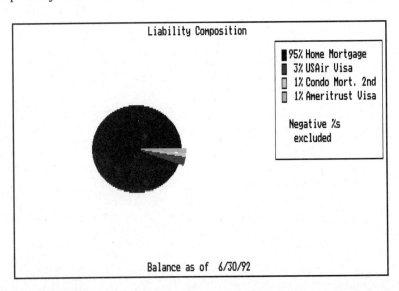

Liability Composition

- 95% Home Mortgage
- 3% USAir Visa
- 1% Condo Mort. 2nd
- 1% Ameritrust Visa

Negative %s excluded

Balance as of 6/30/92

The Liability Trend Graph

The *Liability Trend* graph not only shows how your liabilities are comprised, but also how your liabilities have increased or decreased over time. To create a Liability Trend graph, follow these steps:

1. Access the Net Worth Graphs menu as explained in "Creating Graphs," earlier in this chapter.

2. Select the **Liability Trend** graph option from the Net Worth Graphs menu. Quicken displays the Liability Trend graph window.

3. In the Graph Ending Balances for Months field, type the starting month and year that you want the graph to cover. Type the ending month and year in the Through field. You can use the + (plus) and – (minus) keys to change the dates by one month at a time.

4. Press Ctrl-Enter or F10 to display the Liability Trend graph.

The Liability Trend graph shows how your liabilities are comprised and any increases or decreases in liabilities over time. The composition of your liabilities is represented by each stacked bar that appears in the graph. Each liability account is shown in a different color or pattern within the bar. With the Liability Trend graph, you easily can see how your debts fluctuate over a specified period of time. If you see that your liabilities are increasing, you should investigate the reasons. The stacked bar will show you if the increase is a result of new loan (such as a new car loan or a home improvement loan) or increased credit card debt.

Creating Budget versus Actual Data Graphs

You can use net budget and actual graphs to compare your actual income and expenses to your budgeted income and expenses. The budget reports that you learned how to create in Chapter 12 also tell you how your budget compares to your actual income and expense. The budget and actual graphs provide a visual comparison that enables you to quickly assess how successful (or unsuccessful) you are in sticking to your budget.

You can use budget and actual graphs to compare actual amounts to budgeted amounts, identify areas where you are over budget, identify areas where you are under budget, show the relative contribution of budgeted amounts to your whole budget, and see how your budget has changed over a period of time.

Common questions that you can answer by creating budget and actual graphs follow:

- Am I sticking to my budget?

- How much more can I spend and still stay within my budget?

- In which areas am I over budget?

- In which areas am I under budget?

- What income and expense items make up my budget?

- How has my budget changed over time?

After you create each budget and actual graph, you'll be able to answer these questions, and more.

Quicken provides six different graphs that you can create to analyze your budget versus actual data:

Graph	Description
Monthly Budget and Actual	A bar graph of your monthly budget and monthly budget categories over a specified period of time.
Monthly Actual Less Budget	A line graph of your remaining monthly budget amounts (actual minus budget) over a specified period of time.
Categories Over Budget	A double-bar graph of only the categories that were over budget over a specified period of time.
Categories Under Budget	A double-bar graph of only the categories that were under budget over a specified period of time.
Budget Composition	A pie chart that shows each budget category as a pie piece that makes up your total budget (the pie) over a specified period of time.
Budget Trend	A stacked bar graph of your monthly budget categories over a specified period of time.

You cannot display budget and actual graphs unless you have first created your budget. Refer to Chapter 15 to learn how to create a budget. Budget and actual graphs are created from the categories that you assign to transactions and the categories that you establish budget amounts for. Quicken graphs categories only. Any subcategories that you assign to transactions or enter a budget amount for are included within the categories in the budget and actual graphs.

This section shows you how to create each type of graph. You can change the transactions that Quicken includes in graphs by using the Filter option (see "Filtering Graph Transactions," later in this chapter).

The Monthly Budget and Actual Graph

The *Monthly Budget and Actual* graph is displayed as a double-bar graph that compares your budgeted expenses to your actual expenses. Note that you also can compare budgeted income to actual income using this graph. To create the Monthly Budget and Actual graph, follow these steps:

1. Access the Budget and Actual Graphs menu as explained in "Creating Graphs," earlier in this chapter.

2. Select the **Monthly Budget and Actual** graph option from the Budget and Actual Graphs menu shown in figure 17.16. Quicken displays the Monthly Budget and Actual graph window.

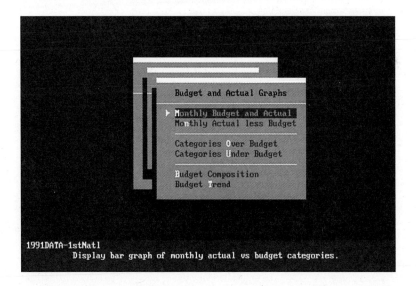

FIG. 17.16

The Budget and Actual Graphs menu.

3. In the Graph Months From field, type the starting month and year that you want the graph to cover. Type the ending month and year in the Through field. You can use the + (plus) and – (minus) keys to change the dates by one month at a time.

4. Press Enter or Tab to move to the Show Income, Expense, or Both Categories field. By default, Quicken graphs expense categories only (the setting is E). However, if you want to graph both income and expense categories, press B. If you want to graph only income categories, press I.

5. Press Ctrl-Enter or F10 to display the Monthly Budget and Actual graph (see fig. 17.17).

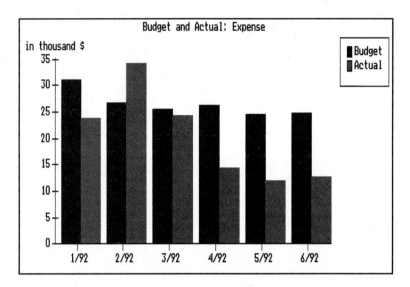

FIG. 17.17

The Monthly
Budget and
Actual graph.

The Monthly Budget and Actual graph compares budgeted amounts to actual amounts over a period of time. If you're sticking to your budget, you should see that the budget bar is higher in the graph than the actual bar. If you graph expense categories only, the Monthly Budget and Actual graph helps you pinpoint which months you were over budget so that you can go back and look at expenses for those months to determine why spending was so high.

The Monthly Actual Less Budget Graph

To see how well (or not so well) you're doing at sticking to your budget, you can create a *Monthly Actual Less Budget* graph that appears as a line graph that shows your remaining budget amounts over a specified time. To create the Monthly Actual Less Budget graph, follow these steps:

1. Access the Budget and Actual Graphs menu as explained in "Creating Graphs," earlier in this chapter.

2. Select the **Monthly Actual less Budget** graph option from the Budget and Actual Graphs menu. Quicken displays the Monthly Actual Less Budget graph window.

3. In the Graph Months From field, type the starting month and year that you want the graph to cover. Type the ending month and year in the Through field. You can use the + (plus) and – (minus) keys to change the dates by one month at a time.

4. Press Enter or Tab to move to the Show Income, Expense, or Both categories field. By default, Quicken graphs expense categories only (the setting is E). If you want to graph both income and expense categories, press B. If you want to graph only income categories, press I.

5. Press Ctrl-Enter or F10 to display the Monthly Actual Less Budget graph (see fig. 17.18).

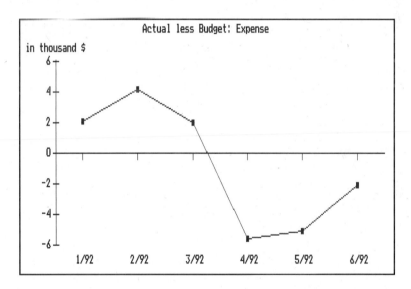

FIG. 17.18

The Monthly Actual Less Budget graph.

The Monthly Budget Less Actual graph shows what remains of your budget, by month, over time. If you're graphing expense categories only, the line in the graph appears above the horizontal axis if you have spent less than you budgeted. If the line appears below the horizontal axis, you spent more than you budgeted.

The Categories Over Budget Graph

The *Categories Over Budget* graph helps you quickly see which areas of spending you're having problems with. Follow these steps to create a Categories Over Budget graph:

1. Access the Budget and Actual Graphs menu as explained in "Creating Graphs," earlier in this chapter.

2. Select the **Categories Over Budget** graph option from the Budget and Actual Graphs menu.

   Quicken displays the Categories Over Budget graph window shown in figure 17.19.

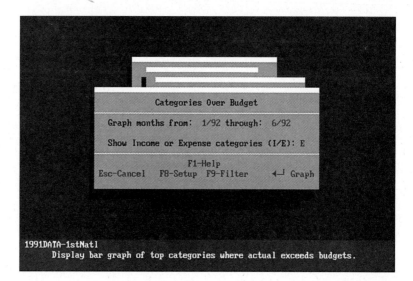

FIG. 17.19

The Categories
Over Budget
graph window.

3. In the Graph Months From field, type the starting month and year that you want the graph to cover. Type the ending month and year in the Through field. You can use the + (plus) and – (minus) keys to change the dates by one month at a time.

4. Press Enter or Tab to move to the Show Income or Expense Categories field. By default, Quicken graphs expense categories only (the setting is E). If you want to graph only income categories, press I.

5. Press Ctrl-Enter or F10 to display the Categories Over Budget graph (see fig. 17.20).

The Categories Over Budget graph shows you the categories that were furthest over budget for the time period that you specify (Quicken cannot include every category over budget in the graph—there's not enough space). The farther away from zero an over-budget category is on the graph, the more attention you need to pay to that particular category to determine whether your budget amount is not realistic or whether actual spending or income needs to be brought into line.

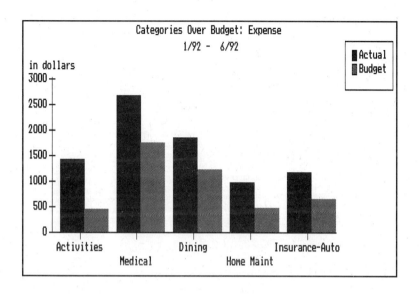

FIG. 17.20

The Categories Over Budget graph.

The Categories Under Budget Graph

To see the categories where you are under budget over a specified time, you can create the *Categories Under Budget* graph. This graph is displayed as a double-bar graph that compares budgeted amounts to actual amounts for under-budget categories. To create a Categories Under Budget graph, follow these steps:

1. Access the Budget and Actual Graphs menu as explained in "Creating Graphs," earlier in this chapter.

2. Select the **Categories Under Budget** graph option from the Budget and Actual Graphs menu. Quicken displays the Categories Under Budget graph window.

3. In the Graph Months From field, type the starting month and year that you want the graph to cover. Type the ending month and year in the Through field. You can use the + (plus) and – (minus) keys to change the dates by one month at a time.

4. Press Enter or Tab to move to the Show Income or Expense Categories field. By default, Quicken graphs expense categories only (the setting is E). If you want to graph only income categories, press I.

5. Press Ctrl-Enter or F10 to display the Categories Under Budget graph.

The Categories Under Budget graph shows you the categories that were furthest under budget for the time period that you specify (Quicken cannot include every category under budget in the graph—there's not enough space). If you graph income categories only, negative values in the graph indicate that you earned more than you thought you would when you created your budget.

The Budget Composition Graph

The *Budget Composition* graph is displayed as a pie chart that shows what expenses (or income items) make up your total budget. To create a Budget Composition graph, follow these steps:

1. Access the Budget and Actual Graphs menu as explained in "Creating Graphs," earlier in this chapter.

2. Select the **Budget Composition** graph option from the Budget and Actual Graphs menu. Quicken displays the Budget Composition graph window.

3. In the Graph Months From field, type the starting month and year that you want the graph to cover. Type the ending month and year in the Through field. You can use the + (plus) and – (minus) keys to change the dates by one month at a time.

4. Press Enter or Tab to move to the Show Income or Expense Categories field. By default, Quicken graphs expense categories only (the setting is E). If you want to graph only income categories, press I.

5. Press Ctrl-Enter or F10 to display the Budget Composition graph (see fig. 17.21).

The Budget Composition graph, displayed as a pie chart, shows the relative contribution of each of your budgeted income or expense categories to your total budget.

The Budget Trend Graph

To see which expense categories make up your total budget and how your total budgeted expenses increase or decrease over time, you can create the *Budget Trend* graph. Follow these steps:

1. Access the Budget and Actual Graphs menu as explained in "Creating Graphs," earlier in this chapter.

2. Select the **Budget Trend** graph option from the Budget and Actual Graphs menu. Quicken displays the Budget Trend graph window.

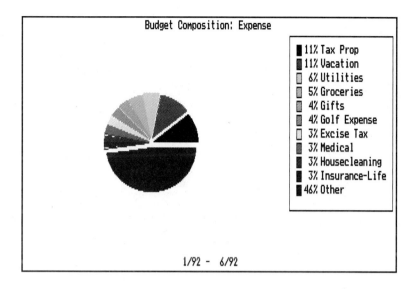

Budget Composition: Expense

- 11% Tax Prop
- 11% Vacation
- 6% Utilities
- 5% Groceries
- 4% Gifts
- 4% Golf Expense
- 3% Excise Tax
- 3% Medical
- 3% Housecleaning
- 3% Insurance-Life
- 46% Other

1/92 - 6/92

FIG. 17.21

The Budget
Composition
graph.

3. In the Graph Months From field, type the starting month and year that you want the graph to cover. Type the ending month and year in the Through field. You can use the + (plus) and – (minus) keys to change the dates by one month at a time.

4. Press Enter or Tab to move to the Show Income or Expense Categories field. By default, Quicken graphs expense categories only (the setting is E). If you want to graph only income categories, press I.

5. Press Ctrl-Enter or F10 to display the Budget Trend graph (see fig. 17.22).

The Budget Trend graph shows how your budget is comprised and your budgeting trend over time. The composition of your budget is represented by each stacked bar that appears in the graph. Each budgeting category is shown in a different color or pattern within the bar.

Creating Investments Graphs

You can use investment graphs to analyze your investment portfolio. With investment graphs, you can see how your portfolio is distributed (stocks, bonds, options, Treasury Bills, and so on), see the changes in your portfolio value over time, and analyze the price trends of your security holdings.

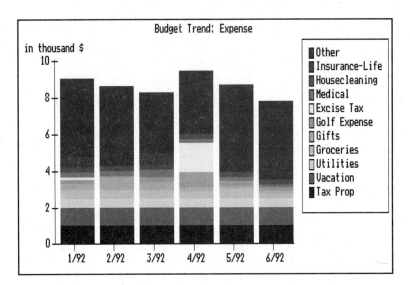

FIG. 17.22

The Budget
Trend graph.

  If you don't track your investments using Quicken's investment accounts, you will not be able to create investment
graphs. Refer to Chapter 16 to learn how to use Quicken's
investment accounts.

Common questions that you can answer by creating investment graphs
follow:

- Is my investment portfolio value increasing?

- How diversified is my investment portfolio?

- Are the prices of my individual holdings increasing?

- Should I sell a security because the price trend of the security is
downward?

After you create each investment graph, you'll be able to answer these
questions, and more.

This section shows you how to create each type of graph. You can
change the transactions that Quicken includes in graphs by using the
Filter option (see "Filtering Graph Transactions," later in this chapter).

Quicken provides three different graphs that you can create to analyze
your income and expenses:

Graph	Description
Portfolio Composition	A pie chart showing each individual security as a pie piece that makes up your investment portfolio (the pie) over a specified period of time.
Portfolio Value Trend	A stacked bar graph that shows the total market value of your investment accounts (or if you filter transactions, the market value of specific securities, types, or goals), by month, over a specified period of time.
Price History	A line graph showing the price trend of securities that you have updated in the Update Prices and Market Value window. Refer to Chapter 16 to learn about updating security prices.

The Portfolio Composition Graph

The *Portfolio Composition* graph displays as a pie chart and shows you just how your portfolio is comprised and the relationship of each of your investments to your total investments. To create a Portfolio Composition graph, follow these steps:

1. Access the Investment Graphs menu as explained in "Creating Graphs," earlier in this chapter.

2. Select the **Portfolio Composition** graph option from the Investment Graphs menu shown in figure 17.23.

   Quicken displays the Portfolio Composition graph window shown in figure 17.24.

3. In the Graph Balances As Of field, type the date you want to use to show balances. Quicken uses this date to look for investment account balances and uses the balances found on that particular date in the graph. You can use the + (plus) and – (minus) keys to change the dates by one day at a time.

4. Press Enter or Tab to move to the Display the Balances field. Press the number that corresponds to the balances you want to display in the graph. Press 1 to display your portfolio allocation by security, 2 to display your portfolio allocation by account, 3 to display your portfolio allocation by type, or 4 to display by goal.

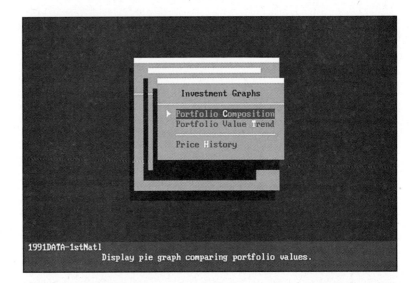

FIG. 17.23

The Investment
Graphs menu.

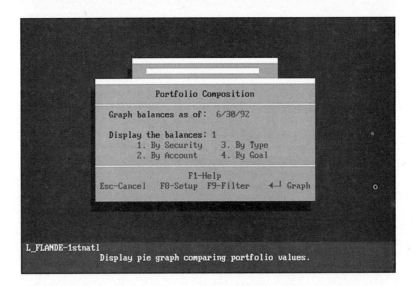

FIG. 17.24

The Portfolio
Composition
graph window.

If you want to see how your total investment portfolio is allocated, create a Portfolio Composition graph displayed by security (press 1). When you display the graph by account, Quicken combines all your investment accounts and shows the relationship of each individual account to your total accounts. Displaying the graph by type shows the relationship of each type of security that you hold to your total portfolio. When you display the graph by goal,

Quicken shows the relationship of each security goal to your total portfolio.

5. Press Ctrl-Enter or F10 to display the Portfolio Composition graph (see fig. 17.25).

The Portfolio Composition graph shows you some valuable information about your investments. You can see how diversified your investments are by displaying the graph by security type (stocks, bonds, CDs, mutual funds, unit trusts, and so on). You also can use the Portfolio Composition graph to show the allocation of securities to meet investment goals (such as funding college, retirement, growth, income, and so on), by displaying the graph by goal.

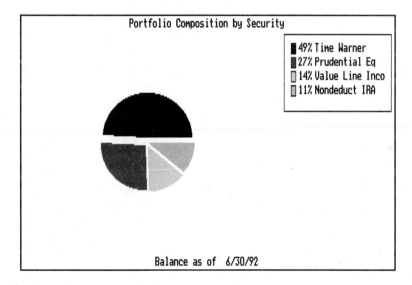

Portfolio Composition by Security

■ 49% Time Warner
▨ 27% Prudential Eq
□ 14% Value Line Inco
▨ 11% Nondeduct IRA

Balance as of 6/30/92

FIG. 17.25

The Portfolio Composition graph.

The Portfolio Value Trend Graph

You can create a *Portfolio Value Trend* graph to help you see how your investments are increasing or decreasing over time and which investments comprise your total portfolio. Follow these steps to create a Portfolio Value Trend graph:

1. Access the Investment Graphs menu as explained in "Creating Graphs," earlier in this chapter.

2. Select the **Portfolio Value Trend** graph option from the Investment Graphs menu. Quicken displays the Portfolio Value Trend graph window.

3. In the Graph Ending Balances for Months field, type the starting date that you want Quicken to use to graph security or investment account balances. In the Through field, type the date that you want balances graphed through. You can use the + (plus) and – (minus) keys to change the dates by one month at a time.

4. Press Enter or Tab to move to the Display the Balances field. Press the number that corresponds to the balances you want to display in the graph. Press 1 to display your portfolio allocation by security, 2 to display your portfolio allocation by account, 3 to display your portfolio allocation by type, or 4 to display by goal.

   If you want to see how the value of your individual securities have changed over time, create a Portfolio Value Trend graph displayed by security (press 1). When you display the graph by account, Quicken combines all your investment accounts and shows the value of your accounts over time. Displaying the graph by type shows the value of securities, grouped by type, over a period of time. When you display the graph by goal, Quicken shows the value of securities, grouped by goal, over time.

5. Press Ctrl-Enter or F10 to create the Portfolio Value Trend graph (see fig. 17.26).

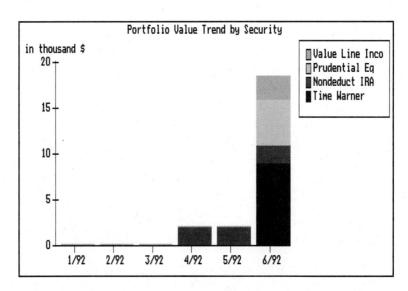

FIG. 17.26

The Portfolio Value Trend graph.

The Portfolio Value Trend graph shows you how your portfolio is growing (or not growing) over a period of time. Within this graph, you also can see how each individual security (if you display the graph by security) is moving. If your total portfolio value is not moving upward, the Portfolio Value Trend graph helps you determine which securities are holding down the value of your portfolio.

The Price History Graph

The *Price History* graph helps you see how the prices of securities that you hold in your portfolio have increased or decreased over time. To create a Price History graph, follow these steps:

1. Access the Investment Graphs menu as explained in "Creating Graphs," earlier in this chapter.

2. Select the **Price History** graph option from the Investment Graphs menu. Quicken displays the Price History graph window.

3. In the Graph Price From field, type the starting date that you want Quicken to use to graph security prices. In the Through field, type the date that you want security prices graphed through. You can use the + (plus) and − (minus) keys to change the dates by one day at a time.

4. Press Enter or Tab to move to the Adjust Prices for Splits field. Press Y if you had stock splits and want Quicken to adjust the prices to take the split into account.

   For example, if you bought 100 shares of stock and paid $10 per share (for a total price of $1,000), and subsequently the stock split 1 for 1 (you received one share for every one share that you held), you now have 200 shares of the stock. The per share price of the stock that you now have is $5, which is determined by dividing the total price of the stock ($1,000) by the total shares (200).

5. (Optional) If you want to select which securities Quicken graphs in the Price History graph, press F9. Quicken displays the Select Securities to Include window shown in figure 17.27. Use the up- and down-arrow keys to highlight the security that you want to select and press the space bar to include the security in the Price History graph. Press the space bar again to exclude a security from the graph, or press F9 to select all securities in the Select Securities to Include window. When you are finished selecting securities to include, press Enter to return to the Price History graph window.

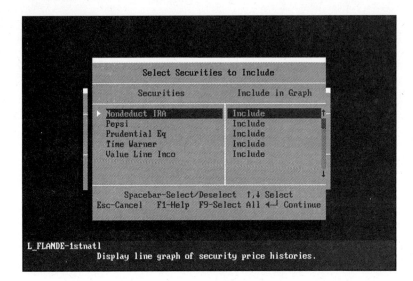

FIG. 17.27

The Select
Securities to
Include window.

6. Press Ctrl-Enter or F10 to create the Price History graph (see
   fig. 17.28).

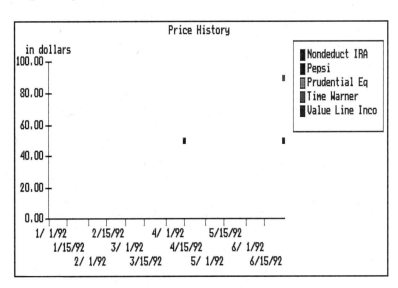

FIG. 17.28

The Price
History graph.

Filtering Graph Transactions

You can choose which transactions Quicken includes in graphs by filtering transactions. Filtering graph transactions is similar to filtering report transactions (you learned how to filter report transactions in Chapter 12).

To filter graph transactions, follow these steps:

1. From the graph window that you use to create a graph (for example, the Monthly Income and Expense graph window), press F9 to select the **Filter** option.

   Quicken displays the Filters window shown in figure 17.29. Note that Quicken enters the title of the report option in the Filters window. If you select the **Filter** option from the Monthly Income and Expense graph window, Quicken displays the Income and Expense Filters window because this type of graph is an income and expense graph.

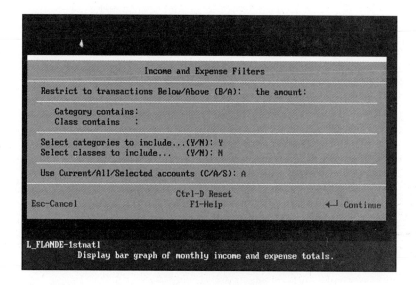

FIG. 17.29

The Income and Expense Filters window.

2. Press Enter or Tab to move to the field where you want to set a filter option. Because each graph you create presents different filtering options, table 17.1 describes the available options.

3. When the Filters window is complete, press Ctrl-Enter or F10. If you chose to select categories, classes, accounts, securities, security types, or investment goals, Quicken displays the appropriate window next so that you can make your selections. When you are finished making your selections, press Enter to return to the graph window that you are using to create a graph.

Table 17.1 Filtering Options

Filtering Option	Function
Restrict to Transactions Below/Above the Amount	Enables you to include only those transactions that fall below (B) or above (A) the amount that you enter.
Category Contains Class Contains	Enables you to specify which categories or classes to include in graphs. You can enter partial words or phrases and also use special match characters for Quicken to search.
Select Categories to Include Select Classes to Include	Enables you to select which categories or classes to include in graphs. When you select to include categories or classes, Quicken displays the Select Categories to Include window or the Select Classes to Include window so that you can make your selections.
Use Current/All/Selected Accounts	You can tell Quicken which accounts to use in graphs: the current account (C), all accounts (A), or selected accounts (S). If you want to select accounts, Quicken displays the Select Accounts to Include window so that you can make your selections.
Display the (2-12)	By default, Quicken displays 10 items in a graph. If you want to display a different number of items, enter a number from 2 to 12.
Categories with Accounts with Budget Categories with	Enables you to include categories, accounts, or budget categories with the highest balance (1) or the lowest balance (2).
Summarize Remaining Categories or Accounts into "Other"?	Balances for categories that are not displayed are lumped into an Other category in graphs. Press N if you don't want to show the Other category in the graph.

Filtering Option	Function

For investment graphs, other filtering options are available as follows:

Select Securities to Graph	Enables you to select the securities to include in the graph. If you want to select securities, Quicken displays the Select Securities to Include window so that you can make your selections.
Select Security Types to Graph	Enables you to select the security types to include in the graph. If you want to select security types, Quicken displays the Select Security Types to Include window so that you can make your selections.
Select Investment Goals to Graph	Enables you to select the investment goals to include in the graph. If you want to select investment goals, Quicken displays the Select Investment Goals to Include window so that you can make your selections.

Chapter Summary

In this chapter, you learned about Quicken 6.0's new graphing feature. You learned about the different types of graphs that Quicken creates (line graphs, pie charts, and so on) and how to create graphs to analyze your income and expenses, net worth, budget versus actual data, and investments. You also learned how to filter graphs to include only the categories or accounts that you want. Graphing your financial information sometimes provides more insight to help you make decisions about your finances.

The next chapter describes more new Quicken 6.0 features: the financial planning calculators. You learn about planning your investments, planning for retirement, planning for college, and refinancing your mortgage.

Financial Planning with Quicken

You already know how to use Quicken to write checks, keep your Register, reconcile your bank account, track your assets and liabilities, manage your credit cards, create a budget, prepare for income taxes, monitor your investments, and create graphs to show comparative data. But what about using Quicken for financial planning? And what is financial planning?

Financial planning is the process of setting future goals and developing plans to meet those goals. For example, in order to retire with enough money to meet expenses (and have a little fun) through the remainder of your life, you first must determine how much money you will need, and then develop and implement a financial plan so that you have that amount of money at retirement age. You also need to develop a financial plan for the things that you would like to acquire, such as a first home, new car, vacation home, trip to Europe, and so on. And if you have children, you will want to plan for college expenses *now*, even though your children are young.

Now, with Quicken 6.0, you don't need other software programs to help you with planning your financial needs for the future. Quicken 6.0 includes all new financial planning calculators that are convenient and easy to use. Quicken's financial planning calculators are easy to access from the Register or the Write Checks screen and make calculations as quickly as you can enter the data. Financial planning calculators include the following:

- *Loan Calculator:* Amortizes fixed-rate and variable-rate loans. You learned about this calculator in Chapter 10.

- *Investment Planning Calculator:* An investment planning tool that calculates the expected growth of an investment, how much money you need now to have a certain amount in the future, or how much money you need to contribute periodically to an investment to have a certain amount in the future. You learn about the Investment Planning Calculator in this chapter.

- *Retirement Planning Calculator:* Calculates how much your current retirement account will yield in annual, after-tax income at retirement age given your estimated tax rate, yearly contributions, predicted inflation rate, and the expected annual yield. With the Retirement Planning Calculator, you also can determine how much you need to have now or how much you need to contribute to your retirement account on a yearly basis so that you have the money you need when you retire. This chapter explains how to use the Retirement Planning Calculator.

- *College Planning Calculator:* Calculates how much money you need to have today, or how much you need to save each year, to send your kids to college in the future. You can even use this tool to help you determine how much annual tuition you can afford—state supported school, Ivy League, or other. You learn about the College Planning Calculator in this chapter.

- *Refinance Calculator:* The Refinance Calculator is somewhat different from the other financial planning calculators. It helps you determine the benefits of refinancing your existing mortgage. You can calculate the difference in your monthly payment at various interest rates and how long it will take to recover the closing costs incurred when you refinance your mortgage. This chapter shows you how to use the Refinance Calculator.

In this chapter, you learn how to do the following:

- Use each of the financial planning calculators described (except the Loan Calculator, which was covered in Chapter 10)

- Change the calculation that Quicken makes in each financial planning calculator

- Display payment schedules based on the calculations that the financial calculators make

- Print payment schedules

Planning Your Investments

Most of us have some amount of money saved or invested (no matter how large or small) that we would like to see grow. Whether you're saving for a new car, a down payment, or a European vacation, you want your money to grow quickly so that you don't have to wait so long to acquire the things you want. Although Quicken cannot make your money grow any quicker than the investment vehicle it's currently maintained in, you can monitor your investment growth and play out "what-if" scenarios using Quicken's new Investment Planning Calculator. You can see how much your investment will grow given different interest rates, inflation rates, and yearly contributions.

Using the Investment Planning Calculator

With the Investment Planning Calculator, you can calculate the following variables:

- The expected growth of the money that you currently have saved or invested over a certain time period and based on a specific interest rate and expected inflation rate.

- How much money you need *now* to accumulate a certain amount of money in the future.

- How much money you need to save on a yearly basis to accumulate a certain amount of money in the future.

To access the Investment Planning Calculator, follow these steps:

1. From the Register or the Write Checks screen, press Alt-A to access the Activities menu.

2. Select the **Financial Planning** option from the Activities menu to display the Financial Planning menu (see fig. 18.1).

3. Select the **Investment Planning** option from the Financial Planning menu. Quicken displays the Investment Planning Calculator, shown in figure 18.2.

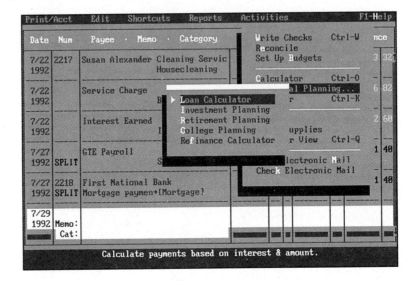

FIG. 18.1

The Financial
Planning menu.

Notice the calculation check mark in the far left column of the Investment Planning Calculator. The calculation check mark determines which calculation the calculator will perform when you enter data. In figure 18.2, the check mark appears next to the Future Value field. Therefore, when you enter data in the other fields in the Investment Planning Calculator, Quicken calculates the future value, or the amount that your investment grows to or is worth in the future.

To change the calculation that Quicken makes, press the F8 function key to move the check mark to the Present Value field, the Additions Each Year field, or the Future Value field.

Performing Investment Planning Calculations

To calculate the future value of an investment based on the amount that you have invested today, follow these steps:

1. Access the Investment Planning Calculator.

2. Press F8, if necessary, to move the calculation check mark to the Future Value field.

3. Press Enter or Tab to move to the Present Value field, and enter the current value of your investment or your savings account.

```
 Print/Acct    Edit    Shortcuts    Reports    Activities        F1-Help

 Date  Num   Payee  ·  Memo  ·  Category    Payment  C   Deposit    Balance

 7/22 2217┌──────────────────────────────────────────────┐  -1,433 32
 1992    │            Investment Planning               │
─────────│                                              │──────────
 7/22    │  Present Value                : 0.00          │  -1,436 82
 1992    │  Additions each Year          : 0.00          │
         │  Number of Years              : 1            │
─────────│  Annual Yield                 : 8%           │──────────
 7/22    │                                            2 │  -1,432 60
 1992    │ √ Future Value                = 0.00          │
         │    (in today's dollars)       : 0.00          │
─────────│                                            0 │  1,101 40
 7/27    │  Predicted Inflation          : 4%           │
 1992 SPLI│  Inflate Payments Yearly (Y/N) : N           │
─────────│                                              │──────────
 7/27 2218│                                              │     101 40
 1992 SPLI│                                              │
─────────│  F7-Change Periods       F8-Select Calculation│──────────
 7/29    │  Esc-Cancel          F1-Help    F9-Show Payments│
 1992 Memo└──────────────────────────────────────────────┘
      Cat

 1stnatl
                                        Ending Balance:  $101.40
```

FIG. 18.2

The Investment Planning Calculator.

4. Press Enter or Tab to move to the Additions Each Year field. Enter the amount of additional investments or savings that you plan to make each year.

5. Press Enter or Tab to move to the Number of Years field. Enter the number of years you plan to make contributions to your investment account or savings account. If you want to change the time period from yearly to quarters, months, or weeks, press F7 until the time period that you desire is displayed. If you change the time period, make sure that you enter the amount of additional investments or savings (in step 4) based on the new time period.

6. Press Enter or Tab to move to the Annual Yield field. Enter the rate of return that you expect from this investment (do not type a percent sign). If, for example, you're calculating the future value of a savings account, enter the interest rate that the account currently pays.

7. Move next to the Predicted Inflation field and enter the current or expected inflation rate. Do not type a percent sign.

8. In the Inflate Payments Yearly field, press Y if you want Quicken to adjust the additions made to your investment or savings account based on the inflation rate. Press N if you want the additions to remain constant.

When you have entered all variables in the Investment Planning Calculator, Quicken calculates the future value of the investment and enters the result in the Future Value field. Quicken converts the future value amount to today's dollars (the amount that your investment is worth today) and enters the result under the Future Value field. Figure 18.3 shows that a savings account worth $10,000 today is worth $16,288.94 10 years from now if the savings account earns 5 percent annually and inflation is 4 percent.

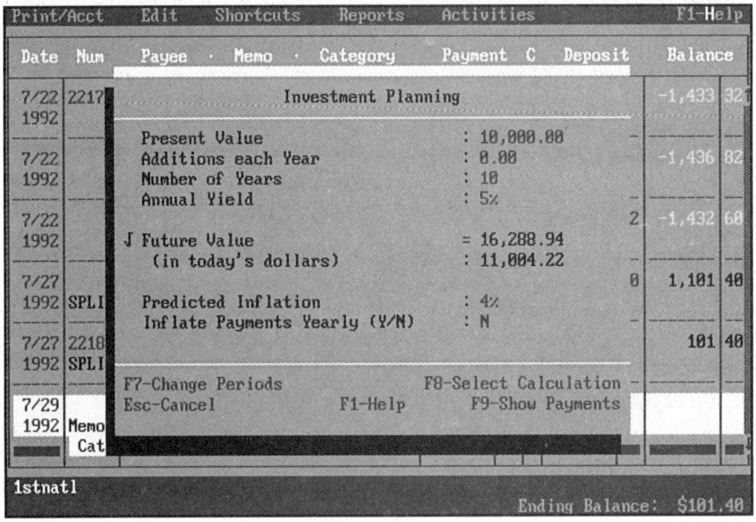

FIG. 18.3

Calculating the future value of an investment using the Investment Planning Calculator.

To calculate how much money you need *now* to accumulate a certain amount of money in the future, follow these steps:

1. Access the Investment Planning Calculator.

2. Press F8, if necessary, to move the calculation check mark to the Present Value field.

3. Except for the Present Value field, fill in all other fields in the Investment Planning Calculator as explained for calculating the future value of an investment.

4. Move to the Future Value field and enter the amount of money that you would like to have in the future (your financial goal). If your goal is to have one million dollars in 10 years, enter *1000000* in the Future Value field. (Quicken converts the amount that you enter in the Future Value field to today's dollars and enters the result under the Future Value field.)

Based on the variables that you enter in the Investment Planning Calculator, Quicken calculates the amount of money that you need today to reach your financial goal and enters the result in the Present Value field. Figure 18.4 shows that you need to have $613,913.25 invested now (at 5 percent with 4 percent inflation) if you want to have one million dollars in 10 years.

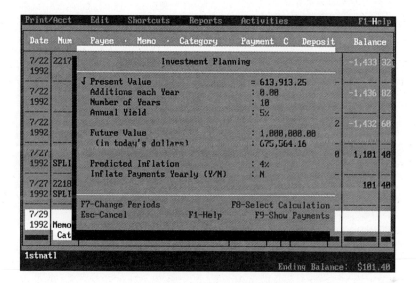

FIG. 18.4

Calculating the amount of money you need to have invested now to meet your future financial goal.

To calculate how much money you need to save on a periodic (yearly, quarterly, monthly, or weekly) basis to accumulate a certain amount of money in the future, follow these steps:

1. Access the Investment Planning Calculator.

2. Press F8, if necessary, to move the calculation check mark to the Additions Each Year field (this field may be labeled Additions Each Year, Quarter, Month, or Week based on the period that you are using. Remember, press F7 to change the periods used in the calculation).

3. Except for the Additions Each Year field, fill in all other fields in the Investment Planning Calculator to calculate the future value of an investment. Leave the Present Value field blank if you have no current savings or investments.

When you're finished entering all variables in the Investment Planning Calculator, Quicken calculates the amount of money you need to save or invest each period. Figure 18.5 shows that to have $50,000 in five years (with no current savings), you need to save or invest $8,869.82 each year.

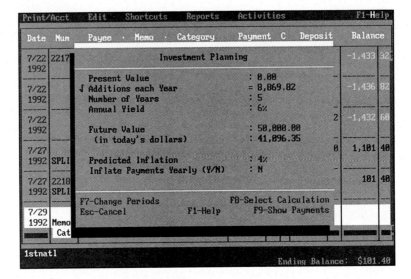

FIG 18.5

Calculating the periodic savings or investments required to accumulate a certain amount in the future.

Planning for Your Retirement

Most people aspire to stop working someday so that they can enjoy their later years. However, just because you stop working doesn't mean your expenses also stop. So how do you plan to pay for living expenses after the paycheck stops? You may believe this topic to interest only readers who are retiring soon, but this is not the case. The irony is that the easiest time to prepare for retirement is when the time you stop working is still a long way off, and the hardest time to prepare for retirement is when retirement is right around the bend.

Preparing a Living Expenses Budget

The first step in planning for retirement is to estimate living expenses. Obviously, the further away your retirement, the less precise are the estimates. Even if retirement is 20 years away, however, your current spending can provide a useful benchmark for estimating future expenses. The general rule of thumb is that retirement expenses are roughly 80 percent of current living expenses. Generally, three reasons account for this calculation:

■ Housing expenses may go down, either because you owned a home and paid off your mortgage or you moved to a smaller house or apartment.

■ Children grow up and, usually, cease to be financial responsibilities.

■ Work expenses, such as special clothing, transportation, tools, dues, and so on, stop because you stop working.

Be careful, however, that you don't drastically reduce your planned living expenses. Remember that certain expenses also may increase because you age or retire. Medical expenses—such as the insurance an employer paid previously—may increase. Entertainment and vacation expenses may increase because you have more free time on your hands. Consider also that retirement may mean new hobbies or activities with attendant costs.

In any event, the reports that Quicken provides should prove immensely helpful. In particular, Quicken's Itemized Category report should be useful because the report shows the ways you currently are spending money. (Refer to Chapter 12 if you have questions about how to print a particular report.) Figure 18.6 provides a worksheet you can use to estimate the living expenses you may have during retirement. You can fill in the first column, the one that records your current expenses, using the Itemized Category report.

Using this information and the ideas already touched on, you can fill in the second column to come up with an estimate of retirement expenses. Remember that Quicken's calculator provides a convenient way to compute the total expenses for retirement.

Once you determine your estimated retirement living expenses, you have the number you need to enter as your after-tax income for retirement in the Retirement Planning Calculator.

Estimated Living Expenses Worksheet		
Expense	Current	Retirement
Housing		
Mortgage or rent		
Property taxes		
Property insurance		
Maintenance		
Food		
Transportation		
Work		
Hobby		
Vacation		
Recreation		
Healthcare/Insurance		
Clothing		
Other		
Total Expenses		

FIG 18.6

A worksheet you can use to estimate living expenses.

Keep in mind two more things about estimating retirement living expenses. First, don't adjust the expense estimates for the inflation that probably will occur between now and the time you retire, because the Retirement Planning Calculator addresses the ravages of inflation by factoring an inflation rate into its calculations. Second, don't worry about taxes in your worksheet, the Retirement Planning Calculator also factors a tax rate into its calculations.

Estimating Tentative Retirement Income

Estimating tentative retirement income is the second step in planning a retirement income. In general, a person's retirement income essentially consists of three components: Social Security, investment income, and pension income. To tally these three sources, you need to do the following:

1. Contact the local Social Security office and ask for the form called *Request for Earnings and Benefit Estimate Statement.*

2. Complete the Request for Earnings and Benefit Estimate Statement by following the directions on the form. You need to enter your Social Security number, information about your earnings, and when you plan to retire. After you complete the form, send it to the address given. In a few weeks, you will receive an estimate of what you may receive in Social Security benefits when you retire.

3. If you qualify for an employer's pension, contact the pension fund administrator or trustee and ask for whatever information you need to estimate your future retirement benefits. The administrator should be more than happy to give this information to you. In fact, the pension fund trustee is required to give you the information.

4. Add any other income sources that you may have when you retire, such as rental income from properties, annuities, and so on.

Now you have the information you need to determine your estimated retirement income. Add the amounts from steps 2, 3, and 4. This is your total retirement income. You use this number in the Retirement Planning Calculator.

Using the Retirement Planning Calculator

Now you're ready to use the Retirement Planning Calculator to calculate any of the following variables:

- How much your current retirement account will yield annually when you retire based on yearly contributions, expected annual yields, and estimated income tax rates.

- How much money you need *now* to accumulate the money you will need when you retire.

- How much you need to contribute each year to your retirement account to ensure that you have enough money when you retire.

To access the Retirement Planning Calculator, follow these steps:

1. From the Register or the Write Checks screen, press Alt-A to access the Activities menu.

2. Select the **Financial Planning** option from the Activities menu to display the Financial Planning menu.

3. Select the **Retirement Planning** option from the Financial Planning menu. Quicken displays the Retirement Planning Calculator, shown in figure 18.7.

Notice the calculation check mark in the far left column of the Retirement Planning Calculator. The calculation check mark determines which calculation the calculator will perform when you enter data. In figure 18.8, the check mark appears next to the Present Savings field. Therefore, when you enter data in the other fields in the Retirement Planning Calculator, Quicken calculates the present savings, or the amount that you need to have presently to meet your projected retirement income goals.

```
                    Retirement Planning

J Present Savings     = 0.00       Tax Sheltered (Y/N)    : Y
  Annual Yield        : 8%
  Yearly Payments     : 0.00       Inflate payments (Y/N) : N
  Current Tax Rate    : 28%        Retirement Tax Rate    : 15%

  Current Age         : 30
  Age At Retirement   : 65
  Withdraw Until Age  : 79

  Predicted Inflation : 4%

  Retirement Income
  Other Income (SSI,etc.): 0.00
  After-tax Income    : 0.00
    (in Future dollars) : 0.00


F8-Select Calculation                        F9-Show Payments
Esc-Cancel                  F1-Help          F10-Continue
                                                            0
```

FIG. 18.7

The Retirement Planning Calculator.

To change the calculation that Quicken makes, press the F8 function key to move the check mark to the Yearly Payments field, the After-Tax Income field, or the Present Savings field.

Performing Retirement Planning Calculations

Now you're ready to perform the various retirement calculations with the Retirement Planning Calculator.

To calculate how much your current retirement account, plus annual contributions, will yield annually when you retire, follow these steps:

1. Access the Retirement Planning Calculator.

2. Press F8, if necessary, to move the calculation check mark to the After-Tax Income field.

3. Press Enter or Tab to position the cursor on the Present Savings field. If you have a retirement account or a savings account established, enter the amount in the account(s).

4. Press Enter or Tab to move to the Tax Sheltered field. If your current retirement account is tax-sheltered—not subject to federal income taxes due to a tax law provision, such as a 401(k) plan or IRA—press Y. Otherwise, press N.

5. Press Enter or Tab to move to the Annual Yield field and type the rate of return that you expect from your retirement or savings account. Don't enter percentages as decimals. To enter 5 percent, for example, just press *5*.

C P A
T I P   As a frame of reference in picking appropriate real rates of return, you may find several pieces of data helpful. Over the last 60 years or so, inflation has averaged a little more than 3 percent, common stocks have averaged 10 percent, long-term bonds have averaged around 5 percent, and short-term treasury bills have averaged roughly 3.5 percent. Therefore, when you subtract inflation, stocks produced real returns of 7 percent, long-term bonds produced real returns of about 2 percent, and treasury bills essentially broke even. Accordingly, if half of the retirement savings is invested in long-term bonds yielding 2 percent and the other half invested in common stocks yielding 7 percent, you may want to guess the return as somewhere between 4 and 5 percent.

6. Press Enter or Tab to move to the Yearly Payments field. Enter the amount that you plan to contribute to your retirement or savings account on a yearly basis. Typically, for an IRA account, the yearly contribution is $2,000. For 401(k) plans, you can contribute a maximum (in 1992) of $8,728.

7. Press Enter or Tab to move to the Inflate Payments field. Here is where Quicken factors in rates so that your yearly contributions keep up with inflation. The *inflation rate* is the annual percentage rate that prices increase. The $2,000 that you contribute this year will not be the same as contributing $2,000 10 years from now. Press Y if you want Quicken to increase your yearly contributions for inflation, or press N to keep your contributions constant.

8. Press Enter or Tab to move to the Current Tax Rate field. Quicken uses this rate to calculate the income tax effect on the earnings from your yearly contributions if your retirement account is not tax sheltered. Type your current maximum tax rate without the percent sign. Because tax rates continually change, be mindful that you may need to modify retirement planning results to take into consideration higher or lower tax rates.

9. Press Enter or Tab to move to the Retirement Tax Rate field. Type your estimated tax rate when you retire. This may be tough to project because you really don't know where tax rates will be in the future. The best estimate, however, is today's tax rates given your future level of income.

10. Move to the Current Age field and type your age.

11. Next, move to the Age At Retirement field and type the age that you're eligible or would like to retire.

12. Then, in the Withdraw Until Age field, type the age that you hope to live to. Use some common sense here. If your family history shows a long life span for men, be positive and enter an older age than the average here. If your family history shows just the opposite, be realistic and enter the average life span age here.

13. Press Enter or Tab to move to the Predicted Inflation field. Type the current inflation rate without the percent sign.

14. Press Enter or Tab to move to the Other Income field in the Retirement Income section of the Retirement Planning Calculator. Here's where you enter your estimated retirement income (Social Security, pensions, other income) that you determined in the last section. Enter your annual retirement income and press Enter.

After you have entered all the variables, Quicken's Retirement Planning Calculator calculates the unknown variable, or in this case, the after-tax retirement income (in today's dollars and future dollars). Figure 18.8 shows after-tax income of $22,447.46 in today's dollars and $64,724.30 in future dollars based on the following variables:

Present savings	$25,000 (tax-sheltered)
Annual yield	5%
Yearly payments	$2,000 (inflated)
Current tax rate	28%
Retirement tax rate	15%
Current age	35
Age at retirement	62
Withdraw until age	80
Predicted inflation	4%
Other Income	$18,000

You also can calculate the amount of present savings you need to yield the desired after-tax retirement income. To calculate how much money you need *now* to accumulate the money you will need when you retire, follow these steps:

1. Access the Retirement Planning Calculator.

2. Press F8, if necessary, to move the calculation check mark to the Present Savings field.

3. Except for the Present Savings field, fill in all other fields in the Retirement Planning Calculator as explained in the previous steps for calculating after-tax retirement income.

4. Move to the After-Tax Income field and enter your projected retirement income goal. (When you enter your income goal in today's dollars, Quicken converts today's dollars to future dollars and enters this amount under the After-Tax Income field.)

Figure 18.9 shows that if you want to have $50,000 in after-tax retirement income ($144,168.42 in future dollars), you must have present savings of $747,485.42 with yearly contributions of at least $2,000 (granted, of course that you're 35 now, retire at age 62, and live to be 80).

Lastly, you can use the Retirement Planning Calculator to calculate how much you need to contribute each year to your retirement account to ensure that you have enough money when you retire. To perform this calculation, follow these steps:

1. Access the Retirement Planning Calculator.

2. Press F8, if necessary, to move the calculation check mark to the Yearly Payments field.

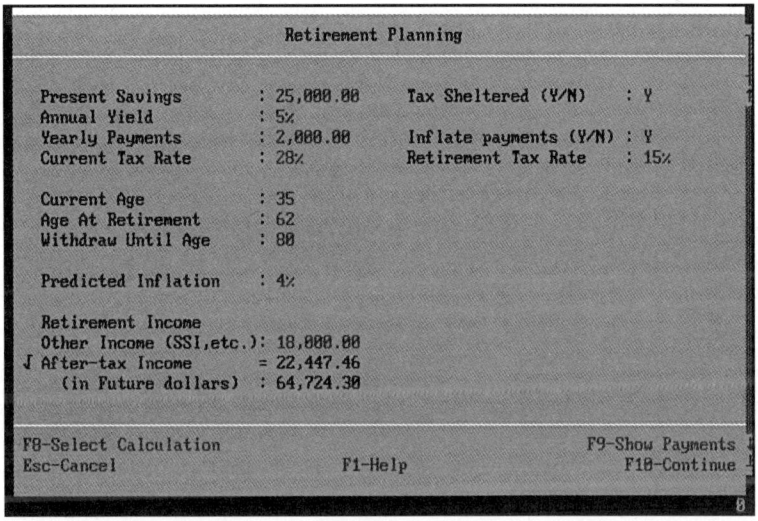

```
                        Retirement Planning


   Present Savings      : 25,000.00   Tax Sheltered (Y/N)    : Y
   Annual Yield         : 5%
   Yearly Payments      : 2,000.00    Inflate payments (Y/N) : Y
   Current Tax Rate     : 28%         Retirement Tax Rate    : 15%

   Current Age          : 35
   Age At Retirement    : 62
   Withdraw Until Age   : 80

   Predicted Inflation  : 4%

   Retirement Income
   Other Income (SSI,etc.): 18,000.00
 √ After-tax Income      = 22,447.46
     (in Future dollars) : 64,724.30


   F8-Select Calculation                        F9-Show Payments
   Esc-Cancel                      F1-Help          F10-Continue
                                                              0
```

FIG. 18.8

Calculating after-tax retirement income using the Retirement Planning Calculator.

3. Except for the Yearly Payments field, fill in all other fields in the Retirement Planning Calculator as explained in the previous steps for calculating after-tax retirement income.

4. Move to the After-Tax Income field and enter your projected retirement income goal. (When you enter your income goal in today's dollars, Quicken converts today's dollars to future dollars and enters this amount under the After-Tax Income field.)

Quicken calculates the amount you need to contribute yearly to your retirement account to yield the desired after-tax retirement income.

```
                        Retirement Planning


 √ Present Savings      = 747,485.42   Tax Sheltered (Y/N)    : Y
   Annual Yield         : 5%
   Yearly Payments      : 2,000.00    Inflate payments (Y/N) : Y
   Current Tax Rate     : 28%         Retirement Tax Rate    : 15%

   Current Age          : 35
   Age At Retirement    : 62
   Withdraw Until Age   : 80

   Predicted Inflation  : 4%

   Retirement Income
   Other Income (SSI,etc.): 0.00
   After-tax Income      : 50,000.00
     (in Future dollars)  : 144,168.42


   F8-Select Calculation                        F9-Show Payments
   Esc-Cancel                      F1-Help          F10-Continue
                                                              0
```

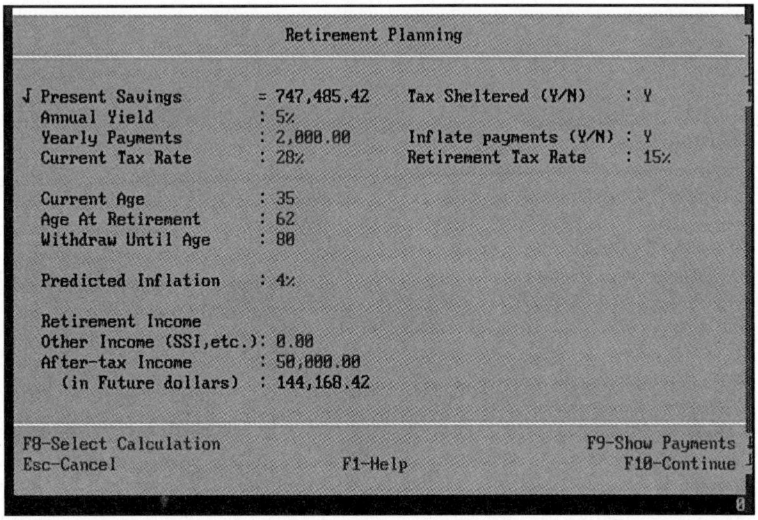

FIG. 18.9

Calculating present savings required to yield a desired after-tax retirement income using the Retirement Planning Calculator.

More Tips on Retirement Planning

Planning for retirement can be frustrating and difficult. Before you decide that you can never quit working, however, consider the following suggestions and observations.

First, invest retirement money in tax-deferred investments, such as individual retirement accounts, 401(k)s, annuities, and so on. Consider these kinds of investments even if you don't receive an immediate tax deduction because paying income taxes on the interest or investment income you earn greatly reduces the real interest rate you enjoy.

Suppose that you choose to invest in a mutual fund you expect will return around 7.5 percent annually. If you don't have to pay income taxes on the interest, you may be left with a real interest rate of around 4.5 percent (calculated as the 7.5 percent minus the 3 percent historical inflation rate).

If you have to pay income taxes, however, the story is different. Suppose that your highest dollars of income are taxed at the 28 percent tax rate. To subtract the income taxes you pay, multiply the 7.5 percent by (1 – 28 percent). This means that the real *adjusted-for-income-taxes* interest rate is 5.4 percent. When you calculate the real interest rate by taking this 5.4 percent interest rate and subtracting the 3 percent inflation rate, the annual real interest rate amounts to a measly 2.4 percent—less than half the amount you receive if you use an investment option that allows you to defer income taxes.

In this example, using investment options in which you can defer the taxes more than doubles the return, which makes a huge difference in the amounts you accumulate over the years you save.

A second consideration is that the longer you postpone retirement, the more retirement income you typically enjoy when you do retire. This tactic isn't much of a revelation, of course, because it makes intuitive sense. However, the difference postponed retirement makes may surprise you. If you postpone retirement, you have several things working in your favor.

Social Security benefits may increase because you begin drawing benefits later or because the average earnings are higher. Any retirement savings you accumulate have a few more years to earn interest, and you probably can save more money. Finally, pension plans usually pay benefits based on years of service, so working a little longer can increase this source of retirement income. You can rework the numbers by using the Retirement Planning Calculator described in this chapter to see specific results for your case.

A third and final point to consider relates to a fundamental assumption of the Retirement Planning Calculator. The calculator assumes that you live off only the annual investment income, Social Security, and pensions. This means that you never actually spend the money you save, only the interest those savings earn. If you have $100,000 in savings that earns $5,000 in annual interest, for example, you spend only the $5,000, and you leave the $100,000 intact. As a practical matter, however, you probably can spend some of the $100,000. The trick is to make sure that the $100,000 doesn't run out before you do.

Planning for College

Financing a college education is no small investment. You can no longer wait until your kids are in high school to start thinking about where you're going to get the money to send them to college. With rising tuition costs, most people must save and invest for several years to have enough money to pay for college.

With Quicken's new College Planning Calculator, you can determine how much you need to save each year for college, as well as how much tuition you can afford in the future based on the amount that you can afford to save today. You also can calculate how much you need to have invested or saved currently to have enough to pay tuition when your child reaches college age.

 Quicken's College Planning Calculator assumes that you will continue to save until your child graduates from college. If, for example, your child is 8 years old, there are approximately 10 years remaining until he or she starts college. But, there are 14 years until your child graduates from college. Therefore, the College Planning Calculator calculates present savings, current tuition, and yearly payments based on 14 years of savings, not 10.

Using the College Planning Calculator

To access the College Planning Calculator, follow these steps:

1. From the Register or the Write Checks screen, press Alt-A to access the Activities menu.

2. Select the **Financial Planning** option from the Activities menu to display the Financial Planning menu.

3. Select the **College Planning** option from the Financial Planning menu. Quicken displays the College Planning Calculator, shown in figure 18.10.

```
 Print/Acct    Edit    Shortcuts    Reports    Activities           F1-Help

 Date  Num    Payee  ·  Memo  ·  Category    Payment  C  Deposit    Balance

 7/22 2217                     College Planning                   -1,433 32
 1992
                  Current Tuition (annual)    : 0.00         —
 7/22             Years Until Enrollment      : 18                 -1,436 82
 1992             Number of years enrolled    : 4
              √ Present Savings               = 0.00         —
 7/22             Annual Yield                : 8%           2     -1,432 60
 1992
                  Yearly Payments             : 0.00         —
 7/27             Predicted Inflation         : 4%           0      1,101 40
 1992 SPLIT       Inflate Payments Yearly (Y/N) : N

 7/27 2218        All calculations assume saving until student       101 40
 1992 SPLIT        graduates from college.

 7/29         F8-Select Calculation              F9-Show Payments
 1992 Memo:   Esc-Cancel              F1-Help          F10-Continue
      Cat:

 1stnatl
                                             Ending Balance:  $101.40
```

The College Planning Calculator.

Notice the calculation check mark in the far left column of the College Planning Calculator. The calculation check mark determines which calculation the calculator will perform when you enter data. In figure 18.10, the check mark appears next to the Present Savings field. Therefore, when you enter data in the other fields in the College Planning Calculator, Quicken calculates the present savings, or the amount that you need to have presently to meet tuition costs when your child reaches college age.

To change the calculation that Quicken makes, press the F8 function key to move the check mark to the Yearly Payments field, the Current Tuition field, or the Present Savings field.

Performing College Planning Calculations

To calculate how much you money you need *now* to have enough to fund your child's college education, follow these steps:

1. Access the College Planning Calculator.

2. Press F8, if necessary, to move the calculation check mark to the Present Savings field.

3. Move to the Current Tuition field and enter the current annual tuition for the school that your child plans to attend. Check with the school's bursar's office to find out the current cost of tuition.

4. Press Enter or Tab to move to the Years Until Enrollment field. Type the number of years between now and the time your child reaches college age.

5. Press Enter or Tab move to the Number of Years Enrolled field. Type the number of years that you will be funding your child's education. Normally this is 4. However, if your child plans to get a graduate degree and you plan to pay for that, enter the total undergraduate years and graduate years.

6. Press Enter or Tab to move to the Annual Yield field. Enter the annual rate of return that you expect to receive on your investment or college savings. Do not enter the percent sign.

7. Move to the Yearly Payments field and type the amount, if any, that you will invest or save each year.

8. Press Enter or Tab to move to the Predicted Inflation field and enter the expected inflation rate from now until your child begins college. This is tough to estimate, so you can just use the current inflation rate unless you have some source that estimates inflation in the future.

9. In the Inflate Payments Yearly field, press Y if you want to inflate the yearly payment or press N if you want the payments to remain constant.

When you have entered all variables in the College Planning Calculator, Quicken calculates the amount that you need to have now to fund your child's education based on the current tuition level, the annual yield, and the number of years from now until your child starts college. Figure 18.11 shows that you need to have $74,451.65 today to pay for your four-year-old's annual tuition of $25,000 (in today's dollars).

To calculate the amount that you need to set aside each year to fund your child's college education, follow these steps:

1. Access the College Planning Calculator.

2. Press F8, if necessary, to move the calculation check mark to the Yearly Payments field.

3. Except for the Yearly Payments field, fill in all other fields in the College Planning Calculator for calculating the present savings needed.

4. Move to the Present Savings field and enter the amount, if any, that you have saved or invested for college.

Quicken calculates the amount that you need to set aside each year and enters the result in the Yearly Payments field. Figure 18.12 shows that if you have no other savings for college, you need to save $9,955.57 each year to send your 10-year-old to a $25,000 (in today's dollars) per year college.

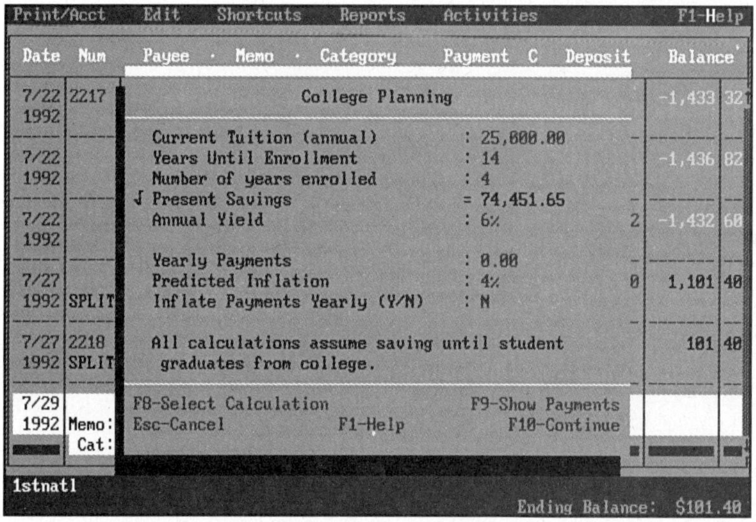

FIG. 18.11

Calculating present savings for college using the College Planning Calculator.

You can use the College Planning Calculator to determine how much tuition you can afford based on the amount that you can afford to save each year. To make this calculation, follow these steps:

1. Access the College Planning Calculator as explained previously.

2. Press F8, if necessary, to move the calculation check mark to the Current Tuition field.

3. Except for the Current Tuition field, fill in all other fields in the College Planning Calculator for calculating the present savings needed.

4. Move to the Yearly Payments field and enter the amount that you currently can afford to save for college each year.

Quicken calculates the annual tuition amount that you can afford based on the yearly payments that you entered. Figure 18.13 shows that you could afford a $5,784.34 per year school if you save $2,000 each year for 10 years.

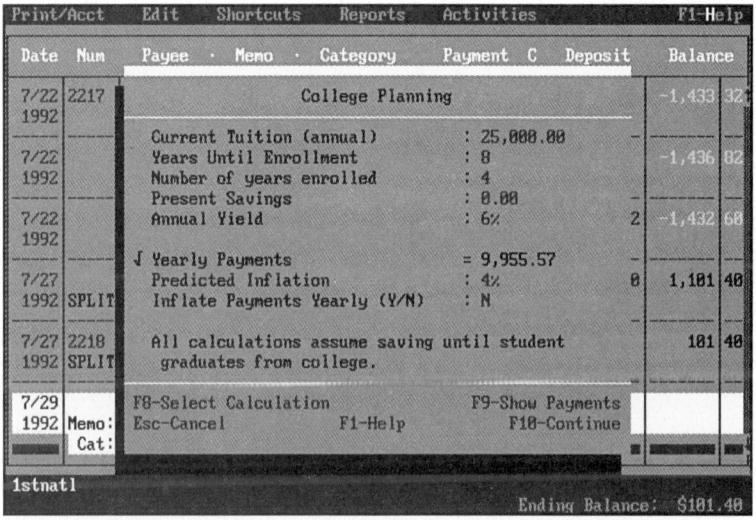

FIG. 18.12

Using the College Planning Calculator to calculate annual savings for college.

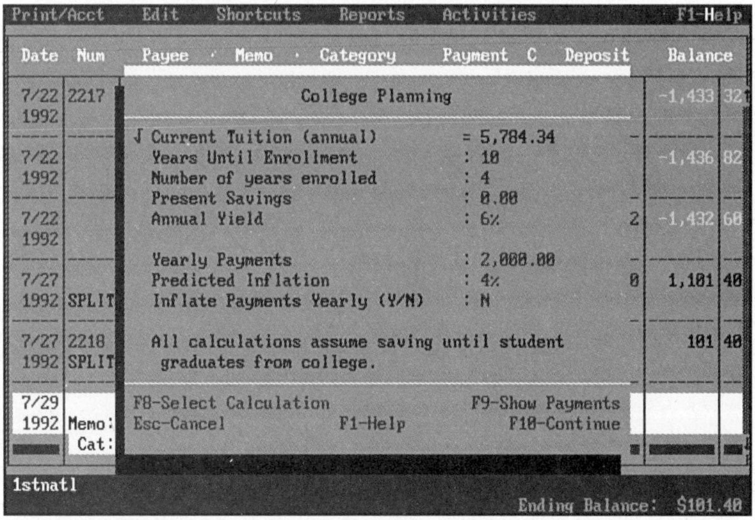

```
Print/Acct    Edit    Shortcuts    Reports    Activities         F1-Help

Date  Num    Payee  ·  Memo  ·  Category    Payment  C   Deposit    Balance

7/22  2217                      College Planning                  -1,433 32
1992
                   Current Tuition (annual)    : 25,000.00    —
7/22               Years Until Enrollment      : 8                 -1,436 82
1992               Number of years enrolled    : 4
                   Present Savings             : 0.00         —
7/22               Annual Yield                : 6%           2   -1,432 60
1992
              √ Yearly Payments              = 9,955.57     —
7/27               Predicted Inflation         : 4%           0    1,101 40
1992  SPLIT        Inflate Payments Yearly (Y/N) : N

7/27  2218         All calculations assume saving until student        101 40
1992  SPLIT          graduates from college.

7/29          F8-Select Calculation              F9-Show Payments
1992  Memo:   Esc-Cancel           F1-Help       F10-Continue
      Cat:

1stnatl
                                             Ending Balance:  $101.40
```

FIG. 18.13

Using the College Planning Calculator to determine the tuition you can afford.

```
Print/Acct    Edit    Shortcuts    Reports    Activities         F1-Help

Date  Num    Payee  ·  Memo  ·  Category    Payment  C   Deposit    Balance

7/22  2217                      College Planning                  -1,433 32
1992
              √ Current Tuition (annual)      = 5,784.34     —
7/22               Years Until Enrollment      : 10                -1,436 82
1992               Number of years enrolled    : 4
                   Present Savings             : 0.00
7/22               Annual Yield                : 6%           2   -1,432 60
1992
                   Yearly Payments             : 2,000.00
7/27               Predicted Inflation         : 4%           0    1,101 40
1992  SPLIT        Inflate Payments Yearly (Y/N) : N

7/27  2218         All calculations assume saving until student        101 40
1992  SPLIT          graduates from college.

7/29          F8-Select Calculation              F9-Show Payments
1992  Memo:   Esc-Cancel           F1-Help       F10-Continue
      Cat:

1stnatl
                                             Ending Balance:  $101.40
```

Tips on Saving for College

Tuition and fees at state colleges have risen an average of 9 percent a year since 1980. Costs have risen 10 percent at private schools. At these rates, it's estimated that a four-year degree for a newborn will cost between $95,000 and $290,000, or even more. So there's no question that you must think about saving for college *now* (when your children are young) so that you can keep up with these rising costs. The following are some things to consider to help you decide how you're going to meet rising college costs head on.

- If you're funding college for a young child, consider a multiphase investment plan. Phase 1, when your children are young, should include mutual funds that invest in stocks. Stocks are your best bet for growth at a level that exceeds the high rate of increasing college costs. Although the stock market can drop, it usually bounces right back and over the long run, stock values rise.

  Begin phase 2 of your college investment plan as your child becomes closer to college age (12 to 14 years old, for example). You will not want the volatility of the market to impact your capital or earnings at this point. Consider gradually moving your money into capital preservation investments, such as Series EE Savings Bonds, Treasury securities, and certificates of deposit (CD). You also could switch to a mutual fund that divides your money between stocks and bonds.

  Phase 3 should begin when your child reaches age 14 or so (then you know college is only four years away). At this time, preserving your investment becomes more important. Begin moving a portion of your funds (maybe 25 percent to cover the first year of college) into a guaranteed four-year investment like a CD. The next year, move another 25 percent, and so on.

- Automated savings plans are available that take money directly from your bank account each month and deposit it into a savings plan or investment account. This makes saving a little less painful and virtually effortless. Consider the amount withdrawn from your bank account a fixed payment, like your mortgage or car loan payment. That way, you will not be tempted to think of other ways to spend it.

- Don't get hooked into investing your money in bonds that don't mature until after your child reaches college age. If you buy a 30-year bond when your child is born, for example, you will be forced to sell it after only 18 years and risk losing some of your capital. Make sure that bond maturity dates coincide with the dates you will need the money for college.

- Some states (about half) are offering special college savings bonds, also known as *baccalaureate bonds*. These bonds are *zero-coupon bonds*, which means that they don't pay interest over the life of the bond, but sell at a large discount from their maturity value. The face value of college savings bonds increases from year to year. College savings bonds usually come in maturities of 5 to

21 years and are exempt from federal income tax and from state and local taxes if you live in the issuing state. Check with your state's finance department to see if these bonds are being issued in your state and which brokerage firm you can call to place an order.

■ Remember that you can take out a home-equity loan to pay for college when the time comes. Hang on to your home, instead of trading up. The longer you keep it, the more equity you'll have.

Refinancing Your Mortgage

In this day and age of rising and falling mortgage interest rates, refinancing has become quite popular. It is estimated that 3 million homeowners will refinance in 1992—twice as many as in 1991. Although refinancing your mortgage may save on your monthly payment, refinancing is rarely achieved without incurring additional costs (closing costs and mortgage points). Don't be fooled into thinking that refinancing is the answer just because you can secure a lower interest rate. Mortgage lenders usually charge closing costs and points to refinance a mortgage. If your existing mortgage is not very old and you incurred closing costs to obtain your mortgage, it may not be prudent to refinance unless the refinance rate is significantly less than your current rate. Quicken's Refinance Calculator can help you determine if it's cost effective for you to refinance your current mortgage. The Refinance Calculator shows you your new monthly payment amount (based on the refinance rate), how much you save per month by refinancing, the total closing costs that you will incur if you refinance, and the amount of time that it will take to recoup those closing costs with your monthly savings from refinancing.

Many mortgage lenders will refinance only 80 percent of your home's current market value or less. If the value of your home has not appreciated and your current mortgage balance is greater than 80 percent of the market value of your home, you may not be able to find a lender to refinance your mortgage.

C P A
T I P

Using the Refinance Calculator

Use the Refinance Calculator if you're considering refinancing your existing mortgage; it may save you some wasted time spent with mortgage companies if you find that the refinance rate they are offering isn't cost effective. You may also find, though, that refinancing makes a lot of sense and results in significant savings.

To use the Refinance Calculator, follow these steps:

1. From the Register or the Write Checks screen, press Alt-A to access the Activities menu.

2. Select the **Financial Planning** option from the Activities menu to display the Financial Planning menu.

3. Select the **Refinance Calculator** option from the Financial Planning menu. Quicken displays the Refinance Calculator, shown in figure 18.14.

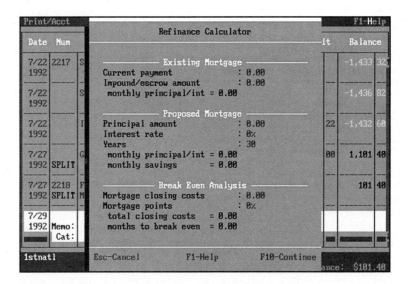

FIG. 18.14

The Refinance Calculator.

4. In the Existing Mortgage section of the Refinance Calculator, enter your current payment amount in the Current Payment field and the escrow amount for insurance, property taxes, and so on in the Impound/Escrow Amount field. Quicken subtracts the escrow amount from your current payment and enters the result in the monthly Principal/Int field. This is the portion of your monthly payment that relates to the principal balance of your mortgage loan and the mortgage interest due.

5. Move to the Proposed Mortgage section of the Refinance Calculator. This is where you enter the data for the new mortgage. In the Principal Amount field, enter the amount that you would be refinancing and press Enter. Remember that this amount is not the same amount as your original mortgage because you have paid down some principal since the time the mortgage originated.

In the Interest Rate field, enter the refinancing rate and press Enter. Don't enter a percent sign. Enter 8.75% as *8.75*, for example. Next, in the Years field, enter the number of years that you plan to extend the refinanced mortgage loan and press Enter. This is usually 30 or 15 years.

Quicken calculates the new monthly principal and interest payment and your monthly savings (your old monthly principal and interest payment minus the new monthly principal and interest payment).

6. In the last section of the Refinance Calculator, Break Even Analysis, enter any cost you will incur by refinancing. In the Mortgage Closing Costs field, enter the amount that the mortgage bank is charging to refinance your mortgage and press Enter. Move to the Mortgage Points field and enter the percentage point(s) that you are being charged. Usually this is anywhere from 1 percent to 4 percent, but this can vary from lender to lender and also is based on the size of the loan.

Quicken calculates the total closing costs to refinance and determines how many months it will take you to break even (how many months it will take you to recover the closing costs using the monthly savings from refinancing).

Figure 18.15 shows a monthly savings of $118.37 when refinancing a mortgage of $125,000 at 7 percent. With closing costs of $2,250, it will take exactly 19 months to break even or recover the closing costs using the monthly savings.

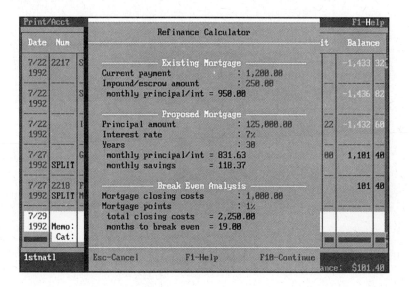

FIG. 18.15

Using the Refinance Calculator to determine monthly savings and recovery of closing costs when refinancing a mortgage.

C P A
T I P

When you refinance your mortgage, in essence, you're giving up deductible interest by refinancing at a lower interest rate. Currently, mortgage interest on up to two residences is generally fully deductible (subject to the 3 percent reduction for itemized deductions if your adjusted gross income is greater than $100,000—$50,000 if filing separately). You may end up paying more in taxes a few years down the road than you would if you hadn't refinanced. Consider the income tax implications before you make the decision to refinance.

Tips on Refinancing

Use the Refinance Calculator to help you determine whether refinancing is a viable option for you. Also consider the following:

- Although the Refinance Calculator shows that you will save on your monthly payment by refinancing your mortgage, in the long run, refinancing could cost you more. If you extend your current mortgage over a longer time period than it is originally set to come due, you may end up paying more in interest than you would have had you stayed with the original mortgage at the higher rate. If you currently have a 30-year mortgage at 10.5 percent, for example, but have made payments for 6 years, your mortgage comes due in 24 years. If now, you refinance for another 30 years, even though the refinance interest rate is lower, you have in effect created a 36-year loan with an interest rate change in year 6. Many times, this scenario results in lower monthly payments, but more interest paid over the term of the loan. You can prevent this result, however, by refinancing at a lower rate and shortening the mortgage term. Just continue to make your old payment and apply the excess (the amount of the old payment that exceeds the new payment) to the principal. Your loan will be paid off quicker and you will avoid paying more in interest.

- When you're shopping for mortgage interest rates, be sure that you lock in the rate or have the rate guaranteed by the mortgage company or bank. Just one-half point rise in interest rates could make a difference in your decision to refinance. Most lenders, however, require that you file an application before they will give you a locked-in rate.

■ Mortgage points charged to refinance are not fully tax deductible in the year you refinance. Deductions for points paid to refinance a mortgage (unlike points paid up front when you purchase a home) must be spread over the life of the loan. Therefore, if you paid $2,400 in mortgage refinancing points for a 30-year loan, you can deduct only $80 each year. Two exceptions exist for deducting points on refinancing. If part of the loan is used for renovations, the points attributable to that part of the loan are fully deductible. Also, if you refinanced previously and did not fully deduct the points incurred to refinance, you can deduct them in the year that you pay off the loan (you pay off the existing loan when you refinance a loan).

■ Carefully scrutinize mailings that you receive from mortgage brokers. On the surface, it may sound like they're offering a great deal, but what you don't know is how much they charge in *up-front fees* (fees that are charged even though the loan never closes). Be suspicious if you read or hear about up-front money for appraisals, credit checks, and application fees that are greater than $500. And be sure that your money is refundable if the loan doesn't close and that this provision is stated clearly in writing.

Displaying and Printing Payment Schedules

Each financial calculator, except the Refinance Calculator, enables you to display the payment schedules based on the current calculation. To display payment schedules, simply press F9 from the financial calculator. Quicken displays a window similar to the one you see in figure 18.16 for a calculation from the Investment Planning Calculator.

To remove the payment schedule from the screen, just press Esc and Quicken returns to the financial calculator currently in use.

You can print a payment schedule if you would like a hard copy of Quicken's calculations. You might want to show payment schedule data to your financial planner, estate planner, or your accountant.

To print a payment schedule, follow these steps:

1. From the financial calculator that you currently are using and that you want to see payment for, press F9 to display the Payment Schedule window.

2. Press Ctrl-P to display the Print window. The Print window is similar to the Print Register window.

3. Press the number that corresponds to the printer you want to print to or the **Print To Disk** option and press Enter. If you select to print to a disk file, Quicken displays an additional window for you to enter the DOS file name, lines per page, and width.

FIG. 18.16

The Investment Planning Payment Schedule window accessed by pressing F9 from the Investment Planning Calculator.

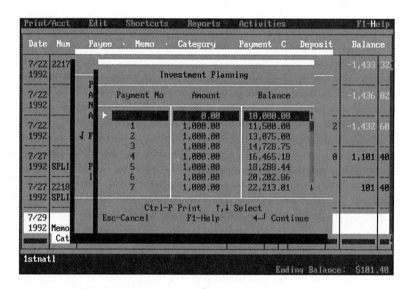

Chapter Summary

This chapter concludes Part III of *Using Quicken 6 for DOS*, "Analyzing Your Finances with Quicken." In this chapter you learned how to use Quicken 6.0's new financial calculators to plan your investments, plan for your retirement, plan for college, and analyze mortgage refinancing options.

The next chapter begins Part IV, "Managing Quicken." You learn how to manage your Quicken files and customize the Quicken program in this part of the book. The next chapter deals with managing Quicken files. You learn how to add, edit, and delete files, back up and restore files, shrink the size of files, import and export data, and assign and use passwords to prevent unauthorized access to your Quicken files.

Managing Quicken

P A R T

IV

O U T L I N E

Managing Your Quicken Files

Up to now, you worked with only one Quicken file. Quicken enables you to add additional files so that you can maintain separate accounts for more than one household or business. With multiple files in the Quicken system, you can work easily with several different sets of accounts by switching from one file to another. With Quicken, however, you can work with only one file at a time.

In this chapter, you learn how to perform the following tasks:

- Add a new Quicken file
- Edit Quicken files
- Delete a file
- Select a file to use
- Change the location of Quicken files
- Search for Quicken files in other directories
- Back up your Quicken data
- Restore data
- Use Quicken's backup reminder

■ Shrink Quicken files by archiving or starting a new year

■ Export and import file data

■ Assign passwords

■ Change or eliminate passwords

Working with Quicken Files

Quicken assigns a DOS file name to each file. As you learned in Chapter 1, the name for the first file added to the Quicken system is based on the name you enter when you install Quicken. Each Quicken file consists of four data files with the same DOS file name, but with different extensions—QDT, QNX, QMT, and QDI. You can find these data files in the directory where you store Quicken data (C:\QUICKEN). Quicken stores in files the financial information you enter in the Register. You can delete unneeded files to free memory and make Quicken even more efficient.

Quicken stores accounts you define in files and enables you to have more than one file. The obvious question, then, when you begin defining new accounts is to which file an account should be added. You usually find these decisions fairly easy to make.

The general rule is that you store related accounts together in a separate file. Accounts are related when they pertain to the same business or the same household. If you use Quicken for home accounting and for a commercial printing business, you use two files: one for home and one for business. If you use Quicken for three businesses—a consulting practice, a small publishing business, and a restaurant—you use three files, a file for each business.

Adding a New File

As part of installing Quicken, you create at least one file by using the **Create New File** option from the Use Tutorials and Assistants menu or the **Select/Set Up File** option from the File Activities menu. Chapter 1, "Preparing To Use Quicken," explains how you use both these options to create the first Quicken file. You may, however, need to add new files even after the installation.

To add a new file to the Quicken system, follow these steps:

1. From Quicken's main menu, select the **Set Preferences** option. Quicken displays the Set Preferences menu.

2. From the Set Preferences menu, select the **File Activities** option. Quicken displays the File Activities menu, shown in figure 19.1.

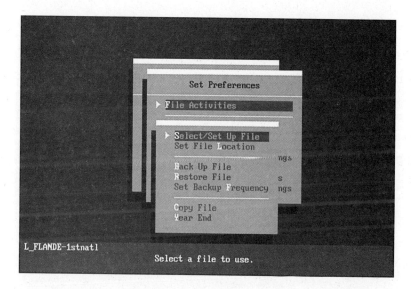

FIG. 19.1

The File Activities menu.

3. Choose the **Select/Set Up File** option from the File Activities menu. Quicken displays the Select/Set Up New File window (see fig. 19.2).

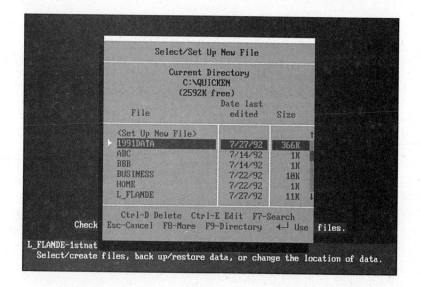

FIG. 19.2

The Select/Set Up New File window.

T I P   You can press Ctrl-G from the main menu to access the Select/Set Up New File window.

4. Highlight the <Set Up New File> line and press Enter to display the Set Up New File window shown in figure 19.3.

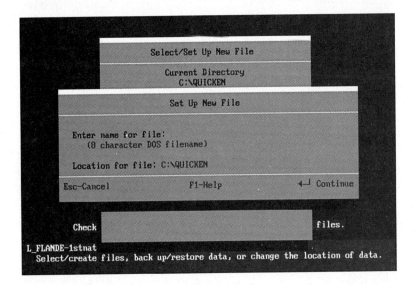

FIG. 19.3

The Set Up New File window.

5. Enter the name for the new file that you want DOS to use. The name you enter must be a valid DOS file name. Refer to the DOS user's manual if you have questions about DOS file-naming conventions.

6. When the file name is correct, press Enter or Tab to move the cursor to the Location for File field. By default, Quicken stores data files in the Quicken program directory. If you want the file stored in a different directory, enter the new directory path name.

7. When the file location is correct, press Enter. Quicken displays the Standard Categories window where you select the standard category list that you want to use in the new file.

From here, you select the standard categories to use in the new Quicken file and then set up an account to use. Refer to Chapter 1 to learn how to select categories and set up an account.

Editing File Names

You also can use the **Select/Set Up File** option to edit the names of existing files. You may want to edit a file name, for example, if you named the file incorrectly. If you name files based on the business name, changing the name of the business also may mean that you want to change the name of the file. Suppose that the file name for the business Acme Manufacturing is ACME_MFG. If the business name changes to Acme, Incorporated, you can change the file name to ACME_INC.

To edit a file name, follow these steps:

1. From the Quicken main menu, select the **Set Preferences** option. Quicken displays the Set Preferences menu.

2. From the Set Preferences menu, select the **File Activities** option. The File Activities menu appears.

3. From the File Activities menu, select **Select/Set Up File**. The Select/Set Up New File window appears.

4. (Optional) To edit a file in some directory other than C:/QUICKEN, press F9. Quicken displays the Set File Location window for specifying another location for Quicken's files. Press Enter.

 NOTE If you don't know the directory that holds a file, you can search all directories by pressing the F7 function key and Quicken searches the drive that you specify. See "Searching for Data Files," later in this chapter, to learn how to search for data files.

5. Use the up- and down-arrow keys to highlight the file that you want to edit from the Select/Set Up New File window.

6. Press Ctrl-E. The Rename a File window appears.

7. Edit the file name in the Enter New File Name field. Be sure that you enter a valid DOS file name.

8. Press Enter to save the name change and return to the Select/Set Up New File window. To edit additional file names, repeat steps 1 through 7.

Deleting a File

Quicken enables you to delete files that you inadvertently added or that you no longer use. Usually, never delete a file because when you do, you are essentially deleting all the accounts in the file. If you no longer are tracking any of the accounts in the file, you can delete the entire file. This may be the case if you set up a special file for learning to use Quicken and you no longer use the file. You also no longer need the file used for a business if you sell the business.

To delete a file, display the Select/Set Up New File window and follow these steps:

1. (Optional) If you want to delete a file in some directory other than C:\QUICKEN, press F9. Quicken displays the Set File Location window, which you can use to specify some other directory as the location in which to look for Quicken files. Press Enter.

2. Use the up- and down-arrow keys to highlight the file that you want to delete from the Select/Set Up New File window.

3. Press Ctrl-D. Quicken displays the Deleting File window (see fig. 19.4). This window gives the name of the file that Quicken is ready to delete and asks you to confirm the deletion.

4. Type *yes* to delete the file. If you don't want to delete the file, press Esc.

5. To complete the deletion and return to the Select/Set Up New File window, press Enter. To delete additional files, repeat steps 1 through 5.

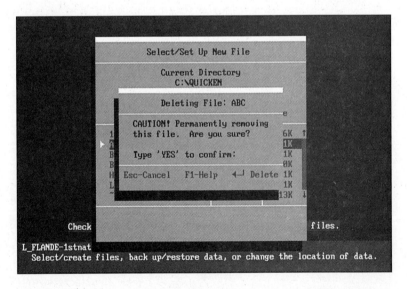

FIG. 19.4

The Deleting File window.

Selecting a File

When you work with more than one file, you need to tell Quicken the file in which you want to work. To select a Quicken file, follow these steps:

1. Access the Select/Set Up New file window.

2. Use the up- and down-arrow keys to highlight the file that you want to use.

3. Press Enter to access the file. Quicken displays the Select Account to Use window so that you can select an account to use to begin your work in the selected file.

Locating Files

If you accept the program defaults, Quicken stores data files in the C:\QUICKEN directory. You have the option, however, of having Quicken locate the files somewhere besides the default location when you specify where the files for a data file are to be located (when you are setting up or shrinking a data file). If you locate Quicken files in a place other than the default directory, you need to tell Quicken where these files are.

To inform Quicken of the location of a data file that you have relocated, follow these steps:

1. Select the **Set Preferences** option from Quicken's main menu. The Set Preferences menu appears.

2. Select the **File Activities** option from the Set Preferences menu. The File Activities menu appears.

3. Select the **Set File Location** option from the File Activities menu. Quicken displays the Set File Location window shown in figure 19.5.

4. Enter the drive and directory where the Quicken data files are located.

   The drive and directory you enter must be a valid DOS path name. The drive letter must be valid and followed by a colon. (The Quicken 6.0 installation program creates the directory QUICKEN.) If you use a directory and subdirectory together, the combination must constitute a valid path name. The subdirectory specified must be in the directory specified. (For more information on directories, subdirectories, and path names, see the DOS user's manual.)

5. Press Enter to save the file location.

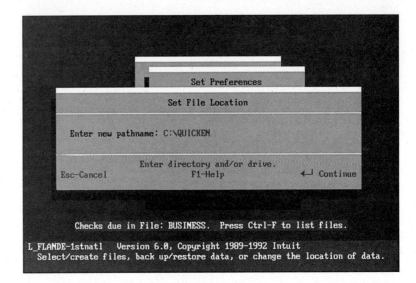

FIG. 19.5

The Set File
Location window.

Searching for Data Files

Quicken 6.0 provides a new feature, Search, that you can use to search
for and open a Quicken data file from any drive (including a floppy disk
drive). This is useful if you want to locate a data file that you know is
somewhere on your hard disk but you don't know which directory
it's in.

To search for a Quicken data file and open the file, follow these steps:

1. From the Quicken main menu, select the **Set Preferences** option.
   The Set Preferences menu appears.

2. From the Set Preferences menu, select the **File Activities** option to
   display the File Activities menu.

3. Choose the **Select/Set Up File** option from the File Activities
   menu. Quicken displays the Select/Set Up New File window.

4. From the Select/Set Up New File window, press F7 to display the
   Search for Quicken Files window shown in figure 19.6.

5. Type the drive in which you want Quicken to look to locate your
   Quicken data files. Press Enter.

   Quicken searches the drive that you specify and, in the Existing
   Quicken Files window, lists all Quicken data files found in the
   drive (see fig. 19.7).

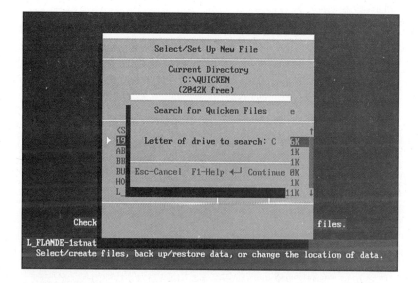

FIG. 19.6

The Search for
Quicken Files
window.

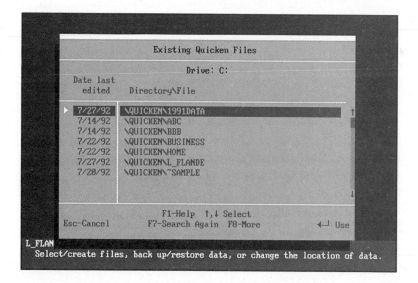

FIG. 19.7

The Existing
Quicken Files
window.

6. (Optional) To see the size or complete path of any file in the list,
use the up- and down-arrow keys to highlight the file and press F8.
Quicken displays the File window that shows the date of the last
entry into the file, the file's size, and the full path where the file is
located. Press Esc to return to the Existing Quicken Files window.

7. To open a file that Quicken finds in the specified drive, use the up-and down-arrow keys to highlight the file that you want to open and press Enter. Quicken opens the file and displays the Select Account to Use window so that you can select an account on which to work.

Backing Up and Restoring Files

You need to understand the importance of backing up files. Although you may be a careful computer user, everyone loses data (including this author—a whole three months worth!) at one time or another. Avoid losing important financial data by backing up your files regularly.

Backing up means that you make a second copy of all Quicken data files (including Q3.DIR). Back up these files so that if the original Quicken data files are damaged, you can use the backup copies to restore the damaged files to original condition. You can back up and restore by using DOS file commands or one of the popular hard disk management programs. For convenience, you may find the Quicken backup and re-store options easier to use. This section discusses these backup and restore options.

Backing Up Files

You need to make two important decisions about backing up files. First, you must decide how often you need to perform a backup. Although opinions on the subject vary, a good habit to form is to back up data files after completing a session in which you enter or change financial data. When you finish entering the first set of account transactions, for example, back up all the data files.

Most people back up financial records daily, weekly, or monthly. After you spend time working with Quicken and become familiar with data file restoration procedures, you can estimate more accurately how often you need to back up files.

Second, decide how many old backup copies to keep. Usually, two or three copies are adequate. (This rule of thumb is the grandfather, fa-ther, and son scheme.) Suppose that you back up the data files every day. On Thursday, a coworker accidentally deletes the data file. If you keep two old backup copies besides the most recent backup copy, you have backups from Wednesday, Tuesday, and Monday. If the Wednes-day copy is damaged (an unlikely but possible situation), you still have the Tuesday and Monday copies. The more recent a backup copy, the easier data is to recover, but using an old backup copy still is easier than reentering all the data from the original documents.

Store these data file backup copies in a safe place. Do not keep all backup copies in the same location. If you experience a fire or if someone burglarizes your business or house, you may lose all the copies—no matter how many backups you keep. Store at least one copy at an off-site location. If you use Quicken at home, you can keep a backup copy in your desk at work; if you use Quicken for business, keep a backup copy at home.

To back up your Quicken files, follow these steps:

1. From Quicken's main menu, select the **Set Preferences** option. The Set Preferences menu appears.

2. Select the **File Activities** option from the Set Preferences menu. The File Activities menu appears.

3. Select the **Back Up File** option from the File Activities menu. Quicken displays the Select Backup Drive window shown in figure 19.8. Insert the backup disk into Drive A or B and type the appropriate drive letter in the Drive Letter of Backup Disk field.

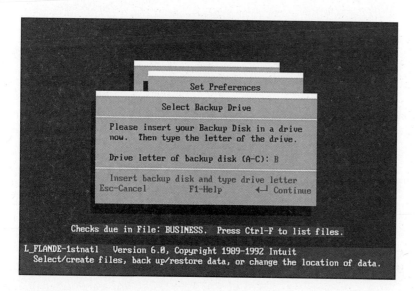

FIG. 19.8

The Select Backup Drive window.

4. Press Enter. Quicken displays the Select File to Back Up window. This window is similar to the Select/Set Up New File window shown in figure 19.2—only the title is different.

5. Use the up- and down-arrow keys to highlight the file that you want to back up and press Enter.

The message `Backing Up` then appears as Quicken copies the selected file to the backup disk. When Quicken finishes backing up, the message `File backed up successfully` appears.

6. Remove the backup disk from the disk drive and store the disk in a safe place.

 NOTE If the file you are trying to back up cannot fit on the disk, an error message alerts you that the disk is full, and you must press Esc to cancel. The warning message `File not backed up` appears. If the disk is full, press Esc, insert a different backup disk, and repeat steps 1 through 6.

T I P You can press Ctrl-B from the main menu to display the Select Backup Drive window. Then continue with steps 4 through 6 to back up a selected file.

T I P To back up the current file and exit Quicken, press Ctrl-E from the main menu.

To back up the current Quicken file, follow these steps:

1. From the Register or the Write Checks screen, select the **Back Up File** option from the Print/Acct menu.

2. Quicken displays the Select Backup Drive window.

3. Insert the backup disk into drive A or B and type the appropriate drive letter in the Drive Letter of Backup Disk field.

4. Press Enter to begin the backup process.

5. When Quicken finishes backing up, the message `File backed up successfully` appears.

6. Remove the backup disk from the disk drive and store the disk in a safe place.

Restoring Backed-Up Files

Eventually, someone or something may accidentally delete or destroy a data file. A computer can malfunction; a coworker may spill the contents of the pencil sharpener or a cup of coffee on the floppy disk that contains the Quicken data files. If you recently backed up these files and if you were diligent about printing copies of the Register, you should experience no serious problems. You can restore the Quicken files by using the backup copies.

To retrieve the data you copied with the **Back Up File** option, follow this procedure:

1. From Quicken's main menu, select the **Set Preferences** option. The Set Preferences menu appears.

2. From the Set Preferences menu, select the **File Activities** option. Quicken displays the File Activities menu.

3. Select the **Restore File** option from the File Activities menu. Quicken prompts you to identify the backup disk drive and to insert the backup disk. After you insert the backup disk and press Enter, Quicken displays the Select File to Restore window. Quicken reads the files from the backup disk that you inserted into Drive A or B and displays the files in the Select File to Restore window.

4. Use the up- and down-arrow keys to highlight the file from the Select File to Restore window that you want to restore and press Enter.

   NOTE Quicken alerts you that the restoration operation will overwrite the existing file (see fig. 19.9). To continue with the restoration, press Enter.

When the file is restored, Quicken displays the `File restored successfully` message.

You cannot restore the currently selected file. If you try to restore the currently selected file, the message shown in figure 19.10 alerts you to this error. If you originally set up only one file, you need to set up a second, dummy file that you can select as the current file before you use the restore option.

5. Using the most recent printed copy of the Register, reenter each transaction that you entered between the time you backed up and the time you lost the data. You need to reenter transactions for each account.

6. Back up these files in case another accident causes you to lose the Quicken files again.

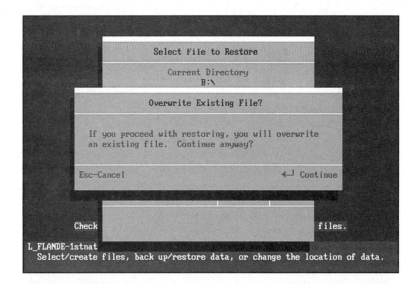

FIG. 19.9

The Overwrite Existing File? message.

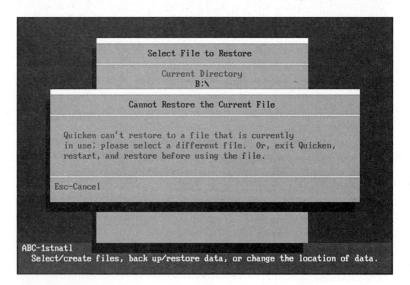

FIG. 19.10

The Cannot Restore the Current File message.

Using the Backup Reminder

Without regular backups, you may lose financial records. Obviously, backing up files is important. Because backing up is this important, Quicken provides a backup reminder feature that you can set so that Quicken periodically reminds you to back up a specified file.

To use the backup reminder feature, first select the file for which you want to be reminded to back up—you need to take this step because backup reminders attach to specific files—and then follow these steps:

1. From Quicken's main menu, select the **Set Preferences** option. The Set Preferences menu appears.

2. From the Set Preferences menu, select the **File Activities** option. The File Activities menu appears.

3. Select the **Set Backup Frequency** option from the File Activities menu. The Backup Frequency Reminder window appears (see fig. 19.11).

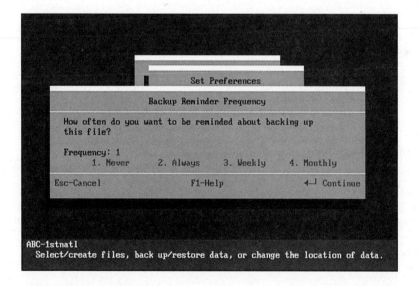

FIG. 19.11

The Backup Reminder Frequency window.

4. Indicate how often you want to be reminded to back up the current file. Press 1 if you never want to be reminded to back up. Press 2 to be reminded every time you exit the Quicken program (and you have entered transactions or changed the data file in any way). Press 3 to be reminded once a week. Press 4 to be reminded once a month. After you make your selection, press Enter.

After you set a backup frequency reminder, Quicken monitors backups you make of a particular file. If the time arrives for you to again back up a file, Quicken displays a message upon exiting the program that tells you to back up a particular file.

> **NOTE** Remember that the backup reminders attach to specific files. Accordingly, if you decide to use this handy feature, you probably want to set backup frequencies for each file so that you don't forget to back up a file.

> **C P A**
> **T I P** If disaster strikes data files that you didn't back up, you must re-enter each Register transaction. Up-to-date printed copies of each Register can show what you need to reenter. If you don't have up-to-date copies of each of the Registers, you need to reenter each transaction, using the original source documents—checks, deposits receipts, and so on. Of course, you don't ever want to reenter data from original documents, so regularly back up the files and store the backup disks in a safe place.

Shrinking Files

Theoretically, Quicken enables you to store up to 65,353 transactions in a file's Registers. Practically, these limitations are much lower. Using a hard disk, you may not be limited by disk space, but you probably do not want to work with thousands or tens of thousands of transactions in Registers.

Quicken provides a twofold solution for dealing with the problem of ever-growing data files: Quicken enables you to create archive copies of files and to create fresh copies of files that include only transactions that fall after a certain date. This twofold solution means that you can break down large files into smaller, more manageable files.

When To Shrink Files

For most users, the most convenient time to shrink the files is after completing the annual income tax return and after any year-end reporting. At this time, all transactions from the prior year should have cleared the bank, and you have printed all necessary Quicken reports.

Now, an archive copy of the files can provide a permanent copy of the data you used to prepare the year's financial reports. A fresh copy of the file also enables you to start a new year without a load of old, unnecessary data.

How To Shrink Files

Because you can shrink only the currently selected file, you need to use the **Select/Set Up File** option to select a file to shrink. If you don't select a file before attempting to shrink files, Quicken warns you before shrinking the files.

When you are ready to shrink files, take the following steps:

1. From Quicken's main menu, select the **Set Preferences** option. The Set Preferences menu appears.

2. From the Set Preferences menu, select the **File Activities** option. Quicken displays the File Activities menu.

3. From the File Activities menu, select the Year End option. The Year End window appears (see fig. 19.12).

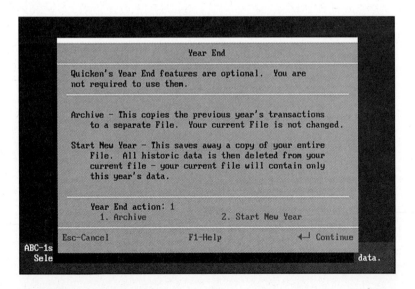

FIG. 19.12

The Year End window.

4. Identify the year-end action you want to take. Press 1 **(Archive)** to create a year-end archive copy of the current file. Press 2 **(Start New Year)** to create a fresh copy of the file that includes only transactions from the current year. After you enter your selection, press Enter.

NOTE   If you press 2 to create a fresh file copy, Quicken may include some transactions from previous years, such as investment transactions and any uncleared transactions. You need to keep these transactions in a working copy of a file because the investment transactions are needed for investment recordkeeping and the uncleared transactions are needed for bank reconciliations.

C P A   If you create a separate set of Quicken data files for each year, consider including the year number in the account group name. You can name the data files from 1992 as QDATA92, the data files from 1993 as QDATA93, the data files from 1994 as QDATA94, and so on. Including the year number in date file names enables you to easily determine which year's records are contained in a particular data file.
T I P

5. If you select the **Archive** option in step 4, the Archive File window shown in figure 19.13 appears. By default, Quicken names the archive file with the current file name and the previous year, locates the file in the Quicken program directory, and includes transactions only through the end of the previous year. If any of these default settings are incorrect, move the cursor to the incorrect field, and then make the necessary corrections. When the Archive File window is complete, press Ctrl-Enter or F10. Quicken creates the archive file copy and then displays a message that asks if you want to work with the archive file or the current file. Press 1 to use the current file; press 2 to use the archive file.

6. If you select the **Start New Year** option in step 4, the Start New Year window appears (see fig. 19.14). Enter the file name you want Quicken to use for the new file in the Copy All Transactions to File field. Indicate the date that, if a transaction date falls before, controls the transactions that get deleted from the file in the Delete Transactions from Current File Older Than field. If you only want the file to contain transactions dated from 1/1/92 to 12/31/92, for example, enter 1/1/92 in this field. All transactions dated before 1/1/92, such as 11/2/91 or 4/15/91, are deleted from the file. When the Start New Year window is complete, press Ctrl-Enter or F10. Quicken creates the new file copy and then displays a message that asks if you want to work with the old file or the file for the new year. Press 1 to use the old file; press 2 to use the new year file.

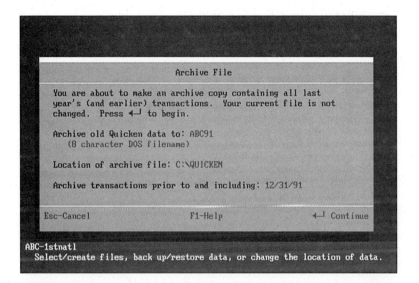

FIG. 19.13

The Archive File window.

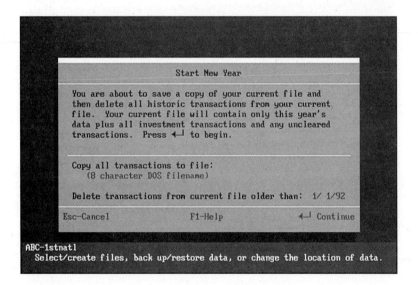

FIG. 19.14

The Start New Year window.

Copying Quicken Files

You can make a copy of your Quicken file, perhaps to give to your accountant to use with his Quicken program. Before you begin to copy a file, select the file to copy from the Select/Set Up New File window to make this file the current file.

To copy the current Quicken file, follow these steps:

1. From Quicken's main menu, select the **Set Preferences** option. The Set Preferences menu appears.

2. From the Set Preferences menu, select the **File Activities** option. Quicken displays the File Activities menu.

3. From the File Activities menu, select the **Copy File** option. Quicken displays the Copy File window shown in figure 19.15.

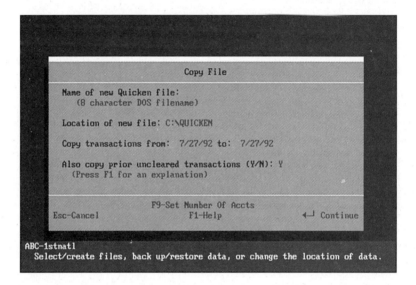

FIG. 19.15

The Copy File window.

4. Type the DOS file name for the new Quicken file in the first field and press Enter.

5. In the Location of New File field, type the path (drive and/or directory) where you want to locate the new file. Press Enter.

6. In the Copy Transactions From and To fields, type the beginning and ending dates for transactions to be copied and press Enter.

7. In the next field, press Y if you want to copy prior uncleared transactions or N if you do not. Press Enter.

8. (Optional) Press F9 if you want to set the maximum number of Quicken accounts that can be created in the new file (up to 255). Quicken sets the maximum amount to 64.

9. Press Ctrl-Enter or F10 from the Copy File window to start copying the file.

When the copy procedure is complete, Quicken displays the File Copied Successfully window, shown in figure 19.16. To reload the original file, press 1; to load the new file copy, press 2.

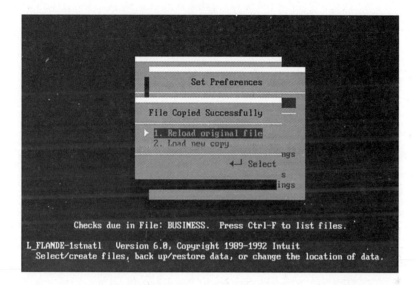

FIG. 19.16

The File Copied
Successfully
window.

Exporting and Importing Files

Exporting is the process by which a software program makes a copy of a file in a format that another program can read. You may want to export the information stored in the Quicken Register so that you can retrieve and use the information in a database program, such as dBASE, or in a spreadsheet program, such as 1-2-3.

Importing is the process by which information created by one software program is retrieved by a second software program. You may want to import into Quicken the information created by an accounting program, such as DacEasy, so that you can use Quicken's reports to summarize the information.

Exporting and importing represent two sides of the same coin: exporting creates a file by using the information stored in the Quicken Register, and importing retrieves information from another file into the Quicken Register. Although most Quicken users never need to export or import files, Quicken provides the tools to do both. The **Export** and **Import** options are available from any Register or the Write Checks screen.

Exporting Files

The **Export** option enables you to create an ASCII text file from Register transactions. You then can use this ASCII file in another software program. Most word processing, spreadsheet, and database applications commonly enable you to import ASCII text files from Quicken.

To execute an export operation, follow these steps:

1. At the Register or the Write Checks screen, press Alt-P to display the Print/Acct menu (see fig. 19.25).

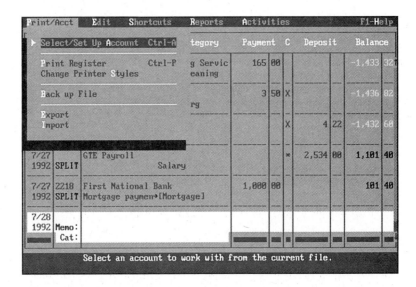

FIG. 19.17

The Print/Acct menu.

2. Select **Export** from the Print/Acct menu. Quicken displays the Export Transactions to QIF File window shown in figure 19.18. *QIF* stands for Quicken Interchange Format, which describes the special format in the ASCII file.

3. In the DOS File field, enter the DOS file name to use for the new ASCII file. You also can include a path name.

4. (Optional) To limit exported transactions to within a certain range of dates, fill in the Export Transactions From and To fields. You can use the + (plus) and – (minus) keys to change the date one day at a time.

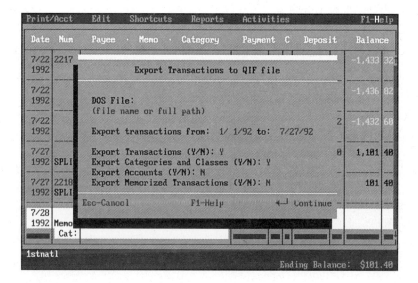

```
Print/Acct    Edit    Shortcuts    Reports    Activities         F1-Help

Date  Num   Payee  ·  Memo  ·  Category    Payment  C   Deposit    Balance

7/22 2217                                                        -1,433 32
1992                 Export Transactions to QIF file

7/22                                                             -1,436 82
1992         DOS File:
             (file name or full path)                     -
7/22                                                     2   -1,432 60
1992         Export transactions from:  1/ 1/92 to:  7/27/92

7/27         Export Transactions (Y/N): Y               0    1,101 40
1992 SPLI    Export Categories and Classes (Y/N): Y
             Export Accounts (Y/N): N                      -
7/27 2218    Export Memorized Transactions (Y/N): N              101 40
1992 SPLI
             Esc-Cancel           F1-Help           ↵ Continue  -
7/28
1992 Memo
     Cat:

1stnatl
                                          Ending Balance:  $101.40
```

The Export
Transactions to
QIF File window.

5. (Optional) Quicken enables you to export transactions, categories, classes, accounts, and memorized transactions. To change the default settings for these items, move the cursor to the Y/N answer fields in the Export Transactions to QIF File window. Then, press Y for Yes or N for No.

6. To start the export operation, press Ctrl-Enter or F10 after you complete the Export Transactions to QIF File window.

Quicken creates an ASCII file that contains the exported transactions. At the beginning of the file, Quicken prints a line to identify the type of account from which transactions were exported. This information begins with an exclamation point and the word *type*, and is followed by the actual type name. Transactions exported from a bank account, for example, show Bank as the first line.

The following example is the actual ASCII information that Quicken uses to record each transaction in the Register:

```
D7/24/89
T-1,000.00
  CX
  N*****
PBig National Bank
L[Savings]
^
```

The first line begins with D and shows the transaction date. The second line begins with T and shows the transaction amount as –1,000.00. (The amount is negative because the transaction is a payment.) The third line begins with a C and shows the cleared status. The fourth line shows the transaction number set to asterisks because the check isn't yet printed. The fifth line begins with P and shows the payee. The sixth line begins with L and shows the Category field entry. If you split a transaction, Quicken creates several L lines. The last line shows only a caret (^), which designates the end of a transaction.

Other kinds of exported data—categories, classes, accounts, and memorized transactions—work in a similar way. Each kind of data starts with a header to identify the exported data: *!Type:Cat* for category list, *!Type:Class* for class list, *!Account* for account list, *!Type:Memorized* for memorized transaction list, and so on. Then, each field in the data type that describes an item starts with a code. Suppose that you want to export the class name *West* and the description *Western*. The ASCII file looks like the following example:

```
!Type:Class
N West
D Western
^
```

 NOTE   The codes for category, account, and memorized transactions are not mentioned here. You easily can obtain this information from the Quicken user's manual.

The **Export** option doesn't produce the same ASCII file as the **Print to Disk** option described in Chapters 4, 6, and 12. The **Export** option creates an ASCII file with each transaction field on a separate line. You may use this option if you are trying to import the Quicken data into another software program, such as an accounting program, that uses the information. The Print Register's **Print to Disk** setting creates an ASCII text file that looks like a printed Check Register. You may use this option to create a list of certain Quicken transactions that you can retrieve by a word processing program, edit with the word processor, and then print or use in a document.

Importing Files

The **Import** option retrieves files stored in the Quicken QIF format. This format is the same one Quicken uses when exporting data. The steps for importing parallel those for exporting data.

To import files, follow these steps:

1. At the Register or the Write Checks screen, press Alt-P to display the Print/Acct menu.

2. Select the **Import** option from the Print/Acct menu. The Import from QIF File or CheckFree window appears, as shown in figure 19.19.

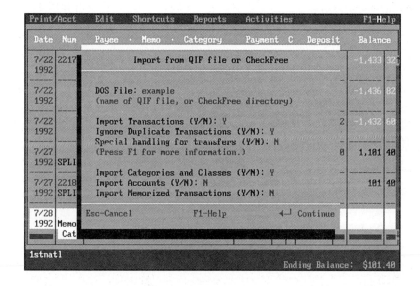

```
Print/Acct    Edit    Shortcuts    Reports    Activities              F1-Help

 Date   Num    Payee  ·  Memo  ·  Category    Payment  C  Deposit    Balance

 7/22  2217         Import from QIF file or CheckFree             -1,433 32
 1992
 ─────       ──────────────────────────────────────────────
 7/22       DOS File: example                                    -1,436 82
 1992       (name of QIF file, or CheckFree directory)
 ─────
 7/22       Import Transactions (Y/N): Y                      2  -1,432 60
 1992       Ignore Duplicate Transactions (Y/N): Y
            Special handling for transfers (Y/N): N
 7/27       (Press F1 for more information.)                  0   1,101 40
 1992 SPLI
 ─────       Import Categories and Classes (Y/N): Y
 7/27  2218  Import Accounts (Y/N): N                               101 40
 1992 SPLI   Import Memorized Transactions (Y/N): N
 ─────
 7/28       Esc-Cancel             F1-Help          ←┘ Continue
 1992 Memo
      Cat

1stnatl
                                          Ending Balance:  $101.40
```

FIG. 19.19

The Import from QIF File or CheckFree window.

3. Enter the DOS file name of the file you want Quicken to import. You also can include a path name.

4. To move the cursor to the Import Transactions field, press Enter or Tab. To import transactions, press Y for Yes and then press Enter.

5. Move to the Ignore Duplicate Transactions field. If you are importing data that you previously exported, press Y to prevent duplicating transfer transactions when importing from multiple accounts.

6. (Optional) To move the cursor to the Special Handling for Transfers field, press Enter or Tab. To import transactions with account transfers included in the Category field, press N for No and then press Enter. If you are importing from CheckFree, enter a Y here to include transfers, such as credit card bill payments.

7. (Optional) To move the cursor to the Import Categories and Classes field, press Enter or Tab. To import categories and classes, press Y for Yes and then press Enter.

8. (Optional) To move the cursor to the Import Accounts field, press Enter or Tab. To import accounts, press Y for Yes and press Enter.

9. (Optional) To move the cursor to the Import Memorized Transactions field, press Enter or Tab. To import memorized transactions, press Y for Yes and then press Enter.

10. To import the file, press Ctrl-Enter or F10 when the Import from QIF File or CheckFree window is complete. Quicken imports the file and records the transactions in the Register.

11. If the imported file does not contain categories, you may be prompted to add categories.

12. Upon completion, Quicken tells you that the import was successful.

Using Passwords

Anytime you deal with financial information, you must maintain the information's integrity and safeguard the system that stores the information from unauthorized entry. Using passwords in Quicken enables you to control the access or restrict transactions from being modified in your Quicken files.

Passwords represent an internal control mechanism. With Quicken, you can use passwords to limit access to the data files in which you store financial records.

Assigning Passwords

You can use two kinds of passwords in Quicken: *file* and *transaction* passwords. The file password that you assign to the current file provides access to the Registers, Write Checks screen, Reports menu, and the View Graphs menu in a Quicken file. If you want each file in your Quicken system to use a password, you need to set up a password for each file. The transaction password restricts anyone without access to the password from changing or deleting transactions prior to the date that you specify.

Assigning a File Password

File passwords prevent unauthorized users from accessing any Register, the Write Checks screen, the Reports menu, and the View Graphs menu. To assign a file password to the current file, follow these steps:

1. From the Quicken main menu, select the **Set Preferences** option. Quicken displays the Set Preferences menu.

2. Select the **Password Settings** option from the Set Preferences menu. The Password Settings menu appears, as shown in figure 19.20.

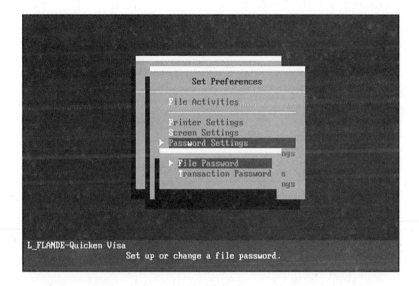

FIG. 19.20

The Password Settings menu.

3. Select the **File Password** option from the Password Settings menu. Quicken displays the Set Up Password window shown in figure 19.21.

4. To define a file password, type the combination of letters and numbers you want to use as a password. You can use up to 16 characters. Press Enter.

> **NOTE** Quicken doesn't distinguish between the use of upper- and lowercase letters in establishing or using pass- words.

5. Quicken asks you to retype the password to confirm that you know exactly what you entered in the Confirm Password window (see fig. 19.22). Type the password, exactly as you entered it in the Set Up Password window, and press Enter.

Quicken returns to the Password Settings menu. Press Esc twice to return to the main menu. After assigning the file password, Quicken asks you for the password before enabling you to view or modify transactions in any of the accounts within the data file that you assigned the password to. Figure 19.22 shows the file password set to SNF86. The next time you try to access the Write Checks, Register, or Reports screen in the data file with the password *SNF86*, Quicken requires that you enter this password. Figure 19.23 shows the Password Required window in which you type the password. As an additional precaution, Quicken doesn't display the password as you type.

Assigning a Transaction Password

Transactions passwords prevent unauthorized users from changing or deleting transactions dated prior to a date that you specify when you assign the password.

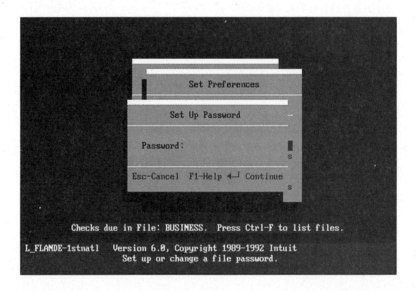

FIG. 19.21

The Set Up Password window.

To assign a transaction password to the current file, follow these steps:

1. From the Quicken main menu, select the **Set Preferences** option. Quicken displays the Set Preferences menu.

2. Select the **Password Settings** option from the Set Preferences menu. Quicken displays the Password Settings menu.

3. Select the **Transaction Password** option from the Password Settings menu. The Password to Modify Existing Transactions window shown in figure 19.24 appears.

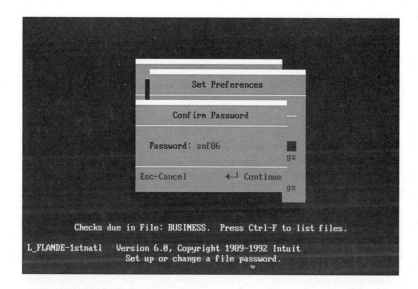

FIG. 19.22

The Confirm
Password
window.

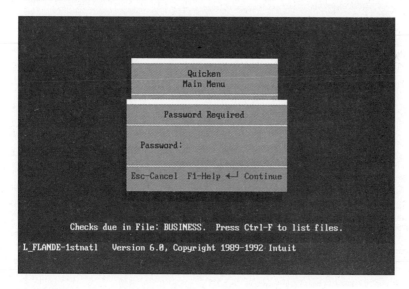

FIG. 19.23

The Password
Required window
to enter a file
password.

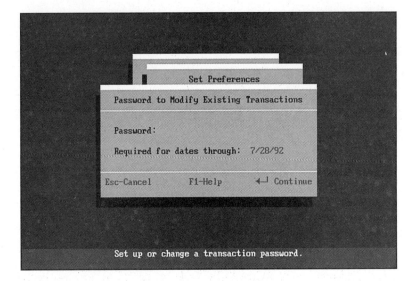

FIG. 19.24

The Password to
Modify Existing
Transactions
window.

4. Enter the password that you want to assign to transactions in the Password field. You can enter up to 16 characters, including spaces. Press Enter.

5. In the Required for Dates Through field, enter the date through which the transaction password is required.

6. Press Enter to assign the password and display the Confirm Password window. Type the password to confirm the password that you entered in the Password to Modify Existing Transactions window. Be sure that you type the password exactly as you entered it the first time and press Enter.

Quicken returns to the Password Settings menu. Press Esc twice to return to the main menu. If you want to record a transaction dated earlier than the date specified when you assigned the transaction password, Quicken requires that you enter the transaction password in the Transaction Password Required window, shown in figure 19.25. As with file passwords, Quicken doesn't display the transaction password as you type.

Changing or Eliminating a Password

You can change the assigned password. You must enter the existing password, however, before Quicken enables you to change it. This precaution prevents unauthorized persons from entering the Quicken system and changing the password and then accessing your data file. You also can remove passwords to eliminate password protection from your file and transaction data.

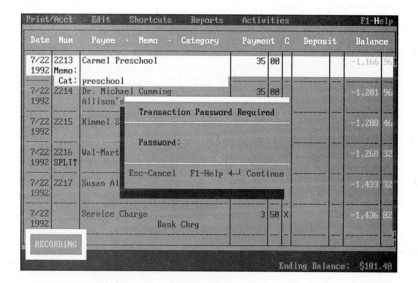

FIG. 19.25

The Transaction Password Required window.

To change or eliminate a password, follow these steps:

1. From the Quicken main menu, select the **Set Preferences** option. Quicken displays the Set Preferences menu.

2. Select the **Password Settings** option from the Set Preferences menu. Quicken displays the Password Settings menu.

3. Select the **File Password** or the **Transaction Password** option (whichever password you want to change or eliminate) from the Password Settings menu. Quicken displays the Change Password window or the Change Transaction Password window as shown in figures 19.26 and 19.27.

4. To change the file password, type the old and new passwords in the Change Password window and press Enter. You now can use the new password. To eliminate the file password, type the old password in the Old Password field in the Change Password window and leave the New Password field blank. Press Enter to eliminate the file password.

To change the transaction password, type the old and new passwords in the Change Transaction Password window and press Enter. You also can change the date through which the transaction password is required. To eliminate the transaction password, type the old password in the Old Password field in the Change Transaction Password window and leave the New Password field blank. Press Ctrl-Enter to eliminate the transaction password.

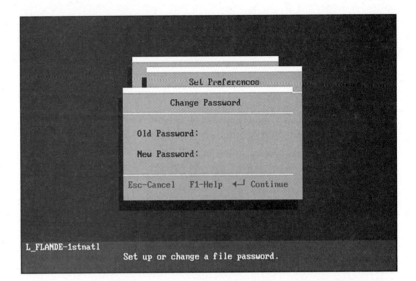

FIG. 19.26

The Change Password window.

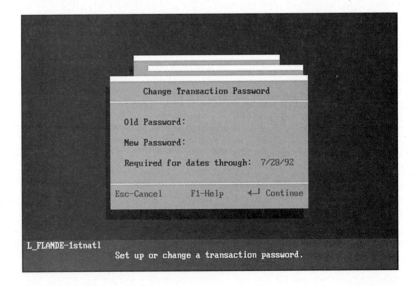

FIG. 19.27

The Change Transaction Password window.

When using passwords, consider the following precautions:

C P A
T I P

- Make sure that you do not lose or forget the password. If you lose the password, you lose your data. Record the password in a safe place.

- If you are worried about someone accessing Quicken and then writing computer checks, initiating electronic payments, or modifying the account information, use nonsensical passwords of at least six characters. The passwords you create with this procedure are extremely difficult to guess.

- Be sure that you don't use a seemingly clever password scheme, such as month names or colors, as passwords. If you set the transaction password to *blue*, the curious user may not take long to figure out the main password.

Chapter Summary

This chapter described the steps and the logic for taking care of Quicken data files. This chapter identified the Quicken files and explained how to back up and restore files, how to shrink files, and how to tell Quicken where the files are located. This chapter also described how to export information from Quicken and how to import information from other programs into a Quicken Register. And finally, this chapter covered the use of passwords to protect your Quicken data from unauthorized access.

In the following chapter, you learn how to customize Quicken to work the way you want the system to work. In Chapter 20, you learn how to change screen colors, background patterns, how Quicken displays the Register, and how to set transaction, check, and report settings. You also learn how to use Quicken's built-in reminder system called Billminder to help you remember checks that you need to print or transaction groups that become due.

Customizing Quicken

When you install Quicken, the program sets the transaction, check, and report options that control how transactions and checks are entered, how items in reports are listed, and how the program works. You can change these options, however, so that Quicken works to suit your needs. If you don't want to assign a category to every transaction, for example, you can turn off the transaction setting that warns you if a transaction has no category. If you don't want the extra message line to appear on checks in the Write Checks screen, you can turn off the check and report setting that controls whether the extra message line appears.

If you have a color monitor and are bored with the default screen colors, you also can change to five other color schemes, and now with Quicken 6, you even can change the on-screen background patterns.

Quicken enables you to use another option, Billminder, which is a reminder system displayed each time you start the computer, even before you start Quicken. Billminder reminds you of actions you need to take, such as printing checks or recalling transaction groups.

In this chapter, you learn how to perform the following tasks:

- Customize transaction settings
- Customize check and report settings

■ Change screen settings, including screen colors, background patterns, the register display, menu access, monitor speed, and screen graphics

■ Use Billminder

■ Deactivate Billminder

■ Start Quicken with parameters

Customizing Transaction Settings

Quicken includes nine transaction settings that you can change so that the program processes transactions in the way you find most helpful. The transaction settings in Quicken are described in the following section.

To change transaction settings, perform the following steps:

1. From Quicken's main menu, select the **Set Preferences** option. Quicken displays the Set Preferences menu.

2. From the Set Preferences menu, select the **Transaction Settings** option. Quicken displays the Transaction Settings window (see fig. 20.1).

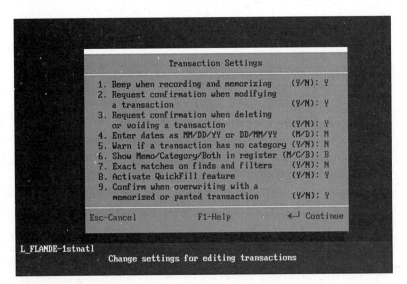

FIG. 20.1

The Transaction Settings window.

3. (Optional) The cursor should already be positioned on the Beep When Recording and Memorizing setting. Press N to turn off the beep that Quicken tells the computer to make when the program records and memorizes transactions; leave the setting at Y to keep the beep. (You may want to consider this option if you enter many transactions. You also use this setting to turn on the beep if you previously turned the beep off.)

4. (Optional) Use the arrow keys or the Tab key to move the cursor to the Request Confirmation When Modifying a Transaction setting. To turn off the confirmation messages, press N. This setting turns on and off the pop-up confirmation messages that Quicken displays before you record a modified transaction.

5. (Optional) Use the arrow keys or the Tab key to move the cursor to the Request Confirmation When Deleting or Voiding a Transaction setting. To turn off the confirmation message, press N. This setting turns on and off the pop-up confirmation messages that Quicken displays before you delete or void a transaction.

6. (Optional) Use the arrow keys or the Tab key to move the cursor to the Enter Dates as MM/DD/YY or DD/MM/YY setting. If you want dates to appear in month/day/year format—August 21, 1992 appears as 8/21/92, for example—press M for month first. If you want the dates to appear in day/month/year—August 21, 1992 appears as 21/8/92—press D for day first.

7. (Optional) Use the arrow keys or the Tab key to move the cursor to the Warn if a Transaction Has No Category setting. If you want Quicken to display a reminder message that asks you to confirm transactions you enter without a valid category, press Y. You do not need to use categories if this switch is set to Y, but you do need to confirm that you do not want to use a category. If you plan to assign categories to all transactions, set this switch to Y for Yes. (Chapter 9, "Organizing Your Finances," describes how to use categories in greater detail.)

8. (Optional) Use the arrow keys or the Tab key to move the cursor to the Show Memo/Category/Both in Register setting. This setting determines the information that appears on the memo line of the register when the transaction isn't selected. Press M to tell Quicken that you want only the memo to appear; press C to designate that only the category should appear; press B to designate that both the memo and category should appear. Because you do not have enough room to fully display both the Memo and Category fields, if you press B, Quicken abbreviates the two fields.

9. (Optional) Use the arrow keys or the Tab key to move the cursor to the Exact Matches on Finds and Filters setting. If you want Quicken to search only for the exact data you specify as a search argument when using the **Find** option or to include items on a report that exactly match a filter, press Y. (Refer to Chapter 5, "Automating the Register," for more on the **Find** option. Report filters are described in Chapter 12, "Creating and Printing Reports.")

10. (Optional) To move to the Activate QuickFill Feature setting, use the arrow keys or the Tab key to move the cursor. If you don't want Quicken's new QuickFill feature to search through the memorized transaction list or the last three months of transactions in the register when you make an entry in the Payee field or the Category field and fill in the transaction for you, press N to turn off QuickFill. Refer to Chapter 5, "Automating the Register," and Chapter 7, "Automating Check Writing," to learn more about Quicken 6's new QuickFill feature.

11. (Optional) Use the arrow keys or the Tab key to move the cursor to the Confirm When Overwriting with a Memorized or Pasted Transaction setting. To turn off the confirmation message, press N. This setting turns on and off the pop-up confirmation messages that Quicken displays before recording a memorized or pasted transaction over an existing transaction.

12. After the transaction settings are the way you want them, press Ctrl-Enter or F10. Quicken returns you to the Set Preferences menu.

Customizing the Checks and Reports Settings

Quicken includes seven checks and reports settings that you can change so that the program prints checks and reports to best fit your needs. The checks and reports settings in Quicken are described in the following section.

If you want to change any of the checks and reports settings, first perform the following steps:

1. From Quicken's main menu, select the **Set Preferences** option. Quicken displays the Set Preferences menu.

2. From the Set Preferences menu, select the **Checks & Reports Settings** option. Quicken displays the Checks and Reports Settings window shown in figure 20.2.

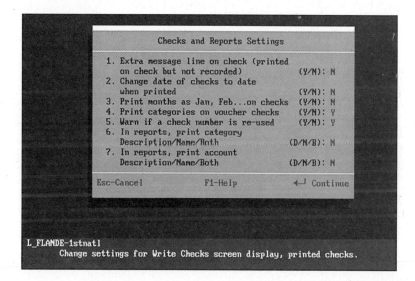

```
              Checks and Reports Settings

       1. Extra message line on check (printed
          on check but not recorded)           (Y/N): N
       2. Change date of checks to date
          when printed                          (Y/N): N
       3. Print months as Jan, Feb...on checks  (Y/N): N
       4. Print categories on voucher checks    (Y/N): Y
       5. Warn if a check number is re-used      (Y/N): Y
       6. In reports, print category
          Description/Name/Both                (D/N/B): N
       7. In reports, print account
          Description/Name/Both                (D/N/B): N

    Esc-Cancel            F1-Help          ◄┘ Continue


L_FLANDE-1stnatl
     Change settings for Write Checks screen display, printed checks.
```

FIG. 20.2

The Checks and Reports Settings window.

3. (Optional) The cursor should be positioned on the Extra Message Line on Check setting. To see and use the extra message line that appears to the right of the address box on the checks, press Y. To remove the extra message line, press N. The extra line message is explained in Chapter 6, "Writing and Printing Checks."

4. (Optional) Use the arrow keys or the Tab key to move the cursor to the Change Date of Checks to Date When Printed setting. If you want Quicken to print the current system date as the check date when printing checks, press Y. When the check date you enter differs from the check printing date, the check's date changes.

5. (Optional) If you want Quicken to print the three-character abbreviation for the month on checks, move the cursor to the Print Months as Jan, Feb...on Checks setting. Then press Y.

6. (Optional) Use the arrow keys or the Tab key to move the cursor to the Print Categories on Voucher Checks setting. If you want what you enter in the Category field or in the Split Transaction window fields to appear on the voucher portion of checks, set this setting to Yes by pressing Y.

   You don't need to print the Category field information on the voucher stub unless someone to whom you pay a check needs to know the income and expense categories you assigned to the check transaction. If you decide not to use the Category fields to record categories, and instead use the fields for information, such as the invoices a check pays, you can print this information on the check stub. This setting doesn't apply unless the checks have voucher stubs.

7. (Optional) Use the arrow keys or the Tab key to move the cursor to the Warn If a Check Number is Re-used setting. If you want Quicken to display a pop-up message when you use a check number you have used previously, set this field to Y for Yes.

8. (Optional) Use the arrow keys or the Tab key to move the cursor to the In Reports, Print Category Description/Name/Both setting. This field determines whether the category name, category description, or both appear on reports. You have three choices: pressing D designates that only the description appears; pressing N designates that only the name appears; pressing N designates that both the name and description appear. D is the default setting and the one you probably want to use.

9. (Optional) Use the arrow keys or the Tab key to move the cursor to In Reports, Print Account Description/Name/Both. Press D if you want the account description to appear on reports. Press N if you want the account name to appear. Press B if you want both pieces of information to appear.

10. When the checks and reports settings are as you want, press Ctrl-Enter or F10. Quicken returns you to the Set Preferences menu.

Changing the Screen Settings

You can change the "look and feel" of Quicken by changing the screen settings. Quicken enables you to change the following screen settings:

■ Screen colors

■ Screen patterns

■ EGA/VGA 43-line display (displays Registers and reports in compressed format)

■ Monitor speed

■ Menu access (changes the method for choosing menus and menu options)

■ Screen graphics (specifies the graphics driver)

■ Register view (changes the number of text lines displayed in an unselected transaction)

The following sections explain how to change each of these screen settings.

Changing Screen Colors

Quicken gives you control over the colors the program uses on menus and screens. If the monitor is monochrome, you can choose monochrome, reverse monochrome, or shades of gray. If the monitor is color, you can choose a navy and azure combination, white and navy, red and gray, purple and white, or green and yellow. Go ahead and have fun experimenting with the various color combinations. When you change screen colors, your data file is not affected in any way.

To change the screen colors Quicken uses, take the following steps:

1. From Quicken's main menu, select the **Set Preferences** option. Quicken displays the Set Preferences menu.

2. Select the **Screen Settings** option from the Set Preferences menu. Quicken displays the Screen Settings menu (see fig. 20.3).

3. From the Screen Settings menu, select the **Screen Colors** option. Quicken displays the Change Color Scheme window, as shown in figure 20.4.

4. Use the up- and down-arrow keys to highlight the color combination you want to use and press Enter. Alternatively, press the number of the color scheme you want to use: 1 for **Monochrome**, 2 for **Reverse Monochrome**, 3 for **Navy/Azure**, 4 for **White/Navy**, and so on.

The default color option for a monochrome monitor is **Monochrome**, but also try **Shades of Gray** to find the combination that works best. If you have a monochrome monitor and the screen display is unclear or portions of the screen don't show, you probably defined the monitor type as color. The default color scheme for a color monitor is Navy/Azure, but try each of the other color schemes to find the combination that works best. If you are color-blind, for example, one of the other color schemes may be easier to see.

Changing Screen Patterns

Now with Quicken 6, if you have a color monitor or a one-color monitor that can display shades of gray, you can change the background pattern that appears at the main menu.

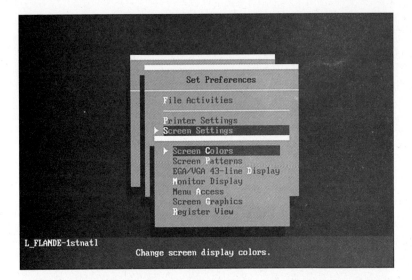

FIG. 20.3

The Screen
Settings menu.

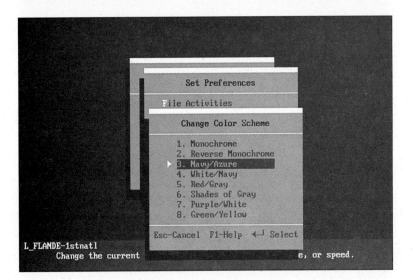

FIG. 20.4

The Change
Color Scheme
window.

To change the screen patterns, follow these steps:

1. From Quicken's main menu, select the **Set Preferences** option.
   Quicken displays the Set Preferences menu.

2. Select the **Screen Settings** option from the Set Preferences menu.
   Quicken displays the Screen Settings menu (see fig. 20.3).

3. From the Screen Settings menu, select the **Screen Patterns** option. Quicken displays the Change Background Patterns window, as shown in figure 20.5.

4. Use the up- and down-arrow keys to highlight the background pattern that you want to display and press Enter. Alternatively, press 1 for **Modern**, 2 for **Traditional**, 3 for **Squares**, and so on.

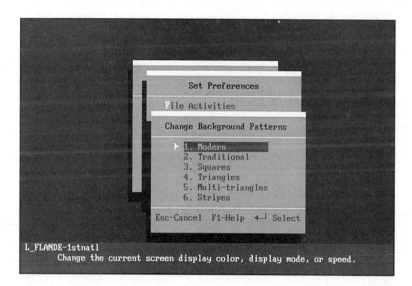

FIG. 20.5

The Change Background Patterns window.

The default background pattern is Modern, but you can try the other patterns to find the selection you like best. Changing screen patterns has no effect on the Quicken data.

Changing the Number of Lines Displayed

If the computer uses an Enhanced Graphics Adapter (EGA), you can display 43 transaction lines in the Register by changing the EGA/VGA 43-line Display screen setting. If you have a video graphics adapter (VGA) monitor and card, by changing the setting you can display 50 transaction lines in the Register. By default, Quicken displays only 25 transaction lines in the Register. If you have an EGA or VGA monitor, try this option. Having more Register information on-screen is helpful. If the compressed version of the Register strains your eyes, set the EGA/VGA 43-line Display screen setting back to N.

All the figures in this book use the standard, uncompressed versions of the Register and report screens.

To change the Register line display from 25 to 43/50 lines, take the following steps:

1. From Quicken's main menu, select the **Set Preferences** option. Quicken displays the Set Preferences menu.

2. Select the **Screen Settings** option from the Set Preferences menu. Quicken displays the Screen Settings menu.

3. Select the **EGA/VGA 43-line Display** option from the Screen Settings menu. Quicken displays the Display Mode window shown in figure 20.6.

4. Press 2 and then press Enter.

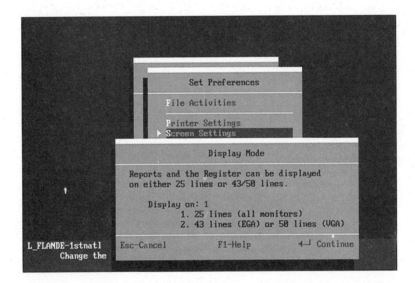

FIG. 20.6

The Display
Mode window.

When you return to the Register, Quicken displays 43 transaction lines in the Register if you have an EGA monitor or 50 lines if you have a VGA monitor. You can change the display back to 25 lines by following the preceding list of steps, except select the **25 lines** option rather than the **43/50 lines** option.

Changing Monitor Speed

The **Monitor Display** option on the Set Preferences menu enables you to choose between slow and fast for the screen-update speed. Quicken initially assumes that you want the fast option. If Quicken ascertains that your monitor can handle the fast update speed, the program doesn't enable you to change the setting to slow. If Quicken determines that the monitor cannot handle the fast speed, Quicken enables you to change the speed to slow.

If the monitor cannot handle the fast-speed setting, you may see little flecks and patches—sometimes known as *snow*—on-screen. If you notice snow on the monitor, set the monitor speed to slow.

To set the monitor speed to slow, follow these steps:

1. Select the **Set Preferences** option from Quicken's main menu. Quicken displays the Set Preferences menu.

2. Select the **Screen Settings** option from the Set Preferences menu to display the Screen Settings menu.

3. Select the **Monitor Display** option from the Screen Settings menu. Quicken displays the Monitor Display window.

4. Press the number of the speed setting: 1 for **Slow** and 2 for **Fast**. Press Enter.

Changing Menu Access

Before Versions 5.0 and 6.0, Quicken used the function keys rather than Alt-letter key combinations to display menus that appear on the Write Checks and Register screens. If you are a former Version 3.0 or 4.0 user and want to continue using the function keys, Quicken Version 6 enables you to do so.

Changing the way that menus and menu options are selected is explained in Chapter 2, "Getting Around in Quicken." Refer to Chapter 2 to learn how to change the menu access from the Alt-key style to the function-key style.

Specifying Graphics Options

One of Quicken 6's new features is the graphing capability. You learned how to create graphs in Chapter 17. To display graphs, however, you must tell Quicken which graphics driver you installed, whether you want the text area of the graph larger, and whether you want graphs displayed in black and white rather than in color.

To specify graphics options so that you can create graphs with Quicken, take the following steps:

1. From Quicken's main menu, select the **Set Preferences** option. Quicken displays the Set Preferences menu.

2. Select the **Screen Settings** option from the Set Preferences menu to display the Screen Settings menu.

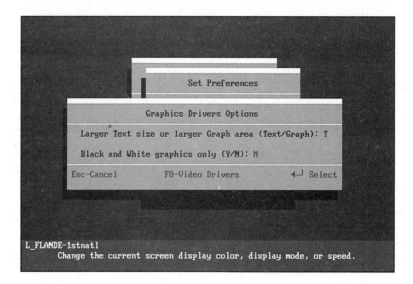

FIG. 20.7

The Graphics Drivers Options window.

3. From the Screen Settings menu, select the **Screen Graphics** option. Quicken displays the Graphics Drivers Options window, as shown in figure 20.7.

4. In the first field, press T to display the text in graphs in a larger size. Quicken displays graph labels in larger text but with coarser resolution overall. Press G to display a larger graph area with labels in smaller text. Press Enter.

5. In the Black and White Graphics Only field, press Y if you want graphs to appear in black and white. Otherwise, leave the setting at N to display graphs in color.

6. Press F8 to display the Select Graphics Driver window shown in figure 20.8. Use the up- and down-arrow keys to highlight the graphics driver installed on the computer. Press Enter to select the highlighted graphics driver.

7. Quicken returns to the Graphics Drivers Options window. Press Ctrl-Enter or F10 to save the option settings.

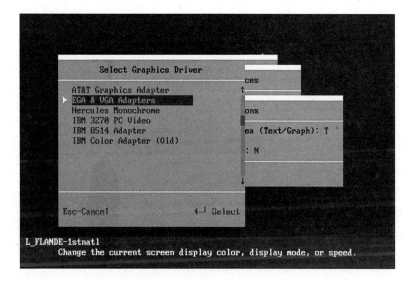

```
              Select Graphics Driver              ces
    AT&T Graphics Adapter                          1
  ▶ EGA & VGA Adapters
    Hercules Monochrome                           ons
    IBM 3270 PC Video
    IBM 8514 Adapter                              ea (Text/Graph): T
    IBM Color Adapter (Old)
                                                  : N


    Esc-Cancel                    ◄┘ Select
L_FLANDE-1stnatl
       Change the current screen display color, display mode, or speed.
```

FIG. 20.8

The Select Graphics Driver window.

Changing the Number of Text Lines in Transactions

You can change the number of text lines Quicken displays for unselected transactions in the Register. Usually, the Register shows unselected transactions on two lines; selected transactions are shown on three lines. To compress the data in the Register screen so that you see more transactions, change the number of text lines in unselected transactions to one line per transaction by changing the Register View screen setting. Changing this setting is the same as selecting the **Register View** option from the Activities menu at a Noninvestment Account Register (see Chapter 5, "Automating the Register," for more information about the **Register View** option from the Activities menu).

To change the number of text lines in unselected transactions, follow these steps:

1. From Quicken's main menu, select the **Set Preferences** option. Quicken displays the Set Preferences menu.

2. Select the **Screen Settings** option from the Set Preferences menu to display the Screen Settings menu.

3. From the Screen Settings menu, select the **Register View** option. Quicken displays the Register View Mode window as shown in figure 20.9.

NOTE Changing the number of text lines in unselected transactions by changing the Register View Screen setting doesn't yield the same results as changing the number of lines displayed by changing the EGA/VGA 43-line Display Screen setting. When you set the display to 43 or 50 lines, unselected transactions appear on two lines in the Register but in smaller print. Therefore, more transactions appear in the Register screen at one time. When you change the number of text lines in unselected transactions with the Register View Screen setting, only one line of text appears for each unselected transaction in the Register. The print size remains the same. When transactions are displayed on one line only, the memo or category assigned to the transaction doesn't appear.

4. Press 2 to compress transactions to display only one line in the Register when the transaction is not selected or highlighted. Press Enter.

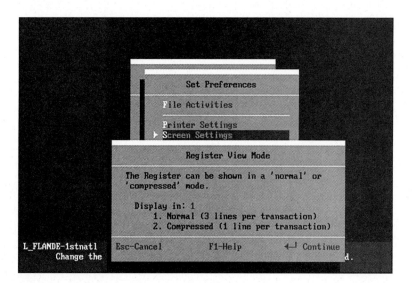

FIG. 20.9

The Register View Mode window.

Quicken returns to the Screen Settings menu. When you return to the Register, all transactions—except for the selected transaction—are displayed on one line.

T I P

To change the Register view back to normal (noncompressed) mode so that unselected transactions again appear on two lines, select the **Register View** option from the Activities menu or press Ctrl-Q.

Using Billminder

Billminder is Quicken's reminder system that checks the data files and displays messages each time you start the computer. Billminder reminds you about actions you need to take, such as printing checks, recalling transaction groups that are due, and so on.

When you install Quicken, the program asks whether you want to also install Billminder (see Appendix A, "Installing Quicken"). If you answer Yes, the program adds an additional line to the computer's AUTOEXEC.BAT file so that Billminder executes each time you turn on the computer. When you turn on the computer, Billminder knows where to look to check the data files (unless you subsequently move the Quicken program).

NOTE If you didn't install Billminder when you installed Quicken, you can perform a reinstallation and install Billminder. When you reinstall Quicken, the program files are overwritten, but data files are not disturbed. When Quicken displays the Use Billminder window during the reinstall process, press 1 to install Billminder.

Getting Billminder Messages

If you installed Billminder when you installed the Quicken program, you simply turn on the computer, and Billminder loads and then searches the Quicken data files for checks to print, transaction groups that are due, electronic payments to transmit to CheckFree, and actions to take in investment accounts. Billminder displays a message similar to the one you see in figure 20.10 each time you turn on the computer.

To remove the Billminder message, press Enter and the DOS prompt appears.

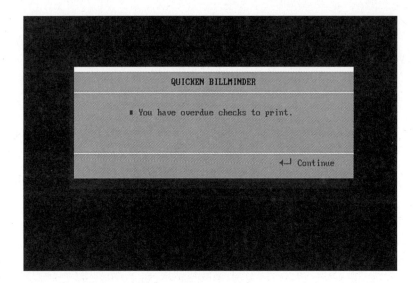

FIG. 20.10

A Billminder
message.

Changing the Directory

If you moved Quicken files from the directory where you initially installed Quicken, you must tell Billminder where to look for these files.
Billminder cannot recognize a directory that doesn't contain the
Quicken configuration file (Q.CFG), and therefore, cannot check data
from within the directory. Make sure that the directory that holds the
Quicken program files also contains the Q.CFG file. To check the directory from the DOS prompt, change to the directory in which you moved
the Quicken program files, type *dir*, and then press Enter to display the
list of files contained in the directory.

To change the directory in which Billminder looks for Quicken files,
change the Billminder line in the AUTOEXEC.BAT file to include the
new directory. To learn how to edit AUTOEXEC.BAT files, consult your
DOS manual. The Billminder line differs between DOS Versions 3.0 and
higher and DOS Versions lower than 3.0.

Changing Automatic Reminder Settings

Quicken enables you to control how many days in advance Billminder
reminds you of postdated checks, transaction groups that are due,
electronic payments to be transmitted, and actions to be taken in
investment accounts. By default, Billminder reminds you three days

in advance of items you need to take action on. You can change the advance notice time period from 0 to 30 days.

To change the automatic reminder settings in Billminder, follow these steps:

1. From Quicken's main menu, select the **Set Preferences** option. The Set Preferences menu appears.

2. Select the **Automatic Reminder Settings** option from the Set Preferences menu. Quicken displays the Automatic Reminder Settings window shown in figure 20.11.

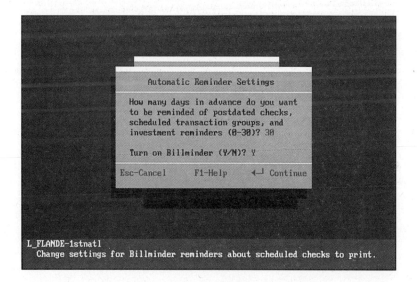

The Automatic Reminder Settings window.

3. Enter the number of days in advance that you want to be reminded of postdated checks, scheduled transactions, electronic payments, and investment actions. You can enter any number of days from 0 to 30.

4. Make sure that the Turn on Billminder field is set to Y so that Billminder is active and ready. To return to the Set Preferences menu, press Ctrl-Enter or F10.

Disabling Billminder

If you don't want to use the Billminder feature, you can disable (or turn off) this feature at any time.

To disable Billminder, follow these steps:

1. From Quicken's main menu, select the **Set Preferences** option. Quicken displays the Set Preferences menu.

2. Select the **Automatic Reminder Settings** option from the Set Preferences menu. Quicken displays the Automatic Reminder Settings window shown in figure 20.11.

3. Move to the Turn on Billminder field and press N.

4. Press Ctrl-Enter or F10 to disable Billminder.

You can turn on Billminder again by returning to the Automatic Reminder Settings window and changing the N setting in the Turn on Billminder field to Y.

Starting Quicken with Parameters

Quicken enables you to start the program with parameters. (*Parameters* are codes you type following the *q* you type to start the program.) These parameters enable you to select an account and to select the menu-access method—both as part of starting Quicken. Although the parameters may sound complicated, these parameters really are not difficult. The following sections describe how to use the parameters that Quicken provides.

Selecting an Account

To start Quicken, type the letter *q* at the DOS prompt. You can specify the account to select from the last Quicken file used by following the letter *q* with the name of this account. To start Quicken and simultaneously select the account named CHECKING, for example, at the DOS prompt type the following text:

Q CHECKING

If an account isn't in the current file, you also can identify the file as a second parameter. If you want to select the account CHECKING in the file named QDATA, type the following text at the DOS prompt:

Q CHECKING QDATA

Leave a space between the *Q* and *CHECKING* and between *CHECKING* and *QDATA*.

Selecting an account when you start Quicken isn't difficult and can be quite handy. You do need to remember one trick, however. If the account is two words, you need to enclose the account in quotation marks so that Quicken doesn't think one part of the name is the file name. In the case of an account named *1st National* in the QDATA file, you enter the parameter in the applicable one of the two following forms:

> Q "1ST NATIONAL"
> Q "1ST NATIONAL" QDATA

You also can specify the path of the file, which you need to do if the file is not in the Quicken program directory.

Selecting Menu Access

You also can start Quicken with a parameter that selects the menu-access method. As noted in "Changing Menu Access," earlier in this chapter, in early versions of Quicken, you used function keys to access the menus; in the current version, you use Alt-letter key combinations. One way to control menu access is by using the **Menu Access** option on the Screen Settings menu (see fig. 20.3). You also can control menu access by using the /f and /i command parameters. To start Quicken with function-key access, for example, type *q /f*.

Using Versions 4.0 and 3.0 Key Definitions

Quicken 6.0, 5.0, and 4.0 use slightly different key definitions of the Home and End keys than earlier versions of Quicken use. Table 20.1 summarizes the different definitions.

Although Version 6.0 key definitions are more consistent with the standard uses of the two keys, you may want to use Version 3.0 key definitions and the /a parameter. To use the Version 3.0 key definitions for the Home and End keys, for example, type the following command at the DOS prompt:

> Q /A

Leave a space between the letter *q* and the character sequence */a*.

After you start Quicken by using the /a parameter, Quicken continues to use the Version 3.0 key definitions until you tell Quicken to stop. To tell Quicken to stop using the Version 3.0 key definitions and return to the Version 6.0 definitions, use the /s parameter. For example, type the following command at the DOS prompt:

Q /S

Table 20.1 Key Definitions		
Key(s)	**Versions 4.0, 5.0, and 6.0**	**Versions 3.0 and earlier**
Home	First character in field in the Register	First transaction
End	Last character in field in the Register	Last transaction
Home Home	First field on-screen	Not used
End End	Last field on-screen	Not used
Ctrl-Home	First transaction in the Register	Same as Home
Ctrl-End	Last transaction in the Register	Same as End

One other command-line parameter exists. However, you probably never will need to use this parameter. The /e parameter tells Quicken not to use the computer's expanded memory. Usually, Quicken uses the computer's expanded memory for overlays and reports. If you have problems with expanded memory, however you can use this command-line parameter until you fix the problems.

Chapter Summary

You can customize the Quicken program so that transactions are recorded the way you want and checks and reports are printed to best fit your needs. In this chapter, you learned how to change transaction settings and checks and reports settings to get Quicken to work the way you want. You also learned how to change screen settings, such as screen colors, background patterns, menu access, and so on. And finally, you learned how to use Quicken's built-in reminder system, Billminder, to help you remember to take actions such as printing checks that you have written or recalling transaction groups that are due.

The following chapter begins the final part of *Using Quicken 6 for DOS:* "Putting Quicken to Use." In this part, you learn how to use Quicken for home finances or in small business. The next two chapters provide helpful hints for using Quicken to meet your needs.

Putting Quicken To Use

PART

V

OUTLINE

Using Quicken for Home Finances

I f you read the first four parts of this book, you know the mechanics of using Quicken. Using any software—particularly an accounting program—takes more than understanding how the software works, however. Like most people, you probably have questions about where Quicken fits in, how Quicken changes the way you keep financial records, and when to use different Quicken options. This chapter answers these kinds of questions.

Where Quicken Fits In

Where Quicken fits into personal financial management or home finances depends on what you want to get from Quicken. You can use Quicken for your home finances in these ways:

- To track income tax deductions
- To automate recordkeeping

■ To monitor how closely you are following a budget

■ To calculate what-if scenarios, such as how much you will save if you refinance your home mortgage or how much you need to save each year to send your two-year-old to Harvard

Tracking Income-Tax Deductions

When tracking income-tax deductions, you need to make sure that transactions that produce an income-tax deduction are entered into one of the Quicken Registers. You also need to be sure that you use a category marked as tax-related.

This process is not as difficult as it sounds. First, although you currently may make payments that represent income-tax deductions from a variety of accounts, often you can change the way you make payments so that every transaction that produces an income-tax deduction is recorded in one or two accounts. If you currently make charitable contributions in cash and with a credit card, rather than set up a cash account and a credit card account, you can change the way you do things and start writing checks on an account you are tracking with Quicken. In this way, if you use Quicken for tracking income-tax deductions only, you need to set up only one account—a bank account is probably the easiest method—and use this bank account only for charitable contributions.

Second, you may not need the power of Quicken to track and tally income-tax deductions. The organization to which you make a tax-deductible payment may track and tally the tax deduction for you. Consider the case of a home mortgage. At the end of the year, the bank sends you a statement (Form 1098) that identifies how much you have paid over the year in interest, principal, and, if applicable, for items such as property taxes and insurance. Similarly, a charity may send a statement that shows all contributions for the year. A bank or brokerage firm also may indicate the total individual retirement account contributions. Although you may need to track and tally certain income-tax deductions, you may not want to go to all this work if an organization tracks these deductions for you.

Automating Recordkeeping

As a rule, any financial recordkeeping you now perform manually is probably a candidate for Quicken. People go to different lengths in their efforts to keep clean, precise accounting records. The obvious candidate for Quicken is tracking activity in bank accounts—particularly checking accounts. You may be someone, however, who also tracks investments carefully, tracks personal spending in a precise manner, or keeps records of personal assets or liabilities. In all these cases, Quicken can make the job easier.

Consider the following three cautions when automating financial record-keeping. First, as with income-tax deductions, don't go to a great deal of effort to account for items that someone else already tracks for you. You probably don't need to use Quicken if all your investments appear on the same monthly statements from a broker or a mutual fund manager. You probably don't need to track other items, such as a monthly pension fund or 401(k) contributions, when your employer pays professional accountants to track these finances.

The second caution to consider is that keeping financial records isn't fun. Keeping records is tedious, requires attention to detail, and can take much time. For these reasons, carefully consider whether you need to keep financial records for a specific asset or liability. You can track the value of a home or car, but often, tracking these values isn't worth the effort. Whenever you go to the work of keeping a detailed, transaction-by-transaction record of an asset or liability, the resulting information should enable you to better manage your personal finances. If the information doesn't help you manage your finances, the data isn't worth collecting and storing.

The third caution to consider is to remember that in a Quicken Register, you record transactions that change the balance of an asset or liability. The values of possessions, such as a home, stocks, or bonds can change without a transaction occurring. Therefore, you cannot point to an event and say, *This event needs to be recorded.* Not surprisingly, you usually have difficulty tracking changes in the value of something when you don't have actual transactions to which you can point and then record. Accounts that you most likely will want to track are your bank accounts (including checking, savings, and money market accounts), your credit card accounts if you don't pay the balance each month, and cash accounts if you use cash a lot of the time to pay for expenses.

Monitoring a Budget

As suggested in Chapter 15, one of the most powerful home accounting uses for Quicken is to monitor how closely you are following a budget. Although the budgeting tools that Quicken provides are superb, the process of using Quicken to monitor monthly spending can be a challenge. Because you probably spend money in several ways—using checks, credit cards, and cash—the only way to really track your monthly spending is to record all three spending groups in registers. Otherwise, you see only a piece of the picture. Recording all three groups can involve a great deal of work.

To simplify monitoring a budget, consider several budgeting ideas:

- Focus on discretionary items

- Aggregate spending categories

- Consider the spending method

Focusing on Discretionary Items

In Chapter 15, budgeting is described as a three-step process:

1. Setting financial goals.

2. Using financial goals as a guide to developing a financial game plan or budget that covers how you want to spend your money.

3. Using the financial game plan or budget to monitor spending in order to track how closely you are progressing toward your business goals.

Quicken helps you with the third step, using the budget to monitor spending. You then need to monitor only discretionary spending and not spending fixed by contract or by law. Keep this spending difference in mind when you define categories and set up accounts. Some spending may not need to be monitored at all. Consider a mortgage payment or a rent payment: although you certainly want to include these major expenditures in a budget, you probably don't need to monitor whether you are spending money on these payments. The spending is fixed by a mortgage contract or a rental agreement. You cannot, therefore, spend less than the budgeted amount unless you want to be evicted from your home. You also will not spend more than the budgeted amount because you have no reason to do so (unless you're trying to pay down your mortgage over an accelerated time schedule).

 NOTE The Quicken monthly budget report is the principal tool you use to monitor a budget. (Refer to Chapter 15 for more information.)

Other examples of fixed spending are loan or lease payments for a car, income and Social Security taxes, and child care. Which spending categories are fixed in this case depends on the specifics of the situation.

In general, you probably don't need to closely monitor categories already fixed—or locked in—by a contract, by law, or by the terms of employment. You do need to include fixed spending in the budget because you want to make sure that you have enough money for the item, but this kind of spending doesn't need to be monitored. The rule is that for purposes of monitoring a budget, focus on monitoring discretionary spending.

Aggregating Spending Categories

When you monitor discretionary spending, working with a handful of categories rather than a big clump of specific categories is the easier method. Take the case of spending on entertainment. You can choose to track spending on entertainment by using just one category, which you name *Entertainment*. You also can break down the spending into all the various ways you spend entertainment dollars, as shown in the following list:

- Eating at restaurants
- Going to the movies
- Renting videos
- Seeing plays at the theater
- Playing golf
- Attending sporting events

Tracking exactly how you spend entertainment dollars takes a certain precision and usually takes effort for two reasons. The first reason is that you end up recording more transactions. A credit card bill that contains charges for only the six spending groups listed needs to have one transaction recorded if only one general category is used, but a split transaction with six separate amounts must be recorded if all six specific categories are used.

The second reason is that you budget by category, so the more categories you use, the more budgeted amounts you need to enter. If you feel you must have the detail that comes with using many, specific categories, consider using subcategories that at least minimize the work of entering budgeted amounts.

Consider these general rules for aggregating spending categories:

- Lump together items that are substitutes for each other.
- Lump together items of similar importance, or priority, to you and the other members of the family.

Both rules stem from the idea that if you overspend in a category, you should consider reducing further spending in this category. A couple of examples may help you use these rules in budgeting. Suppose that you lump together the six spending groups listed previously into one general category. Suppose that you go golfing with friends over three straight weekends so that you also have no money left for restaurants and the theater—favorite activities of your spouse—or no money left for movies, videos, and sporting events—the favorite activities of your kids. In this case, don't lump all six categories together because not spending money in one category may not be a practical remedy for overspending in another category. A sensible solution is to budget for golf as one category, for the theater and restaurants as a second category, and for the movies and sporting events as a third category. You then can make sure that overspending on golf doesn't occur. If your spouse overspends on the theater, a reasonable response is to minimize or curtail spending on restaurants. If the children insist on seeing two videos, they must forego a trip to the ballpark and the movie theater.

Considering the Spending Method

Researchers have proven that the method people use to spend money—credit cards, checks, or cash—affects how they spend. In general, people spend more when they use a credit card than they do when spending cash or writing a check, and people often spend less when they use cash than when they write a check. This phenomenon doesn't directly affect how you work with Quicken but, in terms of monitoring a budget, consider this information before you decide which accounts you set up to monitor spending.

You can find a budget more manageable if you choose an easily controlled spending method. The accounts you set up to monitor spending should recognize this reality. Remember that Quicken enables you to set up special accounts for bank accounts, credit cards, and cash. For monitoring the spending categories you want to watch, choose a spending method that makes staying within a budget easier.

Reviewing What-If Scenarios

With the new financial calculators in Quicken 6.0, you can use the program to review what-if scenarios for investments, retirement, refinancing, or college. Use the Investment Calculator to calculate the growth of an investment using various interest rates, over various time periods, and making various contributions each year.

The Retirement Calculator can show you how soon (or how long) you can retire. You can calculate the growth of your "nest egg" using various interest rates over various time periods. You also can vary the contributions you make each year until retirement. This feature is particularly useful in calculating the future value of an IRA or Keogh account in the year you retire.

And if you have children, you're probably concerned about saving money for college. Not only do we want our kids to go to college, we want them to go to an academically outstanding college (which means expensive!). Use the College Calculator to determine how much you need to save each year, given various interest rates, time periods, and tuition levels.

The Refinance Calculator helps you make the decision of whether to go through the hassles and expense of refinancing your home mortgage or staying with your current mortgage. The Refinance Calculator shows you what your savings will be, based on the refinance rate, and how long it will take you to recover the closing costs and points you have to pay.

How To Use Quicken

With the information covered so far, you are in a good position to know when and where to use Quicken for your home finances. This section covers a few tips that elaborate on the preceding discussion and covers bank-account reconciliation, tracking credit card spending, and recording tax-deductible cash outlays.

Using Quicken for Bank Accounts

Usually, you can use Quicken for any bank accounts you want to reconcile on a monthly basis. You also can use Quicken for checking accounts for which you want to print checks. Finally, you may want to track certain bank accounts used for income-tax deductions or budget-monitoring reasons.

You probably don't need to use Quicken—unless you want to—for bank accounts that don't need to be reconciled. You probably don't need to use Quicken for certificates of deposit or for savings accounts with no activity other than monthly interest or fees. If you want to reflect your net worth accurately in Quicken net worth reports, however, you must set up an account for each bank account that has money in it.

Using Quicken for Credit Cards

You don't need to use Quicken to track credit card spending for credit cards for which you pay off the balance at the end of the month. When you write the monthly check to pay off the credit card company, you can record the spending categories by splitting the transaction.

For credit cards that you don't pay off on a monthly basis, but still need to track income-tax deductions or monitor spending, you can set up and use Quicken accounts. For credit cards for which you want to use the reconcile feature, you also need to set up and use Quicken accounts.

If you set up accounts for credit cards, you need to enter each credit card transaction into the Register. Therefore, you need to collect the credit card slips, and then periodically enter the amounts into the Register.

If you have a Quicken VISA card and want to use the IntelliCharge feature to track credit card activity (see Chapter 11), you must set up a credit card account and designate the account as an IntelliCharge account.

Using Quicken for Cash

If you spend cash on items that are tax deductible, you can use Quicken to track these deductions. If you are using Quicken to monitor cash spending so that you can compare actual spending with budgeted spending, you also can use Quicken to track this information. Essentially, every time you withdraw cash from the bank, you increase cash (and decrease your bank account balance). Every time you spend money, you need to collect a receipt for the expense. You then periodically enter these cash transactions into the Register.

One practical problem with tracking cash spending is that you cannot get a receipt for small items, such as candy, a newspaper, or tips to a bellhop. Therefore, you need to keep a record of these small transactions, or you need to adjust the register's cash balance periodically to match the actual cash on hand. You can give this kind of adjustment category a descriptive name, such as *Sundries* or *Misc*.

For credit card and cash transactions, collect in an envelope the credit card and cash receipts you need to enter. On a periodic basis (such as once a week or month), enter the receipt amounts in the appropriate Register, mark the receipts as entered, and label the outside of the envelope with a descriptive name, such as *credit card and cash receipts from week beginning 11/1/92*. If you have a large number of receipts, number the receipts, and then use these numbers as the transaction numbers in the Register so that you can specifically tie a transaction in the Register to a receipt.

Tracking the Adjusted Basis of Your Home

By law, the gain on the sale of a home is taxable unless you purchase another home of equal or greater value within a certain time frame, or unless you can use the one-time $125,000 exclusion to eliminate the gain. The gain on the sale of a home is calculated roughly as:

(sales price) – (original cost + cost of improvements)

The sales price and the original cost are set and are connected to the purchase and to the sale. One way to reduce the calculated gain—and therefore to minimize the income tax on the gain—is to track the cost of improvements.

Improvements don't include repairs or maintenance, such as fixing a roof, painting the walls, or sealing an asphalt driveway. These are simply repairs and don't increase the value of the asset, your home. Over the years, however, you probably will make a series of improvements that, if tracked, may reduce the gain. These improvements may include the landscaping you put in after you buy the house, bookshelves you add to the family room, and the extra bathroom a remodeler puts in upstairs. Figure 21.1 shows an example of a Register used to collect this kind of information. (Remember that the account-transfer feature means you may never need to access the Register for the asset, House, because you can record the cost of the improvement when you write the check to pay for the improvement.)

Tracking the Nondeductible Portions of an IRA

One of the record-keeping nightmares from the last decade's ever-changing tax laws is the nondeductible individual retirement account (IRA) contribution. Essentially, although you may not qualify for an IRA deduction, you still may have the option of contributing to an IRA. An IRA contribution can be beneficial financially because without the income taxes on the investment earnings, the account grows faster.

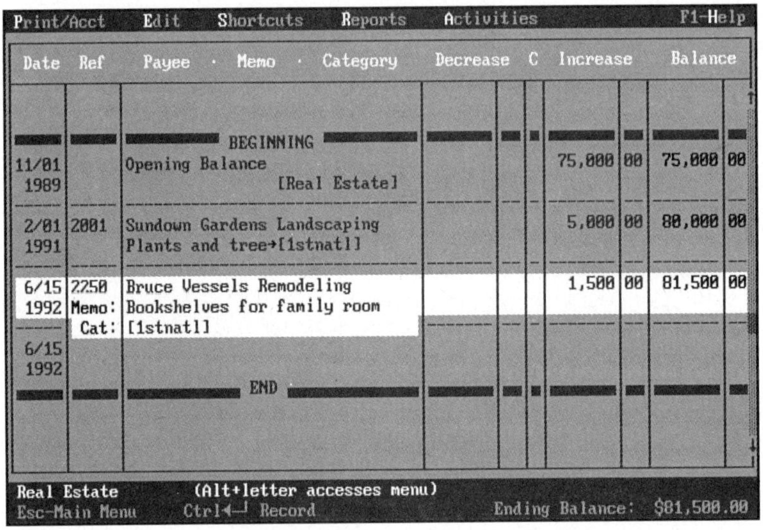

FIG. 21.1

A Quicken Register provides a convenient format to collect the costs of improvements to a home.

Over long periods, you can accumulate a great deal more money—even though the original contribution didn't generate a tax deduction. If, for example, you contribute $25 a month over 35 years, you may accumulate $94,916 if you pay no taxes, but $47,231 if you pay the 28 percent federal income tax (these calculations assume a 10 percent annual yield). In other words, you may accumulate almost twice as much money by not paying income taxes on the earnings. Nondeductible IRA contributions enable you to defer income taxes on money earned until you withdraw the money.

The problem with nondeductible IRA contributions is that the nondeductible portion of your contributions is not taxed when you withdraw the money; you need a way to track the nondeductible contributions. For most people, Quicken is an excellent solution. The basic process is to set up an investment account for nondeductible IRA contributions. Whenever you make a nondeductible contribution, record the payment as a transfer to the account you use to track nondeductible IRA contributions. Over the years, you build a detailed record of all the nondeductible contributions you make. Figure 21.2 shows an example of an Investment Register that tracks the asset *Nondeduct IRA*.

When To Perform Quicken Tasks

One final question that you often have with using Quicken is when to perform the various Quicken tasks. Table 21.1 divides these tasks into three groups: tasks to perform on a daily and weekly basis, tasks to perform on a monthly basis, and tasks to perform on an annual basis. Consider the information in table 21.1 as a rough guideline; as you use Quicken, you learn what works best for you.

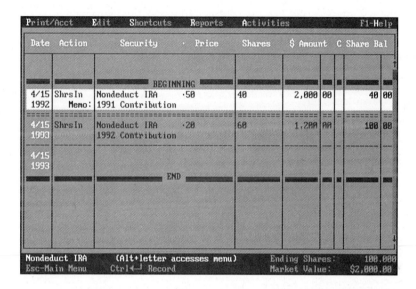

FIG. 21.2

Using Quicken to track nonde-ductible IRA contributions.

Table 21.1 When To Perform Quicken Tasks

Daily and Weekly Tasks

Record transactions in the Registers.

Print checks.

Print a temporary copy of the month's Register.

Back up the files.

Monthly Tasks

Print monthly reports, including a budget report so that you can analyze actual versus budget results.

Reconcile accounts.

Print a final copy of the month's Register.

Throw away the daily or weekly copies of the Register because all this information is contained on the final copy of the month's Register.

Back up the files.

File or store the month's bank statement, Register, reports, and backup files.

continues

Table 21.1 Continued

Annual Tasks

Print annual reports.

Print a permanent copy of the transaction report that subtotals by tax-deduction category. (This report is your permanent record for income-tax purposes.)

Back up files for the year.

Create new year's budget and enter the budget.

Shrink the file.[*]

---

[*] *When you shrink the file, you don't want to lose the transaction detail in accounts that you maintain on a long-term basis for income tax purposes, such as for ultimately calculating the gain on the sale of a home or for determining the total nondeductible IRA contributions. So that you do not lose detail in the shrink file operation, do not mark transactions in these Registers as cleared, and set the Include Only Cleared Transactions switch to Yes. Chapter 19 describes how to shrink files.*

Chapter Summary

This chapter covered information you ultimately learn on your own through trial and error. This chapter discussed where Quicken fits into your home finances, how to use Quicken for home accounting, and when to use the various Quicken options and features. You now can more easily incorporate Quicken into your personal financial management activities.

If you're a small business owner, the next chapter shows you how you can use Quicken for business accounting.

Using Quicken in Your Business

You may be surprised to learn that more people use Quicken as a business accounting package than as a home finance package. The reasons for this usage are logical: you don't need to know double-entry bookkeeping (as you do for many other small-business accounting packages), and you use a simple and familiar tool, the Check Register. Because Quicken isn't a true full-fledged business accounting package, however, this chapter covers some of the special techniques and procedures for using Quicken in business.

The procedures for using Quicken are well-documented in this book. For this chapter you are better armed if you know how to enter transactions into a Register, set up accounts, define categories, and print reports. If you are not familiar with these features of Quicken, review the material covered in the first four sections of the book.

This chapter begins by discussing the overall approach for using Quicken in a business. This discussion is followed by short sections that detail these basic accounting tasks:

- Tracking receivables

- Tracking payables

- Accounting for fixed assets

■ Preparing payroll

■ Tracking inventory

■ Job costing

This chapter is not intended to be an exhaustive list of all the business uses of Quicken. Different types of businesses require different accounting procedures, accounts, and reports. You need to modify your accounts, categories, subcategories, and so on to fit the needs of your particular business situation.

 NOTE With the tools that you have been provided so far in *Using Quicken 6 for DOS*, you should be able to create a Quicken system that works for you. Notice, however, that Quicken is not designed to track inventory on an item-by-item basis. If your business requires specific inventory tracking, Quicken is not for you.

When you combine basic bill paying and check writing—described throughout this book's chapters—with the details of the six basic accounting tasks described in this chapter, you should have the information you need to perform business accounting with Quicken. If you find that you need something more than Quicken to handle your business finances, read "An Introduction to QuickBooks," later in this chapter. QuickBooks is a program, also published by Intuit, that is specifically designed to meet the needs of small business users.

Understanding the Basics

Using Quicken for business accounting is easier if you understand the following three basic concepts: what Quicken accounts track, what should be recorded in a Register, and how categories are used.

Knowing What Quicken Accounts Track

You can use Quicken accounts to track the values of business assets or liabilities. You need to set up one account for each business asset or liability you want to track.

A *business asset* is anything you own. Common examples of business assets include the cash in a checking account, the receivable a customer or client owes you, an investment in stock, inventory you resell, a piece of furniture, a piece of equipment, real estate, and so on.

A *business liability* is a debt that you owe. Common examples of business liabilities include the loan on a car or delivery truck, payroll taxes you owe the government, the mortgage on the building, the balance on a bank credit line, and so on.

Assets and liabilities have something in common: at any time, you can calculate the value of the asset or liability. Usually, you are not interested in the day-to-day or week-to-week change in a particular asset but rather the value at a specific time.

All the accounts you set up for a business must be included in the same Quicken file. If you perform accounting for several businesses, each business needs a separate file. If you use Quicken at business and at home, you need to create a file for each (see Chapter 19 to learn how to create multiple Quicken files).

 Quicken enables you to define up to 255 accounts within a file.

Defining a Transaction

A *transaction* is any activity that affects the balance in an account or the value of an asset or liability. No change ever affects only one asset or liability, however, so each time you record the change in the value of some asset or liability, you also need to record how the change affects other accounts, or income or expenses categories. You actually perform double-entry bookkeeping without thinking or worrying about debits and credits.

When you transfer money from a checking account to a savings account, for example, you record the decrease in the checking account balance with one transaction and the increase in the savings account balance with another transaction. Similarly, when you write a check to pay for utilities, you record the decrease in the bank account that the check is written from, and you assign an expense category to classify the transaction—such as *Utilities*. To accurately reflect all your transaction activity, you must assign a category or a transfer account to all transactions.

This discussion of transactions may seem redundant, but you need to verify that all assets and liabilities are true assets and true liabilities. You also need to verify that items you want to record as transactions in a Register are true transactions and not assets or liabilities.

Suppose that you want to track receivables and record customer payments on these receivables. You must set up an account each time you create an individual receivable. If you bill Johnson Manufacturing $1,000 for a service, you must set up an account for this receivable. The temptation with a group of similar assets, such as receivables, is to group all receivables as one asset by using one account. Using the grouping approach, however, obscures information on specific accounts. You cannot tell whether Johnson Manufacturing still owes the $1,000 or how the $1,000 original receivable value has changed. Changes in the value of this asset, such as when you receive the customer's payment, need to be recorded as transactions in the Register.

The key to using Quicken as a small-business accounting system is knowing your assets, liabilities, and transactions. Throughout this chapter, you find many tips and suggestions to assist you in this analysis.

Knowing How Categories Are Used

The term *bottom line* refers to the figure at the bottom of a profit and loss statement that shows whether you made a profit or lost money in business. The reason you use categories in Quicken is to calculate the bottom line to determine whether you are making or losing money. You use two kinds of categories to perform this calculation: *Income* and *Expense*. Income categories are assigned to business revenues, or *inflows*. Common income categories include sales of products or services, income from rental properties, interest and dividends from investments, and so on. Expense categories are assigned to the costs of doing business, or *outflows*. Examples of expense categories include the cost of advertising, insurance, utilities, and employee wages.

Income and expense categories have something in common: both categories enable you to accumulate business inflows and outflows over a period of time, such as for the week, month, or year. You can use the income and expense category information to tell whether you made or lost money during the last week, month, or year. (Income minus expenses equals net income or net loss.)

When you use Quicken categories to track only cash inflows and outflows (bank and cash accounts), you are using *cash-basis* accounting. Cash-basis accounting means that you record income only when you receive money, and you record expenses only when you pay money. This system makes sense. When you make the bank deposit or write a check, you are categorizing the transaction as income or expense.

When you use Quicken categories to track other assets and liabilities, however, you move toward *accrual-* or *modified accrual-basis* accounting. Accrual-basis accounting means that you record income when you earn it, and you record expenses when you use the goods or services from which the expenses stem. If you use Quicken to account for customer receivables, you recognize the sale transaction as income when you record the receivable. If you use Quicken to account for fixed assets and depreciation, you categorize the expense of using the asset when you record depreciation.

Accrual-basis accounting gives you better estimates of income and expenses to better measure profits. Accrual-basis accounting also results in better record keeping because you keep Registers for all assets and liabilities, not just cash. If accurately measuring profits is important to the business, try to use accrual-basis accounting. If you use this method, you have a better idea of whether you're making money.

**C P A
T I P**

Tracking Receivables

To track customer payments and receivables, you first need to set up an asset account for receivables. You can set up just one receivables account and aggregate all receivable activity or you can set up a receivables account for each customer or client. If you set up separate receivable accounts, it will be easier to track receivable balances by customer or client and to generate an aging report that gives you useful information as to the outstanding balances for each customer or client at any given time. You may name an aggregate receivable account *Receivables* or *Acc Rec*, for example. For separate receivable accounts, you could use the customer name in the account name, such as *Jones Rec* or *Smith Rec*.

Each time you make a sale to a customer on credit (the customer does not pay for the goods or services at the time of sale), you must record an increase in the receivables account. Figure 22.1 shows the Receivables Register with a transaction for a sale to Johnson Manufacturing for $1,000.

After you record the receivable, you can record customer payments on the receivable and monitor receivables—topics covered in the following sections.

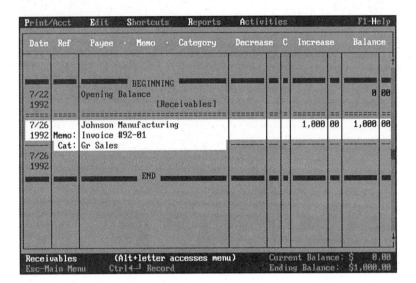

FIG. 22.1

A sale transaction in the Receivables Register.

C P A
T I P

Although businesses prefer that customers pay cash at the time of sale (to the extent that they sometimes extend discounts for cash payments), business owners find that extending credit to their customers increases sales and is therefore good for business. Be cautious, however. One major cause of business failure is lack of control over accounts receivable. If you extend credit to everyone without investigating their credit history, you may get stuck with many bad debts and a large amount of receivables on your hands. Remember: receivables are an asset but are of no value if they are uncollectible!

Recording Customer Payments

To record customer payments, select the bank account you use to deposit the check and record the deposit in the usual way. To categorize the transaction, record the deposit as a transfer from the actual receivable account. If you receive a $500 check from Johnson Manufacturing for partial payment of the $1,000 receivable created by Invoice 92-01 (see fig. 22.1), for example, you enter the deposit in the Register for the bank account into which you are depositing the money, as shown in figure 22.2. (Remember that Quicken lists the categories and transfer accounts in the Category and Transfer list and displays the list when you press Ctrl-C or when you select **Categorize/Transfer** from the Shortcuts menu.)

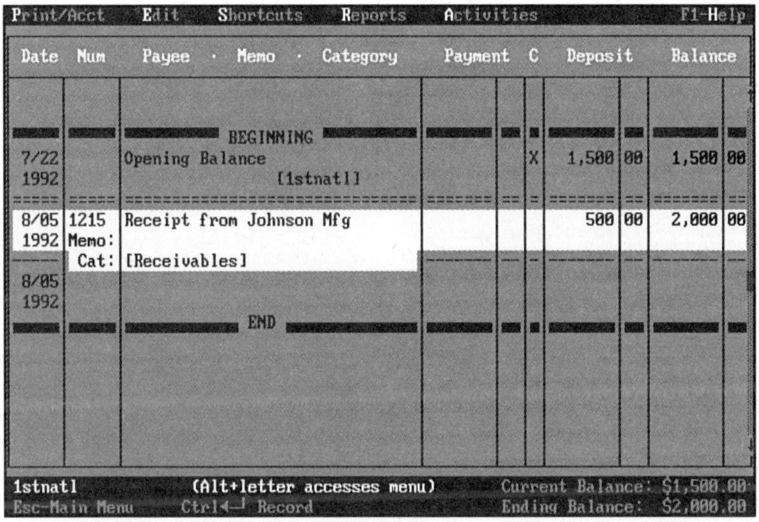

```
 Print/Acct    Edit    Shortcuts    Reports    Activities           F1-Help

  Date  Num    Payee  ·  Memo  ·  Category    Payment  C  Deposit    Balance


 ███████ ██████ ███████ BEGINNING ████████████   ███ █ ████████ █ ████████ ██
  7/22         Opening Balance                     X  1,500 00   1,500 00
  1992                        [1stnatl]
 ─────── ────── ──────────────────────────────── ─────── ══ ═ ═══════ ══ ═══════ ══
  8/05  1215   Receipt from Johnson Mfg               500 00   2,000 00
  1992  Memo:
        Cat: [Receivables]
 ─────── 
  8/05
  1992
 ███████ ██████ ███████ END ███████████████████   ███ █ ████████ █ ████████ ██



 1stnatl           (Alt+letter accesses menu)     Current Balance: $1,500.00
 Esc-Main Menu     Ctrl◄┘ Record                  Ending  Balance: $2,000.00
```

FIG. 22.2

Recording a $500 partial payment on the $1,000 receivable.

Quicken records a $500 reduction in the account you use to track the $1,000 receivable. Figure 22.3 shows the Receivables Register after you record the $500 partial payment from Johnson Manufacturing as a deposit to the bank account. Quicken records the transaction as a decrease in the receivables account.

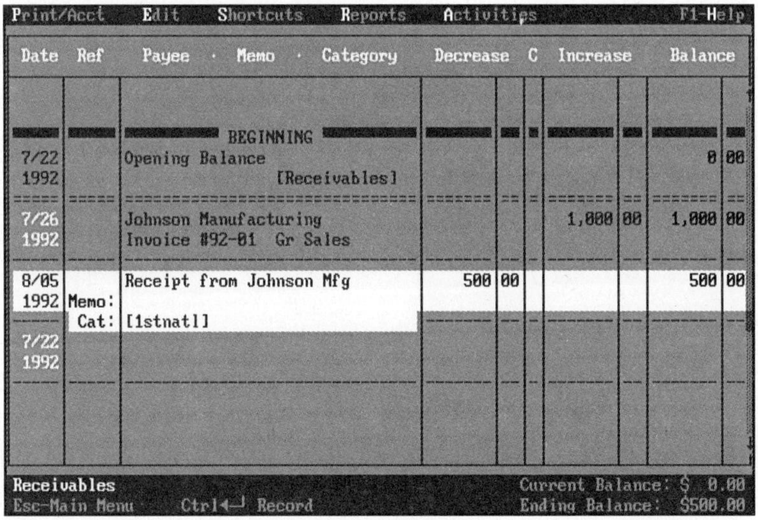

```
 Print/Acct    Edit    Shortcuts    Reports    Activities           F1-Help

  Date  Ref    Payee  ·  Memo  ·  Category    Decrease  C  Increase   Balance


 ███████ ██████ ███████ BEGINNING ████████████   ███ █ ████████ █ ████████ ██
  7/22         Opening Balance                                        0 00
  1992                        [Receivables]
 ─────── ────── ──────────────────────────────── ─────── ══ ═ ═══════ ══ ═══════ ══
  7/26         Johnson Manufacturing                       1,000 00   1,000 00
  1992         Invoice #92-01  Gr Sales
 ─────── 
  8/05         Receipt from Johnson Mfg            500 00               500 00
  1992  Memo:
        Cat: [1stnatl]
 ─────── 
  7/22
  1992



 Receivables                                     Current Balance: $  0.00
 Esc-Main Menu     Ctrl◄┘ Record                  Ending  Balance: $500.00
```

FIG. 22.3

Quicken records the second half of the transfer transaction.

Tracking Customer Receivables

Another basic receivables accounting task is tracking how much customers owe you and how long customers have owed you. The age of a receivable usually determines the collection efforts you make. You probably don't worry about receivables that aren't yet due. You may call customers with receivables more than 30 days past due. You may even turn over to a collection agency or an attorney receivables more than 60 or 90 days past due. To create a summary report that shows accounts receivable balances grouped by age, follow these steps:

1. Select the **Create Reports** option from the main menu or press Alt-R from the Register or the Write Checks screen to access the Reports menu.

2. From the Reports menu, select the **Summary** option. Quicken displays the Create Summary Report window (see fig. 22.4).

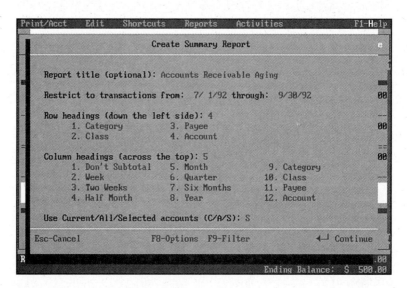

FIG. 22.4

The Create Summary Report window completed for a receivables aging report.

3. To complete the screen to show receivables balances only, enter a report title (such as *Accounts Receivable Aging*) and a range of dates in the Restrict to Transactions From and Through fields that begins with the date of the oldest receivable and ends with the current date.

4. Set the Row Headings field to 4 for **Account**. Next, set the Column Headings field to whatever time intervals you want to use to age receivables. (Usually, businesses age receivables on a monthly basis.)

NOTE An *aging* refers to segregating receivables into different age groups. Aging receivables tells you how long receivable balances have been outstanding. Ages are calculated as the difference between the invoice date and the current date.

5. Set the Use Current/All/Selected Accounts field to S for Selected, and press Enter.

   Quicken next displays the Select Accounts To Include window (see fig. 22.5). Exclude all accounts that are not receivables.

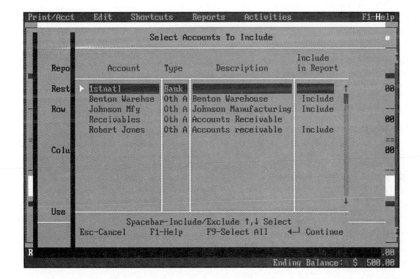

FIG. 22.5

The Select Accounts To Include window.

6. To exclude these accounts, highlight the account you want to exclude and press the space bar. The space bar acts as a toggle to select between include and exclude.

7. After you complete the Select Accounts To Include window, press Enter, and Quicken displays the Accounts Receivable Aging report summary (see fig. 22.6).

The summary report shows how much money each of the receivables customers owes you and also the ages of the receivables. Robert Jones, for example, shows a receivable balance of $1,000 in July because the date of this account's first transaction is in July, and as $500 at the end of September because you received a partial payment on the receivable in August.

```
                    Accounts Receivable Aging
                    7/1/92 Through 9/30/92

    BUSINESS-Selected Accounts                        Page 1
    7/22/92


    Account                                           OVERALL
    Description      7/92         8/92        9/92     TOTAL
    --------------   ----------   ----------  ------   ----------

    Benton Warehse      0.00      5,000.00      0.00   5,000.00
    Johnson Mfg     2,500.00          0.00      0.00   2,500.00
    Robert Jones    1,000.00       -500.00      0.00     500.00
    ------------    ----------    ----------  --------  ----------

    OVERALL TOTAL   3,500.00      4,500.00      0.00   8,000.00
                    ========      ========   ==========  ========
```

FIG. 22.6

The Accounts
Receivable Aging
report shown
on-screen.

T   I   P   The Quicken user's manual offers another approach for recording
receivables and two other approaches for recording payments on
the receivables. The manual suggests that you record all receivables,
or at least all of a specific customer's receivables, in one account.
Regarding recording payments, the manual suggests that you enter
the payment as a decrease transaction in a large Receivables Register or as a negative transfer amount for a specific receivable transaction by using the Split Transaction window. (If you have more
questions about these approaches, refer to the user's manual.) The
benefit of the manual's two approaches is that you don't use as
many accounts—the limit is 255. These suggestions, however, have
the following problems:

■ If you record invoices and payment transactions in a large
Register, you have difficulty determining how much money a
customer owes you or has paid you on a specific invoice.

■ If you use the Split Transaction window to record payments on
an invoice, a second problem arises. To apply a payment to five
invoices, you must go into the Receivables Register and edit
five transactions to show the payment. Bank reconciliation also
is more difficult because you recorded the payment as five
deposits rather than as one payment.

Tracking Accounts Payable

Accounts payable are liabilities to vendors for goods and services used in a business, and any other liabilities the business owes but are not due until a future date. To record your payables, you must set up a separate accounts payable account in Quicken. Because an accounts payable account is a liability of your business, it should be set up as an Other Liability account type (account type 5 in the Set Up New Account window). If you're not using the accrual system of accounting earlier in this chapter), don't worry about setting up accounts payable accounts.

To set up an accounts payable account, add a liability account, name it *Accounts Pay* or *A/P*, and enter zero as the starting balance. Because the accounts payable account is a liability, it will be shown in the Liabilities section of the Balance Sheet.

Take advantage of all early payment discounts by paying invoices on the early payment date. Pay all other invoices so that the payment is received on the due date. You may even consider using aggressive accounts-payable management by taking a 2 percent discount on any early payment, even if the vendor offers no such discount. Most vendors will be glad to receive 98 percent of the invoice amount early, rather than waiting for 100 percent in 30 or more days.

C P A
T I P

After you have established your accounts payable account, you can begin entering transactions for purchases or services. To track your accounts payable, follow these steps:

1. Access the Register for the accounts payable account.

2. Enter a transaction for each credit purchase or service. Use the purchase invoice to enter this information. Use the same dates as the purchase date shown on the invoice. Enter the amount of the purchase or service in the Increase field. Use the Memo field to enter descriptive information about the credit transaction— invoice number, payment terms, and so on. Then, assign a category or subcategory to the transaction and record the transaction.

Figure 22.7 shows the Accounts Payable Register with a credit transaction entered.

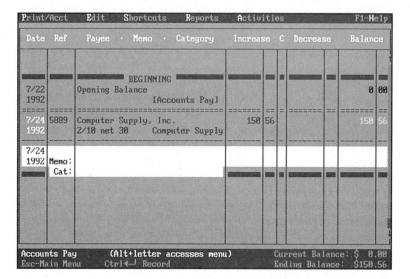

FIG. 22.7

The Accounts Payable Register with a credit purchase transaction.

To record the transaction when you pay for credit purchases that you have entered in the accounts payable account, follow these steps:

1. Select the account that you use to write checks, and access the Register.

2. Enter the payment transaction as usual. In the Category field, enter the accounts payable account. Quicken enters the account in brackets to show that this is a transfer transaction (you're transferring funds from your bank account to decrease the balance in the accounts payable account). Record the transaction. Quicken enters the corresponding transaction in the Accounts Payable Register. Figure 22.8 shows the Accounts Payable Register after a payment is made. (Remember, you can press Ctrl-X to go directly to the corresponding transfer transaction.)

Often, vendors provide incentives to their customers to pay their invoices early. Such incentives can include a 2 percent discount from the invoice amount if paid within 10 days of the invoice date. Otherwise, vendors require the full amount paid within 30 days. (Note that there are many other discount terms provided by vendors.) If you take advantage of an early payment discount, split the transaction for the payment to the vendor and assign the discount to a subcategory called *Discounts* under the Category *Purchases* (you will need to add this subcategory to the Category and Transfer list).

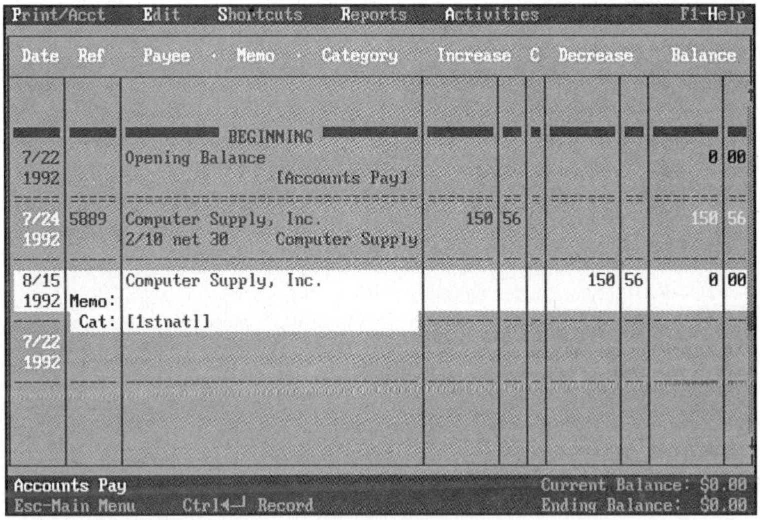

```
 Print/Acct    Edit    Shortcuts    Reports    Activities         F1-Help

  Date  Ref    Payee  ·  Memo  ·  Category    Increase  C Decrease   Balance


            ▅▅▅▅▅▅▅ BEGINNING ▅▅▅▅▅▅▅
  7/22         Opening Balance                                         0 00
  1992                       [Accounts Pay]
 ══════ ═════ ══════════════════════════════ ════════ ══ ════════ ══ ══════
  7/24  5889  Computer Supply, Inc.            150 56                 150 56
  1992         2/10 net 30      Computer Supply
 ────── ───── ────────────────────────────── ──────── ── ──────── ── ──────
  8/15         Computer Supply, Inc.                      150 56        0 00
  1992  Memo:
        Cat: [1stnatl]
  7/22
  1992


 Accounts Pay                                Current Balance: $0.00
 Esc-Main Menu    Ctrl◄┘ Record              Ending Balance:  $0.00
```

FIG. 22.8

The Accounts Payable Register after a payment is made.

Accounting for Fixed Assets

Accounting for fixed assets represents another activity most businesses need to address. You may own furniture, equipment, and even real estate that needs to be depreciated. Although you can depreciate different assets, the mechanics of recording depreciation are consistent.

NOTE If you need to record depletion for natural resources, such as timber, or if you need to record amortization expenses for intangible assets, such as copyrights or patents, the procedures are the same as those described for depreciation.

Understanding Depreciation

Suppose that you purchase a delivery truck for $12,000. You plan to use the truck for five years and then sell the truck for $2,000 (its salvage value). The rationale for depreciating the truck is that over the five years, you need to include the expense of the truck when measuring profits. Depreciation is a way of allocating the cost of an asset over two or more years. Several methods are available to make this allocation, but a common method is *straight-line* depreciation. Straight-line depreciation works in the following manner: if you buy the truck for $12,000, intending to sell the truck five years later for $2,000, the overall cost of using the truck over the five years is $10,000. To calculate the yearly cost, divide the $10,000 by five years, and $2,000 is the annual depreciation expense to include in the calculations of profits.

On balance sheets, assets are listed at their adjusted basis (an amount equal to the original cost, minus the depreciation already taken). Continuing with the delivery truck example, at the end of year one the balance sheet lists the truck at $10,000—calculated as $12,000 original cost minus $2,000 of depreciation. Similarly, at the end of years two, three, four, and five, the balance sheet lists the truck at the original cost minus the depreciation taken to date. After the end of year five, when the truck is listed at $2,000—calculated as $12,000 minus $10,000 of depreciation—you stop depreciating the asset because you don't depreciate the asset below its salvage value.

**C P A
T I P**
Other depreciation methods exist, and the methods the federal tax laws prescribe often are confusing. In essence, however, how you use Quicken to record depreciation works the same way no matter what depreciation method you use. This chapter cannot give you complete information about how to calculate the depreciation on assets, but if you want more information on the tax laws, call the Internal Revenue Service and ask for Internal Revenue Service Publication 534. For more information on how to calculate depreciation according to generally accepted accounting principles, which is different from depreciation calculated for the tax laws, consult a certified public accountant.

Recording Fixed Assets and Depreciation

To record fixed assets and the depreciation expense related to fixed assets, set up an account for each asset that must be depreciated. Enter a descriptive account name, set the account type to 4 for Other Assets account, and enter the purchase price as the initial balance. Figure 22.9 shows the Set Up New Account window with the $12,000 delivery truck entered as an Other Asset account.

If you have groups of similar assets with similar life spans, you usually can depreciate these assets as a group. You probably don't need to depreciate individually each piece of furniture you buy during the year; you can aggregate and depreciate all the furniture together, as one asset.

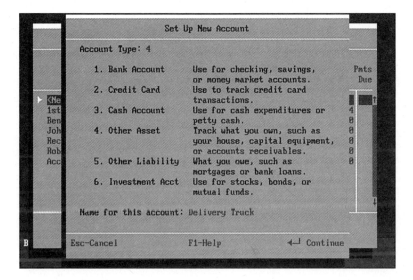

FIG. 22.9

The Set Up New Account window to add a new account for a $12,000 delivery truck.

To record depreciation, you can enter a decrease transaction for $2,000 each year and assign the Depreciation Expense category to the transactions. If you did not set up a category for depreciation, Quicken prompts you to add the category when you try to assign it to the depreciation transaction. Remember that Quicken does not use a transaction in calculating net income unless the date is within the range you specify on the Create Report screens. Therefore, you can enter all five years of depreciation at one time by using transaction dates in each of the five years. Figure 22.10 shows the fixed Asset Account's Register for the delivery truck with depreciation expense recorded for 1992, 1993, and 1994.

Preparing Payroll

One of the more common business applications of Quicken is to prepare employee payroll checks and reports. Suppose that you want to prepare a payroll check for an employee who earns $1,000 every two weeks. The employee's Social Security tax is $62, the Medicare tax is $14.50, the federal income tax withholding amount is $100, and the state income tax withholding amount is $40. You also can assume that the employer's matching share of Social Security is $62, the matching share of Medicare is $14.50, and you must pay $10 for federal unemployment tax.

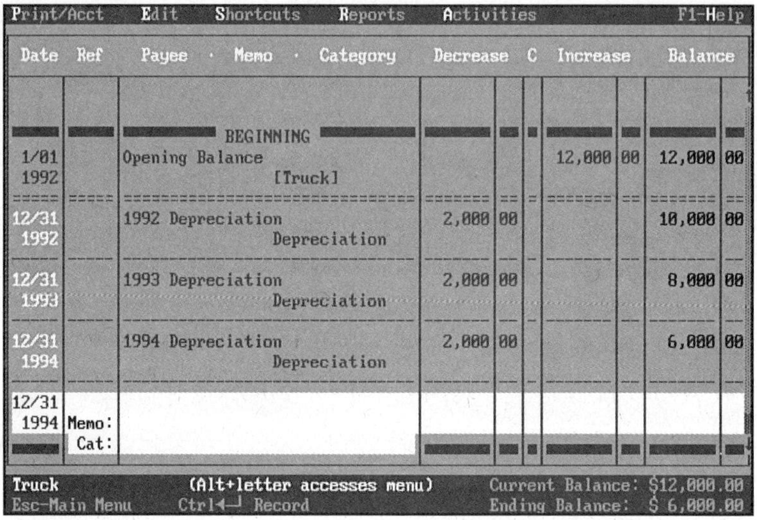

FIG. 22.10

The Delivery Truck Register that shows the asset depreciation transactions for three years.

NOTE   If your payroll is becoming burdensome, consider using Quicken's add-on utility program called QuickPay. QuickPay calculates and processes your payroll and even enters the employee's paycheck information in the Write Checks screen for you. Refer to Appendix B, "Using QuickPay with Quicken," to learn more about this payroll-preparation utility.

Getting Ready for Payroll

To record this payroll transaction, set up a liability account for each of the payroll tax payable accounts. In the Set Up New Account window, enter the account type as 5, for Other Liability, and enter the initial amount (the amount you already owe) as the starting balance in the account. In this example, the amount includes the federal income tax withholding, state income tax withholding, the employee's Social Security and Medicare amount, your matching Social Security and Medicare taxes, and the federal unemployment tax. To define each of the payroll tax accounts, use the Set Up New Account window.

You also need to set up a category for each of the employer's payroll expenses: the employee's gross wages, the employer's matching share of the Social Security and Medicare tax, and the federal unemployment tax. You don't set up categories for the employee's withholding for

Social Security tax, Medicare tax, federal income tax, or state income tax, however, because these amounts are expenses of the employee—not the employer.

> Make sure that you keep up with the changing FICA (Federal Insurance Contribution Act) tax rates and the unemployment tax rates for your state. You also should be aware of limitations on 401(k) plan contributions each year. At the beginning of the year, consult with your accountant or tax advisor for this information.
>
> **C P A**
> **T I P**

Paying Employees

To record the payroll check, enter the payroll transaction (see fig. 22.11) in the Write Checks screen or the Register. If you write payroll checks using the same bank account you use to write other checks, enter the Memo description as *payroll*, or payroll and the pay date, so that you can use the Memo field as the basis for including transactions on reports. Select the **Split Transaction** option by pressing Ctrl-S to assign multiple categories and accounts to the payroll transaction. You don't need to fill in the net paycheck amount in the Amount field in the Write Checks screen because Quicken calculates the net amount for you by subtracting any negative amounts that you enter in the Split Transaction window for withholding from the positive amount that you enter for wages. If you use checks with vouchers—a good idea for payroll—the employee's gross wages and the employee's deductions should appear on the first 16 lines of the Split Transaction window so that the payroll transaction is detailed on the voucher. The employee then can see how much of his gross pay was withheld for federal, state, Social Security, and Medicare taxes.

> **NOTE** You can turn on the Print Categories on Voucher Checks setting (from the Checks and Reports settings) so that Quicken prints voucher information on checks. To learn how to turn on this setting, see Chapter 20, "Customizing Quicken."

Enter the other wages expenses (such as the employer's matching share of Social Security, Medicare, and federal unemployment tax) starting on line 17 of the Split Transaction window so that these expenses don't appear on the payroll check's voucher (see fig. 22.12). (Entries made to lines 16 through 30 of the Split Transaction window are not printed on check vouchers.)

After you complete the Split Transaction window, press Ctrl-Enter or F10 to return to the Write Checks screen or the Register. Figure 22.13 shows a completed payroll check. The net wages amount is $783.50, which is $1,000 in gross wages minus $100 in federal withholding, minus $40 in state tax withholding, minus $62 in Social Security, and minus $14.50 in Medicare.

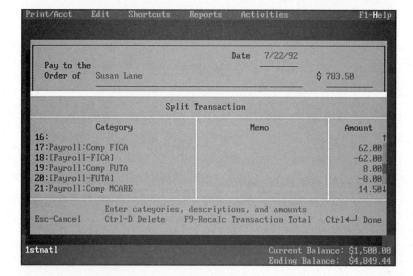

FIG. 22.11

The gross wages and employee deductions should be entered on the first 16 lines of the Split Transaction window.

FIG. 22.12

The other wage expenses start on line 17 of the Split Transaction window.

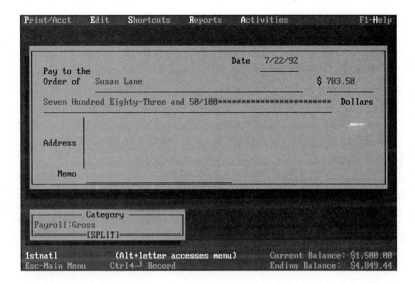

Print/Acct   Edit   Shortcuts   Reports   Activities   F1-Help

Date   7/22/92

Pay to the
Order of   Susan Lane $ 783.50

Seven Hundred Eighty-Three and 50/100**************************** Dollars

Address

Memo

Category
Payroll:Gross
[SPLIT]

1stnat1   (Alt+letter accesses menu)   Current Balance: $1,500.00
Esc-Main Menu   Ctrl↵ Record   Ending Balance: $4,849.44

FIG. 22.13

The completed
payroll check.

Using the Create Payroll Support Assistant

As you may recall from Chapter 1, the Use Tutorials/Assistants menu, which you access from Quicken's main menu, provides several utilities that make working with Quicken easier. One of these utilities, the **Create Payroll Support** option, makes setting up payroll quick and easy. In essence, the **Create Payroll Support** option sets up the categories and accounts you need to prepare payroll in your state. When you select this option, Quicken displays a message screen that tells you what the **Create Payroll Support** option does and that the process takes about 20 seconds. To continue, press Enter. Next, Quicken prompts you for the state's two-letter abbreviation, such as IN for Indiana or NY for New York. (If you don't know the state's two-letter abbreviation, press Enter without making an entry. Quicken displays a window that lists state names and abbreviations, and you can select one of the states on the list.) After you enter or identify the state's two-letter abbreviation, Quicken creates each of the accounts and categories needed in your state.

NOTE   The accounts and categories that Quicken sets up differ from the generic accounts and categories used for illustrating payroll. Quicken sets up accounts and categories specific to the state that you enter.

C P A
T I P

You may know that most payroll deductions and taxes are calculated as a percentage of gross wages. Social Security deductions and matching payroll taxes are calculated as 6.2 percent, and up, of the gross wages to a ceiling amount ($55,500 in 1992). Medicare deductions and matching payroll taxes are 1.45 percent of the gross wages amount to a ceiling amount ($130,200 in 1992). With this feature of payroll preparation, you often can have Quicken calculate most of the payroll deductions and payroll taxes by using the percentage-split feature.

To use the percentage-split feature to calculate payroll deductions and taxes, enter the transaction as usual, except enter the gross wages amount in the Check Amount field in the Write Checks screen or the Payment field in the Register. Then, press Ctrl-S to open the Split Transaction window. Enter a line for each payroll deduction or payroll tax item. In the Amount field, enter the percentage used to calculate the deduction or tax (such as *6.2%* for Social Security tax and *1.45%* for Medicare). Enter the Payroll:Gross amount as *100%*. After you enter the percent and press Enter, Quicken calculates the amount by multiplying the percentage by the amount entered in the Check Amount field or the Payment field. Enter the exact amounts in the Split Transaction window for any deductions or taxes that you derive from withholding tables, such as Employer's Circular E for federal income tax withholding.

A minor problem with this approach, however, is that the check amount isn't really the gross wages amount that you entered. The check amount should be the net of the gross wages amount minus payroll deductions and taxes. This problem isn't difficult to fix. You may recall from Chapter 7 that to make the split transaction lines equal the check amount, Quicken adds another split transaction line to balance the transaction. Just delete this line by highlighting it and pressing Ctrl-D. Then, press F9 to direct Quicken to recalculate the check amount. The amount that Quicken calculates should be equal to the net payroll or paycheck.

Finally, Quicken enables you to create memorized transactions that use percentages rather than amounts. If you use the previously described approach, you can use this capability to make preparing payroll checks even easier.

Paying Payroll Taxes

When you pay the government, you already have recorded the expense of the taxes and are carrying as a liability the payroll taxes you still owe. When you write the check to the government, the entry made in the Category field should be the payroll tax liability account. If you write a check to pay the $10 in federal unemployment taxes, you enter the category as *[Payroll-FUTA]* because Payroll-FUTA is the name of the liability account you use to track the amount you owe in federal unemployment tax.

You also use the same approach to record paying all the other payroll tax liabilities you owe. You write a check to the government agency and categorize the transaction as a transfer from the payroll taxes liability account.

In real life, of course, you may have several more payroll tax expenses and liabilities for items, such as state and local income taxes, state unemployment insurance, and disability insurance. The accounting procedures you follow to record and pay each of these liabilities, however, are the same as the procedures described in the preceding paragraphs.

You should segregate the payroll taxes that you withhold from your employees' gross wages. The best approach is to set up a separate bank account to collect and disburse payroll taxes. Do not, for any reason, *borrow* money from the payroll taxes bank account. Although the act may seem innocuous, this money is not yours to spend. This money belongs to your employee or the federal government; you only hold the money in trust.

C P A
T I P

Completing Quarterly and Annual Tax Reports

The final aspect of preparing payroll relates to the filing of the quarterly and annual payroll forms and reports to federal, state, and local government. A series of federal reporting requirements exists for W-2s, W-3s, 940s, and 941s. Depending on where you live, you also may have several state and local payroll forms and reports to complete. You may be able to retrieve the numbers for these forms by printing a summary report based on the bank account you use to write payroll checks (see fig. 22.14).

To print the summary report, select the **Summary** report option from the Reports menu. You may want to subtotal the report by category. If you write payroll checks on the same account you use to write other checks and include *payroll* in the Memo field, you can use the **F9-Filter** option to specify that only transactions with *payroll* appear in the summary report.

Completing the W-2 and W-3

You use the gross wages figures as the total wages amounts on the employees' W-2s. You use the transfers from withholding figures as the federal income tax withholding amounts. You use the transfers from employees' FICA as the Social Security and Medicare taxes withheld amounts.

The W-3 summarizes the W-2 forms you complete. You enter the employer totals for the individual amounts from each employee's W-2. You can use the totals from the summary report for these employer totals.

> **NOTE** One difference between the transaction report shown in figure 22.14 and the one you use to prepare the W-2 and W-3 forms is that the range of transaction dates encompasses the entire calendar year.

```
                         Payroll Summary Report
                         7/1/92 Through 7/31/92

     BUSINESS-Selected Accounts                                    Page 1
     7/22/92

     Payee              Payroll-FICA      Payroll-FUTA    Payroll-FWH
     -------            -------------     -------------   -----------

     Mark Stephens          -111.60             -6.60          -98.00
     Opening Balance           0.00              0.00            0.00
     Susan Lane             -124.00             -8.00         -100.00
                        -------------     -------------   -------------

     OVERALL TOTAL          -235.60            -14.60         -198.00
                        =============     =============   ===========

              -24.66         0.00              0.00          -5.89    -246.75
                0.00         0.00              0.00           0.00       0.00
              -29.00         0.00              0.00         -40.00    -301.00
           ----------      -------           -------       --------   --------

              -53.66         0.00              0.00         -45.89    -547.75
           ==========      =======           =======       ========  =========
```

FIG. 22.14

A transaction report that subtotals by category.

Completing Other Forms and Reports

The federal and the state governments have other tax forms and reports you must complete. You use the 940 form to calculate and report annual federal unemployment tax liability. You also use the 941 form each quarter to calculate and report federal income and Social Security taxes withheld and the employer's share of the Social Security taxes. Again, you may be able to use a summary report similar to the report shown in figure 22.14 to complete the quarterly return.

 NOTE For the Employer's Annual Unemployment Tax (form 940), the range of transaction dates must encompass the entire year. For the Employer's Quarterly Federal Tax (form 941), the range of transaction dates must cover the quarter.

Typically, the Internal Revenue Service provides a great deal of help and information about federal payroll taxes. You may want to take advantage of the IRS help guides. Specifically, you need the Employer's Tax Guide (also known as Circular E). If you don't already have this document, call the nearest IRS office and request a guide. If you are a sole proprietor, you also may want to request the information packet "Your Business Tax Kit for Sole Proprietor," which provides information about the taxes you pay as a sole proprietor. Some IRS locations provide free small-business tax education seminars. You also can call the state revenue office and request all information they have on the state income and payroll taxes.

C P A
T I P

Preparing Inventory Accounting

A good inventory accounting system answers two questions: How much inventory do you currently hold and how much inventory did you sell over the year? A perpetual inventory system can answer both questions. Unfortunately, Quicken does not provide the tools to maintain a perpetual system. A perpetual inventory system tracks every change in inventory as the changes occur, in dollars and in units. As a result, you always know exactly how much inventory you hold, in dollars and in units. Because Quicken tracks only dollars, not units, you can answer only the second question: How much inventory did you sell over the year? You can answer this question with a simple periodic inventory system.

Understanding Periodic Inventory Systems

A periodic system works in the following way: At the end of every year, you count the inventory you are holding and add up the cost of the inventory. Calculate the cost of the goods, or inventory, you sold by taking the inventory purchases you made over the year and subtracting the change in inventory.

Suppose that you sell antique cars and each car costs $10,000. You held 3 cars in inventory at the beginning of the year, purchased 10 cars over the year, and have 4 cars in inventory at the end of the year. Using the equation described previously, you can calculate the value of the inventory you sold over the year as follows:

> Car purchases: ($10,000 * 10) = $100,000
> Change over year:
>   Ending: ($10,000 * 4 cars) = $40,000
>   Beginning: ($10,000 * 3 cars) = $30,000
> Minus change over year: –$10,000
> Cost of inventory sold over year: $90,000

You know that during the year you bought $100,000 of cars and that you are holding $10,000 more inventory than you held at the end of the previous year, which means that you did not sell all the cars you bought.

Implementing a Periodic Inventory System

If you want to enjoy the benefits of a periodic inventory system, you can use Quicken to construct a simple, but crude, inventory system.

The following steps describe how you implement a periodic inventory system using Quicken:

1. Set up an Other Asset account for the inventory you buy and sell. The name can be *Inventory*. Select 4 as the account type. The starting balance is the starting inventory balance. (If you are just starting a business, the starting inventory balance can be zero if you have not yet begun to purchase inventory.)

2. When you purchase inventory, don't categorize the purchase as an expense—transfer the total purchase amount to the inventory account (enter the inventory account in the Category field; Quicken enters it like this: [Inventory]).

3. At the end of your fiscal year, select the inventory account and use the **Update Account Balance** option from the Activities menu to reset the inventory account balance to whatever the physical count shows at the end of the year. Assign the Cost of Goods Sold category to the adjustment transaction. You may have to add the category Cost of Goods Sold as an expense category.

Figure 22.15 shows an Inventory Account Register after a month of purchases and the adjustment transaction that calculates the actual Cost of Goods Sold amount.

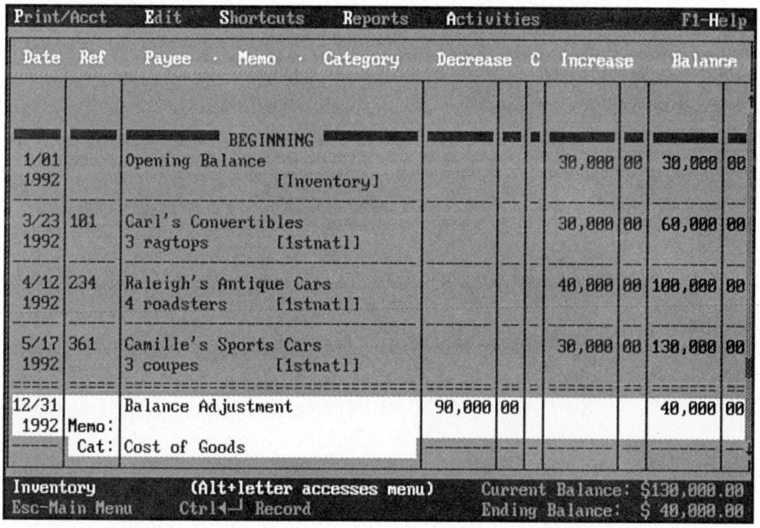

FIG. 22.15

An Inventory Account Register with sample transactions for purchases of inventory and an adjustment transaction.

Reviewing the Problems of a Periodic System

As you know, a periodic inventory system is not without problems. Make sure that you can live with the problems of a periodic inventory system before you spend a great deal of time and energy to implement this kind of system.

Although you have accurate measures of cash flow, you have an accurate measure of profits only through the last adjustment transaction. If you need to measure profits frequently, you must take frequent physical counts of the inventory and make the inventory adjustment transaction.

You don't know the details or components of the cost of goods sold because you get the cost of goods sold from an adjustment transaction.

As a result, you don't know the portion of cost of goods sold that stems from sales to specific customers or the portion that stems from breakage, shoplifting, or spoilage. This loss of information can be especially troublesome if the business has more than one kind of item sold, such as books, tapes, and CDs. You may have to set up separate accounts for each kind of item in your inventory and be sure that you segregate all purchases by using the **Split Transaction** option.

Except when you make physical counts of inventory, you also never know how much inventory you actually have on hand. You cannot use this inventory system, therefore, to see the items you need to reorder or how many units of a specific item are presently in stock.

Job Costing

Job costing refers to tracking the costs of a specific project, or job, and comparing these costs to the amount you planned to spend. Home builders, advertising agencies, and specialty manufacturers are examples of businesses with projects you must monitor for actual and planned costs.

The Quicken user's manual suggests one approach for job costing: Categorize each expense into a category and a class. When you print a transaction or summary report, you can choose to subtotal by the classes. If you use classes to represent jobs, for example, the total for a class is the total for a job. This approach, however, is not strong. The following paragraphs describe alternative approaches that help you avoid two problems you encounter when categorizing expenses into categories and classes. (See Chapter 9 for a detailed discussion of categories and classes.)

The first problem with using classes as the basis for a job-costing system is that within Quicken, you budget by categories, not by classes. If you use the class approach, you omit one of the basic job-costing tasks: comparing the amount you planned to spend with the actual amount spent. Fortunately, you can solve this problem by setting up a group of categories that you use only for a specific job. You may even include a code or an abbreviation in the category name to indicate the job.

Suppose that you are a home builder constructing a house on Lot 23 in Deerfield and that you use three rough categories of expenses on all the homes you build: land, material, and labor. You can create three special categories: *D23 land*, *D23 material*, and *D23 labor*, which you can use exclusively to budget and track the costs of the house under construction. Figure 22.16 shows the budgeting report that you can generate to monitor job costs if you follow the approaches described in the preceding paragraph.

A second problem with using classes as the basis for a job-costing system is that you don't always have to categorize as expenses the costs you incur on a job. Often, you need to treat these costs as assets. The costs of building the home on Lot 23 in the Deerfield subdivision should be carried as inventory until the home is sold. When the home is sold, the total costs of the home may be categorized as the cost of goods sold.

```
                         Budget Report
                    7/1/92 Through 7/31/92
BUSINESS-All Accounts                                  Page 1
7/22/92
                        7/ 1/92    —            7/31/92
Category Description    Actual     Budget       Diff
.......................  ........   ........    ......
INCOME/EXPENSE
  EXPENSES
  D23 Labor             16,753.00  20,000.00   -3,247.00
  D23 Land              30,400.00  30,000.00      400.00
  D23 Materials         23,456.00  25,000.00   -1,544.00
                        ---------  ---------   ---------
TOTAL EXPENSES          70,609.00  75,000.00   -4,391.00
                        ---------  ---------   ---------
TOTAL INCOME/EXPENSE   -70,609.00 -75,000.00    4,391.00
                        ==========  ==========  =========
```

FIG. 22.16

A budget report for a job.

During the job, if you categorize the costs of building the home as expenses when you pay the costs, you overstate expenses (which understates profits), and you understate assets (which understates net worth). These understatements of profits and net worth can become a real problem if you have investors or lenders looking carefully at your financial performance and condition. To solve this problem, create a transaction in which you move cost dollars out of the job-cost categories into an asset account.

An Introduction to QuickBooks

If you like using Quicken but find that it just doesn't fit the needs of your small business (because you cannot print invoices and statements, track accounts receivable and payable adequately, or create customer and vendor lists), you may want to look into Intuit's new small business package called QuickBooks. You easily can convert your Quicken data to QuickBooks, so don't worry about having to reenter anything in a new system. Even though you may decide to convert to QuickBooks and convert your Quicken data, after the conversion process, your Quicken data still is intact if you want to use Quicken to perform activities that QuickBooks doesn't do, such as amortize loans and track investments.

Although Quicken fully accommodates the individual user for home finances and many small business users, Quicken does not offer some of the features that you may need to track your business finances adequately. QuickBooks offers small-business owners the ease of use that they're accustomed to in Quicken, as well as features that relate more specifically to business, such as invoicing and accounts payable tracking.

You write checks and enter transactions in your Check Register in QuickBooks just like in Quicken. You also can use QuickBooks to reconcile your bank account using almost the same steps that you use in Quicken. QuickBooks can do several other things just like Quicken; however, QuickBooks does a lot of things that Quicken cannot do, such as the following:

- Initiates most transactions from the Accounts Receivable or Accounts Payable Register because that's where most small-business activities begin. Transactions entered the Accounts Receivable or Accounts Payable Register are entered by QuickBooks in the appropriate checking account. When you record and pay a bill the Accounts Payable Register, for example, QuickBooks enters the payment in the Check Register.

- Tracks your accounts receivable so that you know at any given time how much your customers owe.

- Applies customer payments to invoices and calculates early payment discounts.

- Prepares a deposit summary that you can take to the bank when you deposit customer payments.

- Offers complete invoice writing capabilities that enable you to enter line items with item codes that link invoice transactions to accounts.

- Determines when your bills are due and gives you the opportunity to pay outstanding bills directly from the Accounts Payable Register.

- Uses your chart of accounts to track income, expenses, and balance sheet accounts, instead of the categories and subcategories that are used in Quicken.

■ Uses company lists to store data about your customers, customer types, vendors, vendor types, employees, invoice-line items, projects, shipping methods, payment methods, and payment terms. You can even store invoice memos so that you don't have to retype them each time you write an invoice. Company lists speed up entry in many fields throughout the program. Any time a small black diamond appears in a field, you can display the appropriate list and select an item, and QuickBooks immediately enters the items that you select in the field. Company lists also serve as a database of your customers, vendors, and employees, and you can use these lists to print mailing labels for your customers and vendors.

■ Uses balance sheet accounts that are more representative of business, such as fixed asset and equity accounts.

■ Enables you to define projects or jobs and assign transactions to them so that you can track closely each project, job, client, and so on. (In Quicken, projects are called *classes*.)

■ Enables you to assign password protection to 13 QuickBooks activities. If you assign a password to the check printing activity, for example, QuickBooks requires a password before printing that first check.

■ Uses terminology with which small-business people are familiar. Familiar, however, does not mean that you must be an accounting expert to understand the terminology in QuickBooks. On the contrary—Intuit strived for a program that does not intimidate the nonaccounting user. In QuickBooks, you don't even see common accounting terms, such as debit or credit. You *do* see accounts receivable and payable, invoice, voucher, and so on—the terms that you use or hear on a daily basis.

■ Offers business reports that are designed to appear in the usual and customary business format.

■ Creates an aging status schedule for each customer that shows the portion of the customer's balance that is current and the portion that is 0 to 30 days past due, 31 to 60 days past due, 61 to 90 days past due, and more than 90 days past due.

■ Generates an accounts payable aging report that shows the status of your unpaid bills.

■ Generates a 1099 report that you can use to fill out 1099 forms at the end of the calendar year for those vendors who you pay more than $600 to.

■ Tracks the sales tax that you collect for each government agency and accumulates sales tax data in a report that you can use when it's time to file sales tax returns and pay sales tax.

■ Displays a transaction history for transactions that you select in accounts receivable and accounts payable. A transaction history shows each transaction related to the selected transaction.

■ Enables you to enter notes about customers, vendors, or employees in the QuickBooks program so that the notes are readily available.

As you can see, QuickBooks is designed to handle most small-business activities (with the exception of inventory control). If your small business has significant investments, however, you should know that QuickBooks is not set up to do the following:

■ Track individual investments, their market values, and their gains or losses. If it's important that you closely track your investments, use the investment feature in Quicken, and use QuickBooks for everything else.

■ Look at transaction detail in reports. QuickBooks does not include the QuickZoom feature that Quicken has that enables you to highlight a line in a report to see the transactions that make up the amount shown on that line. If you want to see transaction detail in a QuickBooks report, you must exit the report screen and search through the Registers for transactions.

■ Specify accounts as tax-related. However, this feature is not as important in QuickBooks because most all business accounts and subaccounts are tax-related.

Chapter Summary

This chapter provided you with a basic approach to accounting for any business asset or liability and gave specific suggestions and tips for performing basic accounting tasks. You now have the necessary information to use Quicken as the basis of a business accounting system. If, however, you still feel that you cannot adequately track your business finances with Quicken, this chapter introduced you to QuickBooks, a software product very similar to Quicken but modified to handle most small-business tasks.

This chapter is the last of *Using Quicken 6 for DOS*. In the appendixes that follow, you learn how to install Quicken (which you probably already have done), how to use QuickPay with Quicken.

Installing Quicken

Before you can use Quicken, you must install the program on your hard disk. This appendix provides the steps to install Quicken and explains software and hardware requirements.

Reviewing the Program Requirements

The following sections review some of the software and hardware requirements of Quicken.

Hardware Requirements

To use Quicken, you must have the following hardware:

- IBM PC, XT, AT, PS/1, PS/2, Tandy, or 100% compatible computer
- 512K of memory
- Hard drive

- At least one floppy disk drive, one of which is a high-density 1.2M or 1.44M drive.

- Any printer (except one that uses thermal paper if using checks from Intuit).

- 80-column color or monochrome monitor; you'll need a monitor with a graphics card if you are planning to use the View Graphs feature.

- (Optional) Modem if you plan to pay bills electronically or use IntelliCharge.

Software Requirements

To use Quicken, you must have the following software:

- MS-DOS or PC DOS Version 2.0 or higher (use the VER DOS command to determine the DOS version installed on your computer).

- The Quicken Install Disks (two 3 1/2-inch disks or three 5 1/4-inch disks).

Installing Quicken

If you haven't been using Version 5.0 of Quicken, you should know a few things about the Quicken hard disk installation program, INSTALL, before you use the program. INSTALL (for Quicken 6.0) creates a directory named QUICKEN on your hard disk, in which the program files are stored. Your data files also are stored in the QUICKEN directory, unless you change the system settings (described in Chapter 19, "Managing Your Quicken Files"). In case you are not familiar with the terms, *program files* refers to the files that contain the actual Quicken software instructions, and *data files* refers to the files that contain your financial information.

INSTALL also creates a batch file named Q.BAT so that all you have to do is press Q at the C> prompt to run QUICKEN. If you already have a Q.BAT file—if you have been using Quicken Version 5.0, for example—INSTALL renames the old file Q2.BAT.

INSTALL also verifies that the CONFIG.SYS file's BUFFERS statement equals or exceeds 10 and that the FILES statement equals or exceeds 10. INSTALL resets these statements because Quicken runs with several files open and performs many reads from the hard disk. For more information on the CONFIG.SYS file and the BUFFERS and FILES statements, see your DOS manual. If you do not have a CONFIG.SYS file, INSTALL creates one with the appropriate BUFFERS and FILES statements. If the CONFIG.SYS file you currently have does not have these statements, INSTALL adds them. If the statements exist but are set to less than 10, INSTALL increases the statement settings to 10. INSTALL does not cause any problems by changing your computer's CONFIG.SYS file.

To install Quicken, follow these steps:

1. Turn on your computer and monitor. Make sure that the correct system date and time are set. (Type *date* or *time* at the C> prompt.) DATE is the DOS command for setting the system date. TIME is the DOS command for setting the system time. Refer to your DOS user's manual if you need help using the DATE or TIME command.

2. Insert the Quicken Install Disk 1 into drive A or B. Type *a:install* or *b:install* (depending on which drive you placed your Quicken Install disk into) and press Enter.

   The introductory install screen shown in figure A.1 appears.

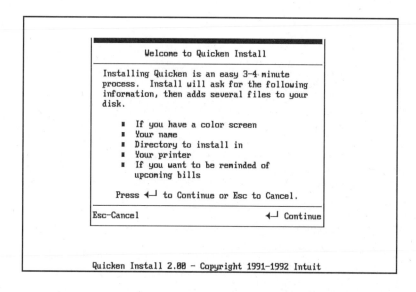

FIG. A.1

The Welcome to Quicken Install screen.

3. Press Enter. Quicken displays the Screen Color window shown in figure A.2.

4. Select the appropriate number to identify your screen type and press Enter. Quicken next displays the Enter Your Name window, shown in figure A.3.

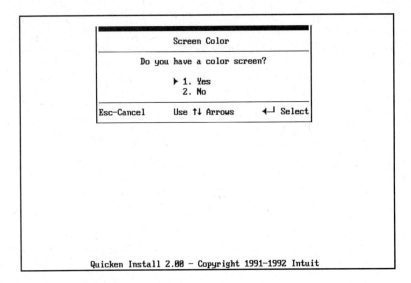

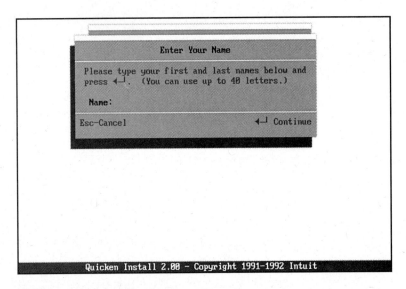

5. Type your name. Then, press Enter.

    Quicken displays the Drive and Directory window to specify
    where you want to install Quicken, as shown in figure A.4. The
    default directory that Quicken creates and installs itself into is
    QUICKEN.

If you previously used Version 5.0 of Quicken and stored the program and data files in \QUICKEN5, installing Quicken Version 6.0
in the \QUICKEN5 directory will not damage the Quicken Version
5.0 data files.

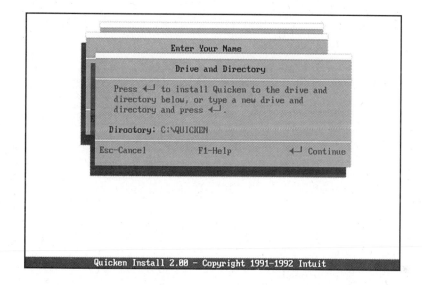

FIG. A.4

The Drive and
Directory
window.

6. If you want to use some other directory, you specify it here by
   typing the default directory. When the correct directory is displayed, press Enter.

   Quicken displays the Choose a Printer list (see fig. A.5).

7. Use the Choose a Printer list to identify your printer. To select a
   printer from the list, use the up- and down-arrow keys to highlight
   the printer that you want to select. If you cannot find your printer,
   select another printer that your printer emulates.

   You should be able to find which printers your printer emulates
   by checking the printer's users' manual. If you cannot find your
   printer on the list and also cannot find a printer your printer emulates, select the **<Other Dot-Matrix>** or **<Other Laser>** options.
   Later, you can define printer settings for printers not found in the
   Choose a Printer list. Chapter 1, explains how to define printer
   settings.

   After you select the printer, press Enter.

   Quicken next asks whether you want the Billminder feature installed, as shown in figure A.6.

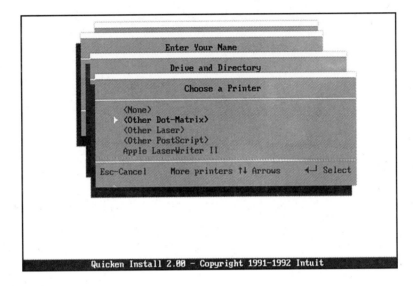

Quicken Install 2.00 – Copyright 1991-1992 Intuit

FIG. A.5

The Choose a
Printer list.

T   I   P   To quickly move through the Choose a Printer list, press the letter
that the name of your printer starts with to move to the first printer
in the list that starts with that letter. Then use the down-arrow key
to move to your printer. To select an HP LaserJet IIp printer, for example, press H to move to the first printer in the list that starts with
the letter H (HP DeskJet), then use the down-arrow key to scroll
through the Hs until you get to HP Laserjet IIp/IIIp.

8. Press Enter to use Billminder or press 2 and press Enter to tell
   Quicken not to use Billminder. The Billminder feature reminds you
   of bills you should pay. When you turn on your computer or when
   you enter Quicken, you are reminded that bills must be paid. This
   handy feature can save you the price of Quicken and this book
   many times over by eliminating or minimizing late-payment fees.

   Quicken displays the Confirm Settings window with all your installation settings listed (see fig. A.7).

9. To accept the settings, press Enter. If one of the settings is incorrect, press Esc one or more times to return to that setting's window. Then, make the necessary changes.

When you press Enter from the Confirm Settings window, Quicken
starts the file-copying part of the installation. As Quicken installs the
program, you see a message on-screen that says Installing Quicken
and a few Welcome to Quicken 6 messages. When necessary, Quicken

prompts you to insert the second (or third if using 5 1/4-inch disks) Quicken Install Disk into drive A or B.

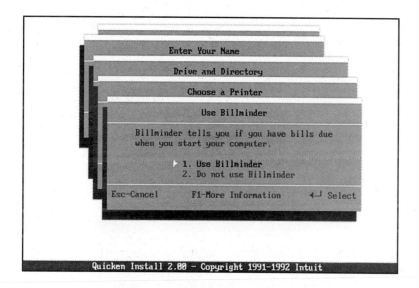

FIG. A.6

The Use Billminder window.

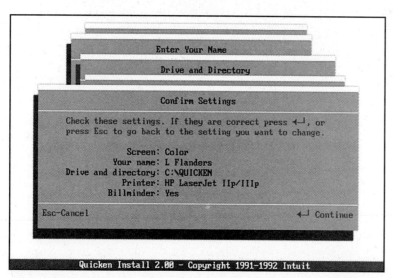

FIG. A.7

The Confirm Settings window.

If Quicken finds data files in an old directory, such as QUICKEN4 or QUICKEN5, a message is displayed asking whether you want these files moved to your new directory. Press Enter to move the data files to the

QUICKEN directory or press 2 for the data files to remain in the old directory. Press Enter.

If the INSTALL program does not find a mouse installed on your hard drive, a message is displayed telling you that you must have a mouse installed if you plan to use a mouse with Quicken. Press Enter to continue.

Finally, Quicken tells you when the installation is complete by displaying a screen with the message Installation Complete (see fig. A.8). To return to the C> prompt, press Enter.

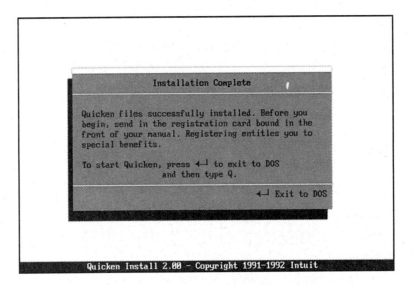

FIG. A.8

The Installation Complete window.

Refer to Chapter 1, "Preparing To Use Quicken," to learn how to start Quicken for the first time.

Using QuickPay with Quicken

If you're a business user of Quicken and the payroll tricks and tips described in Chapter 22, "Using Quicken in Your Business," don't give you the payroll horsepower you need, don't despair. Still another option is available that works seamlessly with Quicken: the QuickPay payroll utility. At the time of this printing, QuickPay 2.0 is the latest version of the program.

QuickPay is a payroll program that works with Quicken. In essence, the QuickPay program calculates the amounts you usually have to calculate outside the Quicken program—including the gross wages and the federal, state, and local taxes—and uses these amounts to prepare and record payroll checks.

The following paragraphs briefly describe how to use the QuickPay utility. Quicken users considering the QuickPay utility and new QuickPay users may find the ensuing discussion useful in deciding whether to acquire QuickPay and in getting started with the program.

The QuickPay utility isn't described here in great detail. This kind of discussion could easily require several chapters—perhaps even an entire book—to cover all the material necessary for every QuickPay user to prepare payroll in his or her state.

Installing and Starting QuickPay

Installing QuickPay is easy. You need just two other items: an installed copy of Quicken 3.0, 4.0, 5.0, or 6.0 and at least 82K of memory more than the minimum amount Quicken requires. Assuming that you meet these two requirements, you simply insert the QuickPay disk into your A drive, make the A drive active by typing *a:*, and then type *install* at the DOS prompt.

QuickPay's installation program next displays a screen telling you where it found Quicken—probably in the QUICKEN directory—and asks you to confirm its discovery. If the identified directory is the correct Quicken program directory, press Enter.

If the identified directory isn't the correct one, enter the correct path name and then press Enter. QuickPay's installation program next copies the QuickPay program files to the Quicken program directory. When it finishes, it returns you to the DOS prompt.

To start Quicken and the QuickPay program, type *qp* at the DOS prompt. The Quicken program starts and its main menu appears and displays the message

        With QuickPay - Version 2.0

at the top of the screen to show that the QuickPay utility is loaded and available (see fig. B.1).

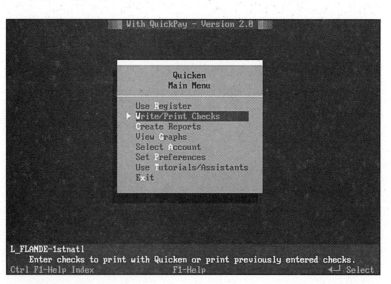

FIG. B.1

The Quicken main menu displaying With QuickPay - Version 2.0 at the top of the screen.

When `With QuickPay - Version 2.0` is displayed at the main menu, the QuickPay program is always available. However, you first must select the Quicken file that you want to use QuickPay in and then access the Write Checks screen to use QuickPay. You learn how to select a Quicken file in Chapter 19 and how to access the Write Checks screen in Chapter 6.

Using QuickPay

Before you can use QuickPay, you must select the Quicken file that you want to use the QuickPay utility in to prepare payroll, and then access the Write Checks screen. When you access the Write Checks screen, Quicken displays the **F7-Payroll** option at the bottom of the screen (see fig. B.2).

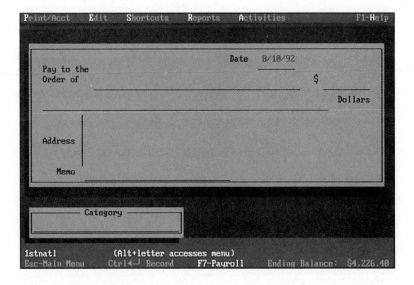

FIG. B.2

The QuickPay **F7-Payroll** option displayed at the Write Checks screen.

From the Write Checks screen, you can begin using QuickPay by pressing F7 to access the QuickPay main menu that you see in figure B.3.

Once you've accessed the QuickPay main menu, you can enter the information for your company and for your employees so that QuickPay can process your payroll.

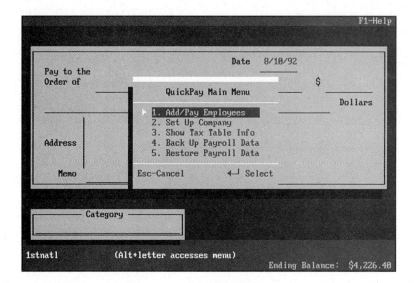

The QuickPay
main menu.

Setting Up QuickPay

Just two steps are necessary to set up QuickPay to process your payroll: describing the employer and describing the employees.

The first step is to describe the employer. When you press F7 to access
the QuickPay main menu, QuickPay displays menu options that you use
to describe the company—**Add/Pay Employees**, **Set Up Company**,
Show Tax Table Info, **Back Up Payroll Data**, and **Restore Payroll Data**.

To describe the employer, follow these steps:

1. Select the **Set Up Company** option from the QuickPay main menu.

2. QuickPay displays the Set Up Company window shown in
   figure B.4.

3. In the Set Up Company window, enter all the employer information that you may use to prepare an employee's payroll check or
   that you may use to prepare any employer payroll tax returns.
   You enter such information as your company name and address,
   your federal and state tax identification numbers, and your state
   unemployment tax.

4. When the Set Up Company window is complete, press Ctrl-Enter
   or F10 to return to the QuickPay main menu.

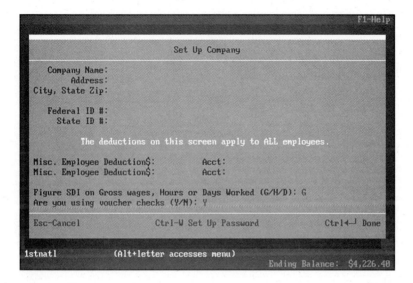

```
                                                              F1-Help

                              Set Up Company

        Company Name:
              Address:
    City, State Zip:

        Federal ID #:
          State ID #:

            The deductions on this screen apply to ALL employees.

    Misc. Employee Deduction$:           Acct:
    Misc. Employee Deduction$:           Acct:

    Figure SDI on Gross wages, Hours or Days Worked (G/H/D): G
    Are you using voucher checks (Y/N): Y

    Esc-Cancel               Ctrl-W Set Up Password        Ctrl↵ Done

    1stnatl          (Alt+letter accesses menu)
                                        Ending Balance:  $4,226.40
```

FIG. B.4

The Set Up
Company
window.

NOTE Menus and screens work the same way in QuickPay as they
do in Quicken, so you shouldn't have any trouble learning
how to move around in the QuickPay program.

The second step for setting up QuickPay to process payroll is entering
information for the employees whom you will pay. To enter employee
information, follow these steps:

1. Select the **Add/Pay Employees** option from the QuickPay main
   menu.

2. QuickPay displays the Add/Pay Employees window shown in figure B.5. This window lists all existing employees and enables you
   to add a new employee to the list, edit or delete existing employees, or sort employees.

3. Highlight the <New Employee> line. QuickPay displays the Add
   New Employee window shown in figure B.6.

4. In the Add New Employee window, enter information necessary to
   prepare a payroll check and to calculate an employee's gross
   wages, any deductions, and any payroll taxes. This information
   includes such items as the employee's name and address, salary
   or hourly pay rate, and Social Security number.

5. When the Add New Employee window is complete, press Ctrl-
   Enter or F10 to return to the Add/Pay Employees window. To add
   other employees, repeat steps 3 and 4 for each employee.

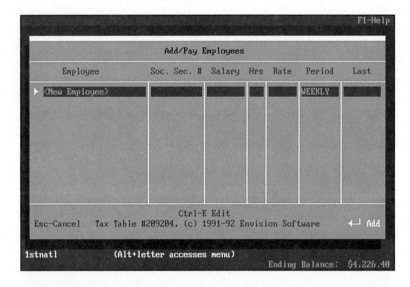

Add/Pay Employees

Employee	Soc. Sec. #	Salary	Hrs	Rate	Period	Last
▶ <New Employee>					WEEKLY	

Ctrl-E Edit
Esc-Cancel   Tax Table #209204, (c) 1991-92 Envision Software   ↵ Add

1stnatl   (Alt+letter accesses menu)

Ending Balance: $4,226.40

FIG. B.5

The Add/Pay
Employees
window.

F1-Help

Add New Employee

```
Full Name:                        Hire Date   : 08/03/92
   Address:                        Release Date:
   Address:
Cty,St Zp:                         Pay FWH: Y        Filing Status:
     Phone:                        Exemptions#: 0    Extra$:
  Chk Memo:
     Class:                        SWH Table:         Filing Status:
       SSN:                        Exemptions#: 0    Extra$:
                                   Joint Filing:      Misc:
 Hourly 1$:         Yr Salary$:
 Hourly 2$:         Commission%:    Employee Ded$:    Acct:
 Hourly 3$:         Pay Period: W   Employee Ded$:    Acct:
                                    Company  Ded$:    Acct:
Pay FUTA: Y  SUI: Y  FICA: Y  MCARE: Y  Company Ded$: Acct:
```

Esc-Cancel   Ctrl-S Other Taxes Ctrl-Y YTD   Ctrl↵ Done

1stnatl   (Alt+letter accesses menu)

Ending Balance: $4,226.40

FIG. B.6

The Add New
Employee
window.

Processing Payroll with QuickPay

After you describe the employer and the employees, you're ready to begin preparing payroll checks. To process payroll for an employee, follow these steps:

1. From the Write Checks screen, press F7 to access QuickPay. QuickPay displays its main menu.

2. Select the **Add/Pay Employees** option. QuickPay displays the Add/Pay Employees window.

3. Use the up- and down-arrow keys to highlight the employee that you want to pay.

4. QuickPay next displays the Compute Payroll window, in which you enter any information specific to the payroll check being prepared—usually just the hours worked, because QuickPay already knows the standard hourly pay rate. Figure B.7 shows the Compute Payroll window.

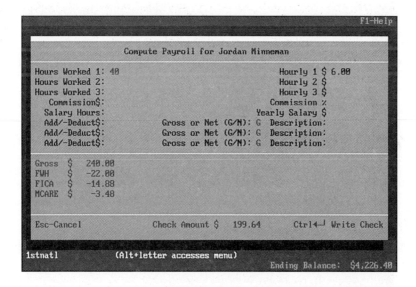

The Compute Payroll window.

5. When the Compute Payroll window is complete, press Ctrl-Enter. QuickPay displays the Quicken Write Checks screen, fills it in as necessary for the employee's payroll check, displays the Split Transaction screen, and fills it in as necessary to record the payroll expenses and deductions. Figure B.8 shows a payroll check filled in by QuickPay.

NOTE If you don't have the appropriate accounts set up in Quicken to process payroll (FWH, FICA, MCARE, and so on), QuickPay sets up these accounts for you as it prepares the first payroll check.

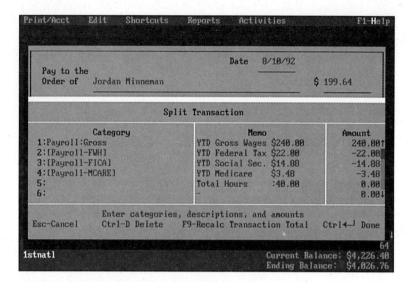

Print/Acct   Edit   Shortcuts   Reports   Activities   F1-Help

```
                                    Date    8/10/92
   Pay to the
   Order of    Jordan Minneman                         $ 199.64

                          Split Transaction

              Category                    Memo              Amount
   1:Payroll:Gross             YTD Gross Wages $240.00        240.00↑
   2:[Payroll-FWH]             YTD Federal Tax $22.00         -22.00▓
   3:[Payroll-FICA]            YTD Social Sec. $14.88         -14.88
   4:[Payroll-MCARE]           YTD Medicare     $3.48          -3.48
   5:                          Total Hours     :40.00          0.00
   6:                                                          0.00↓

              Enter categories, descriptions, and amounts
   Esc-Cancel    Ctrl-D Delete    F9-Recalc Transaction Total    Ctrl◄┘ Done
```

64

1stnatl   Current Balance: $4,226.40
                                           Ending Balance: $4,026.76

FIG. B.8

A sample payroll check filled in by QuickPay.

Tips and Suggestions for Using QuickPay

If QuickPay sounds like something you would benefit from using, here are two suggestions for making your use of this tool as easy as possible:

- Use the Create Payroll Support Assistant, described in Chapter 22, "Using Quicken in Your Business," to create the categories and accounts you will need. QuickPay requires that certain categories and accounts exist. If they don't exist, QuickPay doesn't work correctly. The Create Payroll Support Assistant is the easiest way to be certain that your payroll categories and accounts have the right names.

- Recognize that QuickPay isn't the same thing as a payroll accountant or tax attorney. You cannot expect the QuickPay program or the QuickPay documentation to provide payroll tax knowledge or to answer your questions about how state unemployment taxes are calculated, for example.

Like every other payroll program, the QuickPay program only automates payroll processing. The bottom line is that if you need to prepare payroll but don't understand how the basic process works, you first need to acquire an understanding of payroll processing.

Several options are available if you need to acquire payroll processing knowledge. The Internal Revenue Service and many state taxing authorities offer tax workshops that explain how to calculate federal and state payroll taxes.

The Internal Revenue Service also provides, free to small businesses, several well-written books and booklets that explain all kinds of accounting requirements, including those related to payroll processing. Finally, in a pinch, you always can use outside service bureaus, such as ADP or PayChex, until you feel confident about tackling payroll on your own.

Symbols

A

C

R

T

X-Z